*German Romanticism*
*and Its Institutions*

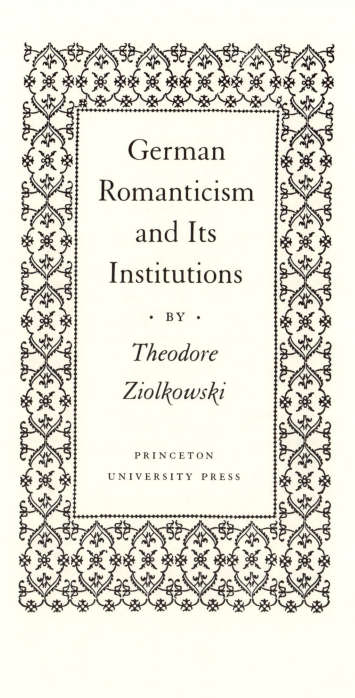

# German Romanticism and Its Institutions

· BY ·

*Theodore Ziolkowski*

PRINCETON
UNIVERSITY PRESS

Published by Princeton University Press, 41 William Street,
Princeton, New Jersey 08540
In the United Kingdom: Princeton University Press, Oxford

Library of Congress Cataloging-in-Publication Data

Ziolkowski, Theodore.
German romanticism and its institutions / Theodore Ziolkowski.
p.   cm.    Bibliography: p.    Includes index.    ISBN 0-691-06801-1
1. Romanticism—Germany.   2. German literature—18th century—
History and criticism.   3. German literature—19th century—
History and criticism.   4. Literature and society—Germany.
5. German literature—Social aspects.   6. Germany—Intellectual life—
18th century.   7. Germany—Intellectual life—19th century. I. Title.
PT361.Z48 1989    830.9′145—dc20    89-8382

This book has been composed in Linotron Granjon

Clothbound editions of Princeton University Press books
are printed on acid-free paper, and binding materials are
chosen for strength and durability. Paperbacks, although satisfactory
for personal collections, are not usually suitable for library rebinding

Printed in the United States of America

Designed by Laury A. Egan

8   7   6   5   4   3   2

FOR MARY WEIGAND

# CONTENTS

## PREFACE

THIS BOOK is in at least two senses a decanal work. It was undertaken and completed during the ten years after I became dean of the Graduate School at Princeton University in 1979. More importantly, it would not have been conceived and carried out in its present form had I not had the experience of being a full-time academic officer during the period of its composition.

I had long intended to write a book on German Romanticism—ever since I completed my doctoral dissertation for Hermann J. Weigand at Yale University on "Hermann Hesse and Novalis" (1957). For the first decade of my career I emphasized the modern pole of that conjunction in my writing. Gradually, in my research and especially in my teaching, I began to shift my attention toward the earlier period. But for many years I could not find an approach that satisfied me. There was no need for simply another "history" of German Romanticism; scholars from Rudolf Haym (1870) to Gerhard Schulz (1983) and Gert Ueding (1987) have provided us with a library of readable and reliable narratives. Yet out of personal interest as well as theoretical conviction I preferred to deal with the literature and thought of Romanticism in its historical context.

When I was offered the opportunity to serve my university in a senior administrative position, many of my friends and colleagues could not understand my decision: for many contemporary academics, university administration signifies retirement from an active life of the mind. I accepted because I realized that I had become interested in the university generally as an institution, and I was eager to find out about that institution at first hand and not simply by observation from my faculty chair or in theory through my reading. At the same time, I was beginning to appreciate through my own research how profoundly the university in which I work is indebted to the institution as it evolved in Germany precisely during the period of Romanticism—that is, between the French Revolution and the defeat of Napoleon. Specifically, I learned from his brief monograph on *The Graduate College of Princeton* (1913) that my predecessor Andrew Fleming West, the distinguished first dean of the Graduate School and creator of the Graduate College at Princeton, was influenced in his conception of graduate education by Fichte's lectures on the scholarly vocation, which I discuss in chapter five. Accordingly, I found myself in the enviable position of being able to combine my scholarly interests and my service to the university in a very practical manner. I was also reassured by the biographical example of such Romantic academics as Fichte, Hegel, and Schleiermacher that it is possible to combine active scholarship with decanal responsibilities. Indeed, it is a principal thesis of this book that most of the major Romantics managed to link successful professional activity in a variety of careers with their writing and, moreover, that their writing was significantly shaped by the institutions they served.

From my desk in the dean's office I began to see my institution in manners that had previously not been clear to me—and, frankly, that had previously not interested me. My thoughts on the history of the university as an institution found expression in a few short pieces for general audiences—commencement addresses, speeches on various occasions, articles for alumni publications, and so forth. Gradually, moreover, my dealings with colleagues outside my own previous and limited frame of reference in the humanities gave me new insights into other fields, as well as a steadying foothold in those nonliterary fictions that my friends in, say, economics or physics regard as reality. My contacts with colleagues in the School of Engineering made it clear to me that they know as little about the history of their discipline and their image in the humanities as I had hitherto known about their work; this encouraged me to explore the manifestations of their activities in literature—a concern that resulted in a paper entitled "The Existential Anxieties of Engineering" (*The American Scholar* 53 [1984]: 197–218). My dealings with our Department of Geology and with the Program in the History of Science drew my interest to the history of geology and mining, and I began to understand the broader implications of the mining images that had caught my attention in Romantic literature. My interaction with colleagues and especially with graduate students in the School of Architecture enhanced my appreciation of the semiotics of buildings, and I began to see that Schinkel's Altes Museum in Berlin in a very important sense embodied the Romantic theories of aesthetics that I knew from various literary sources. Meanwhile, my conversations with friends from the Woodrow Wilson School of Public Affairs as well as the Departments of Politics and Sociology sharpened my understanding of social institutions in general. To put it another way: my own studies in several new fields of learning forced me to go back to school again and, in so doing, to reenact the experiences of the graduate students with whom I have had the pleasure of dealing over the past ten years.

By that time I had begun to understand that an institutional approach would offer precisely the perspective I had been seeking for a major study of German Romanticism. I have tried to clarify the reasons in chapter one. Quite simply, however, this book would never have been written—at least in its present conception and form—if I had not enjoyed the privilege of working within my own institution in a position that gave me the opportunity to deal on a daily basis, for better and for worse, with its administration in general and with its various programs, departments, and schools in particular.

There is one sense in which this work is not decanal. Even though it has grown quite long, it has only seven chapters—not ten. I came early to the conclusion that any one of my principal chapters could easily have developed into a book in itself. But to achieve the goal I wanted—that is, to demonstrate the interaction between the Romantic writers and a constellation of related social institutions—it was necessary to deal with these several institutions and their interrelations in a single volume and, in each case, at sufficient length to establish the fact of their impact on the images, language, and thought of the Romantic generation in Germany.

Initially I planned to limit myself to four institutions: mines, museums, madhouses, and universities—a conjunction that often elicited a snicker from colleagues when I told them about my studies. But by the time I had finished those sections, it became clear to me—from the literary texts as well as the biographical evidence—that at least one more institution was essential to my project: the law. As I worked my way into the history of law, I discovered that the lawyers with whom I chatted usually know as little about the long and distinguished history of their discipline as do the engineers or geologists. Moreover, when American lawyers are concerned with history, it is normally with the history of Anglo-Saxon common law—not with Roman law as it developed in modern Europe. (I am deeply indebted to Professor Gerald Strauss of Indiana University, whose generous responses to my queries on points of early modern German law constitute a model of scholarly collegiality.) In another sense, therefore, this book is intended not just as an analysis of institutions during the

Romantic period but also as a tribute to the fascinating history of several central institutions that still shape our daily lives.

For twenty-four years I have been offering a seminar in German Romanticism every other year here at Princeton, and I have benefited from the opportunity to test my ideas on many generations of graduate students. I have been stimulated by the papers they have written and by the dissertations that have emerged from that Princeton school of Romanticism: I think in particular of Steven Schaber, Ellis Finger, Hermann Weiss, Maria Tatar, Otto Johnston, Walter Wetzels, Clark Muenzer, Graydon Ekdahl, Kathryn Shailer Hanson, Scott Abbott, Katherine Faull Padilla, and Bonnie M. Sachs. In addition, Steven Huff performed knowledgeably as a research assistant in the summer of 1986 when I was working on Kleist and the law. I also wish to express my gratitude for the seemingly endless resources and to the ever cooperative staff of the Princeton University Library, especially Firestone Memorial Library and the Marquand Library of Art, where all the research for this book was carried out.

I have had the opportunity to expose several sections of this book at conferences and in lectures, and I have gratefully incorporated the suggestions I have received. A small portion of the material has already appeared in print. A substantially condensed version of chapter two ("Mines of the Soul: An Institutional Approach to Romanticism") was included in *English and German Romanticism: Cross-Currents and Controversies*, ed. James Pipkin (Heidelberg: Carl Winter, 1985). Two sections of chapter three appeared in other conference proceedings: "Kleists Werk im Lichte der zeitgenössischen Rechtskontroverse," in *Kleist-Jahrbuch 1987*, ed. Hans Joachim Kreutzer (Berlin: Erich Schmidt, 1987); and "The Lure of the Law in German Romanticism," in the *Acta* of the 1987 F.I.L.L.M. conference (Toronto: Univ. of Toronto Press, 1989). A few pages of chapter six ("Schinkel's Museum: The Romantic Temple of Art") were published with eight illustrations in *Proceedings of the American Philosophical Society* 131 (1987). I am grateful to the publishers for permission to adapt that material here in substantially revised and expanded form. All translations, unless otherwise indicated, are my own. I have provided renditions of verse passages cited in German only when the surrounding context does not constitute an adequate paraphrase.

My connection with Princeton University Press now covers exactly a quarter century, and under the directorship of Walter Lippincott the association continues to be as pleasant as it was under that of Herbert Bailey. I want to thank Robert Brown for his enthusiastic and thoughtful stewardship of my manuscript, which brought me the benefit of expert readings by two colleagues whose knowledge of Romanticism I respect enormously: Hans Eichner and Géza von Molnár. Few writers cannot profit from the attentions of an experienced editor, and indeed I have learned memorable lessons about my own style from Janet Wilson's sensible and sensitive scrutiny. Once again, Laury Egan has contributed a design consistent with the spirit of this book as well as the tradition of excellence that has long distinguished Princeton University Press.

My wife, Yetta, has been even more closely involved with this book than with earlier ones: she accompanied me to the mines of the Harz, to the premises of the former Imperial Court at Wetzlar, to Pinel's Salpêtrière in Paris, to Fichte's university at Jena and to Humboldt's in Berlin, to Schinkel's Altes Museum in Berlin, and to other sites mentioned in the book; and in each place she made the photographs (including the one on page two) that have served as visual images of the institutional history that concerned me. She shares the deep affection for a long-standing friend of our entire family that is only inadequately conveyed through the dedication.

Theodore Ziolkowski
Wyman House
Princeton, New Jersey
February 28, 1989

*German Romanticism
and Its Institutions*

Altes Museum (Berlin), 1823–1830, by Karl Friedrich Schinkel

CHAPTER ONE

# *The Institutional Approach*

THE POPULAR IMAGE of the Romantic poet in Germany might well have come straight out of an operetta with words by Eichendorff, stage set by Caspar David Friedrich, and music by Schumann. At the end of act one the hero, a young man who has recently left the university and is now setting out on a journey of education and adventure, pauses on a mountaintop and, looking back at the misty landscape while post horns echo in the distance, takes guitar in hand to extemporize a song about the beauty of nature, the quiet attractions of home, and the vaguely ominous lure of distant lands. This scenario could be based on *Ahnung und Gegenwart* (1815) or any number of other stories by Eichendorff. The scene is indelibly fixed in our imaginations by one of Friedrich's best-known paintings, *The Wanderer above the Sea of Fog* (1818), which has been used as the cover illustration for several books on German Romanticism;[1] but it could just as well be inspired by any of his other paintings of lonely figures gazing reverentially over vast landscapes. And the words that the young traveler sings might be any one of the familiar settings from Schumann's *Liederkreis* of poems by Eichendorff (1842).

The image has variations, of course. If the hero's beloved dies, he may loiter around graveyards like Novalis, waiting for epiphanies. Or if he feels rejected, deceived, and mocked by bourgeois society, as we see him in Offenbach's *Tales of Hoffmann*, he finds consolation ultimately in the embrace of his divine muse.

Now all three facets of the Romantic image reflect a piece of the truth. Eichendorff was fascinated by the ambivalence of a nature at once serene and threatening and by the tension between the security of home and the demonic lure of the unfamiliar. Novalis was philosophically and scientifically convinced that death represented an extension of life, and he saw that tranquil death reflected in the nocturnal side of nature that he por-

· 3 ·

trayed so vividly in his writings. And Hoffmann, like the characters of his fiction, sometimes teetered precariously on the line between reality and imagination, between bourgeois sobriety and the poet's frenzy.

Yet it pays to remind ourselves that these stories and poems (as well as the paintings and songs) are not a reflection of the artists' everyday reality but, rather, a projection of their hopes, aspirations, and beliefs. It is a mistake to identify Eichendorff too closely with the creatures of his imagination, whether it be the problematic Graf Friedrich of *Ahnung und Gegenwart* or the carefree ne'er-do-well of *Der Taugenichts*. We must not imagine that Novalis, despite the mystical experience he underwent at his fiancée's grave and immortalized in his "Hymnen an die Nacht," spent most of his time brooding morbidly in cemeteries. Offenbach—or at least Jules Barbier and Michel Carré, who wrote the play on which his libretto was based—perpetuated a misleading image by introducing Hoffmann himself as the hero of his own tales.

To put the matter most simply: Romantic literature presents us with the image of heroes who have the time and means to lounge on mountaintops, to undertake leisurely *Bildungsreisen*, or to spend their days and nights carousing in taverns. But the authors of these works were not themselves so carefree: they worked for a living. Eichendorff was a minor functionary in the Prussian civil service for thirty years. Novalis was a capable and diligent mining engineer and administrator for the state of Saxony. Hoffmann rose through the ranks of the Prussian judiciary to become a respected judge in the Supreme Court. And these three writers were representative, not exceptions. Most of the figures we associate with German Romanticism could not afford to be men of leisure. They worked as university professors, librarians, civil servants, doctors, lawyers, clerics, journalists, professional scientists, and at a multitude of other jobs. The chapter of Friedrich Schlegel's novel *Lucinde* that is entitled "In Praise of Idleness" ("Lob des Müßiggangs") represents wishful thinking rather than the reality of the man of letters whose collected works (in the critical edition) constitute some thirty-five substantial volumes.

At the same time, it would be a methodological error to read the Romantic writings as simply another example of the polarity between life and art, the bourgeois and the artist, the *vita activa* and the *vita contemplativa*. That polarization is a widely accepted topos of late nineteenth- and early twentieth-century literary scholarship, which seemed unable to think without seeing in all being a duality of Apollonian and Dionysian, of civilization and culture, of spirit and nature, of finitude and infinity, and the other pairings that embellish the title pages of German *Geistes-geschichte* as well as American history of ideas. It has been used alike by friends and critics of Romanticism to characterize the movement. But the Romantics themselves had a more complex view of reality. Indeed, it was one of the principal aims of that generation to overcome the split between mind and matter, rationalism and sentimentalism, reason and emotion, which characterized the eighteenth century. Romanticism discovered history precisely because, in that temporal dimension, the kind of change, development, and synthesis could take place that was exemplified by Fichte's "productive imagination" and the energy of Hegel's dialectics. If Romantic writers projected an idealized life in their works, it did not imply a rejection of the "reality" in which they spent their days. Rather, the relation between life and literature can be regarded more fruitfully as a productive interaction between two complementary realms.

Recently several scholars have begun to help us understand more fully the importance of the professional careers of individual German Romantic writers. Wolfgang Frühwald traced Eichendorff's activities as a civil servant.[2] Gerhard Schulz provided an excellent survey of Novalis's studies in law and mining as well as his administrative career.[3] And Wulf Segebrecht presented new evidence from Hoffmann's legal activities to clarify his view of law and literature.[4] In all three cases it is the implicit or explicit assumption that the popular image of the Romantic poet as isolated from "reality" and incompetent in everyday life is wrong: Eichendorff, Novalis, and Hoffmann were in fact capable professionals in down-to-earth jobs. It is a mistake to view their professional careers as an unpleasant necessity that distracted them from a poetry that they perceived as more important. In all three cases the writers derived a great deal of satisfaction from their professional activities, and the evidence suggests a fruitful interaction between their professional lives and their literary works.

I believe that it is possible to move to a higher level of generalization—from literary biography to literary history—by looking at the Romantics in the context of the institutions that shaped them and that they in turn helped to shape. It is in institutions—family, school, church, professional activity, government—that individuals come together and reveal group characteristics that transcend the specific. These institutions embody the assumptions that individuals share concerning their society and that, as unconscious assumptions and images, enter the works of those who also happen to be writers.

To the extent that institutions change with time, an institutional approach can enable us to set off Romanticism against the periods that preceded and followed it. In the pages that follow, "Romanticism" is not meant to imply any specific and rigorous definition. It is intended, rather, as a historical code word to designate the social, cultural, and intellectual life in German-speaking lands between the French Revolution and the years following the defeat of Napoleon at Waterloo. (Accordingly the term is capitalized throughout in order to distinguish historical Romanticism clearly from typological romanticism, which is not restricted to a specific period.) This book is based on the premise that all the cultural products of a given period are colored by the assumptions of certain shared institutions that transcend such arbitrary classifications as Classicism and Romanticism. Indeed, Anglo-American scholars have never made the distinction between *Klassik* and *Romantik* that characterizes most German literary histories of the period.

To the extent, finally, that institutions respond to local circumstances, an institutional approach can enable us to set off *German* Romanticism against contemporary developments in other countries. As we shall see, for instance, the pace of industrialization produced a radically different attitude toward mining in Germany and England, while the nature of legal training attracted different minds in Germany and France.

## "Institution" in Literary Theory

The term "institution" has become a shibboleth in a decade bent on a "new" historicism and a social history of literature. For that reason it needs to be clarified that I am concerned with institutions from a standpoint appreciably different from that of much contemporary American and German literary theory.

As early as 1946 Harry Levin was disturbed by "the misleading dichotomy between substance and form, which permits literary historians, like Parrington, to dismiss 'belletristic philandering,' and esthetic impressionists, like Mr. R. P. Blackmur, to dispose of 'separable content'...."[5] Reviewing the history of sociological criticism since Taine, Levin postulates that "the relations between literature and society are reciprocal. Literature is not only the effect of social causes; it is also the cause of social effects" (660). To address the "organic character of this relationship" (664), Levin proposes what he calls an institutional method.

· 6 ·

The truth, though it has long been obscured by a welter of personalities and technicalities, is that literature has always been an institution. Like other institutions, the church or the law, it cherishes a unique phase of human experience and controls a special body of precedents and devices; it tends to incorporate a self-perpetuating discipline, while responding to the main currents of each succeeding period; it is continually accessible to all the impulses of life at large, but it must translate them into its own terms and adapt them to its peculiar forms.

Once we understand "how art may belong to society and yet be autonomous within its own limits," he concludes, we are "no longer puzzled by the apparent polarity of social and formal criticism" (664).

The analogy to church and state has been a governing image in American "institutional" literary criticism. In the chapter on "Literary Genres" in the Wellek-Warren *Theory of Literature* (1948), Austin Warren, referring to Levin's essay, wrote that "the literary kind is an 'institution'—as Church, University, or State is an institution. It exists, not as an animal exists or even as a building, chapel, library, or capitol, but as an institution exists. One can work through, express himself through, existing institutions, create new ones, or get on, so far as possible, without sharing in polities or rituals; one can also join, but then reshape, institutions."[6]

While Levin and Warren applied the concept of institution to literary genres, more recent critics have expanded the analogy to embrace the literary establishment as a whole. Frank Kermode, in an essay on "Institutional Control of Interpretation," has argued that literary criticism is controlled by "a professional community which has authority (not undisputed) to define (or indicate the limits of) a subject; to impose valuations and validate interpretations."[7] This institution of literary and critical scholarship displays an "analogy with ecclesiastical and other institutions" (84) to the extent that institutions "confer value and privilege upon texts, and license modes of interpretation" (86). In a number of writings Stanley Fish has advanced the notion of the "interpretive community" as an institution. "The mental operations we can perform are limited by the institution in which we are *already* embedded. These institutions precede us, and it is only by inhabiting them, or being inhabited by them, that we have access to the public and conventional senses they make."[8] Interpretation is an activity that is "determined by the literary institution which at any one time will authorize only a finite number of interpretative strategies" (342). These strategies are not written down but constitute a set of unwritten rules that are understood by the community consisting of graduate students and faculty. It is precisely this community whose history Gerald Graff recently set out to detail in *Professing Literature*.[9] Defining his topic as "a history of academic literary studies in the United States" from 1828 to the present (1), Graff explains: "In calling this book an institutional history, I mean to underscore that its concern is not only with particular scholarly and critical practices, but also with what has happened to those practices once they have become institutionalized in modern universities" (5).

Alvin Kernan, finally, returned to the religious analogy but expanded his understanding to encompass a much broader literary community than Kermode, Fish, or Graff. "Both institutions center on a body of sacred texts, have established a canon of authorized works and an unauthoritative but always troublesome apocrypha, have built up a body of doctrinal interpretation—theology in one case, criticism in the other—and have made strenuous and extensive efforts to define and fix orthodoxy."[10] For Kernan, literature is "a changing, man-made social institution rather than a natural or cultural given" (16). "Like other institutions, literature has developed its established roles, or social identities, chiefly that of the poet, but increasingly in the eighteenth century and afterwards those of the critic, the scholar, the teacher, the reader, the man of letters, the publisher, the reviewer" (22). He appeals for an institutional history of literature that would correspond to the "social histories of great institutions such as the family, the law, systems of punishment, religion, and the state" (29).

For all their shadings of definition, these various "institutional" approaches to literature share one common feature. Whether concerned like Levin and Warren with literary genres or like later critics with the literary establishment, they are looking at literature from *within* the institution or interpretive community. They appropriate the notion of an institution in an effort to help us understand the functioning of generic coherence or the interpretive community or the academic profession. In general, these Anglo-American institutionalists look beyond literature to other social institutions only for purposes of analogy: literature, as Graff has it, is their profession.

We are struck by a conspicuous difference when we turn to the European, and mainly German, scholars who also profess an "institutional" approach to literature.[11] "Institution theory," as defined by such theorists as Peter Bürger and the contributors to the Netherlands-based journal *Poetics*, has at least three characteristics that distinguish it from the views considered above. First, it is concerned not primarily with literature but more generally with "art." Second, the work of art is of interest not as an absolute but as a "commodity." Finally, the entire enterprise of institution theory looks at literature from the outside as simply another social institution of bourgeois society.

The notion of the artwork as commodity goes back at least to Karl Marx. Various German aestheticians appropriated the technological rhetoric quite early. The late nineteenth-century theoretician of literary naturalism, Arno Holz, while not a Marxist, was inspired to determine a fundamental law governing literature that would be as rigorous as Marx's economic laws of society and Darwin's evolutionary laws of nature. In his tract on art and the laws governing it (1891) he concluded: "Art has the tendency to become nature: it does so in accordance with the available means of reproduction and their manipulation"[12]—a view that he summed up in the pseudo-scientific formula "Art = Nature – x." And Walter Benjamin, in the title of one of his most famous essays, analyzed "The Work of Art in the Age of Its Technical Reproduceability" (1936),[13] arguing that such art has been deprived by technology of the "cultic *aura*" that characterizes all true art. But commodity aesthetics received its first full exposition in the so-called Critical Theory of the Frankfurt School. As Max Horkheimer and Theodor W. Adorno formulated it in their *Dialectic of Enlightenment* (1947), Critical Theory begins with the assumption that society is based on the simple exchange of commodities. As cultural products are transformed by this relentless economy into commodities, they are gradually emptied of any binding meaning and taken over by a "culture industry," which mindlessly turns out cultural fetishes for the "new barbarism."[14]

Institution theory, as it developed in the seventies in the wake of Jürgen Habermas's influential analysis of structural changes in public life,[15] accepted commodity aesthetics as an assumption. For Peter Bürger, "There can be no doubt that artworks in a bourgeois society are treated as commodities."[16] Without any reference to, or apparent awareness of, the Anglo-American tradition, he appropriates the religious analogy. "The institution of art/literature in a fully developed bourgeois society may be considered as a functional equivalent of the institution of religion"[17] to the extent that both postulate a radical separation of two realms (human/divine and everyday/poetic), thereby justifying a view of the aesthetic work as autonomous. Carrying the Marxist analysis a step further, Cees J. van Rees, in his introduction to a special number of *Poetics* devoted to "Empirical Sociology of Literature and the Arts," argues that "the value assessment of literary texts (artworks) is the privilege of literary (cultural) institutions."[18] Defining the literary institution as the totality of agents performing specific tasks in the production, distribution, or promotion of literary works, Van Rees explains that "institutional analysis makes it plain that the activities of all literary institutions jointly contribute . . . to the kind of (surplus) value an artwork is thought to possess" (296).

Unlike the American critics, who focus on the institutional nature of the specific work or of the literary establishment itself (academic, critical, publishing, etc.), the German institutional approach extends its field to "social determinants, macrosociological categories" (299). As Bürger argues, his concept of *Institution Kunst* ("art as an institution") is concerned not with the specific social arrangements that mediate between work and public but rather in "the epochal function determinations of art in its social contingency."[19] Although a sociology of theater or publishing has as much justification as, say, a sociology of law, it cannot help us to understand the social function of art. "The addition of investigations of individual cases cannot replace the theoretical framework which in the first place makes possible the study of the social function of art" (175). It is characteristic of the German institutional method that its proponents remain so stubbornly in the realm of the theoretical that they rarely descend to the specific instances of individual artists or works and deal instead with "art in late capitalistic society" on the same level of generality as, for instance, with "the state in late capitalist society" (180).

## "Institution" in Sociological Theory

While we can learn a great deal about the function of genre or the profession of literature from the American institutional critics and while our understanding of the role of art in the society of the past two centuries has been enhanced by the German institutional theorists, the approach that I am proposing here takes a middle ground between those two methods. I intend to deal neither with literature (or the literary establishment) as an institution nor, at the most general level, with the function of art as a commodity in bourgeois society but, rather, with the interaction between the literary work and society as manifested specifically in five social institutions. Let us begin by defining the term "institution" for our own purposes. In his essay on "Self-Reliance" (1841), and with such examples in mind as Caesar's Rome and Luther's Reformation, Emerson observed that "an institution is the lengthened shadow of one man."[20] Modern sociology also acknowledges the role of the individual in the founding of institutions. "It is a curious fact that despite the anonymity of the typical institutional man, institutions are neither brought into existence nor advanced in this way," writes James K. Feibleman. Citing Loyola and the Jesuit order, he continues: "It is the original thinker, the strong man who is able to stand the most alone, who gives the institution life or advances."[21] Let us keep in mind the role of the individual in shaping institutions, for we shall be observing that function repeatedly as we look at German Romantic thinkers in the context of their institutions.

Yet for purposes of analysis it is useful to adopt a more neutral sociological understanding. Generally speaking, most sociologists agree that institutions occupy a place structurally between the individual and the society as a whole. Just as psychology views as its proper object the individual, and anthropology surveys the entire society and culture, sociology is concerned first and foremost with institutions. Talcott Parsons, defining "institution" as "a complex of institutionalized role integrates which is of strategic structural significance in the social system in question," states that "the theory of institutional behavior . . . is essentially sociological theory."[22] Shmuel N. Eisenstadt, in the entry on "Social Institutions" in the *International Encyclopedia of the Social Sciences*, defines his topic as "regulative principles which organize most of the activities of individuals in a society into definable organizational patterns from the point of view of some of the perennial basic problems of any society or ordered social life."[23] And Feibleman begins his study: "By an institution, then, we shall mean that subdivision of society which consists in human beings in groups established together with their customs, laws and material tools, and organized around a central aim or purpose" (20–21).

Sociology is properly concerned with the manner in which institutions are established and organized to satisfy certain basic human needs. For Bronislaw Malinowski an institution is the structure through which a group such as hunters or manufacturers or religious leaders translates its collective purpose into activities.[24] Lloyd Vernor Ballard opens his book on *Social Institutions* with the italicized definition: "*Social institutions are sets of organized human relationships purposively established by the common will*. As such, they may be regarded as the end-products of social processes, since it is their specific function to canalize the conduct of the group in action."[25] A recent German lexicon of sociological terms provides a similar definition: "Institution is what we call the form of order—culturally validated, meaningfully coherent, and publicly guaranteed by law and ethics—in which the communal life of human beings expresses itself."[26] Thus, to anticipate the present enterprise, we can say that society's need for justice organizes itself in the institution of law, the need for education in the institution of the university, the need for health in the institution of the mental hospital, the need for culture in the institution of the museum, and the need for raw material in the institution of the mine. As Feibleman summarizes: "Somewhere between the individual and his culture, perhaps because of his essentially tool-making nature, there interposes itself a structure which is aimed to make the greatest possible allowance for his enterprise yet furnish it with continuity, and the name for this structure is: the institution" (139).

What matters for our purposes is the insight of sociology, as stated by Malinowski, that "a culture functions therefore by means of a system of related institutions" (35). If we hope to understand a society or a culture—e.g., German Romanticism—then we do well to approach it by means of its constitutive institutions and their connections. "It is the institution rather than the human individual or the culture which calls for examination when we try to understand society," as Feibleman puts it (245). "No man contributes to his culture directly, nor even to his society, for that matter. He makes his contribution through the institution which in turn serves the society, which in turn is part of the culture. Thus his work may eventually reach cultural importance, but he does not serve it directly, only via the medium of the institution" (382).

The present undertaking is therefore at once more general than that of the American institutionalists, who limit their interest to literature as an institution, and more restricted in focus than that of the European social theorists, who consider society as a whole in such large units as "art."[27] It is the aim of the following chapters to explore the extent to which German Romantic writers and thinkers, as participants in certain social institutions of their age, were shaped by the assumptions of those institutions and, in turn, helped to shape the institutions into what we now recognize as their characteristically modern form.[28] I propose to approach that goal, first, by tracing the emergence of the institutions in light of the social and intellectual climate of the age and, then, by analyzing representative literary texts for evidences of those institutions.

I hope it will become clear in the course of the following chapters why I chose to focus on the institutions of mine, law, madhouse, university, and museum. In fact, these five institutions forced themselves upon my attention because, wherever I turned in my study of Romanticism (textual analysis, biography, cultural background), I kept running into them. There turned out to be in each case a powerful local (German) and historical reason for broad public interest in the institution. Each emerged from the Romantic era in a form conspicuously different from that with which it entered the age. And each institution embodies a more general concern: e.g., the Romantic obsession with mines reflects institutionally the attitude of the age toward science and technology; the debate about law is informed by the Romantic understanding of society and the state; the nineteenth-century university emerged as the institutionalization of Romantic theories of knowledge and *Bildung*.

In short, these five institutions, for a variety of reasons still to be determined, are central to Romanticism. Individual responses to the institutions may vary widely, but the shared institutions provide *all* contemporaries with certain central and often unconscious assumptions that transcend the artificial and arbitrary divisions into "Romantic," "Classical," and "Neoclassical" that have been imposed on the age by subsequent historians with their compulsion to organize according to their respective ideologies. The question that must be answered through detailed scrutiny of texts and institutions, then, is the extent to which the writings of the Romantics were affected—in theme, substance, vocabulary, imagery—by the institutions they inhabited as members of their society and, conversely, what insights they brought to their institutions from the *Zeitgeist* of Romanticism.

## "Institution" in Romantic Thought

The endeavor, I have come to believe, is thoroughly Romantic in its conception. Romanticism believed in nothing so fervently as in a central force that permeated and colored all the undertakings of the age. Hegel, in the lectures on the history of philosophy that he delivered nine times between 1805–1806 and 1829–1830, established the principle of a "Spirit of the Times," that is: "*one* specific being, character, that permeates all aspects and represents itself in political affairs and in all else as in various elements; it is *one* condition that is coherent in all its parts and whose various aspects, as manifold and random as they may appear, as much as they seem to contradict one another, nevertheless contain nothing heterogeneous to the basis."[29] He elaborates further that the relationship of the various parts—politics, constitutional government, art, religion, philosophy—"is not such that they are the causes of philosophy or, vice versa, that philosophy is their cause; but rather they all have one and the same common root—the Spirit of the Times" (74). In the lectures on the philosophy of history that he delivered fives times from 1822–1823 to 1830–1831 he returned to this idea in terms that precisely anticipate the modern sociological distinction between a society or culture and its institutions. "The State itself is animated by this Spirit in all its particulars—wars, institutions, and so forth."[30] The *Volksgeist*, or national genius, which finds its concrete expression in history, is "the common stamp of its religion, its political constitution, its ethics, its legal system, its morals, even its science, art, and technical skill" (87).

Similarly, Varnhagen von Ense commented in connection with the Prussian reforms that "the impulse and the power of the whole . . . seems coextensive with the spiritual content of the times in the entire breadth of the movement."[31] Novalis, albeit rather more poetically, expressed the same thought in one of the aphorisms of *Blüthenstaub* (1798): "Courts of law, theater, palace, church, government, public assemblies, academies, lecture series, and so forth are, as it were, the special inner organs of the mystical state-individual."[32] Friedrich Schlegel stated his belief in a unifying principle underlying the entire culture of every age in many of his writings. In the preface to *Die Griechen und Römer* (1797) he observed that the clue to seeming puzzles, inconsistencies, or gaps in the history of art can often be found in the ethical and political circumstances ("Sitten und Staatengeschichte") of antiquity: "for the art, the ethics, and the government of the Greeks are so inextricably intertwined that their understanding cannot be disentangled."[33] He put it most poetically perhaps in the poem "Die Gebüsche" (from the cycle *Abendröte* of 1801):

> Durch alle Töne tönet
> Im bunten Erdentraume
> Ein leiser Ton gezogen
> Für den, der heimlich lauschet.[34]

(Through all the sounds of earth's many-splendored dream resounds one gentle tone for him who listens secretly.)

If the spirit of the whole manifests itself in its institutions, then the
appropriate way in which to seek to understand the whole is not on the
abstract level of social theory but through those very institutions. Already
Vico, in the *Scienza Nuova* and elsewhere, had insisted that the literary
scholar must come to grips with institutions in order to understand
works. "Since the ideas of things are represented by words, philology
must first treat the history of things. Whence it appears that philologists
study human government, customs, laws, institutions, intellectual disciplines, and the mechanical arts."[35] But it was a writer of the Romantic
age, Madame de Staël, who systematically adapted that principle to practice in a work with the characteristic title *De la littérature considérée dans
ses rapports avec les institutions sociales* (1800). "I propose to examine what
is the influence of religion, morals, and laws on literature, and what is
the influence of literature on religion, morals, and laws. There exist, in
the French language, treatises on the art of writing and on the principles
of taste, treatises that leave nothing to be desired; but it appears to me
that the morals and political causes that modify the spirit of literature
have not been sufficiently analyzed."[36] In his lectures on the scholarly
vocation (*Über die Bestimmung des Gelehrten*, 1794) Fichte designated the
institution (*Stand*) as the instrument whereby the individual "is able to
restore to society what society has done for us."[37] In a similar spirit the
legal historian Savigny declared in his programmatic statement of 1814:
"In general, everyone will convince himself through a thorough study of
literary history how little among its manifestations can in truth be attributed to separate individuals, independent of the forces and strivings of
the age and the nation."[38] It was this principle that informed his epoch-
making history of Roman law during the Middle Ages—a work truly
exemplary in its Romantic character.

Goethe, too, was representative of the age in his belief that we penetrate most rapidly to the understanding of a historical period through its
institutions. As he observed in *Dichtung und Wahrheit* in an account of
his preparations for writing the historical drama *Götz von Berlichingen*:
"Ultimately the organization of the courts and the armies provides the
most precise insight into the organization of any kingdom."[39] Goethe,
who was himself actively involved in many institutions of the duchy of
Saxe-Weimar, understood that it was only through institutions that the

contributions of brilliant individuals and creative groups could be made productive for society as a whole.[40] One of the most remarkable statements of this conviction may be found in a talk that he prepared in 1795 for the Friday Society in Weimar on cultural activities in that ducal residence ("Über die verschiedenen Zweige der hiesigen Thätigkeit").[41] Having visited an exhibition of the local art academy, Goethe was stirred to reflect on the general benefits of such public institutions. "Neither an artist nor a school of art should be considered in isolation: he is connected with the country in which he lives, with the public of his nation, with his century; if he wishes to have an effect and to earn a position and a living through his work, he must be guided by the times and work for its needs."

In the hope of inspiring the other members of the Friday Society to a systematic study of social institutions and their role in cultural life, Goethe provided a rapid survey of the more prominent institutions that contributed to intellectual and cultural life in Weimar and Jena: from the visual arts (including architecture) to music, theater, and dance; from the physical skills (riding and fencing) by way of gardening and forestry to the educational institutions, journalism, and scientific academies; from the Jena museum to the sciences and technology, including astronomy, mining, and topography. In his concluding sentence Goethe promises for the next gathering "a few general observations." It would be valuable to have those observations from Goethe's hand, but he never returned to his undertaking in any systematic way. However, from his various statements it is clear that he both shared and exemplified the views of the age on the central function of social institutions as the vehicle through which the individual makes his contributions to society and which, in turn, have an undeniable effect upon the individual by training and shaping his assumptions, his thought, and his very means of expression.

This lesson has not been lost on modern students of Romanticism. At the turn of the century Ricarda Huch, in her epoch-making book, *Die Romantik: Blütezeit, Ausbreitung und Verfall* (1899–1902), depicted Romanticism as a phenomenon ranging from literature by way of philosophy and religion to science, medicine, and politics. A decade later Friedrich Meinecke spoke for historicism when he wrote that we can never do justice to Romanticism "if we see in it nothing but a literary movement with various secondary effects; rather, it had an effect on the totality of life—not only on the life of the individual but also on his relationship to the great forces of religion, society, and the state."[42] This same tendency to understand Romanticism as a movement in which pervasive powers or forces manifest themselves in various non-literary forms has been evident in the interdisciplinary symposia that have been held periodically since the end of World War II.[43]

All too often, however, the very critics who acknowledge the Hegelian *Zeitgeist* pervading all aspects of Romantic culture qualify their insights by the assumption that this unity was sought only in the realm of the spirit. It was the central thesis of Henri Brunschwig's important book, *La crise de l'état prussien à la fin du XVIIIᵉ siècle et la genèse de la mentalité romantique* (1947), that the Romantics turned to literature and its "escape into the miraculous" because they had no other outlet for their energies in a closed society. And this view has been frequently reiterated. As Roger Cardinal puts it, "Romanticism sprang up within this context of physical constriction and enforced speculativeness; its adherents turned from the finite, immutable, real world of philistine conservatism to orient their thoughts in the one direction where progress was possible, that of the ideal and the infinite."[44] Isaiah Berlin has made the same assertion, dividing German Romantics into a "left wing," who "looked upon the traditional forces of authority or hierarchical organization as the most oppressive of social forces," and the others, who "despised public life in principle, and occupied themselves with the cultivation of the inner spirit."[45]

I have no wish to deny the Romantic tendency toward inwardness, which Novalis in *Blüthenstaub* called "the mysterious inward way" ("der geheimnisvolle Weg nach Innen").[46] But I believe that we accept Romanticism too uncritically on its own *literary* terms if we fail to take into account its interaction with the "real" world of education, technology, law, and the other institutions in which its chief representatives were educated, lived, and worked. The Romantic writer, in short, stood *between* reality and the ideal, oriented not only toward the infinite and the miraculous but also toward the social actuality of his times. As the following chapters reveal time and again, the Romantics sought to realize their dreams not only in their poetry but also through their institutions. Without an appreciation of this complementarity and tension between literature and life we run a serious risk of misjudging the era and its achievements.

# CHAPTER TWO

# The Mine:
# Image of the Soul

## THE ROMANCE OF MINING IN GERMANY

GERMAN LITERATURE of the Romantic age is crawling with so many miners—sporting their leather aprons, black jackets, green felt caps, and uttering the traditional salutation *Glück auf!*—that the unwary reader might well believe he had blundered into a surrealistic library in which the history of literature is interspersed at random with the history of technology. The most familiar example occurs in Novalis's *Heinrich von Ofterdingen* (1802), where the old Bohemian miner expatiates on the merits of his profession before leading Heinrich and his traveling companions on a spelunking expedition into the nearby caves. But there is no shortage of cases, ranging from the mysterious man of the mountains in Ludwig Tieck's early tale "Der Runenberg" (1802) to the mining community in his late novella "Der Alte vom Berge" (1828), from the pious miner in Achim von Arnim's *Die Kronenwächter* (1817) to the various young students of mining who people the tales that constitute Henrich Steffens's *Die vier Norweger* (1828). And miners are not limited to Romantic fiction. Zacharias Werner's drama *Martin Luther, oder: die Weihe der Kraft* (1807) begins in a mine and ends with a miners' chorus; Theodor Körner's "romantic opera" *Die Bergknappen* (1811) takes place entirely among miners and mountain sprites; and the first act of Clemens Brentano's "historical-romantic drama" *Die Gründung Prags* (1815) culminates when Libussa, presented by miners with a block of silver, has an ecstatic vision (in five strophes of *ottava rima*) of the gold, silver, and mineral mines that will enrich her empire. Körner wrote several poems in praise of mining and the miner's life; Joseph von Eichendorff deals with the demonic as well as the devout aspects of mining in his verses; and one of Brentano's most powerful lyrics comprises the lament of a miner from the depths of his mine shaft.

The legend of the mines at Falun—concerning the young miner who, on his wedding day, vanishes in the copper mines and whose body, perfectly preserved in the vitriolated water, is discovered fifty years later and identified by his now aged fiancée—preoccupied the imagination of the age so obsessively that it generated not just classic prose versions by Johann Peter Hebel and E.T.A. Hoffmann but also at least a dozen verse narratives. Arnim and Brentano's anthology, *Des Knaben Wunderhorn* (1806–1808), contains songs from the realm of mining (e.g., "Der unterirdische Pilger"); the Grimm brothers' collection of *Deutsche Sagen* (1816–1818) begins with three tales about mining; and perhaps the best known of their *Kinder- und Hausmärchen* (1812–1815) concerns a young woman who goes to live with seven dwarfs who mine gold and other ores in the mountains. The fact that virtually every major writer as well as numerous lesser ones took up the figure of the miner and the image of the mine helps to distinguish German Romantic literature not only from German literature of the ages preceding and following but also—despite such isolated examples as "the lonely Miner" of Wordsworth's *The Excursion*—from contemporary English Romantic literature.

If we begin by asking why the image of mining appealed so strongly to young writers in Germany between 1790 and 1820, one reason suggests itself immediately: an astonishing number of them were actually trained as mining engineers. The exemplary figure here, as in so many respects, was Goethe, although he had not studied mining formally; he was a jurist by training. But when, as a young administrator in the duchy of Saxe-Weimar, he was charged with reopening the silver mines at Ilmenau, he devoted himself energetically to the technological as well as the administrative aspects of the assignment.[1] The experience not only complemented his lifelong interest in geology; it also inspired one of his finest poems ("Ilmenau"), furnished an important setting for *Wilhelm Meisters Lehrjahre*, which takes place partly in Ilmenau and features a comic dialogue among miners (bk. 11, ch. 4), and in *Wilhelm Meisters Wanderjahre* provides a new profession for Jarno (now known as Montan), who is Wilhelm's host at a miners' festival (bk. 11, ch. 9).[2] Novalis, also a jurist by training, began his career as an administrator in the royal saltworks of Saxony—an office that included certain mines in its purview. Realizing that he needed more technological training to do his job, he enrolled in 1797 in the royal mining academy at Freiberg and then worked until his death in 1801 as an inspector of saltworks and mines.[3] Clemens Brentano studied mining for one semester at Bonn in 1794 and then worked for a year as an apprentice for his uncle, *Bergrat* Karl von Laroche, director of the saltworks at Schönebeck near Magdeburg, before he went on to Halle in 1797 as a student of cameralistics. Eichendorff attended courses on mining as part of his cameralistic studies at Halle. Henrich Steffens and Theodor Körner both studied at Freiberg, as did such contemporaries as Alexander von Humboldt, Franz von Baader, and Gotthilf Heinrich Schubert.

Indeed, it is safe to say that it would have been difficult, between 1790 and 1810, to assemble a group of intellectuals in any of the centers of German Romanticism without including at least one or two guests who were somehow involved with mining. Alexander von Humboldt spent several years as an *Oberbergmeister* in the Prussian Department of Mines before setting out on his scientific expeditions. During his years as a mine inspector he published several works on the subject, invented a safety lamp as well as rescue apparatus, and founded a free school for miners. Baron Karl vom Stein began his career in the Prussian civil service as an administrator of mines in Westphalia. Franz von Baader pursued an active career as a mining engineer (until in 1820 he retired as director of the Bavarian mines) while he was developing his mystical theology. Johann Friedrich Reichardt, who had been royal composer and *Kapellmeister* at the court of Frederick the Great, retired to Halle, where from 1796 he was inspector of the saltworks while conducting one of the most influential salons of the day at his home at Giebichenstein. Mining was so fashionable a subject that Dorothea von Schlözer, the first woman to earn a Ph.D. at Göttingen (in 1787), was examined for her degree not only on Horace, algebra, and architecture but also on mining (*Berg-Werks-Wissenschaft*).[4]

This fascination with mining carried over from the scientists and engineers to those who had no professional commitment to the subject. Jean Paul, who grew up in the mountain region on the Bavarian-Bohemian border, spent his life among miners and frequently used mining as an ironic image for human life; he liked to designate himself, as in the novel *Hesperus* (1795), as the "chief miner" (*Berg-Hauptmann*) whose job it is to explore those human mines.[5] Hölderlin, who had no direct connection with mining, also employed the mine as an image of the human soul. Thus in *Hyperion* (1797) the young hero tells his friend Bellarmin that he can no longer remain in Greece and intends to flee to some valley of the Alps or the Pyrenees: "in the depths of the mountain world the mystery of our heart shall rest, like the precious stone in its shaft."⁶ Similarly Joseph Görres, in the introduction to his anthology *Die teutschen Volks-bücher* (1807), compares the essential spirit of the people to a "dross-free King of Metal" ("schlackenlosen Metallkönig") that remains evident through all the contaminations of time and circumstance.⁷

The descent into a mine rapidly became a requisite of the walking tour that every German student undertook. On the Whitsuntide excursion that Tieck and Wackenroder made in 1793—an event often cited to mark the beginning of the Romantic movement in Germany—the two young friends visited iron mines in Upper Franconia and recorded the event in ecstatic letters to their parents.⁸ In 1799 Friedrich Carl von Savigny, the future founder of the historical study of law, dressed up in miner's garb and descended to a mine at Freiberg, where he experienced an archetypal epiphany on the mysteries of life beneath the surface of the earth. "The sense of a subterranean existence, the unusual attire, the special jargon, and the singular greeting—everything works harmoniously together to transpose one forcefully into the unique circle of life and feeling of these people."⁹ Heinrich von Kleist passed through Freiberg a year later and, seeing the famous mines in the distance, was sorely tempted to visit them; but the urgent business that had prompted his mysterious trip to Würzburg prevented him from doing so. However, when Eichendorff traveled from Halle to Hamburg in 1805, he paused in the Harz Mountains long enough to don miner's attire and, lamp in hand, make the now ritual descent "down into the underworld" ("in die Unterwelt hinab"), where "with pious reverence" he contemplated the desolate night of the great caverns and listened with awe to the monotonous dripping that shaped the stalagmites into astonishingly human forms.¹⁰

That same year Adolph Müller in Halle was also dreaming of a trip to Freiberg to experience "the subterranean hieroglyphs and their interpretation." "Anyone who wishes to do so can investigate all life and all organized cultivation [*Bildung*] down below; although down there everything has ceased to live, or rather has just made a pause in life, one can now observe the moment at rest."¹¹ Müller never got to Freiberg, but in 1806 he did go on a field trip to the mines in the Harz with his professor, Henrich Steffens. Small wonder that Friedrich Gottschalck's *Taschen-buch für Reisende in den Harz* (1817), a guidebook widely consulted by students as well as such foreign travelers as Washington Irving, strongly recommended the descent into the silver mines near Clausthal.[12] When Heinrich Heine made his journey to the Harz region in 1824, he followed Gottschalck's advice and ventured down into two mines clad in what he called "the dark delinquent's costume" and creeping on all fours.[13] Recovering from his initial anxiety, he emerged from his tour with a favorable impression of the miners' character and culture. Yet at this point, thirty years after the earliest Romantic descents, the mystery is coupled with irony as Heine watches himself reenacting what had by then become a ritual—even down to the mixed sensation of anxiety and reverence.

. . .

So far our roll call of miners in German Romantic literature, as well as the list of writers who studied mining or visited mines, suggests little more than a symptom. If the fact is to be meaningful, we must go beyond statistics to ask why there should have been, in Germany, this sudden surge of interest in mining and whether that interest has any literary significance.

To no small extent, of course, popular interest in mining was stimulated by the exciting developments in geology, a science enjoying from 1790 to 1820 what the author of a standard history of the subject called its "Heroic Age."[14] Geology was the most popular science with the British public in the early nineteenth century—the only one cultivated to any extent at Oxford and Cambridge.[15] In Germany the lively dispute between the so-called Neptunists and Vulcanists concerning the formation of the earth was so much in the public mind that Goethe felt free to introduce it as a major topic in the second part of his *Faust*. The widespread interest in geology stemmed in part from its disturbing implications for one's understanding of the cosmogonical teachings of the Bible—the controversy between Genesis and geology. But it was not the least of geology's charms that it could be pursued out-of-doors and not in gloomy laboratories, a circumstance that appealed to the new Romantic appreciation of nature.

The European public had only recently, in the second half of the eighteenth century, discovered the pleasures of mountain-climbing, an effort undertaken initially in pursuit of the sublime.[16] Just as mountain elevations had become the favorite goal for hikers in English excursion poems, the mountain similarly provided the generic locus for the meditations of the classical German elegy as it was developed by Schiller, Goethe, and their contemporaries. Inevitably the initial obsession with the outsides of mountains was transferred to their inner recesses, and it became a vogue to arrange tours and picnics in such reasonably accessible spots as the Beatus Cave above Lake Thun.[17] The Swiss landscape painter Caspar Wolf gained the nickname *Höhlenwolf* because in the 1770s he painted so many caverns for an eager public. The speleological motif showed up with increasing frequency in the art of the later eighteenth century. Indeed, it sometimes became an obsession. At the turn of the century the Swiss speleologist Carl Lang set out to explore all the famous mines and caves of Europe, which he regarded as "halls and chambers consecrated to tranquillity."[18]

While the scientific interest in geology and the cultural fascination with caves contributed to public receptivity for mining, its development was driven mainly by the requirements of the Industrial Revolution.[19] For centuries the demand for metals had been restricted principally to agricultural and military needs: for plowshares, scythes, arrowpoints, swords, and other tools and weapons. As new industrial uses were found for metals—in machines, bridges, railways, and buildings—the demand for ores increased dramatically. In the 1790s the perfection of the steam engine expedited the expansion of mining because it solved the problem of water control in mines and facilitated the underground hauling and raising of ores. At the same time, the coal industry began to expand rapidly as it was discovered that coke could be used rather than charcoal in the smelting and manufacture of iron.

The Industrial Revolution proceeded at different rates of progress in various countries, with the result that mining took on a wholly different character from place to place. England, whose national economy was the first in the world to be fully industrialized, was almost a century ahead of Germany in experiencing the Industrial Revolution. During the 1790s coal triumphed over wood as the principal fuel for the production of iron and steel, with the result that by 1800 the United Kingdom was already producing over eleven million tons of coal per year. This technological fact had a pronounced impact on British poetry.[20] When John Dalton in 1755 addressed a long descriptive poem to "Two Ladies, At their Return from Viewing the Mines near Whitehaven," he described "nature's fierce intestine" with images of stench and terror:

> Welcome to light, advent'rous pair!
> Thrice welcome to the balmy air
> From sulphurous damps in caverns deep,
> Where subterraneous thunders sleep,

Or, wak'd, with dire Aetnaean sound
Bellow the trembling mountain round,
Till to the frighted realms of day
Thro' flaming mouths they force their way.[21]

Dalton, to be sure, was undertaking a subject that had not, according to
a contemporary reader, been attempted before in verse. In fact, the topic
was so novel that Dalton supplied his text with notes almost half as long
as the 335-line poem, and he had to invoke all the powers of mythological
analogy to render poetic the "dark mansion of despair." Similarly, when
Richard Jago in *Edge-Hill* (1767) eulogized the landscape of Warwick-
shire, he felt compelled to justify the utilitarian products of the local
mines:

Hail, Native British Ore! of thee possess'd
We envy not Golconda's sparkling mines,
Nor thine, Potosi! nor thy kindred hills,
Teeming with gold. What though in outward form
Less fair? not less thy worth. To thee we owe
More riches than Peruvian mines can yield,
Or Montezuma's crowded magazines
And palaces could boast, though roof'd with gold. [22]

And in 1785 Anna Seward, the "Swan of Lichfield," described the "out-
raged groves" of "violated Colebrook":

Grim WOLVERHAMPTON lights her smouldering fires,
And SHEFFIELD, smoke-involv'd; dim where she stands
Circled by lofty mountains, which condense
Her dark and spiral wreaths to drizzling rains,
Frequent and sullied; as the neighbouring hills
Ope their deep veins, and feed her cavern'd flames;
While to her dusky sister, Ketley yields,
From her long-desolate, and livid breast,
The ponderous metal.[23]

For the romance of mining, British poets like James Thomson and Christopher Smart had to look to the more exotic realms of India and South
America. At home, anticipating Blake, they perceived little but "dark
Satanic mills" or infernal places where, as in Keats's "Isabella" (strophe
14), "many a weary hand did swelt / In torched mines and noisy facto-

ries." It is consistent with this attitude that Lord Byron, when he went to inspect his property in Lancashire in 1811, was pleased that he "never went within ken of a coalpit."[24]

Given the national predisposition against mining, it is no wonder that Henry Crabb Robinson, who probably knew Germany better than any other Englishman of his day, was not charmed when he toured "the celebrated mine-mountains of the Harz" with Brentano's younger brother Christian.[25] At Saint Andreasberg, he reports in 1801, "I gratified my curiosity by descending a mine, learning thereby that it is a fatiguing and particularly uninstructive and uninteresting spectacle. Generally speaking, I know no sight which so ill repays the labour. . . . I could hardly be angry with the vulgar inscription of an English 'my lord' in the album: 'Descended this d——d old hole.'" Robinson, we must remind ourselves, was visiting the very mines that Wackenroder, Tieck, Novalis, Savigny, Eichendorff, and countless others were rapturously descending in those same years. But he was looking at the mines with English expectations and with eyes accustomed to industrial mines of coal and iron.

Germany, in contrast, was the slowest of the major Western nations to develop a modern iron industry. The 1790s, in the words of one economic historian, were still the "pre-Homeric age of industrial Germany."[26] Until the mining reforms of 1766—the so-called *Revidirte Bergordnung*—coal miners were regarded as an inferior order, ineligible to enjoy the legal rights and privileges of true miners.[27] The huge deposits of coal in the Ruhr, which made possible Germany's spectacular industrialization in the second half of the nineteenth century, still lay undiscovered. Accordingly, German coal production in the first decade of the century, in contrast to the eleven million annual tons in England, was almost too trivial to be recorded (.3 million tons). As late as 1850, in fact, Germany's coal production amounted to less than half of that of England in 1800.

Germany, however, had been the main source of precious metals in Europe until the discovery of America, and that fact determined the character of mining in such regions as the Harz Mountains and the Erzgebirge well into the nineteenth century. When German writers thought of mines, they did not think of coal and iron, but of gold, silver, and other valuable metals that lay beneath their hills and mountains—metals that could often be recovered without despoiling the landscape and whose usefulness was not so much for the factory as for the craftsman.

The center of German mining since the twelfth century had been the town of Freiberg in Saxony, twenty miles southwest of Dresden, whose unusual variety of veins and ores made it the finest site in Europe for metallurgical study.[28] Even after the discovery of America reduced the importance of the German mines, Freiberg continued to be a center for the study of mining technology and mineralogy. The classic Renaissance treatise on the subject—Agricola's *De re metallica* (1556)—was written with specific reference to the mines around Freiberg. Appropriately, in 1765 the world's first mining academy was founded there and provided the model for those gradually established all over Europe: at Chemnitz (1770), at Saint Petersburg (1783), at Paris (1790), and elsewhere. It is symptomatic not only of the new popularity of mining but also of the reputation of Freiberg's teachers and curriculum that students flocked from every country in Europe to study there. In addition to the writers already mentioned, the enrollment register shows students from Italy, Spain, Portugal, Norway, Denmark, Poland, Russia—and of course from England.[29] Robert Jameson, the noted Edinburgh geologist, studied at Freiberg and subsequently inspired his own pupil, Thomas Carlyle, to learn German—for the purpose of translating German treatises on mining and geology![30] Indeed, during the Romantic period Freiberg was a cosmopolitan center to a degree that became true for German universities only later in the nineteenth century. Until the end of the century the most eminent American mining engineers went to Freiberg for their training.[31] And still today, with some four thousand students, the Bergakademie is an active center of technological training in the German Democratic Republic.

The moving force behind Freiberg's rise to eminence was Abraham Gottlob Werner, a distinguished mineralogist whose family had been associated with mining for three centuries and who taught at the Academy from 1775 until his death in 1817.[32] Werner's special interests were *Geognosie*, or the study of the structure and composition of the earth, and *Oryktognosie*, or the classification of minerals. Following his epoch-making work on the taxonomy of minerals, *Von den äusserlichen Kennzeichen der Fossilien* (1774), Werner published very little. His ideas—including most importantly his advocacy of Neptunism, the theory that minerals were formed as deposits or precipitates from the primeval ocean covering the earth—became well known because his electrifying teaching converted many generations of "montanistic apostles" who spread his doctrines all over Europe: Stein, Humboldt, Baader, Novalis, Steffens, Schubert, and Körner, to mention only those names familiar in cultural history.[33] Many of his students, including Steffens in his autobiography, recorded their impressions of Werner. But he received his most lasting tribute from Novalis, who immortalized him in two literary works: as the teacher in *Die Lehrlinge zu Sais* and as the old miner in *Heinrich von Ofterdingen*. Thomas Carlyle's exposure to Werner's ideas by way of Robert Jameson produced an allusion to him in the opening paragraphs of *Sartor Resartus* (1,i,4). (A respected friend of Goethe's, he also figures centrally in chapter eight of Thomas Mann's novel *Lotte in Weimar* [1939], where "Herr Bergrat Werner aus Freiberg" is the favored guest at Goethe's dinner table.)

What needs to be stressed is the fact that Werner's geological interest—more specifically, his lithological passion—was intimately connected with his practical experience as a mining engineer. Despite his advocacy of Neptunism, Werner had little patience with the grand cosmogonic theorizing that occupied most other geologists of his generation. Instead, he wanted to help miners locate minerals through *Geognosie* and identify them accurately through *Oryktognosie*. As a result of Werner's powerful influence, the study of geology in Germany maintained an unusually close connection to mining technology. Owing to one man's magnetism, many German writers and thinkers became passionately interested in mining. But mining had different associations in Germany, where it was taught in a picturesquely situated academy by a distinguished scientist. Instead of coal mining, iron production, and industrialization, with all the attendant social problems that were agitating the Luddites and that would eventually lure Karl Marx and Friedrich Engels to England, mining aroused in the German Romantic mind the archetypal image of the descent into mysterious subterranean caverns under the guidance of wise old men in search of hidden lore symbolized by glittering stones and precious metals.[34]

## THE BELIEF IN THE GENERATION OF STONES

It may seem surprising, in the light of all that has been said, to ascertain how little the practical realities of mining affected the descriptions of Romantic fiction, drama, and poetry. The old miner in *Heinrich von Ofterdingen* sprinkles his speech with a few technical terms that are usually footnoted in modern editions. The well-digging chapter in *Die Kronenwächter* describes the procedures in terms consistent with the woodcuts in sixteenth-century editions of Agricola's *De re metallica*. And Hoffmann made careful use of contemporary travel books for his depiction of the world-famous copper mines at Falun. Steffens comments briefly on the bleakness of the miners' life at Freiberg before realism is displaced by euphoria. His first impression of the mining capital, as recorded in his autobiography, was so depressing that he did not initially look forward with any eagerness to his residence there. That mood of despondency is captured at one point in *Die vier Norweger*. "It was a gloomy evening, thick clouds had covered the sky, a dreary fog had settled over the entire region, which lay before me, desolate, ominous, and treeless; the bare slag heaps, between which, lonely and quiet, exhausted miners crept about in their filthy, threadbare, black garb, made me think of the entrance to Tartarus, so paralyzed, dead, lonely it all seemed."[35] In general, however, there is nothing in German Romantic literature to match the realistic detail of such eighteenth-century topographical poems as Dalton's, Jago's, or Seward's. The mine in German Romanticism is a mine of the soul, not a technological site. The question becomes, therefore, what was there in the romantic vision of mines that made them suitable and attractive—indeed, irresistible—as an image of the human condition?

Northrop Frye has pointed out that "the metaphorical structure of Romantic poetry tends to move inside and downward instead of outside and upward."[36] Whereas eighteenth-century poets in England and Germany sought out heights for their view of the sublime, their younger Romantic successors probed the depths. Blake's Jerusalem is situated in the center of the world; in *Prometheus Unbound* the erupting volcano is a controlling image; the geography of *Kubla Khan* features underground streams. In a larger sense, of course, the descent into these interior spaces can be seen as a specific example of the general pattern of descent and return familiar from the descents to the underworld known in literature, from the *Odyssey* by way of the *Aeneid* down to the *Divine Comedy*, and that accounts for the Romantic fascination with the theme of Orpheus.[37] But the English poets, as we have seen, did not make use of the image for inside and downward that dominated German Romantic literature. Mining entered the German Romantic consciousness and played such a conspicuous role there as an image of the inward way because of the unique nature of the institution as it existed in Germany at the time. And it imprinted on the literature of the period a set of images and associations that are quite specific to that institution.

From classical antiquity to the eighteenth century it was widely believed that stones and metals grow beneath the earth like organic matter[38]—a notion indebted to the archaic belief in a *Terra Mater* and a *monde sexualisé*.[39] Strabo in his *Geography* (bk. 5) reported that iron renewed itself in the mines on the island of Elba just as did salt in the mines of India. He assured his contemporaries that the stones grow back in the quarries at Rhodes and the marble at Paros. Indeed, the belief was so firmly held that as recently as the seventeenth century exhausted mines were closed down from time to time in order to allow the minerals to replenish themselves. This ancient belief, which survives in the folklore of mining communities today, is still evident in the German miners' slogan: *Es wachse das Erz!* ("May the ore grow!").[40] The theory was argued by analogy. Why shouldn't stones grow in the earth since, after all, they grow in all other realms of nature? The body produces *calculi* in the form of kidney or bladder stones; the oyster generates pearls just as, according to legend, the dragon nurtures in its forehead the precious *draconites*. Ancient and medieval scientists thought that onyx and amber grow in plants, while coral, sand, and stalactites give evidence that water precipitates stones. For centuries, finally, it was held that meteorites as well as certain fossils (e.g., *glossopetrae*) and primitive implements (known in German as *Donnerkeile*) were stones brought forth by the air.

Through the ages three main theories evolved to account for the generation of stones in the earth. In classical antiquity the most familiar was the Aristotelean theory of celestial influences: the rays of the sun and other heavenly bodies, penetrating into the crust of the earth, cause the elements to recombine in such a manner as to produce stones. This doctrine, which was accepted by Thomas Aquinas, Albertus Magnus, and most other scholastics of the Middle Ages, held sway until it was gradually supplemented in the sixteenth century by the theory of the so-called "petrific seed," according to which minerals generate themselves very much like plants. Sometimes the theory was combined with the notion (borrowed from Theophrastus and Pliny) that stones are either male or female to give a frankly sexual explanation of mineralogical reproduction. Finally, the theory of "lapidifying juice" emerged. As explained by Agricola in his treatise *De ortu et causis subterraneorum* (1546), the *succus lapidescens* circulating through the earth's crust transmutes various substances into stone, just as the blood in the human body transforms substances into kidney stones. Agricola answers those who dispute the growth of stones by inviting them to inspect abandoned mine shafts, which have often become quite narrow even though the miners must originally have laid them out to be adequate in width. "They have become so narrow as a result of the increase of matter, from which stone has developed. . . . Through similar increase lead also augments itself, for when it lies in a damp spot it grows."[41] As further evidence, Agricola cites the observation that leaden roof tiles become so heavy after a number of years that they must be replaced by lighter copper ones. The belief that minerals and metals grow and, in the process, become increasingly refined—with the result that all the baser metals tend toward silver and gold—provided the rational basis for alchemy. The theory seemed to be corroborated by the fact that a noble metal like silver was often found in lead ore—that is, in the very process of sublimating itself from lead to silver. Indeed, Roger Bacon reported that a certain silver mine that had been closed for thirty years was found, upon being reopened, to have become a gold mine.[42]

The belief in the generation of metals and minerals did not disappear with alchemy. In the standard German encyclopedia of the eighteenth century the article "Mineralisches Reich, Regnum minerale" explains the generation of minerals according to the ancient theory of celestial influence, to which has been added the theory of petrific seed. "The minerals also have their genesis and seed (like the animals and plants) from God and through the influence of the stars."[43] When the stars cast their rays upon the earth, their powers are sublimated, distilled, and spread throughout the planet. In the process they encounter "a fertile moisture" ("eine fette Feuchtigkeit") and coagulate into tangible bodies from which, according to the degree of purity of the site, various metals are "born." The proof of this, the author argues, can be seen in the fact that metals in the earth, as long as they are still in the process of growth, become increasingly "ripe" or "mature" ("immer zeitiger").

Despite the findings of modern geology, the ancient notion of multiplying minerals had a strong appeal for the Romantic consciousness, which believed in constant process and transformation—in a universe in which there are no distinct categories but an uninterrupted scale along which mind and matter are essentially identical. As Schelling put it in a famous statement at the end of his *Ideen zu einer Philosophie der Natur* (1797): "Nature aspires to be visible spirit while spirit aspires to be invisible nature." ("Die Natur soll der sichtbare Geist, der Geist soll die unsichtbare Natur seyn.") In such a world, according to the premise underlying Fouqué's tale *Undine* (1811), in which a water sprite marries a human being, the elements of nature constantly strive upward to achieve a soul. For those who held this pervasive Romantic belief, the conception of a mineral kingdom eternally *in statu nascendi* and constantly sublimating itself into ever nobler forms was intensely exhilarating. Indeed, the scientific work through which Steffens established his reputation, his *Beyträge zur innern Naturgeschichte der Erde* (1801), was intended expressly as a representation of the earth as a place where the transition from the inanimate to the animate was continually taking place.[44]

In the standard textbook of Romantic *Naturphilosophie*, Gotthilf Heinrich Schubert's *Ansichten von der Nachtseite der Naturwissenschaft* (1808), the discussion of metals provides the transition from inorganic nature to the organic world. Here, Schubert says, we see the shapes of the upper world reflected in the realm of metals. "In general, as I have shown elsewhere, the transition from the kingdom of minerals to that of plants and animals must in every respect be sought in the metals."[45] Their combustibility hints at their chemical affinity with organic matter just as their color and shapes imitate the higher organic world. "The whole kingdom of metals," he concludes, "seems to have arisen at the boundaries of the two worlds, from the decline and deterioration of the anorganic, and to bear within itself the seeds of the new organic age."

It would be difficult, and probably unproductive, to seek to determine in any detail the extent to which individual Romantic writers continued to believe literally in the semi-organic nature of metals and the kingdom of minerals as an intermediate zone where organic and inorganic meet. It is clear enough that in the literature of the age the belief continued to function powerfully as a governing metaphor. Novalis, as a trained mining engineer, was acquainted with the most modern theories of mineralogy. Yet in his literary works we find repeated signs of his familiarity with the ancient conception of an organic realm of metals. In *Heinrich von Ofterdingen* the metaphors used by the Bohemian miner imply an organic conception of mineralogical life. Speaking of the miner's profession and its hardships, for instance, he mentions "the precious growths that blossom for him in these frightful depths" ("welches köstliche Gewächs blüht ihm auch in diesen schauerlichen Tiefen").[46] In another place the miner reflects on the fabled times when nature was still unified and "when every seed slumbered within itself ["jeder Keim noch für sich schlummerte"] and, lonely and untouched, vainly longed to unfold the dark ripeness of its immeasurable existence."[47] When Heinrich, infected by these ruminations, is left alone in the hermit's cavern, he wonders: "Is it possible that beneath our feet a world of its own is stirring in a great life? that unheard-of births are taking place in the depths of the earth, distended by the inner fire of the dark womb to gigantic and immense shapes?"[48] In one sense, finally, the great *Märchen* that Kingsohr relates at the end of book one is an elaborate allegory of the seething life stirring in the realm of metals and minerals and capable of rejuvenation through electromagnetic means.

The young Tieck shares Novalis's belief in the subterranean stirrings of mineral life, as in *Kaiser Oktavianus* (1804), where the poet is enabled through his visionary powers to penetrate the realms where metals, minerals, and precious stones grow:

> Aufgeschlossen sind die Reiche
> Wo das Gold, die Erze wachsen,
> Wo Demant, Rubinen keimen
> Ruhig sprießen in den Schaalen.
> (161-62)

(Disclosed are the realms where gold and ores grow, where diamond and rubies sprout and quietly germinate in their pods.)

Two decades later he is capable of using the same notions for the sake of humor. In "Der Alte vom Berge" (1828) the old miner who maintains that minerals grow "like a rampant field of potatoes" is not only superstitious but also drunk. "There is life and activity in the ores and mountains," Kunz shouts. "Everyone knows that they grow and pass away, and that—just as up here the sun and the moon shine and there is rain and mist, frost and heat, down below there is vapor and weather that strikes and appears and, in the gloom, invisibly brews and takes shape . . . and as the fumes move and rise, they create ore, or stone, quicken into silver or gold or flow off into the veins, both near and far, as crystallized and shattered iron and copper."[49] In the mixture of anxiety and irony that characterizes the tone of Heine's *Die Harzreise* (1824), finally, the author is made uneasy by the sense of constant activity in the depths of the mine, where he hears a continual rushing and humming. "From time to time one also arrives at excavated passages, called galleries, where one can see the ore grow."[50]

These widespread literary allusions to the growth of metals might be little more than a footnote in the history of science, but they point to something central. The transition from inorganic to organic also represents for the Romantic mind the transition from the unconscious to consciousness. The mine in the German Romantic view is not simply a cold dark hole in the ground; it is a vital, pulsing place into which man descends as into his own soul for the encounter with three dimensions of human experience: history, religion, and sexuality.

## THE DESCENT INTO HISTORY

The ancient belief in the generation of stones was not inconsistent with the new understanding of geology as history and process rather than a static state fixed since Creation. In the late eighteenth century people began to look at stones as sources of historical information. The rhetoric of the age spoke of *lapides literati* and "graphic granite" in which the history of the ages was recorded.[51] Poets peering at quartz crystals saw Hebrew and Arabic characters; the Scottish geologist James Hutton, the Father of Vulcanism, even made out runic inscription in them. In his volumes on *Le Spectacle de la nature* (1783) the abbé La Pluche maintained that "the stones and metals have truly preserved for us the history of the world."[52] No one handled this language of lapidary metaphor more fluently than Novalis, who spoke of the "historical lithology" ("historische Oryktognosie") through which philosophers order reality into understanding and, in another place, of the "philosophical mineralistics" ("eine philosophische Mineralistik") that deals with all nature.[53] *Die Lehrlinge zu Sais* constitutes a textbook as well as a lexicon of expressions exploring nature, and specifically geology, as a "cipher language" (*Chiffernsprache*) that man must learn to decode. Novalis's enthusiasm communicated itself to his friends. In the second tale of Steffens's *Die vier Norweger* the narrator, Julius, recalls his student years at Jena, where he knew "the ethereal Novalis,"

who visited nature and history like an alien yet closely related guest, who brought greetings and memories from the ancient communal home, and whose language, resonating like strange music, sounded so wondrous to us because it suddenly revealed the most profound keynotes, that which was long-forgotten, that which lay hidden in history, in nature, in our own childhood, like a lovely mystery, so that the exposed depths of our own existence seized us with a joyous tremor.[54]

Many members of their circle, he continues, were unable to comprehend so powerful a human phenomenon; others were strangely moved. "I believe, in fact, that Novalis's fanciful view of the nocturnal occupation of miners had no little influence on my own decision to choose mining as a career."[55]

If, as Novalis and many of his friends believed, stones, metals, and rock strata amount to transcriptions of the earth's history, what better place to study that history than in the mines and caverns of the earth, where the entire record is preserved and exposed? At this point the ancient conception of mines and mountain caverns as places of lapidary activity encounters a second folkloristic notion—that in the interior of mountains time stands still. The belief in *Bergentrückung*, or the "subterranean translation" of gods, heroes, and wise men, is a primitive form of immortality familiar since antiquity, from Greece through the Islamic countries to pre-Columbian Mexico.[56] This belief, which developed into the Renaissance image of the *spelunca aevi*, or cavern of eternity,[57] was especially widespread among Germanic peoples.[58] Probably the most familiar of the legends concerns Tannhäuser and the Mountain of Venus. But similar tales arose in connection with the Pied Piper of Hameln, who led the children of the town into the Koppelberg, or the spectral host (*Wütendes Heer*) of Germanic myth, which emerges from time to time to terrorize the countryside. Often the legends are attached to popular rulers—from Arminius, Charlemagne, and Holger the Dane down to Barbarossa and his grandson, Frederick II—who are reputed to sleep within the mountain, often with a beard that has grown through the table or wound itself around the chair, until the time arrives for them to venture forth to liberate their people from some such scourge as the Turks or the Antichrist.

The common denominator linking these legends, despite local variations, is the timelessness of the mountain retreat—whether the Hörselberg, popularly identified with the Mountain of Venus; the Kyffhäuser, reputedly the retreat of the Hohenstaufen emperors; or some other mountain. It is not only the inhabitants who live there forever without aging. Visitors to those realms can also spend hours, days, years, even centuries inside them without realizing that time is passing in the world outside. But when they finally emerge, they discover—like Tannhäuser or the three miners in the first of the Grimms' *Deutsche Sagen*—that they have suddenly aged.

These associations reverberate in the legend of Falun and other Romantic works. But they are particularly conspicuous in *Heinrich von Ofterdingen* and enable us to understand why, in the pivotal fifth chapter, Novalis introduces the figure of the miner. He not only exposes the hero to the study of nature but also has the important function of mediating Heinrich's encounter with history in the person of the hermit residing within the mountain. As explicitly as Wordsworth's *The Prelude*, Novalis's novel represents "the growth of a poet's mind." But this process is not depicted in its full autobiographical extent; only the most decisive stages are symbolically portrayed. For this reason the encounters that Heinrich experiences in the course of the brief journey that constitutes part one of the novel assume a special significance. When he sets out on the journey from Eisenach to Augsburg, Heinrich is as unblemished a tabula rasa as is possible for a young man of twenty who has grown up at the court of Hermann of Thüringen. He has never ventured beyond the immediate vicinity of Eisenach; he has read few books and not a single poem; he has not even, so we are assured, attended a great festival or celebration. Only a short time later, however, he has experienced the entire world in a series of symbolic encounters. In chapter two (as well as its extension in chapter three) the chorus of merchants exposes Heinrich to the world of everyday reality and, through their collective narrative, to the realm of art. The Crusaders of chapter four exemplify the world of war, while the captive Zulima acquaints him through her reminiscences with the spirit of the Orient. In chapter five, finally, Heinrich is introduced to the realm of nature and the dimension of history—an experience, we learn at the end of the chapter, that "lifted him rapidly out of the narrow circle of his youth and onto the peaks of the world. The hours immediately past lay behind him like long years, and he had the sense that he had never thought and felt differently" (263).[59] By these words we are given to understand that the experiences of this chapter occupy a special place in the growth of this poet's mind. We must therefore approach it with particular attention.

The chapter, by far the longest of part one, falls into several distinct sections. The opening pages are dominated by the (unnamed) Bohemian miner, who is portrayed as a pious, modest, dignified old man whose rational view of nature has nothing in common with the superstitiousness of the peasants and their unreasoning fear of the caverns in the surrounding mountains. The account of his youth in Bohemia and his training as a miner in Eula (Czech *Jilova*) includes various details from Novalis's own life: e.g., his teacher is named Werner and comes from Lausitz; he becomes engaged to the daughter of a teacher; and he first discovers gold on a date (the sixteenth of March) that we know to be the birthday of Novalis's fiancée, Julie von Charpentier. The old man's idealized portrayal of his career as a miner culminates in a passage contrasting the avaricious world of commerce on the surface of the earth with the pious pursuits underground. "How peacefully the poor, self-sufficient miner labors in his deep solitudes, removed from the restless tumult of the day and inspired solely by the desire for knowledge and the love of harmony" (245). The old man sees in mining a "solemn image of human life" (246), which can be rich or poor, straight or twisted, broad or narrow, but which inevitably leads the patient and constant man to his true goal. This paean leads smoothly into the two great songs, the first expressing the miner's love of his craft and the second an allegory of gold-mining.

At this point the miner invites the assembled guests at the inn—the traveling merchants and the local peasants—to explore the nearby caverns with him, and as the group strolls through the moonlit night, Heinrich is overwhelmed by the power of the miner's revelations. "The words of the old man had opened within him a concealed door. He saw his small room built alongside a lofty cathedral, from whose stone floor the somber primeval world arose, while toward it from the tower floated the bright happy future singing in golden angelic choirs" (252). This initial association of mining (that is to say, the realm of nature) with history is intensified, as they step into the first cavern, by the discovery on its floor of piles of teeth and bones. Whereas the superstitious peasants are frightened by the discovery, the miner points out reasonably that the fossils are relics of prehistoric times. Suddenly they hear singing in the distance and, shortly thereafter, come upon an aged hermit, who warmly welcomes the unexpected guests to his retreat. The hermit, who turns out to be Duke Friedrich of Hohenzollern (died 1200), has now, following a lifetime of action as a soldier, discovered the more contemplative satisfactions of history, which he pursues amidst his books in the caverns. "The true sense for the history of mankind develops late in life, and more under the quiet influences of memory than under the more vivid impressions of the present" (257). Youth, he says, reads history only out of curiosity, while maturity sees in history a consoling and edifying friend. "Only old and pious people, whose own history is at an end, ought to write of history" (258). Any first-rate historian, moreover, must be something of a poet because only poets know how to link events skillfully and appropriately.

A strong sense of affinity emerges in the dialogue between the two old men. The miner has come to appreciate history through geology, while the anchorite expresses a profound respect for the miner's craft. " 'You are inverted astrologers,' " he tells the miner.

"While they steadfastly observe the heavens and wander through its immeasurable spaces, you turn your gaze upon the earth and probe its structures. They study the powers and influences of the constellations, and you investigate the powers of the rocks and mountains and the manifold effects of the layers of earth and stone. For them the sky is the book of the future, while for you the earth reveals monuments of the primal world." (260)

Appropriately this conversation, which has focused upon the processes and movements at work in nature and in history, culminates in reflections on the future. When the recluse and the miner go off with the other travelers to explore further caverns, Heinrich remains behind alone with the hermit's books. Among them he discovers an inscrutable volume in Provençal, whose language he cannot understand but in whose illustrations he recognizes himself, along with his family and friends as well as many other people in strange costumes and unfamiliar places. The chapter closes with this mysterious anticipation of the future, and the old miner disappears from the narrative.

Novalis was by no means the only Romantic writer who made the association between the descent into the mine or mountain cavern and the discovery of history. In his autobiography Henrich Steffens suggested that his *Beyträge zur innern Naturgeschichte der Erde* amounted to an explicit attempt to combine the ideas of Schelling and Werner into a "natural history." "All existence was to become history. . . . History itself had to become wholly nature if it hoped to assert itself as history vis-à-vis nature, that is: in all dimensions of its existence."[60] However, in no other literary work of the period is the purely historical aspect of the mine so explicit as in *Heinrich von Ofterdingen*. Indeed, it may be regarded as one of Novalis's principal achievements that he succeeded at least poetically in reconciling the tension between *Naturphilosophie* and *Geschichtsphilosophie* that characterized later Romantic thought, as in the opposition of Schelling and Friedrich Schlegel.[61]

## The Descent into Moral Ordeal

The descent into the mine of the soul can lead not only to knowledge of history but to that sinful knowledge that produces anguish. Although Novalis was primarily concerned with mining as an image of history, he was fully aware of the ancient ambivalence concerning mining as a profession. From classical antiquity through the eighteenth century, thoughtful men had often been contemptuous of mining because, they argued, it encouraged avarice, vanity, and violence. In the *Metamorphoses* Ovid reproved those wicked men who, not content with the wealth on the surface of the earth, dig into its bowels to uncover forbidden treasures, bringing forth destructive iron, gold, and their inevitable consequence, war.

> *iamque nocens ferrum ferroque nocentius aurum*
> *prodierat, prodit bellum, quod pugnat utroque*
> (1, 141–42)

Pliny begins the five mineralogical books of his *Historia naturalis* (bks. 33–37) with disclaimers concerning the misuse of metals and the corruption of virtue by their pursuit. And Seneca in his *Naturales quaestiones* (v.15.3–4) speaks scornfully of men who, turning their backs on the light, plunge into caverns that know no difference between night and day and, abandoning even the upright stance of human beings, grovel in the filth for the gold that then enslaves them. The *locus classicus* from Seneca survived into the eighteenth century, when it was recapitulated by various writers, notably Rousseau in his *Rêveries du promeneur solitaire.*[62] The remarkable passage in the seventh promenade betrays not only the structure of Seneca's argument but even his phrases. "The mineral kingdom has nothing pleasant or attractive about it; its riches enclosed in the bosom of the earth seem to have been removed from the regard of men so as not to tempt their cupidity."[63] These treasures, he continues, are merely a supplement to the true riches that are easily within man's grasp but of which he tires as he becomes ever more corrupt. "He ransacks the entrails of the earth, he searches in its core at the risk of his life and at the expense of his health for imaginary benefits." Fleeing the sun that he is no longer worthy of beholding, he buries himself alive. "The wan visages of the unfortunates who languish in the foul vapors of the mines, dark blacksmiths, frightful cyclops, are the spectacle that the vaults of the mines, in the womb of the earth, substitute for that of verdure and flowers, of the azure sky, of amorous shepherds and robust workers on its surface." From Rousseau it is an easy step to Blake's "dark Satanic mills" and the indictments of the English Romantics.

The moral arguments against mining were very much alive in the sixteenth century, and Agricola spends most of book one of *De re metal-*

*lica* recapitulating them in order to refute them.[64] In modern times, for instance, copper and tin have become culpable because muskets are made of their alloy, bronze, which is also used to construct instruments of torture. In addition, the discovery of metal-bearing mines exposes the dishonesty of men: magistrates who dispossess the rightful owners, scheming superintendents who lie about the true value of a seam, furtive foremen who hide the best sections for themselves, and so forth. Yet all these potential evils are outweighed by the benefits that mining brings. Metals were also produced by the Creator, he reminds us. Removing metals from the earth is no more wicked than taking fish from the sea. Agriculture and the crafts would be impossible without tools made of metal. Gold does not create avarice, nor iron, war; it is the wickedness of men that does so. Therefore the miner, if he is to resist these temptations, must be the best of men. Agricola enumerates the various arts and sciences that the mining engineer requires in order to pursue his trade: not only such obvious skills as astronomy, surveying, arithmetic, architecture, and drawing but also medicine to protect his workmen against injury and disease, and even philosophy as a basis for understanding the origin, causes, and nature of subterranean things. Book one culminates in a paean praising the moral qualities of the miner, whom Agricola ranks higher than the peasant, the burgher, and most other classes.[65]

Novalis was of course familiar with the works of Agricola, who was the famous man in the tradition of Freiberg mining, praised by Werner as the Father of Mineralogy and cited by Novalis in his own notes. Indeed, the Bohemian miner in *Heinrich von Ofterdingen*, with his lofty conception of mining, exemplifies Agricola's glowing assessment of the profession. Although Novalis was fully aware of the ambivalence that had surrounded mining at least since Agricola, the strategy of his novel— in which mining represents the symbolic introduction to the world of nature and the transition to the dimension of history—required that it be presented in all its glory with little trace of iniquity. If we turn to other writers of the period, however, we find that the mine is regularly used as a place of trial where the individual struggles with the forces of good and evil—either literally or metaphorically, within his own psyche.

A simple yet vivid example is evident in Eichendorff's short poem "Der Schatzgräber" (1834).[66] It is worth noting that the miner in this poem is designated by a name—"treasure-digger"—that Novalis's pious miner indignantly rejects. In this poem, which is so straightforward as to require little exegesis, the foolish miner, burrowing monomaniacally for

precious metals in the deserted mine shafts by night, becomes an object
of contention between the angels above and the dark powers of the underworld. Misled by his passion for false wealth, the miner is finally
killed by a cave-in.

> Wenn alle Wälder schliefen,
> Er an zu graben hub,
> Rastlos in Berges Tiefen
> Nach einem Schatz er grub.
>
> Die Engel Gottes sangen
> Derweil in stiller Nacht,
> Wie rote Augen drangen
> Metalle aus dem Schacht.
>
> "Und wirst doch mein!" und grimmer
> Wühlt er und wühlt hinab,
> Da stürzen Steine und Trümmer
> Über den Narren herab.
>
> Hohnlachen wild erschallte
> Aus der verfallnen Kluft.
> Der Engelgesang verhallte
> Wehmütig in der Luft.

(When all the forests lay sleeping, he began to burrow, tirelessly digging in the mountain depths for treasure. God's angels sang meanwhile in the still night; metals gleamed like red
eyes from the shaft. "Thou shalt be mine!" and more furiously
he grubs down until stones and rubble plunge upon the fool.
Jeering laughter resounded wildly from the collapsed abyss.
The song of angels faded away sadly in the air.)

The mine as the locus for the struggle between the powers of good and
evil is also predominant in various works by Theodor Körner, who is
fond of the image of the "labyrinth" to designate the place of human
contest. For Körner, a one-time Werner pupil at Freiberg, the miner is a
heroic figure who daily descends into the labyrinthine realm of death to
wage pious battle for precious treasure that he brings back up into the
world of light for the benefit of his fellow man. The poem "Bergmanns-
leben" (1810) begins with such heroic tones:

In das ew'ge Dunkel nieder
Steigt der Knappe, der Gebieter
Einer unterird'schen Welt.
Er, der stillen Nacht Gefährte,
Athmet tief im Schooß der Erde,
Den kein Himmelslicht erhellt.
Neu erzeugt mit jedem Morgen
Geht die Sonne ihren Lauf.
Ungestört ertönt der Berge
Uralt Zauberwort! *Glück auf!*[67]

(Into the eternal gloom descends the miner, ruler of a subterranean world. Companion of the still night, he breathes deep
in the womb of earth that no heavenly light illumines. Newly
born each morning, the sun follows its course. Undisturbed
resounds the mountains' ancient charm: *Glück auf!*)

But, the poem continues, the dark spirits of the underworld cannot harm
the miner, for he is aided in his efforts not only by the lovely naiads of
the water streams but also by Vulcan and Proserpine's husband. Aided
by these benevolent powers and by their own faith, the miners are able
to recover the precious metals and stones from "the earth's dark womb"
("der Erden dunklem Schooße") until, one day, they return to her for the
eternally long night. The same images reappear in Körner's "Berglied,"
in which the doughty miners clamber down to the ore-impregnated pits
("zum erzgeschwängerten Grunde") and into the gloomy grave of the
earth.[68] Far beneath the surface, where life begins, they boldly explore
the labyrinths of the shafts ("Der Gänge verschlungenes Labyrinth/
Durchschreiten wir kühn und verwegen"). Even though the peoples may
be battling above—Körner was writing at the time of the Napoleonic
wars—the miner is safe and secure in his depths. To be sure, the mines
have their hazards, which the miner resolutely confronts. Through his
efforts he provides the world above with the treasures by which his own
pure heart has never been corrupted. When the great payday arrives
("der große Lohntag") and the working shift of life ("des Lebens
Schicht") has passed, the miner's spirit will rise from the darkness of the
world into the light of heaven, where the angelic miners' crew ("die
Knappschaft des Himmels") will greet him with the familiar salutation
*Glück auf!*
    In two other works Körner expresses the Romantic belief in the activ-

ity constantly taking place within the earth. In his dramatic poem "Der Kampf der Geister mit den Bergknappen" (also written in 1810 while he was a student in Freiberg) the pious miner is challenged by the king of the mountain ("des Berges Fürst"), the cobold, who claims for himself all the treasures of the mine:

> Was kletterst du nieder aus glänzender Luft
> Zum finstern Schooße der Erde?
>
> Was suchst du in der grausenden Kluft,
>    Die des Tages Leuchte nicht klärte?
> Halt ein, Verwegner, und hemme den Streich;
> Denn weiter nicht dringst du in's Geisterreich.[69]

(Why do you clamber down out of the glittering open air into the dark womb of the earth? What are you seeking in the terrifying abyss that the light of day never brightened? Halt, foolhardy mortal, and check your pace; for you shall penetrate no further into the kingdom of the spirits.)

When the miners refuse to give way, the cobold summons his henchmen, who swiftly—in an obvious allusion to the belief in the growth of minerals—construct a wall shutting off the miners in the bowels of the earth. When the miners repeatedly succeed in breaking down the barriers, the cobold conjures up fires from the earth, and the miners are forced to retreat. Suddenly the Queen of the Waters appears with her fairies to extinguish the flames and drive away the cobold, who observes that man conquers whenever the forces of nature are at odds:

> Nur wo die Kräfte vereinigt quellen,
> Ist das geheime Schloß ihrer Macht.
> Doch, wo Elemente sich feindlich bekriegen,
> Da muß der Mensch, der Sterbliche, siegen.

(Only where the forces rise up in unity is the secret fortress of their power. But when the elements are embattled in hostility, mortal man must prevail.)

The flames withdraw into the depths of the earth, while the waters, rejoicing, join forces with the miners, who help them to stream up into the light of day. In his "romantic opera" *Die Bergknappen* (1811), finally, Körner expanded the basic conflict of his dramatic poem into a much longer libretto with a subplot in which Runal, the spirit of fire, kidnaps Röschen, the daughter of the chief miner. But Alberga, the queen of the mountain sylphs, vanquishes Runal, whom she banishes back into the depths from which he had emerged to torment the pious miners.[70]

In Zacharias Werner's drama *Martin Luther, oder: die Weihe der Kraft* (1807) the image, while still hinting at the conflict between good and evil, displays a more interesting complexity.[71] The play begins in a mine at Freiberg, where the miners are singing their work song:

> Glück auf! Glück auf!
> Wir fördern es herauf
> Das blinkende Erz, wir fördern's herauf!

(*Glück auf!* We bring it forth, the glittering ore, we bring it forth!)

At first we do not appreciate the full implications of the image, which at this point can be read quite literally. The setting is appropriate, however, for mining is an activity closely associated with Martin Luther, whose father was a miner. Suddenly a miner rushes in to announce that a ban has been placed on Dr. Luther, and the miners hurry out of the shaft. During the remainder of the long play, which concerns itself with the events immediately preceding and following the Diet at Worms, it becomes apparent why the action begins with the miners' song: both Luther and his father, Hans, repeatedly use mining as an image for the search for true religion. The implications are developed especially in the long scene (II, 1) in which Hans visits Luther to inquire about his son's new teachings. He has heard such garbled reports that he has made up his mind to ask his son directly. Luther explains his teachings in mining terms instantly accessible to his father. Have you discovered a new shaft or simply uncovered an old one? Hans inquires. It's an old one, replies his son, that the miners have allowed to fall into disrepair:

> 's ist ein verfall'ner Schacht, die Bergleut' haben
> Ihn selber zugestürzt, aus Faulheit, seht Ihr,
> Und Mißgunst, lieber darben wollen sie,
> als graben, und das Erz zu Tage fördern.
> Verkommen lassen sie's!——

(It's a collapsed shaft; the miners ruined it themselves out of laziness, you see, and rancor. They would rather starve than dig and bring the ore to the light of day. They allow it to go to waste.)

Hans, continuing the analogy, says that in that case the ore is going to waste. The prince ought to liberate the mine so that men might dig for themselves. Luther points out that he has done just that, but the false miners object that the ore belongs only to the mountain spirit, who from time to time sends up bits and pieces for the world above:

> Das sag' ich auch, und weil ich just die Hacke
> Von ungefähr zuerst ergreif', und grabe,
> Und allen Leuten zuruf': Grabt doch auch!
> Warum verlieh' der Herr Gott denn Euch Hände?
> Da liegt der Schacht, dicht vor Euch; grabt doch nur!
> Weil ich das thue, seht!—so machen jene,
> Die von der falschen Knappschaft, groß Geschrei,
> Und nennen einen Pfuscher mich, und bilden
> Den armen Leuten ein, das schöne Erz,
> Das sey nur für den alten Berggeist unten;
> Sie sollten nur im Sande d'rüber kriechen,
> Da würden sie schon manches Stückchen finden,
> Das er heraufspeit—Ist das nicht zu toll?

(That's just what I say, and because I happen to be the first to seize the pick and to dig and to call out to everyone: You should dig too! There lies the shaft, right in front of you. Just dig! Because I do that, look!—they raise a great outcry, those from the false mining crew, and call me a bungler and persuade the poor people that the lovely ore is only for the old mountain spirit below. They should just crawl around in the sand above, and there they would find many a bit that he spews up. Isn't that crazy?)

Hans cautions his son that one must not joke with the papal *Berggeist*, but Luther assures him that resoluteness will protect him. When Hans asks if the ore about which Martin is making such a stir is worth the trouble, Martin assures him that it is genuine. And if from time to time a bit of gravel shows up, he takes it to the smelting furnaces:

> Wahrhaftig, ja!—es hielt mir oft schon Probe.
> Kommt manchmal etwas Kies auch—hätt' ich's nur—
> Zum Schmelzwerk erst gebracht!

Such passages as these, as well as various briefer allusions, make it amply clear that mining symbolizes in this play the religious activity of the Reformation. The final words of the play, like the first ones, belong to the miners:

Das blinkende Erz
Wir fördern es herauf!

But now we understand not only that they have made their decision to side with Luther, the miner's son, in his forthcoming battles against Rome but also that the Reformation, like mining, is concerned with the excavation of truth and treasures long hoarded by jealous powers of darkness.

The fact that Luther came from a mining family provided a convenient association between mining and religion for other writers of the Romantic age, as we see in Arnim's Reformation novel, *Die Kronenwächter* (1817). Although the pious miner appears in only one chapter, the mine again provides the locus for the test of character.[72] In the second book, following a magical blood transfusion that has restored his ebbing strength, Berthold has become mayor of Weiblingen and, at age forty, a personage of considerable esteem. Eager for even more power and influence, however, he allows himself to be persuaded by Dr. Faust to excavate a well near his house even though the construction seems for many reasons ill advised. Indeed, even though Faust has divined by magical means where water is to be found, the initial attempts to dig the well not only fail; they almost cost the lives of several inexperienced workers who do not know how to build proper supports for the excavation. Berthold is frustrated in his impatience.

Then one day a mysterious stranger appears, dressed in a leather apron, black jacket, and green cap, who greets Berthold with the words *Glück auf!* A miner, he has been sent by none other than Martin Luther to return a horse borrowed earlier by the reformer. Berthold regards his arrival as an omen. The miner assures him that it is child's play, in comparison with real mining, to dig a well. Specifying the equipment he needs, he sets to work and makes rapid progress, even though the local artisans have difficulty understanding the orders he issues in his unfamiliar dialect and jargon. Following a dispute with a local citizen, the miner is tempted at one point to forsake the entire undertaking, but Berthold persuades him to continue, arguing that one more day's work would probably suffice to open the well. The miner reluctantly returns to the excavation, singing a pious song. A short time later he does tunnel through to the underground spring and drowns in the waters released in the process. Berthold, ashamed of what has happened, bribes the other workers to remain silent; he tells the townspeople nothing of the tragedy—only that the spring divined by Faust has been discovered. Arnim exploits the full ambivalence of mining, whose poles are vividly exemplified by Dr. Faust and Martin Luther. As in Werner's drama, mining can represent the search for truth. While the miner is working in the depths, Berthold thinks of Luther himself, the pious miner's son who set his life at stake, in response to the world's longing for profound knowledge, to discover a source of faith. Yet the pursuit beneath the earth is dangerous, and even the pious miner is threatened and eventually destroyed by the forces released in the course of the impious task conceived by Dr. Faust— not in the interests of truth and the public good, but to gratify the personal vanity of Berthold.

Arnim's friend and brother-in-law, Clemens Brentano, the onetime student of mining, frequently used mining as an image: in his novel *Godwi*, in his drama *Die Gründung Prags*, in his epic cycle *Romanzen vom Rosenkranz*, and elsewhere.[73] Thus in his "cantata" on the founding of the University of Berlin, *"Universitati Litterariae,"* the students greet the new institution as a "Mount of the Muses full of glory" ("Ein Musenberg voll Gloria"), founded by the master-professors, whose shafts it will be their task, like miners, to explore with lighted lamps for noble jewels.

> Glück auf, Glück auf! die Hoffnung lacht,
> Seid rüstig, ihr Gesellen,
> Geöffnet ist ein neuer Schacht,
> Wir wollen ihn bestellen.
> Glück auf, Glück auf! ihr Meister all,
> Die ihr den Bau gegründet,
> Wir grüßen euch mit lautem Schall,
> Die Lampen sind gezündet.
> Glück auf, Glück auf! wir fahren ein
> nach edelem Gesteine,
> Ein jeder soll gewärtig sein
> Daß er es redlich meine.[74]

(*Glück auf!* Hope smiles brightly. Be hearty, journeymen, a new shaft has been opened. Let us cultivate it. *Glück auf,* all you masters who founded the site, we greet you with loud acclaim. The lamps are lighted. *Glück auf!* We are marching in after noble stone. Let each of us take care that he has honest intentions.)

But mining as a religious image was elaborated most fully and poignantly in the great poem of crisis that Brentano wrote in 1816. We know from autobiographical documents that Brentano found springtime a terrifying season—a time of change when the old has vanished while the new has not yet emerged. The spring of 1816 was for Brentano a doubly agonizing period because he was on the point of conversion following a youthful period of agnosticism. The anxieties of spring coupled with religious uncertainties against the background of his own experiences as a former mining student combined to produce one of his finest poems, "Frühlingsschrei eines Knechtes aus der Tiefe," which refers to the cry of a miner threatened by vernal floods in the depths of his shaft.[75]

Like those works in which the mine represents the locus of the struggle between the forces of good and evil, Brentano's poem begins with the outcry of the miner who fears that he will perish in the pits without the aid of his master:

1.

Meister, ohne dein Erbarmen
Muß im Abrund ich verzagen,
Willst du nicht mit starken Armen
Wieder mich zum Lichte tragen.

(Master, without your mercy I must despair in the abyss if you will not bear me with your strong arms back into the light.)

It becomes rapidly apparent, however, that the miner, in describing the floods in his subterranean galleries, is talking metaphorically about the circumstances of his own soul.

2.

Jährlich greifet deine Güte,
In die Erde, in die Herzen,
Jährlich weckest du die Blüte,
Weckst in mir die alten Schmerzen.

(Every year your goodness reaches into the earth, into our hearts; each year you awaken the blossoms and awaken in me the old pains.)

Within a few strophes the description of the floods in the mine is enlarged to refer to the fear that floods the poet's heart:

5.

Und in meinem Herzen schauert
Ein betrübter bittrer Bronnen,
Wenn der Frühling draußen lauert,
Kömmt die Angstflut angeronnen.

(And in my heart a sorrowful, bitter fountain flows, and when springtime lurks without, the tide of fear comes streaming in.)

By means of a wordplay possible in German, the water welling up from the mine, and hence from the depths of the poet's unconscious, becomes the biblical deluge (*Sündflut* = "sin flood").

8.

Andern ruf' ich, schwimme, schwimme,
Mir kann solcher Ruf nicht taugen,
Denn in mir ja steigt die grimme
Sündflut, bricht aus meinen Augen.

(To others I cry: Swim, Swim. But the same warning cannot help me, for within me surges the furious tide of sin and bursts from my eyes.)

In the final strophes Brentano introduces a wider group of mining images to designate spiritual processes. The miner, no matter how frantically he bails, is unable to penetrate through the waters to the firm base of pure crystal. The walls continue to collapse, the waters rise ever higher, and the space in the gallery grows more confined. At this point matters have become so desperate that the miner can no longer help himself: he appeals to his master to rescue him from his depths just as the poet appeals to Jesus to redeem him from his depths of despair.

16.

Und so muß ich zu dir schreien,
Schreien aus der bittern Tiefe,
Könntest du auch nicht verzeihen,
Da dein Knecht so kühnlich riefe!

17.

Daß des Lichtes Quelle wieder
Rein und heilig in mir flute,

Träufle einen Tropfen nieder,
Jesus, mir, von deinem Blute!

(And so I must cry out to you, cry from the depths of bitterness,
even if you are unable to forgive your servant for crying out so
boldly. That the source of light may again flow pure and holy
in me, let fall a drop, Jesus, of your blood upon me.)

In Brentano's powerful poem we find perhaps the most remarkable
interiorization of mining imagery in all of German literature—an intensity matched only by Heinrich von Kleist in the concluding lines of his
tragedy *Penthesilea* (1808). When the queen of the Amazons realizes that,
in her frenzy, she has killed her beloved Achilles in the most gruesome
manner, she wills herself to death in an extended metaphor that is stun-
ning in its rigor. In this final speech Penthesilea descends, in her imagination, into the mine of her soul, where she excavates a destructive feeling, as cold as ore, which she purifies in the forge of her grief into a piece
of steel. She imbues the steel with the corrosive poison of remorse and
then, on the anvil of hope, shapes it into a dagger with which she stabs
herself:

Denn jetzt steig ich in meinen Busen nieder,
Gleich einem Schacht, und grabe, kalt wie Erz,
Mir ein vernichtendes Gefühl hervor.
Dies Erz, dies läutr' ich in der Glut des Jammers
Hart mir zu Stahl; tränk es mit Gift sodann,
Heißätzendem, der Reue, durch und durch;
Trag es der Hoffnung ewgem Amboß zu,
Und schärf und spitz es mir zu einem Dolch;
Und diesem Dolch jetzt reich ich meine Brust:
So! So! So! Und wieder!—Nun ists gut.

(scene 24)

## THE DESCENT INTO SEXUALITY

In addition to history and religious struggle, there remains a third experience to which the Romantic individual is exposed in the mine of his
soul: sexuality. Since antiquity mines and caverns—dark, moist places in
the earth where the generation of stones and metals is ever occurring—
have been associated with erotic encounter, the proper place for satyrlike
couplings.[76] One of the best-known examples, in addition to the *Minne-*

*Grotte* that figures in the legend of Tristan, is Tannhäuser's Mountain of Venus—a popular medieval legend rediscovered and retold by several writers during the Romantic period. It is recounted, for instance, in the "Tannhäuserlied" of *Des Knaben Wunderhorn*. Tieck provided an elaborate retelling in his early two-part tale entitled "Der getreue Eckart und der Tannenhäuser" (1799). Brentano used the legend as the basis for his *Romanzen vom Rosenkranz*. Heine composed a cycle of three poems called "Der Tannhäuser" (1836) and discussed the theme at the conclusion of his essay *Elementargeister* (1837), which provided the source for Wagner's operatic version.

It is well known that Novalis tended to couple religion and eroticism in his imagery. Erotic overtones are evident even in *Heinrich von Ofterdingen*, when the Bohemian miner sings a song representing the miner as Master of the Earth who explores her womb, measures the subtle build of her limbs, and is enflamed by his passion as though the Earth were his bride:

> Der ist der Herr der Erde,
> Wer ihre Tiefen mißt,
> Und jeglicher Beschwerde
> In ihrem Schoß vergißt.

> Wer ihrer Felsenglieder
> Geheimen Bau versteht,
> Und unverdrossen nieder
> Zu ihrer Werkstatt geht.

> Er ist mit ihr verbündet,
> Und inniglich vertraut,
> Und wird von ihr entzündet,
> Als wär sie seine Braut.[77]

(He is the Master of the Earth who measures her depths and forgets every complaint in her womb—who comprehends the secret structure of her rocky limbs and unflaggingly goes down into her workplace. He is bound to her and intimately engaged and is enflamed by her as though she were his bride.)

If Novalis for all his chasteness leaves little to the imagination, Heine takes the familiar sexual imagery and twists it into what amounts to a salacious joke. The two mines that he descended during his journey through the Harz were called "Carolina" and "Dorothea." "First I climbed down into Carolina," Heine begins innocently enough—"the dirtiest and most unpleasant Carolina I have ever met."[78] The joke is made especially piquant by the fact that the mines bear the names of two women prominent in Romantic circles—Dorothea Schlegel and Caroline Schelling. Following this introduction, Heine's description of the activities in the mines, which involve lubricity and spasmodic motion, takes on clearly sexual overtones.

The popularity of the Tannhäuser theme, the erotic religiosity of Novalis's mining song, and Heine's sly puns are symptomatic to the extent that they establish the association in the Romantic consciousness between mining and sexuality—that *regressus ad uterum* suggested by the very act of descent into the tellurian depths of Mother Earth. An early example is provided by Tieck's "Der Runenberg" (1802), which constitutes virtually a lexicon of romantic notions of mining, looking at one moment like a mad inversion of the fifth chapter of *Heinrich von Ofterdingen* and at the next like an anticipation of Eichendorff's "Der Schatzgräber." In general, it is the negative associations of mining that predominate in the narrative, in which the familiar religious struggle is secularized wholly into the erotic. The mine functions again as the place of struggle where the hero—whose exemplary name is Christian—wages his battle with the powers of darkness; but unlike the pious miners who triumph in the works of Körner, Werner, and Brentano, Tieck's hero is doomed to despair.

The first sentence establishes the tone of mild depression that governs the story as well as the link between mountains and alienation: "A young hunter was pensively sitting deep in the mountains beside a fowling place while the murmuring of the waters and the forest resounded in the solitude."[79] The son of a gardener from the northern plains, he was dissatisfied with his father's life and his attempts at fishing and business. Aroused by his father's tales of the mountains with their mines and miners, he resolved to visit them. For the past three months—in this story as elsewhere, Tieck is unnecessarily specific about trivial dates but vague about their significance—he has been working as a huntsman in the service of a forester. But on this evening he suddenly becomes melancholy as he thinks about the various contrasts that have characterized his life—between plains and mountains, plants and stones, temporality and timelessness, religion and thoughtless abandon, community and alienation. As he casually pulls out a root—it turns out to be a mandrake—he is startled by a great chthonic scream. Suddenly he sees a stranger standing behind him, and they strike up a conversation as they walk. Upon parting, the stranger points out to Christian the mysterious Rune Mountain, which he has never noticed before. The stranger goes down the mountain to an old mine shaft, where he lives, as he puts it, with the ores as his neighbors. Christian, in turn, makes his way up Rune Mountain. The spirit of the mountain in Tieck's tale is not embodied by a historical figure, as in *Heinrich von Ofterdingen*, nor by obscure forces of evil, as in Eichendorff's "Der Schatzgräber" or Brentano's "Frühlingsschrei," but by a dark, full-bodied woman who exhibits all sorts of mineralogical associations: she is standing in a room decorated with multicolored stones and crystals; her nude body glows like marble; and she hands Christian a marvelous tablet of precious stones whose colors and lines seem to communicate a mysterious message.

The parallels are by no means as straightforward as those in the other works we have considered. But the stranger in the mountains is clearly supposed to be a miner of sorts with connections to the dark powers of nature (the mandrake root); and he directs Christian to his symbolic encounter with a spirit of the mountain, whose appearance arouses associations with knowledge, avarice, and lust. These, in any case, are the sensations that pursue Christian as he leaves the mountains and descends into the flatlands, where he marries a girl who contrasts in every respect—Elisabeth is fair-haired, slim, devout—with the voluptuous beauty of the mountains. In the next years Christian raises a family and becomes a prosperous and respected citizen of the town; yet his moodiness increases to a point at which his father and his wife see in it clear signs of madness. When his father warns him against the evil of gold, "this accursed metal" ("dieses verfluchte Metall," 74), Christian confesses that "the red glitter penetrates deep into my heart" (75). He can feel, hear, and see nothing but the blandishments of the "glow of delight." As his increasingly horrified parent listens, Christian tells him how the stones talk to him and what wondrous meanings lie written in their markings. In a curious inversion of the usual theory, Christian explains that the organic world of plants is nothing but "the corpse of former splendid realms of stone" ("der Leichnam vormaliger herrlicher Steinwelten," 77) and that the garden world of his father is hostile to him because of his love for the magnificent symbols of the mineral kingdom.

Shortly thereafter, Christian, overcome by his madness, leaves wife and family behind and rushes off into the mountains, where he disappears into an old mine shaft—a symbolic act that clearly represents a sexual coupling with the seductive, maddening spirit of the mountains. "There must still be marvelous, immeasurable treasures in the depths of the earth," he speculates. "If only one could discover, raise, and acquire them! If only one could press the earth to oneself like a beloved bride ["wie eine geliebte Braut"], so that she might bestow upon him in fear and love her most precious possession!" (79). The remainder of the story—Christian's reappearance years later and his final interview with Elisabeth, who has meanwhile remarried and become miserable and impoverished—is incidental to the main theme. Tieck wrote his tale as though he were trying, at all costs, to pack in every Romantic association with mining: the mine as the locus of struggle for the pious ("Christian") soul, the fatal lure of precious metals, the sexuality of the mineral realm, the lore of speaking stones, the descent into the mine as the embrace of the beloved. As critics we can question the success with which Tieck was able to exploit this lavish potpourri of associations to justify Christian's madness. As literary historians, however, we must take the story as powerful evidence of the importance that mining and its associations had assumed in German Romantic circles.

From "Der Runenberg," it is an easy step to E.T.A. Hoffmann's "Die Bergwerke zu Falun" (1819), in which we recognize a culmination of the Romantic obsession with mines.[80] According to old Swedish accounts, in 1719 in the copper mines at Falun, at a depth of 130 meters, the perfectly preserved body of a young man who had perished in a collapse in 1670 was discovered. Although the tale was current throughout the eighteenth century, it was first widely publicized in Germany by G. H. Schubert in his *Ansichten von der Nachtseite der Naturwissenschaft* (1808), which provided Hoffmann's direct source. Schubert tells the story briefly in chapter eight, where he is discussing the transition from inorganic nature to the organic, and he cites it as evidence of the fact that human remains perish more quickly than the remains of the great primeval animals and that, therefore, it is impossible to ascertain whether or not man was present on the earth at the time of the great flood that destroyed the first wave of organic life. Since Schubert's motivation is scientific, his account is economical and straightforward, beginning with the conclusion. "In a similar manner that remarkable corpse—of which Hülpher, Cronstedt, and the Swedish learned journals report—disintegrated into a kind of ash after it, seemingly transmuted into hard stone, had been placed under a glass covering in a futile attempt to secure it from access to air."[81] Having anticipated the conclusion, Schubert quickly sketches the essentials of the story. The body of the former miner was discovered, saturated with vitriol, when miners were trying to dig an opening between two shafts. Though pliable at first, it became as hard as stone as soon as it was exposed to air. It had lain in the vitriolated water for fifty years, and no one would have identified the still perfectly preserved body had not an aged woman on crutches recognized the features of her fiancé, who had perished half a century earlier. Schubert stresses in particular the contrast between the two lovers: "On their silver [sic] wedding anniversary the still youthful bridegroom was rigid and cold while the gray old bride was filled with warm love."[82]

The classic prose version by Johann Peter Hebel, "Unverhofftes Wiedersehen" (1811), though it transposes the events to the recent past, stays conspicuously close to the details of Schubert's account.[83] But the tale, which was greatly admired by Goethe, has been heightened dramatically in three ways. First, instead of beginning with a scientific *Q.E.D.*, Hebel starts with the publication of the marriage banns in the church—"at which Death announced himself." Following the young man's disappearance, Hebel inserts a famous passage, occupying roughly a quarter of the brief narrative, which accounts for the passage of time, as the city of Lisbon is destroyed by earthquake, the Seven Years War begins and ends, America obtains its freedom, and other events transpire in the great world of history. Finally, the entire episode is narrated from the bride's point of view: her grief and loyalty following her betrothed's disappearance, her joy at recognizing him again, her loving preparations for his burial, and her final promise to be reunited with him soon in their "cool wedding bed."

If we skip a number of uninspired verse treatments of the theme—including one that Arnim included in his novel *Die Gräfin Dolores* (1810)—and turn to Hoffmann's version, we note first of all that it is much longer: the two hundred fifty words of Schubert's terse report and the eight hundred words of Hebel's anecdote have grown to almost ten thousand words in Hoffmann's full-fledged novella. But we are dealing with anything but a simple expansion: Hoffmann has radically altered the proportions of the plot. It is no longer the bride's story; indeed, Hoffmann allows her scarcely as many lines for her grief and joy as does Hebel. The story is almost half over before Elis Fröbom even meets Ulla Dahlsjö; and the culminating events—the wedding day, the disappearance, the recovery of the body fifty years later—constitute little more than a brief postscript to the story that fascinates Hoffmann. His interest has shifted from the unusual incident itself to the motivation that governs the young man. Why did Elis Fröbom become a miner? What attracted him into the mines on his wedding day? Here we see all the Romantic elements once again at play. Although Hoffmann got the basic plot from Schubert's *Ansichten* and although *Heinrich von Ofterdingen* supplied a trivial bit of the secondary plot—the young miner's engagement to the mine owner's daughter—Hoffmann's tale is essentially an analogy to Tieck's "Der Runenberg." In both cases a young man from the flatlands has become disenchanted with his former life; under the guidance of a mysterious old miner he goes off into the mountains, where he falls under the spell of a demonic woman of the mines; her allure is so compelling that in both cases the hero leaves a happy marriage (or at least the promise of one) to join the temptress in her mountain retreat. In Christian's case the decision leads to madness; in the case of Hoffmann's hero, to his death in a mine disaster.

At the beginning of the story Elis Fröbom, a young sailor from a maritime family, has made up his mind not to return to his ship. "His entire life at sea seemed to him like a confused, purposeless drifting," we are told, and he is disgusted with the drunken revels of the sailors in port.[84] In Göteberg Elis meets a mysterious miner, who points out that his introspective, pious, and childlike temperament would be better suited for mining than for the wild, inconstant life of a sailor. At this point Elis shares all the common prejudices against mining prevalent since Seneca, in which men descend into hellish regions and grovel like moles for ores and metals simply out of lust for profit. But the old miner gives him such a glowing portrayal of the miner's life as a search for knowledge, and of the mine as a place where the stones and fossils are vibrant with life, that Elis begins to believe he was destined from the earliest premonitions of his childhood for the enchantments of that subterranean world. When the old miner disappears, Elis falls asleep and dreams of exquisite underground passages where he encounters a handsome woman who is identified as the Queen of the Mines. Waking up, Elis is obsessed with the notion of going to Falun and becoming a miner. As he sets out on his journey, he seems to see the mysterious old miner beckoning him along the way from time to time.

Elis's first glimpse of the great pits at Falun is terrifying, and Hoffmann makes skillful use of contemporary travel accounts to give a technically accurate description of what was then still the largest copper mine in Northern Europe. But the miners' celebration that he witnesses following the local assembly day, his warm welcome by Pehrson Dahlsjö, a local mine owner, and his attraction to Dahlsjö's daughter Ulla overcome Elis's initial apprehensions. Beginning as an apprentice in Dahlsjö's mines, Elis soon becomes so skilled that he advances rapidly in the profession and is promised the hand of his beloved Ulla. During this period, however, two developments take place. Working alone in the shafts one day, Elis encounters the old miner, who accuses him of disloyalty to the kingdom of metals. Shaken by the experience, Elis learns that the old miner is allegedly the ghost of a certain Torbern, who perished years before in a great cave-in and now haunts the mines. In particular, he is known to go forth on expeditions to recruit young miners when times are difficult. Secondly, in reaction to the unsettling encounter, Elis begins to have visions again of the Queen of the Mines and feels himself torn between his passion for her and his pure love for Ulla. "He felt himself divided into two halves; it seemed as though his better half, his genuine self, descended into the center of the earth and rested there in the arms of the Queen, while he sought his gloomy bed in Falun" (244). His friends and family note his growing malaise: he tells them, for instance, of mysterious messages that the Queen engraves in the stones and that he alone is able to decipher. But they assume that his trouble will pass when he is once married.

On his wedding day—which is to take place on Saint John's Day, or Midsummer Night, a date charged with magical meaning in folklore[85]— Elis appears early at his bride's home, dressed in his wedding attire, and announces that he is descending into the mine in response to a vision in order to obtain a precious glowing stone for Ulla's wedding gift. Despite her pleas, he disappears. A few hours later miners arrive to announce that there has been a disastrous cave-in; Elis's body is not recovered. When the body is found fifty years later, it appears at first to be petrified (*versteinert*) in a reification of the Romantic wish to be united with the animate stone. But when the aged Ulla appears—she is said to be "stone-old" (*steinalt*)—almost immediately she expires over the corpse, which itself begins to disintegrate. Although Hoffmann makes no further comment, he indicates clearly that Elis's belief in the eternity to be found in the Mine Queen's stony realm is truly madness.

In Hoffmann's tale we find a recapitulation of all the popular Romantic beliefs concerning mining. The descent into the mine, where the stones are said to live, is explicitly designated as a descent into the soul.

Old Torbern promises knowledge, but it turns out to be not the true knowledge of history but the sinful knowledge of sensuality, which leads to madness and death. In a period of less than thirty years the romance of mining has run its full course in Germany, from spiritualization to demonization. It is symptomatic and even symbolic that Hoffmann wrote his story in 1818, only a year following the death of Abraham Gottlob Werner, the guiding spirit most responsible for the brief but intense vogue that mining enjoyed in German Romantic literature and thought—indeed, who provided the model for the mysterious old miners that people the works of the period.

But soon the nature of mining in Germany and even Freiberg itself changed so radically that the old reality was reduced to a literary image. In 1818 the Academy had to be enlarged—in order, paradoxically, to accommodate the extensive library and rich collections that Werner bequeathed to his beloved institution. And in 1829 the traditional curriculum, which had remained relatively intact for decades, began to be extensively revised in an effort to reflect the new technological realities of mining engineering. During the first quarter of the nineteenth century mining had changed very little in Germany. But from 1825 on, new methods were adopted there in response to increasingly massive industrialization. Essentially—in addition to scientific advances in such mining-related fields as hydraulics—two improvements altered mining technology to such an extent that it was no longer comparable to mining as known to Novalis and his contemporaries. Iron rails expedited the movement of ores below and above ground, and improved steam engines assured the efficient functioning of pumps, elevators, conveyances, and the like. Mining became noisy, and it became dirty. Beginning in the second quarter of the century, coal mining grew at an unprecedented pace. The old mineral mines in the Erzgebirge and the Harz, the sources of Romantic inspiration, remained important, to be sure, but the mining industry gradually shifted westward to the Ruhr Valley, where little of the romance of mining remained in the heavily industrialized society of mid-nineteeth-century Germany.

## MODERN RECURRENCES OF THE ROMANTIC IMAGE

Mining entered German literature of the Romantic age and played such a conspicuous role there because of the unique nature of the institution as it existed in Germany at the time. It ceased to play that role when the institution itself began to change. It would be surprising, however, if an image that lived so compellingly in German culture—its law, its language, and its folklore—should simply vanish without a trace. And indeed it did not. In that form of popular culture known as *gesunkenes Kulturgut* the Romantic image of mining is evident in the detailed wood carvings of miners in their traditional garb that are manufactured in the Erzgebirge and exported by the hundreds, as well as in the gingerbread figures of miners traditionally baked at Christmastime in the same region of Saxony. The examples of popular culture mirror the works of porcelain, gold, glass, and pewter from earlier centuries, in which mining provided an iconographically important motif.[86]

On another level, mining survived in literature, which leads a life of its own long after the demise of the institutions that initially produce the images. The Romantic writers, as we have seen, knew mining at first hand, either from their own studies or from their friends and their walking tours. Among modern writers this is usually no longer the case: they are acquainted with mining purely as a literary image. Or, to put it more precisely, when modern writers do know mining at first hand, their works tend to turn into naturalistic documents of a sort not uncommon in France since Zola's *Germinal* (1885) and in the United States since Frank Norris's *McTeague* (1899) and Upton Sinclair's *King Coal* (1917).[87]

In Germany, however, and in occasional non-German authors like Jules Verne in his mining novel, *Les Indes Noires* (1877), or Richard Llewellyn's *How Green Was My Valley* (1940), the old associations live on, revitalized by three thinkers whose thought was profoundly influenced by Romantic ideas: Johann Jakob Bachofen, Sigmund Freud, and Carl Gustav Jung, in whose systems the mine plays a significant symbolic role explicitly as an image of history, sexuality, and psychic discovery. In the matriarchal theory developed by Bachofen, whose influence on German thought around the turn of the century cannot easily be overemphasized, the mine and the mountain interior occur repeatedly as the locus of the *magna mater*. In his distinction between the female *sanctum* and the male *sacrum*, for instance, Bachofen stresses that the former is related to the chthonic forces of the earth. Walls were sacred to the ancients, he argues, because classical antiquity revered walls rising from the depths of the earth as a birth produced by the womb of *magna mater*, which had lain in the dark chambers until it was aroused by the effect of masculine power and brought forth to the light.[88]

From Bachofen it is only a short step to psychoanalysis. In *The Interpretation of Dreams* (1900) and elsewhere Freud analyzed the descent into a mine shaft or mountain cavern as the act of coitus.[89] This standard Freudian interpretation enabled Emil Franz Lorenz, in a reading of the legend of Falun, to designate the mine or cavern as "the most familiar" symbol of the womb and the descent into the mine as an "incest fantasy."[90] In Jung's works, finally, the figure of the wise old man is often associated with mountains and mines[91]—a relic, no doubt, of ancient and medieval legends concerning the subterranean translation of great rulers and wise men, as well as an inversion of legends concerning demons who inhabit the earth.[92] In their view of mines as the locus of chthonic power, sexuality, or wisdom these modern thinkers were stimulated in no small measure by the Romantic writers they read and interpreted. In turn, the Romantic notions received increased significance and credibility from the attention by such powerful minds as Bachofen, Freud, and Jung. The attendant publicity no doubt contributed to the resurgence of the image in twentieth-century German literature.

There is no shortage of literary works in which mining functions in its traditonal capacity as an exploration of the psyche. In one of the great mythological poems that conclude his *Neue Gedichte* ("Orpheus. Eurydike. Hermes") Rilke describes the progress of the three figures up from Hades, moving "like quiet silver ores as veins through its darkness" ("wie stille Silbererze gingen sie/als Adern durch sein Dunkel").[93] The governing image that opens the poem makes explicit the metaphorical action being described: "Das war der Seelen wunderliches Bergwerk"—an ambiguous phrase meaning "That was the wondrous mine of souls," as well as "That was the wondrous task carried out in the mountain by these souls." In the tenth of his *Duineser Elegien* (1923) the youth's guide through the vast landscape of Laments explains that her family was once a great race, whose fathers mined the mountain ranges for precious ores. Sometimes, she says, one still finds among men "a bit of polished primal grief" ("ein Stück geschliffenes Ur-Leid") or "wrath petrified into slag" ("schlackig versteinerten Zorn").[94] When she leaves him at the foot of the mountain, the youth ascends "into the mountains of Primal Suffering" ("in die Berge des Ur-Leids") to seek the mines where formerly mankind excavated its own humanity—a reenactment of the quest undertaken by countless Romantic heroes.

Similar passages in which the mine represents the human psyche can be found in Kafka ("Ein Besuch im Bergwerk"), Hesse ("Iris"), and

Thomas Mann, who includes in his *Doktor Faustus* a few lines from a poem entitled "Der Bergmann," a Brentano-like work allegedly written by the character Ines Rodde, in which the miner descends the shaft of his soul and discovers the precious ore of suffering glittering in the dark:

> Ich bin ein Bergmann in der Seele Schacht
> Und steige still und furchtlos dunkelwärts
> Und seh' des Leidens kostbar Edelerz
> Mit scheuem Schimmer leuchten durch die Nacht.[95]

The most extensive example is no doubt the reworking of the legend of Falun that Hugo von Hofmannsthal wrote in 1899 as the last of the great lyrical dramas of his youth, whose sole source was Hoffmann's tragic tale.[96]

If for Rilke, Kafka, Hesse, Mann, and Hofmannsthal the descent into the mine represents primarily, though hardly exclusively, the descent into the womb of consciousness and self-awareness, for other modern writers the image held different associations. In all three stories of the collection *Drei Frauen* (1924) Robert Musil portrays rational, analytical heroes who, undergoing a mid-life crisis, are forced to come to grips with the irrational and mystical aspects of life in the form of woman. In "Grigia" (1921) the hero's name, Homo, leaves little doubt about his exemplary function. Left alone when his wife and son go off to a spa, Homo, a geologist by profession, accepts an invitation to participate in an expedition to reopen the ancient Venetian gold mines in the Tyrolese Alps. High in the mountains in a community described as being almost prehistoric, and disenchanted with his career and family, Homo succumbs to the frankly sexual attractions of a local peasant woman whom he calls Grigia—the name that she herself has coined for her cow. Repeatedly Grigia is portrayed in terms that remind us of the animal or plant world: she reminds Homo of flowers and stones; her language strikes him as "magical" in its simplicity; when they are caught in the mines, she squeals like a pig and bucks like a horse. Even their couplings are more like those of animals than human beings. When Grigia's husband becomes suspicious, Homo arranges to meet her one last time. They take refuge in an abandoned mine shaft, where they copulate on the floor. Suddenly the opening is closed off when Grigia's jealous husband, who has followed them, rolls a boulder in front of it. After she recovers from her initial animal fright, Grigia discovers a small crevice through which she is able to escape. Homo realizes that he, too, could probably force his way through the crack. "But at this moment he was perhaps already too weak to return to life, he no longer wanted to, or he had fainted."[97] In Musil's story, as in Hofmannsthal's drama, the hero finds himself through the descent into the mine. But instead of mystical illumination, what Homo finds in this mine shaft—which symptomatically is "abandoned"—is that sexual, indeed animal, aspect of his own nature that had hitherto been repressed by the rationalism of his Western personality. Musil is much closer to Tieck than he would have cared to admit.

Hermann Broch's unfinished novel—variously entitled "The Temptor," "The Bewitchment," and "Demeter" (written in the mid-thirties and revised in 1950–1951)—also takes place in a gold-mining village in the Austrian Alps, where the atmosphere, as observed by a retired doctor from Vienna, is pronouncedly primeval. In this village, although the mines were exhausted centuries earlier, the inhabitants still perform annually an ancient ritual in which they consecrate a "mountain bride" (*Bergbraut*) to pacify the dragon within the mountain and then, each fall, symbolically sacrifice the bride to the spirit of the mountain. Like his contemporary and countryman Musil, Broch is obsessed with the primitive-sexual aspects of the mountains and their mines. One working title of the novel, "Demeter," suggests the principal theme of the book—an analysis of the transformation of a matriarchal society into a patriarchal one, as the authority of Mother Gisson is undermined by the Hitler-like vagabond, Marius Ratti, who stirs up the villagers by his promises to reopen the gold mines.[98] Within the major framework of a novel, however, Broch goes much further than Musil was able to do within the minor form of the novella. He is interested in the phenomenon of mass psychology whereby not just a single individual but an entire community can be caught up by the powers of irrationality and led, by a false *Führer*, to carry out in reality the human sacrifice that hitherto had been merely symbolic. In this novel, then, which Broch also called his "mountain novel" ("Bergroman"), we find the familiar elements of the mine as the locus of temptation and the struggle between good and evil. Through the descent into the mine, men recapture primal aspects of their natures and are incited to violence, while the forces of matriarchal tranquillity and civilized decency look on in powerless horror and awe.

Musil served during World War I in the gold-mining mountains of South Tyrol, and Broch spent weeks in the gold-mining country of the Salzkammergut during his arrest by the Nazis in the thirties. Yet both of these writers, albeit technologists by training, knew mining only at second hand. Postwar Germany has produced a writer who, himself at one time a miner, has invoked once again the old Romantic associations in the service of a harsh critique of modern civilization. Following World War II, Günter Grass worked in a potassium mine near Hildesheim, and the experience left its imprint on his fiction. The culmination of the image in modern German literature surely occurs in his novel *Hundejahre* (1963), where a mine is used as the setting for the concluding chapter. Toward the end of the narrative the childhood friends, Walter Matern and Eddi Amsel, meet after having gone their separate ways for many years. Amsel, who now calls himself Brauchsel and whose artistic talent since childhood has manifested itself in his uncanny ability to construct scarecrows of the most ingenious variety, persuades Matern to accompany him to the Harz region, where they visit Brauchsel's enterprise in an abandoned potash mine.

In these scenes Grass's mastery of the technical details and vocabulary of modern mining is evident. Like their Romantic predecessors, Brauchsel and Matern clad themselves in miner's garb—but it is a contemporary uniform of denim coveralls, yellow hardhats, and carbide lamps. During their descent, which is accomplished in fully automated and speedy elevators, only the greeting *Glück auf!* is traditional. But what Matern witnesses in the subterranean galleries, as they move downward through thirty-two chambers, is a grotesque exaggeration of the Romantic motif presenting the mine as the locus for the encounter with history and one's own soul. Here, more than six hundred meters below the surface of the earth, Brauchsel-Amsel has set up a huge factory, where workmen assemble automated scarecrows by the hundreds, which represent every aspect of German culture—in lifelike parodies of its philosophical, sociological, political, theological, religious, and other thinkers—as well as every period of German history from medieval times to the present. On the basis of his catalogues, which he mails out all over the world, Brauchsel does a lively export business with this dead Germanic past—especially, he notes, in Argentina and Canada. When the former Nazi Matern, overwhelmed by this burlesque of history and his own past, calls the enterprise "Hell, Inc.," Brauchsel replies quietly—echoing generations of miners from Agricola to Theodor Körner—that the real hell is six hundred meters above them.

*Hundejahre* represents the ultimate inversion of *Heinrich von Ofterdingen*. Here the descent into the mine leads to the traditional encounter with history—but a history exposed in all its senseless brutality by an absurd caricature of the mysterious old miner. It is absolutely consistent that Günter Grass, a writer more resourceful in his exploitation of traditional myths and themes than any writer in Germany today, should have returned for the culminating scene of this powerful novel of twentieth-century Germany to an image so central to the German Romantic consciousness. For Grass has been obsessed more than most of his contemporaries with that archetypal Romantic exercise: the exploration of the mines of the soul.

CHAPTER THREE

# The Law:
# Text of Society

## THE LURE OF THE LAW IN GERMANY

READERS with a juristic turn of mind might well come away from a survey of German literature believing that the masterpieces of the Romantic age were composed to provide exemplary cases in textbooks of law. The action of Goethe's *Faust* (pt. 1, 1808) is predicated on an agreement concluded between Faust and the devil's henchman. Without the assistance of Mephistopheles we would have none of the stage business for which the legend is famous: no rejuvenation of the aged scholar, no ride on a wine keg or the other hijinks in Auerbach's cellar, no seduction of Gretchen, no Walpurgis Night. Yet for over a century the debate has continued regarding the nature of the agreement.[1] Is it a wager or a pact? Should it be interpreted according to the law of the sixteenth century or the legal practices of Goethe's own time? Is an agreement legally binding if it involves one's soul, which after all is the property of God? If it is binding, then have all the conditions been fulfilled at the end of Faust's life? Does he escape through a weasel clause in the language or by divine intervention? This is the stuff of which seminars are made!

The story of Kleist's *Michael Kohlhaas* (1810) could serve as a handbook of sixteenth-century legal procedures, as the hero's fanatic pursuit of justice leads him from the courts of Saxony to the tribunals of Brandenburg and finally to the Imperial Chancery of the Holy Roman Empire.[2] Yet the entire sequence of horrendous escalations culminating in Kohlhaas's execution for breaching the public peace of the empire is triggered by a seemingly trivial civil suit involving the misappropriation of two horses.

E.T.A. Hoffmann's classic tale, "Das Fräulein von Scuderi" (1820), involves a change of venue: from the Reformation Germany of Luther, Faust, and Kohlhaas to the Golden Age of Louis XIV's France. But the issues are again legal. A series of brutal armed robberies has taken place in the streets of Paris. When the goldsmith Cardillac is found murdered, suspicion falls on his apprentice, who is also the fiancé of his daughter. It requires all the legal skill of the brilliant advocate, Pierre Armand d'Andilly, to save the innocent young man from the inquisitions of the ruthless *chambre ardente* and all the psychological insight of Madame de Scudéry to expose the true culprit—Cardillac himself, who had become so compulsively attached to his own fabrications that he went to any lengths to recover them from their purchasers, until finally he was killed in self-defense by one of his intended victims.

Now any first-year law student would immediately be able to classify these cases within familiar categories: we are dealing basically with contracts, torts, and felonies—along with criminal and civil procedures. As might be expected, these famous literary cases have often drawn the attention of German legal scholars. But interest in the law is by no means restricted to lawyers alone, nor is it exclusively a modern phenomenon: it can be traced back to the earliest stages of human culture.[3] At the mythic beginnings of many national traditions stand those lawgivers bearing suspiciously similar names who are reputed to have received the law from the hands of deities: Manu, the ancestor of humanity in Hindu mythology, who formulated the code of Brahman law; Menes, the first king of Egypt and founder of Memphis; Minos, the fabled legislator-king of Crete, whose moderation and justice were rewarded by the office of supreme judge of the underworld; and of course Moses, who encountered the Lord on Mount Sinai and brought down the two stone Tables of Law that have governed the people of Israel ever since.

While mythic lawgivers stand at the beginning of human history, great legal codes often mark the earliest stages of written documentation. We are acquainted with the late archaic civilization of Sumeria and Akkad largely through the Code of Hammurabi, which the ruler of Babylonia had inscribed upon an eight-foot pillar of black stone. The first five books of the Old Testament, the Pentateuch, or Torah (meaning "law"), are taken up extensively by laws and legislation: especially the Covenant Code (Exodus 20.22 to 23.33) is based on preexisting sources that represent the oldest civil ordinances of the Israelites. The facts of early Greek history are accessible to us largely through the constitutions that were engraved on wooden or stone tablets and set up on revolving axes in the council halls of Athens and other city-states. The Twelve Tables, promulgated in the early years of the republic (451–450 B.C.) as a compromise in the struggle between patricians and plebeians, embody the foundations of Roman law. Although the original bronze tablets that stood in the Forum were destroyed by the Gauls, the text was preserved because for centuries, as Cicero reports, every schoolboy in Rome had to memorize the laws. The legal tradition of the Franks, as incorporated in the *Lex Salica*, is one of the principal sources for our understanding of ancient Germanic society. The close sequence of civilization and law tempts the observer of history to one compelling conclusion: if in the beginning was the word, then the lawyers did not lag far behind.

Inevitably, a subject so central to human culture found its reflection in many works of world literature.[4] The Greek obsession with the law, evident in Plato's *Republic* and Aristotle's *Politics*, dominates classical tragedy from the beginning. Perhaps the most familiar example is Sophocles' *Antigone*, in which divine, or natural, law is brought into violent conflict with the positive law of the state when the heroine, in defiance of an edict prohibiting the burial of traitors, renders funeral honors to her brother Polynices and is punished by death. The fascination with law that motivates many of Shakespeare's plays is representative of the rising bourgeois society of the Renaissance all over Europe. The legal dilemma underlying *The Merchant of Venice*—whether or not a pound of human flesh is suitable mortgage for an otherwise unsecured loan—was treated in a number of works before Shakespeare appropriated the material for his tragicomic masterpiece. (Legal scholars for the past century have tended to take Shylock's side in the affair, believing that, while perhaps "the quality of mercy is not strain'd," Portia's legal reasoning most certainly is.) The very real concern about czarist law, which Dostoyevski had experienced at first hand, permeates *Crime and Punishment* as well as *The Brothers Karamazov*, which devotes almost one quarter of its thousand pages to the trial of Dmitri Karamazov for the alleged murder of his lecherous father. In *The Trial* Franz Kafka carries the device of legal process to its absurd metaphysical extreme when his hero, Joseph K., finds himself arrested, tried, and executed for a crime of which he is never informed or accused. And the literary infatuation with the law has continued unabated into the present.[5]

In one sense the three German works described at the outset reflect this human obsession with law. But one fundamental difference needs to be stressed. *Faust, Michael Kohlhaas*, and "Das Fräulein von Scuderi" are not just about law: unlike most of the other works mentioned so far, they were actually written by trained jurists.[6] Goethe, who came from a family of lawyers, studied jurisprudence at Leipzig and then at Strassburg, where in 1771 he received the degree of licentiate. Following a year of practical training, he spent the summer of 1772 as an intern (*Praktikant*) at the Imperial Chamber of Justice at Wetzlar, an experience roughly equivalent to that of clerk to a justice of the U.S. Supreme Court. Back home in Frankfurt am Main, he practiced law for two more years and handled—competently if not brilliantly—some twenty-eight cases before moving to Weimar in 1775.

Unlike Goethe, Kleist never completed a course of legal training. Having abandoned the military career traditional in his family, he studied law as well as the natural sciences during his three semesters in Frankfurt an der Oder (1800–1801) and then worked for a time as an intern in the Office of Public Finance and Economic Affairs in Berlin. After a hiatus of several years, Kleist was reassigned to the office of provincial administration in Königsberg, where again he attended lectures in law and public administration at the university before giving up government service altogether. However, his interest in the law did not cease, and in his career as a journalist he commented frequently on the legal reforms taking place in Prussia.

Hoffmann was one of the most dedicated jurists of his generation. He, too, studied in Königsberg and then immediately entered the Prussian legal administration, serving from 1800 to 1806 in several posts in Poland. Following Napoleon's defeat of the Prussians, the entire Prussian provincial administrative system was dismantled; for the next eight years Hoffmann eked out an existence in musical and theatrical positions in various German towns. But as soon as the French withdrew in 1814, he returned to the Prussian legal service, functioning as a widely respected judge in Berlin until his death in 1822.

What matters in the present context, however, is the fact that Goethe, Kleist, and Hoffmann were not exceptions. Indeed, they were exemplary for an age in which many writers studied jurisprudence at the university and often went on to practice law in one fashion or another. To mention just a few of the more conspicuous names: the educational reformer Wilhelm von Humboldt, the arch-Romantics Wackenroder and Novalis, the Heidelberg Romantics Görres, Arnim, and Eichendorff, the brothers Grimm and the philologist Friedrich von der Hagen, the scholar-balladeer Uhland and the historian Friedrich von Raumer, the dramatists Zacharias Werner, Grillparzer, Grabbe, and Hebbel, the aesthetician Karl Solger—and of course Heinrich Heine. In the *laudatio* pronounced by the distinguished jurist Gustav Hugo when Heine received his degree at Göttingen in 1825, the dean cited several of these names and others as well to emphasize the frequent felicitous conjunction of literature and law in German letters. *Quasi vero tandem inter nostrates neque Wielandus Göthius Sprickmannus Stolbergii Bürgerus Hoffmannus, neque sexcenti alii juris artem cum poesi junxissent.*[7] Now this list, which could easily be augmented, is quite astonishing. For probably no other country can claim so many writer-lawyers during this period—or, for that matter, any other period.

In a commencement address that he delivered at Brown University in 1897, Oliver Wendell Holmes, Jr., recalled the "black and frozen night" that obscured the world of law when he entered upon its study.[8] "One saw that artists and poets shrank from it as from an alien world. One doubted oneself how it could be worthy of the interest of an intelligent mind." That attitude has in large measure prevailed in Anglo-Saxon lands. Sir William Blackstone, one of the greatest legal minds in England, felt impelled to compose "The Lawyer's Farewell to his Muse" in 1744 when he went down from Oxford to enter the Inns of Court at London:

> Companion of my tender age,
> Serenely gay, and sweetly sage,
> How blithsome were we wont to rove
> By verdant hill, or shady grove.
> \* \* \* \* \* \* \* \* \* \* \* \* \* \* \* \* \* \* \* \* \*
> But now the pleasing dream is o'er,
> These scenes must charm me now no more,
> Lost to the field, and torn from you—
> Farewell!—a long, a last adieu!

> Me wrangling Courts, and stubborn Law,
> To smoke, and crowds, and cities draw;
> There selfish Faction rules the day,
> And Pride and Av'rice throng the way:
> \* \* \* \* \* \* \* \* \* \* \* \* \* \* \* \* \* \* \* \* \* \* \* \* \* \*
> No room for Peace, no room for you—
> Adieu, celestial Nymph, adieu![9]

And to turn to the Romantics: can anyone seriously imagine Wordsworth or Coleridge shrouded in barrister's gown and arguing before the bar? Shelley or Keats functioning as government officials? Or Byron presiding in peruke on the bench? More likely they would have agreed with Mr. Bumble in *Oliver Twist*: "The law is a ass—a idiot."

A few British novelists—notably Fielding and Scott—managed to combine legal activity with writing. But their contemporaries in the United States broke away as soon as possible from what Washington Irving called "this wrangling driving unmerciful profession."[10] The poets who have succeeded in combining law with literature are so rare that the occasional exception—e.g., Wallace Stevens—stands out prominently. More often they reject the profession, like William Cullen Bryant, whose early poems record his struggle to reconcile himself with his unhappy career.

Much the same is true in France, where Balzac is the notable exception: his training in a law office is apparent in many of his novels. A student has counted one hundred and eighteen characters associated with the law in the *Comédie humaine*.[11] But Flaubert, like Frédéric Moreau in *L'Education sentimentale*, failed his law exams. The many writers who had diplomatic careers—Chateaubriand, Lamartine, Stendhal—entered government service by routes other than the law—usually by way of the military. Stendhal allegedly liked to warm up for his writing each day by reading a few paragraphs from the Code Civil; and it is often said that the style of that great document exemplifies the lucidity prized by French writers. But one searches in vain for a generation of writer-jurists of the sort that dominated the scene in Germany during the Romantic age. What accounts for this striking difference?

## The History of Legal Study in Germany

It can be attributed in the first place to the fact that the study of law in Germany was a university course and not, as in England, France, and the United States, a period of practical training to be pursued in law offices, Inns of Court, or professional schools that replace or follow the university.[12] In England, to be sure, a certain kind of law was always taught at Oxford and Cambridge, but it was the history of Roman and canon law—not the common law required for legal practice. The first chair for the history of English law was not established at Oxford until 1758 (the

Vinerian) and at Cambridge until 1800 (the Downing). In the United States the first school of law—in contrast to practical apprenticeships in law offices—was founded at Harvard in 1817. And in France, following the abolition of the universities in 1794, all professional training took place in the newly established *écoles spéciales*.

In Germany, in contrast, law was always studied at the university, where it constituted one of the four traditional faculties. This explains the allusion in the opening monologue of Marlowe's *Doctor Faustus* as well as Goethe's *Faust*, where the aged scholar complains that he has attained advanced degrees in philosophy, medicine, theology, and law without being any wiser than before. The law faculty at a German university around 1800 embraced far more than specialized legal training of the sort available in the Inns of Court, the French *écoles spéciales*, or an American law school. While the reality no doubt fell short of the ideal, jurisprudence aspired to attain that synthesis of philosophy, history, and rhetoric that Vico proclaimed in his writings—most notably perhaps in the prologue to his *Diritto universale* (1720–1722).[13] For this reason, among others, nineteenth-century students with interests as diverse as Johann Jakob Bachofen, Karl Marx, and Max Weber received their university training as students of law.

Goethe's academic adviser in Leipzig, Councillor Böhme, persuaded him that jurisprudence was a better *studium generale* and a more useful introduction to the classical philology that Goethe wanted to pursue than the faculty of philosophy.[14] That Goethe took this lesson to heart is suggested by number XLI of the fifty-six theses that he defended when he took his law degree at Strassburg: *Studium Juris longe praestantissimum est*[15]—an assertion that echoes other tags from Justinian's *Digest* that were commonplace in European thinking of the age: *Jurisprudentia est divinarum, atque humanarum rerum notitia* or *Jurisprudentia est vere philosophia*.

The faculty of law at a German university amounted more or less to a faculty of social sciences equivalent to the Kennedy School of Government at Harvard, Princeton's Woodrow Wilson School of Public Affairs, or the London School of Economics. Rather than training the aspiring lawyer in practical skills and procedures, the law faculty taught through history and theory general principles of law that could be applied to individual cases.[16] Any student who sought a career in public administration, or cameralistics, would also normally enroll in the law faculty. And we should remind ourselves that in Germany, prior to the Napoleonic reform, there were hundreds of principalities that required a steady supply of administrators. Indeed, it was his law degree from Strassburg that qualified Goethe for the various administrative functions—from public works and war to theater and education—that he exercised in the duchy of Saxe-Weimar in the course of almost fifty years. In addition, law was the traditional course of study for sons of the nobility, who undertook that training not only with the expectation of government service but also in preparation for the management of their family estates.

For various reasons the law faculties at German universities developed slowly. Until the end of the seventeenth century they constituted only a small fraction of the faculty and student body; students desiring a legal curriculum often went to Italy and Holland for their training. But during the eighteenth century enrollments surged dramatically in Germany as the demand for trained jurists became more urgent and as ambitious young bourgeois sought careers in government.[17] For the century as a whole, the enrollments in law amounted to thirty-five percent of the student population in Germany, and at certain universities with a reputation for law—e.g., Strassburg—the proportion was well over fifty percent. At Heidelberg the enrollments in law grew from only twelve percent in 1704–1710 to over seventy-five percent a century later. Indeed, the study of law was so popular in eighteenth-century Halle that one professor of classics was driven to the lament: *ius, ius, ius—et nihil plus*.[18] When the University of Göttingen, newly established in 1737 and poorly subsidized, needed to attract wealthy students in order to compete with the older and more heavily endowed institutions, the minister of education made an important decision.[19] He played down theology, which tended to attract needy students, and set about engaging the best law faculty in Germany by means of high salaries. To entertain the rich young men who would be attracted by the law faculty, he followed the example of the *Ritter-Akademien* and appointed masters for fencing, dancing, riding, modern languages, and the other social graces. To care for the horses he also engaged the best equerry in Germany, who marched in academic processions just behind the full professors but ahead of the associate professors. The plan succeeded: Göttingen soon had the largest proportion of wealthy noblemen of any German university and a law faculty that became the envy of Europe.

As a result of these factors, German literature has always featured a considerable number of those literary lawyers whom Eugen Wohlhaupter, in his three-volume bio-bibliographical compilation, calls *Dichterjuristen*. Medicine still lacked respectability; theology became a less attractive subject for thoughtful young men during the Enlightenment; philosophy normally led to no other career than lowly schoolmasterships. A young nobleman with literary ambitions or a young bourgeois who hoped to support himself in a government post while writing had few alternatives other than the study of jurisprudence. At the same time, the legal scholar in Germany enjoyed a prestige and authority to a degree unparalleled in England, France, or the United States, owing to the fact that law in Germany was determined by professors (*Professorenrecht*) rather than by practical lawyers and judges (*Juristenrecht*).

However, even by German standards the number of jurists was unusually great during the Romantic period. Why should this be so? During the eighteenth century, although enrollments had continued to grow decade by decade for the reasons noted, no one boasted that law was an intellectually exciting or challenging field of study. According to a Latin tag common at the time, all that was required to be a competent jurist was a mind of iron, a seat of lead, and a purse of gold:

*Ferrea mens, podex sit plumbeus, aurea pera,*
*Juris-Consultus sic potes esse bonus.*[20]

The hero of Goethe's *Die Leiden des jungen Werther* (1774), like the author himself, is a lawyer who spends a good deal of his time advising people about the settlement of their estates.[21] However, when Werther accepts an administrative position as secretary to a legate (presumably at the Imperial Chancery), his supervisor, a "punctilious fool," expects him to write his reports in a precise chancery style rather than with quick inspiration.[22] Torn apart by this tension between his poetic aspirations and professional reality, Werther finally submits his resignation, aware that his mother will be dismayed that her son is giving up a promising career that was supposed to lead him to the security of a privy councillorship. Two decades later Wackenroder, forced by his lawyer-father to take up the study of law, complained to his friend Tieck:

My time is taken up by unworthy matters and distractions. Ach! Jurisprudence! When shall I be able to compel myself to belabor my memory with the terminology, definitions, distinctions, and so forth! What a curious web is Roman law of words and words and words, with which the simplest matters are entwined! And what a job the judge has! An incident that can shatter hearts and that drives minds mad, an affair of passion, or the human soul—how does he regard it? He searches among the various barbaric names that the Romans have given to the complaints to find the one that fits the case; and now the clockwork is wound up; it takes its course and unwinds.[23]

Most students of the period would have agreed with the student Hoffmann, who wrote to his friend Hippel in 1795: "My studies proceed slowly and gloomily. I have to force myself to become a jurist."[24] In the late eighteenth century the study of law, however useful it might be for purposes of career, remained essentially a mindless *Brotstudium*, as Mephistopheles characterized it in a satirical scene of *Faust* that Goethe wrote shortly after completing his own studies:

> Ich weiß, wie es um diese Lehre steht.
> Es erben sich Gesetz' und Rechte
> Wie eine ew'ge Krankheit fort,
> Sie schleppen von Geschlecht sich zum Geschlechte
> Und rücken sacht von Ort zu Ort.
> Vernunft wird Unsinn, Wohltat Plage;
> Weh dir, daß du ein Enkel bist!
> Vom Rechte, das mit uns geboren ist,
> Von dem ist leider! nie die Frage.
> (*Faust* I, 1971–79)

(I know all about this subject. Laws and rights are passed along from one generation to the next like a congenital disease, and spread gradually from place to place. Reason turns to nonsense, beneficence to torment. Woe that you are an epigone. Never a word, sad to say, about the rights that are born with us.)

Shortly after the turn of the century, however, the situation changed: jurisprudence suddenly emerged as an exciting field of study that attracted many of the best minds of the generation—a transformation due to the unique circumstances surrounding the law in Germany.

Although both English and German law are rooted in ancient Germanic common law as represented by the early medieval *leges Germanorum*, the two systems as they evolved over the centuries are appreciably different.[25] English law developed in the relative isolation of an island kingdom and, as a result, assumed the status of a common law for all of England. Being written down from the beginning in the Anglo-Saxon vernacular, it was unaffected even by the mild contamination that affected Germanic common law on the continent when it was translated into Latin, as in the *Lex Salica*. Ever since English common law received its first major systematization toward the end of the twelfth century in Glanvill's treatise on legal procedure, it has displayed a remarkable continuity through the works of such jurists as Bracton, Coke, and Blackstone. Brought to America by the British colonists, it provided the basis for the legal system of the United States. Until the Revolution young Americans often traveled to England to learn the law; some of the finest commentary has been written by American jurists like Oliver Wendell Holmes, Jr., whose magisterial study, *The Common Law* (1881), sums up in its opening paragraph the essence of common law as opposed to Roman law: "The life of the law has not been logic: it has been experience."

In German-speaking countries, in contrast, Germanic common law underwent a number of transformations.[26] For almost a thousand years it developed autonomously in scores of different political entities, with the result that medieval Germany was ruled by several overlapping systems of law: notably municipal, provincial, and imperial. These systems functioned according to a hierarchy of validity summed up in an old proverb that dictates the priority of provincial law over local law and of imperial common law over both: "Stadtrecht bricht Landrecht, Landrecht bricht gemeines Recht." (In fact, this deliberately ambiguous legal proverb could be used by either side, imperial or populist, in a jurisdictional conflict since the grammar permits exactly the opposite reading: that is, that local law breaks [transcends] territorial law, and territorial law breaks imperial law. But the point of overlapping legal systems is illustrated by either interpretation.)

The original common law was modified on the continent by two major waves of exposure to Roman law. First, through the very act of translation into Latin, Germanic law underwent a certain process of modification as Roman legal terms were adapted to describe Germanic procedures. Second, in constant exposure to the only truly international law of the Middle Ages—the canon law of the Church—secular lawmakers came to admire and appropriate some of the procedures that had been refined in the development of that sophisticated system. By the end of the Middle Ages secular law in the Holy Roman Empire amounted to a chaos of competing legal systems in a variety of languages and dialects. As the medieval traveler moved across Central Europe, he changed laws more frequently than he had to change language or even coinage.

By the end of the fifteenth century the situation clearly required reform. The emerging economic system of the Renaissance demanded personal security for businessmen as they traveled about Europe, as well as a system of contracts that would be binding from one city or state to another. This is made clear in *The Merchant of Venice* when Antonio explains why the duke must enforce Shylock's savage contract:

> The duke cannot deny the course of law:
> For the commodity that strangers have
> With us in Venice, if it be denied,
> Will much impeach the justice of his state;
> Since that trade and profit of the city
> Consisteth of all nations.
>
> (III.3)

Initiatives in this direction were first undertaken in Italy, where the new spirit of enterprise manifested itself earliest. It was at Bologna, Padua, and other North Italian universities that formal instruction in secular law began according to a system based upon commentaries on Justinian's sixth-century compilation of the *Corpus juris civilis*. This Roman law, as revised by the so-called glossators—*jus commune*—gradually made its way north of the Alps as German students returned home with their new learning. The process through which the emerging national states adapted Roman civil law to their local circumstances, is known as the Reception, and it constitutes, along with the Renaissance and Reformation, one of the "three R's" that characterize early modern society in Germany.

Various factors favored the Reception of Roman legal tradition, rather than the reform of common law, as a new basis for the German legal system.[27] First, it served the self-interest of the Germans who had gone to Italy to study Roman and canon law. Germanic common law did not recognize lawyers as advocates: a man seeking justice or accused of a crime might have advisers in the persons of wise or experienced friends, but in legal situations he had to represent himself in court. The early jurists trained in Roman law were therefore interested in introducing a system of law that recognized the trained advocate. (Goethe understood and satirized this often blatant self-interest in the figure of the jurist Olearius in the first act of *Götz von Berlichingen* [1773].) The interests of the lawyers were paralleled, second, by the concerns of the general public, which had long found the local laws inadequate in many cases and, as we have seen, complicated as one moved from place to place. Third, the study of Roman law in Latin was supported by the Humanists, who were beginning to emerge as an intellectual force in Germany and who were committed to any development that helped to restore what they regarded as the values of classical antiquity. Finally, the emperor and the ruling aristocracy were favorably disposed toward any system of law that would help to centralize their authority and work against the particularization that made governance a chaotic nightmare. All of these more or less self-serving motives could be subsumed loftily under the ideological appeal known as *translatio imperii*—the view that the imposition of Roman law was tantamount to restoring the continuity of the Holy Roman Empire and its institutions.

By the beginning of the sixteenth century German-speaking Europe was governed by a legal system known as the *usus modernus pandectarum*, which consisted of an amalgam of Roman law, canon law, and Germanic common law. To preside over questions of law that affected the entire empire—notably to suppress private wars and to enforce the virtually sacred policy of public peace that Michael Kohlhaas was guilty of breaching—Emperor Maximilian established in 1495 an Imperial Chamber of Justice (*Reichskammergericht*) that was based on Roman law and that for the next three hundred years constituted the highest court of appeal in Germany. Unlike the medieval courts of law, which moved from place to place with the ruler, the Imperial Chancery—along with its steadily swelling archives—was located in one place: first at Worms, then Speyer, and finally from 1683 to 1806 in Wetzlar, where Goethe came to know it.

In several informative pages of his autobiography Goethe describes the historical background that led to the establishment of the *Reichskammergericht*—a period that he knew from his legal studies as well as the research for his drama *Götz von Berlichingen*. Goethe appreciated both the urgent need for an Imperial Chancery—to enable the state to ensure the security of persons and property—and the weaknesses inherent in its organization from the start: inadequate resources to achieve the prescribed goal. Inevitably, therefore, the system became more and more cumbersome until, when Goethe worked there in 1772, it was about to collapse under its own weight of three centuries. "There had not been an adequate inspection for one hundred and sixty-six years," he observed in *Dichtung und Wahrheit*. "A massive swollen chaos of dossiers lay there and grew from year to year because the seventeen assessors were not capable of keeping up even with current business. Twenty thousand cases had piled up; annually some sixty could be handled; and double that number was added."[28] So cynical was Goethe about the entire institution that on August 7, 1806, when he learned on a trip from Karlsbad to Weimar that Emperor Franz II had abdicated, he noted in his diary that a quarrel between the footman and the coachman excited more interest among the passengers than the collapse of the Holy Roman Empire.

During the century of its decline modern Roman law was paralleled, and eventually threatened, by another system that gradually grew into complete autonomy: so-called natural law. Notoriously the term "natural law" has been used to designate a number of systems of thought.[29] Most simply one might define natural law as any philosophical or ideological system on the basis of which an age attempts to rationalize and justify its existing positive law. In antiquity and in the Christian Middle Ages this legitimation was sought in transcendent authorities. Cicero believed in a divine *ratio* that could be abstracted from a comparative study of the legal practices governing the various peoples with whom the Romans had to deal. Thomas Aquinas perceived behind the secular laws of the thirteenth century a *lex aeterna* that expressed the will of God. Citing Goethe again, we hear an echo of this traditional understanding of natural law— that it is whatever nature teaches all beings—in the first of the fifty-six theses that he defended to obtain his legal license: *Jus naturae est, quod natura omnia animalia docuit*.[30]

But the rationalism of the seventeenth and eighteenth centuries shifted the emphasis: an anthropocentric natural law no longer sought the basis of universal human rights in God or nature but exclusively in human reason. Rather than regarding human laws as the secular expression of a higher will, Hugo Grotius and his followers in Germany—Pufendorf, Thomasius, Christian Wolff, and others—sought to deduce an ideal system of law from pure reason.[31] As natural law grew away from positive law, it became less and less a juristic and increasingly a philosophical activity. Thus in 1796 Fichte published a volume on the grounds of natural law (*Grundlage des Naturrechts*), and in 1797 Kant brought out his "metaphysical rudiments of legal theory" as the first part of his *Metaphysik der Sitten*. This meant, on the one hand, that natural law became a widespread topic of intellectual discourse—a discourse in which everyone, whether legally trained or not, felt qualified to take part. For examples we need go no further than the effusions about Rousseau in the letters of Hölderlin, Kleist, and other young Romantics. On the other hand, natural law was gradually discredited in the eyes of jurists and others because a natural law that has detached itself from all positive law and all historical reality often came to mutually contradictory conclusions. For instance, Thomas Hobbes maintained that a martial state of *bellum omnium contra omnes* was the necessary prerequisite for the original social contract, while Rousseau believed that the social contract emerged from a paradisiacal primal condition. In any event, popular and increasingly irresponsible theorizing about natural law produced toward the end of the eighteenth century a veritable flood of publications, whose extravagances Schiller ridiculed in his poem "Die Weltweisen":

> "Der Mensch bedarf des Menschen sehr
> Zu seinem großen Ziele,
> Nur in dem Ganzen wirket er,
> Viel Tropfen geben erst das Meer,
> Viel Wasser treibt die Mühle.
> Drum flieht der wilden Wölfe Stand
> Und knüpft des Staates daurend Band."
> So lehren vom Katheder
> Herr Pufendorf und Feder.[32]

("Man needs his fellow man to achieve his great goal; man can be effective only as part of the whole; it takes many drops to make the ocean; it takes much water to move the mill. Therefore flee the condition of wild wolves and knot the lasting bond of the state." Thus teach from their lecterns Herr Pufendorf and Herr Feder.)

In the account that Eichendorff wrote of his studies at Halle and Heidelberg he recalled that in the first decade of the century "the jurists were teaching a so-called Natural Law, which was valid nowhere and never could be valid."[33] It was joked at the time that every book fair brought forth a new theory of natural law.

### THE CODIFICATION CONTROVERSY

These developments eventually produced in Germany of the Napoleonic age a series of legal controversies that were followed with considerable interest by most educated contemporaries. The first stage of the controversy pitted the advocates of an increasingly sterile natural law against two groups of opponents. Legal positivists insisted on the reality of existing laws, in contrast to the abstractions of the natural-law theorists. Meanwhile, the newly emerging historical school of legal science opposed natural law out of the conviction that law cannot be invented by reason but only given through history.

No sooner had natural law been discredited in Germany than a second battle flared up between the legal positivists and the historical school—the so-called codification controversy.[34] An impulse toward codification had motivated various enlightened despots of the eighteenth century, notably in Bavaria and Prussia. In 1746, shortly after ascending to the throne, Frederick the Great commissioned his chancellor, Samuel Cocceji, to produce a *Corpus Juris Fridericiani*, which was supposed to be a standardized legal code for Prussia grounded in natural law as well as local constitutions and intended to transpose Roman law into a natural order and proper system.[35] Frederick's project was opposed by the nobility because of its attempt to bring Enlightenment notions of human rights out of the lecture halls and into everyday life. And it was interrupted almost immediately by the Seven Years War. As a result, it took more than thirty years before a new chancellor, Heinrich Casimir von Carmer, with the assistance of his brilliant colleague Carl Gottlieb Svarez, was able to lay before the public a complete draft of the new code. From 1784 until 1788 the titles were published individually, and competent jurists were invited to append their comments. The characteristic combination of natural law and positive law was evident in the announcement of a competition for the best commentary to accompany the code. A textbook in two parts was required: natural law was to be treated in Latin and the theory of Prussian positive law in German.[36]

Friedrich Wilhelm II was by no means so sympathetic to the progressive ideas of the Enlightenment as his predecessor, and between the draft of the 1780s and the final text of the *Allgemeines Landrecht* (ALR), as formulated by Svarez and enacted in 1794, a number of changes took place. For instance, the authors were careful not to jeopardize support for the new code by challenging the principle of serfdom that was so crucial to the aristocracy (pt. II, title 7). Carmer and Svarez, who were not so much reformers as bureaucrats, were concerned not with creating new laws but with codifying the existing ones. However, for all its basic conservatism, this great document of Prussian Enlightenment constituted a challenge to tradition simply by the fact of codification, which in effect took the interpretation of law out of the hands of established authority and handed it over to the people. Written in a clear, crisp German—with only one sentence for each of its more than 19,000 paragraphs—the ALR rapidly permeated the consciousness of Prussian citizens. Through the public debates around 1790, through the so-called "Crown Prince Lectures" that Svarez delivered in 1792 for the legal education of the future Friedrich Wilhelm III, and through legal training and practice, general familiarity with the new code spread so quickly and thoroughly that, only twenty years later, Achim von Arnim regarded it as equal in cultural importance to Luther's translation of the Bible.[37]

A second great code, which succeeded in transcending the boundaries of an individual state, was the French Code Civil of 1804. This document, known for a time simply as the Code Napoléon, was widely admired as the embodiment of revolutionary principles of liberty and equality. Patterned extensively after the *Corpus juris civilis* rather than natural law, it amounted to a simplified and modernized version of Justinian's vast compilation. (Indeed, it accomplished the astonishing feat of encompassing the totality of French law in a slender volume of 2,281 articles.) Acclaimed eagerly by liberal thinkers, it spread rapidly across most of Europe and into Latin America. Napoleon realized that a common legal system was essential if he hoped to consolidate and unify the territories linked initially only by military conquest. In the annexed German territories on the left bank of the Rhine the code was adopted immediately in 1804 and provided the basis of law until the end of the nineteenth century.[38] Again, however, there was from the start a good deal of opposition to its spread in other territories, especially from the conservative German aristocracy, which saw in the code a subversive tool of the rising middle class. In 1806, when Franz II abdicated as emperor of the Holy Roman Empire and the apparatus of the Imperial Chancery was abolished, the various principalities had to decide whether to accept one of the existing codes, to create a new national code, or to fall back into a judicial chaos encompassing scores of particular local systems of incompatible customary law.

It was the debate stemming from this legal crisis that transformed jurisprudence into a lively issue that engaged the attention of thinking men and women in Germany. This controversy embraced virtually every important theme of the Romantic period. The first factor was nationalism: the Code Napoléon was viewed by many as a French creation, imposed by the hated enemy in place of the cumbersome but cozy compromise of Roman law and local common law that had been in effect for three centuries. But the argument went further. First, the codifiers wanted their law in the vernacular: like all revolutionaries from Plato by way of Thomas More to Thomas Jefferson and Karl Marx, they envisioned a society in which citizens would be able to interpret a rational law for themselves without the interference of lawyers. Their opponents, in contrast, felt that the law was too delicate an instrument to be left to the laymen: the Latin in which Justinian's *Corpus juris civilis* was preserved functioned as a necessary barrier between the expert and an ignorant public. The so-called Romanists regarded it as futile to attempt in a few short years to write any new code that could deal with all the subtleties identified, explored, and resolved in more than a millennium of often brilliant exegesis. While the codifiers believed in the emerging bourgeois values of liberty and equality, their opponents objected to the French code because it made no allowance for such central concepts of Roman law as aristocratic privilege, feudal right, and primogeniture. Codification was modern and rational; Roman-German law had grown organically, it was argued, in a historical process that was viewed as well-nigh sacred.

It is hardly astonishing that a controversy involving such explosive issues as the nationalistic antagonism between German and French, the philosophical argument between history and theory, the political struggle between aristocratic privilege and bourgeois rights, and the educational tension between learned Latin and the middle-class vernacular should have engaged the finest minds of the age. We have already mentioned some of the writers who studied law and the leading thinkers who dealt with the philosophy of law. We should also recall that many of the leading thinkers in Germany during these decades were concerned with the philosophy of law: Kant in *Die Metaphysik der Sitten* (1797), Fichte in his 1812 lectures on *Rechtslehre*, and Hegel in his *Grundlinien der Philosophie des Rechts* (1821). Moreover, at the very center of the controversy stood two of the most highly respected civil jurists of the period, Anton Friedrich Justus Thibaut (1772–1840) and Friedrich Carl von Savigny (1779–1861).

By the beginning of 1814 it was evident that a crisis was imminent: Napoleon had just been defeated and the pressure for codification removed. How should Germany prevent the chaos that would result in the vacuum left behind by the removal of military rule? There were essentially three possibilities: to retain the Code Napoléon, to create for Germany a new code, or to revert to the old system of Roman law supplemented by local customary law. The debate was catalyzed by a pamphlet, *Über den Code Napoleon und dessen Einführung in Deutschland*, published early in 1814 by August Wilhelm Rehberg, a royal councillor in the kingdom of Hannover. Rehberg, a staunch conservative inflated by chauvinism, contemptuously rejected those "philosophical enthusiasts who want to introduce total freedom and equality among men"[39] and argued that Germany, eschewing the artificial unity of Roman law, should revert to a patchwork of particularized legal systems. Rehberg's reactionary proposal was immediately attacked by Thibaut—first in a review and then in a pamphlet entitled *Ueber die Nothwendigkeit eines allgemeinen bürgerlichen Rechts für Deutschland* (Heidelberg, 1814).

The most charismatic teacher in the outstanding legal faculty at Heidelberg, where in 1808 three-quarters of the 440 students (including Goethe's son August) were studying jurisprudence or cameralistics, Thibaut was keenly aware of the dangers and opportunities inherent in the historical moment. He considered it inevitable that Germany would reject the political unity imposed on her by Napoleon along with its potential advantages, but he was convinced that it would be a tragedy if the nation should also forsake the benefits of a unified system of law. "I am of the opinion that our civil law ... requires a total, immediate change and that the Germans cannot become content in their civil circumstances otherwise than if all German governments seek with unified forces to effect the promulgation of a single law code valid for all Germany and removed from the whim of the individual governments" (67).[40]

The old German law was so incomplete that of any hundred questions put to it, ninety must be answered from Roman or canon law. Roman law, in turn, a product of Rome's period of most abysmal decline, was so vast and complex that not even the most learned scholar could master it in its entirety. What was needed, therefore, was a new code written specifically for Germany. "A simple national code of law, executed with German vigor in the German spirit, will be accessible in all its parts to every mind, even the average one, and our lawyers and judges will finally be in a position where the law will be available to them for every case" (74). Such a code will also benefit scholars and students inasmuch as it will bring together, for the first time, the legal theories of the universities and its actual practice in the courts. A common code of law, finally, will provide a legal and ethical unity for the nation transcending the inevitable political separation of states.

Fully aware of the difficulties inherent in such a project, Thibaut anticipates two kinds of opposition—public and covert. Among the latter he cites principally the concern among rulers that a code of law might undermine their authority and the fear that unscrupulous advisers would use the occasion to stir up among rulers a distrust of the German people. Here Thibaut is prepared to rely on the good sense of the rulers to see that the people themselves constitute the greatest source of national strength. Chief among the public concerns is the belief that law must reflect the spirit of the people according to time, place, and circumstances—a view advocated ever since Montesquieu. Thibaut refutes this view with what might be called a "worst-case" scenario, asking us to imagine what sorts of laws would be written by a people responding to the least noble and rational of its impulses. With similar common sense Thibaut anticipates and addresses the other arguments being advanced at the time, producing in the process the most compelling and urgent exposition of the need for a common code of law for the entire German nation.

Such were Thibaut's authority and persuasiveness that he might have carried the day even against the rallying forces of conservatism, which were seeking to recapture the privileges lost under Napoleon, had his opponent been anyone but Savigny, the most brilliant jurist of the day. Though both were historians of Roman law, the differences were striking. Thibaut's genuinely republican sentiments stemmed from his family circumstances. Growing up in Hannover as the son of an officer of Huguenot descent, he was essentially modest in temperament, Protestant in his beliefs, and bourgeois in his aspirations. For Thibaut the law was not a sacred mystery to be practiced, like the Mass, by priestlike specialists in a churchly Latin for the benefit of the devout, but a right accessible in plain German to all citizens in equal measure. It was this "Jacobin" doctrine, noted in 1807 by Eichendorff, that he professed quietly and steadily to many generations of students—first at Kiel and Jena and then at Heidelberg, where he taught from 1805 until his death in 1840, as much beloved for the evenings of choral music that he conducted every week in his house as he was respected for his dedicated pedagogy.[41]

Savigny, in contrast, was intemperate and single-minded in his convictions. Conservative, wealthy, and married into a devoutly Catholic family (the Brentanos), he was perfectly well satisfied with matters as they had been since the Middle Ages. He loathed the revolutionary French and everything they stood for—including especially their detested code. But he hated all codes and insisted to his brother-in-law, the poet Arnim, that the Prussian code also was "eine Schweinerei."[42] A professor who demanded absolute loyalty from his students, he used his chair at the newly established University of Berlin to indoctrinate the youth of Prussia. While he and Thibaut had been friendly acquaintances in their early years, he was later piqued because Thibaut had accepted the position at Heidelberg that had initially been offered to Savigny, and their dispute contains more than a touch of personal rivalry.

Even before Thibaut's response to Rehberg, Savigny had been arguing against codification in his lectures. His epoch-making first book on the Roman laws of possession, *Das Recht des Besitzes* (1803), which had quickly established the young scholar's reputation, begins with the assertion that "the characteristic law of a people can no more be reduced to a stable concept than can its language, because its essential nature consists rather in continual growth and development" ("in ununterbrochener Bildung und Entwickelung"). At the time he was preparing a statement of his own, which he now rushed into print under the title *Vom Beruf unsrer Zeit für Gesetzgebung und Rechtswissenschaft* (Heidelberg, 1814). All of Savigny's passion and brilliance went into this document, which stands as one of the most crucial and representative statements of German Romantic ideology. Savigny argues that Germany has no need for codification and, indeed, no capacity for that great task. All that is needed is a thorough understanding of Roman law—not according to the principles of rational jurisprudence, which had recently contributed to the deterioration of law in Germany, but according to the historical principles of a new science of law for which Savigny coined the term *Rechtswissenschaft*, which occupies the most prominent place on the title page of his brochure.

Savigny acknowledges the urgent need for a generally accepted civil law now that the threat of suppression by the French has been warded off and the Napoleonic code—which Savigny abhors as a disease that "consumed everything around it like a cancer" (98)[43]—has been disposed of. He argues, however, that rational jurisprudence is mistaken in its belief that law can be produced by the prescriptions of authority. History teaches us that everywhere law has a specific character, unique to its people, like language and customs—that law is everywhere unified by the feeling of its people and exists in an "organic connection" of law and folk (103). The true seat of law, he insists, is the shared consciousness of the people ("ein gemeinsames Bewußtseyn des Volkes," 105). Common law ("Gewohnheitsrecht") emerged always from custom and popular be-

lief—through quietly working inner forces rather than through the ca-
price of individual legislators (ch. 2). Till recently such a common law—
that is, Roman law as modified by local law—had prevailed in Germany
(ch. 5). Although Savigny concedes that the system involves both the de-
lays cited by Goethe and excessive variety, he insists that this combination
is best suited for Germany. He rejects the view that every age is equally
well qualified to formulate its own laws (ch. 6). Indeed, the capacity for
legislation ("Gesetzgebung") varies as greatly from age to age and from
country to country as do the arts. His own age lacks precisely the two
senses essential to the gifted jurist: the sense of history, needed to comprehend the uniqueness of every age and every form of law, and the sense
of system, needed to understand each concept in its context and relation
to the whole.

Savigny devotes the lengthy middle section of his book (ch. 7) to a
detailed analysis of three new codes—the Code Napoléon, the Prussian
*Allgemeines Landrecht* of 1794, and the Austrian *Allgemeines Bürgerliches
Gesetzbuch* of 1811—and exposes what he considers the inadequacies of
each as proof that the present age has no calling to undertake a new code
of law. The defects in the juristic education of an entire generation are
manifest not just in specific shortcomings but in the character of the
whole enterprise.

What is needed, rather, is a new science of law—*Rechtswissenschaft*—
that addresses Roman law, Germanic law, and the modifications of both
great systems (ch. 8). We need to study the Roman jurists until we can
actually think as they did and thereby educate a new school of jurists in
Germany capable of creating a living common law ("lebendiges Gewohnheitsrecht," 175) that will enable jurists to settle new controversies on the
basis of old precedent. While he compares the French code to "a political
disease that has been survived" (176), he says that too much confusion
would result if the Prussian and Austrian codes should be discarded at
this time (ch. 9). Although the codes need to be retained as a practical
expedient, the teaching of law in the universities should focus on Roman
law taught according to Latin textbooks, for the goal of university juristic
education is not practical training but the knowledge and understanding
of law and its assumptions. A new code would divide Germany into three
areas: Austria, Prussia, and the other lands (ch. 10). Instead, all should
share and study the common sources of law ("die Urquellen unsres
Rechts," 187).

While he agrees with Thibaut on the goal of national unity (ch. 11), he disagrees on the possibility of a code by committee: a book of law should be an organic whole rather than an aggregate of separate decisions. At present Germany lacks both the jurists capable of conceiving a truly popular code and a language in which to write it. The goal should therefore be to establish a basis for a secure system of law and to serve the community of the nation (ch. 12). "I see the proper means in an organically progressing science of law, which can be common to the entire nation" (192). The problem does not lie, as the codifiers argue, in the ancient sources of Roman and common law, but in the nation itself. Recapitulating his title, Savigny sums up by stating that Germany has at present no true calling for legislation but an enormous talent for the study of law.

The codification controversy was by no means limited to these two most articulate spokesmen. The battle was waged in the leading journals, and many jurists and public figures joined the fray.[44] Gustav Hugo, professor of ancient Roman law at Göttingen, weighed in on the side of Savigny and the traditionalists, while the respected criminal lawyer Anselm von Feuerbach came to the support of Thibaut. The two principals continued the battle to the end of their careers. In 1838, only two years before his death, Thibaut defended the position of the codifiers against the charge of anti-historicism by Savigny and his followers in an article entitled "Über die sogenannte historische und nicht-historische Rechtsschule." Savigny restated his opposition to codes in the preface to a second edition of his monograph in 1828, and as Prussian minister of justice from 1842 to 1848 he was in a particularly favorable position to prevent any effective movement toward codification.

For all practical purposes the debate was won in 1814. Savigny's arguments as well as his rhetoric appealed to the forces of restoration mustering themselves at the Congress of Vienna. In the realm of jurisprudence Germany returned in effect to the status of the years before 1806, and this situation prevailed until the end of the nineteenth century. It was not until 1896 that a newly unified Germany finally adopted a civil code valid for the entire nation—the *Bürgerliches Gesetzbuch*—which took effect on the first day of the new century.

## THE ATTRACTION OF NATURAL LAW

It is hardly surprising, in the light of all that has been said, to find that legal issues are so frequently evident in German literature of the period from the French Revolution until the defeat of Napoleon. During this age of great social and political upheaval the law was a matter of general and urgent concern for all citizens. A number of dramatic events—including the promulgation of the Prussian *Allgemeines Landrecht* in 1794, the imposition of the Code Civil in 1804, the abolition of the Holy Roman Empire and its Imperial Chancery in 1806, and the Congress of Vienna in 1814–1815—kept the question of law before the public eye. A series of legal controversies involving natural law, codified positive law, and traditional Roman law claimed the intellectual attention of the nation for two decades. And many writers, as we noted, were professionally qualified to follow these controversies with interest and understanding. Indeed, it could even be argued that it is not possible fully to appreciate the implications and subtleties of much contemporary literature without at least a general sense of the larger juristic context within which the works were created. It is frequently useful to ask, therefore, where a writer of the period stands with respect to the controversies: naturalist, positivist, or historicist.

Generally speaking, the writers attracted to natural law were heirs of the Enlightenment who approached questions of law from a philosophical standpoint indebted to Kant. The law that concerned them was not positive or historical but law at the level of broad human rights. Kant's own obligation to natural law is evident in many of his writings,[45] as, for instance, in his widely influential "philosophical project," *Zum ewigen Frieden* (1795), published in the year of the Treaty of Basel.[46] In a supplement entitled "Von der Garantie des Ewigen Friedens" Kant writes that "what accomplishes this security (guarantee) is nothing less than the great artist Nature (*natura daedala rerum*)" (217).[47] "When I say of Nature: She wishes this or that to happen," Kant continues, "that does not means that she imposes a duty upon us to do it (for only the non-compulsory practical reason can do that), but she does it herself, whether we wish it or not" (223). "Nature desires irresistibly that law [or right] maintain the supreme power" (225). It is this fundamental assumption that law and human rights are inherent in nature that underlies particularly the early Romantic philosophy of law.

Wilhelm von Humboldt's monograph on the limits of government, *Ideen zu einem Versuch, die Gränzen der Wirksamkeit des Staats zu bestimmen* (1792), was not published until 1851 and therefore had no public impact during his lifetime, but it is a representative document of Kantian thinking about law. It is Humboldt's fundamental thesis that "true reason can wish for man no condition other than one in which each individual enjoys the most unrestrained freedom to develop out of himself in his uniqueness" (69).[48] Humboldt's understanding of the state and its laws is derived with absolute rigor from that classically conservative conviction and leads to the first principle of his essay: "The state should restrain itself from all concern for the positive well-being of its citizens and go no further than is necessary for its internal security and its security against external enemies; it should not restrict their freedom for any other purpose" (90). Accordingly, in the section on criminal law (ch. 10) Humboldt concludes that "in order to assure the security of the citizens the state must prohibit . . . or limit those actions whose results affect the rights of others" (156); but any further restriction of private liberties lies beyond the proper limits of government. Similarly, the principles governing the establishment of civil laws (ch. 11) are restricted to cases in which the individual undertakes actions that go beyond his own property and affect others (171–72). Humboldt concludes by stating the principle of human reason that should govern any political change: "In order to accomplish the transition from present circumstances to new ones that have been decided upon, let every reform, insofar as possible, proceed from the ideas and the minds of men" (216)—and not, in other words, from the vast corpus of existing positive laws either Roman or German. He reminds us, finally, that "in the purely theoretical principles established above I proceeded in every case from the nature of man" (216).

A similar faith in the principles of natural law is still evident in the works of certain writers around the turn of the century before natural law had been discredited by the excesses of its advocates. Schiller's *Wilhelm Tell* (1804) is set against the struggle of the Swiss cantons to maintain their independence from the governors of the Austrian emperors who attempted to impose harsh new laws upon them. In the famous scene on the Rütli, where the representatives assemble to plan their resistance, the appeal to natural law is based not on early fourteenth-century legal principles but on Kant's ethics and Rousseau's vision of a beatific primal society:

> Nein, eine Grenze hat Tyrannenmacht,
> Wenn der Gedrückte nirgends Recht kann finden,
> Wenn unerträglich wird die Last—greift er
> Hinauf getrosten Mutes in den Himmel
> Und holt herunter seine ewgen Rechte,

Die droben hangen unveräußerlich
Und unzerbrechlich wie die Sterne selbst—
Der alte Urstand der Natur kehrt wieder,
Wo Mensch dem Menschen gegenübersteht.

(II.2)[49]

(There is a limit to the tyrant's might. If man oppressed can
nowhere find his right, if the burden becomes intolerable—he
reaches calmly into the heavens and fetches down his eternal
rights that hang above, inalienable and inviolable like the stars
themselves. The ancient primal state of nature returns when
man confronts his fellow man directly.)

Hölderlin was as much taken by Rousseau and natural law as was his
fellow Swabian, Schiller. While he was composing his early hymn to
mankind ("Hymne an die Menschheit," 1791), Hölderlin wrote to his
friend Neuffer that he had been "letting [himself] be instructed by the
great Jean Jacques in the matter of human rights."[50] Several years later
he wrote to his brother Karl that mathematics is the only science that can
match the perfection of natural law. "I now occupy myself frequently
with this splendid science and find, to state it once more, that this subject
and the theory of law as it can and must become are the only pure sciences in the entire realm of the human spirit that are perfect to this degree."[51] (It should be stressed that formal legal training played no part
whatsoever in Hölderlin's seminary education.) It is hardly surprising,
therefore, to find similar sentiments reflected in his poetry of the early
years. In his "Hymne an die Menschheit" the motto from Rousseau's *Du
Contrat Social* is followed, in the third strophe, by a paean to "brotherly
rights" ("Wir reichen uns die Bruderrechte gerne"). And in his "Hymne
an die Freiheit" (1792) the spirit of Liberty recounts the myth of her
origins:

"Als die Liebe noch im Schäferkleide
Mit der Unschuld unter Blumen ging,
Und der Erdensohn in Ruh und Freude
Der Natur am Mutterbusen hing,
Nicht der Übermut auf Richterstühlen
Blind und fürchterlich das Band zerriß,
Tauscht ich gerne mit der Götter Spielen
Meiner Kinder stilles Paradies."

("When love in her shepherd's garb still walked among flowers with innocence, and the son of earth clung in peace and joy to nature's motherly breast, and arrogance on its seats of judgment did not yet tear apart the bond blindly and terribly, I gladly exchanged the quiet paradise of my children for the sports of the gods.")

But this tranquil condition gradually gave way, she continues, to a state of turmoil, and "law's rod" ("des Gesetzes Rute") arose to imitate what formerly love alone had created.

A similar thought is evident, now applied to aesthetics, in the ode "Natur und Kunst," which juxtaposes Jupiter, the god of laws, and his father, Saturn, who lived in an age when it was still not necessary to issue commands and prohibitions:

> Du waltest hoch am Tag und es blühet dein
> Gesetz, du hältst die Waage, Saturnus Sohn!
> Und teilst die Los' und ruhest froh im
> Ruhm der unsterblichen Herrscherkünste.
>
> Doch in den Abgrund, sagen die Sänger sich,
> Habst du den heilgen Vater, den eignen, einst
> Verwiesen und es jammre drunten,
> Da, wo die Wilden vor dir mit Recht sind,
>
> Schuldlos der Gott der goldenen Zeit schon längst:
> Einst mühelos, und größer, wie du, wenn schon
> Er kein Gebot aussprach und ihn der
> Sterblichen keiner mit Namen nannte.[52]

(You reign on high and your law blossoms; you hold the scales, son of Saturn! And you distribute the lots and rest happily in the glory of the immortal arts of rulership. But the bards relate that once you thrust your own sacred father into the abyss and that down below, where those who are unruly before you properly belong, the god of the golden age has long lamented in innocence: once without cares and greater than you, even though he uttered no commandments and none of the mortals called him by name.)

Heinrich von Kleist was educated in a Prussian military system that was based on the natural law of Pufendorf. (Pufendorf's version of natural law was favored in Prussia because it emphasized duties rather than rights.) Accordingly the twenty-two-year-old wrote to his sister Ulrike: "We two, who care so little for the ceremonies of religion and the prescriptions of conventional fortune, must hold all the more holy the laws of reason. The state demands no more from us than that we not transgress the ten commandments. But who imposes on us the virtues of love for our fellow man, of tolerance, modesty, morality, if not reason?"[53] Kleist's early exposure to natural law was continued at the University of Frankfurt an der Oder, where he attended the lectures of Professor Ludwig Gottfried Madihn, a representative of the most trivial late eighteenth-century variety of natural law.[54] However, Kleist's naive version of natural law was unable to maintain itself when he arrived in Paris in 1801 and discovered that life in the capital of the new republic was flagrantly at odds with the teachings of Rousseau. France, he writes, is riper for downfall than any other European nation. Looking at the splendid libraries that house the volumes of Rousseau, Helvetius, and Voltaire, he wonders what good they did. Has a single work achieved its purpose? He bitterly questions the notion of natural law that he had unquestioningly accepted. "Let no one say that a voice within us secretly and clearly confides in us what is right. The same voice that calls out to the Christian to forgive his enemy also commands the savage to roast him, and with reverence he gobbles him up."[55]

Schiller died in 1805, and Hölderlin was subsiding gently into madness by 1806. Kleist, however, lived long enough to witness both the discreditation of natural law and the national indignity of the Prussian defeat in 1806. Those experiences, as we shall see, significantly altered his view of law and his treatment of it in his works.

This is the appropriate place, finally, to consider that remarkable and anomalous work that is linked to Romanticism most intricately through its inversions: the *Nachtwachen von Bonaventura* (1804). The author may poke fun at the sentiment of Novalis's *Hymnen an die Nacht* and at the subtleties of Fichte's speculative system. But the list of his topics amounts to a catalogue of the principal themes and motifs of the age. It is hardly surprising, then, to discover that two of the sixteen "nightwatches" that constitute the book (nos. 3 and 7) are devoted to questions of law. At one point the narrator, Kreuzgang, seems to be exposing his own beliefs when he laments the fact that the common people—"beggars, vagabonds, and other poor devils like me" (61)[56]—have conceded the power of law to the princes and rulers. "I was truly unable to find a corner of ground where I could let myself down, so completely had they divided and fragmented every hand's breadth among themselves, refusing to acknowledge natural law as the single general and positive law and, instead, maintaining in every nook and cranny their own special law and their own special faith."

But it is not so much his aim to advocate natural law as to attack other manifestations of law, and he does so with the knowledge and skill of the trained advocate. Kreuzgang, we learn in the course of his nocturnal ruminations, was a foundling who was brought up by a shoemaker with a taste for the writings of those poetic cobblers Hans Sachs and Jakob Böhme. He worked as a writer, actor, puppeteer, and even served time in a madhouse (as we shall see in the next chapter) before settling down to his job as nightwatchman in an unnamed German town. At some point in his career he also found time to study the three professions ("Brotfakultäten," 84), and from his references—which include Justinian and Charles V's criminal code, the *Constitutio criminalis Carolina* of 1532 (19), but never the *Allgemeines Landrecht*—we can assume that he studied not in Prussia but in a part of the Holy Roman Empire that still practiced law according to the *usus modernus pandectarum*. At one point, when he is trying to dissuade a young actor from what appears to be a suicide attempt, he lists all the advantages of this world in comparison to the beyond. "What do you expect to gain over there, friend? Better laws perhaps? What ours down here have going for them is their age!" (103).

In any case, Kreuzgang has been admitted to the bar because, when summoned to answer to more than fifty charges of slander for his satires against church and state, he responds, "I appeared before the court as my own advocatus diaboli" (62), and makes a skillful presentation with citations from the *Corpus juris civilis* as well as modern studies (Adolf Dietrich Weber, *Über Injurien und Schmähschriften*, 1793). The first part of his statement is a typical satiric inversion: he argues that criminals might well lodge the same complaint against judges as do poets against critics: that they have knowledge of theory but not of practice. What a huge advantage for the state, he continues, if members of the court could familiarize themselves with crime on a practical level and actually help bring it to light by mingling among thieves, visiting bordellos, and acting as partners in adultery. In the second part of his statement he proceeds to his specific defense against the crime of *iniuria oralis*. Pointing out that he is accused of singing his slander, he argues that this fact alone provides grounds for dismissal because singers belong to the caste of poets, who, according to the latest literary theory, have no purposefulness and must therefore be permitted to slander and blaspheme as much as they like. In addition, poetic inspiration is akin to drunkenness, and drunkenness, as a gift of the gods, frees the accused from guilt. "But I intend to formulate my defense even more convincingly and therefore refer you to the writings of our most distinguished modern professors of law, in which it is bindingly demonstrated that justice has nothing to do with morality and that only an act affecting *external* rights can be imputed as a crime in the eyes of the law" (64). But, Kreuzgang concludes triumphantly, since his alleged injury was only moral, the accusation must be rejected as inadequate according to contemporary legal theory. He cites an authority to prove that no injury can be committed against persons who have forsaken the right to their honor. "So by analogy I may also conclude that, because you yourselves as *jurisconsulti* and members of the court have renounced morality, I may heap any possible moral slander upon you here in the public place of law" (65). Kreuzgang rejects as inadequate any judicial decision emerging from the court. But the judges, unpersuaded by his rhetoric, decide that Kreuzgang is suffering from insanity and sentence him to the madhouse.

If in the seventh nightwatch Kreuzgang appears in his capacity as a jurist and renders his professional opinions on contemporary law and justice and the legal-philosophical question of their relationship to morality, these views represent the theoretical summary of attitudes already expressed in another scene. In the third nightwatch Kreuzgang, in the course of his rounds, witnesses an assignation between two lovers. Proceeding to the house designated by the woman, Kreuzgang catches sight of "a creature in a dressing gown at a desk, and initially I was in doubt as to whether it was a human being or a mechanical figure, so totally had every human element been expunged so that only the expression of work remained" (18). Immersed in great piles of dossiers, the creature was working away like someone buried alive and sat there without any evident emotion amidst the coffin of files like a marionette. "Now the invisible string was pulled, the fingers rattled, seized the pen, and signed three papers in succession—they were death sentences. On the table lay Justinian and the Criminal Law, like the personified soul of the marionette" (19). As Kreuzgang watches, this cold jurist works away like a mechanical death machine. When the young woman enters, he realizes that this legal marionette is her husband, who had hoped to give his horrified wife pleasure by setting so many executions on her birthday "because in the books that you read so many people die" (20).

Kreuzgang, following the wife as the two go off to their separate bedrooms, sees her lover appear. Determined to expose the two sinners, Kreuzgang blasts a note on his horn and then conceals himself on an empty pedestal. When the three people come rushing out of their rooms, the husband believes that Kreuzgang is a statue of Justice with which his wife had surprised him. But Kreuzgang points out that Justice is still in the sculptor's workshop and that he is only a provisional substitute. "For Justice is cold as marble, and has no heart in her stony breast" (21). The lovers faint at the sight of the talking statue, while Kreuzgang conducts a zany adultery hearing—ironic to the extent that the husband does not understand that he has been deceived by his wife, Karolina. Referring to the harsh laws against adultery in the *Peinliche Halsgerichtsordnung* of Charles V that was lying on the judge's desk, Kreuzgang continues: "If we, as members of the court, should seek to deduce grounds for leniency from moral principles and wanted at least to avert the punishment of beheading that *Carolina* has imposed on him ..." (23). "Why should Karolina suddenly have become so cruel?" the judge responds. "Just a little while ago she trembled when I spoke of execution." Kreuzgang is not surprised that the judge has confused the two Carolines. "Your living Karolina, as the torment and cross of marriage you have to bear, can easily be confused with the Carolina of capital crimes, which also is not exactly a bed of roses. Yes, I would even like to claim that a marital Caroline is much worse than the imperial one because in the latter at least there is never any mention of *lifelong* torture" (23).

While the *Nachtwachen* can hardly be regarded as a paean to natural law, the frequent allusions as well as the two extended sections on law—which touch upon natural law, Roman law, and the philosophy of law—provide further evidence for the powerful interest in jurisprudence that we have observed in the first decade of the nineteenth century. Moreover, the casual skill with which law is handled for purposes of humor (anticipating Heine two decades later) suggests strongly that the anonymous author may well have had the legal education that characterized so many of his contemporaries.[57]

## The Commitment to Traditional Law

While many German writers of the late eighteenth century accepted the theory of natural law, most writers of emerging Romanticism were sympathetic to Savigny's advocacy of traditional law—not just out of opposition to the French but also for a variety of other reasons ranging from their discovery of history to a reaffirmation of the principle of monarchy and the newfound ideal of the organic *Volk*. Indeed, the motivating impulse behind the commitment to traditional law can be detected in almost every case in a personal conservatism reacting against the perceived threat to order. No one exemplifies this attitude better than Savigny himself. In 1799, as a twenty-year-old student of law, he wrote: "Now, when the old forms are threatened by general destruction, it is more essential than ever to seek out a standpoint that is grounded *within us* and independent of what is positive and conventional. . . . And when (what I hope and wish) the spirit of violent revolutions shall have been extinguished, that loftier standpoint will be no less necessary."[58]

The collection of aphorisms that Novalis called *Glauben und Liebe* was written in 1798, much too early to have been influenced by Savigny. As a legally trained administrator, Novalis was familiar with the Prussian legal code. But his aphorisms betray a faith in traditional law that anticipates Savigny. "A true royal couple is for the entire human being what a constitution is for reason alone. One can be interested in a constitution only as one is interested in a letter of the alphabet. If the sign is not a beautiful image, or a song, then attachment to signs is the most perverse of all inclinations.—What is a law if not an expression of the will of a beloved, venerable person?"[59] "There will come a time, and soon, when people will generally be convinced that no king can exist without a republic and no republic without a king, that the two are as indivisible as body and soul, and that a king without a republic and a republic without a king are only words without meaning" (490). Soon, however, the expression of commitment to the traditional laws became much more explicit. The patriotic songs that Friedrich Schlegel wrote soon after the defeat of the Prussians at Jena-Auerstedt and the abrogation of the legal system of the Holy Roman Empire make frequent appeal to the old German law and custom. The poem "Freiheit" (1807) argues that the German virtues can thrive only under German law:

> Wo nach altem Rechte
> Fromme Sitte gilt,
> Da sind edle Mächte
> Noch der Freiheit Schild.
> Jeder stark alleine,
> Stärker im Vereine,
> Ist des Ganzen Bild.[60]

(Wherever pious custom reigns according to ancient law, noble powers are still the shield of freedom. Each one strong in himself and stronger in union—that is the image of the whole.)

And according to the aphoristic poem "Deutscher Sinn," nothing undermines the true German as insidiously as foreign customs and "the frivolous play of foreign laws" ("fremder Rechte loses Spiel").[61]

In the lectures on politics that he published under the title *Die Elemente der Staatskunst* (1809) Adam Müller proclaimed a typically conservative belief in a "living" monarchic law. "An incomplete living law is, according to all my assumptions, better than the most logical, artificial, but dead law. Therein consists the great advantage of every monarchic constitution: the law is not merely mechanically expounded but really embodied in a person" (lecture 9). In his lecture on "The Spirit of Roman Law-Making" (lecture 13) Müller displays an enormous appreciation for the achievements of Roman law and maintains that "in the study of law the Roman system, if it is explained historically and without any particular preference along with the other systems of legislation, has a great value: in the study of law a fundamental rational calculation, as it emerges everywhere from Roman laws, should assert its claims." But precisely because he believes in the historicity of law Müller argues that Roman law can no longer be of value to us, now that its living spirit is gone. "Of what meaning for us is a legal system whose motivating sovereign idea of Roman freedom died out almost two millennia ago—an idea that to be sure can still affect our understanding but in no way our desire and the totality of our private life!" All the great legal conceptions were tied, he summarizes, to a particular locale: Mosaic religion to Palestine, Greek ethics to the sea-girt land between the Ionian and Aegean, and Roman freedom to the city of the seven hills. It is essential for Germany, along with all other peoples, to find the system of law that is consistent with its own genius.

We hear a similar sentiment in the words of Alexander von der Marwitz, the brilliant young classicist and darling of Rahel Varnhagen's circle, who, after his studies at Halle with F. A. Wolf, returned to Berlin to prepare himself for service in the Prussian government. As he wrote to his university friend Adolph Müller:

I am here to get an appointment in the near future, and to that end I am now studying law with great diligence—in the historical manner, naturally, and as much as possible in its vital connection with the forms of state and society. Viewed thus as a mirror in which the

spirit of the people [*Völkergeist*] has imprinted and apprehended itself in its organic relationship to the whole full life of past generations, the theory of law is full of meaning and interest.[62]

Among the patriotic poems that Ludwig Uhland, himself a jurist,
wrote immediately following Napoleon's defeat, there is a paean to
Themis, the goddess of justice, as "Die neue Muse" (1816). The poem
begins with recollections of the days when Uhland was studying law
against the dictates of his heart ("Als ich mich des Rechts beflissen / Gegen meines Herzens Drang"), but it goes on to make the point that in
these serious times nothing is so moving and inspiring as the thought that
law and justice prevail and summon the peoples to action:

> Andre Zeiten, andre Musen!
> Und in dieser ernsten Zeit
> Schüttert nichts mir so den Busen,
> Weckt mich so zum Liederstreit:
> Als wenn du, mit Schwert und Waage,
> Themis, thronst in deiner Kraft,
> Und die Völker rufst zur Klage,
> Könige zur Rechenschaft![63]

(Other times, other muses! And in these grave times nothing
so stirs my breast and arouses me to the battle of songs as when
you, Themis, with sword and scales, reign in your power, and
summon the peoples to indictment and the kings to their reck-
oning.)

And during that same year Uhland composed a popular eleven-strophe
poem celebrating "Das alte, gute Recht."

> Wo je bei altem, gutem Wein
> Der Württemberger zecht,
> Da soll der erste Trinkspruch sein:
> *Das alte, gute Recht!*[64]

(Wherever a Württemberger carouses with old, good wine, let
the first toast be: *The old, good law!*)

(It should be pointed out that Uhland meant by this term not so much
Roman law as, rather, the German common law traditional in his native
Swabia.)[65]

The case of Goethe is also instructive. The reader of his autobiography is astonished to arrive at the account of the summer in Wetzlar, eager to learn the details underlying *Die Leiden des jungen Werther*, only to be told: "What happened to me in Wetzlar is of no great significance." Instead of the anticipated love story, surely one of the most familiar in world literature, we get a detailed and thoughtful account of the late medieval circumstances that occasioned the establishment of the Imperial Chancery: an account that makes unambiguously clear the importance that Goethe—in the spring of 1813, when this section of *Dichtung und Wahrheit* (bk. 12) was written—attributed to the subject of law. Indeed, as he wrote these pages on the Imperial Chancery, Goethe borrowed many volumes from the library at Weimar in order to refresh his memory and to check his facts. He does not refer at this point to the codification controversy that was coming to a head. As a trained jurist, he followed with interest the controversy whose principals were personal acquaintances of his. He had known Thibaut during his tenure in Jena and had sent his son to study with him in Heidelberg. But we know that Goethe was opposed to the idea of codification from the time of his fifty-six theses of 1771, of which number XLIX states: *Legum corpus nunquam colligendum*. And he was by temperament disposed toward the brilliant young Savigny, whom he encountered several times during his lifetime. We can deduce his own conservative views from his dissatisfaction in 1816 when Archduke Karl August became the first German ruler to grant his state a new constitution. In legislation, as he wrote elsewhere in his autobiography, Goethe "had no sense for anything positive but wanted to have everything explained historically, if not rationally."[66]

· · ·

It was not simply the "old, good law" espoused by Savigny—whether Roman or German—that was admired by most of his contemporaries: the charismatic scholar himself, regarded by his admirers as the "Kant of Jurisprudence," came in for his share of praise. Not surprisingly, he figured prominently in the works of his own two poetic brothers-in-law. Clemens Brentano's exposure to the systematic study of law, as to all other subjects in which he dabbled at several universities, was fleeting (two semesters at Halle in 1797). However, as the brother-in-law of the most brilliant jurist of the day, who had married his sister Kunigunde, Brentano absorbed a good bit of the romance that was then attached to the study of law and its history. Like Brentano, who was less than a year older than he, Savigny came from an old Frankfurt family. Because as an orphan Savigny had been raised by a friend of the family in Wetzlar, the two young men did not meet until 1799 in Jena. An unlikely friendship immediately thrived between the erratic poetic prodigy and the earnest young scholar, who became known in the Brentano family as the "study machine."[67] During the early years the two young men spent a great deal of time together. Following Savigny's marriage to Kunigunde in 1804, the friendship mellowed into a less intense relationship as Savigny's research took him to Paris. But a few years later, during Brentano's difficult second marriage to Auguste Bußmann, Savigny provided both moral support and legal advice.

From the very first, references to Savigny crop up in Brentano's writings. In the paralipomena to his novel *Godwi* (1800–1802) Brentano addresses a sonnet "To S....y," who is depicted as present at the deathbed of the poet Maria.[68] And in the autobiographical prologue to his "historical-romantic drama" *Die Gründung Prags* (1815) Brentano lists "the lofty, radiant Savigny" among the luminaries of his hometown, Frankfurt am Main.[69] However, Brentano's finest tribute to Savigny occurs in his unfinished epic, *Romanzen vom Rosenkranz*, which was written from 1803 to 1812, much of it while Brentano was living in Savigny's house in Marburg (1803) and then in Landshut (1808–1809). Brentano acknowledged his indebtedness to Savigny, and particularly to his erudition regarding medieval Bologna, which provides the principal setting for the romances. The complicated genealogical plot does not need to be recounted here: in the course of the story the brilliant young jurist Jacopone, an orphan who has grown up in a monastery, marries Rosarosa, without realizing that she is his half-sister. Rosarosa, who learns the terrible secret on her wedding night, insists that they maintain a chaste marriage and reveals the reason to her beloved Jacopone only on her deathbed. What matters in the present context is the fact that the description of Jacopone and his work is based extensively on Savigny.[70] So learned, it is said, that he could have restored the Twelve Tables if they had been lost, he is compared favorably to the greatest lawyers of antiquity.

> Er verstand wohl die Gesetze
> Gleich dem griech'schen Hermodore,
> Die zwölf Tafeln hergestellet
> Hätt' er, wären sie verloren.
>
> Und wie Flavius gelernet
> Auswendig die Aktionen,
> Kannte auch wohl alle Leges,
> Alle Formuln Jakopone.

Mutius hat er gelesen,
Und den Brutus wohl erwogen,
Den Manilius versteht er,
Ist Sulpicio gewogen.
(795)

(He understood the laws as well as the Greek Hermodor; he
would have restored the Twelve Tables, had they been lost.
Like Flavius, he learned the Acta by heart and also knew all
the *leges* and all the formulas, did Jacopone. He read Mutius
and carefully considered Brutus; he understands Manilius and
is displosed toward Sulpicius.)

The dissertation that brought him his early fame is devoted to the same
topic—an inside joke—as Savigny's famous treatise on possession (*Das
Recht des Besitzes*, 1803):

Er hielt streng bei den Gesetzen
Und schrieb dissertationem
Die ihn bracht' zu hohen Ehren:
De bonorum possessione.
(795)

(He adhered rigorously to the laws and wrote a dissertation
that brought him high honors: De bonorum possessione.)

If he had lived at the time of Justinian, we hear, he would have been
named along with the other authors of the codices and pandects. Bologna
is fortunate to have him hundreds of years later as the star of her famous
law faculty. The names and works cited in the first twenty strophes of
the eleventh romance demonstrate effectively that Brentano had soaked
up a good deal of at least superficial knowledge concerning his brother-
in-law's research into Roman law of the Middle Ages.

In age and appearance—thirty years old with brown locks flowing
gracefully around a lofty forehead—he is the image of Savigny:

Und kaum dreißig Jahre zählt er;
Um die hohe Stirne Locken
Wallen braun aus dem Barette,
Und sein Bart ist schön geordnet.
(797)

(He is scarcely thirty years of age; around his high forehead the locks flow brown from his scholar's cap, and his beard is beautifully trimmed.)

And his flamboyant lecture manner is that which delighted the students of Marburg, Landshut, and Berlin:

> Wenn er im Ornate stehet
> Und kreieret die Doktoren,
> Fließet ihm die stolze Rede
> Gleich dem zweiten Cicerone.
> (797)

(When he stands in full array and confirms the doctors, his proud oratory flows like that of a second Cicero.)

Although the *Romanzen vom Rosenkranz* were first published posthumously many years later, it is clear that at the time of their composition the history of Roman law, as well as Savigny's impressive contribution to that subject, was a sufficiently compelling topic to warrant scores of strophes and a central figure in Brentano's lengthy romance.

Savigny's other poetic brother-in-law was not so unreserved in his attitude.[71] Achim von Arnim, who was married to Bettina Brentano, was to defend the Prussian legal code against Savigny's attacks. To be sure, Arnim was not an advocate of codification for its own sake. But if a code already existed, summoned up by the will of the people, then he saw no reason to do away with it. "The code has for our people in a legal sense the same importance as, in a religious context, Luther's translation of the Bible," he wrote in 1814.[72] Yet he recognized Savigny's legal genius and was instrumental in attracting him in 1810 to accept a chair at the newly established University of Berlin. And in a series of poems celebrating four of Savigny's birthdays on February 21 (1820, 1825, 1826, and 1830) Arnim acknowledged his standing.[73] Because of police regulations prohibiting public gatherings in 1820—a result of the same persecution of "demagogues" that was to involve E.T.A. Hoffmann—the students and friends of the "master of the chair of the historical school of Roman law" must gather surreptitiously for their torchlight celebration.

> Heimlich, wie ein Werck der Nacht,
> Wird ein Vivat dargebracht
> Unserm Meister von dem Stuhle

## CHAPTER THREE

Der Historisch römschen Schule!
Denn es will die Polizei
Nirgends solch ein Lustgeschrei!

(Stealthily, like a deed of night, a Vivat is offered to our master of the chair of the historical school of Roman law. For the police do not wish anywhere such an outcry of joy.)

The age, Arnim laments, is withering away in suspicion and strife. But the younger brothers of today's students will attend the university in the future, and there will again come a time when Right is honored and the new law and the old will achieve a splendid unification.

Wird das Rechte einst geehrt,
Öffentlich wird dann gehört
Unser Wunsch, der heimlich schallte
Und das Neue und das Alte,
Dringt zu schöner Einigung
Lebe dann im Geiste jung!

(If someday the right is honored, then our wish, which now resounds secretly, will be heard publicly, and the new and the old will come together in a lovely union. Therefore live youthfully in spirit!)

Six years later Arnim produced another birthday poem, which is allegedly spoken by "Italic doctors" who have come to Germany in order to learn from Savigny—in whom they recognize an image of the masters who once taught in Bologna—how Italians thought in the days when its lovely sky was guarded by the stars of freedom.

Wir lernten Deutsch, von Dir zu lernen,
Wie einst Italien gedacht,
Als von der Freiheit Segenssternen
Sein schöner Himmel war bewacht.

(We learned German in order to learn from you how once Italy thought, when her fair sky was guarded by the blessed stars of freedom.)

Savigny's wisdom, which is venerable in his scholarship, remains alive and vital in his activities as an adviser and councillor.

Sie zeigt im Rath sich neugeboren
Und alt in Deiner Wissenschaft,

Des Meisters Wort geht nicht verloren
Dein lebend Wort übt Wunderkraft.

(It displays itself as new in council and venerable in your scholarship; the master's word is not lost; your living word exerts a
wondrous power.)

The literary effect of the renewal of traditional law was not exhausted
by paeans to "das alte, gute Recht" or by tributes to Savigny. During
thirty years of government service—first in provincial administration in
East Prussia and later with the central administration in Berlin—Joseph
von Eichendorff displayed a conservatism that can be traced back to such
teachers as Joseph Görres in Heidelberg and Adam Müller in Vienna, as
well as to his lifelong admiration of Goethe.[74] His opposition to written
constitutions, expressed in a number of essays on constitutional guarantees written in the early 1830s, is absolutely consistent with that youthful
conservatism.[75] In his posthumously published autobiographical writings
he was able to look back at the turmoil of his youth with the understanding of experience and maturity. In "Der Adel und die Revolution" he
sketches the intellectual and cultural situation in Germany during the
final decades of the eighteenth century to show how unprepared people
were for the forces unleashed by the French Revolution. "Nowadays one
can hardly imagine the fright and the immense confusion that the sudden
blast spread through the entire realm of Philistria when the mine in
France really exploded."[76] Under the impact of the calls for freedom and
equality, "the Old was suddenly shattered according to general opinion;
the golden thread from the past was violently torn. But no one can live
among ruins; things had to be rebuilt necessarily on different funda-
ments, and from that point on there began the desperate experimentation
of those who considered themselves artists of statescraft, which down to
the present has kept society in a constant feverish turmoil."

The immediate impact of that turmoil is most keenly evident in the
novel that Eichendorff wrote from 1810 to 1812 while completing his
study of law in Vienna. Here in *Ahnung und Gegenwart* (1815) it is the
ethical power of law that sustains the hero, Graf Friedrich, in a world
that seems to be falling apart. *Ahnung und Gegenwart* is perhaps the most
gossamerlike of the Romantic novels produced in profusion in imitation
of Goethe's *Wilhelm Meisters Lehrjahre*. There is no need to recapitulate
the twistings of the plot, which leads the characters through a geograph-
ically impossible landscape and compresses a complicated action involving doubles, mysterious encounters, and genealogical secrets into little

over a year, at the end of which all the characters who have not already died are miraculously brought together and all the mysteries resolved. We meet the young count just when he has left the university and follow him through a series of adventures that expose him to social life among the rural aristocracy and urban aesthetes, to the power of love, to the disenchantments of friendship, to the claims of political reality, to the horrors of war, and finally to his retreat into the solitude of a monastery. However, it is the search for law that represents the goal of his quest and the guiding force for much of the work.

During the first part of the story Friedrich is a typical Romantic youth—poetically gifted, enthusiastic, devout, pure of spirit, and utterly naive in his aspirations. When he arrives at the royal residence (bk. 2) and presents his letter of introduction to the governmental minister recommended to him by trusted friends, he is initially put off by the minister's "frosty, British manner, with which he was acquainted to the point of disgust from Jean Paul's novels."[77] It is of course characteristic that at this point Friedrich's experience and judgments are still largely conditioned by literature. In reaction to the minister's cool politeness he gushes forth with his notions concerning the state, public affairs, and patriotism. The minister dismisses him with the calm words: "I beg you: devote yourself for a time with exclusive industry to the study of jurisprudence and the cameral sciences." Dismayed by this disparaging encounter, Friedrich departs. Shortly thereafter he is astonished to discover that the minister has recommended him to the prince as a man suited for the demands of the new era. It is one thing, the prince tells him, to live alone and to develop one's own personality in piety, "but it is greater to discard all joys, all one's own wishes and endeavors for the sake of Right—everything" (163). Encouraged by these words, Friedrich hurls himself into the study of government—a new realm for him—spending entire nights working among his books. Gazing for the first time in his life into this great mirror of the world, he is smitten by "its beauty and loftiness and the sacred law" (164–65). Obsessed by his new discoveries, he is suddenly disgusted by "the false poets with their dovelike hearts who, forgetful of the heaven-crying warnings of the era, squandered their national strength in idle play" (165).

Within a short time Friedrich finds himself surrounded by a circle of capable new friends, men of broad experience, who have come together in the residence out of common interest. "An identical ideology seemed to link all the members of this circle as brothers. They worked industriously, hoping and believing that they could free a space for the old law in this narrow age" (166). As the weeks pass, Friedrich devotes himself with doubled energy to his studies: "all his thoughts and efforts were directed to his fatherland" (175). With increasing dismay, however, he realizes that his colleagues lose their commitment as winter gives way to spring and summer, and he stands almost alone in the vacuum of loyalty and will among his former friends. Even the prince, distraught by love affairs, complains that he is not capable of sustaining his ideals. During the war Friedrich encounters, on the opposing side, an officer who had belonged to his political fraternity. "Have you forgotten everything that we were preparing in those good days?" Friedrich asks him. "I was serious about my proposals. I was an honest fool, and I prefer to be that rather than clever without honor" (218). However, because he has committed himself to the wrong—that is, to the losing—side, Friedrich loses all his possessions and properties, and he comes to the realization that he has again reached a crucial point in his life. "Poetry, his onetime sweet companion, no longer sufficed; all his most serious, heartfelt plans had shattered on the envy of his age" (226).

Unsatisfied by poetry, betrayed by law and politics, unfulfilled by human love, Friedrich turns increasingly to religion. It is this process of development that qualifies the novel as a *Bildungsroman*.[78] At the end the three friends meet once again before going their separate ways: Leontin, departing for the political reality of the new world, and Faber, still committed to a life of poetry, represent earlier stages of Friedrich's own career. But Eichendorff makes it clear that Friedrich's decision to enter the monastery is not simply a flight from reality and the abjuration of his earlier ambitions. Rather, he has come to the realization that the times are not yet ripe for his goals. "It is not yet time to build as long as the bricks, still soft and unripe, fall apart under our hands. In this misery there appears to me to be, as always, no other help than religion. For where is there—in the confusion of poetry, piety, Germanity, virtue, and patriotism that now, as in the Babylonian confusion of language, buzz vacillatingly back and forth—a secure middle point from which all of this might come to a clear understanding, a living whole?" (296).

Friedrich urges a return to "the divine truths of religion" as an act of preparation and purification, so that the spirit of God will again find a place in public life. "Not until then will it be time to act directly and to reintroduce the old law, the old freedom, honor, and glory into the reconquered kingdom" (297). Thus the young law student Eichendorff, confused by the developments of the Napoleonic era but consoled by his religious faith and secure in his belief in traditional forms of law and order, states his case for the ethical force of law. Clearly a young man of these convictions would have little sympathy for the teachings of the natural-law jurists who dominated the thinking in the universities. Only the teachers of Roman law made a notable exception here and there (as he put it in "Halle und Heidelberg") "because their subject matter compelled them to immerse themselves in the positive aspects of a grand past. Thibaut's significant accomplishments in this field are well known, and just at that time the mild-mannered, serious Savigny, who was never a member of that group, was breaking new paths in every direction" (1047).

. . .

One of the most fruitful products of the juristic controversy was the oeuvre of the brothers Grimm.[79] The sons of a lawyer, Jacob and Wilhelm Grimm began as students of law in Marburg with the goal of pursuing administrative careers. It was in Savigny's private library that the brothers were first exposed—in the form of Tieck's *Minnelieder* and Bodmer's edition of the *Minnesinger*—to the older German literature to which they were to devote their lives. But those studies still lay in the future. Under the charismatic influence of Savigny, at the time a brilliant young instructor scarcely older than his students, Jacob was initially inspired to dedicate himself to Roman law—an ambition consistent with the opposition that he had already conceived to the Prussian legal code. So talented a disciple was Jacob that in 1805 Savigny summoned him to Paris to assist in the archival research for his monumental history of Roman law in the Middle Ages. At Wilhelm's suggestion Jacob began to search in the Bibliothèque Nationale for manuscripts of medieval German literature. The results were so exciting—he became acquainted, among other items, with the Manesse manuscript of Middle High German poetry—that Jacob, on his return to Germany, discontinued his study of law and shifted his interests toward Middle High German literature. The turn to native German materials was also inspired in no small measure by the brothers' chagrin at the subjugation of Germany by the French in 1806 and the implicit threat to German culture. It was Jacob Grimm's explicit intention—and his grand achievement—to apply to the study of medieval literature precisely the methods that Savigny had developed for the study of Roman law: essentially an intensive analysis of the sources based on a thorough knowledge of the philological and historical circumstances and in a comparative context. To this end the brothers gave up all plans for legal careers and devoted themselves—first briefly as administrative assistants and then as librarians in Cassel—to their new researches.

The immediate result was their epoch-making work in older German literature and folklore: Jacob's study *Über den altdeutschen Meistergesang* (1811), editions of the Hildebrandslied and the Wessobrunn Prayer (1812), their collection of fairy tales (*Kinder- und Hausmärchen*, 1812–1815) and of sagas (*Deutsche Sagen*, 1816). It was by way of his studies of medieval Germanic poetry that Jacob gradually came to his interest in ancient German law. In 1813 he began systematically collecting materials on law, and toward the end of December of that year he wrote to Savigny in a tone of great excitement about his discoveries: "It is hard to imagine that any jurisprudence has ever been so poetic as this."[80] He had come to the realization that many of the old poetic texts revolved centrally around legal questions: for instance, the volume of *Deutsche Sagen* contains a group of "legal sagas" dealing with robbery, murder, boundary disputes, illegal punishments, the execution of innocents, and other legal matters. Grimm gradually saw that these cases could be interpreted only in the context of pre-Reception German law—and not according to subsequent Roman law. At the same time, he became aware of the poetic form of much German law and of the inextricable links between poetry and law in medieval German thought.

The first product of this new insight was Jacob's essay "Von der Poesie im Recht," which appeared in 1815 in the second volume of Savigny's journal, *Zeitschrift für geschichtliche Rechtswissenschaft*. Grimm begins by saying that it is appropriate to examine the reciprocal relationship between poetry and law because German antiquity provides such a wealth of important monuments of both kinds from similar periods and from the most varied parts of the territory inhabited by Germanic peoples. No other people can display such a supply of laws and legal practices from earliest times. Indeed, with the exception of Roman law, no other legal system in Europe rests on such a broad firm basis as German law. In contrast to Roman law, however, German law was never developed into an artful form, never taught systematically, and never cultivated by scholars. Yet it is accessible in all its youthful vigor because it is preserved in the form of poetic utterance. "It is not difficult to believe that law and poetry arose from the same bed," the essay continues, because in both one encounters a non-historical element that transcends mere statute.[81] "Their common source is based on two essentials: wonder and faith" ("auf dem wunderbaren und dem glaubreichen"). The only justice in which the people have faith is that which is handed down from the most ancient pious lore, just as the people are happiest with legends and tales that they have absorbed with their mothers' milk. "But whatever springs from one source is also always related and interwoven; poetry will accordingly contain the law just as the law embraces poetry within itself" (154).

This insistence on the essential similarity and common source of poetry and law brings Grimm to the point that accounts for his interest and characteristic approach. "Everything that is initially and internally related will, on careful investigation, always justify itself from the structure and nature of language itself . . . and the established relationship between law and poetry reaches down into the most profound grounds of all languages" (155). To collect the evidence in the German language alone would demand an extensive investigation, and therefore, Grimm states, he will restrict himself in this preliminary report to a few representative examples from various areas. The collecting went on, of course, and by 1828 Jacob Grimm was able to publish his still standard collection of legal antiquities, *Deutsche Rechtsaltertümer*, which appropriately was dedicated to Savigny.

Though Savigny was and remained essentially a "Romanist"—that is, a historian of Roman law—he encouraged the work of these early "Germanists," a term coined originally to designate historians of German law. To that end he founded in 1814 the *Zeitschrift für geschichtliche Rechtswissenschaft* and introduced the new journal with an essay that still exemplifies the ideals of the organic approach to the study of law. The brothers were of course sympathetic to Savigny in the great codification controversy of 1814. On October 29, 1814, Jacob Grimm—who, as mentioned earlier, had been opposed to codification at least since 1805—wrote Savigny a long and highly detailed response to the publication of *Vom Beruf unsrer Zeit für Gesetzgebung und Rechtswissenschaft*. As late as 1846, at the first meeting of "Germanists" in Frankfurt (*Frankfurter Germanistenversammlung*), Grimm still publicly supported the continued study of Roman law as a living source of German law.[82]

The Grimm brothers were essentially historians in the Romantic quest for what they conceived as the national spirit of the Germans, which they detected in old written documents of every sort—but especially in poetry and law. As they observed in the preface to the 1819 edition of their *Kinder- und Hausmärchen*, it was their principle in retelling the popular tales to preserve what they called "the spirit of the people" ("der Geist des Volkes"). But the path of their career is exemplary for the lure of the law in German Romanticism. They began studying law because it was traditional in the family and because they aspired to administrative positions in the government. Coming under Savigny's spell at Marburg, they shifted their attention from cameralistics to Roman law. Although they gradually turned away from Roman antiquity to their own German past, it was through their application of Savigny's techniques of *Rechtswissenschaft* to Germanic poetic and legal texts that they created the field that has grown into what we now know as medieval studies.

. . .

If Eichendorff exemplifies the Romantic turn to law as ethical power and if Jacob Grimm's career shows how Savigny's example led to the systematic study of the German Middle Ages, another group of typical Romantic works suggests the extent to which a single characteristic legal problem could become obsessive to a generation brought up on law. We noted at the outset that Goethe's *Faust* is predicated on a contractual agreement. Goethe was of course familiar with the problem of contracts, so central to Roman civil law, from his student days. Indeed, three of his fifty-six theses dealt with the nature of contracts, and one (no. IV) was concerned specifically with the difference between contracts and pacts.[83] However, the contractual scenes in *Faust*—not only the agreement between Faust and Mephistopheles but also the opening wager between Mephistopheles and God—were not written until the final stages of composition from 1797 to 1806—in other words, during the years when the legal controversy was beginning to heat up. Adam Müller also addressed the centrality of contracts in *Die Elemente der Staatskunst* (lecture 13). "I challenge any authority on Roman law to show me in it any trace of true reciprocity of legal circumstances apart from the theory of contracts. And yet these are the two basic characteristics of any law and any legislation: first, the innermost reciprocity, the contractual nature of all circumstances of life, material as well as personal, for the sake of right; second, the wisest discipline, subordination, hierarchy of all conditions of life for the sake of exercising law" (157). Whatever the reason—the discussion of contracts, Roman law, the influence of *Faust* following the publication of part 1 in 1808—several works of the period depend essentially on contracts as the prerequisite of plot.

One of the most popular contemporary legends concerned the hunter who makes a contract with the devil in order to obtain bullets that never miss their mark—a story that became well known from its telling in the

*Gespensterbuch* published in 1810 by Johann August Apel and Friedrich Laun and then attained worldwide fame through its treatment in Carl Maria von Weber's "Romantic opera" *Der Freischütz* (1821).[84] In the various versions of this legend the contract is mentioned as the basis of the action but plays no further role. But in Chamisso's *Peter Schlemihls wundersame Geschichte* (1814), which appeared during the year of the codification controversy, the question of contracts arises on several crucial occasions. The story begins when the impecunious Peter Schlemihl bargains with a mysterious stranger in a gray coat to give up his shadow in exchange for a purse whose supply of gold coins is never exhausted. At this point there is no mention of a formal contract—only an agreement by handshake. However, as soon as Schlemihl discovers the inconvenience and embarrassments of life without a shadow, he is eager to make the agreement retroactive. The man in gray, who has been called a "Biedermeier Mephisto,"[85] is quite amenable: Schlemihl may even retain the wonderful purse. "I request only a triviality as a memento. Just be good enough to sign this piece of paper for me."[86] It is of course the traditional infernal contract that he wants Schlemihl to sign in blood. "By the power of this signature I bequeath to the bearer of this document my soul after its natural separation from my body." Schlemihl refuses in horror. But following months more of misery from his shadowless life, he is grievously tempted when the man in gray again offers him the parchment for his signature. He is on the very point of signing with his own blood when he falls into a deep faint and is saved.

At their final encounter Schlemihl again discusses the situation with the man in gray and asks if Herr John, the wealthy businessman at whose house they first met, had signed a contract. The man in gray replies that a signature was not necessary with such a good and trusted friend. When Schlemihl insists on knowing what happened to Herr John, the man in gray reaches into his pocket and pulls out by the hair the pale, distorted figure of the man, whose cadaverous lips mutter: "*Justo judicio Dei judicatus sum; Justo judicio Dei condemnatus sum!*" (451). Horrified, Schlemihl hurls down the cursed purse and rushes away to spend the rest of his life in isolation from mankind, pursuing his scientific researches by means of the Seven League Boots that enable him to reach the most remote parts of the world. While critics have written a good deal about the symbolic meaning of the lost shadow—with interpretations ranging from nationality to honor to material wealth unjustly acquired—it has not been sufficiently remarked that the contract upon which the fiction depends reflects a legal obsession of the age.

Finally, in E.T.A. Hoffmann's "Die Geschichte vom verlornen Spiegelbilde," which was written in 1814 in direct response to *Peter Schlemihl*, the motif of the infernal contract occurs again. In Hoffmann's version, familiar to many from its treatment in Offenbach's *Tales of Hoffmann*, it is not a shadow but a mirror image that the young German traveler in Italy, Erasmus Spikher, sacrifices to win the love of the courtesan Giulietta. Spikher flees from Florence to escape punishment for his murder of an Italian rival, and back in Germany he suffers humiliations for the absence of his reflection. When Giulietta appears in the company of the sinister Signor Dapertutto, Spikher is assured that he may have his heart's desire simply by signing—in blood, of course—a simple contract in which he assigns to Dapertutto all power over his wife and child. Spikher has already dipped his pen into the blood and is prepared to sign the document when an apparition of his wife materializes and appeals to him to desist. Like Schlemihl, Spikher rejects the paper and pen but, isolated from human society by the fatal absence of his mirror image, says farewell to his family and sets out to roam the world in solitary despair.

It would be going too far to attribute the obsession with the infernal contract during this brief period of German literary history specifically to the codification controversy—even though both Chamisso and Hoffmann were acquainted with Savigny in Berlin. It is more reasonable to speak of a climate of opinion that rendered thoughtful people open to questions of law of every sort. Thanks to the inspiration of Savigny and the exciting work of Jacob Grimm, there was a new interest in law as a historical phenomenon. At the same time, this new historicist awareness of the relativity of different legal systems attracted writers to speculate about the conflicts that arise from the encounter of one system with another. Thus Goethe, Chamisso, and Hoffmann treated with variations the meaning of traditional contracts in non-traditional circumstances. Or, to take a completely different example, Clemens Brentano was centrally concerned in both parts of his "Geschichte vom braven Kasperl und dem schönen Annerl" (1817) with the problem of legality versus mercy or of divine and secular justice.

In the first half of the story we hear about the case of a young soldier who, discovering that his father and stepbrother are thieves, hands them over to justice and then commits suicide because he is convinced that his own honor has been sullied. But because he kills himself out of despair, and not from the forgivable cause of melancholy, the law requires that his body be turned over to "the anatomy" for dissection. His grand- mother implores the narrator to write a plea that will persuade the duke to waive the sentence and permit Kasperl to be buried by the side of his beloved Annerl. Only at this point do we hear the second half of the story: Annerl, seduced by a nobleman who promised her marriage, suf- focated her child and then turned herself over to the courts. Having re- fused the pardon vouchsafed if she would name her seducer, she has been sentenced to be executed by the sword this very morning. The narrator succeeds in reaching the duke, who listens to the story and grants a par- don. But the pardon fails to arrive in time, and Annerl is beheaded—a motif familiar to Brentano at least since he and Arnim included the poem "Weltlich Recht" in the second volume of *Des Knaben Wunderhorn* (1808). The seducer poisons himself out of a sense of his own guilt. The old grandmother has the satisfaction of seeing Kasperl and Annerl buried together, for the duke, moved by the stories, grants the request. In the last paragraph we learn that an allegorical monument designed by the duke and his fiancée is to be erected and dedicated in their cemetery. "It represents false Honor and true Honor, who side by side before a cross bow deep to the ground; Justice stands on one side with raised sword; Mercy stands on the other side and casts her veil forward. People claim to recognize in the head of Justice a similarity with the duke and in the head of Mercy a resemblance to the countenance of the princess."[87]

The story is a masterpiece precisely because its subtleties lend dimen- sions of mystery to the basic plots. The monument, for instance, embodies the motifs of a song that we have earlier heard being sung by the duke's mistress (whom, as a result of the affair, he elevates in rank so that he can marry her). The beheading of Annerl is made to seem inevitable because of the fairy-tale motif of the executioner's sword that lusts for her blood. (Brentano had a fixation concerning executions and blood that would interest psychiatrists: see his poem of 1817–1818 entitled "An das Blut am Abend vor dem Gericht.") And the entire secular plot takes place against the background of the heavenly Last Judgment, which is cited repeatedly in the refrain of a song:

> Ihr Toten, ihr Toten sollt auferstehn,
> Ihr sollt vor das Jüngste Gerichte gehn.

(You dead, you dead shall be resurrected; you shall appear be- fore the Last Judgment.)

In the last analysis we are dealing with a story that depends for its effect on the powerful claims of secular law and divine mercy. In 1815 Brentano experienced a profound spiritual crisis and, under the influence of Luise Hensel and her neo-pietist circle, underwent a gradual reversion to Catholicism that led, in 1817, to his much publicized general confession and, from 1818 to 1824, his voluntary exile to the village of Dülmen, where he attended the stigmatized nun Anna Katharina Emmerick.[88] We are entitled to imagine that Brentano, as he moved into the mysticism of his later years, was making a symbolic statement about the relative merits of two kinds of justice—the secular law proclaimed by his famous brother-in-law and the divine mercy of the God that he was about to embrace.

At the same time, it pays to remember that Brentano was obsessed by legal conundrums in several of the other tales that he wrote around the same time. "Die Schachtel mit der Friedenspuppe" (1815) encapsulates one plot within another like the image of the title, which refers to a fateful box in which a Prussian nobleman brings back a doll from Paris following the fall of Napoleon. It turns out that the box had been used shortly after the Revolution to hold the body of a dead child in a case of child substitution used by a man in order to defraud his nephew out of his inheritance. The Prussian magistrate's investigations of an attempted case of manslaughter involving two Frenchmen lead to the unraveling of the old crime and to a tardy restoration of justice. As in "Kasperl und Annerl," the occasion is again immemorialized at the end by a symbolic funeral monument erected in Prussia by the restored French nobleman. Brentano uses the substitution of infants to provide a happy ending to the otherwise bleak tale "Die drei Nüsse" (1817). Here an apothecary in seventeenth-century Lyons, furiously jealous of his beautiful wife, kills a young man whom he takes to be her lover. When it turns out that the young soldier is his wife's brother, not her lover, the apothecary flees. But eight years later, driven by his conscience, he returns to Lyons and submits to judgment and death by decapitation. It turns out, however, that the mayor of Colmar, to whom the lovely widow tells her story when she attempts to establish a new life for herself, is himself her true brother: the dead soldier, who in fact was devoted to her with a more than proper brotherly passion, had been substituted—for otherwise undisclosed reasons—for her true brother at birth. In short, if we look beyond Brentano's most famous tale to others that he wrote around the same time, we see in almost every case that he uses various configurations of the same motifs—including decapitation, changelings, symbolic monuments, and various others mystifications—to construct plots that depend for their tension on the conflict between secular law and individual conscience or divine justice—that is, between Savigny's law and God's law.

## THE SATISFACTIONS OF THE PRUSSIAN LEGAL CODE

It would be misleading to suggest that the support for Roman law and its famous advocate was entirely unanimous. We have already had occasion to note that even Savigny's brother-in-law, Arnim, defended the Prussian legal code, which he called a document as powerful in law as was Luther's Bible translation in religion. Karl Marx, who studied the Pandects with Savigny in Berlin in the winter term of 1836–1837, wrote his father (November 10–11, 1837) that his study of Savigny's *Das Recht des Besitzes* had confirmed him in his fundamental realization that form and content cannot be separated in social analysis,[89] and he became an indefatigable opponent of the historical school of law.[90]

There were also violent personal reactions. As a Jewish Francophile from the Rhineland (like Karl Marx) as well as a liberal bourgeois, Heinrich Heine had every reason to approve of the code promulgated by his hero, Napoleon. Ever since he had encountered Savigny as a student of law in Berlin in 1821, Heine in his poetry and prose seized every opportunity to ridicule "that elegantly immaculate, fulsome troubadour of the Pandects" ("dem elegant geleckten, süßlichen Troubadour der Pandekten," in "Die Menge tut es" [1855]). Thus on the first page of his early *Briefe aus Berlin* (1822) Heine warns us that he is going to speak "today about the dress balls and the churches, tomorrow about Savigny and the buffoons who parade through the city in strange processions, the day after tomorrow about the Giustiniani Gallery, and then again about Savigny and the buffoons. Association of ideas shall always prevail."[91] In the second letter, accordingly, he mentions "a great North German jurist who allows his black hair to flow down from his shoulders as far as possible, who gazes toward heaven with pious loving eyes, who aspires to look like a Christ-image, who incidentally has a French name, is of French descent, and yet behaves in such a mightily German manner" (19). And in the fifth chapter of *Die Bäder von Lucca* (1829) Heine portrays the contemporary juristic situation in Germany hilariously as a mad quadrille in which the dancers are Gustav Hugo, Thibaut, Savigny, and

Savigny's rationalist opponent Gans. Again Savigny comes off the worst because, while Heine's Italian interlocutors have heard of him, they insist that he is a woman.

While many writers of the period took an interest in the legal controversies of the age and expressed themselves on the issues, few incorporated legal matters into their works as compulsively as did Heinrich von Kleist.[92] Indeed, with the sole exception of the brief narrative "Das Bettelweib von Locarno," he did not produce a single literary work in which legal questions do not play a constitutive role, from the motivating inheritance contract in *Die Familie Schroffenstein* to the "law of marriage" in *Amphitryon*, from the marriage contract in "Die Marquise von O . . ." to the meticulously depicted legal procedures in *Michael Kohlhaas*. In his plays and stories we can see a wealth of legal practices from the most varied periods and lands: Germany in the late Middle Ages, the sixteenth and seventeenth centuries; Italy in the Renaissance and eighteenth century; South America in the seventeenth and Haiti in the early nineteenth century—with Roman *jus gentium* and Germanic common law, with military law and trial by ordeal, with secular and ecclesiastical courts. In his fascination with the phenomenon of historical law Kleist is a true contemporary of Savigny and the Romantics.

Nevertheless, he does not share the reverence that we noted for Roman law. This is due in part to the fact that Kleist came so late to jurisprudence and the Latin in which it was written that he never felt at ease with the complexities of Roman law. But the crucial difference here is that Kleist as a Prussian was educated and worked administratively in a state ruled by the modern Prussian legal code. Although in his youth he went through a period of infatuation with natural law, he soon rejected that naively embraced theory, which rarely shows up in his works except to be criticized—as in the story "Das Erdbeben in Chili," where the seemingly paradisiacal society briefly established when the existing positive laws are disrupted by a natural disaster turns out to be a dream that cannot be sustained. Subsequently and despite his rejection of "the law" to which he was exposed as a student in Frankfurt an der Oder, Kleist was able to return to jurisprudence when as an administrator in Königsberg he attended lectures on laws of demesne as well as the Roman Institutions and Pandects. Indeed, the legal mode of thought always came easily to him, as is evident from the essay "Über die allmähliche Verfertigung der Gedanken beim Reden." When he is grasping for an example of typical examination questions, an example from legal instruction immediately occurs to him: "What is the state? Or: What is property?"⁹³

We should not forget that many of his friends and acquaintances—including Ludwig von Brockes, his companion of the mysterious journey to Würzburg, his co-editor Adam Müller, and Savigny, whom he later met socially in Berlin—were jurists. Despite the gaps in his education, Kleist lived in a juristic culture and always had an opportunity to inform himself about the most important developments in the field of legal scholarship and the philosophy of law. In this connection it has been persuasively suggested that the plot of *Der zerbrochne Krug* is based not on incidents in seventeenth-century Holland but rather on legal scandals in eighteenth-century Prussia.⁹⁴ Moreover, it has been demonstrated that Kleist's distinctive narrative style was decisively influenced by the contemporary guidelines for *Relationen*, or legal briefs, that he mastered as a student and used as an administrator.⁹⁵

Already in a letter of May 1799 Kleist distinguished pedantically between the "laws of reason," or natural law, and the positive laws of the state, which assure "our property, our honor, and our life."⁹⁶ With this reference to property, honor, and life Kleist is recapitulating the first part of the *Allgemeines Landrecht* (titles 8 to 22 deal with questions of property) as well as the last title of the second part, which deals with crimes against life and also insults to honor. Kleist was in government service during the years when the Prussian legal code was being vigorously debated. As a soldier he was subject to the articles of war in which the special duties of the military were established. It is not likely that the young cadet was indifferent to the controversies concerning the new legal code—above all from the standpoint of the nobility, whose privileges were being challenged. (But like Achim von Arnim, who lived in a similarly precarious situation, Kleist had little reason to worry about the loss of aristocratic privileges.) After leaving the army, he entered the Prussian civil service. Notoriously Kleist had a highly ambivalent attitude toward any "office." After unhappy beginnings around 1800 in the technical deputation of the Office for Manufacturing and subsequently in the Finance Department in Berlin and Königsberg (1805–1807), he left government service for good. But his experiences in the course of fifteen years in Prussian service had taught him where power resides in the state: in the code of laws. In his new career as a publicist he sought to remain close to the law. In 1807 he toyed with the idea that his publishing enterprise in Dresden would get the rights to the German edition of the Code Napoléon and, further, that he would be chosen by the French government to disseminate their publications in Germany.[97]

It is unimportant for our purposes that these unrealistic hopes came to naught. What matters is Kleist's shrewd recognition of the significance of the French codification as well as his calculating hope to profit from the spread of the Code in Germany. The second important initiative was the founding of the *Berliner Abendblätter*, for which Kleist nurtured the hope that it would become a "semi-ministerial" newspaper.[98] In his announcement of the new journal he promises as its great attraction to evaluate "the changes in the national legislation."[99] Although Kleist was often critical of the great Prussian reforms, for him the issue of legislation—and that means of course the ALR—counted as "first and foremost the most immediate and worthy object of general interest." Accordingly he enthusiastically supported Adam Müller's demand (in the *Berliner Abendblätter* of October 4, 1810) that in the future no one be permitted to enter the Prussian judicial or administrative system who is not equipped with "a thorough and complete understanding of the national universe"—in which of course he took the ALR for granted.

Summing up, one could argue that Kleist's intellectual development from about 1799 until his death constituted a steady development away from natural law and toward an ever firmer relationship to positive law in the form of the Prussian legal code. His early letters reveal at least a superficial acquaintance with both: with a popular natural law, in the sense of Pufendorf, as well as with the spirit of the new Prussian legal code. But after the "legal crisis" in Paris that we noted earlier, his attitude toward natural law became ever more critical. (The famous "Rechtsgefühl" to which he appeals is a subjective conviction that should not be identified with the more general philosophy of natural law.) At the same time he became increasingly interested in positive law as it was being formulated from 1794 on in Prussia as the ALR and in France as the Code Civil—two documents in which he recognized the basis of social order.

What significance do these facts and speculations have for our understanding of Kleist's works? Legal historians have taught us that Kleist, though his intuition was sometimes sensational, can nonetheless scarcely be regarded as a specialist in the history of law, where he repeatedly makes mistakes.[100] Yet it should hardly come as a surprise that this autodidact did not have available the knowledge of a legal historian. The wonder is that he succeeded despite his lack of systematic study in grasping so intuitively the legal situation of his various fictional settings.

Where did he get his material in cases when he needed a specific article of law? Let us take as a simple example *Amphitryon*, in which positive law plays less of a role than in any other play by Kleist. In the early scene where Jupiter and Alkmene appear for the first time following their night of love, Jupiter wants to assure himself that Alkmene has given herself to him out of passion for the beloved and not from a sense of duty toward her husband:

> Du weißt, daß ein Gesetz der Ehe ist,
> Und eine Pflicht, und daß wer Liebe nicht erwirbt,
> Noch Liebe vor dem Richter fordern kann.
>
> (vv. 446–48)

(You know that there is a law of matrimony and a duty and that anyone who fails to win love can still demand it before the judge.)

Kleist had apparently forgotten—or had never known—that the mythological Amphitryon went off on his military expedition precisely because Alkmene had—according to ancient Greek law—*legally* denied him his conjugal rights until he had avenged the death of her brothers. So Kleist did not get the "law of marriage" from the classical source and also not from Molière's *Amphitryon*, which is distinctly indebted to natural law.[101] Kleist's Jupiter can more easily be comprehended as an enlightened despot who clings to the Prussian legal code, where we read in the section on the Rights and Obligations of Married Couples with respect to their persons: "Married couples may not persistently deny one another their marital duties" (II 1 §178)—a conception that is clearly different from the classical as well as the French situation.

In general, whenever Kleist requires for his plot a legal fact—regardless of the historical period in which the work is set—he reaches to the source that he knew best: the *Allgemeines Landrecht* of 1794. This can be demonstrated over and over: in the civil laws that come into play in "Die Marquise von O ..." and protect the Count F. from the death penalty for what amounted to his rape of the unconscious marquise; in the laws of inheritance that invalidate Kunigunde's false claim to the Graf von Strahl's property in *Das Käthchen von Heilbronn*; in the procedural rules violated by the village magistrate Adam in *Der zerbrochne Krug*; in Michael Kohlhaas's rights to restoration of his property by the Junker Wenzel von Tronka (as well as his harsh punishment for crimes against the s〔 〕 of the state!); or for the crime against his pupil for which Jeronimo is imprisoned at the beginning of "Das Erdbeben in Chili." Kleist's practice amounts in almost every case to extrapolation from the codified positive law of his own modern Prussia. We should formulate our conclusions carefully. The possibility cannot be excluded that Kleist was familiar with older legal forms from his various sources or his own historical research—especially with respect to such institutions as trial by ordeal and vehmic courts. But it often appears as though the specific legal formulations that are constitutive in the works are articulated in the ALR. And we may certainly assume that the juristic expectations that Kleist takes for granted in his readership are consistent with the principles of the Prussian legal code.

This brings us to a broader generalization. In his attitude toward positive law Kleist differed radically from most of his literary contemporaries. Indeed, it can be argued that the confirmation of positive law amounts to a principle of organization in most of Kleist's plots. Again and again we find that at the conclusion of his works the legal system that was in effect at the beginning and then upset is once again reinstated. In "Das Erdbeben in Chili" Don Fernando and Donna Elvire continue to live with their adopted son under the same laws that plunged Jeronimo and Donna Josephe into despair at the beginning. In "Die Verlobung in St. Domingo" Herr Ströhmli returns with his family to Europe, where the same laws are in force that governed Haiti until the "ill-advised steps of the national convention" undermined the state of law and opened the way for the inhuman "laws" of the rebellious slaves. In "Der Findling" Piachi is protected against the death for which he longs by the same church law that had earlier robbed him of his possessions. In "Der Zweikampf" the validity of divine judgment and the Imperial Court are upheld despite all appearances. And in *Michael Kohlhaas* the law is fulfilled twice—the law of the land, by which Kohlhaas is granted his justice, and the imperial law prohibiting crimes against public peace, by which he is condemned. And the same paradigm is valid for the dramas. In *Der zerbrochne Krug* the law of the land is fulfilled despite the confusions and evasions of the wily magistrate. And Prinz Friedrich von Homburg reaches his supreme epiphany in the recognition that he intends to ennoble through a voluntary death the sacred law of war that he had violated. (The fact that he is subsequently pardoned is irrelevant for our purposes.)

Kleist was driven by the same rage for order that motivated many of his contemporaries at the time of the crisis in Prussia and the Romantic revaluation of all values. As a Prussian he believed that he could find this social order in the ALR and, by analogy, in the positive law of any society that he portrayed in his works. Accordingly the existing law is almost always confirmed at the end.[102]

This does not mean, of course, that the law always functions as it is ideally supposed to. However, it is not the law but its human agents who are inadequate. The negative figures and forces in his stories and dramas are those that seek to undermine the law or corrupt it for their own purposes: the unscrupulous village magistrate, the Junker von Tronka and his scheming relatives in *Michael Kohlhaas*, and the representatives of ecclesiastical power who attempt to subvert the positive law of the state for their own sinister purposes, as in "Das Erdbeben in Chili" or "Der Findling." What is doubted or made ambiguous is not the law but the spiritual meaning of the world, in which law alone provides a semblance of order.

In contrast to many of his contemporaries Kleist shows no longing for "the old, good law" of Roman or Old German jurisprudence. And after the naive enthusiasms of his youth, he rejected the natural law of Rousseau with its implication that mankind living in a primal state without the restraint of law would be a paradise. As a man experienced in the practical workings of the Prussian legal system, Kleist understood that a society without laws is chaotic and that, given the ambivalent nature of man, it is best for the law to be available not just to the experts, who seek to exploit it for their own purposes, but to every citizen in the form of a straightforward legal code.

· · ·

Of the many Romantic jurists, none was more intimately involved with law than E.T.A. Hoffmann (1776–1822).[103] With the exception of the eight-year period from December 1806 to October 1814, when he was prevented by the French occupation of Prussia from practicing his profession, Hoffmann worked in the Prussian legal service for his entire career. Following his study of law at Königsberg from 1792 to 1795, he passed the first state examination and was appointed to the position of clerk (*Auskultator*) in the East Prussian government, serving first in Königsberg and then in Glogau. Shortly after his second examination in 1798, which brought a promotion to the grade of *Referendar* (a junior magistrate), Hoffmann was transferred to Berlin, where he served at the *Kammergericht* (Prussian Supreme Court). Following the third and final examination in 1800, he was appointed for a probationary period as judge in Posen and, two years later, promoted to a regular position as legal councillor, first in Plock (1802–1804) and then in Warsaw (1804–1806). However, just at the point when he had established himself firmly within the Prussian judiciary, the South Prussian government was suspended at Napoleon's command, and for the next eight years Hoffmann had to eke out an existence in other jobs—notably as conductor and theater director, first in Bamberg and subsequently in Dresden. Almost immediately after Napoleon's defeat, Hoffmann returned to Prussian service at the *Kammergericht* in Berlin—initally as an unpaid assistant and then with a modest remuneration. In May 1816, finally, he received full membership as a judge in the Criminal Senate with a yearly salary, a position that he held until December 1821, when shortly before his death he was appointed to the Superior Appeals Court (*Oberappellations-Senat*) of the Supreme Court.

Like most of the other Romantic jurists, Hoffmann complained steadily about his job—especially in letters to his close friend Theodor Gottlieb von Hippel, who was also a jurist. On May 1, 1795, while preparing for his first examination, he wrote to Hippel: "My studies proceed slowly and gloomily—I have to force myself to become a jurist."[104] After the move to Bamberg, he again wrote to Hippel to say how wrong for him his earlier career had been and how he was thriving in his new life as an artist.[105] Even after his return to the *Kammergericht* in Berlin, his letters are full of complaints about what Hoffmann called *Juridica*.[106] On November 1, 1814, when he had been back for only a month, Hoffmann confessed to Hippel that it was his strong desire to remain in Berlin, "but the destiny of a councillor at the *Kammergericht* is not particularly enviable."[107] Half a year later he reminded his friend "that it was never my idea to return to the judiciary because it is too heterogeneous from art, to which I am sworn."[108] Indeed, the very building that housed the *Kammergericht* reminds him of the rock of Prometheus to which he is chained.[109]

At the same time, Hoffmann passed all his examinations with distinction and, throughout his career, received the highest evaluations from his supervisors and the greatest praise from his colleagues for his diligence, his skill, his precision and thoroughness, the clarity of his presentation, and his deep penetration into the spirit of the law ("tiefes Eindringen in den Geist der Gesetze").[110] The law into whose spirit Hoffmann had penetrated was of course the Prussian legal code, which came into effect during the years when he was studying law. Indeed, the ALR is cited in the earliest briefs that he drafted (with good marks from his superior) as a probationary clerk in Glogau in 1798, and he refers to the ALR again in one of the last cases he handled—a copyright dispute regarding a piano transcription of Weber's *Der Freischütz*—only three weeks before his death.[111] In addition, the ALR is cited frequently in his literary works, as in the introductory framework of *Die Serapionsbrüder*, where Theodor ( = Hoffmann) recalls a social club in Posen with an elaborate set of rules based meticulously on the form of the ALR with its title and paragraphs.[112] In short, Hoffmann's ritual complaints about his work as a judge have no bearing whatsoever on his knowledge of the law in general and the Prussian legal code in particular or on his meticulous and conscientious fulfillment of his responsibilities as a civil servant in the Prussian government.

It is hardly surprising, then, to find a conspicuous interaction between institution and art, between Hoffmann's activities as a jurist and his endeavors as a writer. This interaction is evident, first of all, in the style of his legal briefs, which anticipates and then parallels the clarity of exposition in his narratives. But it is particularly obvious in the material of his tales, which teem with criminal cases, judges, and trials. That Hoffmann was clearly aware of this tendency in his work emerges from the statement that he prepared in his own defense in February 1822, when he was accused of libel against the director of the Prussian Ministry of Police. "One might ask," he writes, "how I happened to put these juristic censures in a fairy tale, and I can only respond that no writer desists from his métier but delights in depictions from it."[113] Hoffmann goes on to recall other writers in whose work their legal profession is constantly evident: the satirist G. W. Rabener, the humorist Theodor Gottlieb von Hippel (the uncle of Hoffmann's friend), and of course Walter Scott, who "as one of the leading law officers in Edinburgh has to do with trials in almost every one of his novels." Hoffmann concludes his argument by noting that he, too, has described trials in several of his works—for instance, in his novel *Die Elixiere des Teufels* and in stories included in the collection *Nachtstücke*. Accordingly it should hardly be remarkable that he does so in the fairy tale *Meister Floh*. We shall return to the libel suit surrounding the late work *Meister Floh* in another connection. For the present, let us survey the role of law in the earlier works that Hoffmann mentions.

Crudely generalizing, we can say that the tales Hoffmann wrote during his years in Bamberg and Dresden—essentially the stories collected in *Fantasiestücke in Callots Manier* (1814–1815) and including the sequence of episodes revolving around the musician Johannes Kreisler as well as such narratives as the tale of the dog Berganza, *Der goldne Topf*, and the so-called "Adventures of Silvester's Eve"—are concerned primarily with the personality and relatively introspective problems of the artist. It was only with his return to Berlin and his legal functions that Hoffmann's tales began to show an increasingly pervasive interest in society generally and the social aspects of the artist's life. It is not until these works, written in the years after 1814, that Hoffmann's juristic experience begins to make itself felt. This is the case with *Die Elixiere des Teufels* (1815–1816), even though it is based extensively on Hoffmann's experiences in Bamberg and with South German Catholicism. The adventures of the sinful Capuchin monk Medardus are just as exuberant and exotic as those of M. G. Lewis's *The Monk*, the Gothic romance upon which it is explicitly based. And the tricky complications of plot and genealogy—with their incestuous relationships, mysterious doppelgänger, portraits of saints that resemble living figures, ecclesiastical and court intrigues, and the constant threat of madness—turn out to owe more to an ancient curse on the family and the temptations of an omnipresent devil than to the rationality of the eighteenth century in which the novel is set. Yet midway through the work, almost as its centerpiece, we find a long, detailed account of the judicial investigation following the arrest of Medardus on the charge of murders that he has in fact committed. The investigation is divided into two parts. The judge who first interrogates Medardus on the morning following his arrest—"a withered little man with fox-red hair and with a hoarse, ridiculously squeaky voice" (202)[114]—is portrayed as an incompetent who chatters away so indiscreetly that the wily monk has time enough to concoct an elaborate fiction and false identity as an alibi. For the next ten days Medardus is left alone in his cell; but when he is summoned for the second interrogation, he is confronted by a different judge—"a rather young man who, as was apparent to me at first glance, was much superior to the former one in skill and penetrating sense" (209).

He was rather square-set for his years, his head almost hairless; he wore spectacles. His whole being radiated so much goodness and geniality that I felt that any but the most hardened criminal would be able to resist him only with the greatest difficulty. He stated his questions casually, almost in a conversational tone; but they were considered and phrased so precisely that only specific answers could follow.

This judge pursues his interrogation with such calm, methodical system that Medardus becomes confused about his own previous testimony and, when confronted with a witness who identifies him, breaks out in a fury. "Up to this point the judge had remained in calm composure, without altering his gaze and tone; now for the first time his face contracted itself to a dark, penetrating earnest expression. He stood up and peered sharply into my eyes. I must confess that even the glittering of his glasses held something unbearable, terrible for me; I could speak no further" (212). By the time the interrogation has ended, Medardus is completely broken. "The words of the judge penetrated my soul like glowing spikes. Everything that I had alleged seemed shallow and insipid" (215).

Shortly after he is returned to his cell, the guards come and fasten him to the wall with chains because the evidence against him as a triple murderer is so overwhelming. In his despair Medardus even dreams that he is undergoing a second trial—an ecclesiastical inquisition in which he is suspended by his hands in such a manner that his limbs are broken out of his joints (219–20). By the time Medardus is summoned for further interrogation, he has prepared himself for death. "In my mind I had organized my confession in such a manner that I hoped to provide the judge with a brief narrative that included every smallest detail" (222). At this point the unexpected occurs: the "real" culprit has been found, and at the command of the ruling prince Medardus's trial has been abrogated. In a daze Medardus signs the necessary release forms and prepares to leave. The young examining magistrate follows him and confides that he has been especially interested in this case and is pleased that Medardus has turned out not to be the criminal monk. But he wants to verify the results of his own investigation: Medardus concedes that he is not the Polish nobleman he had pretended to be. But when Medardus hesitates before answering whether or not he is a monk, the magistrate interrupts and tells him not to go on. "What I believed at the outset and still believe has been confirmed. I see that puzzling circumstances are at play here and that you yourself are involved in a mysterious game of fate with certain persons of the court. It is no longer my task to explore further, and I would regard it as inappropriate inquisitiveness to want to entice anything more from you about your person or the no doubt quite unusual circumstances of your life" (224).

At this point the young judge disappears from the novel for good, and the story continues. But in these twenty pages, which constitute his first extensive description of a legal process, Hoffmann has communicated a good deal. First, he has given us vivid portrayals of two different types of examining magistrates, and it is tempting to recognize in the effective young magistrate not only Hoffmann's vision of personified justice but also certain characteristics of his own style as a judge. Second, he has provided a lively and detailed account of the actual process of legal interrogation, including, in particular, the dramatic interplay between the magistrate and the accused. Finally, he has hinted at the inadequacies of a law that permits the criminal to be pardoned by princely authority even when the shrewd judge suspects secrets that still remain to be uncovered. But in a monarchy there are some matters that it is better even for the court not to know.

That Hoffmann shared the Romantic interest in the history of law is suggested by "Ignaz Denner," a tale from *Nachtstücke* that was written in 1814, the year of the codification controversy. Like many of Hoffmann's ghost stories and fairy tales, the action of "Ignaz Denner," which takes place many years before the narrator's present, is "explained" by an earlier tradition involving a devilish curse on the family of the hero's wife. As a result of this curse, the virtuous huntsman Andres becomes involved against his will and almost unwittingly with a gang of robbers who infest the forests around Fulda. The story culminates in his arrest for armed robbery in connection with an attack on the castle of the Graf von Vach, and despite his protestations of innocence he is found guilty, tortured until he confesses, and then saved at the last minute from the hangman's noose when a witness appears who is able to testify that Andres was in Frankfurt at the time the robbery and murder took place.

Of interest in our context is the care with which Hoffmann explores the nature of evidence and its uncertainties. The reader knows from the narrative that Andres was in fact in Frankfurt on the stated occasion in order to collect an inheritance for his wife. But because he wanted to surprise her with it, he had told no one of his journey except the murdered count and his clerk. Subsequently, even the inheritance money is used as evidence against him when it is assumed that it is loot from the plundered castle. No one in the castle is able to testify in his favor because the count and his clerk have both died, and the banker in Frankfurt, who had referred Andres to the merchant holding the inheritance, could no longer recall his visit. The merchant himself was on business trips to France and Italy while the investigations were taking place and consequently learned about Andres's condemnation only at the very last minute. For reasons of their own—including resentment at his reluctance to work with their gang—the robbers testify that Andres was with them during the attack. "But all this would not have convinced the judges of the unfortunate Andres's guilt as much as the statement of two of Graf von Vach's huntsmen, who claimed to have seen and recognized Andres in the light of the flames just as the count was struck down by him."[115] It is not until the incontrovertible witness to his innocence appears that the other testimony is finally put into proper perspective. In the meantime, persuaded by the evidence that Andres is truly guilty, the judges determine to put him to the torture in order to produce a confession.

In "Ignaz Denner" Hoffmann leaves unspoken the implications about the reliability of evidence and witnesses that clearly stem from his own experience as an investigating criminal magistrate. But in a later story, "Die Marquise de la Pivardiere" (written 1820, published 1821), he expresses his judicial opinion in a similar case. This story has its source in Pitaval's *Causes célèbres*, the eighteenth-century collection of criminal cases that excited the interest of writers in Germany from Schiller to Ernst Jünger. Again it is not the details of the original story that concern us here: the marquise is accused of murdering her husband with the assistance of her confessor, the Augustine priest Charost, with whom she had been in love twenty years earlier. We know from the narrative that her husband has been living in bigamy with an innkeeper's daughter in Auxerre, that she rejects him scornfully when he attempts to return to her, and that he in turn leaves home again in shame and secrecy. However, following her husband's disappearance, the marquise, suspected of his murder, takes refuge with a friend. Her flight arouses more suspicion. The investigating magistrate, Bonnet, interrogates two of the marquise's maidservants, who claim to have witnessed the murder. The marquise surrenders herself freely, and Charost is also arrested. Despite their protestations of innocence and the absence of a body, they are found guilty. They have just been sentenced to torture when suddenly the doors of the courtroom burst open and the marquis de la Pivardière appears and explains that he had fled out of fear that he would be punished severely for his bigamous relationship. It was only much later that he heard of the accusations and the trial of his wife for his alleged murder. Even now, however, the matter is not settled. Because of the testimony of the two maidservants the marquis himself is doubted: his identity is not accepted until two of his sisters and the abbess of their monastery spend three weeks with him and prove his identity.

At this point the story as related in the *Causes célèbres* is completed, and the marquise and Charost are acquitted. But Hoffmann the judge continues for several pages because his professional interest has now been aroused. First, there is the technical question of the corpus delicti. "According to all the rules of law the court had to assume that the proof concerning the person of the marquis de la Pivardière had been conducted as fully as possible. But the marquise and Charost were not accused of the murder of some person in general but of the murder of the marquise de la Pivardière; if therefore the life of the marquise could be established completely, then that accusation had to be false."[116]

However, the acquittal of the marquise opens new questions. "If the accusation was false, then the persons on whose testimony it was based must have borne false witness." This gave cause, in turn, for a trial of the two maidservants. On reexamination of their testimony in the light of the marquise's demonstrated innocence, their statements—concerning armed men entering the courtyard, noises in the marquis's room, laments, and a shot—turn out to be accurate, but the women had drawn the wrong conclusions from the incidents. The rumors about the marquise and her confessor, producing a false interpretation of circumstances that in and of themselves were perfectly innocent, gave rise to the accusation. "Bonnet was (as no judge ought to be) passionate to the highest degree, full of prejudices, deluded in every manner and, in addition to everything else, at odds with the family of the Augustine Charost" (272). Accordingly he began with the firm assumption that the marquise was having an illicit love affair with Charost and that they determined to get rid of the marquis when he returned unexpectedly. "Bonnet did not hesitate to threaten the maidservants Mercier and Lemoine with death if they did not confess everything, and he got every response from them that he wanted. The method for accomplishing this is very easy" (273).

Several people who had spoken separately with the two women testified that they had complained about Bonnet's method and wanted to appear before a different judge so that they might tell the truth—namely, that they only suspected murder but could certainly not prove it. Even the court scribe testified that Bonnet had threatened to cut off Mercier's fingers if she did not immediately confess a circumstance that he had dreamed up. To make his point even more forcefully, Hoffmann added a framework to the story to show how quickly all of Parisian society is prepared to accept the guilt of the marquise until her husband shows up safe and sound—and then those willing to believe the worst of her suddenly concede that her husband was actually a ne'er-do-well. In short, the experienced judge exhibits effectively and in multiple instances the ambiguity of evidence and the need for the most scrupulous and cautious interpretation.

As if the textual evidence of his stories were not adequate, Hoffmann has provided us with an unambiguous statement of his intention to deal in literary form with the chief juristic faults that he knows. In the document for his defense in the *Meister Floh* affair Hoffmann notes that he used the opportunity of his fairy tale "to expose two of the greatest criminalistic mistakes: first, when the investigating magistrate simply inquires blindly without knowing the circumstances of the crime that has actually been committed; and second, when in his soul a preconceived opinion has taken fast from which he will not desist and which alone serves him as the guiding principle for his procedure."[117] Even though Hoffmann is referring here specifically to *Meister Floh*, the points are both quite relevant to "Ignaz Denner" and, particularly, "Die Marquise de la Pivardiere." In the second tale the court makes the first mistake by assuming a crime in the absence of an adequate corpus delicti; and the magistrate, Bonnet, is blinded so totally by his prejudices and emotions that he willfully distorts the available evidence and forces proof where none is available. In both tales the plot of Hoffmann the writer is informed by the experience and convictions of Justice Hoffmann.

It is not only as raw material for legal commentary that Hoffmann tells his tales. They also display other legal dimensions. "Das Majorat" (from *Nachtstücke*) is a tale predicated upon the right of primogeniture, a law precious to the Prussian aristocracy. Hoffmann makes his own position clear when his spokesman in the tale confesses that he finds "quite odious any institution that favors the firstborn so preponderantly and places the other children in the background."[118] He also expresses his own veneration for the law, an institution to which every member of society, specifically including the nobility, must submit. When the young baron becomes impatient at the executor of his father's estate, the attorney reprimands him:

"Not so fast, baron!—You may not seek to give orders here before the opening of the will; for the present I and I alone am the master here and I know how to meet force with force.—Remember that, by virtue of my power of attorney as executor of the paternal testament, by virtue of the arrangements agreed upon by the court, I am entitled to deny you residence here in R. .sitten, and I advise you, in order to avoid any unpleasantness, to betake yourself quietly to K." The seriousness of the magistrate, the decisive tone with which he spoke, gave his words a suitable emphasis. (640)

What is new in this tale is not the detail of legal administration or the plot based upon primogeniture but the fact that the framework draws extensively upon Hoffmann's own youth. Hoffmann's great-uncle, the Royal Councillor Christoph Ernst Voeteri, was justiciar, or estate attorney, for various East Prussian noble families. In 1794, while Hoffmann was still studying law at the university, he accompanied his uncle on several trips to the estates, serving as his official legal secretary. The story that the young narrator tells involves a love triangle of the sort that occurs almost routinely in Hoffmann's tales: the young law clerk falls in love with the young wife of an older man who (in fact or merely in the young man's imagination) mistreats her. In this case the narrator is saved from compromise and embarrassment by his uncle, who reveals to him the mysterious family circumstances of past generations that explain the present action. But in the course of the action we get a depiction, portrayed with fond detail, of the visit to the estate by the narrator and his uncle V., the quarters in which they live during the stay on the estate, and in particular the responsibilities of the justiciar. "On the next morning the work began. The estate inspector came with his accounts, and people signed up who wanted to have a quarrel moderated or any sort of affair arranged."[119]

The aspiring young jurist is repeatedly impressed by "the respect, indeed the childlike reverence that the baron displayed toward my elderly great-uncle" (290), who sits at table beside the baroness. The narrator himself, not unlike the young Hoffmann, "spoke full of enthusiasm of lofty, sacred art and finally did not conceal the fact that I—regardless of the dry, boring juristics to which I was committed—played the piano with relative skill, sang, and also even have set many a song to music" (591). In sum, it is not just the plot of the story, which revolves around questions of inheritance, but also the entire atmosphere that is juristic in a manner unlikely in any writer but one who is at home in legal culture. And it is surely no accident that so many characters in his tales, even when legal issues play no role, are jurists: Councillor Krespel, Advocate Coppelius (in "Der Sandmann"), and the anchorite Serapion, to mention only a conspicuous few.

Hoffmann uses the profession of law for comic purposes as well. In the late tale "Meister Johannes Wacht" (written 1822, published posthumously in 1823) the titular figure, a master carpenter in Bamberg, is an otherwise good-natured and decent man with two obsessive prejudices: he is anti-Catholic and has nothing but contempt for lawyers. Early in the tale the first prejudice prompts him to drive off a suitor for his older daughter's hand. But most of the tale is devoted to his schemes to prevent the marriage of his younger daughter to a lawyer. Wacht, without realizing it, believes in a simple kind of natural law. "Wacht, namely, was absolutely convinced that everything parading under the name of jurisprudence is nothing other than human statutes cooked up by phony brooding and that it serves only to confuse the true right that stands inscribed in the breast of every virtuous person."[120] Accordingly when Jonathan, the younger son of his deceased friend and partner, becomes a lawyer and requests his daughter's hand, Wacht flies into a fury:

> "What," exclaimed Father Wacht in a voice that made the walls resound, "you miserable good-for-nothing, nature has neglected your body but has endowed you with splendid gifts of the mind, and you want to misuse these in a shameful manner like a sly scoundrel and turn the knife against your own mother? You want to do business with justice, as though with a cheap and vile ware on the open market, and weigh it out with a false scale to the poor peasant, the oppressed burgher, who whined in vain before the upholstered chair of the rigid judge, and let yourself be paid with the bloody coin that the poor soul, bathed in tears, extends to you? You want to fill your brain with false statutes and deal in lies and deceit as though it were a profitable handicraft with which you feed yourself? Has all your father's virtue abandoned your heart?" (643–44)

For Master Wacht it would be "the most dreadful misfortune to see his dearest child bound to a lawyer—in short, to Satan himself" (658). The story goes on to show how Jonathan, by a resourceful bit of legal work, restores her rightful inheritance to a Hungarian countess and receives a substantial reward, which he then uses to rehabilitate his profligate brother—an action that finally gains him Wacht's affection and the hand of his beloved Nanni. " 'Lawyer, let me penetrate into the depths of the law as it has come alive in your breast so that I may survive before the eternal Judgment as you shall one day survive' " (678). Jonathan, who displays as a young lawyer all the signs that he will mature into a jurist with the integrity and capability of Councillor V. in "Das Majorat," represents another exemplar of Hoffmann's respect for the law and its finest practitioners.

In the lengthy fairy tale *Klein Zaches* (1819), finally, the entire situation is essentially a juristic one, although the plot does not revolve around law. As in all of Hoffmann's *Märchen*, the story that takes place on the level of everyday reality is "explained" by another series of events that occur on the mythic level. In this case, when Prince Paphnutius decides to "introduce the Enlightenment" to his land and drive out all the fairies along with their "dangerous trade with the miraculous,"[121] two get left behind: the fairy Rosabelverde, who continues her life as the canoness Fräulein von Rosengrünschön, or simply Rosenschön for short; and the magus who lives on as Doctor Prosper Alpanus. It is Fräulein von Rosenschön's misguided gift to the horrid monster-child, Little Zaches—in his presence everything excellent said or done by anyone else is magically attributed to him—that motivates the plot, which ends only with the death of Zaches, or, as he has come to call himself, Zinnober. However, Zinnober's entire career takes place in the realm of law and administration. He arrives at the university as a student of law and is regarded by his professor as the most brilliant student; when he takes an exam for a position with the minister of external affairs, the responses of the truly qualified candidate are attributed to Zinnober, who gets the job; he is soon promoted to the position of special privy councillor and, in due course, displaces his superior, the minister of external affairs, in the affections of the ruler, who awards him for his invaluable service to the state the Order of the Green-Spotted Tiger with twenty buttons. In sum, the story offers Hoffmann a rich opportunity to make a number of satirical comments on the administrative merit system and its rewards as it sometimes functions—a system, that is, that enables superiors to get the credit for the work of their staffs and office toadies to rise above their capable colleagues. More generally, however, it shows once again that, regardless of the details of the plot and whether in more realistic narratives or in his fairy tales, Hoffmann felt most comfortable in a juristic or cameralistic culture and setting.

In Hoffmann's eyes, despite all his epistolary complaints, the law was a noble institution, and he had nothing but respect for the finest of its advocates, who ensure that society functions smoothly and equitably. He not only reflected that ideal in his literary oeuvre; he aspired to it with a notable degree of success in his own juristic career. For that reason he had nothing but contempt for those who sought to exploit, corrupt, or otherwise abuse the law and its highest principles. In his last major work, the fairy tale *Meister Floh* (1821–1822, published 1822), his juristic and literary careers were to come together in a fateful conjunction.

Following the Congress of Vienna and particularly in reaction to the national assembly of students on the occasion of the Reformation Commemoration at the Wartburg in 1817, the conservative forces of many German states took action to stop the spread of what they regarded as threatening liberal ideas of democracy. The so-called Karlsbad Decrees, promulgated in 1819 by Austria, Prussia, and other German states, were ostensibly a response to certain acts of radical terrorism, but they amounted in fact to a general suppression of liberalism and insurgent nationalism. In Prussia Friedrich Wilhelm III granted to the Ministry of Police in Berlin under its director, Karl Albert von Kamptz, extraordinary powers to pursue suspected "demagogues" and established for that purpose a special commission for the investigation of treasonous organizations and activities (*Immediatkommission zur Ermittlung hochverräterischer Verbindungen und anderer gefährlicher Umtriebe*). Under Kamptz's enthusiastic persecutions, a number of liberal spokesmen were arrested and jailed on the basis of shockingly inadequate evidence, including Georg Ludwig Roediger, a leader of the Jena national fraternities (*Burschenschaften*); the jurist Dr. Ludwig von Mühlenfels; and Friedrich Ludwig Jahn, who was known as the *Turnvater* because of his passionate espousal of physical exercise for the young.

The most scandalous case involved the *Turnvater*. At the time of his arrest in July 1819 and before any investigation or trial, Kamptz placed in the Berlin newspapers a notice in which he announced Jahn's guilt for exhorting the youth of Berlin to revolutionary activities.[122] In November Jahn brought a countersuit against Kamptz for defamation of character ("als einen *Pasquillanten*"). Soon after Hoffmann was appointed to the *Immediatkommission* on October 1, 1819, he succeeded in freeing Roediger from his illegal detention. He next took on Jahn's suit against

Kamptz, whom he detested for his brutal and illegal methods. As the investigating magistrate, Hoffmann summoned Kamptz, his own superior, to appear for questioning. On December 28, 1819, Hoffmann was ordered by the minister of justice, Friedrich Leopold von Kircheisen, to desist from the procedure against Kamptz on the grounds that it disrupted the proper *Ordo cognitionum* and could produce distressing "anomalies."

In his response of January 10, 1820, Hoffmann cited the ALR in support of his contention "that even an order received from higher authority could not free the accused from the punishment of slander." And on February 28 Hoffmann, speaking for the *Immediatkommission*, recommended to Kircheisen Jahn's immediate release from detention. In March, however, a royal command from the king himself put an end to the matter; Kamptz continued his persecutions; and the *Immediatkommission* was subordinated to a ministerial commission that reined in its efforts toward independent investigation.

Hoffmann was profoundly distressed by these developments. On June 24, 1820, he wrote to Hippel:

> You can well imagine my mood when, before my eyes, there emerged a whole web of dreadful caprice, insolent disregard of all laws, personal animosity! I do not need to assure you that, like any just man inspired by true patriotism, I was and remain convinced that bounds must be set to the chimerical activities of a few young hotheads.... It was time to punish and guide with all rigor in a legal manner. But instead measures were applied that were directed not only against deeds but against ideologies.[123]

Indeed, when the *Immediatkommission* recommended the release of Mühlenfels later that summer, Kamptz was able to thwart their order. Seeing that the work of the *Immediatkommission* had been almost totally undermined by Kamptz and his supervisory commission of ministers, Hoffmann sought his discharge, which was approved in the summer of 1821.

Precisely at that time Hoffmann began to write *Meister Floh*, a work that was to enable him to carry on his campaign against Kamptz in literary form.[124] In the fairy tale concerning the idiosyncratic bachelor Peregrinus Tyß, the wise Master Flea who counsels him and provides him with a magical eyeglass enabling him to see the innermost thoughts of others, his courtship of the bookbinder's daughter Röschen, and the mythic framework that bestows a higher meaning on the earthly action, there is no obvious legal or political dimension. But in December 1821 it suddenly occurred to Hoffmann how he might have his literary revenge for Kamptz's schemes. He introduced two episodes into his text concerning a Privy Councillor named Knarrpanti, the "factotum" at the court of a prince so minor that the author even forgets his name. During Knarrpanti's sojourn in Frankfurt, where the story takes place, a rumor spreads through the city that an elegant young lady has been abducted from a Christmas party given by a wealthy banker. When the police investigate, it turns out that no young lady is missing; the rumor is declared groundless and the matter is dismissed.

When Knarrpanti hears the rumor, he decides that the missing girl is a princess who disappeared from the court of his prince and appeals to the magistrate to assist him in his inquiries. The judge reminds him that the rumor had been proved untrue, that no one had been abducted, and that therefore there could be no investigation of a culprit. But Knarrpanti assures him that he has already succeeded in discovering the culprit.

> In response to the reminder that a deed must have been done if there is to be a doer, Knarrpanti said that, if only the criminal has been detected, the committed crime will turn up by itself. Only a superficial, frivolous judge is not capable, even if the main complaint cannot be determined because of the stubbornness of the accused, of establishing one thing or another by inquiries, which would attach some sort of blemish to the accused and justify the arrest.[125]

The suspect that Knarrpanti has in mind is none other than the respected citizen of Frankfurt Peregrinus Tyß, who had been seen on that Christmas Eve carrying a beautiful young woman into his house. Knarrpanti argues that the circumstance that no young lady is missing proves nothing; the young woman might have escaped from the house and be ashamed to bring any charges. All he needs are the criminal's papers, and the crime can be demonstrated. Reluctantly the judge issues a warrant for Tyß's arrest and the confiscation of his papers.

In the second episode the judge's representative has determined that the papers do not contain a single word that would suggest any crime of the sort cited in the complaint. But Knarrpanti is not shaken in his convictions: in a diary that Tyß kept as a young man he discovers a number of passages that refer specifically to abduction and concludes that he is an abhorrent person, "a veritable Don Juan." Even when it is shown that the word "abduction" always occurs in a literary context, as for instance in a reference to Mozart's *Entführung aus dem Serail*, Knarrpanti remains steadfast, arguing "that even the context did not improve things because it was precisely the cunning slyness of criminals to disguise such utterances so that at first glance they might be regarded as entirely indifferent, wholly innocent" (107). When the legal experts point out that there was no corpus delicti, "the wise Councillor Knarrpanti maintained that he did not give a damn about the delictum if he only had a corpus in his hands, and the corpus was the dangerous abductor and murderer Herr Peregrinus Tyß." Realizing that everything he says is twisted and used against him by Knarrpanti, Tyß decides to say nothing and to base his case on the absence of any specific crime of which he may be accused. Knarrpanti, prepared with more than a hundred questions with which he intended to elicit some guilt, is unconcerned. "Above all they were aimed at finding out what Peregrinus had *thought* both generally throughout his entire life, as well as on this or that specific occasion, as for example when writing down those suspicious words in his papers" (108). Thinking itself, in Knarrpanti's opinion, is "a dangerous operation" that becomes all the more dangerous in dangerous people. And he is eager to ask Peregrinus if he does not understand that all the mysterious passages in his papers rightfully arouse the suspicion that the things he neglected to write down must have contained much more suspicious matters, even a complete confession of the crime.

With the aid of Master Flea's magical eyeglass Peregrinus is able to see that Knarrpanti himself does not believe that he actually abducted the princess; but he could not pass up an opportunity to turn a rumor to his own advantage and to reawaken the interest and respect of the court in his abilities. "Praised be the art of bestowing upon the most indifferent matter a touch of spiteful significance. It is a gift that nature granted to me and by means of which I get my enemies off my back and remain myself in the best well-being" (110). Because Peregrinus understands Knarrpanti's thoughts and intentions, he is able to outwit him during the interrogation, and the remarkable hearing is brought to a conclusion. Knarrpanti is urged to leave Frankfurt and to deliver his dossier to his ruler as proof of his sagacity and zeal. But he cannot fail to notice that all the citizens of Frankfurt hold their noses as a sign of disgust when he passes.

In this way Hoffmann planned to take his revenge on Kramptz for his unethical behavior, which he regarded as a shame to the profession of

lawyer, and specifically for his practice of inventing a crime where none
has occurred, as well as his tendency to be driven by hatred and emotion
rather than by reason and love of justice. But it was not to be. In early
January, before Hoffmann had mailed this portion of his manuscript to
his publisher in Frankfurt, the rumor of his lampoon against Kramptz
had spread through the literary circles in Berlin. Hearing of this, Kamptz
dispatched an officer to Frankfurt, who got permission from the City
Council to inspect the manuscript. As a result, on Febuary 1 the authorities in Berlin demanded the deletion of eight pages, and despite the publisher's initial objections, the tale, as it was finally published in April,
lacked the offending passages concerning Knarrpanti/Kamptz (which
were not recovered from the government archives and restored to the
text until the beginning of this century).

Hoffmann was not to get off so lightly. At the end of January Kamptz
submitted to Friedrich von Schuckmann, the minister of interior, a complaint against Hoffmann based on his perusal of the censored pages. Specifically, he charged Hoffmann with lèse majesté for lack of respect for
the king and his own superiors, with violation of the official oath of secrecy, and with libel of the crudest sort against a government official in
the exercise of his duty.[126] Because of his severe illness, which led to his
death within five months, Hoffmann was unable to follow the summons
for an official inquiry. On February 23 he prepared the written statement
that we have already cited, in which he identified the two major defects
that he recognizes in public servants of the law and justified his use of
literary works to deal with these juristic criticisms. He of course denied
that Knarrpanti was intended as a lampoon in any specific sense of Police
Director Kramptz. The case dragged on, not abrogated by the king, as
was Jahn's complaint against Kramptz, and only Hoffmann's death on
June 25, 1822, caused it finally to be laid *ad acta* by Chancellor Hardenberg.

*Meister Floh* provides the most dramatic example of the interaction of
law and literature in German Romanticism. It could have been written
only by a man who, as a jurist, had participated in events similar to the
ones described and who, as a writer, had reached the point of maturity
and detachment that enabled him to deal with these events with brilliant
irony. Hoffmann's document of defense, in turn, constitutes perhaps the
noblest statement by a *Dichterjurist* on the dignity of the law and the
proper interaction of institution and art.

We should remind ourselves once more that the law to which Hoffmann subscribed was not a vague natural law or the traditional law of the past, whether Roman or German, but the positive law of the Prussian legal code, which he cites repeatedly in his opinions and which, in his story "Das öde Haus," he called "the lawbook of a highly enlightened state."[127] Yet whatever its manifestation—natural, German, or Roman, common or codified—the law constituted a remarkable force in Germany during the age of Romanticism—a force that not only produced some of the most brilliant legal thought of the nineteenth century but also cast its unmistakable spell on many of the finest and most representative literary works of the times.

# The Madhouse:
# Asylum of the Spirit

## THE INSTITUTION OF THE MADHOUSE IN GERMANY

IN 1805 the first institution in any German-speaking country for the "psychic treatment" of the mentally ill was established in Bayreuth by order of Karl August von Hardenberg, minister in the cabinet of Friedrich Wilhelm III of Prussia. Literary wags might have whispered that the establishment was necessary simply to accommodate the madmen who were showing up with alarming frequency in the fiction of the age. Early cases were evident in Goethe's exemplary *Bildungsroman*, *Wilhelm Meisters Lehrjahre*, as well as the tales of Ludwig Tieck—such as "Der blonde Eckbert" and "Der Runenberg"—which often seemed to depend upon demented heroes for their action. Only two years earlier Jean Paul had completed his novel *Titan*, which featured several of the most fascinating lunatics in German literature; and, as though to confirm the point, Jean Paul himself had recently moved to Bayreuth, where the director of the new asylum soon became one of his close friends. The year 1804 witnessed the appearance of the most brilliant Romantic hymn to madness, published anonymously under the title *Nachtwachen von Bonaventura*. And E.T.A. Hoffmann was soon to settle in nearby Bamberg, where he would begin to create a gallery of literary maniacs who could easily people an entire ward of the new sanitorium.

The Psychische Heilanstalt für Geisteskranke in Bayreuth constitutes a landmark in the history of German psychiatry because its establishment represented the first official acknowledgment of the belief that the insane could be treated and cured, not merely stored away out of sight. As such, it marked the culmination of the shift from a long-standing Enlightenment policy of the administrative sequestration of unreason to a modern effort to emancipate the insane from older modes of mechanical coercion and to integrate them through the techniques of Prussian "therapeutic idealism" back into the society from which they had so long been "alienated."[1]

The debate leading up to this shift—a broad-based dialogue involving philosophers as well as physicians, public health officials as well as ministers of state—took place mainly in the years following the French Revolution. This development was not lost on contemporary writers, who promptly used their craft in an effort to educate their readers to the exciting new social concern. The frequent incidence of insanity in German literature of the age has often been noted.[2] But it has perhaps not been adequately stressed that the gradual shift in the literary use of madness—from motif to metaphor—reflects a change in the writers' attitude toward the psychiatry of the day: from a general acceptance of the prevalent theories and treatments to a position appreciably different from the ideas of emerging psychiatry—or, to put it another way, from the psychologization of literature to the literarization of psychology. The formal institutionalization of psychiatry through the establishment of the Psychische Heilanstalt at Bayreuth marks the symbolic point at which the administrative-professional and literary-philosophical interests began to diverge.

Since earliest times the Christian West had provided places of asylum for the mad, which over the centuries evolved into a system of reasonably humane and complementary institutions.[3] Initially it was the Church, consistent with its commitment to charity and "hospitality," that assumed principal responsibility for the insane. Certain places of pilgrimage achieved a particular renown for efficacy with the mentally disturbed. Since the fourteenth century the shrine of the Irish martyr St. Dymphna in the Flemish town of Geel has attracted the emotionally ill. Originally left in the care of local families who provided simple room and board for their wards, the patients are today treated in the modern asylum that has been established there. Michel Foucault has suggested that the celebrated Ships of Fools, which sailed the Rhine in the fourteenth century, might have originated as vessels bearing the insane to Geel and other pilgrimage sites.[4] In many regions local bishops established hospitals, frequently known as Hôtels-Dieu, where the mad could be cared for along with the sick, the poor, the elderly, the orphaned, and the afflicted of every kind. Simultaneously many monastic orders, in accord with their rules of charity, took in—along with the sick and the needy—the mentally deficient, who often benefited therapeutically from a daily regimen regulated according to the principles of obedience, poverty, and chastity. Certain orders specialized in the care of the insane: notably the Hermanos de la Caridad, who under various local appellations—Frères de la Charité, Fatebenefratelli, Barmherzige Brüder—were largely responsible after the Reformation for care of the insane in the Mediterranean countries as well as in Austria and Catholic Germany.

As towns and cities began to thrive during the later Middle Ages, the new concentrations of population produced the sick and the indigent in numbers too great to be accommodated by the existing ecclesiastical foundations. Accordingly municipal hospitals began to arise all over Europe in which the multitudes dependent on public welfare could be deposited. As citizens became less willing to tolerate the disturbances created by the more unruly insane, from the fifteenth century on certain characteristic forms arose that relocated many of them outside the city—either to towers constructed along the city walls (e.g., the Tour aux Fous in Caen) or into movable wooden cages (known in Germany as *Tollkasten* or *Dorenkisten*), which could be set up outside the city gates at strategic points along the highways where those incarcerated could beg from passersby or be displayed by their keepers for a fee. When the mysterious disappearance of leprosy in the decades following 1500 left many lazar houses standing empty, these often vast facilities were appropriated as places of incarceration for the insane and vagrants of every description.

Following the Reformation, it became necessary for state governments also to assume a certain responsibility for the needy, the sick, and the insane. In Protestant lands the dissolution of the monasteries removed one of the hitherto most important facilities. As their patients were thrown onto the mercy of the public, towns and cities increasingly restricted the use of municipal facilities to their own citizens. As a result, the entire rural population of many states, including roving bands of vagrants, was left with no provision for medical care. The four hospitals that Philip the Magnanimous of Hesse set up from 1533 to 1535 in abandoned monasteries provided the model for a new system of state institutions for the care of the infirm. Paradoxically, as a political response to this Protestant innovation, rulers in certain Catholic territories also established new regional hospitals—e.g., the famous Juliusspital founded by Bishop Julius Echter of Würzburg in 1579—that accepted as patients citizens from the entire bishopric, including Protestants as well as Jews.

This promising beginning in Germany, which through an overlapping system of ecclesiastical, municipal, and state institutions assured specialized and decentralized care for patients of every sort, was interrupted by the ravages of the Thirty Years War. When the Germans began to restore their disarrayed public institutions, it was not to their own traditional forms that they looked but at the new system of *hôpitaux généraux* that had spread across France following the creation of the great model in Paris in 1656. The Hôpital Général in Paris resulted not from any new medical theories but from an extensive administrative reorganization of existing facilities as well as the construction of several new ones in an effort to produce a single centralized system for the care of the sick, the orphaned, the poor, the elderly, the insane, the criminal, and the many other derelicts that the Age of Reason preferred to keep hidden away out of sight. This vast welfare complex in Paris had several places of sequestration for the insane: the "curable" insane were treated in the Hôtel-Dieu in the city, while "incurables" were shipped out to the suburbs—men to Bicêtre and women to the Salpêtrière, newly converted from a royal powder factory.

In imitation of the French *hôpitaux généraux* eighteenth-century German states began establishing those multi-purpose institutions with names that sound as though they had been coined in a nightmare by Jean Paul: in 1714 the *Waisen-, Toll-, Kranken, Zucht- und Arbeitshaus* (Orphanage, Madhouse, Hospital, Jail, and Workhouse) in Pforzheim; in 1716 the *Armen-, Waysen-, Zucht- und Tollhaus* in Waldheim; in 1749 the *Toll-, Zucht-, Waisen- und Findelhaus* in Mannheim; and in that same year the old *Zucht- und Arbeitshaus* in Ludwigsburg got a new *Doll-Haus* (*sic*), to which in short order a *Waisenhaus* was added. This characteristic homogenization of functions is confirmed in the standard encyclopedia of the period, where the brief entry under "Toll-Haus" refers the reader to the much longer rubric for "Zucht-Haus" ("Correctional Institution"), which lists potential candidates under thirteen categories: loafers, beggars, idle apprentices, furloughed soldiers, vagrant students, gypsies, disobedient children, gluttons, bankrupts, captured Turks, prisoners without bail, slanderers, and criminals for whom the state wished to spare the expense of execution.[5]

When differentiation of function did take place, it tended in North Germany to separate patients according to their potential to create a public nuisance: that is, it kept vagrants and the insane together in institutions known jointly as *Zucht- und Tollhaus*, like the ones in Celle (1710), Schwabach (1780), and Bayreuth (1788). In the Catholic South a different development occurred. In the great hospital reform that Joseph II undertook in Vienna in 1784, the small charitable foundations were amalgamated into one great Allgemeines Krankenhaus (after the model of the Hôpital Général), to which a special high-security facility for the insane—the so-called Fools' Tower (*Narrenturm*)—was attached in the rear. This pattern was adopted in other cities of the empire, including Prague, where in 1790 an insane asylum was built onto the existing general hospital.

At the end of the eighteenth century, then, Europe was familiar with a variety of institutions for the care of the insane, ranging from the complex *hôpitaux généraux* in France and Germany to the more highly specialized *Zucht- und Tollhäuser* in North Germany and the Fools' Towers attached to general hospitals in the German-speaking South. But the common denominator in every case was that "great confinement" of which Michel Foucault has written so eloquently. These were not primarily places where the insane were put in order to be treated for their own good but locales where they could be kept isolated together with other undesirables for the benefit of a fearful society. Indeed, the rejection of madness went so far that in 1737 the figure of the fool, or Hanswurst, was formally banned from the German stage in a famous ceremony of Caroline Neuber's theatrical troupe. The sequestration that strikes us today as surprisingly inhumane for the Age of Reason is due to at least three factors that prevailed until the end of the century: an almost total ignorance concerning the nature of mental illness; a profound dread of the insane, who represented in their being the precise opposite of reason; and the belief that madness is essentially incurable.[6] It was these attitudes that the first generation of writers in the 1790s sought to overcome through their works. Then at the end of the century a great sea change swept over Europe. In a shift that has been called "the greatest single step in the history of psychiatric treatment"[7] the madhouse for the sequestration of the insane was converted into an asylum for the treatment of the mentally ill.

In part the transformation was prompted by powerful social impulses that were dramatized by spectacular events. In France this impulse was primarily socio-political. When Philippe Pinel reputedly struck the chains from the inmates at Bicêtre and Salpêtrière, he was striking a blow for liberty in the spirit of the other educational and medical reforms associated with Pierre Cabanis and the Idéologues.[8] The fact that it was not Pinel at all but J. B. Pussin, the governor of the asylum, who carried out that humane act is immaterial.[9] What is symptomatic is the fact that the Age of Revolution would expect nothing less than such an act of liberation from its leading medical hero and therefore attributed that deed to his legend, which has been immortalized in several paintings as well as a statue still standing at the entrance to the Salpêtrière. In England a religious spirit colored the reforms. Just before the Revolution in France, England was shaken by the madness of George III, which, intermittent since 1765, finally became vivid and violent in 1788–1789.[10] Because of the political squabbles surrounding the Regency Act the episode grew into a cause célèbre. The world looked on in fascination as Francis Willis succeeded in treating the monarch with the techniques of so-called "moral management," which had been first described in 1758 in William Battie's *Treatise on Madness* but gone unheeded for thirty years. When the Quaker tea merchant William Tuke founded his Retreat outside York in 1792, this center for the humane care of the insane rapidly became renowned and provided a model for other such facilities. In Germany still another factor came into play.

The Prussian "therapeutic idealism" can best be understood if it is seen as one facet of the general liberalization of Prussian institutions that took place during the first decade of the nineteenth century, notably during the period between the defeat at Jena-Auerstedt and the War of Liberation.[11] In the few short years from 1806 to 1813 the brilliant ministerial team of Stein and Hardenberg achieved an impressive series of reforms that included the liberation of the peasants from serfdom, the civil emancipation of the Jews, the abolition of cabinet government together with a reorganization of the administrative system, the reintroduction of municipal self-government, the equalization of the tax burden, the secularization of church estates, the restructuring of the army under Scharnhorst, and the reform of the educational system under Wilhelm von Humboldt. Unlike the reforms taking place in France, these reforms were not driven by popular demand but, rather, imposed from above by a group of liberal aristocrats whose faith in the ideal of a welfare state had to overcome a general indifference among the bourgeoisie.

For a variety of reasons the momentum for reform of the institutions of confinement got under way earlier than most of the other reforms. In the German territories occupied by the French and subject to the principles of regional administration implicit in the Code Napoléon certain improvements in universal health care were already taking place in cities along the Rhine. Following the *Reichsdeputationshauptschluß* (Imperial Decrees) of 1803, the monastic centers in Cologne were dissolved and incorporated into a centralized Bürgerhospital, but the accommodations for the insane still followed older models: the wooden cages with straw-covered floors attached to the back of the hospital were purely for con-

finement, not treatment. At that time Stein, then president of the West-
phalian Chamber, was in charge of the reforms stemming from the secularization of church properties. His orders during that year often refer
to asylum reform.

That the first "Prussian" reform in mental care was realized in Bayreuth was the result of historical accident.[12] When Markgrave Alexander
of Ansbach-Bayreuth, childless and weary of administrative burdens, decided in 1791 to cede his tiny principality to his future heir, Friedrich
Wilhelm II of Prussia, Hardenberg was appointed governor of the new
Prussian province. As a result, he became familiar with local circumstances in the rather remote southern district (which in 1810 reverted to
the Bavarian crown). Ansbach and Bayreuth had not been brought together under the rule of a single markgrave until 1769. Up to that point
the two principalities had been independent and had maintained separate
facilities of every kind, including their own institutions for criminals and
the insane. Bayreuth's combined *Zucht- und Arbeitshaus* in the suburb of
St. Georgen was completed in 1735, and the one in Ansbach was opened
in the town of Schwabach in 1763. Following the unification of the two
principalities, the markgrave built separate "madhouses" (*Tollhäuser*) in
Schwabach and Bayreuth so that the mentally ill could be segregated
physically from the other prisoners. Although this was a remarkably progressive move in an age that tended generally to confine the insane along
with other vagrants, the madhouses were still essentially places of confinement in the traditional eighteenth-century sense. However, when
Hardenberg—inspired by the same early impulses to reform that were
stirring Stein in Westphalia—was looking around in 1803 for an opportunity to initiate reforms in the Prussian system of mental care, the province of Ansbach-Bayreuth lent itself ideally to that experiment: one of the
two "madhouses" could be maintained as a storage facility for the "incurably" mad, while the other could be transformed into a "Psychic
Cure-Institution for the Mentally Ill," an institution widely regarded as
the beginning of the modern treatment of the insane in German-speaking countries.

## VIEWS OF MADNESS IN THE LATE ENLIGHTENMENT

The administrative decision to reform an institution, whether motivated
by social, religious, or rational impulses, is simply the first step. The mad-

ness and treatment of George III, the highly publicized establishment of the Retreat outside York, the "liberation" of the insane in Paris—all these incidents called attention with dramatic vividness to the plight of the mentally ill. During the years around the Revolution there was greater public interest in madness than ever before. Indeed, the *Irrenhausbesuch* became de rigueur in travel accounts during the closing years of the century in Germany.[13] Doctors, theologians, pedagogues, society ladies, and young men on their *Bildungsreise* included a visit to the madhouse, or to the insane ward of the local hospital, among the obligatory sights in every city. Exemplary is the following passage describing Würzburg from the travel diary of Sophie Becker, who accompanied her friend Elise von der Recke on a trip through Germany in 1784–1786.

> After dinner we viewed the Residence, a large, truly princely edifice, which also has a small but select picture gallery. From there we inspected in passing the cathedral and finally the hospital, also a very lovely building, which affords rather the appearance of prosperity and delight than that of a habitation for those sick in body and soul. In addition to containing a number of the poor, the sick, and the mad, whose number I cannot estimate, it also has a school and an anatomy theater.[14]

The sequence—palace, gallery, cathedral, hospital, madhouse, school— locates the asylum clearly among those institutions that the well-bred person must know for the sake of general enlightened understanding. The famous Julius Hospital in Würzburg attracted many visitors, including Heinrich von Kleist, who described it at length in a letter of September 13, 1800, to his fiancée. Regardless of the particular circumstances— that is, the writer and the location—the description invariably ends with a comment on the value of the visit to the madhouse as a stage in one's knowledge of humankind. Kleist, to be sure, is struck by a typically Enlightenment horror at the state of unreason: "O rather a thousand deaths than a single life like this," he exclaims at the sight of an eighteen-year-old youth made insane by "an unnatural vice" (masturbation). "In this terrible manner nature avenges the outrage against her own will!"[15] But Carl Friedrich Pockel, in his account of a tour of the madhouse and prison at Celle (*Meine Beobachtungen im Zellischen Zucht- und Irrhause*, 1794), states as his purpose "to arouse the attention of readers regarding certain manifestations of the human soul."[16]

Once public interest and the administrative impulse to reform have assured that the building is there, in Paris or York or Bayreuth, many questions remain. Who goes into it? How is it organized? Who runs it? According to what principles are the patients to be treated? During the years from 1790 until 1820—that is, during the age of Romanticism—the theories followed one another in rapid succession. Is madness caused by humors or by such social factors as the Revolution? Should its classification be etiological or symptomatic? Is it essentially psychic or somatic? Should it be treated "morally" or medically? Who is the appropriate person to care for the insane: physician, layperson, theologian, professional governor, or mad-doctor?[17] There was agreement on virtually nothing except the necessity for reform.

The scientific passion of the seventeenth and eighteenth centuries had produced a wealth of data and observations concerning madness that cried out for synthesis and systematization. The prevailing chaos and disorder became a leitmotif inspiring many of the writings on the subject of madness during this period. Alexander Crichton speaks in the preface to his *Inquiry into the Nature and Origin of Mental Derangement* (1798) of the "loose facts, which abound in the writings of medical men, metaphysicians, and philosophers of different ages and of various countries."[18] In the introduction to his *Traité médico-philosophique sur l'aliénation mentale ou la manie* (1800) Philippe Pinel notes the "confusion et désordre" that characterize all earlier attempts to describe the phenomena of mental illness.[19] And Immanuel Kant, in his *Anthropologie in pragmatischer Hinsicht* (1798), worried that "it is difficult to bring any systematic order into that which is by its very nature incurable disorder" ("wesentliche und unheilbare Unordnung").[20] Yet the attempt must be made—in part, as Kant continues, because any thorough understanding of human nature demands at least a sketch of mankind in its state of utmost degradation. Moreover, madness was perceived to be increasing at an alarming rate. Crichton remarks that the mental disorders of which he intends to speak "are common in civilized nations and are daily becoming more frequent, and are universally lamented, as constituting the greatest calamity to which mankind is subject" (i, ii). Pinel is more specific: it is one of the central themes of his *Traité* that the tempest of the Revolution itself ("des plus grands orages de la révolution") had brought forth an outbreak of mania in all its forms (9).

• • •

The works just cited exemplify three of the methods that the late Enlightenment invoked in an attempt to classify the phenomena of madness to which public interest and administrative attention had newly been directed. Crichton's *Inquiry* combines the findings of continental research with an English tradition in physiology extending back through Thomas Arnold to William Cullen.[21] Cullen, who coined the term "neurosis" to designate diseases without a fever, had divided neuroses into four categories: comas (e.g., apoplectic strokes); *adynamiae* (e.g., enervating diseases); spasms (e.g., such convulsive attacks as hysteria); and *vesaniae* (e.g., conditions of intellectual impairment).[22] Crichton's lengthy *Inquiry* is devoted principally to the last category—that is, the order of *vesaniae* under the class of neuroses—which at the end of the study is set forth in a nosological table patterned after contemporary taxonomic categories (II, 342–45). Crichton remarks that in his table the genera and species alone are mentioned since "the varieties are extremely numerous, and, if they were to be defined, would swell the volume beyond all reasonable bounds" (II, 341). Even so, his three genera with their species fill several pages. *Delirium*, defined as "general derangement of the mental faculties, in which diseased perceptions are mistaken for realities," is broken down into *mania furibunda* (delirium with raving and fury), *mania mitis* (delirium with appearance of gaiety), and *melancholia* (delirium with dejection and despair). *Hallucinatio*, or Illusion, defined as "error of mind, in which ideal objects are mistaken for realities," has as its species: *hypochondriasis*, *daemonomania*, *vertigo*, and *somnambulismus*. *Amentia*, or "diminished power of the mental faculties," finally, manifests itself as *fatuitas* (imbecility), *memoria imminuta* (difficulty of recalling thoughts), *perceptio imminuta* (difficulty of forming distinct representations), *vis idearum associandi imminuta* (deficiency of arranging one's thoughts), *vis fingendi imminuta* (total want of genius), and *vis judicandi imminuta* (want of judgment and common sense).

The uncertainty of the age in the face of madness is indicated by the fact that Crichton's nosology, which concludes his book, is arranged according to symptoms. But the *Inquiry* itself is organized according to the causes of insanity, as Crichton understands them. In the preface he informs the reader that the order into which he has arranged the various "diseased affections of the human mind" is "founded on the analogy which the causes of mental derangement have with each other" (I, xiii). He discerns four classes: physical or corporeal causes, over-exertion of the mental faculties, disproportionate activity of some faculties, and the passions, or their influence. This order, in turn, determines the organization of the book itself.

Crichton (1763–1856), who in the course of his medical studies had traveled widely on the continent, became better acquainted with foreign research than most of his contemporaries in England. Indeed, he spent much of his career (1804 to 1819) abroad as personal physician to Czar Alexander, during which time he was significantly involved in Russian scientific affairs. At the time of writing, however, Crichton was established as physician at the Westminster Hospital in London, where he also lectured on chemistry, pharmacology, and general medicine. Those scientific interests no doubt constitute the source of his impulse to arrange the symptoms of madness into the then conventional taxonomic categories. When he wrote his *Inquiry*, he had not had a great deal of clinical experience with the insane. In his preface he frankly acknowledges that many of the cases cited as illustrations were extracted from the eight volumes of the German *Magazin für Erfahrungsseelenkunde*. "In this work I found what I had not yet met with in any other publications, a number of well-authenticated cases of insane aberration of mind, narrated in a full and satisfactory manner, without a view to any system whatever" (1, v). Crichton therefore made it his task to impose upon the cases, which had been sent in to the editor by different contributors without much comment, a set of categories based on the current taxonomy.

• • •

Pinel's *Traité*, by way of contrast, which is commonly regarded as the beginning of modern clinical psychiatry, stands at the other extreme. Pinel (1745–1826) came late to psychiatry.[23] The son of a provincial surgeon in Southern France, he arrived at medicine by way of theology and mathematics. As a young man in Paris he spent most of his time in scientific study, earning his living as a tutor and translator (e.g., of Cullen's work). It was not until his forties that Pinel became interested in mental illness as a result of witnessing the mania of a friend. After 1784 he worked for several years in a private pension for the "alienated," an experience that provided the basis for his first writings. In 1793 he was appointed physician in Bicêtre, and his real career began.

As an empiricist whose intellectual roots go back to Locke and Condillac, Pinel believed that the only source of knowledge is direct observation. As a mathematician he was committed to the statistical analysis of material, which he provided in tables scattered through his work. The general plan of his *Traité* announces that he intends to apply to the study of medicine the same "esprit d'observation," precise terminology, and methods of classification that have served science so effectively (1). All his attempts to apply to the patients at Bicêtre the classifications of earlier studies had produced nothing but an impression of confusion and chaos. The arbitrary and incomplete nosologies of Sauvages and Cullen, he continues, were meant more to impress the reader than to simplify his work. Pinel informs his audience that he chose, therefore, the method that constantly succeeded in all the other branches of science: "to regard each object successively with attention and with no other design than to assemble materials for the future" (2). Rather than relying on earlier studies, Pinel proceeded empirically and clinically: he began by undertaking a general survey of all the patients in the asylum, examined the condition of each in order to determine the nature of their disturbances, and kept a journal on all patients.

Since intermittent or periodical mania is the most common form of insanity and also the easiest to observe, his essay begins with a discussion of that form of the affliction, including various factors that can affect seizures—the seasons, the weather, bodily cycles, and so forth. Since the cases cited in the first section were often successfully cured by "moral" or psychological management, Pinel goes on in section two to discuss more extensively and systematically the "traitement moral des Aliénés," beginning with an attack on the chauvinism and sense of superiority that prompts the English to vaunt their skill in treating the insane. In fact, he argues, Willis's widely acclaimed successes have nowhere been expounded systematically according to any general principles; Arnold's compilations are better suited to retard than to accelerate the progress of science; and Crichton's two volumes amount to little more than observations cribbed from a German journal, a few ingenious elaborations of modern physiological theories, and a table of the moral and physical effects of the human passions.

Pinel then expounds a number of cases in which he successfully treated various types of insanity through appropriate physical and moral responses. Since "moral management" depends on the conviction that insanity is curable, Pinel devotes the third section to a refutation of the popular prejudice that insanity is the result of organic lesions of the brain, drawing upon his own extensive anatomical research. The long central section four, finally, constitutes a nosology of mental derangement based upon Pinel's own observation of symptoms. The five major categories that he distinguishes are: melancholia (delirium centered exclusively on a single object), mania without delirium, mania with delirium, dementia (the loss of the faculty of thought), and idiotism (the obliteration of all intellectual and affective faculties). The fifth section describes in detail the enlightened system of "police intérieure" required for the management of the asylum. (Like most revolutionary thinkers, Pinel took for granted that freedom must be carefully organized.) The *Traité* concludes with a discussion of the circumstances under which the moral treatment can be supplemented by medical means.

• • •

It would be difficult to find a sharper contrast to Crichton's encyclopedic systematization and Pinel's clinical pragmatism than Kant's reductive rationalism. Kant, as we noted earlier, regards madness as inherently chaotic and hence inaccessible to any true systematization. Indeed, his entire *Anthropologie* is based on the assumption, stated in his preface, that it is impossible for man, even under the best of circumstances, to come to any true understanding of himself through (self-)observation (401). Accordingly we will probably never understand the true nature of madness because it is too dangerous to undertake experiments with one's own mind in order to observe the effects. We hear the Enlightenment's full horror of madness in Kant's cry: "A feigned madness could easily become true madness" (532). Nevertheless, despite this horror, it is necessary for the man of reason to study madness even though it resists rational organization. In the first place, "anthropology"—which Kant defines as "a systematically ordered theory of the knowledge of mankind" ("eine Lehre von der Kenntnis des Menschen, systematisch abgefaßt," 399)— requires an appreciation of man in every human state, from the loftiest heights to the depths of degradation in madness. In the second place, since madness is wholly psychological and not physiological, medical doctors—*pace* Crichton and Pinel—lack competence. Accordingly all queries fall to the responsibility of philosophers—including the legal question of determining whether or not an individual can be held responsible for acts committed in a moment of alleged insanity.

Kant begins his *Anthropologie* with the assumption that man's distinguishing characteristic is the consciousness of self that enables him to broaden his experience through cognition of the phenomena surrounding him. Because this capacity for cognition (*Erkenntnisvermögen*) is the most important human characteristic, Kant is appalled by any diminution in or interference with that power. Accordingly the long penultimate chaper in the section on cognition culminates in a discussion of "Debilities and Illnesses of the Soul with Respect to Its Capacity for Cognition" (512–37).[24] Kant devotes several pages (§43) to the milder forms of debility, differentiating carefully between slow-wittedness (*obtusum caput*), stupidity (*stupiditas*), ignorance (*Unwissenheit*), and simplemindedness (*Einfältigkeit*). He talks further (§44) about debility of the mind through distraction, which can be either intentional (dissipation) or involuntary (absentmindedness). An otherwise healthy mind can sometimes display debility that might be called situational: e.g., the immature child, the subject vis-à-vis his ruler, the scholar lost in his work (§45). Finally Kant cites various colloquial designations for mental weakness in order to distinguish rigorously among them (§46).

Mental illnesses (*Geisteskrankheiten*) are divided into two classes: *hypochondria* and the disturbed mind (*mania*). The hypochondriac can be a simple *malade imaginaire* or someone subject to sudden changes of mood (*raptus*) or imagined misery (*melancholia*). All these forms, nevertheless, stop short of true mental illness (§47). With delirium (§48) Kant finally reaches what can properly be called madness or mental disturbance. Although it is difficult to organize that which is essentially disorder and although madness is basically incurable, he proceeds to divide madness into three categories: tumultuary, methodical, and systematic.

"Tumultuary" is Kant's term for feeblemindedness (*amentia*): that is, the incapacity to organize one's thoughts into any reasonable order. "Methodical" insanity incorporates *dementia* or *Wahnsinn*—that is, the subject respects all the formal laws of thought but fills that thought with imagined contents rather than real perceptions. Kant distinguishes between *Wahnsinn* (*dementia*) and *Wahnwitz* (*insania*), which he calls a disturbed capacity for judgment. That is to say, the mind is deceived by analogies between things that are superficially similar and, as a result, the imagination confuses logical association with the jumbling together of disparate things.

*Aberwitz* (*vesania*), finally, is Kant's name for the madness that he calls "systematic": that is, the sickness of a deranged reason. This type of madness transcends all claims of experience to seize upon principles that are beyond the test of reality and, in doing so, believes that it is comprehending the incomprehensible: the squaring of the circle, the *perpetuum mobile*, the mystery of the Trinity.

To sum up: madness represents for Kant a disturbance of human reason and the capacity for cognition. "The only general characteristic of madness is the loss of commonly shared perceptions (*sensus communis*) and the substitution of a logical idiosyncrasy (*sensus privatus*)" (§50). Since Kant regards madness as incurable, madmen belong in a Fools' Hospital

(*Narrenhospital*), a place where people . . . must be constrained to order by an external reason" (513).

. . .

It should be evident from these brief outlines that Crichton, Pinel, and Kant, though motivated by the same passion for order and classification, represent three wholly different attempts to categorize the phenomena of madness to which the late eighteenth century was devoting so much attention. Crichton begins with the presumed causes of mental derangement—the physical causes of delirium, the morbid degeneration of mental faculties, the effects of the passions—and then organizes his material, which includes illustrative cases adduced from his wide reading, into a nosological scheme patterned after the taxonomies current in natural science. Pinel speaks only generally about causes—e.g., heredity, predisposition, the turmoil of the revolutionary years—and concentrates on cases that he has observed at first hand in his own clinical experience in order to discuss the success or failure of his "moral" treatment. Kant, finally, rejects any discussion of causes (he believes that madness is hereditary through the mother) and does not concern himself with treatment (since he is convinced that madness is incurable). He concentrates instead on the organization of madness into categories dictated by the faculties of reason. In his contempt for clinical experience he anticipates the split between theory and practice, between academic and clinical psychiatry, and between the study of neuroses and psychoses that so fatefully characterized German psychiatry for much of the nineteenth century. In short, these representative eighteenth-century thinkers were responding to the phenomenon of mental illness with the tools of the age: encyclopedic knowledge and taxonomic sophistication, clinical precision informed by incisive observation, and "anthropological" interest in human nature coupled with the tools of rational analysis. The principal common denominator—beyond the general contentiousness that marks all these works—is the conviction that insanity is fundamentally a disturbance of human reason—that is to say, an "alienation" of man from himself and from society.

The works by Crichton, Pinel, and Kant exemplify the state of the study of madness in the last decade of the eighteenth century. On the one hand, the discipline was still in exceedingly early stages. In fact, it had as yet no proper name, since the term "psychiatry" was not coined until 1808 (by Reil). Altogether these early thinkers were severely hampered by a lack of precise terminology. Since the term "psychosis" had not yet been defined in its modern sense—it was first used by the poet-physician Ernst von Feuchtersleben in his *Lehrbuch der ärztlichen Seelenkunde* (Vienna, 1845)[25]—the first psychiatrists were unable to make the distinctions commonly accepted today between psychoses and neuroses. Indeed, they did not make the fundamental distinction between mental illness and mental deficiency, since, as we noted, they tended to list idiocy, imbecility, and feeblemindedness along with functional or organic forms of mental illness. Instead, they tried to make do with terms handed down from classical antiquity—mania, melancholia, dementia—with all the vague associations attached to those terms by folklore and the theory of the vapors. On the other hand, these same works demonstrate vividly that madness had emerged from the obscurity of the "great confinement" to become a phenomenon of considerable interest to thinkers in a wide variety of fields: scientists like Crichton, philosophers like Kant with their interest in "anthropology" and law, clinical practitioners like Pinel, religious leaders like William Tuke, and public administrators like Stein and Hardenberg.

## THE IMPACT OF MADNESS ON THE ARTS

It would be remarkable indeed if a phenomenon so far-reaching in its fascination had not also had an impact on the arts, and that is conspicuously the case.[26] William Hogarth created one of the best-known images of the madhouse in the engravings of his popular series *The Rake's Progress* (especially *The Rake in Bedlam*, 1732–1733). And the genre was extended in Daniel Chodowiecki's illustrations for Matthias Claudius's account of "Der Besuch in St. Hiob zu ..." (1783), Henry Fuseli's engraving *The Mad House* for the English edition of Lavater's *Essays on Physiognomy* (1792), Thomas Rowlandson's *The Hospital for Lunatics* (1789), Francisco Goya's *Yard of the Madhouse at Saragossa* (1794), down to Wilhelm von Kaulbach's painting of the sanitorium at Düsseldorf (1835). Théodore Géricault's obsession with individual cases of madness in his last and perhaps finest series of paintings of lunatics (1822–1823) is anticipated by the sixty busts of madmen created shortly before the French Revolution by the Austrian sculptor Franz Xaver Messerschmidt. It would have been odd if contemporary writers had not been provoked by the same interest that captivated their contemporaries.

Madness entered German literature with a sudden extravagance in

1795. This is not to say that earlier there had been no mentally unbalanced people in literary works. Two of the classics that figured most conspicuously in the Romantic library of world literature were *Hamlet* and *Don Quixote*. But during the eighteenth century such characters were a rarity in European literature—quite possibly as a consequence of the "great confinement" that made them socially invisible. In the popular Gothic romances, where they might most readily be expected, characters are from time to time plunged into melancholy or madness by (almost always) the loss of a beloved. The effect is virtually instantaneous: there is little interest in the etiology of the disease; and once the madman or madwoman is incapacitated by the affliction, he or she becomes uninteresting as a character and is promptly hustled off the scene.[27] Gretchen in Goethe's *Faust* both exemplifies this type and, to the extent that her madness dominates the end of the play, represents a notable exception. But *Faust*, while it was available in fragmentary form as early as 1790 (*Faust: Ein Fragment*), had not yet become the literary force with which we are today familiar. More representative by far was the attitude expressed in Friedrich von Blanckenburg's theory of the novel, which states that "all true exaggerations, all unnatural depictions of characters, even if they are not exaggerated in the direction of evil, are useful to the author of novels only as Wieland uses Don Sylvio or (to begin with his predecessor) as Cervantes used Don Quixote and others used such unnatural heroes—in order to make them ridiculous."[28]

During the 1790s the situation changed. Herman Meyer, in his study of the figure of the eccentric in literature, notes that both the term and concept of the *Sonderling*, at least in the modern sense of the word, emerged in the final decade of the eighteenth century. Meyer explains this emergence in large measure as a product of subjectivism. "The eccentric appeared wherever the conflict between subjective inwardness and objective reality came into consciousness as a central factor determining spiritual life."[29] But several other factors can probably be adduced as well. First, the general disenchantment with the rationalism that had dominated the century and, especially in Germany, had become progressively more shallow (as we have already observed in connection with natural law) gradually led to a new focus on man's inner life and the struggle of that inner man with the external reality that had obsessed rationalism. Second, the disenchantment with rationalism coincided with the emergence of idealism that, again especially in Germany, was challenging Kant and his followers to concern themselves with man's transcendental being and, in particular, with the relationship between nature and spirit. (This shift toward the psychic aspect distinguished psychology in Germany from the study of mental illness in France, which ever since Pinel had frowned on theory and favored the clinical, the empirical, the somatic.) Finally, this retreat into the inner world—triggered by the new subjectivism, hastened by the disenchantment with rationalism, and justified by the new idealism—paralleled the situation in the historical reality of the day, where Germany's effective departure from the international diplomatic arena from 1795 to 1805 favored a life that sought its meaning not in external affairs but in the inner life of man. Not coincidentally, historians of psychiatry have also pointed out a correlation between the emergence of that new field of study and the period of social and cultural inwardness produced by the factors just cited.[30]

To these commonplaces of intellectual history one more factor needs to be added: the natural rapport between literature and psychiatry. Indeed, one historian of psychiatry has noted the curious circumstance that so many of the early psychiatrists in Germany also wrote poetry.[31] We have already discussed the existence of a literary topos—the visit to the madhouse—that became pervasive in popular travel reports in the decades around 1800. The new literature of psychiatry that was replacing the older theoretical compilations displayed a powerful narrative strain. The case histories that dominate Pinel's *Traité*, for instance, amount in many instances to artfully narrated short stories of the variety that had emerged as one of the most popular genres of the later eighteenth century. Pinel often recounts extended tales, such as the one about the young man who comes to Paris for his studies and, determined to have a brilliant career at the bar, works so hard that he begins to suffer from violent migraines, frequent nosebleeds, and stomach spasms. Disregarding Pinel's medical advice, he deteriorates into extreme states of manic-depressive alienation. One day at the theater he sees the play *Philosophe sans le savoir* and takes it into his head that Pinel has betrayed his confidences to the author. Henceforth on every street he imagines that he is surrounded by disguised actors who study his moves and gestures. Sent by his parents for treatment at the Hôtel-Dieu and then for recuperation in the Pyrenees, he escapes from his keepers and dies of exposure in the woods, clutching in his hand a copy of Plato's dialogue on the immortality of the soul.[32]

Finally, the relaxed narrative genre that was establishing itself as the characteristic form of the Romantic age—the novel with its many characters, adventurous situations, and digressions—lent itself perfectly to the aims of the new psychiatry. That is, the novel provided an ideal opportunity not just to portray figures teetering on the edge of madness for the propagandistic purposes of education but, more importantly, to explore the sources and causes of madness, to chart its growth, and to plot its function within the total context of a fully developed character. The novelists, as we shall see, were interested in what we now know as functional mental illness—that is, insanity that has an identifiable and non-organic cause—and not in congenital mental deficiency that results in cretins, imbeciles, and otherwise feebleminded characters of limited literary interest. But these fictional melancholics, dominated by what Pinel knew as an *idée fixe* and Kant as a *sensus privatus*, are not simply described symptomatically: they become fictionally engrossing precisely to the extent that we see their melancholia come into being and grow. To that extent these fictions reflect the obsessive new interest of the age in madness and the pedagogic impulse of the first generation of writers.

## The Psychologization of Fiction

In 1795–1796 three popular, representative, and influential works were published in which madness suddenly became a phenomenon of considerable literary interest: Spiess's *Biographien der Wahnsinnigen*, Tieck's *William Lovell*, and Goethe's *Wilhelm Meisters Lehrjahre*. What is interesting about this configuration of dissimilar works is that, in their appeal, they cut across the entire spectrum of contemporary tastes and audiences—from late rationalism through Classicism to early Romanticism, from the readers who rented potboilers from the public libraries by way of the mandarins of Weimar culture to the severe young critics of the Romantic journals.

Christian Heinrich Spiess (1755–1799) belongs to a constellation of literary stars that, while virtually unknown today, dominated the popular market in the 1790s and provided a disproportionate number of the roughly 2,500 novels and story volumes that appeared during that decade.[33] In addition to Christian August Vulpius's "Romantic tale of our century," *Rinaldo Rinaldini der Räuberhauptmann* (1799–1800), and Karl Gottlob Cramer's historical novel *Adolph der Kühne* (1792), it was especially Karl "Marquis" Grosse's *Der Genius* (1791), whose complicated machinations involve a secret society deteriorating from idealism to gangsterism, that kept Ludwig Tieck awake all night, reading it to a group of friends.

Spiess, who was born near Freiberg in 1755 as the son of a clergyman and attended the gymnasium just at the time the Mining Academy was being established, studied literature at the University of Prague for a few years.[34] By 1774 his talent for acting had revealed itself, and as a member of the well-known Karl Wahr Ensemble he enjoyed considerable success from Vienna to Petersburg in a variety of roles ranging from young lovers to the tragic father of the brothers Moor in Schiller's *Die Räuber.* During these years he also discovered an aptitude for writing stage works of a rather derivative sort: comedies, a tragedy on the theme of Maria Stuart, and—his greatest success—a historical drama after the fashion of Goethe's *Götz von Berlichingen* with the title *Klara von Hoheneichen* (1792).

It was not until the last fifteen years of his life, most of which he spent as house guest of a nobleman at a castle outside Prague, that Spiess turned out the forty volumes with which he dominated the lending libraries. In 1785 he published a volume of twenty *Biographien der Selbstmörder*, a topic that had been fashionable ever since Goethe's Werther committed suicide in 1774. His greatest success was the ghost story *Das Petermännchen*—a tale of rape, incest, murder, and conjuration from the thirteenth century—with which he established the genre of the horror story (*Schauerroman*) in Germany. His *Biographien der Wahnsinnigen* (1795–1796) turned out to be one of his last works. Only three years later, in one of those cases in which life seems to imitate art, Spiess himself went mad and died. Like a character from one of his own stories, he had fallen in love with the wife of his benefactor (who in turn was deceiving Spiess with his own mistress). When the wife died (allegedly a suicide by poison), Spiess collapsed and passed away at the age of forty-five.

No doubt Spiess was drawn to cases of madness by the tendency to melancholia that he observed in himself, but that is not the main point. Regardless of his personal destiny, his work exemplifies almost typologically the view of madness, its causes and its care, at the end of the eighteenth century as the Enlightenment was about to give way to Romanticism. Spiess undertakes his work with an explicitly didactic intention: it is not so much documentary as propagandistic. "Madness is terrible," he tells us in the preface, "but it is even more terrible that one can so easily become a victim of madness. Overwrought, violent passion, deceived hope, forlorn prospects, often no more than an imagined peril can rob us of the most precious gift of the Creator, our reason ["unsern Verstand"]. And who among mortals can claim that he was not once in a similar situation and, hence, in equal danger?" Accordingly, Spiess continues, he is recounting the biographies of these unfortunates not simply to stir our sympathy but mainly in order to demonstrate "that each of them was the initiator of his misfortune and that it is therefore in our power to prevent similar misfortune" (7).[35]

The four volumes of the original *Biographien der Wahnsinnigen* contained eighteen biographies. Seventeen of these recount individual stories of varying length and complexity. For instance, the tale of "Marie L." is hardly more than an expanded anecdote: Marie is the daughter of a widowed peddler who remarries; the depraved stepmother, in order to cover up her own dalliances with the soldiers billeted in town, opens Marie's bedroom to a soldier, who seduces her. In an ironic inversion Marie is accused by the townspeople of corrupting her stepmother; she goes mad but lives on for years, mocked by the villagers but living in anticipation of the day when her seducer, whom she imagines to be a general, will come back to claim her hand.

Other tales amount to capsule novels. The tale of "Esther L." has all the complexity of a Gothic romance: a lovely, virtuous Jewish girl falls in love with the scion of a noble family, Friedrich, who returns her love. When the two are prevented by the trickery of his family from marrying, Esther takes the fortune she has inherited from her father, converts to Catholicism under the name Karoline, and enters a cloister. Friedrich eventually discovers her whereabouts and rescues her; she converts again, this time to Protestantism, and they get married and live happily until Friedrich is killed in a duel. Esther-Karoline, now pregnant, is recaptured by the nuns, who need her presence in order to profit from the money that she brought to the order. When her child is born and taken from her, she goes mad and consoles herself with various rag dolls. Eventually she escapes from the nunnery during a conflagration and spends the last years of her life being cared for by a princess who knew her and Friedrich at the time of their marriage.

The tale of "Wilhelm M...r and Karoline W...g" represents variation by doubling. Here again the two young people, very much in love, are separated forcibly—this time by the Seven Years War. Karoline's madness, which occurs following the death of her father, manifests itself in the fixed idea that she and her illegitimate child are already dead and in heaven. When Wilhelm finally returns, she is happy to see him but will not let him approach or touch her lest he drag her down from the bliss of heaven to the torments of earthly existence. Wilhelm eventually goes mad himself, and the two gentle lunatics are cared for by the villagers until they die, arm in arm, in a flood. Their daughter grows up and is happily married, but the story closes with the (Kantian) hint that symptoms of the parental melancholy are present in her physiognomy.

It is unnecessary to recapitulate all the plots, which are quite readable: Spiess was an experienced writer who knew how to exploit his material. It is also unnecessary to speculate on the extent to which the stories are fact or fiction. Some, no doubt, are based on actual cases that he heard about in the course of his travels; others have a clearly literary source. For instance, the story of "Jakob W...r," whose love for a servant girl is so ridiculed by his noble friends and relatives that he comes to believe that he has a glass chest through which his heart is visible to all, clearly belongs to the category of stories of which Cervantes's "The Glass Licentiate" (in his *Exemplary Tales*) is the most famous example. What matters for our purposes is the fact that madness in these tales is not peripheral but central: the same compelling fascination that led travelers to visit madhouses prompts them to be interested in the stories of these madmen and madwomen. In addition, the stories display a number of common denominators that reflect the beliefs of the day. First, the individual destinies are acted out against a background of social and political turmoil: the madness is often catalyzed by violent separation caused by forced recruitment or by the intrigues of families opposed to a union. (The theme of violent times is reiterated by Crichton, Pinel, and other contemporaries.) But the responsibility—indeed, the guilt!—always goes back to a case of individual passion.

It should be noted that the people who go mad are not the immoral pleasure-seekers, like the wicked stepmother who has her fun and remains sane. Instead the victims are almost inevitably decent people— usually from the prosperous bourgeoisie that constituted the largest reading audience of the day—who, in good faith, make one small lapse from virtue and then suffer the consequences ever after. These are the people to whom Spiess addresses his cautionary tales, expressing in his preface the hope that "my tales might prevent the credulous maiden, the incautious youth from the execution of a bold plan that could one day deprive them of their reason" (8). To be sure, the fall from virtue is often intensified by the death of a beloved parent, for which the fallen youth feels responsible, but basically madness is a moral delict, for which the individual must bear the guilt. Madness is not merely self-generated by guilt, however; it is also incurable (Kant again), and hence all the more dangerous. In the story of "Konrad G.," for instance, the hero has a sturdy character that remains constant despite two last-minute escapes from execution. His mind finally snaps when he returns to find that his beloved, having been falsely informed of his death, has married another. In the hospital for the insane he is helped by shock therapy: doused with buckets of cold water, he recovers his speech and returns to military duty with no further symptoms. But just as he is on the point of marrying a different young woman, he experiences a sudden relapse, produced by a visual shock, and sinks into incurable madness.

To generalize from Spiess's *Biographien*, then, madness is an incurable affliction that results primarily from illicit passion or despair—but also from heredity—and to which young men and women from good bourgeois homes seem to be particularly susceptible. It is important to take the necessary precautions against madness for another reason, finally, for when someone goes mad, it is basically the family or the community that must care for the patient. In almost all of these stories the patient is dependent upon the patience and generosity of the village, the family, a noble benefactor, or—in the case of Esther L.—the self-serving religious order. Patients can be kept at home only when they are relatively harmless; as soon as they become violent or create a public nuisance, they must be institutionalized. All in all, the book constitutes a precise literary counterpart to Kant's thinking on the subject of madness.

One episode differs from the other seventeen stories in two conspicuous respects: the whole story takes place in a madhouse, and it contains not one extended biography but the briefer accounts of some nine inmates. "Das Hospital der Wahnsinnigen zu P." recounts a tour of the madhouse that the narrator makes in the company of its doctor, a worthy man whose dedication has impressed the narrator during his stay in P. (271–314). Moved by the doctor's accounts of his patients, the narrator requests a tour. As they enter the walled court, they pass through a group of some twenty young men wandering around silently, gesticulating in pantomime, or tearing at the flowers and leaves on the trees. These patients, it turns out, are the curable ones—though by "curable" the doctor means specifically those whose somatic illness can be treated with medication. Almost by definition the curable insane seem to be of little narrative interest, for without pause or anecdote the two men leave them behind and approach the large round tower standing at the rear of the court, from whose small barred windows the rattle of chains is audible. In this prison, the narrator learns, "only innocent men pine who are mostly the hopeless prey of madness and must often be severely chained so that they will not do harm to their benefactors and keepers in an access of rage" (274). This vision produces the most extended and eloquent of the various hymns to reason with which Spiess, a true contemporary of Kant, from time to time interrupts his narrative.

> I never felt as keenly as now what a precious treasure reason is. Only reason separates the presumptuous, proud human being from the rapacious, fierce beast! Without reason man, to be rendered harmless, must be weighed down with chains, like this one, and shut up in a prison cell! Almighty, gracious Creator! Reason is the masterpiece of your omnipotence, a portion of your divine primal matter, and yet—lest I become the accuser of my fellow mortals—and yet we pay so little heed to your invaluable gift! ... O that my voice might equal the strength of my feeling! It would resound like the blast of the trumpets of the Last Judgment through the wide world and cry out to the inhabitants: Man! Heed the value of your reason! Without it you are like unto the lion, which one leads around on display in the narrow barred cage. Without it you are less grateful than a dog that licks the nurturing hand of its benefactor! (274–75)

When the two men enter the tower, they first encounter two patients walking around wordlessly in the hall. These young officers have been reduced to incurable madness by their love for the same woman. Since they are harmless and completely happy in each other's company, they are permitted to dress normally and move about unchained. In the cells that ring the circular gallery around the inside of the tower, however, the situation is different. Here are confined the incurable madmen who, dressed in long linen gowns, need to be chained by the leg to prevent them from harming themselves or others. Accompanied by the daughter of the keeper, who is able to calm the madmen, the doctor and his visitor make their way around the tower, and we hear the story of each inmate. Of the eight tales, half concern madness produced by frustrated or disappointed love: the last case involves a young man whose madness is realized in scenes that he describes in a peep show that he keeps in his room. In every case the episode hinges on the duplicity of scheming women. Another case involves a former treasury official who, believing himself responsible for the loss of 10,000 guilders, turns himself in and goes to prison. When it is discovered that the apparent shortage was due to a simple mistake in calculations, the man is released, but the sudden liberation is too much for his mind to bear; he goes mad and spends his days in the madhouse repeating to himself, with perplexity and frustration, "One plus one equals one?" and gaining momentary relief only when someone insists that the correct sum is two. One venerable man, a Maltese knight, had endured forty-five years of captivity under the Turks with equanimity; when he was released and returned to Germany, his mind snapped upon kissing his native soil again. Another man, a shoemaker, watched his wife and seven children become dangerously ill from plague and starvation. He goes begging to save them; they are all restored, but the strain of the incident causes him to go mad. Finally, one miserly old man loses his mind when he is forced to restore money that he had lent at exorbitant interest rates illegally to an underaged youth.

In all these cases the etiology is essentially the same as in the other seventeen stories: that is, madness is caused by violent passion and emotional shock (often love, but sometimes concern for country and family or avarice); and it is normally incurable. (It is noteworthy that the only curable cases mentioned are somatic—that is, they have physical causes and can be cured by medicament or physical therapy.) The difference here is related to the fact of incarceration. In the first place, we note that the narrator visits a madhouse that displays the segregation by sexes characteristic of the eighteenth century: this madhouse is for men only. In the second place, the fact that these patients are incarcerated means by definition that their cases are more radical, since cases of harmless or mild insanity are kept at home or in the village or the cloister. Appropriately, therefore, the image of animality routinely applied to madness in the Age of Reason shows up repeatedly in these pages. It is only our reason that separates us from animals—from the caged lion, the chained dog. If we lose our reason, then we, too, must be chained and caged like the beasts to whose state we have now descended. The madhouse itself, and by extension the tower along the wall within the madhouse, symbolize the removal of the patient from the society that can still accommodate him or her as long as the madness remains relatively calm and the insane person does not constitute a public nuisance.

Through his *Biographien der Wahnsinnigen*, which peaks (though it does not actually end) in the description of the madhouse at P., Spiess conducts his fascinated readers through the whole scale of symptoms— from the most ethereal fixation (Karoline W...g, who thinks she is in heaven with her child) to the most violent mania of the chain-rattling inmate who attacks his keepers with all the savagery of a beast. In every case, however, the moral to be drawn from these examples is: Beware! For the loss of reason is the most terrible fate that can befall a human being; but that loss in every case is provoked by the individual's own incautious heed of his or her own passions.

. . .

When we turn to Tieck's *Die Geschichte des Herrn William Lovell* (1795), the figure of the German poet Balder seems at first glance to fit perfectly into Spiess's *Biographien der Wahnsinnigen*. Once again we are dealing with a case of melancholy, triggered initially by the death of the beloved, that deteriorates through dementia with hallucinations by way of violent mania to ultimate death. But while Balder bears a superficial resemblance to Spiess's madmen, there are at least two striking differences in his portrayal. First, to the extent that Balder talks and writes extensively about himself, he no longer constitutes simply an object to be contemplated with detachment but, rather, a subject expressing his own history and decline into madness: madness is internalized, and we experience the process as well as observe the product. Second, he is not in the novel merely as an object of curiosity and sympathy but as a living exemplification of one of the possible outcomes of the Romantic *Zerrissenheit* that afflicts Lovell along with so many of the other characters. (To this extent Balder anticipates the Romantic attitude toward madness that we shall consider later.)

On one level the novel resembles the popular Gothic romances of the day, so greatly admired by Tieck, in which the hero becomes the tool of a mysterious secret society that uses him for its purposes.[36] William Lovell, a decent young Englishman with a pronounced inclination toward sentimentality and that almost hysterical enthusiasm that eighteenth-century Germans called *Schwärmerei*,[37] is first misled during his grand tour in Paris and Rome to debauchery that alienates him from friends and family, then ruined financially, and finally reduced to attempted arson and murder—all to gratify the lust for revenge of an old enemy of his family. In all of this we hear the echo not only of Grosse's *Der Genius* but also of Rétif de la Bretonne's *Le Paysan perverti* and Choderlos de Laclos's *Les Liaisons dangereuses*—the latter notably in the multi-perspectival depiction of events and the obsessive analysis of character that was the pride of eighteenth-century *Menschenkenntnis*.[38]

On another level, however, the approaching Romantic revolution constantly breaks through the eighteenth-century veneer. For Tieck is not satisfied that reality can be encompassed by reason alone; when all the rationalizing is done at the end of the novel, there remains a residue of mystery. Unlike the mature writers he was imitating, Tieck was incapable of organizing the world rationally in his own mind. What Kant would have called the "anthropology" of the novel is depressing. Tieck was not yet twenty years old when he began the work and barely twenty-three when it was published; and he was in any case philosophically the least sophisticated of the early Romantic writers. He and his characters see the world not as an orderly whole but—the recurrent images in the letters give it away—as a "chaos" or "labyrinth" or "prison."[39] It is a world, moreover, that represents a constant threat and danger. Death by falling from a cliff is a recurrent theme in Lovell's nightmares, and the image of Icarus is used twice to characterize him. For instance, when we first hear of him—in Wilmont's opening letter—he is said to be an excellent young man who needs to get his feet planted firmly on the ground. "But he thrives in no soil. No eagle is as much at home in the ether and all the heavenly breezes as he. Often he flies so far beyond my sight that I think of poor Icarus—in a word: he is a *Schwärmer*" (238).[40]

Now Tieck, at least in his twenties, tended to see the possible responses to this threatening, chaotic world rather simplistically in terms of polarities; certainly he was incapable of imagining a classical synthesis of personality. Accordingly the novel is not so much plotted as choreographed in such a manner as to make evident the various possibilities of human existence. The ruthless skepticism of the scheming Andrea, who tries to rise above the world and control it, is paralleled by the selfless affection and naive good-heartedness of Lovell's manservant, Willy. The two contending aspects of William's character that generate—to use another of the key words of the novel—his *Zerrissenheit* are embodied in his two closest friends during his continental adventures, the worldly Italian skeptic Rosa, and Balder, the poetic German with the inclination toward melancholy. However, the characters who survive at the end of the novel are neither the satanic manipulators nor the pious souls; Andrea and Willy are both dead, along with Balder and Lovell himself. The survivors are those who have consciously committed themselves to a life of renunciation. Mortimer writes that "only he can be happy who does not nurture excessive expectations from life and is modest in his demands and his goals" (658). Burton replies that "for me life becomes increasingly constricted; I have given up all travels and all my youthful plans and renounced all glittering happiness" (661). In his last letter Rosa invites Lovell to join him at his villa in Tivoli, where "we can enjoy life gently" (695). In the closing lines of the book Wilmont announces his intention of going off to America: "In the English army there must still be a place for a man who's had enough of life and who can at least hope to die for the good of his fatherland" (697).

The world, in short, is a chaos manageable only by those who are willing to give up all human ambition or those who so fully deny their humanity that they can use others as tools to achieve their ignoble ends. But those who persist in trying to fulfill their humanity either lose their way in the labyrinth of the world and end in madness or else fall to their death from the heights they have sought, Icarus-like, to scale. This analysis is absolutely consistent with the view of a young man whose relationship to reality was so severely disturbed that he suffered as a child, by his own account, from conditions of fear and horror and was tormented as a student by attacks of anxiety and premonitions of death.[41] The fear of madness that plagued Tieck during his youth shows up from his earliest writing down to "Der blonde Eckbert" (1797) and "Der Runenberg" (1802).[42] In one of his earliest publications—the final chapter of Rambach's novel *Die eiserne Maske* (1792), which Tieck was commissioned to write—the hero, Ryno, goes mad from guilt and self-recriminations and then, in anticipation of the nightmares in *William Lovell*, dies in a plunge from a seaside cliff.

In view of the general Enlightenment horror of madness and Tieck's personal phobia, it is hardly surprising that the motif of madness shows up frequently in the novel and that a fear of madness is widespread among the various characters—and not just in Lovell, who constantly feels himself to be teetering on the edge of insanity. In one of his letters (310–11) Wilmont relates an elaborate parable of a state in which the subjects (passions) are normally held in balance by their regent (reason); but from time to time, like a ruler unable to come to grips with affairs, reason abdicates and leaves the state to anarchy (madness). On another occasion Mortimer writes about the enthusiast who removes himself from everyday life: "In this way one could go mad in a rather reasonable manner, and no matter how excellent this condition may be in and of itself, from a distance it looks too frightful for me to wish to get any closer to it" (605). Similarly, two of Andrea's disenchanted followers agree that "the desire to act wholly as a free human being leads ultimately back to the worst prejudices or to madness. I prefer to believe in something in order to come to peace with myself" (605–6). Small wonder that the case of Balder turns out to be so endlessly fascinating for the other characters in the novel.

The figure of Balder is so unique that no analogous character can be found in the Gothic thrillers that Tieck's work otherwise so closely resembles.[43] But the melancholic poet would have been right at home in Spiess's *Biographien*.[44] We first hear of Balder when Lovell's traveling companion, Mortimer, writes from Paris that he and William have just become acquainted with "a young, boisterous, peculiar German to whom William has wholly surrendered: his name is Balder and he has also been in Paris for only a short time" (266). Mortimer stresses especially the close analogy between the two young *Schwärmer*. "Two harmonizing tones could not blend together as easily as these two souls: both are enthusiasts, both are poetically inclined, each encounters the other with equal affection." But Mortimer is concerned lest a friendship between two such similar natures consume itself, for where there is no critical perception of strengths and weaknesses, there can be no veneration and love.

The very next letter gives a slightly different view. William begins by confirming his affection for Balder, "a youth whose soul corresponds to virtually all the demands that my extravagant sensibility makes of a friend: he is gentle and feeling, his heart is easily warmed by beauty and sublimity, almost everywhere our kindred spirits meet at a mid-point" (267). At the same time, he continues, there are the nuances of difference necessary to true and permanent friendship. "I do not share his profound inclination to gloomy *Schwärmerei*, this childlike quality with which he nestles up to every character he loves; I am colder and more withdrawn, my fantasy is more at home in sweet, lovely dreams while he is more intimately acquainted with the underworld and its terrors." From the very start, therefore, we are made aware both of Balder's symbolic function as a mirror of Lovell but also of the tendency toward melancholia that will eventually ruin him. By the time they reach Florence, William is concerned about Balder, who is "more reserved and mournful" than ever—so much so that William occasionally is startled by his distracted gaze. At this point William has still not learned the cause of Balder's melancholy, but in the belief that melancholy is "a contagious affliction" ("ein ansteckendes Übel," 323), William begins to think that his own moodiness is perhaps a disease with which Balder has infected him.

After we have heard about Balder from a variety of external witnesses, we finally encounter him in his own words—in his response to a letter in which William has confessed his infidelity to his fiancée. Balder begins with a contemptuous image of the world as a puppet show in which the figures believe that they are moved by lofty emotions, but a quick look behind the scenes exposes the simple machinery that motivates everything. William, he continues, has desecrated the lofty word "love" by confusing it with simple sensuality (290–91). We begin to understand Balder's anger when he goes on to speak of the "few golden hours" of his life when he was privileged to experience true love. But his beloved died, and ever since he has been "sitting at the graveside of my joys. . . . My misery is my consolation." Already at this point we begin to understand the etiology of Balder's melancholy, which began according to the classic Enlightenment theory with the shock following the loss of the beloved.

By the time the friends reach Rome, William is distressed about Balder. "Balder often withdraws from us entirely, he likes to dream away the hours all by himself, my concern is growing with each passing day, for he often is not at all himself anymore" (333). Their longest conversation takes place in the course of a walk during which Balder ignores all the beauties of nature, for all creation reminds him of death. "You are forgetting that we are walking over the corpses of millions of the most varied creatures—that the splendor of nature takes its material from decay—that it is nothing but disguised decomposition" (333). They manage to agree that one's view of reality—whether cheerful or sad—is a matter of perception. But when Lovell objects that Balder's view could lead him into madness, Balder replies with cool equanimity: "Perhaps. But it is still an open question whether I would win or lose by going mad" (334). When William cites human reason as "the divine symbol of mankind," Balder scoffs.

"Reason! O William, what do we call reason? —Many people have gone mad because they worshiped their reason and committed themselves tirelessly to its investigations. Our reason, which comes from heaven, can only walk upon the earth; no one has yet succeeded in discovering any firm truth about eternity, God, or the destiny of the world. We wander around in a great prison, we whine for freedom and scream for the light of day, our hand knocks at a hundred bronze gates, but all are closed and a hollow echo answers us." (334)

And when people are occasionally brought face to face with the divine and are confounded by it, we call their higher wisdom madness and their rapture a frenzy (337). In an effort to distract himself, Balder makes a trip to Naples, but he develops a fever; his companion, Rosa, begins to irritate him; and he finds himself insufferable. He is most at ease, he says, among the phantoms of his own imagination; but wherever he sees happy people, his soul is pierced. "I seem to myself like a masked ghost that moves unknown and gloomy, quiet and taciturn, among people; they have become for me a foreign race" (347).

As Balder's alienation increases, William realizes that his affliction is not simply physical and urges him to dispel the excesses of his imagination and return to the company of human beings. But Balder's fever grows worse from day to day. Reading *Hamlet* in Naples, he finds all his beliefs confirmed. "How sober, impoverished, and unproductive life is; how madness and reason are intermeshed and destroy each other" (349). Then he reports to William how his fantasies materialized one night at midnight when the apparition of a man with white hair passed through his room. A few days later, announcing that Rosa is returning to Rome, he implores Lovell to join him in Naples. "My brain is desolate, a hot aridity burns in my head, everything rushes away, I can't keep hold of a single thought: everything races past me, no sound penetrates into my soul" (357). Balder wonders what will happen to him when people begin to call him mad. "I feel that in many instants I am so close to that state that if I should take only a single small step forward I would no longer be able to return" (358). His terrible dreams deprive him of all energy. Even awake he envisages hordes of monsters that rush past and grin at him. "A blind rage could seize me when I hear the miserable jabbering of the doctors about fever heat and paroxysms. The fools! Because their senses are blinded and dumb, they regard as mad anyone who sees more than they" (357).

The letter concludes with Balder's farewell as he announces his intention to follow the beckoning hand of a tutelary spirit. Before his disappearance, Balder writes one more letter to report how he attended a gathering of friends who had invited him out of sympathy. Disgusted by their condescension, Balder is moved by his enthusiasm to address prophetic words to the assembly, which he calls simply "the masses of flesh" ("Fleischmassen," 385), in which he warns them of the death and decay that will soon mock their vanity. Small wonder that his physician is concerned for his health and prescribes cooling medicaments, all the while shaking his head over his ideas and regarding him as mad "because I am not stupid and phlegmatic" (386). Balder is no longer even afraid of the visions—e.g., of all his ancestors sitting in cloaks at his table—that plague him at night. This time Balder does disappear, and no one knows whether he has run away or killed himself. As Rosa reports, toward the end he had reached the highest stages of rage, cursing strangers and even stabbing at them with knives.

Following this gradual decline from disappointed love by way of melancholia, social alienation, and delirium into raging mania Balder disappears from the novel and appears only twice more. Many months later Lovell unexpectedly receives a letter from him, now living in a lonely forest hut in a mountain range whose name he does not know (it turns out to be the Apennines), where the occasional visitors regard him as a prophet and where his soul has become much calmer. Living in the wilderness with the creatures of nature and a deaf-and-dumb friend, Balder has found a tranquillity that he had not previously known. "In solitude the soul thinks and feels differently; it is not interrupted by the disorderly twittering and rumbling. In open nature everything is related to the soul and tuned to the same note" (500).

His final appearance is described in the letter in which Lovell reports his death. On a trip to Genoa Lovell catches sight of a face behind a barred window that looks like Balder. Making inquiries, Lovell ascertains that it is indeed his old friend, whose story he now concludes. Tiring of his solitude, Balder decided to return to Germany. Arriving in Genoa, he met a young woman and fell in love—for the first time since the loss of his beloved Henriette, which had originally plunged him into melancholy. He had his fortune sent from Germany and married the woman, also from a wealthy family, and enjoyed the first true happiness in years. Then his second wife was taken from him by death. Up to this point Balder had behaved like a completely normal person. But as he tells Lovell that he is not even permitted to visit her grave, he becomes increasingly agitated. When Lovell idly picks up a large red cloak covering some chairs in a corner of the room, he discovers to his astonishment a stake with strong chains. When a few links of the chain fall with a clatter, Balder rages around the room, screaming and tearing at his face. "The rage soon stifled his voice. His face was now blue and swollen, all the limbs of his body moved with an incredible rapidity, in his ghastly movements there was something both vulgar and comical that increased my horror" (652). When suddenly Balder attacks Lovell with maniacal strength and with a horrible laugh, several guards rush into the room with whips and clubs and drag Balder to the corner, where they chain him to the block. When his rage bursts out again, he hurls himself back and forth "like a wild beast," straining against the chains with a glowing visage. Even when the keepers flog him mercilessly, he seems to have no sensations. Unable to bear the sight any longer, Lovell leaves the room, weeping. Two days later, Lovell reports, Balder died in a mad rage in the house where relatives of his dead wife had paid for his care. "Doesn't this unfortunate creature seem to have inherited his madness from his very birth? First he went slowly through all the stages of madness until he was driven by a new love more quickly and rapidly to the last extreme" (653).

We subsequently learn that the evil Andrea, who had also noticed "a lovely disposition toward craziness in him, which it would have been a shame not to nurture" (689), had arranged for the apparition in his rooms that Balder regarded as the materialization of his ghostly visions. But that detail, required by the conventions of the Gothic romance for the rationalization of all apparent mysteries, is psychologically irrelevant. Lovell's analysis makes it quite clear that Tieck had a very precise understanding of the stages of madness as perceived in the late eighteenth century. A hereditary tendency toward madness is initially catalyzed by the loss of a loved one; Balder moves through the stages of melancholy to mania with delusions, from which he gradually recovers with the help of a new love. When he is deprived a second time of the support of love, he is plunged irrevocably into a severe mania with rage, from whose excesses he finally dies. On one level Balder's story represents a close parallel to the tale of "Konrad G." in Spiess's *Biographien der Wahnsinnigen*, who also recovers from a disastrous love experience, only to suffer an irremediable relapse through a second disappointment and shock. Although we do not know with any precision where Tieck got his information, the textual evidence makes it abundantly clear that he was familiar with the etiology and symptomology of madness as understood in the late eighteenth century and that he made brilliant use of the relevant details—though not necessarily the technical vocabulary—to create a case of melancholia that was fully consistent with its description in the writings of Crichton, Pinel, and Kant.

· · ·

While only one figure in *Wilhelm Meisters Lehrjahre* (1795–1796) achieves the same level of explicit insanity as Balder and the various cases in *Biographien der Wahnsinnigen*, Goethe manages to represent in the course of his novel a much broader and more subtly varied spectrum of mental derangement than either Tieck or Spiess. Indeed, we encounter almost every type of mental illness known to the later eighteenth century, from hypochondria and sporadic hysteria by way of melancholia to mania and dementia. The term "insanity" ("Wahnsinn") first occurs in the discussions of *Hamlet*, as Wilhelm and the members of Serlo's troupe prepare for their performance of Shakespeare's play (bk. IV, chs. 13-16). In their conversation Aurelie points out that the beginnings of Ophelia's spiritual collapse can be detected in the moment "when she sees herself abandoned, rejected, and disdained, when in the soul of her insane lover the highest is transformed into the lowest and instead of the sweet beaker of love he hands her the bitter chalice of sorrows" (247).[45] A short time later, in justification of the songs that the author gives Ophelia to sing, Wilhelm points out that the truth of her love emerges "in the innocence of madness" (255) when she sings her songs of love before the king and queen. The introduction of the theme of madness in this context is of course no accident but a precise analogy to the case of Aurelie herself. She identifies so closely with the role of Ophelia—just as she does later with the role of Orsina in Lessing's *Emilia Galotti*—because she, too, abandoned by her lover, spends her entire life fighting against madness, much like the forsaken lovers in Spiess's *Biographien*. "To protect myself against madness I again surrender to the feeling that I love him," Aurelie confesses at one point to Wilhelm (279). But her case is hopeless: weakened by the struggle against madness and by the abandon with which she exposes her feelings in her roles on the stage, she wastes away until, consumed by a fever, she dies.

Aurelie is merely the first in a series of constantly escalating cases of mental derangement that the novel exhibits. A classic case of melancholia is evident in the count, who is so shocked by the apparition of what he takes to be his double—it is actually Wilhelm disguised in his dressing gown and cap—that he undergoes a radical personality change from boisterous insensitivity to religious fervor and goes to live a life of piety among the Moravian Brethren. His wife is even more profoundly afflicted by hypochondria. In a passionate embrace Wilhelm had pressed into her breast the bejeweled portrait of her husband that she was wearing. At the time she simply cried out at the sudden pain. But gradually, tormented by guilt at her husband's melancholia, she comes to believe despite all assurances of her doctor that the moment of passion has left behind a growth in her breast. "And when one tries to dispel this illusion through touch, she claims that only at this moment is there nothing to be felt; she has it fixed firmly in her mind that this illness will result in a cancer, and so her youth, her loveliness, is totally lost for herself and others" (349).

The case of Mignon is more complicated. While she actually dies as a result of one of her frequent heart convulsions, the attacks are produced by sudden emotional shocks. Her peculiar mental condition is characterized by visions (e.g., of the Virgin Mary) and by impeded thought processes that cause difficulties in speaking (587). It is strongly implied that her "sonderbare Natur" (586) is the result of heredity, since she is the product of an incestuous union. Although her mother never appears in the novel as a figure, we hear her story in detail (bk. VIII, ch. 9). The late fruit of a happy marriage, she was sent away by her father to be raised in anonymity lest jokes be made about the passions of elderly parents. When she returns to the region around Lago Maggiore as a lovely young girl, her three older brothers meet her without knowing her identity, and the youngest, though destined for the priesthood, falls in love with her. Before the relationship can be clarified, they conceive a child. The brother is informed of the circumstances and locked up in the monastery. (We will return to his story later.) The young mother is not told the truth in order to protect her against the full horror of incest, but her confessor, wishing to persuade her of the weight of her guilt, tells her that her unknown lover was a priest—an equally serious sin against nature. "The poor mother felt a sad relationship to the child; the treatment of the confessor had so confused her mind that, without being insane, she found herself in the strangest conditions" (587). In this state of mind, she is told that her child has been drowned. Succumbing to a local legend that the lake always coughs up its victims, she spends her days collecting bones along the shore in the hope of reconstituting her child. Through the influence of the confessor she comes to be regarded in the region as an ecstatic rather than a madwoman ("eine Entzückte, nicht ... eine Verrückte," 589). Her physician attempts to heal her fixed idea by mixing the bones of children with the animal bones that she has accumulated. One morning, when her attendant has removed the bones from their box in order to show the doctor what progress the patient is making, she awakens unexpectedly to find the box empty and is convinced that her child has come back to life. In ecstasy she begins to think only of the beyond, and soon wastes away to death, viewed in the entire neighborhood as a saint.

While these cases of melancholia, hypochondria, and mania with delusion fall into the category of insanity according to the nosologies of the eighteenth century, several of the allegedly "normal" figures in the novel display characteristics that attest to Goethe's acute observation and sense of mental health. For instance, when after several years Wilhelm sees his old friend Werner—now his brother-in-law and the manager of the family fortune—it is apparent that Werner's success in business has been achieved at a considerable psychic cost. He has lost weight; his features have become sharp and sallow, and his voice shrill and agitated; he has lost most of his hair, and his chest is collapsed between curved shoulders. All this "left no room for doubt that an industrious hypochondriac was present" (499). Over and over again Goethe indicates how overt virtues have been purchased at the expense of emotional or psychological balance. The attentive reader can easily conclude that Therese—the insufferable little prig in her obsessively tidy little doll's house—needs nothing so much as a good psychoanalyst. It becomes apparent, when she tells Wilhelm her story (bk. vii, ch. 6), that she has been driven into her compulsive orderliness and occasional protective transvestitism by what amounts to contempt for her flagrantly flirtatious and unfaithful mother, coupled with a semi-incestuous love for her father. When she finally relaxes enough to fall in love, it is with a man (Lothario) who comes so close to being a father figure that he has even been one of her mother's various lovers!

In the sixth book, finally, Goethe demonstrates with sublime irony that the "Confessions of a Beautiful Soul" can also be read as a case study of extreme religious hysteria stemming from childhood sexual repression.[46] Repeatedly we are told that any normal relationship with boys and young men was precluded by an abnormal fear that males could destroy not only her virtue but even her health. She grows up "morally and physically isolated" (365), even afraid of glasses and cups that have been handled by men, as well as the chairs in which men have been sitting. When she finally falls in love with a young man named Narcissus, they disagree about the boundaries of virtue and modesty (373). No wonder, as her morbid obsession with purity increases, that their affair breaks up! Her progressive alienation from the everyday world eventually reaches the point at which she lives only in her own overheated imagination (398). While her friends and relatives come to regard her profound religiosity with a cautious respect, there are adequate indications that her case is in no way considered exemplary. Her favorite niece, Natalie, recognizes her disturbance. "A very fragile state of health, perhaps too much preoccupation with herself, and in addition a moral and religious anxiety never permitted her to be for the world what under other circumstances she might have become" (517). Her uncle arranged to keep the children away from her in the conviction that she was a dangerous influence on them (419). In short, the "Confessions" represent within the novel itself what the writings of Count Zinzendorf represent within the "Confessions"—not a model to be emulated but "a psychological phenomenon" (397) valuable for *Menschenkenntnis*.

The most extreme case of mental derangement can be seen in the dementia of the harpist, the partner in the incestuous love affair that produced Mignon. As the novel is organized, we do not learn his full story until the very end, long after his first attacks of madness and his treatment. If we start at the beginning, however, we recall that the harpist was the youngest of three brothers in a wealthy North Italian family. Destined originally for military service, he displayed such "a manner of enthusiastic calm" (580) that he was permitted to exchange places with his older brother and enter the monastery, where, as Brother Augustin, he yielded wholly to "the enjoyment of a sacred enthusiasm, those half-spiritual and half-physical sensations that raised him for a time into the third heaven and soon thereafter plunged him into an abyss of unconsciousness and into empty misery" (581).

From the beginning, therefore, it is clear that we are dealing with an unstable personality with extreme tendencies toward manic depression. After the death of their father, he implores his two older brothers to release him from his churchly vows, for during his visits at home he has caught sight of Sperata and fallen in love with her. At this point the story of Sperata's birth is revealed in order to prevent their union, but Augustin, in his emotional state, refuses to believe it; he announces that Sperata is already his wife and carrying his child. Devoting himself to his love with the same fervor that had characterized his earlier religiosity, Augustin stubbornly insists on the rights of nature above the artificial constraints of social custom. "His unbound free reason exculpated him; his feeling, his religion, all the customary notions declared him to be a criminal" (585). Augustin's mind snaps under these terrible pressures, and he escapes with the intention of fleeing with Sperata. But their priestly adviser has alerted the local boatsmen, who return Augustin to his monastery instead of taking him to Sperata. During the following years, while Mignon is born and grows up, Augustin dwells happily in the monastery. "After many terrible and strange epochs ... he had achieved a remarkable state combining peace of mind and disquiet of body" (590). Constantly on the move, he rested only when he played his harp and sang. All his former passions had resolved themselves into a single *idée fixe*: a fear of death, in which he was tormented by the vision of a lovely boy who sat at the foot of his bed and threatened him with an unsheathed knife. This situation persists for years until the death of Sperata, when the rumor of her sainthood penetrates the walls of Augustin's monastery. With uncanny shrewdness he orchestrates his escape and visits the chapel where the body of his beloved Sperata is on display. Then he disappears for good, never again to be seen by his brothers.

It is this same Augustin, burdened with all the symptoms of dementia as it was known to the late eighteenth century, who shows up among the troupe of actors, where he is taken in by Wilhelm and bound to Mignon by a strange bond of affection. (Mignon and the harpist never realize that they are daughter and father.) For a long time the signs of madness are not evident. Indeed, despite the sense of guilt that plagues him, the harpist is entrusted with a number of practical responsibilities. When Wilhelm is wounded during an attack by robbers, it is the harpist who rushes off in search of medical assistance. Later it is he whom Wilhelm sends out on scouting missions in search of his unknown rescuer (Natalie). It is not until the end of Wilhelm's acting career that Augustin's madness suddenly erupts: when fire breaks out in the actors' lodgings, the old man, agitated by fear and excitement, mistakes Wilhelm's son Felix for the child in his vision who threatens him with a knife; throwing Felix to the ground, he prepares to sacrifice him with a knife until Wilhelm, alerted by Mignon, is able to rescue his son. When Wilhelm searches for the old man after the fire, fearful of finding his remains in the charred ruins, he suddenly hears the familiar voice intoning a song that "contained the consolation of an unfortunate man who feels himself quite close to madness" (334). (It is the famous *Lied* "An die Türen will ich schleichen.")

Uncertain how to deal with the old man, "who displayed such clear signs of madness" (335), Wilhelm turns him over to a country clergyman who has achieved renown for his success in treating the mentally deranged. Since it is against the principles of the clergyman and the physician who advises him to ask direct questions of their patients, they only gradually come to understand the reasons for his insanity—from his songs and from occasional chance remarks. They soon learn, for instance, of his greatest delusion ("Wahn"): that he is everywhere the bearer of misfortune and that his death will be brought about by an innocent boy.

However, they still have hopes of curing their patient despite the severity of the affliction. "I have never seen a mind in such a peculiar state," the physician reports. "For many years he has not taken part in, nor even paid the least attention to, anything that was external to him. Turned wholly within himself, he contemplated his hollow, empty self, which appeared to him as an immeasurable abyss" (436). However, the cure by means of a "moral management" patterned after Tuke seems to succeed. Within a few months the physician presents the harpist to Wilhelm and the company at Natalie's residence: clean-shaven, in normal traveling clothes, he addresses the group with reason and dignity. But the physician must concede that the cure did not come about through normal treatment. "The recovery of this man succeeded through the strangest accident. For a long period of time we have treated him morally and physically according to our convictions: matters were going quite well up to a point; but the fear of death was still great, and he refused to give up his beard and his long gown" (596). Then the harpist came into possession of a vial of opium, which he carried on his person at all times as a talisman. The thought that he could end his sufferings at any moment through poison, paradoxically, set him on the road to recovery. However, consistent with the eighteenth-century belief that dementia is incurable, the harpist soon suffers a relapse. Having chanced upon the manuscript containing the story of his life, he falls back into his dementia and decides to escape his misery by use of his poison. Leaving the room for a moment, he returns to discover that Felix has seemingly drunk the opium. Alerting the household to the danger to the child, he rushes off to the attic and cuts his throat. Even though he is discovered and bandaged before he dies from loss of blood, he refuses to believe the assurances that Felix has not perished. During the night the harpist rips the bandages from his wound and bleeds to death.

Several important features of these various "biographies of the insane" need to be noted. First, in a novel that has such a highly episodic structure they can claim a certain degree of autonomy. Indeed, most of the stories are told in the form of intercalated novellas. The story of Augustin, Sperata, and Mignon is communicated in the form of a manuscript written down and then read to the group by the abbé on the basis of a verbal report from the marchese (one of the three brothers). The "Confessions of a Beautiful Soul" constitute a first-person autobiographical account passed along to Wilhelm and Aurelie by the physician, who also brings Wilhelm up to date on the fate of the count and countess. Aurelie tells

Wilhelm the story of her own life, as does Therese—the story of a German maiden beneath a German tree, she says. On the one hand, then, it is appropriate to analyze the various tales independently just as one reads the separate *Biographien der Wahnsinnigen*.

On the other hand, these episodes are also bound in various ways to the main plot of the novel: the "Confessions" familiarize us with the family relations of the various figures we are to meet in the last two books of the novel, while the tale of Augustin, Sperata, and Mignon acquaints us retrospectively with the circumstances of two figures we have already gotten to know quite well. But the "Confessions" have another function that is at least as important as their plot function. From the very beginning critics have commented on the demonic, irrational nature of that curious pair, Mignon and the harpist, stressing in particular the function of their dark destiny as a countervalence to the rationalism of the Society of the Tower or the idealized humanism of Natalie. From their Italian background they bring an element of primal energy into the controlled world of Enlightenment Germany. In particular, the obsessive dementia of the harpist stands in radical contrast to the order that the other figures of the novel strive to achieve through their various means and plans.[47] But it is an oversimplification, as we have seen, to detect the irrational element only in the two outsiders, Mignon and the harpist. Through the spectrum of mental derangement that Goethe presents to us he suggests emphatically that only a thin line separates the treasured reason of the Enlightenment from the perils of insanity. The balance can be tipped by excessive piety as well as by total exposure of one's persona on the stage, by the trials and disappointments of love as well as an irrational fear of death. Even the seemingly most rational people in the novel—Werner with his business acumen and Therese with her fussily ordered life—are exposed as motivated respectively by hypochondria and sexual repression. In Goethe's novel, in short, mental derangement plays a far more significant role than in Tieck's. There the figure of Balder represented symbolically one facet of the dual tendencies of Lovell's character, teetering between a rationalism verging on skepticism and an enthusiasm tending toward insanity. Here, in contrast, madness represents an entire dimension of human life—the world of the chthonic, the irrational, the unpredictable—that is denied unsuccessfully by sterile rationalism and that by its very existence refutes the absolute claims of reason.

The entire theme of madness, which has emerged as such an important aspect of *Wilhelm Meisters Lehrjahre*, is entirely absent from the first version of the novel *Wilhelm Meisters Theatralische Sendung*, which Goethe wrote during the years 1777 to 1786. Several of the figures discussed above—notably Therese and the Beautiful Soul—are missing altogether in the earlier version. The count and countess are present, but the episodes leading to their melancholia are not related, nor does Aurelie succumb to the mania that precipitates her death. Mignon with her convulsions figures in the earlier version, but there is as yet no explanation for her peculiar condition.[48]

Most importantly, while the harpist belongs to the original conception of the novel, in that uncompleted first draft there is scarcely a hint of the demonic quality and madness that epitomize his character in the *Lehrjahre*.[49] When he first appears to entertain the troupe of actors, all are struck by his remarkable appearance, with his gray hair, trailing beard, and long gown.[50] The entire company, and especially Wilhelm, is immediately enchanted by the songs that he sings. Later that night, too restless to sleep, Wilhelm seeks out the harpist in his miserable inn, where he hears him singing the inexpressibly sad lines of "Wer nie sein Brod mit Thränen aß." The long conversation that follows, we are told, was like a religious convocation in which the harpist—like the liturgist at a Moravian meeting—illustrated his meaning with examples drawn from the texts of various songs. Although Wilhelm is moved to a new sense of the nobility of man and the loftiness of his own destiny, the scene remains on such a level of abstractness that we gain no insight into the background or personality of the harpist, and his brief appearances during the remainder of the story add nothing to our understanding.

The conspicuous addition of the entire psychological dimension to the novel between 1786 and the revision in 1794–1796 reflects both the new public concern with insanity that we have already noted and Goethe's own development.[51] His interest in medicine goes back to his student years in Strassburg in 1770–1771, when, as we know from the autobiographical account in *Dichtung und Wahrheit*, many of his friends as well as most of the companions at his pension were medical students. However, Goethe's serious interest in medicine—stimulated by his newly discovered fascination with science generally and his own medical episodes—dates from the 1780s. During the years when he was revising *Wilhelm Meisters Lehrjahre* he was frequently in Jena and in the company of physicians—Justus Christian Loder, August Karl Batsch, Christoph Wilhelm Hufeland—whose lectures he often attended. And among the students whose progress he monitored with a paternal eye was Johann

Gottfried Langermann, the future director of the asylum at Bayreuth. Nor was his interest purely passive. On June 4, 1795, for instance, the medical student David Veit wrote to Rahel Levin that Goethe had been in Jena again for a visit. "Every time he comes to our hospital and inquires about every detail. He has completely mastered the theoretical aspects of medicine."⁵² (It is symptomatic that at this stage in his life and in the history of psychiatry Goethe could indulge himself, as a scientist and a writer, in such a profound interest in abnormal mental states. Less than twenty years later the public interest in madness and his own fears vis-à-vis insanity caused him to reject impatiently the Romantic fascination with madness.)

This growing interest in medicine is reflected, among other things, in the fact that so many doctors appear in the *Lehrjahre*. On the one hand, there are the many *Wundärzte*, who prefigure Wilhelm's decision, in the *Wanderjahre*, to become a surgeon: the old *Wundarzt* with Natalie, who treats Wilhelm after his skirmish with the marauders; the latter's son who, as a *Wundarzt*, cares for Lothario following his duel and also for Mignon during her last illness; and the *Wundarzt* in the "Confessions," who treats Narziß after his fight with a jealous husband. (In general, the "Confessions" amount to a storehouse of medical lore: the Beautiful Soul's parents suffer from cancer and incapacitating migraine headaches; she refers to God as "the great physician" [393]; and one of the main figures is the wise old *medicus* who plays such an important role toward the end of the novel.) The novel, however, makes the customary eighteenth-century distinction between *Wundärzte*, who were just beginning to emerge to a position of respectability from their earlier lowly state as barbers or druggists, and internists (*medicus, Arzt*). It is the latter who sometimes take an interest in the psychic state of their patients. In the account of Sperata's life it is her physician who suggests that an attempt be made to cure her psychologically by including bones of children among the bones she collects; in the "Confessions" we hear that the old physician "had instructed himself very well regarding the state of my body and my mind; he showed me how very much these sensations, if we nourish them within ourselves independent of external objects, hollow us out and undermine the basis of our existence" (415). It is this same physician who explains to Wilhelm that the harpist was being treated "according to our conviction both morally and physically" (596).

In short, Goethe's novel represents not only the new post-Enlightenment acknowledgment of irrational powers that can undermine our

minds and bodies but also the contemporary approaches to their treatment. The tentative state of mental-health care is evident in the variety
of possibilities described in the novel. In Italy, where the ecclesiastical
care of the insane prevailed longer than elsewhere in Europe, Augustin
is maintained by his order in the security of the monastery. He is supervised by both medical and spiritual authorities, who follow the then modern practice of prohibiting visitors from the outside world, lest they disturb the patient's equanimity: Augustin's brothers are permitted to
observe him from a distance or to listen through the windows of his
room, but not to talk to him. Sperata, whose behavior is diagnosed as
being "confused without being insane" (387)—what Kant would no
doubt call *Aberwitz* or *vesania*—is permitted to remain at home, as befits
the daughter of a wealthy family, under the supervison of an elderly attendant and under the spiritual guidance of her confessor and the medical attention of a physician.

In North Germany, in contrast, Augustin is turned over by Wilhelm
to a clergyman who specializes in the treatment of mental patients and
particularly "the most violent attacks of melancholy" (335). His method
of treatment, as Wilhelm learns in the course of a visit, is essentially the
work therapy that came into fashion toward the end of the eighteenth
century.[53] While the clergyman consults a physician for the purely physical symptoms, his means of treating insanity is straightforward. "One
must stimulate their activity, accustom them to order, give them the idea
that they have their being and their destiny in common with many others" (346)—in other words, reintegrate them into the society from which
they have become "alienated." The spiritual counselor has divided the
harpist's hours in such a way that he gives instruction on the harp to
children and works in the garden. As progress is made, the psychologist
hopes to persuade the patient to give up his beard and long gown, "for
nothing brings us closer to madness than when we distinguish ourselves
from others, and nothing preserves common sense as much as living in
the broadest sense of the word with many people" (347). Wilhelm spends
several days with this eighteenth-century psychiatrist, from whom he
hears accounts not only of deranged persons ("verrückten Menschen")
but also of people who are generally regarded as clever and even wise but
"whose idiosyncrasies border closely on insanity" (347). It is in this company, from the clergyman's doctor-friend, that Wilhelm hears the sad
tale of the melancholy count and countess. And it is no accident that
Wilhelm receives from this physician the manuscript of the "Confessions

of a Beautiful Soul"—an exemplary case of a highly regarded person whose idiosyncrasies, as we have seen, do indeed border on madness.

The earliest readers of *Wilhelm Meisters Lehrjahre* recognized the presence of the irrational and demonic in the novel, especially in the figures of Mignon and the harpist. While Schiller and Körner found vaguely unsettling the "unfathomable" element in their characters,[54] the Romantic critics had no ambivalence about the mysterious duo or generally about the madness in the work. In his great review in the *Athenaeum* (1798) Friedrich Schlegel singled out that aspect as characteristically Romantic, noting that many figures in the novel interest our intellect but remain marionettes or allegorical playthings for the spirit. "Not so Mignon, Sperata, and Augustino, the Holy Family of Nature Poesie, who provide a romantic charm and music for the whole and then perish in the excess of their own glowing souls."[55] A few pages earlier, in his discussion of the fifth book, Schlegel had noted "the not infrequent advances toward madness, which might appear to be a favorite motif and tone of this part." Here, he continues, the novel "is already preparing itself to burrow into the most extreme depths of the inner man." Jean Paul was equally attracted by the mystery associated with the mad couple. He even wishes that Goethe had not felt compelled by the conventions of the genre to dispel the mystery at the end by explaining the genealogies. What is truly miraculous about the novel, he claims in his *Vorschule der Ästhetik* (§5), is not to be found in its fictional tricks but "in Mignon's and the harpist's splendid spiritual abyss, which fortunately is so deep that the ladders of family trees that are subsequently lowered turn out to be much too short."[56]

## THE FICTIONALIZATION OF PSYCHIATRY

If the works by Spiess, Tieck, and Goethe reflect the attitudes on the nature and treatment of mental illness that were prevalent during the last decade of the eighteenth century, then another cluster of works around 1803 exhibits the characteristics of the new "Romantic" psychiatry that was beginning to take shape. This is not to say that Jean Paul's *Titan* (1800–1803) and the anonymous *Nachtwachen* (1804) attributed to "Bonaventura" were directly influenced by Reil's *Rhapsodieen* (1803), the most important document of Romantic psychiatry. Yet they share an undeniable intellectual kinship that distinguishes them from the earlier works with their more rationalist view of madness as an incurable state of alienation from the human condition and human society that can be treated most effectively by "moral management."

Reil's exemplary study of mental illness distinguishes itself by its very title from the scholarly *Inquiries* and *Traités* of the late Enlightenment: *Rhapsodieen über die Anwendung der psychischen Curmethode auf Geisteszerrüttungen* (Halle, 1803). In the course of a brilliant career Johann Christian Reil (1759–1813) achieved distinction in a variety of fields ranging from internal medicine and pharmacology to ophthalmology and brain surgery.[57] (The central lobe of the cerebrum, which he identified, is still known as the Island of Reil.) As a professor at the University of Halle from 1787 to 1810, he was closely associated with Fichte, Schleiermacher, Wilhelm von Humboldt, Henrik Steffens, Goethe, F. A. Wolf, and others—including Johann Heinrich Ferdinand Autenrieth, the physician who attended Hölderlin during the years of his madness in Tübingen. As one of the most famous physicians in Germany, Reil was called in 1810 to assume one of the chairs of medicine at the newly founded University of Berlin. But the career of this profoundly patriotic Prussian— he was reputedly the only man in Germany whose hatred of the French exceeded that of his friend and colleague Fichte—was brought to a premature end: he died in 1813 as a result of typhus that he contracted when he took over the direction of the Prussian military hospital following the battle of Leipzig.

Like Pinel and other contemporaries, Reil came to the field of psychiatry, which was just taking shape around the turn of the century, from another area of medicine. But his *Rhapsodieen* emerged smoothly and consistently from his earlier works. He established his reputation with an essay *Von der Lebenskraft* (1795), in which he argued that life is a continuum extending from matter to mind and characterized essentially by the quality of the "life force" or energy that animates it. From this arch-Romantic theory, which amounts to the physiological counterpart of *Naturphilosophie*, it was an easy progression to Reil's major study of fever (*Über die Erkenntnis und Kur der Fieber*, 1799–1805), which he understood as the deviation of the "life force" of an organ from its normal healthy condition. When the organ affected is the nervous system, nervous ailments are produced, which lead in turn to mental derangements—the topic to which Reil devoted the fourth volume of his *Fieber*. At this point he was still concerned with the theoretical question concerning the psychosomatic relationship between mind and body, between physical experience and mental reaction. In 1799 he came to the typically Romantic conclusion that "the real and the ideal sides of man are manifestations of a single being and organism that develops in two directions and thereby establishes the close dependence of the one side on the other. In this case there would have to be a higher theory of nature to which physiology and psychology are subordinated inasmuch as the former deals with the objective side and the latter with the subjective side of that single fundamental basis [*Urgrund*] of nature."[58] The *Rhapsodieen* add little that is new to the theoretical discussion. They constitute Reil's attempt to carry his diagnosis of psychic disturbance to its logical conclusion: a "psychic method of cure," in which the practices of Pinel and the English "moral management" would be adapted to German circumstances.

When Reil wrote his *Rhapsodieen*, he had had virtually no clinical or practical experience with madness. He was acquainted, and dissatisfied, with most of the important books on the subject, including specifically the three that we discussed earlier. Although he borrowed most of his specific examples from Pinel, as his footnotes indicate, and shared the Frenchman's narrative gift, he expressed little appreciation for the *Traité* as a whole. "Herr Pinel enjoyed the rich harvest for this subject at the time of the Revolution, when according to his own confession the fools in France became more frequent than at any other time. His work on madness is a *coq à l'ane*, sumptuous in individual parts but sickly in context, without principles and originality although he has enough national conceit to arrogate all these qualities to himself. That we shall in the long run receive a systematic theory of the psychic method of cure, I believe; but I don't believe that it will come from the Republic."[59] As this remark suggests, Reil's Romantic temperament, with its predisposition to philosophical speculation, was dissatisfied with the clinical and experimental approach that characterized the theory-hostile French psychiatry after Pinel. He felt the need for a synthetic approach that would combine practice with theoretical principles consistent with the prevalent *Naturphilosophie*. To this end he established two short-lived journals: in 1805–1806 the *Magazin für die psychische Heilmethode* (with A. B. Kayßler) and from 1808 to 1812 the *Beyträge zur Beförderung einer Curmethode auf psychischem Wege* (with J. C. Hoffbauer). It was in the pages of the latter journal (1 [1808]: 169) that he coined the term "Psychiaterie" in an effort to express his conviction that the study of mental illness should not be simply a branch of medicine ("psychische Medizin") or theology or penal practice but a discipline with its own trained practitioners.[60]

In 1803, however, Reil was still concerned primarily with publicizing the plight of the insane in the madhouses of the day, which in Germany had not reached the level of care attained in the finest instances in England and France. To this end he sought to make a case for understanding insanity as a disturbance of the whole individual, and argued the necessity for a new "psychical" method of treatment. His work was initially undertaken in support of the prison reforms of Pastor Wagnitz and, accordingly, should be seen directly in the context of the Prussian reform movement. With his first sentences Reil announces a point of view that differs radically from the prevailing Enlightenment attitude, which distinguished sharply between reason and madness. "It is a remarkable sensation when one suddenly steps out of the turmoil of a great city and enters its madhouse. One finds here the city all over again, represented in the manner of vaudeville, and somewhere in the Fools' system a comfortable genus of its own. The madhouse has its usurpers, tyrants, slaves, blasphemers, and defenseless sufferers, fools who laugh without reason. . . . But those fools in Bicêtre and Bedlam are more open and less harmful than the ones from the great Fools' House" (7–8).

The madhouse—in a metaphor wholly antithetical to the Enlightenment view—is a microcosm of the worldly macrocosm. But it is not merely a distorted mirror image of reality: it is also a product of our society and an inevitable outcome of mankind's increasing alienation from nature. Pinel had suggested that madness of heredity or disposition was often catalyzed by the events of the Revolution. For Reil, as for most other Romantic thinkers, madness is an inevitable product of man's increasing alienation from nature. "We approach madness ever more closely step by step as we advance in the course of our sensual and intellectual culture" (12). Indeed, the equation of madness with civilization was carried by some early thinkers on mental disease to the extreme that they pointed with pride to the number of neurotics as a measure of a country's high level of sophistication.[61]

Through the rhetorical strategy of his introduction Reil establishes a pronouncedly Romantic attitude toward insanity. The madman is no longer an Other, different in kind from the sane, to be hidden away in places of confinement or to be regarded with the rational horror of a Kant, the religious fervor of a Crichton, or the medical solicitude of a Pinel. Rather, the mentally deranged person differs from us only in the degree of his alienation; the mirror of the madhouse may be distorted, but it is no less a mirror of a mankind that comprises all extremes of personality.

The attitude announced in Reil's introduction is consistent with the explanations of the main text. Insanity is not the product of a physical lesion or a hereditary evil but a disturbance in the harmony of interaction between three essential functions of the mind: *Selbstbewußtsein, Besonnenheit*, and *Aufmerksamkeit*, which Reil designates as "this triumvirate of closely related powers of the soul" (53). Self-awareness (*Selbstbewußtsein*) is that power which, by binding the separate parts into a unified consciousness, makes man into an individual human being (54). Presence of mind (*Besonnenheit*) is the power that guarantees continuity in that self-awareness and, at the same time, enables the soul (mind) to ascertain a difference between itself and external reality (98–99). Attentiveness (*Aufmerksamkeit*) is the capacity of the mind to fasten on any object that has been raised by presence of mind into consciousness. These three capacities, which assure human individuality, are rooted in the nervous system (and hence the continuity of the *Rhapsodieen* from Reil's earlier works on the life force and fevers). In cases of mental derangement the nervous system is afflicted at its very core: "it suffers from such a dynamic distemper [*Intemperatur*, or imbalance of temperature] that the normal balance of the three capacities is suspended" (33).

Reil devotes his lengthy chapter 20 to a discussion of the four basic categories of madness that occur when such an imbalance takes place (298–439). It is clear that these categories, despite his contempt for the French, owe a considerable debt to Pinel. The first category—"fixed partial insanity, melancholy"—is virtually identical with Pinel's "mélancholie ou désire exclusif." Here the patient is obsessed with various real or imagined circumstances—past mistakes, starvation, transformations of the body, superstitious beliefs, religious objects, love, surfeit with life, fear of death, self-sacrifice, and others—all of which have the effect of plunging him or her into a state of depression. Reil's second category enlarges what Pinel calls mania with and without delirium to embrace any state of furor or rage. *Narrheit* approaches that "abolition of thought" that Pinel terms dementia. And the last category, *Blödsinn*, is the "abnormal asthenia of reason" that Pinel calls idiotism or obliteration of the intellectual faculties.

When the harmony of the mind has been unbalanced, normal methods of treatment are no longer adequate: medicaments and surgery can treat the effect of madness but not its causes. Any direct cure, Reil concludes, can take place only by means of a "psychic method of cure" through which the "alienated powers of the mind" ("die alienirten Kräfte," 49)— by which Reil means alienated from nature and not, in the Enlightenment sense, from reason—are aroused by appropriate stimuli so that the "distemper" can be given a different direction. "Feelings and ideas, in short, arousals of the soul, are the appropriate means through which the distemper of the vitality of the brain must be rectified" (50). Psychic cures, in turn, are either negative or positive—that is, they can deprive the patient of disturbing stimuli, or they can provide new stimuli of three sorts. The first category contains an astonishing variety of physical stimuli, ranging from food, drink, and sexual stimulation to nausea, cold baths, and torture. The second contains a variety of objects that are used systematically to stimulate the various senses. The third consists of signs and symbols used to provoke the imagination and the thoughts. Reil argues that, from the moment of his initial reception in the asylum, it is essential to prepare the patient to be docile and totally responsive to the psychic cure. "Through violent and painful impressions we compel the patient's attention, accustom him to absolute obedience, and imprint on his heart indelibly the sense of necessity" (223). Accordingly the patient must be removed from friends, relatives, and all familiar surroundings and brought into the unfamiliar setting of the asylum, where he is greeted by beating drums, booming cannons, rattling chains, and frightful Moors. "An entrance with such ominous premonitions can destroy on the spot any thought of intractability" (225).

The book ends with an impassioned plea for asylums that will be true places of care and cure for the insane.

> How little do our insane asylums meet these needs! They are madhouses, not just because of their inhabitants but especially because of the contradiction in which, as means, they stand to the ends that are supposed to be achieved through them. They are neither institutions of healing nor asylums for the incurably insane to whom humanity can pay tribute, but dens in which society deposits whatever it finds troublesome. (454)

Such humane asylums as Reil envisages would not be simply appendages to the poorhouses and prisons but pleasant refuges—perhaps in the form of an extended farm—lying in a tranquil rural setting. He devotes several sections to a discussion of the order of discipline necessary in his asylums, including the external administration (governor) and the internal administration of doctors and psychologists. If such asylums are properly maintained, they can serve as training places for doctors who wish to specialize in the treatment of the insane—an extension of Reil's earlier argument that, in addition to the surgical and medical branches, contemporary medical faculties need to develop a third category: "the doctoral degree in psychic cure" (27).

Reil offers no comprehensive new theory of insanity. But in his Romantic recognition that mental illness is psychic rather than somatic in nature he provided the first systematic discussion of modern psychotherapy and moved the field beyond the eighteenth-century stage at which madness was regarded as the product of a lesion and hence incurable. His volume had the fortune to appear at a crucial moment: just when the liberalization and reform of Prussian institutions was about to get under way in the hands of Hardenberg and Stein and, simultaneously, at the moment when Romantic thinkers and writers were looking for an interpretation of madness that would be consistent with their attempt to overcome the eighteenth-century dualism of mind and matter, nature and spirit, madness and sanity. Reil's *Rhapsodieen* therefore had a profound impact on both cultural and institutional developments in Germany.

. . .

In view of Jean Paul's admiration for the psychically complex figures of Goethe's novel, it is not surprising that several of the main characters of his masterpiece, *Titan*, which was influenced not only by *Wilhelm Meisters Lehrjahre* but also by Tieck's *William Lovell*, display varying degrees of mental illness—even though the psychology of the work, which had a long genesis, combines older rationalist principles with the newer Romantic views. *Titan* (1800–1803), which was written over a period of ten years from 1792 to 1802, boasts even by the standards of Jean Paul's other novels a notoriously complicated plot.[62] In fact most of the mystifications—involving dynastic disputes, concealed parentage, mysterious prophecies, and a variety of other paraphernalia common to the Gothic romances of the period—occur in the opening chapters of the unusually long novel and are rationalistically resolved in the last fifty pages. The main action, which takes place from the spring of 1791 to the autumn of 1792, amounts to a fairly straightforward *Bildungsroman* in the course of which the twenty-year-old Albano, the secret heir to the throne of the principality of Hohenfliess, undergoes a series of experiences that shatter the illusions of youth and lead him to a level of manly maturity at which, all the mysteries of birth and heredity having been cleared up, he is able to assume the responsibilities of his rulership. To put it another way, the process of Albano's *Bildung* involves exposing the dangers of the spiritual excesses that Jean Paul had observed among the early Romantics—first from afar and then directly during two years in Berlin while he was completing his novel—and leading Albano to the kind of mature balance that he admired in Herder during his stay in Weimar, if not in Goethe and Schiller. It is characteristic of the period that the excesses of Romanticism—the false titanism that is ambivalently implicit in the title, along with the positive allusion to the sun deity Titan—bear in three of the four principal cases the unmistakable mark of insanity.

Most of the novel is taken up by one of the most idyllically serene love stories in German literature: the love of Albano and Liane, which lasts for little more than one summer. Liane and her brother, Roquairol, are the children of Minister von Froulay, a ruthless and calculating official at the court of Hohenfliess. Although Albano first meets Liane in the spring of his twentieth year, he has known of the handsome brother and sister for many years, having heard tales about their accomplishments while he was growing up in a village near the capital. When he first meets her, therefore, he is prepared to be smitten, and it turns out to be love at first sight. The following chapters, which recount that first love, belong to the most tender that Jean Paul ever wrote. But the affair is doomed because Liane's scheming parents, unaware of Albano's true identity, have higher aspirations for their daughter. They prohibit the romance and enlist the assistance of the court chaplain, who, swearing Liane to silence, informs her of Albano's true rank, which in turn precludes their marriage. When she returns Albano's letters and refuses his hand, he cannot understand her decision and becomes enraged. Shocked by his behavior, Liane becomes ill and soon dies. At her deathbed Albano learns that she has been true to him in her love and, smitten by regret, must be brought to his senses by a ruse. (His friends persuade Idoine, princess of the neighboring principality of Haarhaar, who bears a remarkable resemblance to Liane, to visit the stricken Albano as an apparition of his beloved and announce that he is forgiven—a technique recommended by Reil for dealing with cases of *idée fixe*.)

This episode, which fills roughly two-thirds of the novel, is more than a simple love tragedy after the fashion of the social dramas of the Sturm und Drang, complicated by the machinations of the Gothic romance. In the person of Liane, Albano encounters what Jean Paul regards as one of the most dangerous aspects of Romanticism: a debilitating *Schwärmerei* that leads through sickness to death. When Albano first lays eyes on Liane, she is afflicted temporarily by one of the seizures of hysterical blindness to which she is subject. Shortly before, just after the death of the old prince, she was paying her respects to the body when her brother, Roquairol, made one of his characteristically brutal remarks concerning the removal of the ruler's heart. "This tyrannical reminder of the autopsy had a terrible effect on the sick Liane, and she had to turn her eyes away from the covered breast because the pain of a sudden lung seizure cut off her breath" (156).[63] In due course Liane recovers from her seizure, but during the entire period of their brief romance Albano is keenly aware of the fragility of her delicate nature. It is her *idée fixe* that she is going to die within a year. Wracked by migraine headaches, from time to time she hears her body resound with music—a phenomenon that Jean Paul documents in a footnote as occurring frequently in cases of migraine and other "illnesses of debility" (342). She suffers from hallucinations and irrational phobias: ever since her first attack of hysterical blindness, for instance, she has been afraid of clouds (348 and 373). Given her physical and psychic frailty, it is no wonder that she is shocked into a second incident of blindness by the emotional stress of having to reject Albano without giving him any reason. As she wastes away toward death, she slips into a state of delirium punctuated by visions of eternity.

If Liane symbolizes what Jean Paul regards as the sickliness of life at court,[64] as well as the dangers of the Romantic death wish (as he had witnessed it in the case of Novalis), her condition—a spiritual inclination to death based on physiological debility with its anxiety states, phobias, hysterical attacks of temporary blindness, and delirium—is clearly recognizable as a psychoneurosis of the type familiar to Pinel and Reil. Although Jean Paul describes her symptoms with clinical accuracy, he does not hint at their cause, apart from the general frailty of her health and psyche. Some suggestion of hereditary illness is evident in the fact that her brother, Roquairol, is also mentally unbalanced to a degree that can be called psychopathic. Years before Albano meets Roquairol, he hears of a symptomatic incident in which the then thirteen-year-old boy, smitten by love for a striking young girl, attempted in imitation of Goethe's Werther to shoot himself in her presence.

Roquairol, one of Jean Paul's most famous fictional creations, has been thoroughly analyzed by both the author and his scholars. In the figure of Roquairol, Jean Paul was depicting the perils of an untrammeled aestheticism of the sort that he saw implicit not just in the lives of the Romantics—Clemens Brentano recognized himself in the portrayal of Roquairol—but also in the aesthetic theory of Weimar Classicism.[65] Exposed prematurely to life by his tutors, Roquairol has already seen and read everything and tends therefore to experience life as nothing more than a series of quotations from great works of art. Growing up without the guidance of a caring father, he lacks any sense of moral restraint on his actions. When he hears of Liane's second attack of blindness and attributes all the blame to Albano, he takes revenge by seducing Albano's innocent foster sister Rabette—not out of love or passion or even hatred but, as he observes, out of ennui (483). When Albano, following the death of Liane, wins the love of Roquairol's childhood infatuation, Linda de Romeiro, his former friend becomes literally insane with jealousy. Taking advantage of his own gift of mimicry and Linda's peculiar affliction of night blindness—a trait that Jean Paul rather ungallantly borrowed from his affectionate Weimar patroness, Charlotte von Kalb, along with several passages from her letters to him![66]—he lures Linda to a rendezvous by forging a note in Albano's handwriting and then, imitating Albano's voice to the night-blind young woman, seduces her. Shortly thereafter, in a self-written play that he performs before an audience of the entire court, Roquairol acts out this seduction scene and then shoots himself in the head before the entire assembly, thus fulfilling the suicide gesture that he had botched as a thirteen-year-old boy.

Now there is a great deal of pure malice in the character of this brilliant, doomed Romantic; Walther Rehm has written an important paper on Roquairol under the title "A Study in the History of Evil."[67] But it is an oversimplification to regard Roquairol as no more than a symbolic figure: his psychological constitution is at least as carefully observed as is that of his neurotic sister, Liane. Indeed, while Jean Paul designates Roquairol as "a child and sacrifice of the century" and as one of "life's burnt-out ruins" ("diese Abgebrannten des Lebens," 262), the term "madness" occurs so frequently in connection with Roquairol that it is clear that Jean Paul regards him as touched by the family affliction. Albano catches sight of Roquairol for the first time when he and his friend Schoppe are watching the funeral procession of the dead prince. The ironic Schoppe has just been provoked by the pomp and circumstance of the crowd to make an observation about "the dulled, heavy madness ["Wahnsinn"] of the human race" (228). The very next sentence introduces Roquairol into the text: "Suddenly a brightly dressed and resplendent rider, Roquairol upon his prancing riding horse, broke through the black chain and profoundly moved our two friends."

From this point on, Jean Paul takes frequent occasion to imply that Roquairol's character, in its fascinatingly brilliant as well as its sinister aspects, is based on severe mental distress. Very early, for instance, Jean Paul observes that different external circumstances might have preserved him—if, for instance, he had been poor and compelled to work. "For that reason the first Christians always gave tasks to their possessed, e.g., sweeping out the churches and so forth. But the idle life of an officer simply made him ever more vain and impudent" (264). Similarly, the disarray of Roquairol's quarters, along with his chaotic life, signals the confusion of his mind (260). His sudden shifts of mood, coupled with his outbursts of violence and his utter amorality, make it clear that we are dealing here with an even more serious case than that of his sister—a case that by modern terminology could be accurately described as severe manic-depressive psychosis but that was known to Pinel and Reil as *manie avec délire*. Such cases, according to current beliefs, were not incurable and often became milder with increasing age. "But sometimes," says Pinel, "the accesses of fury also become more frequent, and that is a fatal omen" (158).

The most exuberant case of madness in the entire novel is embodied by Albano's friend and companion, the "Maltese librarian" Peter Schoppe. From the earliest stages of composition, even before he was clear about name and function, Jean Paul had planned to include in his novel a *Komikus* and *Humorist* who, in a "mad whimsy," confounds the tragic and the comic.[68] Long before he became acquainted with Fichte's philosophy, Jean Paul had written satirically about extreme philosophical egoism, which recognizes no reality outside itself. By 1798, as the character of Schoppe took shape, it was clear to Jean Paul that Schoppe would suffer from the *idée fixe* that he is a dream and fears his mirror images, who represent the ego, or "I," that pursues him. Around this time, too, he decided to identify Schoppe with the figure of Leibgeber from his earlier novel *Siebenkäs*, so that he might make use of the fact that Siebenkäs and Leibgeber are exact look-alikes.

For the first two-thirds of the novel Schoppe plays a relatively minor role. He is Albano's frequent companion, an eccentric whom few people like—especially the loathed Roquairol—because, as Jean Paul puts it, few people can tolerate "a wholly free human being" (318). During these early appearances Schoppe is not insane, but his mental lability is suggested by his manic exuberance, as well as the utter lack of restraint that he imposes on his thoughts and words. Shortly before Liane's death, however, the symptoms begin to become more sinister. First, Schoppe's friends notice a personality change in him as he becomes moody, restless, morose: he has fallen in love with a woman whose identity he refuses to reveal (though it subsequently becomes clear that his bewitching obsession is the unobtainable Linda de Romeiro). Around the same time, for reasons that belong to the dynastic-political aspect of the plot, a mysterious stranger with a skull-like head—completely bald and lacking even eyebrows—suddenly appears before Schoppe one night in a wine cellar and prophesies that he will go mad within the next fifteen months. At this point Schoppe is still able to respond aggressively, saying that he is not at all alarmed at the prospect of madness, a comment that Jean Paul illuminates in a footnote citing an English authority to the effect that servility rarely occurs among the fixed ideas of the asylum (521). Shortly thereafter, when he has gone to the palace to persuade Idoine to play the role of the deceased Liane in order to free Albano from his guilty conscience, Schoppe has the first in a series of upsetting experiences with his own reflection when he is left to wait in the hall of mirrors. Walking back and forth, accompanied by "his peevish following of silent, nimble mirror orangutans," Schoppe is disgusted by these multiplications of himself. " 'Must you disturb me, you I's?' he says," as he envisages a great scale in which his life is measured and in which "his I would vanish from him like the imitation glass I's all about" (546).

At the time these scattered incidents seem not terribly important, and Schoppe remains behind in Pestitz while Albano goes off to Italy. During his absence Albano learns that Schoppe has disappeared for several months and that everybody in town is convinced he is going mad. On his return Albano learns further details: before his departure, Schoppe had spent most of his hours with his Alsatian dog, to whom he addressed long discourses, and he also liked to spend hours before the mirror, holding conversations with his own reflection (689). Finally, a letter from Schoppe himself provides clarification. Having become convinced of his imminent insanity, he no longer wonders whether but only when madness will arrive. In a compulsively systematic manner he lists various symptoms and reasons: his florid literary style with its wild mixture of images; the prophecy of his madness, which has obsessed him ever since; the model of Jonathan Swift, whose madness is not unfamiliar to scholars; his total forgetfulness; his frequent confusion of hallucinations with reality; and other symptoms (697–98). From the same letter Albano learns that Schoppe's mysterious journey was to take him to Spain in search of information that might clarify the genealogical confusions that, at this point in the narrative, are still unresolved.

When Schoppe returns, his condition has gotten worse. From Albano's uncle he had heard of a man resembling the sinister figure who prophesied his madness and who traveled around with a wax museum full of figures of madmen with whom he converses. One night in an inn Schoppe hears noises from the adjoining room. Stepping onto the balcony, he sees that the room is filled with wax madmen, the bald death's head sitting among them and talking. Greeting Schoppe, they call him "Brother" and invite him to join them. Schoppe reports to Albano that he attempted to free himself from their sinister pursuit by shooting the master of ceremonies of that mad assemblage. This incident has clearly driven Schoppe over the brink. When Albano seeks to leave him, Schoppe pleads with him to keep him company: "Otherwise I'll be alone *vis-à-vis de moi*" (766). When Albano fails to comprehend his anxiety, Schoppe looks around fearfully and says, "The I might come," explaining that his impulse to total egoism, complicated by his reading in philosophy, has finally driven him mad.

> "Sir, anyone who has read Fichte and his general vicar and brainservant Schelling as often for amusement as I, must finally take it quite seriously. The ego posits itself and the ego along with that remainder that most people call the world.... The ego imagines itself, it is therefore an 'as though'-subject and at the same time the storehouse for both—damnation! there is an empirical and a pure ego—the last phrase that the mad Swift uttered shortly before his death, according to Sheridan and Oxford, was: I am I—philosophical enough!"

Now the whole story begins to come out. Schoppe confesses that his real name is not Schoppe; he has been changing his name constantly throughout his life so that the true "I" of which he, Schoppe, is merely the dream or reflection will never catch up with him and destroy him. Shortly thereafter they part, but when Albano looks for his friend the next day, no one knows what has happened. Finally Albano learns that Schoppe has been sent off to a madhouse. Having been accused of the murder of the waxmuseum director in Spain and given the choice of madhouse or prison, he chose the former. It turns out that there has been a mistake stemming from the sinister plot against Albano and Schoppe, who in fact has killed no one. But the psychic damage has been done. When Albano goes to the madhouse—a humane institution, where moral therapy is carried out by an enlightened couple resembling Pussin and his wife at Bicêtre—he finds that Schoppe has smashed every mirror in sight, studies books on madness, and discusses the institutional care of the insane with the director. Even when Albano takes Schoppe back to his own apartment, the troubles do not cease: all the mirrors must be covered up lest Schoppe catch sight of a hostile I. He sleeps so poorly that the doctor finally gives him a sleeping potion, but the potion drives Schoppe into a delirious state from which he suddenly springs up and runs away.

At this point the plot becomes fast and complicated. In pursuit of revenge against the Spaniard, Schoppe has made his way back to the palace where once he spoke to Idoine in the hall of mirrors. This time he is driven to such distraction by the "people of I's" surrounding him that he attempts to dismantle the glass. This sets in motion a sequence of incidents that culminate in the revelation of Albano's true identity by means of a hidden portrait. Rushing to find his friend in order to tell him the news, he encounters the evil uncle who has conspired in his misery and threatens to kill him—"for I am a maniac full of *idées fixes*" (798)—but is prevented at the last minute by Albano's arrival. Just at this point Schoppe-Leibgeber's old friend Siebenkäs arrives, and Schoppe is shocked by the unexpected appearance of this double into a fatal seizure. "I have waited long enough! You are the old Ego—come lay your face against mine and make cold this stupid existence" (800).

In the figure of Schoppe, Jean Paul illustrates what he regarded as the dangers of an untrammeled solipsism as embodied politically in the French Revolution and philosophically in the teachings of Fichte—a freedom so excessive that it leads to nihilism. Schoppe's life shows that such a freedom progresses by way of despair and madness to ultimate death. Pinel and Reil had already linked madness to the turmoil of the Revolution and had pointed out the dangers of excessive study to the unstable mind. But it is specifically Jean Paul's symbolic use of madness that sets it apart from the occurrence of madness in earlier works. Here it is not the madness that is primary but the parody of Fichtean subjectivism and the problem of identity. Balder and the harpist are fully developed characters who go mad according to the stages of psychic disintegration as understood by late eighteenth-century psychology. Schoppe, in contrast, is a figure who takes Fichte literally: that is Jean Paul's joke and the thesis that he sets out to demonstrate.[69] But to carry out his joke he needed the symptoms of *manie avec délire* or "partieller Wahnsinn," as it was understood by contemporaries. Indeed, the stages of Schoppe's madness are developed so carefully, with explicit reference to symptoms that Jean Paul—perhaps the most indiscriminately voracious reader of his generation—knew from books on madness as well as Swift's biography, that we can easily recognize a rapidly advancing case of schizophrenia. All of this, moreover, is in the service of Albano's *Bildung*. As his sister Julienne remarks at one point late in the novel: "It is a miracle that my brother, living between two such phantasts as Schoppe and Roquairol, did not become one himself" (632). On the contrary, his experience of the tragedy stemming from the mental illness of the three people closest to him—from Liane's neurosis and Roquairol's psychopathy to Schoppe's schizophrenia—eventually leads Albano to a degree of spiritual integration at which he can deal with reality. The three graves that he visits at the end of the novel symbolize more vividly than any other image the perils of Romantic titanism—perils that he escaped only because he experienced them through his surrogates. "I don't need to wonder why I, too, did not sink down. O enough, enough of me fell into their graves" (821).

Even if the internal evidence did not make it sufficiently apparent, Jean Paul's references in the text as well as the notes demonstrate not only his consuming interest in the phenomenon of madness but also his knowledge of the most important developments of his day. Liane's physician, Dr. Sphex, cites an article in Reil's *Archiv für die Physiologie* on the chemistry of tears in connection with her blindness (159). Schoppe attributes her affliction to an attack of nerves and cites the English physiologist Robert Whytt regarding women who suffer obscured vision as a result of excessive acidity in the stomach (162). The author observes in a footnote that Simon-André Tissot, in his *Traité des nerfs et de leurs maladies* (German translation, 1781–1784), speaks of the pharmaceutical function of haughtiness in producing madness (164). He cites Erasmus Darwin and Thomas Sydenham to illustrate the violent shifts in Roquairol's temperament (264), and on another occasion adduces the Brownian system of irritability and its principal exponent in Germany, Melchior Adam Weikard, to characterize the love of princes as "a fever of lassitude" (502–3). Jean Paul alludes in passing to the Salpêtrière, the Invalid Hospital in Copenhagen, Bedlam, and even to the recent (1798) conflagration of the madhouse in Berlin (235, 270, 705). During Liane's illness Albano informs himself about afflictions of the nerves (183), and Schoppe's table in the madhouse is strewn with English and German texts on insanity that he has borrowed from the asylum inspector (775). It is hardly astonishing, given this informed interest, that Jean Paul became friends with Dr. Langermann, the director of the new madhouse in Bayreuth. More to the point, we see that his obsession with madness as the symptom of the times was in fact undergirded by a solid acquaintance with the psychiatric theories and practices of his day. Yet while the symptomology of madness and the description of its treatment by moral management in *Titan* are absolutely consistent with the theories of Pinel and Crichton, Jean Paul's implication that madness is inherent in society and that the insane person is a mirror image of normality brings him very close to Reil's Romantic psychiatry.

• • •

Jean Paul was one of the first readers of the anonymous *Nachtwachen*, which appeared late in 1804 bearing the publication date 1805. On January 14, 1805, he urged a friend: "Be sure to read the Nightwatches by Bonaventura, that is, by Schelling. It is a splendid imitation of my Giannozzo, but with too many reminiscences and liberties at the same time."[70] With his reference to Schelling's presumed authorship and to one of his own works as a model, Jean Paul contributed what was probably the first in an unending series of speculations on the identity of the anonymous author that has obsessed scholars and, to a great extent, distracted energy and attention from the critical understanding of his fascinating work.[71]

It is no wonder that Jean Paul was attracted to these strange *Nachtwachen*, for—along with all the other tendencies of the times that they satirize so mercilessly—Fichte's ideas come in for their share of ridicule. It seems clear that the anonymous author is paying tribute to Jean Paul's own recently published novel in at least one passage. As the narrator, Kreuzgang, conducts the physician Dr. Oehlmann through the madhouse, they converse with one patient who regards himself as the creator of the world.

"Just look, Herr Doctor," I continued when the Creator of the World had ended, "what furious plans the fellow has for the world. It is almost dangerous for us other fools that we must tolerate this Titan among us, for he has his own absolutely consistent system just like Fichte. But basically he cares less for human beings than Fichte, who merely separates man from heaven and hell and in compensation crams man's classical aspects, as though into pocketbook format, into the tiny I, which any small boy can utter. Nowadays anyone can summon up at will from his own insignificant hull whole cosmogonies, theosophies, world histories and the like, along with the relevant images. That is grand and splendid, to be sure; if only the format were not so small!"[72]

On another occasion—but in the same madhouse—Kreuzgang is alone at night with his only gloomy thoughts.

I had now ceased to think about anything else and was imagining only myself! No object could be found anywhere except for the great terrible I, which consumed itself and, in devouring, constantly bore itself again. I did not sink, for there was no longer any space, nor did I seem to float up. All variation had vanished along with time, and there prevailed a frightful, eternally desolate tedium. (122)

As in *Titan* and the figure of Schoppe, Fichtean speculation is adduced as a clue to and symptom of madness. But "Bonaventura" plays even more exuberantly with madness than does Jean Paul—with a certain degree of knowledgeability, to be sure, but conspicuously as a mirror of the general human condition. At the very end of the book (in the sixteenth nightwatch) when Kreuzgang learns the secret of his birth—that he was sired by an alchemist and a gypsy in an act of conception consummated at the very instant when the devil appeared to them—he is immensely relieved to have discovered finally what he regards as the key to his nihilistic view of the world.

What a bright light was illuminated within me after this speech only psychologists can imagine; the key to my Self was handed to me, and for the first time I opened with astonishment and secret trembling the long closed door—it looked like Bluebeard's chamber, and it would have strangled me if I had been less fearless. It was a dangerous psychological key!

I would like to hand myself over just as I am to skillful psychologists for dissection and anatomization in order to see whether they would be able to read out of me that which I was now really able to read. This trace of doubt, by the way, is not meant to offend the science that I truly esteem because it does not shrink from squandering time and energy on such a hypothetical object as the soul. (136)

In the otherwise highly satirical context of the book this passage amounts to a startlingly genuine statement of regard for the developing field of psychology, despite any mild skepticism regarding the competence of its practitioners. Certainly it represents a declaration of conviction that the human personality is motivated by psychic and not by somatic factors and that he can understand his own moods and behavior if he has the "psychological key" in his hands.

For it is Kreuzgang's "fixe Idee"—the technical term occurs several times in the course of the work—that the world aspires not to order but to chaos. He wants to emulate God by creating first "a good and total chaos from which later, if it occurred to me, a decent world might be organized" (48). It is Kreuzgang's theory that humanity spoiled things by rushing to make order out of chaos and therefore got everything wrong. For that reason he constantly seeks to return to a state of chaos in his own life and view of things. Because of this underlying *idée fixe*, which he now believes was his inheritance from the strange circumstances of his birth, he has always had "a special preference for madness" ("Tollheit," 48).

Kreuzgang's method for creating chaos out of order and getting back to a pre-logical state of affairs is the strategy of inversion that we noted in his view of law.[73] Thus for the street ballads that got him charged with slander he found lots of material in history for cases of murder on a large scale, such as the murder of souls by church and state as well as occasional small episodic delights: "the murder of honor by means of an insidious good reputation, of love by cold heartless knaves, of loyalty by false friends, of justice by the courts, of healthy common sense by the censor's edicts, etc." (62). Because society cannot tolerate these inversions Kreuzgang is sentenced to the madhouse. But there he finds himself at last in his proper element, for the madhouse—in the ultimate inversion—is not only the mirror of society but an asylum of the spirit "because the *idée fixe* of the fools locked up with me was generally a pleasant one" (77). Accordingly it is in the madhouse that Kreuzgang finds "at least *one* blooming full rose in the many thorns of my life" and spends "this one month of bliss among the other winter and autumnal moons" (76–77).

It is Kreuzgang's idea that "humanity organizes itself precisely according to the model of an onion" (77): one must peel away layer after layer in order to get down to the basic individual. Nature, for instance, created one great world religion: but as you strip away the layers, you find first various folk religions for Jews, heathens, Turks, and Christians; then another layer reveals yet other subcategories for the latter. The same principle applies, Kreuzgang continues, in "the general madhouse of the world, out of whose windows so many heads peer, some with partial and some with total insanity" (77). Within this macro-madhouse men have built "smaller madhouses for special fools," and it is into one of these that Kreuzgang is sent for the most pleasant period of his life.

Because his foolishness is regarded as relatively harmless the governor of the institute appoints Kreuzgang to serve as vice-governor, and in this capacity it is his responsibility to guide the visiting physician from time to time through the place. On one such occasion he explains to the doctor that "we all are afflicted more or less by fixed ideas; not only single individuals but entire commonalities and faculties" (78). It is the delusion of academic faculties, for instance, that by the mere imposition of a hat from their factory they can make heads wise—an observation that causes the visiting physician to shake his own doctoral cap. Kreuzgang then leads the physician past twenty rooms, making appropriate comments about each case. No. 2 and No. 3, for instance, are "philosophical antipodes, an idealist and a realist" (79). One (like "Jacob W. . . r," whom we encountered in Spiess's *Biographien*) believes that he has a glass breast, while the other thinks that he has a glass bottom, "for which reason he never posits his I"—an allusion to the first proposition from Fichte's *Wissenschaftslehre*.

The inmates of Bonaventura's symbolic madhouse, in fact, are almost without exception bourgeois intellectuals: No. 4 is there because he is half a century ahead of his times in culture ("Bildung"); No. 5 was committed because he gave talks that were too sensible and comprehensible; No. 6 went mad because he was crazy enough to take seriously the jest of a powerful man; several are "variations on the same old pop song, love" (84), and so forth. Only two cases receive more extensive comment. No. 9 thinks that he is "the creator of the world," and he delivers a sad monologue about his disappointment in the crazy mortals who inhabit his creation (a child's ball that he holds in his hand). No. 20, finally, is Kreuzgang's own room, into which he invites the physician with the comment that, in God's eyes, all men are equal "and simply suffer from different fixed ideas, if not from a total madness, but with small nuances" (84). It is here that Kreuzgang talks about his study in the three *Brotfakultäten*. He gave it up because he found in this highly acclaimed wisdom "nothing but the cover that is hung over life's Moses-countenance so that it will not see God" (85).

This brings Kreuzgang to his own case: "It is my *idée fixe* that I regard myself as more reasonable than the reason deduced in systems, and far wiser than the wisdom taught in the universities." Kreuzgang suggests that he and the physician should collaborate to determine what means might be applied against this madness. How, he wonders, can one rebel against illnesses if one does not agree with the system and, accordingly, regards as illness what others call health, and vice-versa? "Who decides in the last analysis whether we fools here in the madhouse are more masterfully mad or the members of the faculties in their lecture halls? Whether perhaps error is truth, foolishness is wisdom, or death is life—just as, at present, reasonable people think the opposite!—O I am incurable. Even I concede the point" (86).

In the fourteenth nightwatch Kreuzgang relates how it happened that he left the madhouse, where he experienced his only true happiness in life. When he arrived there, he discovered that the inmate in the adjoining room was none other than a young woman he had known during his career as an actor. Playing the role of Ophelia (an explicit allusion to Aurelie in *Wilhelm Meisters Lehrjahre*), she suddenly underwent the transformation that had horrified Kant: she succumbed to her role and, in a "transformation of the real person into a poetic one" (113), went mad and was sent to the madhouse. Most of the chapter consists of the story of the growing love between "Ophelia" and Kreuzgang, her "Hamlet," a story told through interpolated letters. Finally the inevitable happens: Ophelia gets pregnant and then dies over her stillborn child. Kreuzgang is punished for his attempt to propagate the race of madmen by being sent back out in the world of the rational, "for I had brought back from the madhouse an intensified hatred against all reasonable people who now again walked around and beside me with their insipid, vague physiognomies" (124).

It is clear that "Bonaventura" is exploiting madness, in the principal thematic inversion of his nightwatches, in a purely symbolic way. Like Jean Paul, he shows how a belief in Fichte's system must inevitably lead to insanity, but he goes much further in his reification of the notion that reason is mad and "madness" actually reason. Of course, the literary use of madness as a metaphor and the madhouse as a symbol is an ancient topos that extends from the Greeks down to Nietzsche and beyond.[74] What distinguishes the *Nachtwachen* from examples in classical antiquity or the twentieth century are not just the many contemporary allusions (to Novalis, Fichte, Goethe, Jean Paul, Mozart, and others) but also the use of contemporary medical and psychiatric practices. Thus in the extended parody of Novalis's *Hymnen an die Nacht* (sixteenth nightwatch) the young man seeking the image of his deceased beloved in the grave rejects the imputation that he is insane and refers to Karl Phillip Moritz's *Magazin der Erfahrungsseelenkunde*. The first journal of psychology, it served as a source for the notion that certain people have the power to see the dead lying in their graves. Similarly, when Kreuzgang is conducting the physician through the madhouse, several of the cases he describes are based upon Reil's *Rhapsodieen*.[75] No. 1, for instance, has such a high opinion of humanity and such a low opinion of himself that, "in contrast to bad poets," he retains all his bodily fluids because he is afraid that by releasing them he might cause a great destructive flood ("Sündflut," 79). Reil cites this familiar psychiatric phenomenon. "To this category [fixed ideas relating to transformations of the body and the personality] belong the cases of those patients . . . who thought they had so much urine in their bladders that a *Sündflut* would be created if they released it" (339).

But more important than the specific symptoms—some of which, like the "man of glass," have venerable literary antecedents—is the psychiatric "culture" of the work.[76] Thus "Bonaventura" uses Reil's terminology and ideas. We have already had frequent occasion to cite such terms as *idée fixe* or "fixe Idee" and "partieller Wahnsinn." But also the means of cure—not the official ones, but Kreuzgang's more Romantic ones—are very much in the spirit of Reil's therapeutic play. To cure the madman with the urine fixation, for instance, Kreuzgang first thought of providing conflagrations to be extinguished or dried-up riverbeds with mills standing still and hungry and thirsty people on the banks. Finally he thought of a truly radical cure: he conducts him every day through Dante's inferno, which the madman now proposes to extinguish with his accumulated urine. In general, Reil would be compatible with "Bonaventura" because the *Rhapsodieen* provide the theoretical basis for the fundamentally intellectual ailments of the madmen in the *Nachtwachen*. Moreover, Kreuzgang's praise of the gentle and harmless inmates of the madhouse sounds like a quotation from Reil's introduction, which compares the fools in Bicêtre and Bedlam favorably with those "from the great Fools' House" (8). Above all, it was Reil's basic assumption in the *Rhapsodieen*, as we observed, that madness is not the condition of total "alienation" from society but, rather, a state closely linked to society in advanced stages of development.

THE ROMANTIC OBSESSION WITH MADNESS

With Jean Paul's *Titan*, then, and especially with the *Nachtwachen* we are dealing with works that reflect the emerging Romantic view of madness as a special and higher state of altered consciousness and of the madhouse as a mirror of society and a place of spiritual refuge rather than of shameful confinement. These notions are compatible with Reil's psychiatry, which sees madness as an integral aspect of humanity and the asylum as a place of therapeutic play. But this was perhaps the last moment for several decades at which the literary and medical views of madness were still essentially compatible. For with the establishment of the asylum in Bayreuth in 1805 German institutional psychiatry moved off independently in its own direction.

At several points in the *Rhapsodieen* (notably 478) Reil had singled out as one of the few physicians in Germany adequate to the challenge of being a doctor for the insane a young physican named Johann Gottfried Langermann. It is likely that Hardenberg, when he was reviewing candidates to head his new initiative in Bayreuth, knew Langermann not only from Reil's influential volume but also in another connection. Langermann was a friend of his distant relative Friedrich von Hardenberg, or Novalis, and is known to literary history as one of the physicians who ministered to Novalis's fiancée, Sophie von Kühn, during her long struggle with tuberculosis.[77] In any case, Hardenberg's choice fell upon a man whose view of madness and madhouses represented a typically Prussian compromise between Enlightenment and Romanticism, between the rationalist psychologists and Reil, between authority and freedom.

Johann Gottfried Langermann (1768–1832), known as the first German *Irrenarzt* or "mad-doctor," came to psychiatry from a varied background of experience.[78] The son of a peasant near Dresden, he had the good fortune to impress a noble patron, who sent him to school in Dresden, where he excelled in music. He first went to study law at Leipzig in 1789, but gradually his love of philosophy alienated him from the pandects and institutes. When in 1794 he had disagreements with the authorities at Leipzig for his criticism of the university constitution, he transferred to Jena. There he was a passionate auditor of Fichte's lectures while pursuing a degree in medicine, which he received in 1797 with a dissertation on the diagnosis and treatment of melancholia. (It was during this period, as an assistant of Professor Johann Chr. Stark, who was also Schiller's personal physician, that he helped to care for Sophie von

Kühn and became acquainted with Goethe.) Although Langermann had visited nearby asylums for the insane while studying at Jena, his work is not an empirical treatise like Pinel's, based on actual clinical experience, but a theoretical work on the order of Kant's *Anthropologie*—a work inspired in particular by the strong moral impulse of his teachers Fichte and Schiller. Like Kant, Reil understood insanity as a disorder of the soul, produced by the individual's own "idiopathic" passions: people who are psychically strong do not go mad; but he disagreed with Kant's view that insanity is incurable.

Following his degree, Langermann practiced for a time at Bayreuth and then became a doctor in the *Zucht- und Irrenhaus* at Torgau (north of Leipzig). Eventually he returned to Bayreuth and in 1803 was asked by Hardenberg to inspect the facilities for the care of the insane at St. Georgen and to submit a plan for their reform. Langermann addressed himself to the problem with practical experience similar to that of Pinel but with a theoretical background closer to that of Reil.[79] The plan that he submitted to Hardenberg in May 1804 represents the kind of Prussian compromise that might be anticipated from a man of his background, training, and administrative experience. In the first place, Langermann proposed to admit both the curable and the incurably insane. As a doctor he felt that the distinction between the two categories was unclear, and as a Prussian administrator he was aware of the need to protect the public from madmen, curable or not. The recommended therapy depended, as Reil advocated, on exercise of the mental faculties as well as physical activity, but it rejected the utopian notions of democratic organization or anything else that would threaten the moral authority of the institution. Similarly Langermann rejected the traditional Christian notions of therapy that involved the belief in insanity as sin. As a disciple of Fichte and Kant, Langermann insisted on the moral responsibility of the patient, who must be educated by work and mental exercise back to reason—the perfect example of what has come to be known as "therapeutic idealism" and quite remote from any view of madness as symbolic.

The Psychische Heilanstalt für Geisteskranke, which Hardenberg authorized in February 1805 and to which Langermann was appointed director, was therefore not only the first modern mental asylum in Germany but also a typically Prussian institution that represented a compromise between Pinel's Gallic empiricism and Reil's Romantic idealism. Based on the scientific belief in the idiopathic origin of mental illness, the medical belief in the curability of insanity, the philosophical belief in the moral responsibility of rational human beings, and the pedagogical belief in the educability of all, including the insane and the feebleminded, it embodied the administrative belief in a strong central authority and stern disciplinary methods. All of this was reflected in the administrative structure of the institution at Bayreuth, which restricted the powers of the physician by means of a co-director appointed to represent the legal interests of the state and counterbalanced both with a salaried teacher who embodied the pedagogical convictions of the age.

The asylum at Bayreuth, which was paired with a twin *Pflegeanstalt* for the incurably insane, provided the model for the thirty mental hospitals that were established in the following years: Sonnenstein in Saxony (1811), Marsberg in Westphalia (1814), and others in rapid succession.[80] When Ernst Horn in 1806 became assistant medical director of the Charité in Berlin, he began to apply the new methods of psychic treatment of his patients there.[81] Langermann himself, who from 1810 on occupied a variety of administrative positions in the Prussian medical services and finally became director of the entire system, had a profound influence on the development of mental hospitals in Prussia, including notably the new ones that he established at Siegburg and Leubus. The intellectual significance of these institutions needs to be emphasized because until mid-century—when what Karl Jaspers has called "institutional psychiatry" gave way to "university psychiatry" again—these institutions constituted bases such as Reil had envisaged, at which the new discipline of psychiatry was defined, while future practitioners were being trained and the patients treated more humanely than ever before.[82]

However, to the extent that psychiatric research from 1805 until mid-century took place in clinics that were often isolated from the universities, two separate lines of psychiatry developed in Germany: an empirical psychiatry after the fashion of Langermann (and consistent with the French model of clinical psychiatry) and a theoretical psychiatry that developed from the beginnings of Reil and was fueled by *Naturphilosophie*. It was this second line with its theological bent after the fashion of Schelling and G. H. Schubert that appealed to many Romantics with their view of madness as a metaphor. In his paralipomena to *Heinrich von Ofterdingen* (1802), that textbook of Romanticism, Novalis hints at the transformation of mind that his hero will undergo in order to experience other forms of being following his *Bildung* as a man. "In a state of madness Heinrich becomes a stone—[a flower] a resonant tree—a golden ram—Heinrich divines the meaning of the world—His voluntary madness."[83] In his so-called *Stuttgarter Privatvorlesungen* (1810) Schelling elaborated the view that madness is "the most profound essence of the human mind" when it is considered in isolation from the soul and from God.

Madness therefore does not come into being but appears when that which is actually non-being, i.e., without reason, is actualized—when it seeks to be essence, being. The basis of understanding itself therefore is madness. . . . What we call understanding, if it is real, lively, active understanding, is actually nothing but regulated insanity. . . . People who have no madness in themselves are people of empty, unfruitful understanding. Hence the inverted sentence: *nullum magnum ingenium sine quadam dementia*. Therefore the divine madness of which Plato speaks, of which the poets speak.[84]

In the person of Friedrich Hölderlin, whose worsening mental state finally necessitated his confinement in Autenrieth's Tübingen clinic in 1806–1807, the Romantics had before their eyes a walking model for madness as an access to privileged poetic knowledge—a model that provided subsequent generations with material for the legend of the mad poet. Hölderlin's illness was variously diagnosed by his contemporaries as "Hypochondrie," "Manie," or a disturbance of the nervous system resulting from excessive intellectual exertion after the fashion of Kreuzgang's companions in the madhouse.[85] (Today most authorities agree that he suffered from schizophrenia.) As a student in Tübingen, Wilhelm Waiblinger spent many hours with the revered Hölderlin, whose "Life, Poetry, and Madness" he subsequently (1830) depicted in the first biography of the poet. During the years of their daily association he took Hölderlin as the thinly veiled model for the hero of his novel *Phaethon* (1823). On August 8, 1822, he noted in his journal: "I only would like to depict a madman—I cannot live if I do not depict a madman. . . . Hölderlin! Hölderlin!"[86] And two days later he exclaimed: "The *hero of my novel* . . . is *a Hölderlin*—someone who goes mad from intoxication with God, from love, and from striving for the divine."

Almost twenty years later, in the peculiar amalgam of biography and epistolary novel that she concocted about her friend Karoline von Günderode (*Die Günderode*, 1840) from letters written during the period 1804–1806, Bettina von Arnim devoted the last letter of part one to a rhapsody on poetic madness as exemplified in Hölderlin, whose spirit was "often carried away by the holy rhythm and then borne and swept up and down in a sacred madness, in total surrender to the divine."[87] In

Hölderlin one sees how "the spirit rises up from despair into sacred madness, insofar as madness is the loftiest human manifestation, where the soul transcends all verbal expression and the poeticizing God leads it into the light. . . . For me," Bettina concluded, "his utterances are like oracular sayings that he proclaims in a state of madness as the priest of the god."

## FICTION AS A MODE OF PSYCHIATRIC PERCEPTION

The Romantic obsession with madness quickly reached such a state that in 1813, following an evening at the theater, Goethe worried that

> what is monstrous about our culture is this: we elevate our public— against its will and to our detriment—to *irony* by purifying its passions through putting everything on display, even madness and the insane asylums and fools' hospitals. For what can be the result of all this, other than that the public will become acquainted with this force, which is so destructive for the feelings and emotions, simply as a condition, as something pathological vis-à-vis which one feels better, more serene, and with which one finally learns to play?[88]

Little did he know it, but the worst was yet to come. By 1821 Jean Paul, in his preface to the second edition of *Die unsichtbare Loge*, commented that readers of contemporary literature have learned "to venerate madmen as saints."[89] Jean Paul had in mind specifically E.T.A. Hoffmann, and it is certainly true that Hoffmann's works teem with madmen of every variety, from the melancholics who end in suicide—Anselmus in *Der goldne Topf*, Nathanael in "Der Sandmann," and Elis Fröbom in "Die Bergwerke zu Falun"—by way of the "partial madmen" with their fixed ideas—like the jeweler Cardillac in "Das Fräulein von Scuderi," who cannot bear to part with his creations; Viktorin in *Die Elixiere des Teufels*, who believes that he is the monk Medardus; or the lovesick old countess in "Das öde Haus"—to such harmless eccentrics as Councillor Krespel with his wacky house and clothes; Uncle Siegfried in "Die Genesung," who is convinced that nature is punishing mankind by depriving the trees and plants of their verdure; and the curious old man in Berlin who is convinced that he is the composer Gluck.

Yet it is important to make a distinction here. Hoffmann is not simply indulging in the general Romantic glorification of madness. His works represent a position intermediate between the clinical psychiatrists like

Pinel and Langermann and the theorists of the soul like Reil and the philosophers of nature. We can see this most clearly if we look closely at the exemplary story "Der Einsiedler Serapion" (written in late 1818), which stands at the beginning of the collection *Die Serapionsbrüder* (1819–1821) and provides its title. Most of the nineteen stories had already appeared in various newspapers and journals. But it is the fiction of the framework narrative that Hoffmann invented for the book publication that four friends—Theodor, Cyprian, Lothar, and Ottmar—have come together (in Berlin) after an absence of twelve years and agree to meet once a week for conversation and amusement by telling stories. (The fiction is based on the actual weekly meetings of friends—Hoffmann, the jurist Julius Eduard Hitzig, the poet Carl Wilhelm Contessa, and the physician Johann Ferdinand Koreff—that took place from 1814 on in Hoffmann's apartment in Berlin.) On that first evening Cyprian relates the story of a curious adventure that he experienced several years earlier during his stay in "B..." (= Bamberg).

While taking a walk one day, Cyprian gets lost in the woods outside the town and meets a man with a long, wild beard wearing a monk's cowl and a broad straw hat who resembles an anchorite from early Christian times who had stepped out of a painting by Salvator Rosa (23).[90] When Cyprian asks for directions back to town, the weird man chides him for interrupting his conversation with friends, then says he can return to Alexandria with his friend Ambrosius of Kamaldoli, and disappears into the wilderness. From a passing peasant Cyprian learns that the man calls himself Priest Serapion and for several years has lived in a small hut that he built for himself in the woods. Although people say that he is not right in the head, he is a pious and gentle man who harms no one.

Back in Bamberg, Cyprian makes inquiries and hears the full story from an acquaintance, Doctor S** (a tribute to Hoffmann's Bamberg friend, Dr. Friedrich Speyer). The hermit is actually the talented scion of one of the most distinguished families in "M——," who was well on his way to an important diplomatic career when he suddenly disappeared mysteriously. Sometime later a relative happened to encounter him in the Tirol, where he dressed in a brown cowl, called himself Priest Serapion, and traveled from village to village, preaching. Confronted with his true identity, Serapion flew into a raging mania, which could not be cured by the most famous doctors in M——. "He was brought to the asylum in B***, and here, thanks to the methodical treatment, based on profound psychic understanding, of the physician who at that time headed the institution, it was possible to rescue the unfortunate man at least from the frenzy to which he had succumbed" (24–25). (Here Hoffmann is paying tribute to his friend Dr. Adalbert Friedrich Marcus, who was director of the asylum St. Getreu at the time of Hoffmann's sojourn in Bamberg.) Then—whether by accident or the physician's design—the patient managed to escape and finally appeared in the forest some two hours distant from Bamberg. The physician said that he should be left in peace or else he would be plunged again into a frenzy, and the local police took that advice. Serapion built a comfortable hut, made a table and chair for himself, and planted a garden with vegetables and flowers. "Except for the notion that he was the anchorite Serapion, who fled into the Theban desert under Emperor Decius and suffered a martyr's death in Alexandria, his mind appeared not in the least disturbed" (25). But the physician declared him utterly incurable.

Cyprian comes up with the idea that he can eradicate Serapion's *idée fixe*. "I read Pinel—Reil—all possible books on madness that I could get my hands on; I believed that it was perhaps reserved for me, the psychologist from outside, the medical layman, to cast a ray of light into Serapion's darkened spirit" (26). Preparing himself by studying the lives of all eight of the saints and martyrs who went under the name of Serapion, Cyprian makes his way back to the hermit's secluded hut, where he finds Serapion in excellent spirits. There, after refreshments, Cyprian elicits from his host the statement that he is indeed the martyr Serapion who died hundreds of years earlier by a terrible martyrdom. The hermit confides that nothing but a violent headache and aches in his limbs occasionally remind him of the tortures he has undergone.

At this point Cyprian, deciding to initiate his cure, speaks "very learnedly about the disease of fixed ideas that sometimes afflicts people and, like a single dissonance, ruins the otherwise purely tuned organism" (28). He cites various cases (all borrowed from Reil!) of others afflicted by fixed ideas and argues "that the replacement of one's own Ego with some historic person frequently takes shape as a fixed idea in the mind." Seeing that Serapion is listening to him with close attention, Cyprian springs from his seat, seizes the hermit's hand, and cries with a loud voice: "Graf P**, awake from the destructive dream that has captivated you, discard these awful clothes, return to your family, which grieves for you, to the world, which has the most legitimate claims on you!" But Serapion merely responds with a sarcastic smile. Saying that people driven by the devil appear from time to time and attempt to convince him that he is Graf P** from M——, he sets out to refute Cyprian "with your own weapons, that is, with the weapons of reason" (29). If I am really insane, he begins, then only a madman would be crazy enough to believe that he could talk me out of my fixed idea. If such cures were possible, then there would be no more madmen on earth. On the other hand, if I am not mad and am truly the martyr Serapion, then it is equally foolish to try to persuade me that I am Graf P** from M——. And even if he should follow Cyprian to B***, then how could they be sure that it is the South German town and not Alexandria? Perhaps Cyprian himself is caught in an illusion and believes that the Theban wilderness is nothing but a forest. Cyprian stands in shame before the madman. "He had completely defeated me with the consistency of his foolishness, and I understood the madness of his undertaking in its full extent" (31). Noticing Cyprian's change in mood, Serapion now consoles him, saying that he is not an evil man but merely misled by the devil. And indeed, if Cyprian had found in him a starved cynic, deformed by waking and fasting and with the horror of terrible nightmares in his eyes, then Cyprian might have regarded him as mad. But he, awakening from his martyrdom with shattered limbs and bludgeoned head, found a new serenity that permitted him to heal in body and soul. Cyprian is unsettled by this madman who praises his condition as a gift from heaven and wishes him a similar fate.

Then Serapion tells him that his wilderness is anything but inhospitable—that he receives daily visits from the most remarkable people. Just yesterday Ariosto, Dante, and Petrarch were with him, and he is expecting a visit from the church father Evagrius. Climbing to the peak of the nearby mountain, he can see the towers of Alexandria and the most marvelous events as they take place. "Many people have found that incredible and have thought that I am simply imagining that I see taking place in external reality what has shape only as a product of my mind, my fantasy" (33). But that is silly, Serapion continues, for "is it not the mind alone that is capable of embracing all that takes place around us in space and time?" If the mind alone can comprehend an event before our eyes, then it must have taken place. Even Ariosto, in their conversation yesterday, conceded that it is a misunderstanding for the poet to believe that he can pack into his brain everything in life that he has witnessed, thanks to his special powers of vision. As proof of his claim, Serapion proceeds to tell several stories that he witnessed that morning at dawn as he stood on the mountain peak—stories, Cyprian assures his audience, that matched in inspiration and form the finest novellas.

Cyprian finds himself in an ambivalent state. "While his condition, the methodical madness in which he found the salvation of his life, filled me with deep horror, his lofty poetic talent astonished me, his companionability and his whole being, which breathed the calmest resignation of the purest spirit, aroused in me the deepest compassion" (34). Cyprian concludes his account by saying that he had enjoyed many visits with his hermit friend. But when he returned to B*** after an absence of three years, he arrived just in time to pay his last respects to Serapion after his death. His friends initially greet his story with skepticism, attributing it to his overheated imagination. And Cyprian concedes: "You all know my special inclination to traffic with madmen; I always believe that nature grants particularly the abnormal ones insight into her most terrifying depths" (36).

Cyprian's last-quoted statement reaffirms Hoffmann's own obsession with madness, which, as we noted above, provided him with characters for many of his tales. But Hoffmann's attitude goes far beyond the fascination that madness exerted on some of his contemporaries. He was also remarkably well informed on current theories of madness and therapeutic practices, and it was his habit to do careful research, especially on symptomology, before writing any of his stories about madmen.[91] Cyprian's story contains specific allusions to Pinel and Reil as well as references to Dr. Marcus and his highly regarded asylum for the insane at St. Getreu. While Hoffmann was living in Bamberg, he was closely acquainted with Marcus and his circle, which constituted one of the most progressive groups of physicians in Germany.[92] Through Marcus, who was a friend of Reil's, Hoffmann was introduced to the *Rhapsodieen* as well as Reil's other writings, and he also visited the asylum and made firsthand observations of the insane. Indeed, it is possible to list well over twenty authors with whose books and journals on psychological topics Hoffmann was acquainted.[93]

Hoffmann's acquaintance with writings on madness was not superficial. In "Der Einsielder Serapion" he cites analogous cases from Reil and uses such terms as "fixed ideas" and "methodical madness" with technical precision. In other works he does far more. For instance, in the late story "Die Genesung" the description of Uncle Siegfried's fixation—that an angry nature has deprived the world of her green—is made in the most precise terms. "Several months ago poor Uncle Siegfried was afflicted by a serious nervous disorder, from which one fixed idea remained, which, since it is firmly entrenched after the body recovered its health, has degenerated into true madness. . . . All means of resisting this idea remain futile, and you can imagine that the old man threatens to succumb to the inconsolate, destructive hypochondria which naturally accompanies this idea"[94]—a diagnosis that could not have been presented more succinctly by Reil himself.

To take another example, the melancholia of Nathanael and Elis Fröbom is introduced in both cases by a reference to their "gloomy dreams" ("düstere Träumerei").[95] And when Theodor, in "Das öde Haus," begins to behave strangely (believing that he sees the apparition of a lovely girl in his pocket mirror), one of his friends, a medical student, leaves a copy of Reil's *Rhapsodieen* in his room. The book feeds his tendency to hypochondria. "I began to read, the work attracted me irresistibly, but how did I feel when I found myself in everything that was said about fixed madness!"[96] Terrified by his self-diagnosis at the prospect of insanity, he rushes to visit Doctor K., who is famous for his treatment and cure of the insane (a tribute to Hoffmann's friend and Serapion brother, Koreff). The doctor assures him that matters are by no means as dangerous as he believes. Beyond any doubt he has been afflicted by a profound psychological disorder, "but the full clear recognition of this attack of some evil principle provides you with the weapons to defend yourself against it." The doctor recommends the standard treatment in the case of fixed ideas: to remove the offending object if possible. "You see that I want to extirpate merely the fixed idea, that is, the appearance of the face in the window of the desolate house and in the mirror that confounds you, to shift your attention to other matters, and to strengthen your body."[97]

However, Hoffmann's unique standpoint, which coincides neither with institutional psychiatry nor with Reil and the theoreticians, is exemplified in the fact that the cures almost never succeed.[98] The true melancholics like Anselmus, Nathanael, and Elis commit suicide. Viktorin dies without ever recovering from his desperate schizophrenia (melancholia with a fixed idea); Cardillac is killed while trying to carry out his own impulsive *idée fixe*. Countess Angelika, in "Das öde Haus," is plunged into a lifelong madness from which she never recovers and which necessitates her remaining under the close supervision of a private nurse. Gluck, Krespel, and Serapion live out their lives and their fixations in tranquillity. Some critics claim that even the apparently successful cure of Uncle Siegfried in "Die Genesung" is ironically intended because he is closer to the truth in his "madness" than is the surrounding society in the "sanity" to which he is restored.[99] We have already seen that Cyprian fails conspicuously to effect the cure of Serapion that he attempts in accordance with Reil's principles. And in "Das öde Haus" Theodor is cured of his fixed idea not by the efforts of Doctor K. and his animal magnetism but rather by the face-to-face encounter with raging madness in the person of the Countess Angelika, which jolts him into sanity. In short, even though Hoffmann relies heavily on contemporary works for the symptomology of madness—especially in the form of melancholy and partial insanity with fixed ideas—he is conspicuously critical with regard to the prevailing therapeutic notions. Most notably, he implicitly rejects the governing principle that the physician must maintain distance vis-à-vis the patient, keeping a clear distinction between reason and madness.

This rejection of the rationalist separation of reason and madness is related to Hoffmann's belief, as expressed by Cyprian in "Der Einsiedler Serapion," that in the person of the madman nature permits us to penetrate most profoundly into her secrets. That this attitude is not peculiar to Cyprian but is shared by Hoffmann is evident in the preferred structure of his fairy tales, in which the earthly action is paralleled and explained by a mythic action. In *Der goldne Topf* Anselmus is privy to the wondrous myth of redemption narrated in the third and the eighth vigils only because of his madness, which begins with hypochondria and is intensified through various accidents into a state of melancholy from which he never recovers. (The chapter headings, even more than the text itself, contain clues in technical terms to his psychological disintegration.) That myth—which attributes an allegorical role to the people who surround him in reality—is his fixed idea, and his suicide, when he plunges to his death from the Elbe River bridge, represents his attempt to enter his own *idée fixe* and its submerged kingdom of Atlantis.[100] Similarly the mystical underground realm of which Elis Fröbom becomes aware is a fixed idea attributable to the melancholy that characterizes him at the outset. To this extent Hoffmann shares the prevailing Romantic view of madness as a state of altered consciousness that provides access to privileged knowledge.

In another respect Hoffmann is less close to his contemporaries and, notably, the author of the *Nachtwachen*. For the madhouse as an institution is conspicuously absent from his works. There are brief references: Cyprian alludes by implication to the famous asylum in Bamberg directed by Dr. Marcus, and that same institution is cited by name in *Die*

*Elixiere des Teufels.* Toward the end of the novel Viktorin, trapped in the incurable fixed idea that he is the monk Medardus, shows up at the Capuchin monastery where the novel begins and ends. Convinced that the simple remedies of the monastery would not aid this desperate case, the prior "decides to hand the strange man over to the insane asylum at St. Getreu because I hoped that, if restoration should be possible, it would surely succeed for the director of that institution, a brilliant physician capable of penetrating deeply into every abnormality of the human organism."[101] And in "Der Sandmann" Nathanael, following an outburst of violence, is placed for a time in a madhouse but then released as wholly cured just a short time before he commits suicide by plunging to his death from the church tower (in another example of the failure of cure).

Generally, however, the madmen in Hoffmann's tales are more or less at liberty, and if they are under any sort of supervision, it is family care. Uncle Siegfried with his harmless fixed idea about nature in "Die Genesung" is attended at home by his family and their physician, Doctor O ...; the Countess Angelika is kept under close guard by a family attendant in "Das öde Haus"; Nathanael, following his release from the madhouse, remains at home in the care of his mother and fiancée, Klara. Others, with their harmless fixations, are permitted to roam about town and country. The narrator of "Ritter Gluck" is sitting in the well-known establishment of Klaus and Weber in the Berlin Tiergarten when he first encounters the strange figure who turns out to believe that he is the composer Gluck; and the performance of Gluck's *Armida* that "Ritter Gluck" produces takes place in a house that may well be a private asylum. Councillor Krespel, with his fantastic clothes and manners and his even crazier ideas, participates freely in the social life of his town: the house he designs without doors and windows, while not technically a madhouse, is literally a "mad" house because "it afforded from the outside the maddest appearance."[102]

Alternatively, perfectly "normal" social affairs turn into manic occasions. Professor Spalanzani's ball in "Der Sandmann," at which no one ("except very intelligent students"[103] ) notices that his "daughter" Olimpia is actually a mechanical doll, is like a scene from a madhouse. And at the punch party at Rector Paulmann's house (ninth vigil of *Der goldne Topf*) the conversation reaches such a state of craziness that even the host exclaims: "Am I in a madhouse? Am I myself mad?—What sort of crazy nonsense am I chattering?—Yes, I'm crazy, too—crazy, too!"[104] When he tears off his wig and hurls it against the wall, it is a signal for Anselmus and the other guests to shatter the punch bowl along with all the glasses. The point that Hoffmann very effectively makes through scenes such as this—the intrusion of "madmen" into "normal" society and the craziness, in turn, of the everyday world—is that the line that rational psychiatry tried to establish between reason and madness was not tenable. Sometimes madness may reach an extreme of frenzy that needs to be controlled, for the good of the individual and the welfare of society. But in many cases the condition perceived as "madness" by normal society is in fact either harmless eccentricity or even a privileged kind of knowledge and requires understanding rather than confinement—and in any case cannot simply be written off by medicine or law in a mechanical fashion.

Cyprian's tale is first greeted by Ottmar's skepticism and then by Theodor's Kantian horror at the possibility that he himself might succumb to madness in its presence and also that, as Pinel suggests, the victim of fixed ideas may often degenerate to a violent rage and strike out against everyone around like a raging animal.[105] In an effort to create a "gentle transition from madness through spleen to a wholly healthy reason" (38), Theodor volunteers to relate the story of "Rat Krespel." By the time he has finished, Lothar has had second thoughts about the meaning of Serapion, whom he now proposes as an exemplary figure. "Your hermit, Cyprian, was a true poet: he had really envisioned everything that he proclaimed, and for that reason his speech captivated your heart and spirit" (69). He explains that there is an inner reality and that people have the spiritual power to see this reality in full clarity and brilliance, but that all too often the external world in which we live veils or blurs the vision of the inner world. Serapion was blessed with the ability to see this inner world clearly with no interference from the external world of so-called reality. Accordingly Lothar proposes that Serapion should be the patron saint for their own poetic enterprises. "Let each of us test carefully whether he has really envisaged that which he undertakes to proclaim before he ventures to make it public. Let each of us at least strive seriously to comprehend the image that has arisen in his soul fully with all its figures, colors, lights and shadows and then, when he feels truly inflamed by it, to transmit the representation into external life" (71). The proclamation of this "Serapiontic Principle" amounts to the elevation of madness to an aesthetic principle.

· · ·

It was precisely Hoffmann's tendency to locate so many of his works on the borderline between myth and reality, between "madness" and reason, that caused him, as a judge, to have a profound respect for the misty area of uncertainty in legal issues—an uncertainty wholly uncharacteristic of rationalist law whether natural or codified. This Romantic approach to law caused him, in turn, to take a stance between the medical or institutional approach to insanity and the philosophical or theoretical approach. Hoffmann's own position is most clearly stated in the brief that he prepared in 1818—the year when he wrote "Der Einsiedler Serapion"—in connection with the trial of Daniel Schmolling, a thirty-eight-year-old tobacco worker accused of stabbing to death his girlfriend.[106] The facts of the case were not in dispute: according to the dying girl's own testimony as well as Schmolling's confession, he committed the crime and was charged with premeditated murder by the prosecution. The defense conceded all the facts, but the expert witness called by the defense, a physician named Merzdorff, argued that Schmolling should be acquitted on the basis of temporary insanity (*amentia occulta*) and remanded to a mental institution. When the case was handed over to the *Criminal-Senat* of the Prussian Supreme Court for an opinion, it was Hoffmann's responsibility to prepare the decision—a remarkable statement that provides full insight into his views on legal competence in two respects and into his own position vis-à-vis the psychiatric thinking of his day.

The lengthy document begins with an attempt to set out the areas of legal competence. The legal situation was spelled out clearly in the *Allgemeines Landrecht*: "In the case of persons who are incapable of acting freely, no crime takes place and hence no punishment" (20 1 §16). But this shift from punishment according to deed to punishment according to doer merely transferred the uncertainty from the law to the mind of the accused. According to rationalist theories, the law was neatly parceled off into tidily defined areas of competence, and the judge was not expected to question the competence of expert witnesses in their own fields.[107] Hoffmann argues that the physician's area of competence is limited to "knowledge of the physical organism" (90), not the psychic organism, and that the understanding of that spiritual principle is based on wholly different premises. For that reason, he reminds the reader, Kant had claimed the investigation of emotional conditions as the prerogative of the philosophical rather than the medical faculty; Hoffmann himself states that certain men, such as Karl Phillip Moritz (the editor of the influential *Magazin der Erfahrungsseelenkunde*), had displayed a profound psychological knowledge without being physicians. Consequently the physician should be regarded as competent in evaluating a state of insanity only if he can demonstrate the presence of symptoms in the physical organism that might have caused the mental disturbance. In the case of Schmolling the expert witness had been able to demonstrate neither organic causes nor any history of mental disturbance: the only cause adduced was what Schmolling called an "irresistible compulsion" to commit the deed.

Hoffmann cites Reil, Pinel, and other writers on the existence of such compulsions but refuses to cede total authority to them. "Principles established by writers in medicine and psychology can be of value for the criminal judge only when they are based on scientific experience and do not appear as hypotheses grounded merely in philosophical speculation" (98). Otherwise the judge would be distracted into the vague realm of possibilitity and would never reach the point of applying the law. "This would be the case especially when it is a matter of determining the soundness of mind of an accused person with regard to his emotional condition." At that point Hoffmann makes a statement that surely emerges from his life as a writer. "It is not vouchsafed to man ensnared in earthly life to fathom the depths of his own nature, and if the philosopher loses himself in speculations about this dark material, the judge must cling only to that which the most unambiguous experience has established" (99).

Having thus delimited the areas of competence of the medical expert and the philosophical psychologist vis-à-vis each other as well as the criminal judge, Hoffmann goes on to mark out the judge's responsibility. "Man's freedom, regarded metaphysically, can never be of influence on legislation and administration of justice; the moral freedom of man—that is, the capacity to determine his will and its active expression in accord with the ethical principle (*arbitrium liberum*)—is assumed as restricting the application of any punitive sanction; and any doubt regarding it [moral freedom] must be exposed with convincing force to the judge, if he is expected to heed it" (99). The theory of automatic compulsion, he continues, which is said to annul moral freedom, has no physical basis but is justified only by psychological observation. For this very reason the judge has not only the competence but also the responsibility to examine thoroughly any arguments concerning moral freedom. In the following lengthy section Hoffmann does just that, first considering "partial madness produced by a fixed idea" and then "periodic insanity," punctuating his discussion with novelistic examples borrowed from Reil and Pinel. But if the symptoms are lacking, the physician as well as the psychologist must draw his conclusions, as Merzdorff did, from the nature of the deed and the doer's own comments. "This may be permissible for the physician, the philosopher, the psychologist; the criminal judge, who starts with the assumption of the moral freedom of man and demands of him that, determined by the law, he resist the impulse to infringement, will not regard the law as inapplicable" merely because the motive was not evident and the criminal asserts that he was driven by an irresistible impulse (106).

Recapitulating other precedents from psychology, Hoffmann concludes that the condition of *amentia occulta* is a hypothesis without value for the criminal judge. He then examines Schmolling's testimony. "Who does not discover in the defendant's own portrayal, with the clearest outlines, the struggle of an evil intention with the better moral principle?" (111) Accordingly Hoffmann finds no reason to question the moral reason or sanity of the accused and no reason to exclude the penalty of death that has been recommended by the prosecutor. What is of particular interest here is not the decision itself. (In fact, the verdict was subsequently commuted to life imprisonment.) It is rather the process of reasoning by which Hoffmann reached his decision—a careful, well-informed process that betrays not just his detailed acquaintance with the psychiatric thinking of the day but also, more importantly, his delineation of a position midway between the clinical psychiatrists and the psychological philosophers. (Here again, as we observed in connection with Hoffmann's activities as a jurist, he insists on a distinction between deed and opinion.)

This position, which Hoffmann regards as the appropriate and absolutely legitimate one for the criminal judge, is at the same time precisely the position that we have already observed in his tales as the point of view of the writer. In the two decades since 1795 German literature has moved from the tentative intrusion of psychology into fiction that characterized the works of Spiess, Tieck, and Goethe, by way of the total fictionalization of psychiatry by Jean Paul and "Bonaventura," to the point in Hoffmann's tales at which fiction has become an autonomous mode of psychiatric thought. That development reveals, in turn, how the art of the age shaped itself through a tension of interaction with the institution of the madhouse, which itself was being transformed during those years from a hiding place for the incurably mad to a humane asylum for the alienated spirit.

CHAPTER FIVE

# The University:
# Model of the Mind

WHEN HENRICH STEFFENS reaches the point in his autobiography, *Was ich erlebte* (1840–1844), of recording his student years in Germany, he reminds the reader "that in Jena an enthusiasm [*Begeisterung*] from which all German literature received a new impetus was in its first moment of fresh, youthful formation just at the time when I had the fortune to experience its liveliest point of development."[1] Steffens concedes the philosophical differences that separated Fichte and Schelling, the idiosyncrasies of the brilliant young scientist Johann Wilhelm Ritter and other faculty members, and the temperamental vagaries of the writers and intellectuals assembled in Jena during the winter of 1798–1799. But what made that period so exciting, he continues, was "the spirit of unity that prevailed among the originators of such an important transformation in literature. Just as in any organic development the most varied shapes emerge, scarcely distinguishable, from a common point, . . . so, too, all of us believed in those days that we were carrying out a common task, and there arose a covenant of spirits that had a profoundly significant effect" (92).

One of the most rapturous descriptions of Jena just a few years earlier occurs in Johann Georg Rist's autobiography. Recalling the esprit de corps among the students in 1795, he writes: "To lead a free life, dedicated to learning, art, and friendship together—that was the extent of our modest wishes and hopes."[2] "What we desired and strived for," he recalls in the same passage,

> was great and excellent; what we achieved is little. But we do not
> on that account deprecate the lovely dreams of our youth. For those
> dreams were revelations of the great spirit from whose womb we

had progressed, pure and unconfused, through the phenomena of an old world; those dreams nurtured within themselves the ideal toward which man may never cease to strive, even if he finally persuades himself that he will neither attain nor catch sight of it in earthly shape.

A similar tone is evident in Rudolf Köpke's biography of Ludwig Tieck (1855), when he describes the first encounter of Tieck and Novalis, which took place during Tieck's visit to Jena in the summer of 1799.

A. W. Schlegel played the intermediary. In excited conversations they opened, tested, and recognized each other's heart; the barriers of quotidian life fell, and to the ringing of glasses they toasted brotherhood. Midnight approached; the friends stepped out into the summer night. Once again the full moon, the poet's old friend since the days of his childhood, was resting magically and gloriously on the heights around Jena.[3]

Later that year Tieck moved to Jena, where he lived in A. W. Schlegel's house, which was the center of activity for a group including Friedrich Schlegel, Fichte and Schelling, Novalis and Brentano, along with various others.

In blithe spirits they assembled in Schlegel's house for the common midday meal. . . . Here there took place in reality those intellectually lively social gatherings that he portrayed so masterfully in his late stories. . . . Schlegel read his poem on the actress Bethmann. On another occasion Novalis gave a lecture that summoned forth a zealous debate because people believed that he was professing Catholicism. Brentano recited his *Naturgeschichte des Philisters* on an occasion when Fichte was present.[4]

Tieck himself, dedicating the fifth volume of his *Schriften* (Berlin, 1828) to A. W. Schlegel, recalled those glorious days thirty years earlier: "That lovely time in Jena . . . was one of the most radiant and delightful periods of my life. You and your brother Friedrich—Schelling along with us— all of us young and striving—Novalis-Hardenberg, who often came over to visit us: these spirits and their multiple plans, our aspirations for life, poetry, and philosophy, constituted almost uninterruptedly a festival of wit, esprit, and philosophy."

Such scenes as these rapidly made their way into Romantic historiography. Rudolf Haym, in *Die romantische Schule* (1870), refers to Tieck's move to Jena in 1799 and to Friedrich Schlegel's return that same year.

The circle of Romantics had never before been so completely and so closely together. Never before had the interaction of the individual members of this circle been so multifaceted and vital—it was in every respect the true blossoming of Romanticism.[5]

It is hardly an accident that Ricarda Huch picked up the phrase *Blütezeit* to designate the first volume of her work on *Die Romantik* (1899–1902), which opens with a portrayal of that Jena gathering. And Jena has remained the code word for early German Romanticism ever since. As Karl Jaspers states in his monograph on Schelling: "From that brief period in Jena there radiates to us an exuberance of the spirit that appears to be historically unique."[6] In Gert Ueding's recent volumes on German literature during the age of the French Revolution he contrasts "Jena or the Dream of a Romantic People's Movement" with Weimar as the model of Classicism.[7] And in the introduction to his *German Romantics in Context* Roger Cardinal observes that "it is Jena that most deserves the name of birthplace of the Romantic school. For it was here that, in the space of a few years, a meeting of unique talents brought about the rapid and spectacular definition of the movement."[8]

For well over a century, then, Jena has been viewed as the *locus amoenus* in the mythic universe of German Romanticism—the site of the encounter between Tieck and Novalis, of the development of Fichte's *Wissenschaftslehre* and Schelling's *Naturphilosophie*, of collaboration on the journal *Athenaeum*, and of countless other *tableaux vivants* that constitute our image of that incomparable period of German cultural history. But the pervasiveness of the image has distracted our attention from another question that urges itself upon anyone who approaches the subject from a comparative point of view. That is, why did German Romanticism achieve its *Blütezeit* in a university town rather than, say, a political or cultural center? And of all the university towns in Germany, then why in Jena, which was notorious for being the rowdiest of all?

## THE CRITIQUE OF UNIVERSITIES IN EIGHTEENTH-CENTURY EUROPE

The reasonableness of the first question to any foreign observer is immediately apparent if we consider the situation in France and England.

In France, to put it most succinctly, any association during the revolutionary age between a cultural movement and the university would have been impossible for the simple fact that the university as an institution no longer existed. Following two centuries during which conservative universities torn apart by internal religious strife had resisted the philosophical trends of the times and all significant scientific and intellectual activity had moved into the academies, the urgent need for educational reform was obvious. On September 15, 1793, accordingly, colleges and universities throughout France were abolished by the *Convention nationale* and replaced by a group of state-run *écoles spéciales* dedicated to specialized training in specific fields: the École normale supérieure for teachers (projected in 1794 and finally realized in 1831), the École polytechnique for science and engineering (1794), and others that were gradually added. At the same time, literary and scientific inquiry was shifted into the three classes of the Institut national, under which label in 1795 the former Académie française had been reconstituted.[9] By a Napoleonic decree of March 17, 1808, the various special schools were organized into a grand hierarchy known as the Université impériale and, later, as the Université de France. What characterized the French system throughout the nineteenth century, until the universities were reconstituted in 1896, was the priority of secondary education over the higher faculties, the subordination of all education to the practical needs of the state, and the absence of any institution combining the higher faculties into one unified whole.[10] For that reason, while nineteenth-century literary heroes like Julien Sorel or Frédéric Moreau may pass through the seminary or study law, the university as an institution does not play a role either in their lives or in the lives of their creators. (For that we must wait for the brilliant group of *normaliens* who dominated French literature of the twentieth century.)

The situation in England, while not similar, was analogous. During most of the eighteenth century, one historian of the period has observed, undergraduates and fellows in Georgian Oxbridge suffered principally from an excruciating boredom that they sought to alleviate through drinking, gambling, and other pastimes. "This was the inevitable consequence of social and historical conditions which turned a university education into one of the least desirable alternatives for a student making the transition from boyhood to young adulthood."[11] Oxford and Cambridge amounted to little more than an extension of school, focused on training in the classics with compulsory chapel attendance, rather than a broad liberal education. And what, after all, could one expect from dons who were by profession clergymen and not university teachers? Even in the unusual cases when college fellows were not required to be in holy orders, most chose an ecclesiastical career, spending some ten to fifteen years as a don until they had accumulated seniority enough to be offered a college living and a position in the church.[12] In 1809 R. L. Edgeworth's *Essays on Professional Education*, in which he argued that "the value of all knowledge must ultimately be decided by its utility," triggered a debate on higher education that lasted until mid-century.[13] By 1852, when Cardinal Newman published *The Idea of a University*, the view had changed enough to accommodate education rather than religious training, but Newman still regarded the university as a place for the dissemination of knowledge—not its advancement.

> The view taken of a University in these Discourses is the following:—That it is a place of *teaching* universal *knowledge*. This implies that its object is, on the one hand, intellectual, not moral; and, on the other, that it is the diffusion and extension of knowledge rather than the advancement. If its object were scientific and philosphical discovery, I do not see why a University should have students; if religious training, I do not see how it can be the seat of literature and science.[14]

Under these circumstances it was possible for Wordsworth to record in book three of *The Prelude* ambivalent memories of his "gladsome time" at Cambridge. And Keats, during a one-month visit, might write to his sister Fanny, "This Oxford I have no doubt is the finest City in the world."[15] But the university hardly marked an important stage in the careers of the English Romantics who passed through it—often without completing a degree. In view of the conservative career patterns of the dons, it is not surprising that Oxford and Cambridge did not become centers of intellectual or cultural activity during the revolutionary period.

The situation at German universities during the eighteenth century was scarcely better than in France and England. Indeed, the rowdiness that prevailed among students was a common motif in the literature of the times.[16] During the seventeenth century the various versions of the Faust legend tended to criticize the institution with which that notorious learned doctor was said to have been associated.[17] The old chapbook of *Faust* (Widmann's version of 1599 as revised in 1674) has a three-page note (ch. 2, note 1) detailing the assertion "that sometimes young men at universities spend their time badly." The seventeenth-century editor (Pfitzer) warns well-intentioned mothers that the generous allowances they send their sons are often used "to cultivate the ladies instead of the books."[18] As a case in point, Eberhard Werner Happel's academic satire, entitled simply *Der akademische Roman* (1690), recounts the picaresque adventures of a group of German students in Italy and Germany, involving murder, erotic episodes, cheating, brawls, and virtually every sort of scandal. Two entire chapters are devoted to indictments of university education and academic practices: a Swiss traveler complains that bad people are often promoted to the rank of master, licentiate, and doctor contrary to the teachings and rules of the ancients (ch. 9); and another section amounts to a general catalogue of the pedantry and other short-comings of academies (ch. 24).

Suspicion of universities did not cease with the establishment of Halle in 1694 or Göttingen in 1737—two institutions explicitly founded according to modern rational principles of education and in opposition to the appalling conditions prevailing at other universities. Frederick the Great, who was generally contemptuous of German literature and culture, even made fun of the principal institution in his own state of Prussia. In his comedy *L'École du monde* (1748) Bilvesée returns to Berlin from Halle, where he has been sent by his pedantic father, M. Bardus, to study "la métaphysique, la physique et la plus sublime géométrie."[19] But Bilvesée instantly exposes his ignorance when his father inquires: "Eh bien, comment vont les monades?" (313). Bilvesée, having never heard of that philosophical unit, tries to conceal his ignorance with a variety of excuses. As it turns out, he has spent all his time drinking, chasing women, gambling, and brawling, as his servant Martin reminds him.

> "C'est que, mon cher maître, il aurait fallu plus étudier que nous n'avons fait. Je vous l'avais bien dit qu'en courant les rues toutes les nuits, en buvant le jour, en débauchant les filles lorsque nous n'avions rien de mieux à faire, en nous battant lorsque nous avions perdu notre argent au jeu, nous serions mal reçus dans la maison paternelle." (317)

Worst of all, Martin observes, is the fact that his master's essentially good nature was corrupted by the university: "Vous étiez si bon en partant d'ici; fallait-il vous envoyer à l'université, où le mauvais exemple, une dissipation continuelle, une license sans bornes" (319). Bilvesée loses his fiancée to another and is himself finally arrested when he breaks the windows of the bordello where he has been residing for two days. Frederick knew his university![20]

One of the most popular works of the century, the mock epic by Carl Arnold Kortum known as *Die Jobsiade* (1784; continued 1799), relates the "life, opinions, and deeds of Hieronimus Jobs, Candidate in Theology." The thirteenth canto describes how the ignorant and ill-fated Hieronimus arrives at the (unnamed) university to take up the study of theology among students of every discipline and from every land, most of whom, instead of studying, waste their time and money in high living.

Hieronimus, dem's Studiren zuwider,
Mengte sich bald unter die lustigen Brüder
Und betrug sich in kurzer Zeit schon so,
Als wäre er längstens gewesen do.

Dann so gut als der beste Akademikus
Lebte er täglich in Floribus,
Und es wurde manche liebe Nacht
In Sausen und Brausen zugebracht.

Wein, Tabak und Bier war sein Leben,
Er that dabei die Stimme hoch erheben,
Wenn er mit lautem und starken Klang
Das *Gaudeamus igitur* sang.[21]

(Hieronimus, finding his studies repugnant, soon joined the merry brothers and in a short time was behaving as though he had been there forever. Like the best academic, he lived daily in the flower of youth and spent many a night drinking and carousing. Wine, tobacco, and beer were his life; he raised his voice on high when, with loud and strong resonance, he sang *Gaudeamus igitur*.)

Hieronimus acquires a great reputation among his fellows as "a true model of loyal students": he battles with the detested police, proctors, and citizens ("Häscher, Pedellen und Philister"); seduces girls in the neighboring villages; shatters windows at night; brawls constantly; and, for occasional variety, attends lectures once every two months. He makes debts, cheats his creditors, pawns his books and clothes, spends time in the student jail, and is almost expelled. For three years he manages to deceive his parents in the letters in which he appeals for money (ch. 14). When he must finally return home, he has so few possessions left that he pretends that his goods have all been stolen. He buys an academic diploma from one of his professors for cash but cannot read it because it is written in Latin and Greek (ch. 16). It goes without saying that Hieronimus fails ignominiously when he is examined for a church position. Asked about the apostles, for instance, he replies that they are (in student jargon) the large pitchers in which beer and wine are served; he has never heard of St. Augustine, but he knew Augustin, the proctor, who often summoned him to the prorector's office; and so forth (ch. 19). From this point on, Hieronimus's fortunes decline until he dies (at the end of part one) as nightwatchman in his hometown of Schildburg.

The "Philanthropinist" Christian Gotthilf Salzmann provided the most extended attack on contemporary educational practices in his six-volume epistolary novel, *Carl von Carlsberg oder über das menschliche Elend* (1783–1788). Among the various social ills that he addresses we find conspicuously the university. In the first volume Colonel von Brav is summoned to the university town of Grünau to attend to his cousin, Carl, who has been wounded in a duel. (The colonel arrives in a state of distraction, for he has just discovered that his own son has been ravaged spiritually and physically by the masturbation rampant at his preparatory school.) On the day of his arrival he witnesses a student riot that takes place when the prorector attempts, as a result of Carl's duel, to impose a mandate against dueling and to imprison the aggressor. The students, regarding this move as an attack on their academic freedom, assemble at the marketplace singing bawdy songs and then barrage the prorector's house with stones, shattering his porcelain and almost killing his six-month-old child; afterward they seek to free their colleague from the academic jail but are driven off by the municipal soldiers (letter 24).

Following another incident of student boorishness in a tavern (letter 28), the colonel is assured by Carl and his friends that these crude students are not representative. "They look down with contempt at all other classes and call the most skilled, industrious citizens 'Philistines.' They even ridicule the classes that they hope someday to enter, making fun of the professor and the councilman, the minister and the officer. Preachers may never let themselves be seen in the lecture halls unless they want to be hissed at."[22] But they assure the colonel that the academies have improved a great deal in comparison with their state only fifty years earlier. Later in the story Carl is told by his friend Deacon Rollow that the fault does not lie with the men who teach at universities but with the very system of the institution, which was created for the times of the Crusades, when few people could read and write (letter 44). When Carl is expelled for a fight in which he was the innocent party, he challenges the prorector regarding the rules. But the university official defends the existing procedures, asking how otherwise "one can prevent a group of six to eight hundred young men, who lack supervision and wearying work and who are for the most part without moral principles, from leading a lecherous life" (I, 267). Salzmann's view of universities as medieval institutions unsuitable for the modern world was so broadly accepted that for the next two decades reformers had to come to grips with his criticism.

In view of the generally scandalous behavior of students and the notoriety of universities, it is hardly surprising that the new Prussian legal code (ALR), when it was promulgated in 1794, contained an entire section on universities (II 12 §§67–129: "Von Universitäten"). A few of the paragraphs deal with students' rights, but most of the sections concern "Academic Discipline" (§§84–96) and laws governing indebtedness (§§99–126). In general, students were subject to the laws of the land and the municipality; discipline was left in the first instance to academic officers, but their responsibility was spelled out in no uncertain terms. "In particular, brawls, debauchery, and other student excesses leading to public nuisance or to disturbance of the common peace and security must be emphatically punished" (§85)—usually by incarceration during hours when the offender was not expected to attend lectures. However, there were limits beyond which transgressions would not be tolerated. "Repeated crude excesses, insubordination to the academic senate or to its employees entrusted with the execution of academic discipline; instigation to rebellion, rabble-rousing, and the seduction of others must be punished by expulsion" (§89)—in which case the expelled students must immediately leave the town as well as the university.

Under the circumstances reflected in the literary texts as well as the laws, it is hardly surprising that in the course of the eighteenth century there were calls from many sides, as in France and England, for the reform and even the abolishment of the entire institution of the university.[23] First, the new spirit of bourgeois utilitarianism, coupled with the need for economic security following the Seven Years War, caused many citizens of the middle class to turn away contemptuously from the pedantry of what they considered a medieval *Gelehrtenuniversität* and to demand secondary schools in which the general populace could be trained in useful skills. Second, the Prussian state emphasized practical training that would produce young men qualified to fill posts in government and society. The new university at Halle had been created in 1694 expressly to prepare students for technical and utilitarian purposes, not for scholarship or learning as such. Consistent with this aim, the university elected to its chair of law Christian Thomasius, the first scholar in Germany who lectured in the vernacular rather than Latin. Together with his colleague, the pietist theologian August Hermann Francke, Thomasius shaped Halle into the first university with a recognizably modern professional curriculum, which in 1717 added such innovations as chairs in economics and public administration. At the same time, the cause of decentralized education was advanced in Prussia by the establishment of a series of specialized schools in Berlin: the Collegium Medico-Chirurgicum (1724), a mining academy (1770), a school for veterinary medicine (1790), the Pépinière for military doctors (1795), the academy of architecture (1799), and an institute for agriculture (1806).

By the last decade of the century many serious reformers were calling for the abolishment of universities, which were regarded as relics of a past monastic life and utterly unsuited for present realities, while the very title of "professor" had become a cue for ridicule. This call was tied to the shift of intellectual endeavors into the scientific academies that had been established during the eighteenth century, notably in Berlin (1700), Göttingen (1751), and Munich (1759). The educational reformer Johann Heinrich Campe (1746–1818), who began his career as tutor to Wilhelm and Alexander von Humboldt and then went on to assist Basedow at his Philanthropinum in Dessau, published in 1792 his wide-ranging reform proposal: *Allgemeine Revision des gesammten Schul- und Erziehungswesens von einer Gesellschaft praktischer Erzieher*. Campe argues for a radical separation at the secondary level between schools for scholars and schools for other citizens because scholarly learning is useless for professionally active citizens; indeed, it may even be harmful. Accordingly, Campe calls for the abolishment of the universities, which are constitutionally incapable of dealing with the moral turpitude that prevails there: the students believe that they have outgrown all discipline, and the professors have no understanding of ethical training.

A similar proposal was circulated in 1795 by J. G. Gebhard, the preacher in Berlin, to members of the influential Wednesday Club (*Mittwochgesellschaft*), arguing that the educational needs of society are better served by institutions of a different sort and that disciplinary measures are most appropriately administered by the civil courts. Meanwhile, conditions at many universities had become grievous: because there were so many universities—each state, no matter how small, insisted on having its own—they became an intolerable budgetary burden, especially at the end of the century when secularization and mediatization removed the financial basis that had often supported universities. Public support became so weak that, during the Napoleonic era, twenty-two, or over half, of the universities in Germany did in fact disappear in what has been termed the "mass death" of universities.[24] Some had become so peripheral and small that they simply disappeared (Rinteln, Dillingen, Helmstedt); others were suspended by Napoleon (Cologne, Mainz, Trier); still others were eventually incorporated with existing institutions (Altdorf with Erlangen, Wittenberg with Halle, Frankfurt an der Oder with Breslau).

## The Situation in Jena

Now if matters were generally bad at most German universities, with Halle and Göttingen representing mild exceptions, they were notoriously appalling at Jena. When Friedrich Wilhelm Zachariae (1726–1777) wrote his celebrated mock epic *Der Renommist* (1744), he was a student at Leipzig, which under the influence of Gottsched and his followers was acquiring the reputation of being the most fashionable—that is, the most French in tone—university in Germany. It is symptomatic that Zachariae chooses as the anti-hero of his work Raufbold ("Ruffian"), a student who has been expelled from Jena and has come to Leipzig to continue his education.

> Den Helden singt mein Lied, den Degen, Muth, und Schlacht,
> In Jena fürchterlich, in Leipzig frech gemacht.[25]

(My song sings the hero whom sword, boldness, and battle rendered dreadful in Jena and insolent in Leipzig.)

At Jena, we learn, it has been his role to carry a big sword, to brawl in the marketplace, to sing in public, to booze day and night, to cheat his creditors, to curse constantly, and never to study. Following a particularly heinous offense, he is "relegated" and promptly looks up some old friends from Jena who have also sought refuge in Leipzig, where they continue their old ways.

> Ihr Singen war ein Schreyn, und ihre Freude Raufen:
> Sie haßten Buch und Fleiß, und ihr Beruf war Saufen.

(Their singing was a shrieking, and brawling their delight:
they hated book and diligence, and their profession was booze.)

The plot concerns the efforts of the goddess Galanterie, with the assistance of Sylvan—a former Jena student who has been transformed into a Leipzig fop (*Stutzer*)—and the lovely Selinde to reform Raufbold and teach him fashionable manners. Their efforts fail; Raufbold and his friends depart for Halle; and the goddess Galanterie sets out on what we take to be the futile attempt to conquer Jena.

Through Zachariae's work, which enjoyed a huge popular success, the term *Renommist* ("braggart") became inextricably associated with Jena and its students. But there is ample other evidence for the notoriety of the institution. In one of the autograph books that eighteenth-century students carried we find the following typical inscription from 1746 concerning the drinking, sexual, and dueling practices at Jena:

Die Gläser geschwänket, gesoffen, gespien,
Die Jungfern geküsset, ein Vivat geschrien,
Zu Dorfe gelaufen, geschlagen, gewetzt,
Ist, was in Jena die Pursche ergötzt.[26]

(Waving glasses, guzzling, vomiting, kissing the maidens, screaming Vivats, running off to the villages, dueling, whetting—that's what delights the students at Jena.)

Elsewhere we hear of a drinking ritual practiced in Jena in the second half of the eighteenth century: the conferring of the degree of *Doctor cerevisiae et vini* (doctor of beer and wine). For this purpose a special Faculty of Beer, with its own dean, assembled in a local inn. The candidate selected three opponents (in an analogy to oral examinations) and was required to drink as much beer as they consumed. Following the properly accredited consumption of beer, the successful candidate was named *Doctor cerevisiae* and henceforth entitled to inscribe himself in all autograph books with the title *Dc*.[27] It is symptomatic that the archetypal student song—*Gaudeamus igitur*—was first set to music and adapted for modern celebrations in Jena around 1745.[28]

One of the most exhaustive sources for student life in the later eighteenth century is the autobiography (1792–1802) of F. Ch. Laukhard, M.A., who attended the universities of Giessen, Göttingen, and Halle and then taught briefly at Halle before his debts drove him to enlist in the army just before the outbreak of the revolutionary wars. Laukhard, a connoisseur of universities, seized every occasion to visit those at which he was not enrolled. He was fascinated by Jena from his earliest days at Giessen because the ambience of the students in Giessen, we hear, was totally oriented toward Jena: so many students sent down from Jena came to Giessen to complete their studies that they set the tone for the "Brüder Studio" in the much smaller university.[29]

Laukhard was delighted when he had an opportunity to visit Jena. "The tone of the Jena students suited me perfectly; it differed from that in Giessen only through a greater degree of coarseness. The Jena student—in those days, at least—knew no compliments; fine manners were called *Petimäterei* [from *petit-maître*], and a crude tone belonged to proper style" (102). Laukhard finds that, true to its reputation, it is easy to get involved in a duel in Jena, but because each duelist has a good second, they rarely result in dangerous wounds or death. With his new friends he visits the outlying villages and meets a number of "nymphs" who desolate the wallets, the health, and the morals of the youths (103). He also makes contact with the local chapter of his fraternity, the *Amizisten*, but finds its members unusually restrained because shortly before his arrival an official inquiry had been made into their behavior. Jena was the first university at which the fraternities in 1791 published the rules for student conduct known as *Komment*, a volume that provided the basis for all subsequent works of that sort.[30] Small wonder that Goethe, when he went to Weimar in 1775, immediately learned that "the academy at Jena ... had remained somewhat behind the times and was threatened with the loss of very capable teachers."[31]

During his entire career at Weimar Goethe was greatly concerned with the university at Jena—first as a member of the duke's Privy Council, then (following his return from Italy in 1788) as a minister without portfolio, and finally as the celebrated *éminence grise* of the archduchy.[32] Despite—or perhaps precisely because of—his own mixed experiences at Leipzig and Strassburg, Goethe was convinced that a strong university was essential for the intellectual health of Saxe-Weimar and that the institution must be firmly in the hands of the faculty. His attitude emerges clearly from the report that he submitted to Duke Carl August on April 30, 1786, concerning the regional fraternities (*Landsmannschaften*) at Jena. For years, as the literature indicates, these fraternities, of which there were fifteen at Jena, had been a source of great concern to the students, the faculty, the municipal authorities, and the government. On December 30, 1785, in response to a duel with fatal consequences, Carl August had requested from various professors their proposals for dealing with the situation.

Goethe chaired the committee charged with reviewing the proposals and preparing a recommendation.[33] Taking a conspicuously hard line, he began his report by noting that "fraternities and other student organizations can perhaps not be completely eradicated, but they can be weakened."[34] To this end he recommended that the senior administrative council (*consilium arctius*), consisting of the prorector and the four deans, be enlarged to include four respected faculty members. "Why," he asks, "should men who spend their lives in one place and have experience and authority not be able to deal with young people who change at least every three years?" This expanded council should undertake three initiatives: oversee admissions to insure, in particular, that students dismissed by other universities not be admitted; supervise the behavior of students with the assistance of an increased number of proctors; and expel harmful members as expediently as possible. (Goethe notes that the council already had the right to dismiss students for poor academic performance, but he wants to expand its authority to include students accused repeatedly of bad behavior.) He appended to his official report a *promemoria* to the duke in which he explained the importance of letting the fraternities understand that these measures did not stem simply from a few crotchety professors but rather from the duke himself as *Rector magnificentissimus* of the university.

Improvement, however, did not come about rapidly. Professors dependent upon registration fees for their lectures, as well as townspeople dependent upon student trade, hesitated to offend their potential audience and customers. As a result, as Schiller reported to Körner on August 29, 1787, following his first visit to Jena: "That the students here count for something is evident at first glance; and even if you closed your eyes, you would know that you're walking among students because they saunter with the steps of one who has never known defeat."[35] He concedes that "on the whole, the manners of the students here have greatly improved. One no longer hears much about duels, but not a week passes without some incident." Similarly, in the report on German universities that Friedrich Gedike prepared for Friedrich Wilhelm II of Prussia in 1789, he was able to write that "the students of Jena were formerly notorious for their crudeness and wildness. Now the tone has improved to an extraordinary extent. Yet there are still quite a few traces of the former crudeness."[36]

The tensions reached their peak in the years from the French Revolution until 1795.[37] In February 1790 a series of conflicts between students and the local militia led to a fight in which many students were brutally mistreated. (Goethe was sent to investigate the situation, and the duke had to intercede.) Two years later matters again became critical. In response to a truly intolerable situation, a number of students inspired by democratic ideals of the Revolution organized in an effort to do away with duels at Jena, proposing the establishment of a student court that would be empowered to deal with affairs of honor.[38] Many professors, however, as well as the privy councillors in Weimar, objected to yielding any power to the students. The state became involved, and Goethe made extensive notes for a report.[39] In the course of the negotiations, however, there occurred on June 10, 1792, another brawl between students and militia that went to violent extremes. When Carl August sent a committee of inquiry and, at the same time, strengthened the Jena garrison, the students regarded these actions as an assault on their academic freedom. This time the students resisted not by violence but by boycott: on July 19 approximately six hundred students (from a student body of some eight hundred fifty) decided to leave the university and transfer to Erfurt—a move that would have had dire economic consequences for the town of Jena. Goethe observed the procession, which took the students to the outlying village of Nohra, where, following extensive negotiations with the government of Weimar, they decided on July 23 to return to Jena with the promise of no disciplinary measures. On August 22 Goethe's administrative colleague Voigt was able to report to the duke that "our Jena Jacobins are quiet."[40]

The final act took place at the end of 1794 and during the first half of 1795. When Fichte arrived at Jena in May of 1794, he delivered a popular series of public lectures on the responsibility of the scholar. Encouraged by the success of the first series, he decided to continue the lectures in the following winter semester and included in his remarks an attack on the student secret societies (of which there were three in Jena) as an offense to academic freedom. Impressed by his arguments, representatives of the three societies approached Fichte and declared that they wanted to dissolve the societies by pledging an oath in his presence and handing over their books to him. When Fichte had the bad judgment to make an official matter of this informal approach, the students became mistrustful and turned against him. They disrupted his lectures, shattered the windows of his house—according to the old tradition—on New Year's Eve, insulted his wife on the streets, and threatened him with violence. Because his security could not be guaranteed, he obtained from Carl August the permission to suspend his lectures and to withdraw to Osmannstedt until matters could be resolved. In May and July, finally, the student aggression became so outrageous that the government, with the agreement of the prorector and the faculty senate, determined to suppress all resistance. Massive military reinforcements were sent to Jena; many students were jailed; many others were expelled. The influence of the fraternities was shattered for years to come. In their place Fichte's supporters established a Society of Free Men (*Gesellschaft freier Männer*), which marked the beginning of a reform of student life in Jena and, eventually, in Germany.

. . .

It seems unlikely, in light of everything we have reviewed, that a movement as intellectual as German Romanticism should have been associated with any university, much less with Jena. Yet precisely because the students at Jena pushed matters so far that extreme measures had to be taken, the situation there showed the first signs of real improvement. Not overnight, to be sure! When Caroline Schlegel—herself the daughter of a professor at sophisticated Göttingen—first arrived in Jena, she reported: "Just between us, the students still look more barbaric than the ones in Göttingen; it seems to me as though they all had a rather brownish *teint*."[41]

Schiller was also under no illusions: following his inaugural lecture of May 26, 1789, he wrote to Körner that he sensed no receptiveness or "preparatory capability" among the students. Indeed, he felt "that between the lectern and the listeners there is a kind of barrier that can scarcely be surmounted."[42] Almost ten years later Henrich Steffens described in amusing detail how Fichte, "already acquainted with the deficiencies of his listeners," sought to make his *Wissenschaftslehre* comprehensible to them."[43]

"Gentlemen," he said, "pull yourselves together; enter your innermost selves, for we are not talking here about anything external but only about ourselves."—The students seemed truly challenged to turn inward. Some changed their positions and straightened up, others relaxed and closed their eyes; but it was obvious that they were all waiting with great anticipation to see what would now follow this challenge.

Despite Fichte's best efforts to explain the difference between the *Ich* and the *Nicht-Ich*, however, it was obvious to Steffens "that young men, who stumbled so hazardously on their first attempt at speculation, could arrive in the course of their further efforts at a very dangerous frame of mind." Indeed, J. G. Rist, who subsequently became one of Fichte's most devoted apostles, recalls his initial dejection when Fichte's theory undermined his earlier beliefs. "I gradually became ice-cold as I saw everything disappearing around me, the accustomed world with its cheerful colors, the pleasures of the senses and what the heart loved in nature, whose bodily child I liked to call myself. In its place there now appeared a gloomy, formless chaos, a no-thing."[44] And in 1802 Crabb Robinson was amused to sit in Schelling's lectures on speculative philosophy with "more than 130 enquiring Young Men listening with attentive ears to the Exposition of a Philosophy, in its *pretensions* more glorious than any publicly maintained since the days of Plato & his Commentators. . . . I shall smile at the good nature of so great an assembly; who because it is the fashion listen so patiently to a detail which not one in 20 comprehends And which fills their heads only with dry formularies and mystical rhapsodical phraseology."[45]

Yet there were a number of reasons why Jena, despite the student disorders and the inadequacies of the student body, turned out to be an attractive place for scholars and intellectuals.[46] In the first place, it provided an unusual degree of academic freedom. Owing to historical circumstances—complicated dynastic partitions and territorial shifts within the realm of the Saxon Ernestines—Jena was in an absolutely unique situation: it was answerable not to one single state authority but to four so-called *Nutritoren*: Weimar, Coburg, Gotha, and Meiningen.[47] The advantage of this arrangement was the lack of coordination and supervision among the four supporting states: the professors at Jena were usually able to do whatever they liked since official decisions required the agreement of all four courts. The professors boasted about this circumstance, as Schiller reported to Körner following his first visit. "The authority over the *academie* that is distributed among four Saxon dukes makes it a rather free and secure republic in which suppression cannot easily take place. . . . The professors in Jena are almost independent people and don't need to worry about any princely personages. Jena is ahead of all other academies in this respect."[48] Gedike, noting the same situation in his report to Friedrich Wilhelm II, went even further: "A professor cannot receive even a reprimand from any one of the courts, but the four courts must agree on the matter."[49]

Secondly, the lack of centralized princely responsibility had one pronounced disadvantage that, paradoxically, contributed to its appeal: Jena was notorious for its low salaries, especially in comparison with such recent establishments as Halle and Göttingen.[50] In order to compete for faculty, the supporting states had to be willing to tolerate new ideas, and they had to rely heavily on young teachers. It was not without significance, moreover, that Jena, situated within the territories protected by the Treaty of Basel, was not subject—from 1795 until 1806—to the Napoleonic measures that closed down and disrupted so many other universities in southern and western German lands. As a result, toward the end of the eighteenth century Jena often attracted brilliant young scholars at the start of their academic careers—Fichte, Schelling, and Hegel, to mention only the most conspicuous—who tended to move on to other wealthier or more illustrious institutions as their fame grew. During their tenure, however—often as junior faculty without chairs—they contributed mightily to the intellectual excitement of the university.

A third reason for the attractiveness of Jena was the presence of Goethe and Schiller. Schiller became a member of the faculty in 1789 and, though he stopped lecturing in 1793, continued to take an interest in university affairs until he moved to Weimar in 1799. Goethe resided in nearby Weimar but was frequently in Jena on university business, to attend meetings of the Naturforschende Gesellschaft (where he first met Schiller), or to visit other Jena cultural and scientific institutions—hospital and maison d'accouchement, botanical garden, zoological and anatomical collections, library, societies for mineralogy and natural history, and the *Allgemeine Literatur-Zeitung*—of which he wrote solicitously in his report of 1806 to Napoleon's minister of war.[51] Their presence, especially Goethe's, was a magnet for a generation of writers and intellectuals, from Novalis, Hölderlin, and Fichte to the Romantics who assembled in Jena at the end of the decade. As Crabb Robinson observed, in radical contrast to English academies, "The protestant German Universities in general are nothing but places of Union for Men of Letters & Students, with more or less advantages of public Libraries, Cabinets of natural history, And Professors in all the various Sciences & Arts."[52]

Thanks in large measure to Goethe and his administrative colleague Christian Gottlob Voigt, the university made a number of excellent appointments in the years following 1785.[53] The theological faculty was especially strong, with Johann Jakob Griesbach, Johann Christoph Doeder-lein, and H.E.G. Paulus. Gottlieb Hufeland was the outstanding jurist, while Justus Loder, Christoph Wilhelm Hufeland, and Johann Christian Stark brought new vigor to the medical faculty. Carl August's practical interests were largely responsible for the establishment of new chairs in chemistry, botany, and mineralogy, along with facilities for the study of those subjects. But it was especially in the field of philosophy that Jena became the leading German university in the two decades from 1785 to 1806. The university had already established itself as a center of mod-ern—that is, Kantian—philosophical studies in 1785 with the creation of the *Allgemeine Literatur-Zeitung*, which was in effect a journal for the dissemination of Kantian ideas. These views were represented on the faculty by the scholar of natural law Gottlieb Hufeland, by the theologian of ethics Johann Wilhelm Schmid (who was known as "Moralschmid" to distinguish him from his theological colleague Carl Christian Erhard Schmid), and especially by Wieland's son-in-law, the philosopher Carl Leonhard Reinhold. Reinhold's commitment to Kant was so passionate that Schiller reported to Körner in 1787: "In comparison with Reinhold you are a scorner of Kant, for he claims that in a hundred years Kant will have the reputation of Jesus Christ."[54] Reinhold's ardent Kantianism drew the students to his lecture rooms in ever larger numbers, with no fewer than six hundred of Jena's eight hundred students attending in 1793. Indeed, so great was the appeal of philosophical speculation at Jena that Schiller, Woltmann, and other lecturers in history saw their students depart in masses.[55]

Because Reinhold's career was blocked by the two chaired professors of philosophy, he accepted a call to Kiel in 1794, so his position had to be filled. Despite widespread concern about his "democratic" views—he had just published a book explaining the French Revolution—Voigt summoned the thirty-two-year-old Fichte to his first university position, and Jena entered a five-year period of philosophical glory. Fichte had made his reputation with his anonymously published *Versuch einer Kritik aller Offenbarung* (1792), which was at first generally attributed to Kant. Accordingly it was as a Kantian that he was brought to Jena. But with the publication of his *Grundlage der gesammten Wissenschaftslehre* (1794), which was prepared as a lecture guide for his students at Jena, it became apparent that Fichte was no mere popularizer of Kant, as Reinhold had been, but the exponent of a new theory of philosophical idealism. While Fichte's tenure in Jena was not untroubled—owing to his own principled stubbornness as well as fraternity opposition and the authorities' increasing dissatisfaction with his ideas—many students regarded him as the "pride of our century."[56] The Society of Free Men established by his students provided not only a source of opposition to the influence of the *Landsmannschaften* and secret societies but also an occasion for the discussion of democratic ideas.[57] When he was forced to resign in 1799 as a result of the so-called "Atheism Conflict," a petition signed by 260 students was sent to Weimar demanding his reinstatement: "No one can claim, as a leader to the truth that we seek, such a high degree of confidence and devotion of all students as Fichte."[58] Authority prevailed, and Fichte departed for what became a spectacular career in Berlin.

However, the tradition of philosophical idealism at Jena remained unbroken; Fichte's place was taken by his younger colleague Schelling, who had been appointed in 1798 and whose less abstract *Naturphilosophie* had greater appeal for Goethe and Carl August. Even when Schelling departed for Würzburg in 1803, Hegel was still in Jena, where he completed his first great work before his departure in 1806. As a result, the students in Jena bore witness to the birth of three of the most significant phases of German philosophical idealism: Fichte's theory of knowledge, Schelling's philosophy of nature, and Hegel's phenomenology of mind. When Crabb Robinson arrived in Jena in 1802, he reported that "Jena is the most fashionable Seat of the New Philosophy," going on to explain the subtleties of "the Critical School," which "is infinitely divided into sects whose points of difference would not be intelligible to those who are ignorant of the common character of the whole."[59] It is no wonder that the young intellectuals who constituted the first wave of Romanticism were attracted to Jena by this atmosphere of intellectual excitement.

ROMANTIC THEORIES OF THE UNIVERSITY

The university was not simply a gathering ground for Romantic intellectuals. Many of the most creative minds of the age were challenged by the sense of academic ferment—and specifically at Jena—to address themselves to university matters. Indeed, it is symptomatic that so many young intellectuals—like Schiller and Fichte at Jena—used their inaugural lectures as an occasion to discuss the university and to express their views on the nature of the institution that would be the suitable locus for the intellectual excitement of the era.

Schiller was called to Jena on Goethe's recommendation because of the success of his history of the Netherlands: *Geschichte des Abfalls der vereinigten Niederlande von der spanischen Regierung* (1788). As it turned out, his venture into academia was a serious error. He was not properly qualified for the post and spent agonizingly long hours in preparation for his lectures. He was resented by many of the older professors, who scoffed because he was incapable of delivering his lectures in Latin. On the insistence of the chaired professor in history, his title had to be changed from history to philosophy. Because he was a supernumerary professor without salary, he was dependent upon lecture fees; as a result, when his enrollments fell off drastically following the first few weeks—because of competition from the speculative philosophers and his own inadequacies as a lecturer—his finances suffered, and he found it necessary to devote less time to his lectures and more to income-producing writing. By 1793 Schiller gave up teaching altogether, even though he maintained his formal connection with and interest in the university.

His "adventure on the cathedra," began, however, with a spectacular success, as he reported to Körner in a letter of May 28, 1789.[60] As a new professor, Schiller had announced a series of lectures entitled *Introductio in historiam universalem*, to be delivered twice weekly from six to seven in the evening. By half past five on the appointed evening (May 26) the lecture hall was already full of students who had come to hear the famous author of *Die Räuber*. In Jena, as at most other universities, professors had to provide their own lecture halls—normally in their own houses. Schiller had obtained the use of Reinhold's hall, which held about one hundred students. Because of the overflow crowd he requested the use of the largest hall in town, that of Professor Griesbach, and he takes great pleasure in describing the rush of the students down the longest street in Jena to get a good seat in the new auditorium. Schiller held his *Antrittsvorlesung*, therefore, before an audience of about four hundred students. The lecture was a sensation, he reported to Körner. All evening long people in town talked about nothing else, and the students appeared before his lodgings to sing a serenade and to honor him with a triple *Vivat!*

The lecture that created such a sensation was the introduction to his course on universal history, *Was heißt und zu welchem Ende studiert man Universalgeschichte?*, which was delivered on two successive evenings. It is Schiller's central thesis that citizens of the modern world, even in the most mundane situations of bourgeois life, are "the debtors of past centuries" (761).[61] He sees world history as a succession of events leading from the origin of all being down to the present. It is the task of the Universal Historian to select from the entire sum of these events those "which have had an essential, incontrovertible, and easily traceable influence on the *present* shape of the world and the condition of the presently living generation" (762). In sum, Schiller intends to review with his audience the people and events from world history that have contributed to shaping the reality in which the bourgeois citizens of modern Germany live.

The theme that constitutes the culmination of the second evening's lecture was preceded on the first evening by a more general statement on the nature of academic study. Schiller begins by emphasizing the responsibility of the teacher, whose duty it is to bring truth to his students. But in a typical shift he quickly emphasizes the moral aspect of history, which contains within itself the entire moral world. As a result, every student has something to learn from history, regardless of his future career. At this point Schiller makes his famous distinction between the narrowly focused, professionally oriented student, who is studying only in order to make a living (the *Brotgelehrte*), and "the philosophical mind" ("der philosophische Kopf"), who has a nobler purpose. Schiller is contemptuous of the *Brotgelehrte* not merely because he concentrates so narrow-mindedly on his specialized studies and pays no attention to the rest of the world of learning but also—and more importantly—because people trained in that way actually suppress reform and hold up progress.

> Every expansion of his bread-science makes him uncomfortable because it demands new work from him or invalidates past work; every important innovation startles him because it shatters the old school form that he worked so hard to acquire; it places him in danger of losing the entire work of his earlier life. Who has cried out more at reformers than the mob of bread-scholars? Who holds up the progress of useful revolutions in the realm of knowledge more than they? (751).

Because he has acquired his knowledge for a purpose and not for its own sake, he requires affirmation from outside—in the form of public acknowledgment, honors, provisions. "He has searched in vain for truth if truth does not convert itself for him into gold, newspaper praise, princely favors" (751). He cannot tolerate the purposelessness (*Zwecklosigkeit*) that constitutes the prerequisite for objective judgment and feels torn from all context "because he has neglected to relate his activity to the great whole of the world" (752).

The philosophical mind works in wholly different ways, seeking to unify where the bread-scholar differentiates.

At an early point he convinced himself that in the realm of reason, as in the world of the senses, everything is related, and his vigorous drive for harmony cannot content itself with fragments. All his strivings are directed toward completion of his knowledge; his noble impatience cannot rest until all his concepts have organized themselves into a harmonious whole, until he is standing in the middle of his art, his science, and from this point surveying its realm with a satisfied gaze. (752)

He is delighted, not made uncomfortable, by new discoveries because they fill a gap and help him to complete his image of the whole. Even if new learning should destroy the whole structure of his knowledge, he is happy because "he has always loved truth more than his system." Since he is not learning for the sake of a one-track career, he takes delight in every object of his attention. "It is not *what* he does that distinguishes the philosophical spirit, but *how* he deals with what he does" (753).

Schiller ends this introduction by reminding his listeners that they must make the decision for themselves. He intends to address his lectures only to the second type, the philosophical mind, because the bread-student degrades scholarship too much from its lofty purpose and makes too great a sacrifice for too trivial a profit. But for the philosophical mind, he concludes, universal history contains invaluable lessons. "It will kindle light in your reason and a beneficial enthusiasm in your heart. It will disabuse your mind from the common and petty view of moral matters" (765). The students at Jena had not been accustomed to hear university education discussed in these terms, which made serious demands upon their commitment, and the initial enthusiasm is still understandable when we read Schiller's words today. Even if they soon deserted Schiller's lecture hall, his theme was brought home to them with a vengeance by the compelling moral presence who took the lectern in 1794 and developed an entire philosophical system based on what Schiller called, in passing, that "midpoint" (*Mittelpunkt*) from which the philosophical mind surveys and unifies its field of knowledge.

• • •

Fichte's five years in Jena constituted at once the philosophically most creative and personally most tumultuous period of his life. The lustrum that ended with his forced resignation, over strong protests by his student admirers, began with an equally controversial sensation. For his first semester at Jena, Fichte had announced a "private" series of lectures that amounted to the first exposition of his *Wissenschaftslehre*. Concurrently he proposed a series of "public" lectures on the ethics of the scholar— "Moral für Gelehrte" or, in the Latin formulation for the Catalogus praelectionum, *de officiis eruditorum*.[62] The lectures, which began almost five years to the day after Schiller's *Antrittsvorlesung* and in the same hall, met with a similar success. As he wrote to his wife on May 26, 1794: "Last Friday I held my first public lecture. The largest auditorium in Jena was too small; the entire entryway, the courtyard outside was full, they were standing on tables and benches."[63] Four weeks later—for his audience did not desert him—he received both a serenade of "solemn music" and the traditional *Vivat!* And by the time Hölderlin arrived in Jena the following November he could report to his friend Neuffer that "Fichte is at present the soul of Jena."[64]

But despite—or, more likely, because of—the huge success, Fichte was almost immediately undermined by several of his envious colleagues. Thanks to his recent publications on the French Revolution (notably *Beitrag zur Berichtigung der Urtheile des Publikums über die französische Revolution*, 1793), he had arrived in Jena with a reputation for radical sympathies. Accordingly, as Voigt reported to Goethe on June 15, two professors had zealously notified Weimar that Fichte was "a terrible Jacobin" who had proclaimed in his lecture that in ten to twenty years there would be no more kings or princes.[65] (What Fichte actually said in the second lecture was: "The state, like all human institutions that are mere means, tends toward its own destruction: *it is the purpose of all government to make government superfluous*."[66]) Fichte, as soon as he learned of the charges, wrote indignantly to Goethe on June 24 that he was not lecturing on politics but that he had no intention of concealing his ethics: "I have no special *summer* and *winter ethics*."[67] To demonstrate his innocence he proposed to publish the first four lectures verbatim just as he had delivered them. It is those lectures, plus a fifth lecture on Rousseau, that appeared that fall under the title *Einige Vorlesungen über die Bestimmung des Gelehrten* (1794).

Owing to the continuing popularity of his lectures—Fichte, unlike Schiller, was a compelling speaker, and students stood on ladders at the windows to hear him—he planned to continue the series in the following winter semester. But again Fichte encountered difficulties. First, in an honest effort to avoid scheduling conflicts with other professors and in the belief that his essentially ethical topic was suitable for the occasion, he chose the hour of 9 A.M. to 10 A.M. on Sunday mornings. When it was pointed out that this hour conflicted with services in the town church, he shifted the second lecture to the time slot beginning at 10 A.M. By this time, however, the church council, which chose to interpret the scheduling as an intentional offense, had asked the duke—despite student protests—to prohibit the continuation of his Sunday-morning lectures. By the time the matter was straightened out in February 1794 and Fichte had moved his lectures to Sunday afternoons, the university situation had changed. New disorders had arisen in connection with the secret societies, and when Fichte used his lectures to criticize these societies as an offense against academic freedom, the students turned against him and caused him to cancel his lectures for the semester.

Despite all the difficulties in Jena, the subject of these lectures obviously concerned Fichte, for he returned to the same material in 1805 for his *Antrittsvorlesung* at the University of Erlangen: *Über das Wesen des Gelehrten, und seine Erscheinungen im Gebiet der Freiheit* (1806). Essentially the same ideas provided the basis for his lectures "Über die Bestimmung des Gelehrten" at the University of Berlin in 1811 (published the following year in the journal *Die Musen*).[68] Yet the essentials are present in the Jena lectures of 1794. Indeed, to the extent that they were written just at the time when Fichte was making the first public presentation of his *Wissenschaftslehre*, they betray more clearly than subsequent versions their indebtedness to Fichte's philosophical system and represent the social concretization of the abstractions of his theory of knowledge.

Fichte would not be Fichte if he proceeded directly to the matter at hand—that is, the vocation of the scholar. Instead, he begins the first lecture ("Über die Bestimmung des Menschen an sich") by defining the vocation of mankind according to the dialectical terms of his epistemology: "The scholar is a scholar only to the extent that he is opposed to other human beings who are not scholars" (27).[69] Fichte clarifies his meaning through an analogy familiar to the students attending his concurrent lectures on *Wissenschaftslehre*. While it is not true that the pure Ego is a product of the Non-Ego, nevertheless the Ego can become conscious of itself only in its empirical determinations. "The pure Ego can only be imagined negatively: as the opposite of the Non-Ego, whose nature is multiplicity—hence as complete absolute oneness" (29). The loftiest goal of mankind, he concludes, is "the complete agreement of man with himself" (31)—a condition that he designates as "identity." It is for this reason, he continues in the second lecture ("Über die Bestimmung des Menschen in der Gesellschaft"), that man can define himself only within society, which he characterizes as "the relations of reasonable beings to one another" (34). That is to say, we require the conception of rational beings outside and different from ourselves in order to achieve self-identity and self-awareness. Accordingly "the social impulse belongs among the basic impulses of man" (37). The concept of man is an ideal concept because it is unattainable. Indeed, Fichte maintains that "we are still standing on the low step of half-humanity or slavery. We have not yet matured to the sense of our freedom and autonomy" (39).

Up to this point the first two lectures look like nothing so much as modifications of the first principle of the *Grundlage der gesammten Wissenschaftslehre*: that is, "*das Ich setzt sich als bestimmt durch das Nicht-Ich*" (III. §5). At the beginning of the third lecture Fichte recapitulates: the scholar can define himself as a scholar only when he is viewed within the larger society. But the scholar is not just a member of society; "he is also a member of a particular class or institution [*Stand*] within that society" (42). Before he can go on, Fichte realizes, he must come to grips with another problem: how does it happen that there are different classes of men? Physical inequities can be attributed to nature, but social inequality would appear to be a moral dilemma. Fichte proposes to justify class distinctions on purely rational grounds. He reminds us that nature—that is to say, the Non-Ego—is by definition manifold. No part is completely like any other part; "it follows therefrom that it also has a pronouncedly different effect on the human spirit" (43). This, in turn, produces differences among individual human beings. But how does this differentiation relate to the final goal of all society: the total equality of all its members? (44) At this point the *social* impulse of rational creatures offsets the mistake that nature has made: "the one-sided development that nature has bestowed on the individual becomes the property of the whole race; and the whole race in return gives the individual its own development" (44). Reason insures that each individual receives from society that shaping [*Bildung*] that the individual could not win directly from nature. Reason wages a constant battle with nature, in other words, in which society as a whole achieves the goal that the individual alone can never attain.

While the process described hitherto produces different *characters*, it still does not account for different *classes*. At this point Fichte introduces the principle of human freedom: for each individual is free to chose the profession or class for which he feels most suited by nature and in which he wishes to make his contribution to the social whole. We do not have the right to work simply for our own pleasure. We must strive to pay the debt that we owe to society for all that it has provided us. Fichte reminds us that we are indebted to all the great names of history who have worked for us and from whose efforts we have all benefited. In order to repay society for all that it has done for us as individuals, we choose a profession or class that is closest to our inherent abilities through which we can serve society. But we make that choice individually in absolute freedom, for every individual must be a free collaborator in the grand plan, not a compelled and suffering instrument. "Every individual has the duty not only to seek to be useful to society generally but also to devote to the best of his knowledge all his efforts toward the ultimate purpose of society—ever to ennoble the human race, that is, to make it ever free from the compulsion of nature, ever more independent and spontaneous" (49). Out of the inequality of individuals, Fichte concludes, a higher equality arises: "namely, a steady progress of culture in all individuals" (49).

Having disposed of the seeming dilemma of inequity among the various classes, Fichte turns in his fourth lecture to the topic of his series: the vocation of the scholar ("Über die Bestimmung des Gelehrten"). While the goal of society is the development and satisfaction of all human needs, most men are by definition incapable of surveying those needs because they are limited to the standpoint of their own special class or profession. "The concern for this uniform development of all human abilities presupposes the knowledge of his total abilities, the science of all his impulses and needs, the completed measure of his entire being" (52). Among the various human impulses is also an urge to *know*; and it is the cultivation of this talent that has called forth a special class or profession for its satisfaction: the scholar.

Fichte differentiates three different kinds of knowledge that constitute what is known as learning or scholarship. Philosophical knowledge, based on purely rational criteria, studies the abilities and needs of mankind. Philosophical-historical knowledge, based in part on experience, seeks to understand by what means those needs can be satisfied. Historical knowledge, finally, ascertains what stage mankind has reached in its progress and what needs and satisfactions are appropriate for the contemporary world. The true vocation of the scholarly profession, Fichte sums up, is "the supreme surveillance of the real progress of the human race in general and the constant furthering of this progress" (54) as humanity moves toward its perfection.

The scholar, therefore, has essentially a social responsibility: more than any other class he exists through and for society and possesses to the highest possible degree the social talents of receptiveness and the ability to communicate. To the extent that he exists to communicate to other men a feeling for truth, the scholar is by vocation the teacher [*Lehrer*] of mankind (56). But he must not be content with that general message. To the extent that he shows mankind the needs that arise at a given time and in a specific society as well as the means for satisfying them, the scholar is also the educator [*Erzieher*] of humanity (57). The ultimate purpose of every individual as well as the whole society is the ethical ennobling of the whole man. But no one, Fichte perorates, "can successfully work at ethical ennoblement if he is not himself a good person" (57). Accordingly the scholar must in the final analysis be the ethically finest man of his age and should embody the highest possible level of ethical refinement. In lucid awareness of his place in history Fichte states that the course of future races, the world history of nations still to be, will emerge from his works. "I am a priest of truth" (57). He concludes his powerful fourth lecture with the concession that an emasculated and nerveless age cannot tolerate the message he has preached, but he expresses his confidence in the young men sitting before him, who are still young enough to be immune to the enervation of the age.

This was a heady message for the students of Jena, who saw themselves challenged by the most compelling moral presence of the age not merely to lift themselves out of the mire of brutishness that had hitherto characterized their university but also to prepare themselves to be the teachers, the educators, and even the priests of mankind. Small wonder that they flocked to Fichte's lectures by the hundreds and offered him serenades and *Vivats*! But it is equally clear why Schiller was captivated by the lectures, which he recommended to his friends and cited in the fourth of his letters *Über die ästhetische Erziehung des Menschen* (1795). For Fichte, albeit at greater length and with greater rhetorical passion, was addressing precisely the same problems that Schiller had dealt with in his inaugural lecture. The parallels are evident in at least two respects. First, like Schiller, Fichte stresses the role of history: the individual is a link in the great chain extending from the emergence of the first man by way of the full consciousness of his existence down to eternity (49). We are indebted to the past, and in all our actions must be concerned for the obligation that we bear to the future. Indeed, Fichte's use of the vocable *Weltgeschichte* (58) would seem to be an allusion to Schiller's lecture five years earlier. Second, Fichte's understanding of the scholar and his role as opposed to the more specialized social estates is closely analogous to Schiller's somewhat more invidious distinction between the *Brotgelehrte* and the "philosophische Kopf." In both cases we sense a clear anticipation of the academic transformation that Kant was to formulate a few years later in his three essays on *Der Streit der Fakultäten* (1798): the transformation, namely, that catapulted philosophy—that is to say, the arts and sciences—out of a subservient position as mere prerequisite for theology, law, and medicine and into a new superiority over and above all the specialized professional faculties. Most importantly, however, in Fichte's lectures we see emerging the view that all knowledge is a unified whole, that the scholar is the individual whose role it is to understand that unity, and that the university is the place where such understanding most appropriately takes place. We can easily comprehend why a reading of these lectures subsequently persuaded Savigny to become a professor of law rather than a practicing cameralist.[70]

• • •

Fichte—partly for reasons of temperament, partly for reasons of political opposition among his colleagues—failed to achieve the great reforms that he announced in his *Antrittsvorlesung* of 1794. In 1799 his enemies succeeded in driving him out of the university on charges of atheism.[71] His successor, the brilliant young Schelling, addressed himself to issues of the university under wholly different circumstances. When he took the podium in the summer of 1802 to deliver his *Vorlesungen über die Methode des akademischen Studiums* (1803), the precocious twenty-seven-year-old had already published his most important philosophical works—*Ideen zu einer Philosophie der Natur* (1797), *Von der Weltseele* (1798), and *System des transzendentalen Idealismus* (1800)—and was on the point of leaving Jena to accept a chair at the University of Würzburg. In several respects his lectures on university study constitute the most accessible summary of his early philosophy: the theory of "identity" or *Duplizität*.

Rather than working his way systematically, like Fichte, from the vocation of mankind to the vocation of the scholar, Schelling begins his series of fourteen lectures straightaway with the most fundamental question: "Über den absoluten Begriff der Wissenschaft."[72] Schelling worries that the talented young man at the beginning of his academic career is confronted initially with a curriculum that looks either like an undifferentiated chaos or, at best, a broad ocean on which he is afloat without compass or guiding star. Accordingly he argues that universities should provide a course of general instruction concerning the purpose and nature of academic study (4). This concern is doubly important, he continues, because in science (*Wissenschaft*) as in art the particular is valuable only in its relation to the whole. It frequently happens that even a first-rate jurist or physician loses sight of the larger mission of the scholar—Schelling actually uses a phrase ("des durch Wissenschaft veredelten Geistes") that evokes Fichte—in his effort to master his particular field (4). It is philosophy, he maintains, that seizes the whole human being, liberating his mind from the limitations of a unilateral education and elevating it into the realm of the general and the absolute.

Accordingly recognition of the organic whole of the sciences must precede special training in a given field. The individual must understand how his particular field is related to the harmonious structure of the whole and must recognize "the living unity of all sciences" (5). This recognition is especially critical, Schelling claims, in the present age, "when everything in science and art appears to press more urgently toward unity" (5). Such a view, he repeats, can be expected only from the science of all science ("Wissenschaft aller Wissenschaft"), namely, philosophy, whose purpose it is to strive for the totality of all cognition (6).

Following these introductory paragraphs, Schelling establishes the basic principle underlying his entire argument: "the idea of an absolute knowledge that is only One and in which also all knowledge is only One, that primal knowledge [*Urwissen*] that, separating into branches only on various levels of the phenomenal ideal world, expands into the whole immeasurable tree of knowledge" (6). As a corollary Schelling stresses that in this absolute knowledge there can be no distinction between the Real and the Ideal. It is this essential unity and identity of the unconditionally ideal and the unconditionally real that constitutes the first presupposition of all science, since science can deal with the ideal only as it is reflected in the real. (Schelling stresses that he is speaking about *Urwissen* and not about the individual sciences, which have separated from the totality and its primal image [*Urbild*].) Any thought that is not conceived in this spirit of unity and totality is empty and objectionable. "Since all knowledge is only one, and every aspect of it enters the organism of the whole merely as a member, all sciences and kinds of knowledge are parts of the one philosophy—namely, the effort to take part in the primal knowledge" (8). Schelling concludes this general statement with the reminder that the realm of the real is characterized by temporality and necessity—that of the ideal by infinity and freedom.

The last section of this first lecture deals with the principal objection, as Schelling sees it, to his belief in the absoluteness or unconditionality of science: that is, the objection that knowledge is nothing more than a means to which action is the end. At this point he elevates earlier discussions by Schiller and Fichte on the nature of the specialist or *Brotgelehrte* to a level of high philosophical abstraction. If it is in the nature of the absolute, Schelling recapitulates, for the absolutely ideal to be at the same time the real, then this fundamental "duplicity" must find its expression in every act of absolute knowledge. Accordingly "the opposition, in which the two entities within the same identity of primal knowledge occur as knowledge and action, takes place only for the merely finite conception" (10). "Temporal knowledge as well as temporal action posits only conditionally and successively that which in the idea is unconditional and simultaneous" (10). Those who assume that knowledge is nothing but a means toward the end of action, therefore, have no conception of knowledge other than from everyday activity. Such "apostles of utility" (11) will never appreciate philosophy. But the student who has learned from philosophy will understand that "there is no true freedom except through absolute necessity, and between the former and the latter there exists the same relationship as between absolute knowledge and absolute action" (12).

Having dealt with "the absolute concept of knowledge," Schelling turns in his second lecture to the scientific and ethical vocation of the universities ("Über die wissenschaftliche und sittliche Bestimmung der Akademien")—that is to say, from the conception of the totality of the sciences to the special conditions under which the sciences are taught in universities. Science, to the extent that it is a temporal phenomenon, seeks to ground eternity within time. That is, it seeks to come to grips with the ideal through its manifestation in the real. To the extent that it expresses itself through the individual, science is bound by time; yet science is essentially independent of time to the extent that it has a generic existence that is eternal. "It is therefore essential that, like life and existence, so also science communicates itself from individual to individual, from generation to generation" (14). It is in this transmission that science expresses its eternal life.

This thought leads Schelling to the notion of human history, much as was the case with Schiller and Fichte. "It is inconceivable that man, as he

now appears, raised himself by his own means from instinct to consciousness, from animality to reasonableness" (14). The record of what went
before is captured in myths of the gods and the first benefactors of mankind. In earlier times the lofty ideas that motivated men were expressed
intuitively in images and customs; morality was the spirit of the whole
community, and science lived in the light of the public life and organization. Gradually, however, as life became more internalized, science also
was separated from external reality. "The modern world is in all respects,
and especially in science, a dissociated world that lives simultaneously in
the past and present" (15). The study of the sciences as well as the arts
began to become increasingly historical, and the philosopher began to
recognize the intentions of the world spirit in history.

Now it is one thing to make the past into the object of science; it is
quite another to put knowledge of the past in place of true science. For
in the second case the access to true reality is closed off; no idea has
significance for such scholars until it has gone through other minds and
been digested there. And it was in this spirit that the first academies or
universities were established. "Their entire scientific organization would
like to derive itself wholly from this dissociation of science from its primal model through historical learning" (16). In order to simplify their
task, they have separated the great mass of knowledge into separate
branches and "shredded the living organic structure of the whole into the
smallest pieces." It is Schelling's challenge to universities to restore the
unity lost by this particularization and to return to a treatment of all
sciences in a consciousness of the whole and of an absolute science.

The tendency toward particularization has been furthered in part by
the state, which has made universities into instruments to serve its special
needs. Schelling is aware of the trend around the turn of the century to
suspend the universities or to transmute them into technical schools. But
that cannot be done without destroying all progress. External completeness alone does not produce that true organic life of all areas of knowledge to which universities aspire—universities, Schelling adds, that got
their name from that tendency toward unity of knowledge. "Only the
general is the source of ideas, and ideas are the living substance of science" (18). The specialist who knows only his own field and is not capable
of recognizing its general implications is unworthy of being a teacher or
keeper of the sciences. He can make himself useful in various ways, but
he will never advance the cause of science. Such specialists, who appreciate nothing but the utility of learning, regard universities merely as

institutions for the transmission of science. But the teacher who merely transmits, Schelling insists, will often transmit falsely. In science, as in the meanest craft or art, it is necessary to give evidence of mastery before man can practice his art as a master. But that is not at present the case in our universities. Because our universities hitherto have functioned according to a one-sided vision, they are not true universities but only institutions that exist for the sake of learning—not *Wissenschaft*.

As long as bourgeois society pursues empirical goals rather than absolute ones, it can establish no true inner identity. But universities by definition can have nothing but an absolute purpose. At universities nothing should have any value except science, and no differences should be acknowledged other than those created by talent and education. Mindful of the reputation of his own university, Schelling reiterates Fichte's admonition that "privileged idlers" who spread uncouth behavior at universities should not be tolerated (22). The realm of the sciences is not a democracy and certainly not an ochlocracy, but an aristocracy in the noblest sense of the word. Talent requires no protection as long as its opposite is not favored. "The capacity for ideas creates of itself the loftiest and most decisive effect" (23). This force of ideas, Schelling concludes, is the only politics required in institutions for science.

Following the two introductory lectures on the nature of science or knowledge and the nature of the university, Schelling turns to other matters in his remaining twelve lectures. He stresses the need for proper training in study and memory for anyone who intends to enter the university and emphasizes the prerequisites of analytical logic and foreign (especially classical) languages (lecture 3). Then he offers, as a model for the external organization of universities reflecting the inner unity of the sciences, a "general encyclopedia of the sciences" (32). In a survey of the pure sciences of reason, mathematics and philosophy (lectures 4–6), he maintains that philosophy should not constitute a separate faculty as it is the basis for all other faculties to the extent that they profess the action that is the aspect in historical reality that ideal knowledge assumes (lecture 7). Thus theology is the external form that deals with the science of the absolute divine being. Jurisprudence is the real form that deals with the science of history and law. And medicine is the mode that deals with the science of nature and the organism. Lectures 8–13 deal in greater detail with the three faculties, the real and ideal aspects of their subjects, and the relation of the special field to the whole of scientific knowledge. The series concludes, rather surprisingly, with a lecture on the science of art, by which Schelling means the historical aspect of literature and the arts. For universities, he stresses, are not professional art schools. They should deal with the intellectual, not the empirical, aspect of the arts. Yet the essence of art is just as appropriate a subject for the philosopher as are theology, law, and medicine. Art stands in the same relationship to philosophy as does the real to the ideal. While philosophy is capable of resolving the ultimate oppositions of knowledge in pure identity, it remains itself always opposed to art as the ideal vis-à-vis the real. "Each encounters the other on the final peak and each, by virtue of their mutual absoluteness, is the other's image and reflection" (119). The forms of art are the forms of the primal things. Philosophy of art is therefore representation of the absolute world in the form of art. This concern with the absolute forms of art has nothing in common, Schelling notes, with those activities that parade at present under the name of aesthetics, the theory of the fine arts, and others. Yet because art represents a magic and symbolic mirror in which the philosopher views the inner being of his own science, "philosophy of art is the necessary goal of the philosopher" (122). With this surprising twist, which relates the lectures to Schelling's own *Philosophie der Kunst* (1802) and the conclusion of his *System des transzendentalen Idealismus* (1800), Schelling ends his contribution to the philosophy of universities.

It is obvious that the three series of Jena lectures on the nature of the university have certain basic notions in common. First—from the "midpoint" from which Schiller proposed to see all knowledge, by way of Fichte's *Gelehrte*, who surveys all knowledge, to Schelling's ideal conception of *Wissenschaft*—all three see knowledge as a totality, a unified whole, in sharp contrast to the merely voluminous erudition that in their view had characterized education down through the Enlightenment. It is this conception of a unified science that finally led Schelling, with a certain degree of etymological latitude, to define the university as the place where such cognition properly takes place. Second, all three see the universe of knowledge not merely as a synchronic whole, an *encyclopedia*, but also as a diachronic organic process—as a history in which the individual consciously assumes his place. At the same time, the scholar earns his place in the university not merely by recapitulating existing knowledge but, through a process of creative scholarship, contributing to knowledge and (for Fichte, at least) to society. Third, their lofty view of the university leads all three to distinguish sharply and rigorously between the rightful citizens of the world of knowledge and those who do not belong in such lofty surroundings: Schiller's "philosophical mind" as opposed to the *Brotgelehrte*, Fichte's *Gelehrte* as opposed to the specialists, and—in the final abstraction—Schelling's knowledge or science as opposed to temporal action. Fichte and Schelling, finally, placed philosophy at the center of the university curriculum in an effort to provide precisely that unified view of knowledge that would bring together the previously disparate fields of the arts and sciences as well as the professions of law, medicine, and theology.

In every case, of course, the lecturers were speaking to an audience whose experience included both the student riots at Jena (that is, the students who had no place in the ideal academy) and the efforts on the part of some reformers to abolish universities altogether or to convert them into "useful" special schools. In sum, all three lecture series reflected the lively debate of the 1790s concerning university reform. But their implicit conclusion was, in each case, that the university should respond to criticism not by forsaking its mission but rather by giving a new role of central authority to philosophy and the arts, which are capable of restoring meaning to an institution that has been floundering. Schiller, Fichte, and Schelling raised the discussion of *Wissenschaft* and the nature of the university to a theoretical level that was not attained in most contemporary contributions.

## THE JENA MODE OF DISCOURSE

In the light of these lectures it is easy to understand why the early Romantics felt comfortable in Jena. The university as idealized by Schiller, Fichte, and Schelling embodied precisely the principal themes of Romanticism as we have observed them in earlier chapters. The view of the university as the concretization of a unified knowledge within a historical context—for all the differences between Fichte's *Wissenschaftslehre* and Schelling's *Identitätsphilosophie*—finds its analogy in the Romantic view of mining as well as law. The aspiration toward unity is evident both on the microscale of the Romantic metaphor, in which disparate elements were brought together in an illuminating new configuration—what Novalis in *Die Christenheit oder Europa* called "the magic wand of analogy" ("den Zauberstab der Analogie"[73])—and on the macroscale of the Romantic *Enzyklopädistik* to which Friedrich Schlegel, Novalis, and Hegel aspired.

As Novalis put it in numerous jottings in the collection *Das allgemeine Brouillon* (1798–1799), which bears the subtitle "Materialien zur Enzyklopädistik": "The theoretician of knowledge ["der Wissenschafts-Lehrer"] deals only with knowledge as a whole—Has to do only with the sciences as such./ The *WissenschaftsLehre* is a true, autonomous, independent encyclopedics."[74] Elsewhere he notes that encyclopedistics "contains scientific algebra—equations. Relations—similarities—equalities—effects of the sciences one upon the other."[75] Around the same time Friedrich Schlegel observes in a similar tone that "poetry must and will now be reformed and centered through encyclopedia and through religion." "The *encyclopedia* becomes harmonious development in poetry, enthusiasm in religion."[76] Similarly Hegel begins his *Philosophische Enzyklopädie für die Oberklasse* (1808) with the statement: "An encyclopedia has to consider the entire extent of the sciences according to the subject matter of each and according to the basic principle of each."[77] It is wholly consistent with this belief in a unified world of knowledge that Alexander von Humboldt entitled his great lifework, in which he attempted to synthesize and harmonize all our knowledge and understanding of the physical world, *Der Kosmos* (1845–1862).

In short, the impulse toward unity and toward a conception of all nature and reality as a single unified whole that characterizes Romantic thought is reflected perfectly in the new conception of the university as a place in which all knowledge is concretized in faculties unified by the centralizing authority of philosophy and understood in the context of its historical development. When Friedrich Schlegel wrote in his famous *Athenaeum* fragment (no. 116) that "Romantic poetry is a progressive universal poetry," intended to unify all the separate genres of poetry and to reunite poetry with philosophy and rhetoric, he was restating essentially the message of unified knowledge in a historical context that had been expounded by Schiller, Fichte, and Schelling in their lectures on the nature of the university. To the extent that the ancient distinction between the student and the Philistine was translated by the Romantic theoreticians of the university from the social to the intellectual and redefined in such a manner as to distinguish the true scholar-critic-intellectual from the specialized *Brotgelehrte*, these thinkers also created a category within which scholars and intellectuals could feel equally at home.

There is no need to belabor the thematic parallels between this conception of the university and other Romantic ideals. René Wellek has pointed out that one view of the European Romantics on which virtually all scholars and critics have been able to agree is the belief in an organic nature viewed by a unified consciousness.[78] It would be surprising if this fundamental belief did not show up here as well, particularly since that belief in a unified nature began at the universities as philosophical theory and worked its way out from there into the broader public consciousness.

On another level altogether, however, we can observe a less conspicuous but ultimately highly pervasive influence. I believe that we can speak of a Jena mode of discourse that constitutes the common denominator of the seminal writings produced by this generation of early Romantics. I would like to suggest that the mode of these works, quite distinct from that of English and French contemporaries as well as that of the preceding and following literary movements in Germany, is fundamentally the discourse of the academy—"academy" understood here both in the sense of the Platonic academy as well as the university lecture hall. It is a striking fact that many of the basic works of early Romanticism were in fact originally presented as lectures—either at the university or publicly. In addition to the three series of lectures that we have just discussed, let us recall that Fichte's *Wissenschaftslehre* was first made accessible in 1794 as lecture notes for his students at Jena and disseminated by his students at least as rapidly as through his actual publications. The fact that Hegel began his academic career at Jena (1801–1806) is suggested by the circumstance that most of his major works from his Berlin years (1818–1831)— the philosophy of history, of religion, of nature, as well as the aesthetics and the logic—are known to us only from the lecture notes preserved and edited by his students. While Schleiermacher did not teach at Jena, he was in spirit and by association a member of that group. Consistently his dialectics as well as his ethics were developed originally as lectures for his students at Halle and Berlin.

However, it is not just works of philosophy that are indebted to the Jena mode. Arguably the most important critical works of the Schlegel brothers, both of whom began their careers on the faculty at Jena, were presented to the public as public lectures: A. W. Schlegel's *Vorlesungen über schöne Literatur und Kunst* (Berlin, 1801–1803) and his *Vorlesungen über dramatische Kunst und Literatur* (Vienna, 1808); indeed, the impact of the earlier series, in which for the first time Schlegel sought to define the difference between "Classic" and "Romantic," was achieved solely through the public hearing because the text was not published until 1884. Friedrich Schlegel's greatest critical work, his *Geschichte der alten und neuen Literatur*, was presented to the public as a series of lectures in Vienna in 1812. And it can be attributed to the model of Jena discourse that so many other basic works of German Romanticism made their initial impact in the form of lectures: e.g., the onetime Jena student Gotthilf Heinrich Schubert's *Ansichten von der Nachtseite der Naturwissenschaft* (1808), as well as Adam Müller's *Elemente der Staatskunst* (1809).

Related to the *Vorlesung* is the form of the public oration, to which we owe not only Schleiermacher's *Reden über die Religion* (1799) but also such characteristic socio-political works as Fichte's *Grundzüge des gegenwärtigen Zeitalters* (1804–1805) and his powerful *Reden an die Deutschen* (1807), as well as Novalis's "oration" *Die Christenheit oder Europa* (1799). It is immaterial that neither Schleiermacher's *Reden* nor Novalis's "oration" was ever formally delivered before an audience. What matters in the present connection is the authors' conviction that the proper rhetorical mode for the presentation of their ideas was not the essay or the treatise but the lecture or talk or oration—whether in a university lecture hall, in a public forum, or in a small group of friends.

If the *Rede* represents the public aspect of the university *Vorlesung*, then its more intimate hypostasis is the dialogue or symposium, the third popular rhetorical form of the Jena mode. As we shall observe in the next chapter, A. W. Schlegel chose to elaborate his thoughts on the visual arts in the form of a dialogue (*Die Gemählde*), while Schelling (*Bruno*) and Solger (*Erwin*) developed their theories of aesthetics in colloquies. Fichte, dismayed over the lack of public understanding for the various versions in which he had produced his *Wissenschaftslehre*, sought to remedy the situation with his *Sonnenklarer Bericht an das größere Publicum, über das eigentliche Wesen der neuesten Philosophie* (1801), which is cast in the rigorous academic form of a dialogue between "the Author" and "the Reader" in six "Lessons" (*Lehrstunden*). Fichte was especially partial to dialogue around this time. The second book of *Die Bestimmung des Menschen* (1800), in which he sought to outline the implications of "the newer philosophy" for non-academic purposes, consists wholly of a dialogue between the doubting *Ich* (by whom Fichte in his preface explains that he means what we would today call the implied reader) and the spirit of knowledge (*Wissen*). And Schleiermacher, the translator of Plato, made one of his most important statements on the nature of religion in *Die Weihnachtsfeier* (1806), a symposium among a group of friends gathered to celebrate Christmas Eve. In sum, the modes of discourse preferred by the Jena Romantics show the pronounced influence of the lecture hall and the seminar room—spaces ideally suited to the kind of

*Symphilosophieren* of which Friedrich Schlegel, Novalis, and their contemporaries so often spoke.

• • •

It is only against this background, I believe, that we can understand the common denominator linking three otherwise utterly disparate works written in Jena in the closing years of the century. Clemens Brentano's "facetious treatise" *Der Philister vor, in und nach der Geschichte* was first published in 1811 following its reading to the members of the Christlich-Deutsche Tischgesellschaft in Berlin. But the central passages—minus a certain anti-Semitic animus as well as the conservative attacks against Hardenberg's reforms, which were added later—are based on a satirical essay on the "Naturgeschichte des Philisters" that Brentano recited in 1800 in the Schlegel circle while he was still a student at Jena.[79] Brentano's satire is not simply an attack on the Philistine—in itself of course a topic characteristic of the university—but also a travesty of academic style, from its title to the individual parts. The work begins with a list of fifteen theses to be defended and then proceeds to deal with the prehistory of the Philistine, including theosophic views of God and the Creation, the Fall of Lucifer and Adam, and Christian myth down to the time of Ham. "Der Philister in der Geschichte" traces the story from Ham to Goliath and then, following a review of the material, makes a great leap to the present. The central section on "Der Philister nach der Geschichte" begins with a typically Jena strategy—a parody of Fichtean method. (According to Köpke's account, as we noted earlier, Fichte was present when Brentano read his treatise to the circle in Schlegel's house.) Brentano begins by ascertaining that the term "Philistine" was appropriated in modern times by students to apply to a class of people who are nothing but a pale imitation of the mighty Philistines of history.

> Philistine, therefore, was the name for all who were not students; and if we take the word student in the broader sense of one who studies—someone eager for cognition; a person who has not yet sealed shut the house of his life like a snail (the true house-Philistines); a person caught up in the pursuit of the eternal, science, or God; who lets all the rays of light joyfully play in his soul; a worshipper of the Idea—then the Philistines stand opposed to him, and all who are not students in this broader sense of the word are Philistines.[80]

The playful parody of the Fichtean positing of the *Ich* and *Nicht-Ich* continues in the succeeding paragraph.

> If I now call studying an active suffering or a receiving of all cognition, of an infinitely unified, eternal cognition, then I could call the student perfected in his individuality (that is, the Non-Philistine) the person who receives and gives with equal vigor at all points of his being; and such a one I imagine as a sphere; I call him the healthy, the natural, the cultivated man; but in order to approximate my opinion to the image I shall call him that one whose contact with the external world, whose skin (to state it in a leathern manner) breathes in and exhales in equal measure. Goethe appears to me to be among all I know the one whose ideal phenomenon I would in the first instance label such a one.

Following this definition of the student, who is posited in opposition to the Philistine, the treatise continues with the portrayal of a model Philistine with his characteristics (*Philistereien*) and provides a long list of *Philistersymptome*. The treatise concludes with an explanation of the copperplates and a digression on the question as to whether the wife of a Philistine is therefore necessarily a Philistine—indeed, can a woman be a Philistine? In a postscript Brentano notes that the University of Helmstedt displays in its coat of arms an image of Samson strangling a lion, and concludes from that fact that the name Philistine, as the opposite of student, must have been initiated at that university. The final genealogical table of Philistines ends with the question: "Is it possible that the dead are also Philistines?" (1016).

. . .

If Brentano's travesty of the academic dissertation represents a zany spoof of Jena themes and modes, we can see a more serious adaptation of the same discourse in two other works. Novalis was closely associated with Jena for the entire decade of the 1790s. As a student in Jena, he was a devoted follower of Schiller and Reinhold; he also seems to have belonged to a fraternity or secret society and, according to Friedrich Schlegel, to have had a number of duels.[81] While Novalis did not live in Jena at the end of the decade, he frequently came over to Jena from Freiberg, Weissenfels, or Tennstedt in order to be with his friends there; and he participated in the most important gatherings, such as the art symposium in Dresden in the summer of 1798 and the great autumn assembly in Schlegel's house a year later. His appreciation of the university as an institution is expressed in a number of statements, as in the following two aphorisms from *Blüthenstaub*. "Years of apprenticeship are for the poetic disciple, and academic years for the philosophical one. Academy should be a wholly philosophic institution: only One faculty; the entire arrangement organized for the arousal and purposeful exercise of the power of thought."[82] And: "The most intimate community of all knowledge, scientific republic, is the lofty goal of scholars [*Gelehrten*]" (451). Therefore it comes as no surprise that the letter written from Freiberg on February 24, 1798, in which he announces to A. W. Schlegel that he is writing a work entitled (at this time still in the singular) *Der Lehrling zu Sais* states in the very next sentence that he misses the intellectual stimulation of Jena. "I very much lack books—and even more, people with whom I might philosophize, on whom I might charge myself electrically. I am at my most productive in conversation, and that is missing here altogether."[83]

Accordingly it is consistent that the novel fragment *Die Lehrlinge zu Sais*, though written mainly in Freiberg in 1798, betrays the influence of the familiar Jena discourse as well as a number of details that are specifically indebted to town and gown. To make this argument does not invalidate the assumption that in the figure of the teacher Novalis sought to apotheosize his Freiberg mentor, Abraham Gottlob Werner. But the teacher is merely one of the figures to whom the student (*der Lehrling*) is exposed. Indeed, the first chapter begins with a set of allusions that remind us more of Jena than of Freiberg.

It has frequently been remarked that both Schiller and Fichte are evident in Novalis's novel.[84] The entire conception of the temple-school at Sais is indebted to Schiller, whose poem "Das verschleierte Bild zu Sais" appeared in 1795. And the figure of the grave man ("ein ernster Mann") who speaks in the chorus of voices in the second chapter exemplifies not only the thoughts but also the very vocabulary of Fichte. But there are many other hints. The remarks in the second paragraph on incomprehensibility, for instance, anticipate Friedrich Schlegel's essay "Über die Unverständlichkeit," at the beginning of which he notes the widespread belief that "the basis of unintelligibility resides in the lack of understanding" ("der Grund des Unverständlichen liege im Unverstand").[85] Schlegel's essay did not appear until 1800 (in the last number of *Athenaeum*). But if we can take him at his word that he had long intended to write on this subject in order to demonstrate that incomprehensibility is a relative matter, arising often enough from rationality itself, we can also assume that Novalis's *Lehrling* has Schlegel in mind when he says: "From afar I heard it said that unintelligibility is only a consequence of the lack of understanding."[86]

It is of course possible that the influence went in the other direction—from Novalis to his friend Schlegel. In either case, however, the statement is a clear allusion to Jena conversations. We recognize Fichte's terminology at the beginning of the second section: "It may have lasted a long time before it occurred to people to designate the manifold objects of their senses with a common name and to oppose themselves to them" ["sich entgegen zu setzen"] (82). Similarly, the notion that consciousness, which deprived man of his primal unity with nature, is nothing but "a pathological disposition of later men" (82) is a thought familiar to Novalis and his friends from Schelling's *Ideen zu einer Philosophie der Natur* (1797), where reflection is identifed as "a mental illness of man."[87] Other passages play on ideas that we have learned to recognize as topoi in the three series of lectures on the university treated above. Thus the reference to students who desert their teacher in order to return home and learn a trade (80) is consistent with the topos of the *Brotgelehrte* or specialist that, as we saw, runs through Jena discourse, just as is the topos of history, which Novalis's student also recapitulates: "To treat the history of the world as the history of mankind, to find everywhere only human events and relationships, is a migratory idea that shows up in the most various ages in new guise and that appears to have had precedence constantly in wonderful effect and easy conviction" (84).

In *Die Lehrlinge zu Sais*, then, we hear the voices of Novalis's closest Jena associates—Schiller, Schlegel, Fichte, Schelling—as well as echoes of many of the commonplaces shared by the Jena Romantics. But it pays to remind ourselves that the very shape of the work, which amounts for the most part to a dialogue of voices expressing different attitudes toward nature, is indebted to what we have called the Jena mode of discourse. Following the student's brief introductory statement, what we get at the beginning of chapter two amounts to a lecture on the history of natural philosophy from mythic pre-history by way of the Greeks to modern times. Against this historical background various voices speak in turn, setting forth various responses to nature—from the superstitious fear of nature's power and mysteries by way of rationalist domination of nature to the view of nature as a projection of man's mind.

These positions are followed by the tale of Hyazinth and Rosenblüte, which illustrates the view that only love reveals the innermost secrets of nature, and by the chorus of stones in the deserted halls, in which nature gives utterance to its own view of unhappy man who has fallen out of his natural state of unity. Thereupon a group of travelers—represented by four individuals speaking two times each—recapitulates several of the most common Romantic views of nature, again encompassing extremes ranging from Fichtean egotism by way of Schelling's "duplicity" to an all-embracing love. By this point the essentially academic mode of discourse—the situation of the student-narrator, the background lecture, the seminar discussions, the presentations of the competing authorities— has emerged clearly. It is only here—close to the end of the fragment— that the actual scene of the work is mentioned. (Up to this point it is quite conceivable that Jena might be adduced as the locale.) The travelers, it is disclosed, have come to Sais because of its reputation for antiquity. They are not there for religious purposes. Their quest is essentially anthropological: they are in search of traces, especially linguistic traces, of the primal people from whom contemporary humanity is descended. They hope to find useful information in the temple archives, and they also ask permission to audit the famous professor's courses for a few days. The permission is granted, and the fragment closes with the teacher's paean to his profession, which he regards as the task "of awakening, of exercising, of sharpening in young minds [Gemüter] a varied sense of nature and of linking it with the other capacities to higher blossoms and fruits" (107). The true teacher accomplishes this task, he concludes, by forming from the insights he has attained "by experimentation, analysis, and comparison" (109) a "system for the application of these means"—a system that he must apply until it becomes second nature to him. Only then is he competent to undertake his profession. Novalis's definition of the teacher comes remarkably close to the definition of the scholar as we have observed it in Fichte's and Schelling's lectures on the university: the individual who lives for pure cognition and who creates a system for that cognition by which he is able to unify the manifold aspects of his science. In sum, Die Lehrlinge zu Sais can be understood in one sense as an example of Jena discourse—albeit an example that lies at the other extreme of the rhetorical scale from Brentano's travesty.

• • •

Although Friedrich Schlegel was a notably unsuccessful lecturer during his brief tenure at the University of Jena (1800–1801), he shared the local respect for the university as an institution. Indeed, he announced as one of his two Antrittsreden a lecture de officio philosophi—the by now ritual

topic for inaugural lectures in Jena.[88] And even after circumstances—
notably the heavy demands of lecture preparation, the competition with
Schelling for students, the need to write for money—caused him to leave
Jena in 1802, he dreamed of establishing in Paris "une académie centrale
des litterateurs allemands" from which a cosmopolitan European university might be developed.[89]

It was during the years while he was still aspiring to the professoriat
and had not yet been disappointed by the realities of the lecturer's life
that Schlegel wrote most obsessively about the university as an institution.
"The university is something quite arabesque," he observed in 1798, concluding with a typically Romantic metaphor, "a symphony of professors."[90] As Konrad Polheim has observed, the image is Schlegel's short-
hand for his conviction at that time that the university offered the best
opportunity for his goal of uniting art and scholarly knowledge in a single institution.[91] Polheim (379) quotes another aphorism of 1798: "Encyclopedics and criticism are inextricably linked. The theory of the university is identical with the philosophy of encyclopedics. . . . Not logic but
encyclopedics ought to be the deity of the universities." Elsewhere Schlegel noted that "scholars ought to be not merely thinkers and artists, but
also legislators and priests."[92] And several of the aphorisms in the collection *Ideen*, published just as he was beginning his brief academic career,
posit the scholar in relation to the poet and priest. "Fichte is supposed to
have attacked religion?" he begins with reference to the recent atheism
debate. "If interest in the metaphysical is the essence of religion, then his
whole theory is religion in the form of philosophy."[93] Further: "What
can be done as long as philosophy and poetry are separated has been done
and completed. So the time is now at hand to unify the two" (98). And
finally: "Hail to the true philologists! They accomplish the divine, for
they spread an artistic sense over the whole realm of erudition. No
scholar ought to be a mere craftsman" (99).

We should not be surprised, therefore, to find evidences of Jena discourse in the work that has been called "the most concentrated masterpiece of Schlegel's criticism,"[94] his *Gespräch über die Poesie*, written in
Jena from September 1799 to January 1800 just as he was contemplating
the application for his *venia legendi*. Unlike Schleiermacher's *Die Weihnachtsfeier*, Schlegel's work is not so much "a Platonic dialogue in a very
free form"[95] as, rather, a seminar on literature with papers and discussion.
Schlegel proposes in the introductory statement to deal with literature
very much as Novalis had dealt with nature in *Die Lehrlinge zu Sais*: that

is, "to oppose quite different views, each of which from its own stand-point can display the infinite spirit of poetry in a new light" (286).[96] And the seven young men and women who engage in the seminar do represent a variety of Romantic viewpoints on literature. Although some of the figures have taken on thoughts or characteristics identified with specific members of the group—Amalia plays the social role of Caroline Schlegel, Ludoviko is a philosopher who advances Schelling's ideas, and Antonio displays many characteristics of Schleiermacher (who though not in Jena joined the group often enough to belong to it)—the work is not simply a dialogue à clef but a Romantic *summa poetologiae*.

The action (following the author's introductory statement) opens when Amalia, Camilla, Marcus, and Antonio get into a lively discussion about a new theater piece. Hitherto the group of friends had followed the custom, after the fashion of literary societies in Berlin, of reading a dramatic work aloud and then discussing it. But when they noted the deficiencies of that random method of discussion, Amalia suggested that each of them should, instead, write an essay expressing his or her views on literature. On the appointed day, following an introductory conversation in which the various participants have the opportunity to introduce themselves to the reader, Andrea begins with a presentation on "Epochen der Dicht-kunst." It is characteristic that the seminar begins with a paper that takes as its basis the Romantic historicism that we have observed in the three university lectures. The paper begins with a survey of Greek literature from Homer through the principal genres of Attic poetry down to the Alexandrines—a discussion familiar from Schlegel's earlier studies of classical literature. The next section deals rather disparagingly with Roman literature and the millennium of decline that Schlegel saw in medieval Latin literature. Then a second high point is attained with the poetry of the Renaissance: the Italian triumvirate of Dante, Petrarch, and Boccaccio (based not on medieval literature but rather on medieval jurisprudence and theology!) succeeded by Cervantes and Shakespeare. Dismissing French letters as "this sickly mental disease of so-called good taste" (302), Schlegel/Andrea concludes by suggesting that a third period of literary greatness is on the point of being attained in Germany, thanks to Winckelmann's renewal of classical antiquity, Goethe's universality, and the achievements of modern philosophy.

In the discussion following this exposition of the Romantic canon of classic texts, Camilla triggers a number of characteristic responses by noting that Andrea has almost wholly ignored the French. Antonio observes that the French prove that a nation can be great without poetry, while Ludoviko complains that Andrea has anticipated his "polemical work on the theory of false poetry" (304). When Marcus objects that the role of genres and, more generally, the realm of theory are absent from Andrea's report, Andrea retorts that he had intended to remain within the bounds of history. Ludoviko remarks that Andrea's opposition of epic and iambic forms might well reflect the original philosophical oppositions within Greek poetry. And the remaining conversation, which focuses increasingly on the need for a theory of genres and the question of whether or not poetry can be taught, provides the transition to the second seminar report, Ludoviko's "Rede über die Mythologie."

Ludoviko begins by noting that modern poetry lacks a midpoint of the sort that mythology provided for the ancients. But the mythology that we require will not come, as did the mythology of the past, as "the first blossom of the youthful fantasy" (312) but, rather, from the depths of the human mind. "It must be the most artificial of all works of art, for it must embrace all others" (312). If such a modern mythology can work its way out from the depths of the mind, then—Ludoviko continues—we find "a remarkable confirmation of what we seek in the great phenomenon of the age, in idealism!" (313). Idealism, "in practice nothing but the spirit of revolution" (314), reveals the inner unity of the age and must constitute not merely an example for the new mythology but, indeed, a source for it. Referring to Spinoza, Ludoviko observes that all mythology is nothing but "a hieroglyphic expression of surrounding nature in this transfiguration of fantasy and love" (318). The new mythology will amount to a revitalization of ancient mythology by means of Spinoza and modern physics. But we should also be open to other sources. "In the Orient we must seek the loftiest Romanticism" (320). Ludoviko concedes that the new *Wissenschaftslehre* provides a perfect form and "a general scheme for all knowledge" (321), but the new mythology requires more—both the mysticism of Spinoza and the dynamic paradoxes of modern physics, from which "at present the most sacred revelations of nature are bursting forth on all sides" (322).

Ludoviko's presentation prompts an excited discussion on the role of science in poetry and the possibility of a didactic poetry, which leads to Lothario and Ludoviko's agreement "that the power of all arts and sciences meets in a central point" (324), a view anticipated by Plato, Spinoza, and Jakob Böhme. For Lothario, "Every work ought to be actually a new revelation of nature" (327). Only to the extent that it embraces one and all does a poetic work differ from a scholarly study. To this Antonio responds that he could cite scholarly studies that are indeed poetic works in that sense. Lothario suggests that only the epic could satisfy this criterion since, in Ludoviko's sense, drama is merely applied poetry (328). These remarks provide the transition to Antonio's contribution, the "Brief über den Roman."

Antonio begins his "critical epistle" (329) with a defense of Jean Paul, Sterne, and Diderot against the charge that their works are not proper novels. To the contrary, he maintains: "According to my view and my terminological usage, precisely that is romantic which represents to us a sentimental subject matter in a fantastic form" (333). In contradistinction to ancient poetry, which is based wholly on mythology, "romantic poetry rests wholly on a historical basis" (334). Beginning with the tautology that "a romance is a romantic book" ("Ein Roman ist ein romantisches Buch," 335), Antonio develops a position that is virtually identical with Schlegel's own famous *Athenaeum* fragment. "Indeed, I can scarcely imagine a novel as anything but a mélange of narrative, song, and other forms" (336). He argues that a true theory of the novel would have to be itself a novel that would reanimate the sound of fantasy, the chaos of the courtly world, the shade of Dante—a world in which Shakespeare would engage in conversation with Cervantes (337). In this sense Rousseau's *Confessions* amount to a better novel than *La nouvelle Héloïse*, and Gibbon's autobiography constitutes a comic novel of the highest order.

Antonio's presentation prompts Camilla to a tongue-in-cheek praise of the patience and consideration of women because they sit and listen so modestly to the ponderous discussions of the men, who take it as a matter of pride not to be understood by their fellows. Antonio remarks shrewdly that women regard art, antiquity, philosophy, and the like as ungrounded traditions that men try to put over on one another simply to pass the time. Following this brief exchange, Marcus offers his "Versuch über den verschiedenen Styl in Goethes früheren und späteren Werken." Beginning with the notion of Goethe's universality, which Andrea had already cited in his "Epochen der Dichtkunst," Marcus observes that few authors display such a striking difference between their early and late works as Goethe. Rapidly surveying Goethe's career, he cites *Götz von Berlichingen* as an example of the vigor and formlessness of Goethe's early efforts; *Torquato Tasso* for the spirit of reflection and harmony in the works of the second period; and finally *Hermann und Dorothea* for the idealistic attitude and objectivity of the third and most recent phase. He reserves his highest praise for *Wilhelm Meister*, in which the author's individuality is refracted in various beams and distributed among several figures. It reveals a classical spirit that is perceptible even beneath the modern guise. This harmonious combination of the Classic and the Romantic constitutes the loftiest goal of all poetry. Finally, the novel overcomes an underlying tension inherent in its dual conception: as a simple *Künstlerroman* and then gradually as a novel of *Bildung*. A similar duplicity is evident in the two most artful works of Romantic art, *Hamlet* and *Don Quixote*. But Goethe transcends both Shakespeare and Cervantes because his art is progressive, not static. As a result, Goethe emerges as "the founder and the head of a new poetry, for us and for posterity, as was Dante in a different manner in the Middle Ages" (347).

In the concluding discussion, Andrea is pleased that they have finally reached the fundamental question concerning the art of poetry: "Namely, the question of the unification of the classical and the modern, under what conditions it is possible and to what extent it is feasible" (348). Ludoviko protests that the spirit of poetry is identical at all times. Lothario recommends a division into the spirit and the letter, arguing that a unification is possible in spirit (as in the new mythology) but not in the letter or form since classical rhythm and modern rhyme are eternally opposed. Marcus, realizing that any agreement on these matters must be relative, suggests that what really matters is the authenticity of the judgment: namely, that it be based on solid knowledge and presented in such a pure and rigorous manner that the others will be prepared to take it seriously. Lothario hopes, nevertheless, that some sort of science of art is possible—perhaps by way of Andrea's historical approach or Ludoviko's philosophical analysis. The discussion ends with Lothario's plea for a rejuvenation of the mysteries and mythology through the spirit of physics and his claim that such a mythological subject is more suitable than a historical one because the modern treatment of character flatly contradicts the spirit of antiquity. With Camilla's plea for a Niobe, with Marcus's for a Prometheus, and with Antonio's for the story of Apollo and Marsyas, the work comes to a close (351).

It should be clear from the analysis that, all details apart, Schlegel's dialogue on poetics follows the structure neither of a brilliant soirée conversation nor of a Platonic dialogue but of a rigorously planned seminar. The four papers constitute a logically organized sequence—from the historical survey and the theoretical analysis by way of the generic analysis of the novel to the specific example of Goethe and his *Wilhelm Meister*.

(The sequence, in fact, closely parallels Schlegel's own intellectual development from his early essay *Über das Studium der Griechischen Poesie* by way of the *Athenaeum* fragments to his essay "Über Goethes Meister" of 1798.) The papers catalyze a series of lively discussions in which each participant (actually only the five men play an active role) approaches the common topic from an increasingly recognizable point of view. If we disregard the social setting of the work—that is, Caroline Schlegel's apartment—then we easily recognize the basically academic nature of the enterprise in the themes as well as the form of the *Gespräch*.

· · ·

At this time the academic seminar was still in the process of being shaped into its modern form. Historically the seminar originated in the philosophical faculty, specifically in the field of classical philology.[97] Created initially by Heyne in Göttingen in the second half of the eighteenth century in an effort to train theologians for teaching careers, the seminar shifted the emphasis from the rote memorization of material that the lecturer delivered from his lectern to the active participation of students in joint exercises with the professor. In Halle, F. A. Wolf accommodated the seminar to a different purpose: the training of scholars in classical philology in meetings that already display a recognizably modern format. The group met two or three hours per week for the close analysis of specific texts, the presentation of essays and treatises on various topics, and discussions of the material. But Wolf, who was interested in exegesis, rigorously excluded theoretical speculation from his seminars—so much so that some students complained of their sterility. It was really in Fichte's theory that the seminar assumed its central role as the common ground where teacher and student came together for the mutual pursuit of new knowledge, not merely the mastery of existing learning. Fichte's views, while clearly anticipated in his *Antrittsvorlesungen* of 1794, found their full elaboration in the plan for the establishment of a university in Berlin that he submitted in 1807 at the request of Cabinet Councillor Beyme, his *Deduzierter Plan einer zu Berlin zu errichtenden höheren Lehranstalt* (1817).[98]

Fichte's plan has sometimes been ridiculed for certain of its proposals. He wanted, for instance, to divide students, whom like Novalis he calls *Lehrlinge*, into *regulares*—that is, full-time students dedicated exclusively to the pursuit of *Wissenschaft*—and all the others—the *irregulares* or *socii*—whose ambitions were not so pure. (We note again the conventional Jena distinction between the *Brotgelehrte* and the "philosophical mind.")

The *regulares*, who would be fully supported by the state and hence free from need, would live and dine together as an "organic student body" ("organischer Lehrlingskörper," 133) in isolation from the distractions of the surrounding city, be identifiable by a uniform, follow strict rules of order and behavior enforced by the university *Justitiarius*, and finally be entitled to first claim on government positions. The entire endeavor was envisaged in honor of the general Romantic ideal of developing the "philosophical mind" that would be in command of "the entire scientific material in its organic unity" ("der gesamte wissenschaftliche Stoff, in seiner organischen Einheit," 150).

It was in the proposed method of instruction that Fichte departed most radically from existing forms. Questioning the value of lectures in an age of printing, he proposed an entirely new system. He conceded the usefulness of lectures for students in the first year: to provide them with the "philosophical encyclopedia" or general overview of knowledge in its interrelatedness. From the start, however, these lectures would be accompanied by three pedagogical devices (§9). In *examina* the student, or *Lehrling*, is asked questions intended to elicit not factual information but, rather, applications based on an understanding of the premises of the lectures. In the *conservatoria* "the student poses questions and the master asks about the question, and thus an explicit Socratic dialogue arises within the invisibly ever continuing dialogue of the entire academic life" (134). Finally, the *Lehrling* is assigned problems to be resolved in written exercises, through which he demonstrates his mastery of the material, the principles, and the methods of scientific presentation. It is these three devices that Fichte regards as "the first characteristic trait of our method" (152) and that constitute what he calls the "plant nursery of scientific artists" which at its best becomes a *Professor-Seminarium* (142).

Fichte's *Deduzierter Plan*, in its social as well as many of its academic proposals, was too radical a departure from the traditional institution to be accepted as the basis for the new university that was founded in Berlin. It was in Jena, as we know from descriptions of Fichte's teaching by Steffens and others, that Fichte began developing his ideas on teaching. In Jena, to be sure, the ideal of the seminar hardly existed in the reality of instruction at the university, where enrollments in the faculty of philosophy in 1798 constituted only two percent (fourteen to sixteen students) in a student body of 792.[99] But it was reflected quite clearly, I believe, in certain of the literary works that emerged at Jena just at that time. I would like to suggest that it was precisely the coincidence of the rudimentary form of the seminar, the familiar model of the Platonic dialogue, and the lively exchange of the social setting that contributed in a typically Romantic interaction to the first true realization of the academic seminar in the two literary works we have discussed: Novalis's *Die Lehrlinge zu Sais* and, especially, *Gespräch über die Poesie* by the aspiring young *Privatdozent* Friedrich Schlegel with his still very much idealized view of the university as an institution. It is not implausible that Novalis's work—with its close-knit group of *Lehrlinge* living and studying together in the relative isolation of an "organischer Lehrlingskörper"— contributed something to Fichte's vision of the ideal university.

## The Image of Halle in Romantic Memoirs

Unfortunately this educational ideal survived in Jena neither socially nor academically. It was unlikely, in the first place, that an assortment of temperaments as powerful as the ones assembled in Jena could live together for long in any kind of tranquillity. As Steffens wrote to Tieck fifteen years later (November 9, 1814): "As sure as it is that those times— when Goethe and Fichte and Schelling and the Schlegels, you, Novalis, Ritter and I dreamed that we were all united—were rich in seeds of various sorts, there was still something profligate [*ruchlos*] about it all. A spiritual Tower of Babel was to be erected, which all spirits were supposed to recognize from afar. But the confusion of tongues buried this work of arrogance beneath its own ruins."[100] The culmination of Jena Romanticism in the autumn of 1799 was followed within a year by its almost total disintegration. Not long after the arrival of Friedrich Schlegel and Dorothea Veit in 1799, relations between the two temperamental sisters-in-law became strained. In 1800 Caroline Schlegel left August Wilhelm to live with Schelling; the death that summer of her daughter, Auguste Böhmer, set off Schelling's feud with his colleague, the classicist Schütz, who spread the rumor that Schelling caused her death by his medical incompetence. That same year witnessed a scandal surrounding Clemens Brentano's affair with the poet-translator Sophie Mereau, who soon deserted her professor-husband to elope with the young poet. Meanwhile, Tieck left Jena with his family and, following a brief sojourn in Berlin, moved to Dresden. By the time Novalis died in 1801, the glory of Jena was a thing of the past. When Friedrich Schlegel departed for Paris with Dorothea in 1802, almost none of the circle remained.

Not long after the dispersal of the writers, many of the most prominent professors departed.[101] Tensions at the university had been gathering ever since the controversy surrounding Fichte's atheism in 1799 had forced his resignation. (In fact, his own stubbornness helped to produce a dilemma from which even the support of Goethe and Voigt was unable to rescue him.) In 1801 Carl August appointed a special commissioner to supervise matters at the university, especially with regard to finances, the academic constitution, and procedures regarding promotions. This act of administrative high-handedness infuriated a faculty that was already aggrieved at the duke's favoritism, which resulted in salary supplements for certain professors as well as the widespread belief that extensive repairs to the palace at Weimar were being accomplished at the expense of faculty salaries, which were already notoriously low. At the same time, other universities were being restored and strengthened. In Prussia, Friedrich Wilhelm III authorized a massive injection of thalers into the state university at Halle as a step toward the great social reforms of the decade. And through the incorporation of the town and university of Heidelberg, which had languished for the past two centuries under the benign neglect of the Palatinate, into the new state of Baden in 1803, that university underwent a conspicuous rejuvenation and became, as we saw, a center for jurisprudence.

As a result of these internal dissatisfactions and external competitions, Jena witnessed a mass exodus of its most prominent teachers in the first years of the new century. In 1802 the jurist Feuerbach moved to the University of Kiel, while both Schlegels definitively severed their ties with Jena. In 1803–1804 alone the professor of medicine J. C. Loder (along with his important collections) and the classical philologist Christian Gottlieb Schütz (along with his journal, the influential *Allgemeine Litteratur-Zeitung*) moved to Halle; Schelling, the theologian Paulus, the philosopher Niethammer, and the jurist Hufeland departed for Würzburg. In 1806 Thibaut moved to Heidelberg, while Hegel—who had yet to establish his reputation with his *Phänomenologie des Geistes* (1807)—temporarily gave up his academic career to become editor of a newspaper in Bamberg. The Jena that was burned and plundered by French troops and German looters following the Battle of Jena-Auerstedt in October 1806 had already been weakened from within to the point of depletion. It was due almost wholly to the heroic efforts of Goethe that Napoleon did not simply close down the university that fall. Even so, the enrollments dropped from over eight hundred during the glorious last decade of the eighteenth century to barely three hundred students in the years from 1806 to 1810. It was only after the defeat of Napoleon, when Jena became the home of the German national student movement (the so-called *Burschenschaften*) and the convener of the 1817 meeting on the Wartburg, that Jena once again became a university of major significance. But the almost total revision of the image of the university that had taken place at Jena manifested itself in the following decade in at least three different ways: in the tone of autobiographical writings about the university, in the frequency of students as central figures in literature, and in the conception of the University of Berlin.

Few people would have suspected even at the turn of the century that much of the intellectual force of Jena would shift to an institution as notorious as Halle. In 1803 Savigny wrote a short article on German universities that Henry Crabb Robinson translated into English and published in the *Monthly Register* (3 [May, 1803]: 3–6).[102] The young jurist foresaw clearly that "the great political events now taking place in Germany will have a considerable influence on the Universities," to which Germany—in the absence of wealth, political character, and a unifying metropolis—owes "its vast progress in the arts and sciences" and indeed its nationhood. But Savigny would have been surprised at the names of the universities that would rise to prominence. In 1803, he summarized, only four institutions were entitled to be put into a rank of distinction: Jena, Göttingen, Leipzig, and Halle. "During the last fifteen years Jena has been the center of German cultivation," notably because of its achievements in philosophy and the prevailing brotherly spirit among the unified student body. "On the whole, it is here that the character of German Universities is most fairly exhibited." Göttingen represents the antithesis, being wealthy and pedantic. Leipzig is held back by its "antiquated establishments, and its inactive narrow-minded administration." Halle, finally, "is the worst of all the great Universities, coarseness without geniality, a narrow-minded and illiberal study, which, at the utmost, never rises above the idea of practical utility." Savigny could hardly have imagined how markedly the academic map of Germany was to change within only a few years: that Jena would lose its glory, that the despised Halle, along with the unmentioned Heidelberg, would replace it for a few years, and that a still non-existent university in Berlin would by the end of the decade attract him as one of the stars in its brilliant academic constellation.

Paradoxically it was Halle, even more than Heidelberg, that generated a spate of autobiographical accounts in which the new Romantic view of the university is evident. For a few brief years Halle could boast perhaps the most distinguished faculty in Germany: F. A. Wolf maintained the most advanced seminar in classical philology; Schleiermacher was the star of theology; Reil, recently famous for his *Rhapsodieen*, taught medicine; Steffens had been summoned back from Denmark to represent natural science and *Naturphilosophie*. Indeed, while Jena had been noted especially for its philosophers, Halle embodied the Jena ideal of the integrated faculty collaborating in an intellectually unified university. In addition to the scholars, the composer Johann Friedrich Reichardt, former concertmaster at the court of Frederick the Great, made his home at Giebichenstein outside Halle the social center of the intellectual and cultural community. At Jena it had been essentially the participants themselves—the young intellectuals born around 1770—who conceived the vision of the Romantic university. For a generation of writers born in the 1780s, in contrast, the university was already there, at Halle, and they recalled their student years as illumined by a radiance characteristic of a lost Golden Age.

Perhaps the most immediate record of Halle during its brief period of glory is to be found in the letters that Adolph Müller wrote home to his sister and father in Bremen from October 1803 to April 1807. Müller provides not only an informative account of the study of medicine at this time but also a vivid portrayal of the daily life of students during the first decade of the new century—including not just the cudgel battles between rival fraternities but also the expeditions to Dresden and the Harz, the literary life, musical performances, and the theater in nearby Lauchstädt. Müller waxes rhapsodic about his teachers. Professor Wolf is "the wittiest man that I have ever seen," and Schleiermacher is "the model of all culture and social intercourse."[103] He describes mineralogical field trips under the guidance of Steffens, and he makes a pilgrimage to Jena especially in order to visit the physicist Ritter. Astonishingly, for three years (and over three hundred pages) Müller is so totally obsessed by the rich cultural and intellectual life of Halle that he makes no reference to the threatening political and military events. On October 25, 1806, finally, he mentions the battles near and in Halle and catches sight of Napoleon shortly before the university is closed and the students ordered out of the city within twenty-four hours. Müller manages to obtain a position in the library and is permitted to remain in Halle, where he studies Italian and Spanish while waiting for the university to reopen. When it becomes clear that the reopening is going to be significantly delayed, he completes his dissertation in six weeks under the supervision of Reil and leaves Halle—"the most splendid blossom that Germany could produce, now torn asunder by French barbarians and strewn into the winds" (363)—to take up a position at the Charité in Berlin.

What is immediately apparent in these letters is their new tone. Following the caesura of Jena, the German university is no longer the institution against which preachers and educators warn their constituencies. The professor is no longer a figure of ridicule but a model of respect and intellectual accomplishment. The students—at least those who now write about their experiences—are no longer the *Renommisten* and bullyboys of the regional fraternities but young men committed seriously to matters of the mind and the spirit. This change is evident in the memoirs of Varnhagen von Ense (1837–1859). When the sixteen-year-old Varnhagen was sent in 1800 to study medicine at the recently established Pépinière in Berlin, where the students were kept in a semi-military discipline, "I was regarded as fortunate that at such an early age I could enjoy all the advantages of the university without any of its dangers."[104] Six years later—following an interruption of his studies and having gone back to the school bench in order to master the Greek required for regular university matriculation—Varnhagen entered the University of Halle to continue his studies in medicine and philology. As he rode into Halle on April 21, 1806, "I felt as though I were entering a sanctuary (*ein Heiligtum*), a consecrated place" (347)—an emotion quite remote from the feelings of the students who had approached Jena, Göttingen, and Halle only two decades earlier.

Varnhagen devotes two sections of his memoirs (ch. 8 and ch. 10) to his year in Halle, where he knew Adolph Müller as well as all the famous professors, whom he characterizes at length. Although Varnhagen was primarily a student of medicine, his first visit was paid to Privy Councillor Wolf, "who appeared like a king among the scholars, surrounded by such intellectual regard, by such power and greatness of presence" (349–50). Varnhagen, the consummate social being, is of course in possession of letters of introduction to Giebichenstein; he participates in the weekly gatherings at the homes of Schleiermacher and Steffens; and he is invited from time to time to Wolf's house. Following his description of the social life of Halle, which always takes precedence in Varnhagen's scheme of things, we hear about the lectures: ancient history with Wolf, whose method stimulated the auditors to active participation; Paul's Epistles with Schleiermacher; and "philosophical physiology" and experimental physics with Steffens. With his gift of characterization Varnhagen describes the dialectical method of Schleiermacher as well as Steffens's more rhapsodic presentations. Homer and Plato were omnipresent in Halle because Wolf had become famous, only ten years early, through his *Prolegomena ad Homerum* (1795), while Schleiermacher had recently published the first two volumes of his Plato translation. But Varnhagen did not restrict himself to the luminaries. "None of the excellent young people in Halle could escape our attention because, apart from the places I have already mentioned, there were hardly any other assemblies to which intellect and culture would have aspired" (357). Varnhagen and his friend Neumann, somewhat older than the other students and already published writers, enjoyed a position of particular advantage. "The professors treated us like young scholars" (360). Like Müller, Varnhagen remained in Halle for a time after the closing of the university, where he continued to benefit from the company of Wolf, Schleiermacher, and several others. It was during this time that he and Neumann wrote the first few chapters of their parodistic *Doppelroman*, which subsequently was published under the title *Die Versuche und Hindernisse Karls* (1808). But as the professors wandered away to other cities, Varnhagen accompanied Müller to Berlin with the intention of continuing his medical studies there.

Eichendorff begins his nostalgic account of "Halle und Heidelberg" (posthumously published in 1876) with a survey of German universities before the revolutionary age. The universities, he observes, were "the recruitment places and training camps" for the intellectual revolution that had renewed itself from generation to generation—from Luther in Wittenberg by way of Christian Wolff in Halle, Kant in Königsberg, and Fichte and Schelling in Jena: "invisible catastrophes of thought that exerted an essential and more decisive influence on life as a whole than the diplomats could imagine."[105] But the entire structure had already collapsed internally before the storm of the French Revolution swept away the ruins, and what remained was "an imaginary Germany that was neither properly rational nor properly historical" (1046), in which eighteenth-century rationalism competed with the new Romantic ideas.

Looking back from the mid-nineteenth century, Eichendorff reminds his readers that "the universities in those days still had a completely alien appearance, as though they were situated outside the world" (2: 1048), and he takes evident pleasure in describing the student garb and the semi-medieval life, which resembled "a wildly lovely fairy tale" in comparison to which everyday life appeared ridiculous and Philistine, like Sancho Panza beside Don Quixote (1049). Then suddenly, as though it were "a conspiracy of the scholars" (1052), a new intellectual life appeared on the scene. "The confusion that this sudden revolution produced displayed itself most conspicuously perhaps at the university that had the largest enrollments: in Halle, because there the most heterogeneous material also provoked the most decisive battle" (1052). At the head of the Romantics Eichendorff cites Steffens, whose personality and poetically improvised lectures equipped him to be the leader of a youth in search of inspiration. And along with him, Reil, Schleiermacher, Wolf, as well as the Kantian philosopher Kayßler, constituted the intellectual leadership of the university. Opposed to the "Romantic" faculty was "the broad, heavy mass of the orthodox Kantians and the plodding jurists" (1053). When Eichendorff recalls Giebichenstein with its castle ruin, "an utterly appropriate workshop for a young poet's heart," he is inspired to set down the strophes of his poem "Bei Halle":

> Da steht eine Burg über'm Tale
> Und schaut in den Strom hinein,
> Das ist die fröhliche Saale,
> Das ist der Gibichenstein.
>
> Da hab' ich so oft gestanden,
> Es blühten Täler und Höh'n,
> Und seitdem in allen Landen
> Sah ich nimmer die Welt so schön!
>
> (1054)

(A castle stands above the valley and gazes down into the river. It is the cheerful Saale and Giebichenstein. There I have often stood when the valleys and peaks were blooming; and ever since in all lands I have never seen the world so lovely.)

But Old Halle was buried along with the ruins of the Prussian monarchy in 1806. Napoleon, sensing in the student sentiments the first "symptom of a more serious people's will" (1057), suspended the university and drove the students ruthlessly out of town, robbed even of the most necessary clothing. Looking back at those glorious days and regretting the relocation of universities from small towns to large cities, Eichendorff concludes that "our universities were in the last analysis a kind of republic, the sole remaining relicts of German unity, a brotherly union without regard for differences of province, rank, or wealth, where superiority of mind and character raised the lowborn to a position of seniority above princes and dukes" (1076). The point is not that Eichendorff's memory is not consistent with the historical facts of German universities around the turn of the century but rather that the image of the university had been so radically transformed by Romanticism that it was capable of bearing such an idealizing view.

Even Ludwig Börne, though he did not run in the same circles as Müller, Varnhagen, and Eichendorff, was captivated by the magic of Halle. His autobiographical essay, "Die Apostaten des Wissens und die Neophyten des Glaubens" (1828),[106] begins: "I remember with delight those academic years that I lived in Halle." Like Eichendorff, he believes that youth is lovely under any circumstances, "but for academic youths it is doubly splendid." In contrast to Göttingen—venerably learned, wealthy, aristocratic—Halle was characterized by a fresh and vigorous scholarly life. Again Börne reviews and characterizes the most famous professors: Wolf, "whose fame is not greater than his merits"; Schleiermacher, who "taught theology as Socrates would have taught it had he been a Christian"; Reil, who began his lectures on therapy and diseases of the eye with poems by Schiller and Goethe; and Steffens, who inspired his listeners to heights of enthusiasm with his *Naturphilosophie* as the key to heaven and earth. "Stimulated by teachers like these, the blood of academic youth flowed more rapidly and fierily through the veins of the mind." Börne concedes that the manners of the students left something to be desired. But spirit is more moving, he argues, when it arises in unexpected circumstances. He recalls a drinking party at which two students got into an argument over the subtleties of Schelling's philosophy, exchanged insults, "and two days later blood flowed." Börne concludes his memories of Halle with the ritual curse on Napoleon: "Wither the hand that first defiled this lovely life!" But he provides a unique twist. "Napoleon did not stamp out the mind (*Geist*) because he despised it as a worm; rather, he bound it fast because he esteemed it as a lion."

While Müller's letters and the memoirs of Varnhagen, Eichendorff, and Börne portray Halle from the viewpoint of the students, Henrich Steffens's autobiography covers the same ground from the standpoint of a young professor.[107] Steffens was tied into the social network by his marriage to one of Reichardt's daughters. And as a faculty member he knew his colleagues differently than did the admiring students. Again we hear of Wolf, whose absolute authority was generally feared; of Reil, whose practical concerns in medicine did not allow him to follow Steffens into the mysteries of *Naturphilosophie*; and above all of Schleiermacher, "the man who created a new epoch in my life" (179). Whereas Jena was torn apart around the turn of the century by inner tensions and administrative pressures, Halle was doomed in 1806 by military action and by Napoleon, who suspected that the students in Halle had organized themselves against him and was angered that the authorities had not locked them into their colleges (200).

While the closing of the university represented an inconvenience for the students, who could continue their studies at another university, it constituted a severe threat to the careers and economic welfare of the professors. Accordingly Steffens's account of his years in Halle also amounts to the story of his political awakening as he was forced to realize for the first time in his life "that I, too, might be summoned to some sort of political activity" (186). Hitherto the German scholars, in their only recently established position and security, had found it "impossible to imagine that a university could be disturbed in its activity" (188). Even in the fateful summer of 1806 Steffens found that the number of his students had grown. But the truth soon became evident, and Steffens provides us with a dramatic account of the fighting and looting of Halle that took place in the course of the battle between the French and Prussian troops in October. "Our entire future life had been transformed in a terrible manner. No past decision, no matter how carefully weighed, had any significance for the immediate future" (195). The professors sent a deputation to Napoleon, but to no avail. "The troops had departed, the students were driven out of the city in the course of the day. We, the teachers, remained behind in the devastated, desolate town: our office, our activity were annihilated, our future position still uncertain" (201). Among the names of the few remaining students Steffens notes those of Müller and Varnhagen. In the interests of economy Schleiermacher and his sister moved into Steffens's small apartment, where they lived in dire need and scarcely left the house. When the funds were gone, Steffens sold his family silver. The autobiography provides a remarkable account of the radicalization of a generation of professors who only a decade before, in Jena of the 1790s, had come to scholarly maturity convinced of the absolute nature of science. That conviction is radically qualified by the reality of Napoleon and his troops.

In 1808, two years following its suspension by Napoleon, Halle, now reassigned to the state of Westphalia, was permitted to reopen; but the competition from the University of Berlin, newly established in 1810, prevented it from regaining the position it had enjoyed during the eighteenth century and then again for a few brief years following the crisis at Jena in 1803. While Halle was the largest university in Germany, Heidelberg was still one of the smallest, having grown from fewer than fifty students around the turn of the century to around four hundred—principally jurists, as we have seen—in the years before Napoleon's defeat.[108] Among these jurists were three young men who contributed significantly to the image of Romantic Heidelberg that dominated the later nineteenth century. When Otto Heinrich von Loeben, following several depressing semesters in Wittenberg, arrived in Heidelberg in the spring of 1807, he exclaimed that Heidelberg was truly "a premonition of paradise."[109] Heidelberg cannot be described, he wrote to a friend; "one should simply mention its name and then be silent." In Heidelberg Loeben, who assumed the pen name Isidorus Orientalis, soon met the brothers Joseph and Wilhelm von Eichendorff, who had recently arrived from Halle. The poems that these three young students wrote during their year in Heidelberg—both about the place and about one another—helped shape the myth of Romantic student life.[110] Indeed, much of the section concerning Heidelberg in the second half of "Halle und Heidelberg" consists of an extended quotation from his novel *Ahnung und Gegenwart*, in which Eichendorff portrays the Romantic posturing of his friend Loeben.

During the first decade of the century Heidelberg entered the German literary consciousness not through the largely unknown poetic efforts of its students but through the more scholarly vehicles of an older generation of writers: the quintessential Romantic anthology of Arnim and Brentano, *Des Knaben Wunderhorn* (1805–1808); the lectures of the nationalistic philosopher Johann Joseph von Görres, and notably his influential essay *Die teutschen Volksbücher* (1807); and Arnim's *Zeitung für Einsiedler* (1808), which constitutes a repository of the collective efforts of the group.[111] Even the attempts to attract Tieck to Heidelberg as a professor were based not on his poetry but on his edition of *Minnelieder aus dem Schwäbischen Zeitalter* (1803), his current studies of the *Nibelungenlied*, and other enterprises of a scholarly nature.[112] In later years—thanks in no small measure to Joseph Viktor von Scheffel's *Der Trompeter von Säckingen* (1854), with its poem "Alt-Heidelberg, du feine," as well as the Heidelberg songs in Scheffel's collection *Gaudeamus* (1867)—it was Heidelberg's student life that became renowned. It is no accident that when

Bettina von Arnim published the memorial to her friend *Die Günderode* (1840)—who committed suicide in 1806 as the result of an unhappy love affair with the Heidelberg classicist and mythographer Friedrich Creuzer—she dedicated her work with a rhapsodic inscription "to the students": "you who err and seek! who exult to Parnassos, at Castalia's spring. . . . who call yourselves Hermann's race, Germany's disciples! . . . When the fools' breed of Philistines condemns you, remember—you sons of the Muses—that their noisy drum does not deafen the spirit of the radiant Pythian."[113] But in 1806, when her brother Clemens wrote his "Lied von eines Studenten Ankunft in Heidelberg"[114] in imitation of Martin Opitz—"Nach Heidelberg, bin ein Student, / Von Jena komm' ich hergerennt"—the battle between the new generation and the entrenched opposition of rationalists in Heidelberg was far from won. Indeed, by 1808 almost all the Romantic poets—both the older generation of Arnim and Brentano and the younger circle around Loeben and the Eichendorffs—had left Heidelberg for more receptive fields, including notably Berlin.[115]

## THE STUDENT AS HERO

In the first decades of the new century, however, the role of universities in Romantic consciousness manifested itself in another way. Given the fact that the university was a common experience shared by virtually all writers of the period, it is hardly surprising that the student begins to show up with increasing frequency as a figure in literature. There had, of course, been students in earlier German literature, notably the brawling desperados of *Der Renommist* or *Carl von Carlsbad*, where "student" was tantamount to moral depravity and brutishness. With the revaluation of the university as an institution at Jena, however, the role of the student also changed. We have already noted the example of *Die Lehrlinge zu Sais*, where the university is allegorized and idealized. And it is surely no accident that Heinrich von Ofterdingen—before the merchants suggest that he displays the talents to be a poet—has the ambition to "occupy himself with learned matters" and, specifically, with "the science of human history" ("Wissenschaft der menschlichen Geschichte").[116] The merchants assure him that it is not necessary to become a cleric in order to fulfill that ambition and that in Swabia he will encounter "truly intelligent and experienced men among the laity." And Hölderlin, who also sat at Fichte's feet in Jena, concluded the first volume of his novel *Hyperion* (1797) by having his young Greek hero set out for—where else?—Germany in order to become an educator of his people ("Erzieher unsers Volk"). Heinrich and Hyperion do not of course become scholars, but within the next decade students begin showing up in increasing numbers in Romantic fiction.

We have already had occasion to discuss Brentano's *Romanzen vom Rosenkranz*, which deals extensively with university life in thirteenth-century Bologna. But contemporary students play a much more prominent role in the works of Brentano's collaborator and brother-in-law, Achim von Arnim. Arnim's early story "Hollins Liebeleben" (1801) represents a transition because the twenty-one-year old author, having just recently passed through Halle and Göttingen, had not experienced the new university. Accordingly his depiction of student life in "H." is still essentially pre-Romantic. To be sure, Hollin is stirred by a sense of youthful freedom at the first sight of the university town. "Heavens, what a feeling when I saw the first tips of the towers and, ever more, the whole splendid free city of youth emerge from the plain! It has still not died out in me, that inner summons to freedom that spurred me even as a child to the most daring games."[117] He joins a fraternity and becomes one of the best duelists, but he also strives to instill in his brothers his sense of the profundities of philosophy. His friend Odoardo, who has been sent to the university in "G.," warns him against the degrading influence of the fraternities and complains about the rote learning that takes the place of true knowledge. But Hollin plunges so eagerly into student life that he is soon elected chief officer of his fraternity and, as such, must represent it in a duel against another fraternity. In the duel he wounds his opponent, who subsequently becomes his close friend; Hollin withdraws from student life to his solitary studies and forsakes his desire to educate others. Soon thereafter the scene of the novel shifts away from the university town, and the story—heavily influenced by *Wilhelm Meisters Lehrjahre* as well as *Die Leiden des jungen Werther*—takes its rapid course to Hollin's dramatic suicide on stage in the role of Mortimer in Schiller's *Maria Stuart*.

A decade later Arnim returned to university life in two of his best-known works. His lengthy novel *Armut, Reichtum, Schuld und Buße der Gräfin Dolores* (1810) is, to be sure, no university novel. But when the pampered and discontented Countess Dolores first meets Graf Karl, who is to become her husband, the young count is still a student wandering the countryside with a group of his university friends. This circumstance provides the author with the obviously attractive occasion to devote an entire chapter (bk. i, ch. 6) to "Die Studenten," in which he portrays the costume and manner of these "Sons of the Muses" (*Musensöhne*) for the benefit of those who know nothing about the Muses. University life provides a more important scenario in the first part of Arnim's drama *Halle und Jerusalem* (1811), which is dedicated to Brentano and Görres "in memory of good and bad days in Heidelberg." Arnim had been fascinated for several years by the works of Andreas Gryphius, and in his "tragedy in two comedies" he sought to modernize Gryphius's *Cardenio und Celinde* (1657). Arnim has not altered the essential plot, which revolves around the frustrated love of Cardenio for Olympie, his search for happiness and revenge through his attachment to Celinde, and their ultimate quest for redemption (in Arnim's version through a pilgrimage to Jersualem in the second part). But he has transposed the scene from medieval Bologna to contemporary Halle and transformed the hero from a Spanish student into a German *Privatdozent*. The entire work is framed by student activities: in the opening scene a group of students are lounging around the market square in Halle, discussing a duel that is just taking place; and the play ends as other students row their boats along the Saale and sing a choral song of youthful reassurance:

> Mut gewinnt sich neue Zeit,
> Bald wird uns die Welt so weit.

A pronounced academic spirit permeates the whole. At the beginning it turns out that the student whom Cardenio has wounded in the duel is supposed to be the "opponent" in a formal disputation with the philosopher Wagner. (The allusion to Goethe's Wagner was quite timely since the first part of *Faust* had just been published in 1808.) As a matter of honor, Cardenio takes his place in the disputation, where he performs so brilliantly that Wagner dies of apoplexy. Olympie's brother, Baron Viren, is a professor of law who specializes in the pandects and whose favorite reading matter is a "civilistic work on possession" (act ii, scene 2), an allusion to the treatise *De possessione* by Arnim's brother-in-law, Savigny. One entire scene (iii, 2) depicts the meeting of a student secret society from which Cardenio resigns as "master" when circumstances force him to leave Halle. If the student atmosphere is still generally pre-Romantic (as it was at Halle when Arnim studied there), the Romantic conception of learning, which by the time Arnim wrote the play was prevalent, comes through clearly in Cardenio's explanation to Ahasverus (III, 4) why he has decided to give up his academic career. As he packs his belongings, he points to the astronomical charts, "all of which remind me of those rich hours when, in lively splendor, thought tested itself against thought in the contest of eager duelists with ever new thrust." He was so eager for knowledge—notably scientific learning—that every dawn found him at his books.

Much praised as a student, Cardenio became at an early age a teacher to whom all turned with respect and friendship. A good teacher, he was prepared to share doubts with any mind struggling for truth. "It seemed as though science here had taken a new course, the torpid letter was penetrated in the spirit, all life became a joy, and a boldness entered all thought." In those days Cardenio's learning was so acclaimed that even graying heads sought his counsel. Nor was he tied to his room and his books. "Because I never studied except to discover, there remained ample time to train my body to be strong and supple through swimming, wrestling, dancing, fencing." But then Cardenio gradually expanded his focus from science to philosophy and political matters. He began to understand the power of men and the spirit of entire peoples, and under the leadership of a friend he began to enjoy the taste of power and the sense of superiority above others. Working through the secret society, he hoped to train worthy servants for his fatherland, but he also became impatient and irritable at any failure. Suddenly, however, his spiritual empire was undermined by the power of love and jealousy. Cardenio forsakes his academic life for revenge against the man who has cheated him of his beloved Olympie. At this point the academic part of the work ends, and the scene soon shifts to Jerusalem. *Halle und Jerusalem* shares the ambivalence of *Hollins Liebeleben* toward student life. While the atmosphere is still essentially pre-Romantic, we sense in the ambitions of Hollin and Cardenio a new conception of learning: to work through student organizations to train the youth of Germany for a better future. But in both cases the initiative fails.

In Justinus Kerner's *Reiseschatten* (1811) university life is portrayed in the weird distortions that characterize all twelve sections of this fantasy, which is presented in the form of scenes cast on the wall through a camera obscura (hence the allusion to "shadows" in the title). Following the completion of his medical studies at Tübingen in 1808, where he studied with Autenrieth and, as part of his training, observed Hölderlin in his incipient madness, Kerner undertook a one-year trip that led him north to Hamburg and then south through Germany to Vienna and, by the spring of 1810, back home to Ludwigsburg. It is this journey that he purports to portray in his *Reiseschatten*, but most of the scenes and experiences are actually based on his years in Tübingen. (Hölderlin has a walk-on appearance as "the mad poet Holder.") When the narrator arrives in the university town of Mittelsalz, the first person he encounters is a tall, thin fellow carrying a large manuscript in his coat pocket. This personage greets the narrator and tells him that he is none other than the walking stick that the narrator had left behind in Mittelsalz on an earlier visit years before (VIII, 3). In the hands of a local professor, his slumbering genius had been awakened; he absorbed everything the professor read and lectured about and finally learned so much that he was able to pass the exams in classics brilliantly and now writes reviews and lectures as a *Doctor legens*.

The learned cane—a not-so-subtle personification of the wooden lecturing of many German professors—disappears before the narrator can recover from his astonishment, whereupon he enters a lecture hall to listen to "a historico-critical lecture on the destruction of the world by water" (VIII, 4). All the students are sleeping with their eyes open, including a poet, whose vision of a hunter and shepherdess is related. When the poet wakes up with a terrible howl, the entire student body is aroused, and the professor concludes his lecture in the belief that the students had been moved by his vision of the end of the world. The following scenes describe the life in a student boardinghouse, where later the student poet is arrested by the proctor for his disturbances during the lecture and, even worse, for writing poetry. The following scenes (IX, 1–4) portray the trial of the poet by a committee consisting of the *praeses* plus professors from each of the four faculties—a trial that parodies the well-nigh untranslatable pedantic language of academic bureaucracy.

> Die von einem hochpreislichen Senate zur Untersuchung der Kisten und Kästen des der Dichtkunst suspekten *studiosi philosophiae* Kullikeia ernannte Kommission hat sich *sub dato*, nach erhaltenem Befehle, sogleich in das Zimmer Produktens verfügt, alle *contenta* desselbigen aufs genaueste beaugenscheinigt und in Beschlag genommen und lautet ein *visum repertum* hierüber also: . . ."[118]

> (The commission appointed by the most estimable senate to investigate the boxes and crates of the student of philosophy Kullikeia, who is suspected of writing poetry, has as of this

date, having received its charge, immediately betaken itself to the aforesaid student's room, inspected all the contents of same most carefully and taken them into custody, and the inventory of same contains: . . .)

In the course of their search of the premises they finally discover, hidden at the bottom of a barrel, a thick folio containing the works of Hans Sachs plus quarto volumes including the *Nibelungenlied, Des Knaben Wunderhorn*, the saints' lives, Old German lays, and other similarly suspect documents. Finally they detect not only poems written by the accused but also excerpts from the works of Jakob Böhme, Novalis, and "other insane scribblers." The room is sealed, the committee disperses, and the narrator leaves town as his cousin swears to take vengeance for his friend's punishment. Although Kerner's literary oddity does not belong to the mainstream of Romantic writing, his university scenes clearly make use of the conventional opposition between students and Philistines (including the pedantic professors) as well as contemporary *Naturphilosophie*.

By the time we reach the works of E.T.A. Hoffmann, the figure of the student has become well profiled and prevalent. Indeed, some of Hoffmann's most familiar heroes are students, such as Anselmus in *Der goldne Topf* (1814), Nathanael in "Der Sandmann" (1815), Theodor in "Rat Krespel" (1815–1816), and Klein Zaches as well as his mortal enemy, Balthasar, in *Klein Zaches* (1819). The fact that Theodor, the narrator of "Rat Krespel," is a student at the time of the events narrated, is almost immaterial—apart from the fact that his legal studies give him easier access to the eccentric old jurist and retired diplomat, Krespel. But it is anything but immaterial that Anselmus is a *Candidatus theologiae* who has recently completed his studies at Halle. The theological aspect is essential for the structure of the first chapter, which is based closely on motifs from the opening chapters of Genesis: Anselmus's "fall" (out of the innocence of youth into consciousness) is precipitated when he bumps into an old woman with apples on a religious holiday (Ascension Day). A short time later he has his first encounter with the mythic world of the Archivarius Lindhorst when he sees serpents climbing about in the branches of an elder tree. These biblical motifs—a woman with an apple, serpents in a tree, and a "fall" from innocence—as well as the pervasive mythic atmosphere of the work are appropriate in the context of a theologian—a theologian, moreover, who has been primed by his student years to be receptive to the promise of mythic unity, to which he surrenders at the end of the story.

Nathanael, in contrast, is a student of natural science, and his first letters home to his foster brother and sister provide an account of his life at the university of "G." Nathanael's faculty is equally appropriate in his case: Spalanzani's efforts to construct a dancing automaton so lifelike that many observers consider her alive is consistent with his position as a professor of physics at the university. At the same time, it is Hoffmann's implication that Nathanael is susceptible to this delusion, by which he is ultimately driven mad and to his death, because his studies are so one-sidedly scientific that they have failed to provide him with a unifying vision of nature that might have protected him. As we noted in an earlier chapter, much of the action in *Klein Zaches* takes place at the university— "the famous University of Kerepes"—where the deformed Zaches dazzles his professors by magical means. We hear in particular about the lectures of Mosch Terpin, professor of natural science, who explains

how it rains, thunders, lightnings, why the sun shines by day and the moon by night, how and why the grass grows, etc., in such a manner that any child could comprehend. He had compressed all of nature into a small delicate compendium so that he could have it conveniently at hand and could extract from it as from a drawer an answer to any question.[19]

But the idyllic university life, portrayed at length in several chapters, is disrupted when the hideous Zaches arrives to take up the study of law and deludes all his professors, including Mosch Terpin, into believing that he is the most brilliant intellect of all.

It is in the works of Eichendorff that the Romantic student achieves his ultimate apotheosis. The university as such does not appear as a setting in the fiction of the author of "Halle und Heidelberg." But repeatedly the character and background of the hero(es) are adumbrated by reference to his student years. *Ahnung und Gegenwart* (1815), written in part while Eichendorff himself was still a student, introduces Graf Friedrich as a young man who has just left the university to undertake his travels and who is being accompanied for the first few days by "a boisterous group of students." In this case, in other words, we are dealing with a hero who has had all the benefits of the Romantic university, as Eichendorff depicted it in his autobiographical writings, and who is thereby prepared for the adventures of love, society, and politics that he is about to encounter. In his other major novel, *Dichter und ihre Gesellen* (1834), in contrast, two of the principal figures are young men who left the university some years earlier. When Baron Fortunat appears on the first page, riding in the evening sun and singing an old song, he is puzzled at the familiar appearance of the town that he makes out from the hilltops. Then it suddenly occurs to him: "Just as in Heidelberg the houses lay below between the gardens and hills and evening lights, just as in Heidelberg the river resounded from below and the forest from all its heights." Then he realizes that his "faithful Heidelberg comrade" Walter must live in the town that he is approaching. That turns out to be the case, and the mood is immediately established by the nostalgic reminiscences of the two old friends, who decide to set out on a Romantic expedition together.

Eichendorff's fantasy *Auch ich war in Arkadien!* (1834) uses the university motifs in a different manner to express the conservative's amusement at recent developments among the liberal nationalist students and professors. Eichendorff is reporting on a journey that he recently took—the first, he tells us, in many years, since he has been living like a recluse quite apart from the world and its July Revolution. When he was last out in the world, he begins, the cult of Germanity was at its height. So in preparation he lets his hair grow long in the style of Albrecht Dürer, orders an Old German travel outfit from his tailor, and sets out by stagecoach. The academic mood is anticipated when he remarks that the stagecoach itself is a "flying university."[120] However, Eichendorff notices almost at once that his costume is out of fashion because his countrymen had in the aftermath of the 1830 revolutions become quite Frenchified with a soupçon of Polish. Stopping at an inn, At the Sign of the Golden *Zeitgeist*, the narrator observes a curious manner of greeting: people made a quick bow to the left and awaited the response "Freedom of the Press" or "Constitution" or some other liberal shibboleth. At dinner that evening the company is harangued by a large man called "the Professor," who manages to consume the entire roast while delivering a long speech on freedom, tolerance, and the other truths. At a certain point the narrator realizes that the date is Walpurgis Night (April 30), and the remainder of the story amounts to a vision in which "the Professor" takes him by flying horse to the Blocksberg (made famous by Goethe in *Faust*), where they experience a contemporary Walpurgis Night—namely, a great battle among the various current political principles ranging from tyranny by way of constitutional monarchy to democracy and anarchy.

When the narrator wakes up with a hangover in The Golden *Zeitgeist*, he realizes that he, too, had been privileged to experience "the fragrant coasts of that El Dorado for which the people long" (748). While the university does not provide the actual setting here, it amounts to the allegorical setting because Eichendorff uses the phantasmagoria of the Walpurgis Night to embody the unruly intellectual strife of the post-Romantic university that he compared so unfavorably to Halle and Heidelberg in his autobiographical essay. The German university, he writes there, did not remain content with its accomplishments. First it sought to raise itself above the world, to dominate it and rule it more rationally. "To this was added the fact that they had actually played a laudable role in the world theater during the Wars of Liberation and now also claimed the right to continue to play out the remaining acts of the great world drama: in short, to make politics" (1073). But this was an unwise move, the aging civil servant Eichendorff concludes, because youth lacked the necessary knowledge and experience for that challenge. As the universities lost their political innocence and moved into the cities, they were able to provide their students with little more than "an orientation in the labyrinth of the new education" (1075). In this new metropolitan world the ancient meaning of the universities has been wiped out. "The students are indoctrinated increasingly into the general philisterium and become accustomed quite early to address the world diplomatically with glacé gloves" (1076). It is this politicized university that Eichendorff is satirizing in *Auch ich war in Arkadien*—a satire whose necessary counterfoil is a lament for the Romantic university that was doomed virtually at the moment it came into existence.

## THE UNIVERSITY OF BERLIN: INSTITUTIONALIZATION OF THE JENA IDEAL

Following the disintegration of Jena after 1803, the suspension of Halle by Napoleon in 1806, and disenchantment with Heidelberg, which appeared to favor rationalism and professionalism over Romantic ideals, the eyes of the younger generation turned toward Berlin. Ever since the ascension of Friedrich Wilhelm III in 1797, the notion had been entertained of establishing some sort of comprehensive institution that would combine the various educational enterprises of the capital—the Academy of Sciences, the thriving medical school and other professional institutes, the outstanding collections, the lectures by such distinguished scholars as Fichte, Schleiermacher, and A. W. Schlegel.[121] During the last decade of the eighteenth century Berlin had been a center of resistance toward the traditional university—a resistance led, as we have seen above, by rationalist associations like the Mittwochgesellschaft, by the sophisticated court circles, and by such influential officials as Julius von Massow. But by 1807 the situation had changed. Accordingly, when a delegation of professors from the suspended University of Halle, led by the rector T.A.H. Schmalz, visited Friedrich Wilhelm III in August at his residence at Memel and asked that their university be reestablished in Berlin, the king was receptive to the idea, responding (according to a widely cited remark) that "the state must replace through intellectual powers what it has lost in the way of physical powers" ("der Staat müsse durch geistige Kräfte ersetzen, was er an physischen verloren habe").[122] Whether or not Friedrich Wilhelm III actually uttered the words attributed to him in Schmalz's reports, they were certainly not inconsistent with the convictions of the patriotic young king. In any case, they became the rallying cry around which revolved the efforts to establish the new university in the next several years.

Despite lingering reservations among certain members of his court, the king, by a cabinet order of September 4, 1807, authorized his cabinet chief, Karl Friedrich Beyme, to undertake the plans for a "general institution of learning" (allgemeine Lehranstalt) in Berlin. Beyme, who had worked on the Allgemeines Landrecht under Svarez, began discussions with several professors from Halle and, at the same time, commissioned statements on the nature of the new institution from various scholars, including notably Schmalz, F. A. Wolf, and Fichte. Schmalz proposed that the new institution should sever all ties with traditional universities—e.g., no rector, no academic jurisdiction, no separate faculties—and align itself with the Berlin Academy of Science.[123] Wolf responded with a brilliant, disorganized, opinionated, and self-serving set of suggestions that were virtually useless to Beyme.[124] Fichte's Deduzierter Plan, as we have already noted, was too radical in its expectations to provide the basis for administrative action. The publication that did in fact succeed in shaping public opinion and preserving the ties of the new institution to the university of the past was Friedrich Schleiermacher's Gelegentliche Gedanken über Universitäten im deutschen Sinn (1808).

Schleiermacher was not among the scholars from whom Beyme, in the late summer of 1807, had solicited a statement on the nature of the institution to be established in Berlin. But as soon as he heard that Wolf was drafting a proposal, he decided to submit his own plan, which he composed during the winter and published in the spring of 1808. Because it was published and not submitted to Beyme as a private communication (like Fichte's proposal), Schleiermacher's monograph was widely read and eagerly discussed. Indeed, it was the most influential of the various writings that preceded the establishment of the University of Berlin. In the first chapter, "Vom Verhältnis des wissenschaftlichen Vereins zum Staate," Schleiermacher defines the hermeneutical as well as the dialectical relationship between university and state.[125] He begins with the assumption that it is human nature to seek a science that is both unified and total. But since no single individual can achieve this total synthesis of knowledge, scholars must rely on the state to create the institution in which they can come together. Scholars therefore need the state, and the state also needs the knowledge produced by the scholars. But the state has little patience with the pursuit of pure knowledge—or "speculation," as Schleiermacher terms "that aspect of scientific activity that relates primarily only to the unity and the communal form of all knowledge" (231)—seeking instead the practical information that will serve its specific purposes.

In his second chapter Schleiermacher distinguishes among the three principal educational institutions in Germany: schools, universities, and academies. The school, or *Gymnasium*, is the institution where the boy discovers whether or not he has any aptitude for science and acquires the mass of knowledge necessary for any progress in learning. The academy, in contrast, is the institution where the masters of scientific knowledge are assembled among themselves in a configuration that reflects the whole of knowledge. The university, finally, is the institution where the idea of science is awakened in the young men who have been prepared by acquiring preliminary knowledge and who now learn to understand every phenomenon from the standpoint of science and in its larger context with reference to the unity and totality of cognition. This function is suggested by the name of the institution, for the university is the place where "not only manifold—albeit new and higher—pieces of information are collected, but the totality of cognition should be represented inasmuch as man displays the principles and, as it were, the basis of all knowledge in such a manner that the capability arises of working one's way into every field of knowledge" (238). For this reason the student spends less time at the university than the pupil at school, for he is not attempting to master a variety of material but simply to experience the single moment, the highest consciousness of reason, as a guiding principle. At school the progress is linear, from one specific detail to the next. At the university, in contrast, progress is circuitous—from the center out and then back again—inasmuch as "in every field the encyclopedic, the general survey of the whole and its connections, is presupposed as the most essential and is made the basis of the entire instruction" (239). Accordingly "philosophical instruction" is the basis for everything that is accomplished at the university, and "the scientific spirit" embracing "the immediate unity of all cognition" is regarded as the highest principle (240–41). "The scientific mind that has been awakened by philosophical instruction . . . works its way from the midpoint ever more deeply into the discrete—to discover, to relate, to produce original results, and to maintain through its correctness the achieved insight into the nature and the interrelatedness of all knowledge" (241).

The "Nähere Betrachtung der Universität im Allgemeinen" that constitutes chapter three amounts to a detailed critique of the more radical aspects of Fichte's *Deduzierter Plan*—although Schleiermacher does not mention Fichte by name and presumably had not seen the text of his proposal. Schleiermacher takes issue with the idea that students should be precluded from civic duties, and he rejects the separation of dedicated students from less talented or less highly motivated colleagues. He also rejects criticism of the lecture as a means of instruction. "Just as the entire university is a scientific community, the lectures in particular are its sacred aspect [*Heiligtum*]" (250).

The chapter "Von den Fakultäten" presents the familiar Jena view that the philosophical faculty should constitute the center of the university. "In it alone the whole natural organization of knowledge is contained—philosophy in its purely transcendental aspect as well as in its scientific and historical aspects" (259). The other three faculties, in contrast, have their unity not from cognition but rather from external application, and they appropriate whatever they need for this purpose from the various disciplines. "The philosophical faculty alone, therefore, represents what the scientific association for its part would have founded as a university," while the other three faculties respond to external needs. The "true spirit of the university" requires, furthermore, that the greatest freedom must prevail within every faculty, with no prescriptions concerning the sequence of lectures or the coverage of the field. Such enforced repetition leads only to intellectual stagnation. Student and teacher alike are best served when the professor follows his own interests and inclinations. After all, it is his function to inspire his students with his model of active scholarship—not to teach specific facts.

In his last chapter, "Von den Sitten der Universität und von der Aufsicht," finally, Schleiermacher argues that the students must also share in academic freedom. There should be absolutely no pressure on students, for their goal is not learning as such (*Lernen*) but cognition (*Erkennen*). Many will not make proper use of this freedom, but the best will thrive. Like Fichte, Schleiermacher complains about the student tendency to reject everything outside academic life as Philistinism and regrets the practice of dueling. But the first will be obviated if students are no longer isolated so rigorously from the rest of society, and he proposes regularized exercise and training in fencing as an antidote to dueling.

It was largely due to Schleiermacher's pamphlet that the Jena ideas gradually penetrated the Prussian consciousness: the belief in the university as an institution combining all the faculties and unified by a central faculty of philosophy professing an "encyclopedic" approach to knowledge. The force of his arguments overcame the long-standing rationalist prejudices against the traditional university and prepared the ground for the establishment of a university in Berlin.

Initially and for a variety of reasons—including Stein's lack of enthusiasm for the project, disgruntlement among the professors who were not offered positions, and the reopening of the University of Halle in 1808—the enterprise failed. By the late fall of 1808, however, the situation had changed once again. At Napoleon's insistence his archenemy Stein was forced out of office—but not before he had succeeded in reorganizing the Prussian government in such a manner that power was shifted from the former royal cabinet into a new centralized system of ministries. Beyme, appointed to head the Ministry of Justice, had nothing further to do with educational policy. On Stein's recommendation Count Alexander von Dohna was named as minister of the interior. To the newly created Section for Religion and Public Instruction, which reported to his ministry, Dohna—again on Stein's recommendation—summoned as "chief" the forty-two-year-old Prussian envoy to the Vatican, Wilhelm von Humboldt.

• • •

Humboldt, who had spent what he regarded as the happiest years of his life in Rome and had no wish to forsake his studies in Vatican City for the tedium of administration in Berlin, resisted the appointment for several months. But by the end of February 1809 he was finally obliged to accept the position that made him responsible, among a variety of other charges, for the establishment of the new university. The task that Humboldt faced was anything but a simple one. As it turned out, he had only sixteen months—from late February of 1809 until June of 1810—to accomplish the monumental undertaking. In addition, during most of that period the king and his court were in Königsberg, with the result that Humboldt, whose wife and family had remained behind in Rome, had to spend a good deal of his time—from mid-April 1809 until early December of that same year—in the remote Prussian capital, far from Berlin and the local situation. If Humboldt, despite all these difficulties, succeeded in accomplishing the task that Beyme had been unable to bring about and in founding a university that for a time at least represented the fulfillment of the Jena vision, his success was due to at least two factors: the shift in public opinion owing to Schleiermacher's monograph and his own unique views and abilities.

Humboldt had studied law in Frankurt an der Oder and then law and philology (in Heyse's seminar) at Göttingen, but neither of these experiences enhanced his view of the university as an institution. However, during the four years that he spent largely in Jena, from 1794 to 1797, he was in close contact with Goethe, Schiller, Fichte, the Schlegels, and the other leading spirits during the very years when the Jena ideal of the university was being shaped.[126] In sum, his view of education combined the Weimar conception of *Bildung* with the Jena spirit of the university. Along with Fichte and the historian Woltmann, he was one of the founding editors of Schiller's literary journal *Die Horen*. He sat at Schiller's side to listen to Fichte's 1794 lectures on the university. Accordingly it is no surprise to find in Humboldt's own writings on the institution a number of statements reflecting that view.[127]

First of all, Humboldt had to argue that the new institution should be a university and that it should be located in Berlin. In the "Antrag auf Errichtung der Universität Berlin" that he submitted to the king on May 12, 1809, barely two months after having assumed his new position, he states his own position, which is emphatically at odds with the rationalist argument in favor of specialized professional schools and conspicuously echoes many of Schleiermacher's arguments. "I am also convinced that the name *university* will require no justification in Your Majesty's eyes. It is only supposed to indicate that no science is excluded and that the teaching institution will also confer academic distinctions" (31).[128] Humboldt assures the king that "everything antiquated and otherwise detrimental" will of course disappear. But it would be unfeasible to attempt to establish any institute of higher learning that would not be a university because theory and practice cannot be easily separated in instruction; moreover, it would not be easy to insert an entirely new type into the three traditional models that Schleiermacher had identified: school, university, and academy. Humboldt returns to the notion of the university as "one organic whole" in another report to the king on July 24, 1809 (115). Again he insists on "the old and traditional name of *university*," adding that— no matter what title it might bear—it must contain everything that the concept of a university contains. "Beginning with the proper views of general education, it could neither exclude subjects, nor begin from a higher standpoint (since the universities embrace the highest one), nor finally limit itself merely to practical exercises" (116).

His view of the university as a moral institution symbolizing and embodying the unity of all knowledge is summarized in his great fragmentary essay of 1810, "Ueber die innere und äußere Organisation der höheren wissenschaftlichen Anstalten in Berlin," which begins with the claim:

The conception of higher scientific institutions as the summit on which everything comes together that bears directly on the moral culture of the nation is based on the conviction that they are meant to deal with science in the most profound and broadest sense of the word and to contribute to its use as a material of intellectual and ethical development that is prepared to that end not with intent but with purpose. (255)

It is the characteristic of universities that they deal with knowledge never as an accomplished body of facts (as do the schools) but as a problem to be solved; and it is this characteristic that determines the relationship between teachers and students, neither of whom is there for the sake of the other but rather both for the benefit of science (256). The university must be organized according to the principle that knowledge ("Wissenschaft") is an end in itself and to be sought constantly. As soon as knowledge is sought for some other purpose, its ethical value is lost, "for only knowledge that comes from within and can be planted into the inner being is capable of shaping character, and the state is as little concerned as is humanity with knowing and talking but with character and action" (258). If this principle of autonomous science is kept in mind, everything else will take care of itself. "There will then be no lack either of unity nor completeness; the one automatically seeks out the other, and both posit one another—the secret of any good scientific method—in a proper reciprocity" (259).

Humboldt never had call or occasion to express himself extensively or theoretically on the nature of the university. We have from his pen no such monographs as we possess from Fichte, Schelling, and Schleier-macher. Almost all his statements occur in the context of administrative reports during his brief but remarkable tenure as chief of the Section for Religion and Public Instruction. Yet those brief statements make it quite clear that he set about his task motivated by a vision of the university that was indebted extensively to the Jena rhetoric with which he was familiar.

If Humboldt's conception of the university was not unique, his success in achieving the goal at which so many had failed can be attributed in large measure to his magnificent diplomatic and administrative gifts. Having persuaded the king to accept his proposal, he faced the equally difficult task of dealing with the scholars themselves. Yet he managed to attract to his university the most distinguished faculty—and one of the youngest—in Germany: in philology F. A. Wolf, in law Savigny, in theology Schleiermacher, in philosophy Fichte, in medicine Reil—and on and on. This was a faculty for which the Romantics could summon a good deal of enthusiasm and a project that they observed with unabated interest. Indeed, the presence of Savigny, whom Arnim helped to recruit to Berlin, caused his brothers-in-law, Brentano and Arnim, to believe that they also had a certain influence in what they regarded as the new Romantic university. Rarely has the founding of an academic institution been accompanied by as much literary activity as was evident in Berlin in 1810.

Arguing that Berlin should make a virtue of necessity and locate its university in the very heart of the city (rather than in the suburbs and away from what some critics viewed as the temptations of the city), Humboldt had obtained for his institution the Prinz Heinrich Palais, a large, handsome building on the boulevard Unter den Linden across from the theater and only a few hundred yards from the royal palace. Lectures in the Palais had actually begun by the end of 1809, almost a year before the official opening of the university. In December Humboldt reported to the king his success in recruiting Wolf for the faculty—an achievement of great significance for the university, "since no one can match him in philological erudition" (233). Moreover, the large atten-

dance at the lectures on Greek literature that Wolf had immediately undertaken (in Latin), despite the fact that no students had yet been admitted to the university, demonstrated the desire in Berlin for serious
scholarly study—a fact seconded by the attendance at public lectures in
the Palais by Fichte, Schleiermacher, and others.

.   .   .

The university got under way on October 10, 1810, when Schmalz, who
had been appointed rector for the first term, welcomed the faculty senate
to its first meeting. Lectures began formally on October 29. Initially a
ceremony of "proclamation" had been planned for October 15, the birthday of the crown prince. But for a variety of reasons the ceremony was
postponed: the walls of the building were still damp; the faculty was not
yet complete; the university statutes had not yet been promulgated; and
there were too few students to justify the occasion. (At its first meeting
Schmalz announced to the faculty that sixty-one students had already
enrolled, including one prince, one count, and ten noblemen; by the time
the semester began, there were 256 students—almost half of them in the
medical faculty.)[129] In fact, the postponed ceremony never took place, and
so the University of Berlin began its history with little formal *éclat*. But
that fact did not deter the Romantic writers, who set about composing
poems to commemorate the occasion. On October 15 Kleist's *Berliner
Abendblätter* published a poem by Arnim, "Der Studenten erstes Lebe-
hoch bei der Ankunft in Berlin am 15. Oktober 1810," consisting of fourteen quatrains alternating between the solo voice of a "native" (*Eingeborner*) and the "chorus of arriving students."[130] On the festive birthday the
*Eingeborner* greets the pilgrims, weary from their journey through the
sandy soil of Brandenburg, and asks them what drives them abroad
through the wilderness. When they reply that it is the "pious desire for
science" ("fromme Lust / Nach Wissenschaft") glowing in their breasts,
he assures them that their quest is ended: they have found the place
where they can work productively.

> Geendigt ist die Pilgerreis',
> Hier schafft in gutem Willen,
> Hier betet froh in mut'gem Fleiß,
> So wird sich viel erfüllen.

(The pilgrims' journey is ended. Work here with a good will;
pray here in courageous diligence, and much will be fulfilled.)

The chorus of students admires the spacious avenue beside the quiet river
Spree, where science, which unites the entire world, can be resplendent:

> So still, so treu die Spree hier fließt,
> So hell, so weit die Straße grüßt,
> So still, so hell glänzt Wissenschaft,
> Die aller Welt Verbindung schafft.

The *Eingeborner* points out to them the "hero's palace" that has been
consecrated to science and that suggests the courage and vigor with
which science is being renewed in Berlin:

> Hier findet ihr der Wissenschaft
> Ein Heldenschloß geweihet,
> Das deute euch den Mut, die Kraft,
> Womit sie sich erneuet.

The song concludes with praise for the king, whose vision has brought
forth this new palace of learning.

Arnim's poem celebrates the Jena theme—the centrality of *Wissenschaft* and its role as the force that unifies all knowledge—without developing it fully. The poem is primarily a paean to the wisdom of the king,
who decided to create a home for science in his kingdom. The real an-
them of the new university—although the occasion for which it was written never took place—was the "cantata to the 15th of October 1810,"
written under the title *"Universitati Litterariae"* by Arnim's brother-in-
law, Clemens Brentano, possibly at the suggestion of Savigny. Brentano's
cantata, which was advertised in the *Berliner Abendblätter* (on October
13), was set to music by Reichardt and published with a title vignette
depicting the university building in the Prinz Heinrich Palais. (The title,
which is also the concluding line of the lengthy work, refers to the legend
that Humboldt had had embossed in gold above the portal of the university building.[131]) The cantata opens with a chorus of trustees (*Vorsteher*—
the ministers and other government officials), who observe that teaching
is a divine responsibility because Jesus also was a teacher:

> Es ist ein göttlich Werk, zu lehren;
> Er selbst, er hat gelehret
> Die hohen Priester in dem Tempel,
> Da er, ein Kind noch, wandelte
> Auf seiner Erde.[132]

(To teach is a divine task. He himself taught the high priests in the temple when, as still a child, he walked upon his earth.) They are followed by a chorus of teachers who praise the king for establishing the "house of science" ("Haus der Wissenschaft") and take an oath to teach the truth in his honor. Then a combined chorus of scholars and citizens intones a hymn to Friedrich Wilhelm III, who had the courage to undertake this project of *Wissenschaft* in a period of turmoil: "[Du] brichst im Sturm ein Lorbeerreis" (219). These first three choruses are followed by three more sections that praise Germany as the land with a particular mission for teaching and scholarship. First the "voice of the poet" notes Germany's impulse to wisdom:

Mein Deutschland, du stehst ewiglich,
Tief innerlich
Verbindet dich ein hoher Weisheitstrieb.

(219–20)

Then a "chorus of citizens" states that the finest achievements of German rulers have been their universities:

Aber eure schönsten Werke
Hat die neue Macht geehret,
Eurer hohen Schulen Kreis.

And the second triad is concluded by a "general chorus" praising Germany's grandeur in agriculture, defensive arms, and scholarship:

Fleiß ziert Deutschland,
Wenn es nähret,
Treu ist Deutschland,
Wo es wehret,
Groß ist Deutschland,
Wenn es lehret,
Pflug und Schwert und Buch es ehret.

(220–21)

(Diligence adorns Germany when it nourishes; loyal is Germany when it defends; great is Germany when it teaches: it honors plow and sword and book.)

From praise of nation the cantata now moves to praise of Berlin by the Muses, who greet the "royal city" in whose midst "a German Mount of the Muses" ("ein deutscher Musenberg," 221) has arisen. The "voice of the poet" announces the arrival of the students:

Ich sehe eine sel'ge Schar
Von Jünglingen dir nahen,
Ein ernster Rausch durchweht ihr Haar, . . .
(222)

Then the City, the Muses, and the Citizens all welcome the university, the students, and the professors. In a chorus teeming with Brentano's favorite mining images the students proclaim the "Mount of Muses" in which a source of precious ores has been discovered in the heart of their land and whose new veins they intend to mine:

> Glück auf, Glück auf! ihr Meister all,
> Die ihr den Bau gegründet,
> Wir grüßen euch mit lautem Schall,
> Die Lampen sind gezündet.
> Glück auf, Glück auf! wir fahren ein
> Nach edelem Gesteine,
> Ein jeder soll gewärtig sein
> Daß er es redlich meine.
> (1: 224)

(*Glück auf!* all you masters, who have founded the building— we greet you with loud acclaim; the lamps are lighted. *Glück auf!* we enter in search of noble stone. Each of us should take heed that he has honest intentions.)

At this point a "chorus of citizens" proclaims the arrival of the "four wise lofty women" who enter the university building through its open portal: the spirit of theology in her violet garb with Bible in hand; the black-robed spirit of philosophy, her head garlanded with laurel; the purple-clad spirit of law with her scales and sword; and the spirit of medicine in scarlet gown with the staff of Aesculapius. This "divine race" is welcomed by voices from the citizens, and the students of the four faculties welcome their teachers. A "voice from the chorus of the faculties" responds to the greetings. Then the "chorus of the Academy of Sciences" approaches and offers a pomegranate as a symbol of the unity of knowledge:

> Wir nahen uns und bieten euch die Hände,
> Ihr die, was wir gelernt, nun lehren wollt,
> Den Apfel der Granate nehmt als Spende,
> Der Vielheit Einheit in der Schale Gold.
> (226)

(We approach and offer you our hands, you who wish to teach what we have learned. Take the pomegranate as a gift, the unity of multiplicity in a shell of gold.)

The faculty accepts the gift with thanks, and the "voice of the trustees" reminds students and teachers to be grateful to the state for its support:

> So lerne Schüler fromm,
> So werd' Studente dann gelehrt,
> Und Meister lehre treu,
> Das ist, was ernst der Staat von euch begehrt,
> Der Staat, der euch ernährt,
> Der Staat, der von euch lernend, hoch euch ehret,
> Der Staat, der hohe Freiheit euch gewährt.
>
> (227)

(Then let the pupil study piously and let the student be taught and let the master teach loyally—that is what the state earnestly desires of you: the state that nourishes you, the state that, learning from you, holds you in high esteem, the state that guarantees you freedom.)

The students praise the academic freedom ("Du hohe Wissensfreiheit," 227) that has been disclosed to them, and the professors promise to teach them as colleagues, not as pupils:

> Nicht Schüler seid ihr, ihr seid uns Gefährten,
> Wir sind der Fahrt erfahrne Männer nur.
>
> (228)

The "chorus of citizens" asks in conclusion for an exegesis of the "golden inscription" that glitters above the portal, and a "voice from the teachers" explains that the golden words refer to the totality, the universality, unity, and commonality of knowledge to which the palace has been consecrated:

> Der Ganzheit, Allheit, Einheit
> Der Allgemeinheit
> Gelehrter Weisheit,
> Des Wissens Freiheit,
> Gehört dies königliche Haus!
> So leg' ich euch die goldnen Worte aus:
> UNIVERSITATI LITTERARIAE. (229)

Brentano's great cantata clearly represents a poeticization of the Jena view of the university as an institution embodying the unity of knowledge—not separate professional schools—to be pursued in academic freedom by students and faculty working together as colleagues. But Brentano departs from Fichte, Schleiermacher, and Humboldt in his understanding of the dialectical relationship between university and state and of the need for the university to situate itself gratefully within the city and the state that support its enterprise. It is in this acknowledgment of the institution's responsibility to the state that we recognize the shift of emphasis that has taken place since Jena. Humboldt established his university essentially in the spirit of Jena—of Fichte's Jena—as an institution dedicated to the pursuit of pure science. But the younger generation, under the influence of a nationalism generated by the Napoleonic wars, saw things differently. For them the university was an institution by, of, and for the state. While this message is evident as a secondary theme in Brentano's cantata, it emerges in full force in the works of his Berlin associates, Kleist and Adam Müller.

· · ·

The founding of the university was the first public issue addressed in the *Berliner Abendblätter* that Kleist and Adam Müller had recently established.[133] In the second number of the journal (October 2, 1810) Müller began a three-part article entitled "Freimüthige Gedanken bei Gelegenheit der neuerrichteten Universität in Berlin," which makes evident the extent to which the younger Prussian Romantics had moved away from the goals of Jena. Müller begins by noting that in the first lecture catalogue of the new university all civil qualifications and titles are omitted following the names of the professors. Acknowledging only scholarly distinctions, the university seeks to rehabilitate the long-discredited titles "professor" and "doctor"—"and the effort must succeed because names like Wolf, Niebuhr, Savigny, Reil, Fichte, et al. occur in this plainly sublime ornamentation."[134] Müller finds it appropriate that the state should have, in addition to its civil and military ranks, a special and independent ranking for the intellectual estate of professors, who should not be required to take time from their scholarship to compete for civil titles. The first article ends with an appeal for the kind of academic freedom—that is, freedom from censorship in scholarly matters—that had once enabled Göttingen to achieve its greatness.

In return for these benefits, Müller continues on October 3, the university has the responsibility to serve its fatherland. The earlier "cosmopolitan" focus of scholars, which had contributed to its disintegration, must be balanced by a national ("vaterländische") emphasis. "If the scholars want to have an influence in this specific Prussian state, they must first of all serve it. The university is not being founded as a mere feast for the scientific *gourmands* of Europe" (11). Scholars lost their standing because they forsook allegiance to their nations in a quest for recognition abroad. "The immediate purpose of all higher education is the preparation (*Bildung*) of civil servants" (12)—a word that Müller takes in its broadest sense to designate every citizen of the state, and specifically the scholar to the extent that he is a government official. "It is the greatest mistake of education if it educates with idealizing randomness ("ins Blaue"), aiming at nothing but generalities, and for all its humanity and philanthropy does not succeed in taking a position and having an effect" (12). In the absence of a binding Christian faith, which once enabled Bologna, Paris, and Prague to thrive in the late Middle Ages, the scholarly sciences can flourish only if they dedicate themselves freely to the state. Let there be an end to collecting and discovering and emending, Müller exclaims. The last century accumulated a superfluous amount of knowledge. The sciences can now be served by restoring to them the vitality, the practical vigor, the flesh and blood that they lost "in the barbarism of the recent past" (12).

The conclusion (October 4) begins with an attack on "the currently prevailing hypercritical spirit of the scholars that is turned away from all true science, the war of all against all, the fruitless splintering of the literary republic" (15). This deplorable condition can be improved only through the state, which can provide for the dissociated sciences a common, definite, practical goal. Why, he asks, have our schools of higher education produced nothing but virtuosi of jurisprudence and provincial officials? The higher officers of the state have all reached their position by innate talent and practical experience. The answer is simply that the old universities have neglected the study of their fatherland for the sake of the universe. "It is in the highest interest of the state that the candidates for its offices should enter the special court and the special administrative department in no other manner than equipped with a capable complete view of the fatherland-universe" (15–16). The new university in Berlin can demonstrate that the patriotic goal can be accomplished with no loss for the European universe or for the republic of the sciences.

The editors of the *Berliner Abendblätter* continued their scrutiny of the new institution. On October 10 it was noted that "an anonymous essay on the proclamation of the university" (38) could not, for compelling reasons, be published—a reference, it is assumed, to a lost article by Kleist expressing the editors' dissatisfaction with the decision to postpone the opening ceremonies that they had announced so eagerly in their pages.[135] On October 8 Adam Müller weighed in on the debate concerning scholarly advisory panels to the government with a piece ("Ueber die wissenschaftlichen Deputationen," 29–30) arguing, characteristically, that it is more important for state officials to inform themselves about scientific developments so that they will be in a position to control the scholars and not be controlled by them. And on October 27 an anonymous contributor (presumably Schleiermacher) made a "modest query" ("Bescheidene Anfrage," 97–98) as to why *Naturphilosophie* was not represented on the faculty of the university if, indeed, the *universitas literaria* is supposed to embrace not simply a totality of the scientific disciplines but also to represent the principal tendencies of the age. All major forms of philosophy should exist side by side in the faculty and be brought into controversy with one another—and not, as is suggested by the first lecture catalogue of the university, be represented only by Fichtean idealism.

Two points need to be noted with respect to the *Berliner Abendblätter*. First, even if the journal did not have the kind of influence on university policy that its editors hoped, it embodied the broad public interest in the new institution through its articles, its advertisement of Brentano's cantata, and its publication of Arnim's poem. The founding of the university in the face of adversity *was* viewed by the literary, intellectual, and cultural public as a heroic act and as the beginning of a new era in Prussia and Berlin. On November 12, 1810, for instance, Rahel Varnhagen reported in a letter to her husband that "the university, even if it should expire as the mere beginning of a university, is splendid—and truly dear to everyone here according to the capacities of each. It is a product of the mind, conceived, projected, undertaken in the midst of defeat, poverty, yes, fear and disorder! It is a greening of the earth through its own fire. May Phoebus cast his rays *mercifully* and not hurl any arrows upon the bold initiators."[136]

As to the second point, the repressive sentiments uttered by Adam Müller, who wished to keep the new institution under the strict control of the state, were far from representative. Most contemporaries—including specifically Humboldt, Savigny, and Brentano—disclaimed Müller's narrow views, writing them off as the opinion of a man embittered because, for all his efforts, he was never invited to join the faculty of the new university.[137] At the same time, Müller foreshadowed ominous developments. No sooner had the university opened its portals than a conflict began to take place between the Jena ideals of the faculty and the reality of the Prussian state. Indeed, it can be argued that the Jena ideal found its finest realization in the conception of the University of Berlin but that the ideal was compromised from the very instant of its realization.

· · ·

Humboldt, who had accepted with reluctance his position as director of the Section for Religion and Public Instruction, was wearied by his efforts as well as the political intrigue in a time of turmoil and the bickerings of the very scholars in whose interest he was seeking to establish the new university. "You cannot imagine how many difficulties I have had to contend with," he wrote his wife on May 22, 1810, "how the scholars, the most unruly and least easily satisfied class of mortals, besiege me with their eternally conflicting interests, their jealousies, their envy, their desire to dominate, their one-sided views where everyone believes that only his discipline deserves support and nurturing."[138] In June he submitted his request for resignation and actually left Berlin on August 15, almost two months before the formal opening of the university that he had brought into existence. During the first months following his departure—in the period that witnessed the first faculty meeting and the beginning of lectures—his former associate and interim successor, G.H.L. Nicolovius, along with the faculty that he had brought together, managed to pursue a course essentially in the spirit of the free university that Humboldt had envisaged.[139] But on November 20, 1810, Nicolovius was replaced in a major reorganization of the ministry by Friedrich von Schuckmann, a professional civil servant whose abilities were greatly admired by Goethe, who had repeatedly tried to lure him to Weimar. But Schuckmann was also a Prussian authoritarian who put the interests of the state ahead of all else, including the Romantic conception of a pure *Wissenschaft*. Almost immediately he abolished the steering committee (*Einrichtungskommission*) that had been charged with the opening of the university, as well as the promulgation of its statutes, and handed over the entire matter to government administrators. In addition, he struck at the heart of the university's independence by annulling the financial arrangement proposed by Humboldt and tentatively approved by the king, according to which the university would receive the income from secularized domains assigned to it by the state.

Accordingly, during the winter months, as newly recruited faculty members arrived in Berlin and the lectures got under way, Rector Schmalz was engaged in a running battle with Schuckmann and his department to preserve at least some of the privileges under which the new university had been so idealistically inaugurated. Schmalz had been appointed for a term of one year, and despite several threats to resign and leave Berlin, he did manage to complete his term. But in July 1811 the twenty-three members of the faculty senate came together, although no statutes had yet been approved that would govern their procedures, to elect a rector. For various reasons of university politics and personal ambition it required four ballots before a clear majority could be obtained. Eventually Fichte emerged as the first rector of the university to be actually elected by his colleagues. The inaugural address that he delivered on October 19, 1811, before a closed group of faculty and students, represents the culmination of the Jena spirit in Berlin.

Fichte's lecture *Ueber die einzig mögliche Störung der akademischen Freiheit* constitutes perhaps the noblest distillation of his views on the university as an institution[140]—a sentiment poignantly enhanced by the threat that he no doubt already sensed to the institution whose establishment he had supported with such enthusiasm. Fichte begins by greeting the students and informing them with passionate conviction that academic freedom is beyond any doubt the "divine air" in which all benefits of the university thrive. He continues, with an italicized intensity that suggests his own underlying concern, to express his belief *"that at no university in the world is this academic freedom more secure and more firmly grounded than here at our university"* (452). He then proceeds to tell the students what a university ideally should be, using all the rhetoric with which we have become acquainted since his lectures of 1794. "The entire world exists solely in order that in it may be represented the transcendental, the godhead, and specifically so that it may be represented by means of conscious freedom" (452). The transcendental reveals itself to human reason, but it appears in ever greater clarity as reason purifies and enhances itself. Consequently the transfiguration of reason is the sole means through which mankind fulfills its destiny and each generation earns its place in history. "But the university is the institution created expressly for the securing of the uninterrupted continuity of this progress inasmuch as it is that point in which, with circumspection and according to rule, each generation transmits its loftiest cultivation of reason to the following generation" (453). If this is the case, Fichte continues, "then clearly the

university is the most important institution and the most sacred possession of mankind" (453), for within the university humanity lives a contin-
uous life that transcends all temporality. "The university is the visible
representation of the immortality of our race in that it permits nothing
truly essential to perish. . . . It is the visible representation of the unity of
the world as the phenomenon of the deity and of the deity itself" (453–
54).

Following this intoxicating paean, Fichte begins to characterize the
essential organization of the institution. "The entire rational culture of
the generation and the entire means of acquisition and the objects of this
culture must be completely represented in the totality of the teachers as
the representatives of that generation that is transmitting its culture"
(454). The teachers must be complemented by the students, the representatives of the generation to which this loftiest culture is being transmitted.
If these two forces are present, then nothing external is required. Indeed,
external influences can only be detrimental to the purpose of the university, which should be left entirely to itself to pursue its mission. For this
reason the university requires and demands academic freedom in the
broadest sense of the word. Each generation must be able to transmit its
freely achieved culture to the next generation in absolute freedom of
thought. The student, in turn, must be free to commit itself to this communication. Consequently—and here we hear again the tones of Fichte's
*Deduzierter Plan* of 1807—the student must be relieved during the period
of his studies from all civic burdens and demands; he should be answerable only to a special court of laws; and, finally, the temptations that
exceed the strength of still untested youth must be removed from his
path.

Whether the inner conditions governing teachers and students will be
fulfilled at Berlin, Fichte continues, remains to be seen. But he confidently
proceeds to explore the question of the external conditions required for
the success of the university. Fichte protests—too much?—that he is not
concerned about academic freedom of expression in such a liberated age
and kingdom as modern Prussia. Moreover, the personal freedom of the
students is acknowledged and assured by the law (specifically, as we have
already noted, by a section of the new *Allgemeines Landrecht*). But—and
here Fichte comes to the real topic of his discourse—a threat to academic
freedom exists from an entirely different side. What Fichte has in mind
is that old Jena nemesis, the eternal student—"that familiar type of person who, since he is in fact nothing and is otherwise tolerated nowhere

in human circumstances, claims to be a student and attaches himself to universities" (457–58). Fichte is confident that no representative of that deplorable breed is in his audience in Berlin. But he wants to define the danger. These false students, incapable of perceiving the true mission of the university, see only the externalities and regard students as a *class* of people, like nobles, bourgeois, or peasants. They do not understand that studying is a profession, that universities exist simply to accommodate that profession, and that no one can claim to be a student except the person who actively studies. But the false students regard their status as a class with privileges inherent to it and not granted by the state. Fichte takes several pages to catalogue with the full power of his irony the iniquities of these so-called students, who regard themselves as a special class and better than all Philistines. In their delusion these false students have constructed a para-university, a "Lehrgebäude über das Universitäts-Leben" (462), to which they dedicate all their energies. It is this false university, with its drinking and dueling and special rules, that constitutes the greatest internal threat to academic freedom. Fichte reminds his audience of the complaints, so frequently heard in the past, about the growing wildness of German universities and tells them of the crassly mercantilistic reasons, so familiar to him from his own Jena years, that cause local citizens to tolerate boorish student behavior.

Returning to the present, Fichte points out that circumstances in Berlin are completely different and that the students sitting before him are still "pure and unstained by the described errors" (471). These students have the opportunity and the mission to represent, in the midst of a still troubled populace, the image of "minds striving fervently for the loftiest and the most sacred" (472) and, moreover, to spread throughout the German nation a new image of the university as a place of cultivation for the highest purposes. He concludes with words of praise for the king and his statesmen, who had the vision to create the new university, and for his faculty colleagues, to whom the students may confidently entrust the protection of their academic freedom. He sends the students forth into the new academic year in the confident expectation that they will not permit their precious freedom to be undermined by the dangers that he has portrayed. "The sweetest reward of the office bestowed upon me has already been vouchsafed me in this hour—to envision in my imagination your vigorous thriving and to express in your presence our hopes for you as well as our blessings, with which all the hearts around you are beating" (476).

• • •

The ideal of the Romantic university, conceived in Jena and brought by way of Halle and Heidelberg to Berlin, was shattered virtually before its brief moment of realization in the Prinz Heinrich Palais. Only four months after his rectoral *Antrittsrede* Fichte submitted his resignation to the Section for Religion and Education, brought down by the very forces that he had attacked in his speech.[141] A Jewish student named Brogy lodged a complaint against two fellow students who had insulted and attacked him on university grounds in a blatant attempt to incite him to a duel. Fichte, sensing in this incident yet another example of the appalling fraternity morals that he had detested almost twenty years earlier in Jena, went after the offending students with the full authority of his office. He was opposed, however, by the majority of the faculty senate, including Schleiermacher, who took a more relaxed view of student disagreements and sought a compromising resolution. Never a man for compromise, Fichte resigned from his office, but not before the incident had brought dissension into the ranks of a faculty still early in the process of shaping itself. As Solger reported in a letter of March 22, 1812, "We have here a great internal and external war."[142] Fichte, in particular, "is making life bitter for us, not just through his paradoxical whims and true perversities, but also through his obstinacy and egotism." Fichte apparently had the unsettling practice of facing down his opponents by stating: "It is not I as an individual who says and wills this, but the Idea, which speaks and acts through me." The situation was exacerbated by other factors, e.g., the head-to-head competition among the faculty for fee-paying students. Thus Schleiermacher always insisted on holding his main lectures at precisely the same hour as Fichte.[143]

It was therefore a university already weakened by faculty discord and by tension between students and professors that was further undermined by the events leading up to the War of Liberation in 1813. Students and professors alike were caught up in the fervor of patriotism. In the summer preceding the Battle of Leipzig only fifteen students were enrolled in the university, and those professors who still held lectures were often speaking before empty seats.[144] Many professors devoted their energies to patriotic matters. Schleiermacher was one of the founders of a political newspaper, *Der preußische Korrespondent*. Schmalz offered his services to the state as a political publicist, and Fichte volunteered to serve the army as a "philosophical chaplain." The professors of medicine forsook their lecture halls for the military hospitals. And virtually the entire faculty—

including Savigny, Fichte, and Wolf—took part in training exercises of the local militia.

The university to which professors and students drifted back following the defeat of Napoleon was quite different in spirit from the institution that had been founded with such *éclat* only five years earlier. Fichte was dead, carried off by the fever that had ravaged the military hospitals in the winter of 1813–1814, and the remaining faculty members seemed enervated by the events of the past few years. On June 18, 1816, Humboldt wrote in response to the complaints of Nicolovius:

> Your laments are completely justified, but I know of no way to counter them. Like you, I see that the University of Berlin is doing more than declining, but it cannot help even if I speak to the Chancellor about it. The evil cannot be addressed by a step, by a single allocation of money. There must be a spirit, a solicitude, at least a good will that nurtures, protects, elevates. At present precisely the opposite prevails. . . . The spirit has departed from everything. People are sinking back into a vast quotidian morass.[145]

In 1817 the classicist August Böckh observed a resurgence of "narrow-minded professionalism" ("engherziges Brotstudium") among the students.[146]

By the time Hegel was called to Berlin in 1818 the spirit of the Romantic university had wholly disappeared, as he observed in his *Antrittsvorlesung.*

> Until recently it was in part the needs of the day that gave to the trivial interests of everyday life such a great effectiveness. In part it was the great interests of reality, the struggles to save and restore first of all the political whole of the people and the state, which made such demands upon all the capacities of the mind, the powers of all classes, as well as external resources, that the inner life of the mind could not claim any tranquillity.[147]

Hegel has great hopes for the future: "Those conditions appear again to have taken shape in which philosophy may once again claim attention and affection—when this almost silenced science may again raise its voice." The Germans have been able to stem the tide of reality and to preserve their nationality. It is now time for "the free kingdom of thought" to thrive in its autonomy, and Prussia is the state in which Hegel envisages a new blossoming of the power of mind. "Here education

[*Bildung*] and the flowering of the sciences constitute one of the most essential elements even in the life of the state; at this university, the university of the midpoint [note the Jena phrase *Mittelpunkt*], the midpoint of all intellectual formation and all science and truth, philosophy must also find its place and preeminent cultivation." Hegel believed that Germany had become by talent and default the true home of philosophy. "This science has taken refuge among the Germans and continues to live only among them; to us has been entrusted the preservation of this sacred light, and it is our mission to nurture it, to cultivate it, and to ensure that the highest prize that man can possess, the self-consciousness of his being, is not extinguished and does not disappear."

But Hegel's hopes were misplaced. Baron von Altenstein, the minister who replaced Schuckmann in 1817 and called Hegel from Heidelberg to Berlin, was even more authoritarian than Schuckmann and supervised the repressive measures instituted in 1819 by the infamous Karlsbad Decrees. At the same time, as the philosophical core of the curriculum was weakened, the university, prodded by a state that needed to rebuild its resources, poured its funds increasingly into the development of the natural sciences and displaced the humanities from its center. The ideal university, which had existed in the imagination of the Jena Romantics and been realized for a few fleeting months in the pristine *universitas literaria* of Berlin, now became a memory that lived on only in the memoirs, the poems, the novels of those who had briefly experienced it. Yet the university as the Romantics conceived it constituted the appropriate model of the transcendental mind in its totality and unity that provided the principal metaphor of the age.

CHAPTER SIX

# The Museum:
# Temple of Art

## Schinkel's Altes Museum

EVER SINCE its opening in 1830, Karl Friedrich Schinkel's museum in
the Berlin Lustgarten—known since the addition of a new annex as the
Altes Museum—has been treasured as one of the great monuments of
neoclassical architecture. The majestic edifice with its imposing frontal
plane of eighteen fluted Ionic columns constitutes a model of symmetry.
The vertical lines of the seemingly endless colonnade—a rare realization
of the stylophilic ideal proclaimed by neoclassical theorists—contrast dramatically with the horizontal planes of the great open stairway leading
up to the podium and the rectangular attic that masks the dome of the
central rotunda. Yet the design contains mysteries that belie its rationalism. Within the darkness of the portico the viewer can make out the
ascending movement of a recessed double-winged staircase leading into
the open entrance hall. Schinkel confided to his friend Sulpiz Boisserée
that he regarded the museum as his best design,[1] and this view has been
often confirmed by subsequent judges. Henry-Russell Hitchcock calls the
museum not just the finest work of the "great international master of
Romantic classicism" but also, along with the bank interiors of Sir John
Soane, "the masterpiece of the period."[2] Owing to the building's success,
the rotunda became a favorite motif of later nineteenth-century museum
architecture in the United States as well as Europe.[3] Schinkel's inspiration is evident in the work of some of the most distinguished twentieth-
century architects, such as Mies van der Rohe, and Philip Johnson regards
the museum as "Schinkel's most restrained and classical building and
urbanistically the most successful."[4]

Yet Schinkel's building, magnificent as it is, represents much more than the triumph of individual genius. If any structure can be said to exemplify the cultural thought of its time—not only in its design and setting but in its very conception—it is the Altes Museum. The fact that the building was dedicated in 1830 (August 3) on the sixtieth birthday of Friedrich Wilhelm III of Prussia underscores the symbolism of the occasion as a national event. The king had been obsessed for over thirty years with the idea of a national museum.[5] The demand for a unified collection of Prussian art had been in the air ever since the revitalization of the Berlin Academy of Arts in 1786 by Friedrich Anton von Heynitz, the same foresighted minister who two decades earlier had established the mining academy in Freiberg before his decision to move from Saxon to Prussian civil service. Like other enlightened rulers of Europe, Frederick the Great had permitted artists to copy in his private galleries several days a week, and this practice was continued by Friedrich Wilhelm II after his uncle's death in 1786.

On September 25, 1797, Alois Hirt, a historian of ancient architecture who had been appointed professor of fine arts in Berlin the preceding year, delivered a ceremonial address for the king's birthday, in which he pointed out that Prussia was lagging behind many courts of Germany and Europe that had long enjoyed centralized picture galleries and collections of antiquities—not just Vienna and Dresden but also a number of lesser residences. Hirt argued that all antiquities in the various royal collections should be brought together into a single museum and all the best paintings into a single gallery—preferably in Berlin, where they would be available to students and scholars at the academy for copying and study. The king approved the establishment of "a museum for artists and friends of art in Berlin"; and when he died only a month and a half later, Hirt's proposal was passed along to his successor, Friedrich Wilhelm III, with a strong endorsement by Heynitz. On January 18, 1798, Heynitz reported to Hirt that His Majesty acknowledged the desirability of a central museum but felt that the time was not appropriate for its realization because the Prussian treasury had been weakened by the first War of Coalition (1792–1797). However, he commissioned Hirt to work out tentative plans for the future, and thus began the king's commitment to a project that was to embrace in its history almost the entire age of Romanticism in Germany. Even during Prussia's darkest years the king and his most thoughtful advisers—men like Beyme, Hardenberg, and Humboldt—emphasized the importance of establishing and maintaining such intellectual and cultural institutions as the university and the museum despite and even as a response to military and political setbacks.

For the next twenty years circumstances were not propitious for the establishment of a museum. Following Prussia's defeat at Jena and Auerstedt in 1806, the French Commission of Trophies carried off scores of art treasures to complement booty from Italy in the Musée Central des Arts in the Louvre—known after 1804 as the Musée Napoléon. Meanwhile, the Prussians themselves removed other objects from Berlin and Potsdam for safekeeping in remote locations. In 1810 the king authorized a systematic cataloguing of the remaining royal art treasures. The count reported in 1812—80 statues, 133 busts, 29 vases, and 2,244 paintings— made it clear that the Prussian holdings in their ravaged state did not constitute a collection comparable to that of the finest European galleries. Yet paradoxically the wartime depredations contributed to the future quality of the museum because the king's advisers determined to purchase according to a systematic plan as they rebuilt the collections.

Following Napoleon's defeat, the plunder began to be returned from Paris—albeit with great public reluctance in France, as Varnhagen von Ense reported[6]—and in October of 1815 many items were exhibited at the Royal Academy for the benefit of wounded soldiers. Hirt took the occasion to express formally his hope that the paintings would never again be separated. In the succeeding years the original holdings were enriched by the purchase of two major collections from abroad: in 1815 the Giustiniani collection and, in 1821, the Solly collection of religious art. (An attempt failed to obtain for Berlin the Boisserée collection of older German art, which eventually went to Munich.)

With the rapid expansion of the collections by these additions the realization of the long-planned museum became imperative. In late 1822 the king had just approved the renovation of the old Academy building situated on Unter den Linden—the location that Hirt had been advocating since 1798—when on January 8, 1823, Schinkel submitted his radically original plan for a completely new building in the Lustgarten.[7] The plan was quickly approved by the Museum Building Commission and, by a Royal Cabinet Order of April 1823, funded with the budget of 700,000 thalers previously earmarked for the renovation. The single dissenting vote in the commission was cast by Hirt, whose gradually intensifying disagreements with the museum planners led finally in 1829 to his resignation.

Hirt's criticism of Schinkel's plan exposes such a symptomatic shift in the conception of the museum as an institution that it is worth scrutinizing in detail. As a professor at the Academy of Art (and Schinkel's one-time teacher in the history of architecture), Hirt was convinced that works of art should be housed centrally in museums and not separately and inaccessibly in palaces. "Only by making them public and uniting them in display can they become the object of true study, and every result obtained thereby is a new gain for the common good of mankind."[8] Although Hirt pays lip service to the Enlightenment ideal of "public instruction and noblest enjoyment," he did not have in mind a truly public museum in the modern sense. His thinking, rather, was compatible with the recommendations of Goethe's friend and consultant, Heinrich Meyer, who argued that galleries should be available to students all day every day but to *Liebhaber* only at special hours on certain days.[9] Accordingly Hirt proposed that the museum should be open to artists all week long but to the general public only on weekends from 8:00 A.M. to 4:00 P.M. Hirt's consistent preference among various possible locations for the museum was the Academy building itself, where it would be most conveniently accessible to students and scholars alike.

Hirt's conception of the museum as an institution intended primarily for study and a gathering place for scholars emerges from the controversy surrounding the inscription that he composed for it: FRIDERICUS GUILELMUS III STUDIO ANTIQUITATIS OMNIGENAE ET ARTIUM LIBERALIUM MUSEUM CONSTITUIT MDCCCXXVIII.[10] A cohort of consultants—ranging from Ludwig Tieck, Alexander von Humboldt, and the classicist August Böckh to Friedrich Schleiermacher responding in the name of the Historical-Philological Section of the Royal Prussian Academy—objected to Hirt's inscription on a variety of grounds, arguing that the word *omnigenus* was obsolete, that the phrase *artes liberales* was not classical, that the language lacked sonority and rhythm, and, above all, that the word *museum* referred in antiquity to academies and libraries rather than to collections of art. The art critic Carl Friedrich von Rumohr objected that Hirt knew no more Latin than a schoolboy.[11]

In fact, the vocable *museum* does not occur in the standard German dictionaries of the period, from Johann Christoph Adelung's *Grammatisch-kritisches Wörterbuch* (2nd ed., 1793) and Theodor Heinsius's *Volksthümliches Wörterbuch* (1820) to the Grimms' *Deutsches Wörterbuch* (vol. VI, 1885). And although one standard reference work of the eighteenth century, Zedler's *Universal-Lexikon*, concedes that *Museum* can designate both a temple for the veneration of the muses and a room containing art collections (*Kunst-Kammer*), the article states that the word indicates most properly a building in which scholars lived, dined, and studied together.[12] This was certainly the sense in which Goethe intended the word in *Faust*, when Wagner complains that the scholar confined in his *Museum* (1, 530) sees the real world only from afar, on holidays and through a telescope. But this was precisely Hirt's point: that the museum ought to be a refuge for scholars and students. The word *studium* was meant to indicate in no uncertain terms that the museum exists "not merely for pleasure but essentially also for education." Even though it represented an out-of-date attitude by 1828, Hirt's wording won the king's approval and was duly inscribed on the building, where it can still be deciphered today.

Schinkel had a radically different conception of the museum—a conception that reflected the thinking of the revolutionary age that shaped his ideas. Although the twentieth century has come to take for granted the existence of museums dedicated to the arts and open to the public, the institution was still very much in the process of being shaped when Schinkel was at work.[13] Earlier galleries, both royal and ecclesiastical, had often been accessible to the public by special dispensation, but visiting was a privilege, not a right, and could be revoked at any time, restricted for the use of artists at work, or made difficult by surly attendants. We are talking about a period, after all, that was still not remote from the days when Winckelmann had to convert to Catholicism in order to gain access to the classical sculptures in ecclesiastical collections. Thus in Vienna the royal collections were open after 1792 on Mondays, Wednesdays, and Fridays to anyone "with clean shoes"; the British Museum had been technically public ever since 1759, but entry was notoriously limited to holders of the rare tickets of admission.[14]

The first museum accessible to the public as a matter of policy was the Louvre, which opened in 1793 and rapidly became one of the most popular entertainments in Paris—so popular that many visitors complained that it was regarded as a social rather than a cultural gathering place. The collection, augmented by paintings recently looted from galleries all over Europe, was not only the largest collection of art ever assembled but also a conspicuous symbol of French power. But the hasty accumulation of hundreds of treasures in a facility not adequately prepared for them produced an Augean disarray. On a visit to Paris in 1797, Wilhelm von Humboldt noted the deplorable condition of the building and especially the damage to paintings from dampness and improper care.[15]

The lament about the Louvre became a leitmotif in the reports of Germans visiting Paris. In 1801 Heinrich von Kleist remarked that the main gallery was as cluttered as a junkroom (*Polterkammer*), while in other rooms the works lay strewn about, covered with dust, and even misplaced.[16] Two years later Friedrich Schlegel objected to the crowding, the inadequate lighting, and the poor displays.[17] Adolph Müller was appalled in 1808 at conditions in the sculpture gallery, which was open "like a tavern" (*Tabagie*) to anyone who could walk on two legs, while the Raphael Madonnas were "covered mineralogically with chalk," as crude, half-naked workers strutted about with iron bars and tools.[18] And in 1810 Varnhagen, observing that the collection—arranged more like a victory monument than an art gallery—had been damaged extensively by rain, dust, and building materials, experienced a "sensation of profanation."[19] In short, even the establishment of the public museum as an institution did not assure its suitability as a shelter for works of art.

The turmoil of the revolutionary era precluded any significant development of the institution: various private collections were made more freely accessible to the public in accordance with the spirit of the times. But the shaping of the museum into the institution as we know it today took place essentially in Germany during the years from 1815 to 1848. Schinkel's Altes Museum, the first public museum conceived and constructed as such in the state of Prussia, plays a major role in that history. In accord with the explicit wishes of the king, as he noted in his proposal, it was to be an institution for the edification of the nation ("für die Bildung der Nation").[20] The primary purpose of any museum, as he elaborated later in a memorandum composed jointly with Gustav Waagen, the young art historian who was to become the first director of the painting gallery, should be "to awaken in the public a sense of fine art as one of the most important branches of human civilization."[21] All other purposes—including arrangements for artists to copy and for scholars to study—must be secondary to the goal of public education. This set of priorities was confirmed by the rules that Wilhelm von Humboldt, as chairman of the Committee for Arranging the Museum, formulated for the galleries.[22] In specific contrast to most galleries, Humboldt noted, artists would be permitted to work in the new museum only to the extent that their activity did not interfere with free public access to the works of art.

Given this shift in emphasis from the narrowly academic purposes advocated by Meyer and Hirt to the broadly cultural impulse of the new age, the location of the museum in the Academy building no longer remained an important consideration—especially since, as Schinkel pointed out, the walls and foundations of the building had been undermined by corrosion caused by saltpeter from the royal stables, which were housed on the first floor of the same building, and could not bear the weight of the sculptures.[23] In addition, the shift from Hirt's building— which had to contain two academies (science as well as arts) in addition to the museum—to one erected specifically as a museum reflected Schinkel's general disdain for multi-purpose structures and his aesthetic preference for unity of purpose and design. To find a space suitable for a new building designed to house a unique national institution Schinkel proposed a daring solution.

The most elegant thoroughfare in Berlin and, with the opera and the university, the center of its cultural life, was Unter den Linden, a broad avenue extending almost a mile from Langhans's monumental Brandenburg Gate eastward to the palace bridge, which Schinkel had recently completed across the River Spree to the Lustgarten. The Lustgarten, located on a small island created by two arms of the Spree, was bordered on the south by the royal palace, on the east by the cathedral, and on the western bank across the river by Schlüter's arsenal, the most handsome Baroque building in the city. The Lustgarten constituted the geographical heart of the city and certainly its most imposing public plaza. But in 1823 its perfection was marred along the northern edge by a short canal that had been dug a century earlier in order to link the two branches of the river. Schinkel proposed a drastic and dramatic solution: to broaden the western channel to the point where it rejoined the main river farther downstream and, with the excavated earth, to fill in the canal north of the Lustgarten. This plan had two conspicuous advantages: it straightened out a tricky bend in the canal, making it more easily navigable and preventing congestion along a busy stretch of the main channel; and it created on the north side of the Lustgarten a new piece of land that Schinkel regarded as the loveliest site in Berlin, requiring, as he clearly realized, a monumental building.[24] The location had the benefit for city planning of removing an urban eyesore and replacing it with a beautiful edifice. Above all, the location of the site, facing the palace and adjacent to the cathedral, enabled Schinkel to assert architecturally—in signs not lost on his semiotically sophisticated contemporaries—the claim of art to exist on a par with church and state. That Schinkel was fully aware of this symbolism is evident both from the site plans and drawings, in which he represented the Lustgarten as it would appear with its three principal buildings, and from the design itself, which is calculated with an eye to the proportions of Boumann's cathedral (which Schinkel had renovated a few years earlier) and the lines of Schlüter's restoration of the royal palace.

To appreciate the significance of Schinkel's achievement we should pause to note another aspect. Although the public museum as an institution had been taking shape for some thirty years, there was virtually no precedent for the building itself. Almost all existing museums, whether ecclesiastical or secular, had been converted from existing structures— like the Louvre in Paris or the Uffizi in Florence—or added to them, like the Museo Pio-Clementino in the Vatican. The Fridericianum in Kassel (1769-1779) had been built separately, to be sure, but to house collections of every sort, from libraries, natural curiosities, and scientific instruments to antiquities and paintings. During the revolutionary era and the Napoleonic wars there was virtually no major construction activity on the Continent outside of France. The two museum buildings erected before Schinkel undertook his project were also not total museums. The Dulwich Gallery, built by Sir John Soane in 1811-1814, had the distinction of being the first independent building erected to be a picture gallery, but it was still essentially a small (five-room) private collection that also served other purposes. And the Glyptothek currently being built (1816–1830) in Munich by Leo von Klenze was designed for the display of classical sculpture and also contained a few rooms designated for ceremonies of state. Schinkel was, in short, the first architect in Europe to be faced with the challenge of designing and erecting what was in effect a new architectural genre: a public museum dedicated solely to the display of painting and sculpture.

Much to Hirt's disgruntlement, the king approved Schinkel's bold plan—both its location and its design—and on July 25, 1825, the cornerstone was laid on a foundation that had required 3,053 piles to be set in the marshy ground of the filled-in canal at an additional expense of more than 70,000 thalers. Hirt objected, for reasons of economy as well as aesthetics, to the most characteristic features of Schinkel's design—notably the stairway, the colonnade, and the rotunda.[25] These objections expose the fundamental difference of opinion between the Enlightenment academician, who wanted an unpretentious space with no distractions in which to display works of art for the benefit of students and scholars, and the Romantic architect with a keen appreciation of symbolic statement who shared the emerging view of art as sacred and, consistently, of the museum as a sacral space, a temple, a sanctuary—in short, a work of art in itself designed for the contemplation of works of art.

All the architectural features to which Hirt objected can be understood as Schinkel's effort to enhance the sacral aspect of the museum. First, it was the function of the front staircase as well as the great double stairway, looming mysteriously in the darkness of the portico, to exemplify the idea that the visitor must ascend from the everyday world for an encounter with the majesty of art. With the spectacular colonnade, then, Schinkel lent to his building what he called "grandeur" and "character." (The influential Étienne-Louis Boullée, as we know from his posthumously published treatise on architecture, taught his students that the colonnade was the most "majestic" and "agreeable" architectural motif.[26]) As for the rotunda, finally, such a mighty edifice as a museum, he explained in his response to Hirt's objections, requires a central point as the sanctuary (*Heiligthum*) in which the most precious possessions are preserved. "The view of a beautiful and sublime space should make the viewer receptive and produce a mood for the enjoyment and recognition of everything that the building contains."[27] The rotunda as a feature of museum design was not original with Schinkel; it was modeled after the Sala Rotonda in Simonetti's Museo Pio-Clementino in the Vatican (1775), which Schinkel had first seen in 1803–1804 and had again admired on his trip to Rome in 1824. But its function in the Altes Museum was to provide a worthy center that would prepare the visitor spiritually for the encounter with art. While Hirt objected to its excessive size, Schinkel intended it to over-whelm the visitor with its sheer monumentality. It is symptomatic that Schinkel refers to the rotunda as a "pantheon,"[28] a term that betrays his sense of the space as sacred.[29]

If the location of the museum was intended to remind the visitor that he was approaching a national cultural institution equal in standing to church and state, and if its external design was calculated to inspire a sense of religious awe in the presence of art, the arrangement of space and works within the museum was meant to have unique effects of its own. The first intention of the arrangement was to emphasize the integrity of the individual work of art, and the movement from the rotunda to the galleries required Schinkel to solve the fundamental architectural problem of the transition from the monumental to the human scale. When Schinkel visited the Louvre, he was dismayed, as were most other foreign visitors, to find that the vast and cluttered concourse invited the public to promenade rather than to contemplate the works of art and thus transformed what should be a sanctuary of art into "a rendezvous of the beau monde and demimonde of Paris" ("zum Rendezvous der höheren und niederen Pariser Welt")[30]—a condition familiar from Hubert Robert's painting of the Louvre around 1786. At the Uffizi and other galleries it offended his sense of order to find that paintings and sculptures were intermingled in a confusing variety,[31] as is evident in such contemporary representations as Pannini's painting of the Galleria Valenti Gonzaga in Rome (ca. 1740) or Teniers's various depictions of late seventeenth-century galleries.

Schinkel sought to counteract such confusion on both floors of his museum, as Humboldt pointed out to the king in his final report of August 21, 1830—a document that provides the most precise description of the museum in its original installation according to its original premises. The first floor was devoted wholly to sculpture. Rather than situating the statues in the traditional manner along the walls or in niches, where they could be viewed only from one side, Schinkel arranged them alongside the columns that divided the gallery into three sections. Humboldt emphasized to the king the novelty of this arrangement, which existed in no other collection of the day. (In Klenze's Glyptothek in Munich the statues were set up in aedicules along the wall.) "The position alongside the columns provides the statues with a background against which they are effectively set off; at the same time, they receive proper lighting and can be viewed from all sides. In addition, the viewer has the advantage of not having to take in too much at one time."[32] Schinkel also designed a pedestal for each statue, assuring that each work would be seen at the proper height and in the proper proportions.

The same respect for the integrity of the individual work of art was evident in the picture galleries on the second floor. Just as he designed the pedestals for the statues, here Schinkel contrived individual frames for the paintings, taking care to suit the proportions and the period style of each one. Again he sought to counteract any spatial distraction by constructing, at right angles to the outer walls, a series of wooden screens that interrupted the open expanse of the galleries without extending all the way to the ceiling. This device, which strikingly anticipated the movable walls common in twentieth-century museums, provided intimate spaces in which the visitor, "without being overwhelmed by too many works of art all viewed at the same time," could contemplate single works or small groups of paintings "without any disturbance or distraction."[33] Also, as the first visitors noted, the divisions provided glare-free lighting for the paintings.

The disposition of paintings within the galleries, finally, sought to do justice to a collection that had been acquired more systematically than any other major collection of Europe, most of which had been assembled according to the often idiosyncratic taste of individual rulers or randomly as the booty of war. As Schinkel and Waagen put it in their report, "If one visits the famous painting galleries, one soon realizes that they are not arranged according to any rationally considered plan but rather owe their origin to accidents or hobbyhorses."[34] In contrast, the royal gallery in Berlin, as Humboldt appreciated, was "distinguished by the fact that it systematically covers all periods of painting, and the history of art can be traced from its beginnings on."[35] During the later eighteenth century a few galleries had begun to organize their holdings according to the Enlightenment principle of schools—Italian, Flemish, French, German. But usually the paintings within the schools were not organized in any particular order; if they were arranged at all, it was according to subject matter or the decorative principle of symmetry.[36] Schinkel's divisions "make it possible to separate the various schools of painting, which is necessary to bring out the essence of each painting and, at the same time, in such a way as to illustrate the development of art over the centuries."[37]

Schinkel and Waagen were powerfully influenced by their adviser, Carl Friedrich von Rumohr, the man generally regarded as the first modern art historian of Europe.[38] As the king's official consultant, Rumohr insisted on ridding the collection of the second-rate works purchased on the recommendation of his enemy, Hirt. Then he drew up a plan for displaying paintings in a manner that would "combine the aesthetic purpose with the art-historical and the systematic." Specifically, he rejected the conventional "statistical-geographical division," which sets up "schools" according to the birth certificates of the artists, in favor of a loosely historical sequence in which the various national schools came together at significant moments of influence or contact. In their joint memorandum Schinkel and Waagen summarized the criteria according to which paintings were to be hung in the new museum.[39] Each work ought to be, first, "a worthy representative of the time and school to which it belongs." The collection as a whole, in turn, ought to display as fully as possible "the true, principal, and fundamental masters" of each school and should provide an overview of those great masters who are noteworthy for their variety, as well as representative national painters who are at the same time great artists. Finally, the collection should be sparing in pictures by masters of limited individuality, including only one or two examples by minor artists. Humboldt noted in his suggestions for future purchases that the directors of the museum would be greatly assisted by the fact that the collection was already so logically arranged that its lacunae were evident, and therefore purchases could be made systematically—not haphazardly, as had been the tendency hitherto in major European collections.[40] In addition, as Humboldt approvingly observed, the museum provided such novel conveniences as placards that identified the paintings in each alcove by artist and title as well as a catalogue with information to assist the visitor.[41]

In its unique combination of characteristics—including purpose, situation, design, and interior organization—Schinkel's museum in the Lustgarten embodied an institution that had never before existed: a museum dedicated exclusively to art (and specifically including painting as well as sculpture), intended primarily for the education of the nation, located in such a manner as to make a statement about the equality of art vis-à-vis church and state, designed in such a manner as to suggest the religious power of art, displayed in such a manner as to emphasize the autonomous integrity of the work of art, and organized in such a manner as to reveal the historical development of art as a central phenomenon of human culture. It is not to denigrate the importance of the Louvre as an institution or of Klenze's Glyptothek as a building to say that the role and function of the modern museum began to be defined in no small measure as a response to the practical needs of design and organization of Schinkel's building. That Schinkel was able to design such a building without a precedent is testimony to his architectural genius. That he was able to gain official backing, royal support, and intellectual approval for his vast project, however, is testimony to the fact that it was largely in harmony with the spirit of the times. The modern art museum as we know it is in a very precise sense a Romantic institution that emerged under special circumstances in Germany during the early decades of the nineteenth century.[42] Indeed, we know from a scene in Karl Immermann's novel *Die Epigonen* (1836) just how lively were the public discussions of the new museum in the Berlin salons of the 1820s (bk. vi, ch. 4). To put it another way, Schinkel would not have been able to design his new museum as he did if the way had not been paved by the thought of the preceding thirty years on three fundamental issues: the nature of art itself, the conception of painting and the figure of the artist, and a new appreciation of the history of art.

## THE TEMPLE AS IMAGE IN ROMANTIC AESTHETICS

We can approach the first subject by asking a simple question. Given the fact that Schinkel was designing a wholly new type of building, why did he choose among the available architectural styles the neoclassical and, more specifically, the Greek Revival temple—especially in light of the circumstance that the temple as such was utterly unsuitable for the Northern European climate? Owing to a unique historical situation— the almost total hiatus in public building for more than a decade during the revolutionary and Napoleonic wars—any continuity of design and style had been interrupted, and architects could look back at a set of equally plausible possibilities. The three most obvious stylistic modes for architects working in the second decade of the nineteenth century were Grecian, Gothic, and Italianate.[43] In addition, Schinkel's own experience would have suggested other possibilities: for instance, the Baroque pala-tial style that he knew from Schlüter's arsenal or Schlüter's renovation of the royal palace in the Lustgarten. As a student Schinkel had been ex-posed to the radical geometrical shapes espoused by such rationalists as Boullée, Ledoux, and Durand in France and George Dance in England.[44] Finally, some of Schinkel's designs during these same years—for the Kaufhaus (the urban shopping center that he designed in 1827), the Academy of Architecture (built 1831–1836), or the National Library (1835)—display an unadorned functionalism that points directly toward the early twentieth century.

Apart from the readily available forms, Schinkel was also familiar with styles that had previously been used for existing museums and that therefore were associated with the genre: the cinquecento government office building by Vasari that had been converted to accommodate one of the richest collections in Florence (the Uffizi), the palazzo in the same city that housed the Pitti collection, the French Renaissance grandeur of the Louvre, or the eclecticism (combining baroque, neoclassical, and Pal-ladian elements) of the more recent Fridericianum in Kassel. In the var-ious competitions for museum design sponsored by the Académie d'Ar-chitecture the judges had favored buildings (never constructed, to be sure) in a heavy Imperial Roman style à la Piranesi. Indeed, Schinkel's earliest museum design, drawn in 1800 while he was still a student, displays the severe cubism, unrelieved by windows or external decorations, that was characteristic of Boullée as well as his own teacher, Gilly. (Over a century later it provided the inspiration for John Russell Pope's National Gallery in Washington.[45]) When Leo von Klenze was invited by Ludwig I in 1815 to submit a design for the competition for the Glyptothek in Munich, he submitted not one but three: in Greek, Roman, and Renaissance styles. Shortly after the Glyptothek and the Altes Museum were completed in neoclassical style, several important museum buildings in Germany were put up in the increasingly popular Renaissance style: e.g., Klenze's Neue Pinakothek in Munich (1826–1836) and Semper's Dresden Gallery (1847–1855). Given the wide variety of available styles—a characteristic of early nineteenth-century historicism—and the freedom of the architect to pick and choose among them without the constraints of tradition, why did Schinkel settle on the particular style that he chose for his exemplary museum? And why was his design greeted with such general enthusiasm?

Today we are accustomed to the notion that architecture makes a statement about the kind of activity that takes place in a building and the kind of people who inhabit a house—or at least the ideas about the activity and the people held by the architect who designs the building. The symbolic meaning of buildings—and, by analogy, of clothing or literary genres and other forms—was even more apparent at the end of the eighteenth and the beginning of the nineteenth centuries. Pevsner, arguing persuasively that the architecture of the nineteenth century cannot be fully appreciated without taking into account such "evocative or associational elements," quotes a variety of contemporary sources to demonstrate how clearly architects were aware of the images conjured up by their various styles.[46]

The Italian theoretician Francesco Milizia wrote in 1787 that "buildings, like figures in painting and sculpture, must have their own physiognomy. . . . If only artists would inquire into the nature of each monument, they would know how to give it its own character, in such a way that people would recognize it." Around the same time Boullée stated in his treatise that "to put 'character' into a work is to employ properly all the means needed to make us experience no other sensations than those which are supposed to result from the subject."[47] At the other end of the same period Gottfried Semper wrote in 1846 that "the impression made on the masses by a building is partly founded on reminiscences." Conspicuous examples of such evocative styles are the use of Gothic in churches to summon up notions of medieval piety, palazzo forms in banks to evoke the wealthy Renaissance merchants, and Gothic or neo-classical style in academic buildings to suggest the learning of the cloister or the educational ideals of fifth-century Greece."[48] And we know that there was considerable public debate about the style that Schinkel chose. For instance, there was pressure from certain quarters to choose a Gothic model for the museum on the grounds that the Van Eyck paintings would not be comfortable in a Greek home.[49] Brentano's poetic tribute ("An Schinkel," ca. 1816) acknowledged his friend's ambition to advocate a neoclassical ideal (which at that time he was able to express only through his paintings) in opposition to the fashionable neo-Gothicism of the day:

> O zürne nicht, daß ich Dich auf die Zinnen
> Der Tempel führe, die im Geist Du bauest,
> Und unermüdlich gut der Zeit vertrauest,
> Ob einmal wohl ihr Großes geh' zu Sinnen;
> Es ist um Dir die Aussicht zu gewinnen,
> Wo Du der Erde Hoffnungsgrün erschauest
> Und Trost des blauen Himmels niedertauest
> Zu Bildern schöner Kunstzeit auf die Linnen.
> Doch ach die liebe Zeit! mit Wortposaunen
> Bläst sie Dein Bild des Griechenlebens an,
> Und bleckt bei dem Gewitterdom den Zahn,
> Wahrhaftig schön, altdeutsch, recht zum Erstaunen![50]

(O don't be angry if I lead you onto the pinnacles of the temples that you build in your imagination and untiringly entrust to the age in the hope that it will one day have noble ambitions; it is in order to provide for you the prospect from which you may see the earth's green of hope and that you may cover your canvases with the consolation of the blue sky to form images of a lovely age of art. But, alas, the age blasts your image of Greek life with verbal trumpets and displays its teeth at the storm-girt cathedral: "truly lovely, Old German, really aston-ishing!")

Pevsner is no doubt correct when he suggests that Klenze's three de-signs for the Glyptothek were all supposed to embody, each in its own way, the contemporary idea that classical learning is the basis of all proper *Bildung*.[51] But that analysis explains only part of Schinkel's choice for his design. To be sure, the neoclassical style was generally suggestive both of the classical antiquities that the museum was intended to house, and of the ideal of public education so powerfully advocated by Wilhelm von Humboldt in his Prussian educational reform. It is no accident that the great classical landscape that Schinkel painted in 1824 following his return from Italy, entitled *A View of the Flowering of Greece* ("Ein Blick in Griechenlands Blüte"), features in the foreground the construction of a temple. But the fact that Schinkel chose specifically the form of a temple tells the visitor a great deal more: that he is about to enter the presence of works of art that have been elevated to the status of the sacred. Because the classical temple was a popular style for public edifices of various kinds, Schinkel had various contemporary models as possible sources of inspiration.[52]

In 1797 Schinkel's teacher, Friedrich Gilly, created one of the boldest and most original designs of the age in the national monument to Frederick the Great that he conceived in the form of a Doric temple. It was the impression of this design that determined the young Schinkel to commit himself to the study of architecture. Gilly's design was never carried out, but the temple style was specified by Napoleon for such secular buildings as the monument to the Grande Armée (the church of the Madeleine, 1806) and the Bourse (1808). When Ludwig I commissioned a great Walhalla near Regensburg to commemorate the glories of German culture, he demanded an edifice "after the most beautiful patterns of ancient temples."[53] (This eccentric structure was actually built, from 1830 to 1842, by Leo von Klenze following a design drawn in 1814–1815 by another pupil of Gilly, Karl Freiherr Haller von Hallerstein. In its location, as we know from his painting of the site, Klenze repeated and indeed carried a step further the spatial symbolism of the Altes Museum: his temple-like museum is located with clear reference to a nearby castle ruin and village church, above which it rises loftily.)

Although Schinkel had an abundance of contemporary models, he was inspired in his design by drawings of the great sanctuary of Apollo at Didyma in Asia Minor, which he knew from a recently published English volume of *Ionian Antiquities* (1821).[54] What impressed Schinkel about Didyma, which Strabo had called the greatest of Greek temples, was its unique combination of architectural features, for Didyma not only displayed an impressive row of columns but also had a feature that, while common in Rome, was virtually unknown among Greek temples—a powerful stairway leading up to the podium.

In other words, there was no shortage of models. That Schinkel chose a temple at all, however, must be attributed not to mere availability but to the fact that the notion of the temple of art to designate a display of painting had, by 1823, become a commonplace in German cultural thought. With his building Schinkel was reifying an idea and making a powerful statement about the new conception of art.

• • •

Goethe shared this notion. During his two years in Italy (1786–1788) he had gotten to know Alois Hirt, whom he recommended to Herder as a competent *cicerone*. But he warned Herder that Hirt was also a "pedant,"[55] and ten years later, in his fictionalized essay "Der Sammler und die Seinigen" (1799), caricatured Hirt as a fussy "rigorist" always on the lookout for what he called the "characteristic" of every painting. Goethe did not share Hirt's sober academic view of the museum as an unadorned display hall for the convenience of students and teachers. In Rome he had frequented the Caffè Greco near the Spanish Steps, which was known as "a special kind of temple of art" because the German artists tended to congregate there and exhibit their paintings and drawings.[56] In 1798, when Goethe and Heinrich Meyer—who styled themselves, along with Schiller, as the Weimar Friends of Art—were choosing a name for their new (and short-lived) journal of art, they settled on *Propyläen*, which designates the vestibule leading into a temple. As Goethe explained in the opening sentences of his introduction to the journal:

> The youth who is attracted by nature and art believes that he will soon be able by means of lively striving to penetrate the innermost sanctuary [*Heiligtum*]; the man notices, after wandering around for a long time, that he is still outside in the vestibules.
>
> An observation of this sort has prompted our title. Stairway, gate, entrance, vestibule, the space between inside and outside, between the sacred and the profane, can be the only place where we shall normally congregate with our friends.[57]

A similar image occurs in "Der Sammler und die Seinigen" (published in the *Propyläen* in 1799) when the collector is describing his early experiences with art (letter 3). His first real epiphany occurred in the Royal Gallery in Dresden. "With what delight, indeed, with what intoxication I wandered through the sanctuary [*Heiligtum*] of the gallery."[58] In this passage, just as often elsewhere in the story, Goethe is recapitulating his own experience. In a familiar passage in *Dichtung und Wahrheit*, he depicts his initiation into the gallery at Dresden in the spring of 1768 while he was a student at nearby Leipzig. "I entered this sanctuary [*Heiligtum*], and my astonishment transcended every concept that I had imagined."⁵⁹ The rooms, he continues, produced a feeling of ceremoniousness that resembled the sensation "with which one enters a house of God, all the more so because the décor of many a temple, the object of many a reverence was displayed here once again, but only for the sacred purpose of art."

Goethe's reverence for the temples of art, which differed from the more restrained opinions of many of his more rationalist friends (notably Heinrich Meyer and Hirt), was shared by his younger contemporaries. Some of them, to be sure, felt that he did not go nearly far enough. The irrepressible Caroline Schlegel, after reading the first issue of *Propyläen*, wrote to Novalis: "Why do we need the vestibules when we ourselves possess the holiest of holies?"⁶⁰ But that same year her husband, August Wilhelm Schlegel, used images close to Goethe's when he wrote: "If anything of German painting deserves to be set up in the vestibule of Raphael's temple [*Tempel*], then Albrecht Dürer and Holbein surely will stand closer to the sanctuary than the learned Mengs."⁶¹

One of the most memorable and influential passages occurs in the document that set the tone for art euphoria of early Romanticism, Wackenroder's *Herzensergießungen eines kunstliebenden Klosterbruders* (1797). In a chapter rather cumbersomely but symptomatically entitled "How and in what manner one ought to contemplate the works of the great artists of the earth and use them for the welfare of one's soul," Wackenroder exclaims indignantly: "Picture galleries are regarded as annual fairs, where *en passant* the new wares are judged, praised, or disdained; and they should be temples [*Tempel*], where in still and silent humility and in heart-stirring solitude one admires the great artists as the loftiest among mortals and warms oneself during long, undisturbed contemplation of the works in the solar radiance of the most delightful thoughts and sensations."⁶²

Even the ironic Friedrich Schlegel was moved to similar feelings when he first saw the Louvre: "an old and, at least on the side where one enters the museum, anything but imposing building, rather formless and depressing, as might have been suitable in past centuries for despots without genius or cultivation." In any case, as he continues in his report on the paintings in Paris for readers of his journal *Europa* (1803), it is "in no respect designed to be a temple [*Tempel*] of the most magnificent of all plastic arts."[63] Years later Schlegel spoke of the "new temple of art" ("des neuen Kunsttempels") that the crown prince of Bavaria was building in Munich to house his collections.[64]

If the larger galleries lacked the proper temple-like atmosphere, matters could be arranged differently in private homes and collections. When Caspar David Friedrich, at Christmastime in 1808, displayed his controversial painting *Cross in the Mountains*—more generally known as the Tetschen Altar—in his darkened studio in Dresden, "it affected all who entered the room as though they were entering a temple [*Tempel*]. Even the biggest loudmouths ... spoke softly and seriously, as though in a church."[65] Marie von Kügelgen, who provided that account, obviously liked the effect. A few months later when her husband—Friedrich's friend, the painter Gerhard von Kügelgen—completed a copy of Raphael's *Sistine Madonna*, she transformed her parlor wholly into a temple (*Tempel*), as she reported to a friend, "so that even the children enter softly."[66] As is often the case, the parodistic inversion proves how common the topos had become. In his thirteenth vigil the author of the *Nachtwachen von Bonaventura* (1804) describes the "temple of Apollo" ("Tempel des Apollo") in the most satirical terms. "On the mountainside, right into the museum of nature, they had built a small one for art." And into this temple/museum stream the connoisseurs and dilettantes to admire the classical statues, "stone gods as cripples without arms and legs"—"a veterans' hospital of immortal gods and heroes, built in the midst of a miserable humanity."[67]

During the very years when the new museum was being discussed in Berlin, and Schinkel was designing the building to house it, the topos got wide publicity and received, so to speak, the formal seal of philosophical approval. In his four dialogues on art entitled *Erwin* (1815), Schinkel's boyhood friend Karl Wilhelm Friedrich Solger, professor of philosophy at the new University of Berlin, had noted suggestively that "it remains the most general and highest destiny of architecture to provide temples for the deity."[68] Solger expanded this idea more systematically in the series of lectures on aesthetics that he delivered in 1819, the year of his death. Close to the end, in the section dealing with arts other than poetry—the conventional quadrivium of sculpture, painting, architecture, and music—Solger contrasts architecture, in which the object is pure material, with music, in which the concept is pure form.[69] "The main goal of architecture," he continues,

is to construct by means of proportion a harmonic whole that is complete within itself. As far as the object of this art is concerned, essentially it can refer only to the divinity. Therefore it proceeds solely and exclusively from the construction of temples and exists basically for no other purpose. The temple is the representation of the immediate presence of God in the real world, and the temple building, upon which all architecture is based, does not proceed from everyday house construction. All other buildings must be viewed in their relation to the temple building.

Following a discussion of the basic rectangular form of the temple and its colonnades—"The most perfect ancient temples are the oblong rectangles that have columns on all sides"—Solger concludes by asserting that "in the modern world, architecture is the comprehensive art for all other arts" since both sculpture and painting must now be conceived as elements within the whole. "Given this lofty significance of architecture in modern art, the other arts must necessarily be ailing as long as architecture is not in some fashion restored."

Hegel, who arrived in Berlin in 1818, expressed similar thoughts in his lectures. As early as in his *Phänomenologie des Geistes* (1807) he had argued that art is the form of self-consciousness in which Spirit objectifies itself (§699ff.). In the lectures on aesthetics that he delivered at the University of Berlin—in 1820, in 1823, and again in 1826—the introduction culminates in the image of the temple of art. Hegel identifies three fundamental forms of art that he regards as aspects of the idea of beauty: symbolic, classic, and romantic.[70] The first of these he identifies as architecture, whose task it is "to shape external non-organic nature so that it is related to the spirit as an artful outerworld." Architecture paves the way for deity by coming to grips with nature in all its finitude and misshapenness. (We must keep in mind the fact that, for Hegel, deity or god is nothing more or less than the manifest spirit of an ethical nation, as he stated in §712 of the *Phänomenologie des Geistes*.) "Thereby it smooths the place for the god, forms its external surroundings, and builds him his temple [*Tempel*] as the space for inner collection and focus on the absolute objects of the spirit." Through architecture, therefore, the external world is "purified, symmetrically ordered, brought into a relationship with the spirit; and the temple of the god, the house of his community is ready."

It is this temple that the deity himself enters in the form of the second art, the classic art of sculpture. "When architecture has prepared the temple, and the hand of sculpture has placed in it the statue of the god, then this sensuously present deity is confronted in the wide halls of his home, thirdly, by the community." In sum, the temple becomes the museum, the locus for the sacred encounter of the community and with Spirit in its earthly manifestations as painting and sculpture.

## THE SYMBIOSIS OF RELIGION AND ART

The notion of the museum as a "temple of art" is therefore more than a topos: or, to be more precise, as a topos it represents the verbal crystallization of a conviction that lies close to the center of Romantic ideology. Few ideas characterize Romanticism more generally, and set it off from the Enlightenment more distinctly, than the belief in the essential symbiosis of religion and art. It is this belief that gives meaning to the topos of the museum as a temple of art. This is not to be confused with the notion that religion has been displaced by art, a notion much closer to the attitude of Schiller (e.g., in such poems as "Die Künstler" and in his aesthetic essays) and his followers down to later nineteenth-century aestheticism than to the Romantics. Romanticism is permeated from start to finish by the view that art is both a product, and the noblest expression, of religion.[71]

Unlike some Romantic attitudes, this one does not develop slowly: it emerges full blown in the works of Wackenroder and maintains its vigor for the next thirty years. Here I am not talking about such superficial traits as the repeated use of the terms "heavenly" (*himmlisch*) and "divine" (*göttlich*) to characterize the painters and works of art that the art-loving friar eulogizes. Wackenroder's use of those epithets is as mechanical as, say, Goethe's apostrophe to Erwin von Steinbach in his oration "Von deutscher Baukunst" (1772) as "holy" ("heiliger Erwin"). I am referring to the view that art itself, as a manifestation of the divine, is an aspect of religion—a conjunction suggested by the key words of Wackenroder's title: "Effusions of an *Art*-loving *Friar*."[72] In the chapter "Von zwei wunderbaren Sprachen und deren geheimnisvoller Kraft" the narrator declares that there are "two marvelous languages through which the Creator has permitted men to grasp and comprehend heavenly things in their full force"—nature and art.[73] While nature is the direct expression of the deity, art speaks to us through images created by men—"a kind of Creation ["eine Art von Schöpfung"], as it was vouchsafed to mortal beings to bring forth."[74] For this reason, the friar claims, he is stirred by equally powerful emotions when he regards the grand spectacle of nature or returns into "the God-consecrated temple of our monastery" and contemplates the art image of Christ on the cross. The section concludes with the observation that God views nature and the world just as we contemplate a work of art. It is this analogy that justifies the "reverence" for art that is so frequently evoked in the *Herzensergießungen*. In the previously cited chapter on the proper manner of contemplating works of art the friar compares the enjoyment of noble works of art to prayer.[75] Like nature, art is above man: we can only admire and venerate the most splendid works of its initiates. It is all art—not just painting— that deserves this reverence. When Joseph Berglinger, in the biography of the archetypal Romantic artist that concludes the book, attends a concert, he listens to the music "with precisely the reverence [*Andacht*] as though he were in church."[76]

Not surprisingly, *Franz Sternbalds Wanderungen* (1798), a novel planned jointly by Tieck and Wackenroder before the latter's early death, teems with similar thoughts. At one point, for instance, Franz justifies the usefulness of art by pointing out that the Bible is glorified by painting and that religion is sustained by it. "What more can one ask of this noble art?" (23). Later Franz's teacher, Dürer, urges him to read the Bible and the sacred legends: "Then you will surely become a good painter" (60). In other words, art is both the product and the tool of religion.

The fictions of Wackenroder and Tieck were among the most widely read of early Romantic documents, influencing not only the asthetic theories of Philipp Otto Runge but also the life-style of the young painters who came to be known as the Nazarenes. Their naive assumption that simple Christian piety was the absolute prerequisite for the loftiest Christian art was not accepted by everyone, of course; Goethe rejected it with ridicule. But that their association of art and religion expressed a mood of the times and did not create it is suggested by the fact that another central document of German Romanticism was written with no apparent reference to Wackenroder and Tieck. It seems inevitable that a theologian who wrote a book on aesthetics would be concerned with the interrelationship of religion and art, and that is conspicuously the case in Friedrich Schleiermacher's *Reden über die Religion* (1799). In an explanatory note that he added to the third edition of 1821 Schleiermacher ob-

THE MUSEUM: TEMPLE OF ART

served that "today scarcely anyone would deny this affinity between religion and art."⁷⁷ But when he first presented his views to its cultivated
critics ("an die Gebildeten unter ihren Verächtern") in 1799, he felt it
necessary to argue his case at considerable length; the third of the five
orations is devoted essentially to this question.

Schleiermacher begins by stating that the faithful can cultivate religion
only through the free expression and communication of religion itself.
This cannot be done intellectually; but once the "sacred spark" ("der
heilige Funken," 95)⁷⁸ is ignited within a person's soul, it grows into a
vigorous flame. In the cultivation of religion, therefore, it should be the
goal to seek what Scheiermacher calls "accesses to the infinite" ("Über-
gänge ins Unendliche," 102) in order to light that sacred spark. Art is the
means of putting to an end the "slavery" ("Sklaverei," 108) through
which rationality and analysis have bound our souls. Schleiermacher suggests that art can be the means of producing a sudden conversion—that
is, of enabling the individual to rise beyond the finite to a point at which
his sense for the higher things emerges in a moment of sudden, blinding,
luminous epiphany. "I believe that more than anything else the sight of
great and sublime works of art can accomplish this miracle" (112). Art is
therefore the means by which he anticipates the greatest hope for a turn
to religion among its cultivated critics. For the moment, however, art
serves no religion. "Religion and art stand side by side like two friendly
souls, whose inner kinship, even if they already suspect it, is still unknown to them" (113). Unaware of their inner affinity, a triumphant art
stands apart from a dry, rationalistic religion, each professing no need for
the other. If either is set free from its bonds, however, it will hasten with
fraternal loyalty to the other's aid.

The speech ends with a paean to the few distinguished figures—no
doubt his Romantic associates in Jena—whom he sees "returning from
the sanctuary [Heiligtum] initiated into these mysteries" (115). These initiates, clad in their ceremonial garb as the new priests of the goddess of
creative art, will shape a new humanity. Already this new humanity is
emerging boldly, "and you will be the neophytes [Neokoren] when the
new shapes are set up in the temple of time. . . . Let us embrace past,
present, and future, an endless gallery of the most sublime works of art
multiplied eternally through a thousand sparkling mirrors" (115).

It is hardly surprising that such a rhapsodic affirmation, in which a
brilliant young theologian virtually equated art with religion, should
have encountered an enthusiastic response among the young Romantics,

although it was received with considerable hostility by the orthodox theologians and literary classicists (specifically Goethe and Schiller) alike. Novalis, however, greeted Schleiermacher's work joyously, noting in his journals that "Schleiermacher has proclaimed a kind of *love*, of religion—an *Art*-religion—almost a religion like that of the *artist*, which venerates beauty and the ideal."[79] In the essay "Die Christenheit oder Europa," which Novalis wrote in 1799 in immediate response to Schleiermacher's book and which was circulated widely among his friends though not published until 1826, he punningly proclaimed Schleiermacher as the "pulse of the new age," who in his art-religion "has made a new veil for the Holy One" ("Er hat einen neuen Schleier für die Heilige gemacht").[80] Schleiermacher confirmed Novalis's ideas rather than inspiring them. A year before the publication of the *Reden über die Religion* Novalis had written in the aphorisms of *Blüthenstaub* (no. 71) that "poets and priests were in the beginning one and the same, and only later times have separated them. The true poet, however, is always a priest, just as the true priest has always remained a poet. And should not the future again bring back the former state of affairs?"[81] Friedrich Schlegel, in the collection of aphorisms mainly on religion entitled "Ideen," observed that "only he can be an artist who has a religion of his own, an original view of the infinite" and that "religion is not merely one aspect of cultivation [*Bildung*], an element of humanity, but the center of everything else, everywhere the primary and the highest, that which is categorically originary."[82]

Even Schleiermacher was skeptical of the facility with which some of the new converts took up his art-religion. Specifically with reference to August Wilhelm Schlegel, who slipped back and forth all too easily between classical paganism and Renaissance Christianity, he wrote to his friend Brinkmann that Schlegel's apparent religious enthusiasm came to him only at second hand through painting or poetry.[83] In all fairness to Schlegel, it should be recalled that in his glowing review of Wackenroder's volume he noted that "it is undeniable that modern art in its restoration during its greatest epoch stood in a very close league with religion."[84] In any case, that the labile Schlegel took up the cause demonstrates strikingly how rapidly the equation of religion with art had taken over in early Romantic thinking. In Schlegel's poem of 1800, "Der Bund der Kirche mit den Künsten," the poet tells in thirty-three (!) ottava rima strophes how the spirit of the Church comes down from heaven to Mount Parnassus, where the arts are leading a dismal existence now

that Apollo and the deities to whom they formerly dedicated their services are gone.[85] The Church reminds them that the old gods have been
replaced by a new religion with a hierarchy of patriarchs, saints, martyrs,
Virgin Mother, and Holy Son. To the service of this new religion the
four arts—architecture, music, sculpture, and painting—might well devote their energies and win new acclaim. Even monks in their cells, she
continues, will seize the tools of art, and the two greatest practitioners
will be named after the angels Michael and Raphael. Extending an invitation for them to join her in Rome, the city once unparalleled in secular
matters and now in spiritual affairs, the spirit of the Church returns to
heaven while the four sister arts prepare to take up their new challenge:

> So eilt, ihr Schwestern, und verschmäht mit nichten
> Den kleinsten Ort: jedennoch müßt ihr euch
> Vor andern gern der großen Stadt verpflichten,
> Der weltlich einst, nun geistlich keine gleich;
> Und in der Stadt euch auf den Tempel richten,
> Den jene Schlüßel öffnen, die im Reich
> Des Himmels lösen können oder binden.
> Dort sollt ihr mich, euch Beifall winkend, finden.

(So hasten, sisters, and do not despise even the smallest place:
yet you must pledge yourselves above all to the great city which
formerly no other matched in secular affairs and none now in
spiritual matters. And in the city set yourselves upon the temple opened by those keys that in the kingdom of heaven can
bind or loosen. There you shall find me, applauding your efforts.)

It is hardly surprising that such effusions—from Wackenroder to Schlegel—summoned forth the contempt of "Bonaventura" in his *Nachtwachen*: "The ancients sang hymns, and Aeschylus and Sophocles composed their choral odes in praise of the gods; our modern religion of art
prays in critiques and has its piety in its head, just as truly religious people
have it in their hearts" (109).

It was not of course only the writers who thought about these questions. Philipp Otto Runge appeals with notable frequency in his letters
and other writings to the Bible, to the authority of Christ, and to the
mysticism of Jakob Böhme. A letter to his father of December 31, 1802,
is typical. "Unconsciously and in a manner still incomprehensible to me,

I have made a breakthrough, and it is now becoming clear and lucid before my very eyes—it would be impossible for me to know what I know if I now should not wholly rely upon God and on the teachings of Jesus Christ, for this teaching concerns mankind in all matters and is the rock and the cornerstone."[86] For a man so firmly rooted in his faith nothing in life, including his art, is conceivable without religion. "Religion is not art; religion is the supreme gift of God; it can only be expressed more splendidly and comprehensibly by art."[87] Of his close friend Tieck, whose *Franz Sternbalds Wanderungen* profoundly affected his own thinking, he noted approvingly: "through our relationship he has, to my great joy, become much calmer and decisive in himself, to the extent that he will not seek to fathom and comprehend any art that is not grounded in God and our revealed religion."[88] Runge's most elaborate declaration of his principles occurs in a letter to his brother Daniel, in which Runge lists ten requisites of any work of art: the last seven refer to such predictable qualities as subject matter, composition, drawing, color, and the like. But the first three would have come as a surprise to academic painters only a decade earlier: "1) Our premonition of God; 2) the sense of ourselves in connection with the Whole, and from these two; 3) religion and art; that is, to express our loftiest sensations through words, tones, or images."[89]

Runge did not live long enough to perfect his theories in practice before his death in 1810; many of his existing paintings tend in fact to be neoclassical and realistic rather than "Romantic" in the sense of his immediate successors. But through his close friendship, personally in Dresden or through his varied correspondence, with many leaders of the Romantic period—notably Tieck, Friedrich Schlegel, Brentano, Arnim, Schelling, Kleist, the Grimms, Steffens, Görres, and others—his ideas on art, and especially his insistence that true art is necessarily grounded in religion, became well known during the period.

Caspar David Friedrich was in many respects the opposite of Runge, whom he knew only casually though these two most exemplary painters of German Romanticism lived near each other in Dresden. Friedrich has much less to say about the theory of art; he was far too busy with his painting. And he was much less social a person than Runge. But his paintings exemplify more perfectly than any others of the epoch the connection between religion and art: not the explicitly Christian themes that characterize the paintings of the Nazarenes but, rather, the spiritualization of landscape whereby in his paintings the experience of nature is transformed into a religious experience closely akin to Schleiermacher's definition of religion as "contemplation of the infinite" ("Anschauen des Universums").[90] In one of his rare theoretical utterances—a brief note "Über Kunst und Kunstgeist"—his belief reflects that of Runge.[91]

> You should obey God more than men. . . . The sacred Ten Commandments are the pure, unadulterated expression of all our knowledge of the true and the good. Each of us recognizes them unconditionally as the voice of his innermost being; no one can resist them. Therefore if you wish to dedicate yourself to art, if you feel a calling to consecrate your life to art, o! then pay close heed to the voice of your innermost being, for it is art within us.

He cautions the aspiring artist against pedantry and rationalization, which destroy the heart and soul. "You should keep holy every stirring of your heart [Gemüt], every pious premonition; for it is art within us! In the hour of inspiration it becomes visible form, and this form is your image!" Sentiments of this sort would have been judged mad in the academies of Hirt and Meyer.

Given the growing popularity of the notion that art and religion are related, it seems inevitable that the notion should have been taken up and systematized by the philosophers. It is symptomatic that in the *Phäno-menologie des Geistes* (1807) Hegel deals with art in the section on religion (ch. 7).[92] In this great *Bildungsroman* of the spirit on its road from simple consciousness to absolute knowledge, Hegel traces the spirit through various stages. As consciousness first emerges, it develops from simple apprehension of the world through the senses to a more sophisticated perception. This simple classification gradually gives way to consciousness of self, where the self becomes aware of its dependence upon other selves and the concerns of society. To deal with these problems of self-consciousness the spirit develops various strategies. On the first level reason (*Vernunft*) leads the spirit from the observation of nature and community to the recognition of the need for virtue and law in order to survive socially. At the next level (*Geist*) the spirit passes through the stages of ethics and alienation before it arrives at the conception of morality and conscience. At this point, finally, the spirit ascends to the recognition of religion—that is, the experience of a spirit that transcends the individual consciousness and therefore can be thought of as divine.

Following his discussion of natural religion, in which this transcendent spirit is conceived of as light (in Iranian religion) or as plant and animal (in Egyptian religion), Hegel moves to the next stage of religion in the form of art (in classical antiquity). Here, where spirit transforms itself into pure consciousness in the effort to raise its own essence above the real world, art makes its appearance. In this religion of art (*Kunst-Religion*) spirit is worshipped first as "absolute work of art" (*das abstrakte Kunstwerk*) in the form of cultic deities or national spirits exemplified by the utterances of oracles; then as "living work of art" (*das lebendige Kunstwerk*) in the form of personalized deities like Bacchus and Ceres; and finally as "spiritual work of art" (*das geistige Kunstwerk*) as manifested in Greek epic and tragedy. Through the religion of art, spirit has progressed beyond substance (*Substanz*) to the form of the subject itself (*Subjekt*). At this point, when the spirit no longer has need of substance through which to apprehend itself, religion-as-art, which characterized classical antiquity, gives way to revealed religion (*die offenbare Religion*), the final stage before the consummation of absolute knowledge.

Hegel was concerned—at least in this early masterpiece—with the phenomenology of spirit and not with art per se; accordingly he is not distressed when art is displaced along with religion as the spirit reaches the highest stage: absolute knowledge. However, his colleague Solger worried greatly about the situation. He realized, like Hegel, that religion is inherent in the art of classical antiquity. In the third dialogue of *Erwin*, in powerful reminiscence of Novalis's *Blüthenstaub*, he says that all inspired prophets of God, depending on whether they are directed inward to the divine center or outward into the world, are either sacred priests or creative artists (211). But he was no longer sanguine about the relationship between the two. "Art had devoured religion, insofar as religion revealed itself as present," he observes sadly toward the end of his lectures on aesthetics. "Therefore all life of the ancients compressed itself into art and sought to be symbolic."[93] Writing twenty years after Schleiermacher's *Reden über die Religion*, Solger was not confident that modern art had been rejuvenated by religion. "Art will not arise again," the lectures conclude, "until people understand that all modern art is based on religion, that religion in turn expresses itself essentially through architecture and music, and that painting and sculpture obtain their significance only in connection with those arts. Here too, then, art is tied to revelation."[94] In short, while it was generally believed that a symbiosis exists between art and religion and that modern art could no more flourish without its ground in religion than could classical art, there was no confidence that the expectations of Schleiermacher, Wackenroder, Novalis, and Schlegel for the immediate rejuvenation of art through religion had in fact been realized. Writing from Paris in 1826, Schinkel reported sadly that "the idea of the sacredness [Heiligkeit] of art no longer exists" in France.[95] The establishment of a temple for the reverent contemplation of art, therefore, represented not just a confirmation of the sacred nature of past art but also a gesture of hope for the future and an emphatic statement regarding the conception of art at the end of the Romantic period in Germany.

## The Artist as Hero

This, then, was the intellectual and cultural atmosphere surrounding Schinkel in Prussia and greater Germany as he determined which available form to choose for the new museum to be erected on the loveliest site in Berlin, facing the royal palace and next to the cathedral. Given the currency of the topos "temple of art" during the decades after Wackenroder's *Herzensergießungen* and Goethe's *Propyläen*, the temple was the obvious choice for the outer form of the building. If the architectural symbolism of the temple could be missed by few, the statement of the great rotunda that the visitor entered after ascending the winged staircase and passing through the entrance hall, and that Schinkel called a "pantheon," was equally emphatic. The pantheon was beloved by neoclassical architects with their passion for geometrical forms as the "paradigm of spherical purity."[96] In the first place, the Roman Pantheon was the most completely preserved building of antiquity and the only one with an impressive interior space. Secondly, it represented a desirable synthesis to the extent that it combined the features that many authorities—e.g., Hegel in his lectures on aesthetics (pt. III, sec. 1, ch. 2)—regarded as archetypal for the two styles of antiquity: the columns of Greek temples and the vaulted interior of Roman public edifices. Schinkel was fully aware of the structural merits of the rotunda. In his response to Hirt's critique he pointed out that the rotunda is "that form of building that encompasses the greatest space with the least circumference."[97] In addition, he continued, it assures even lighting for works of art. Finally, a large, beautiful, and dignified space is appropriate to hold such "colossal objects" as the finest sculptures. But it had another, equally important symbolic function. The museum was not only the temple dedicated to the abstract deity or spirit of art; it was also a pantheon housing the works of many individual artists. Hence the great rotunda in the center of the building, which Schinkel called the "sanctuary" (*Heiligtum*) of the temple, found its full justification.[98]

Romanticism brought forth not merely a new glorification of art; it also produced a new interest in the figure of the artist.[99] In classical antiquity writers like Xenocrates and Pliny the Elder had included stories about artists in their writings on art, but this interest was largely lost during the Middle Ages, which tended to reduce art to a craft and the "artist" to a craftsman in the service of God. The first "Lives" of artists since antiquity appeared in fourteenth-century Florence, when Filippo Villani, in his chronicle of his beloved city, included accounts of the great painters, whose creative genius made them superior to mere men of science and letters. Leon Battista Alberti in his treatise on painting (*Della pittura*, 1436), as well as Lorenzo Ghiberti in his *Commentarii* (1455), related occasional anecdotes from the lives of specific painters, usually classical. But in these early works the interest in the lives was distinctly subordinate to the theory and practice of painting.

It was not until the middle of the sixteenth century that Giorgio Vasari produced the voluminous work that exemplified the Renaissance passion for pragmatic history with its interest in the individual and his accomplishments. His *Vite de' più eccellente architetti, pittori e scultori* (1550), while introduced by a theory of art, developed the narration of anecdotes concerning the lives of mainly contemporary artists into the focal point of his work. In the seventeenth century the Renaissance preference for the theoretical treatise illustrated by observations on specific painters gradually gave way to the baroque obsession with compendia and the tendency to derive principles of criticism from ad hoc and ad hominem discussions of artists and their works. The prevailing tendency is exemplified by the titles of those works that served as the most popular source books for the age: Gian Pietro Bellori, *Le vite de' pittori, scultori ed architetti moderni* (1672); Joachim von Sandrart, *Teutsche Akademie der edlen Bau-, Bild- und Mahlereykünste* (1675); A. Félibien, *Entretiens sur les vies et les ouvrages des plus excellens peintres, anciens et modernes* (1666–1668); and Roger de Piles, *Abrégé de la vie des peintres* (1699).

If writers down to the end of the seventeenth century had mingled aesthetic theory, art history, art criticism, and "Lives" together in various combinations of emphasis, the rationally tidy minds of the eighteenth century preferred to segregate the various functions and activities neatly into separate compartments. Aesthetic philosophers in the tradition of Shaftesbury, Vico, and Baumgarten displayed little interest in specific works, much less in their creators. Winckelmann, the first and greatest historian of art in the century, tended to lose sight of the individual artist in his constant search for styles that transcended the individual and in his efforts to establish once and for all a history of art in distinction to formal aesthetics or anecdotal "Lives." The new phenomenon of the Salon with its exhibitions of contemporary art produced a separate genre of art criticism based on taste, as distinct from aesthetic theory or art history, whose greatest practitioner for several decades was Diderot. The effect of the autonomous development of these three approaches to art meant a conspicuous neglect during the eighteenth century of interest in the individual artist—a neglect that remains evident in the writings of later idealist aestheticians such as Kant and Schiller.

In this cultural climate, therefore, Wackenroder's *Herzensergießungen* (1797) had the effect of great novelty and originality. He drew extensively on such older sources as Vasari and Sandrart for anecdotes from the lives of Raphael, Leonardo, Michelangelo, Dürer, and other painters of the Renaissance. He also elevated anecdote to a privileged status by attributing spiritual value to the life of the artist, who is able to create great works only because he has lived a good life. It is due in no small measure to Wackenroder's work that the novel featuring a painter as its hero— *Künstlerroman* or, more specifically, *Malerroman*—has been such a conspicuous genre in German literature from early Romanticism through Gottfried Keller's *Der grüne Heinrich* (1855) by way of Hermann Hesse's *Roßhalde* (1914) and *Klingsors letzter Sommer* (1919) right down to Siegfried Lenz's *Deutschstunde* (1968).[100] Wilhelm Heinse's *Ardinghello* (1787) is often cited as the first work in this series, and to the extent that its hero is among other things a painter—as well as a poet, musician, philosopher, and political theorist—the statement is correct. Indeed, the work includes not only scenes involving such figures as Veronese and other painters but also brilliant descriptions of paintings that Ardinghello views in Perugia, Florence, and other Italian art centers. In the last analysis, however, Heinse's epistolary novel is not so much a *Malerroman* as, rather, a novel celebrating a philosophy of hedonism and sensualism to which the enjoyment of painting contributes its share.

With Wackenroder, as we have seen, the emphasis is different. Here art contributes not to our pleasure but to our virtue, occupying a place in human creation next to religion. The artist is not an artist among other things: the true artist is consumed in the core of his being by the divine spirit of art. Accordingly the focus shifts in the *Herzensergießungen* from art appreciation to the process of artistic creativity.[101] As A. W. Schlegel noted in his review, "The author recommends with the greatest warmth the generally neglected history of artists' lives and especially the accomplishment of Vasari."[102] Schlegel particularly appreciates the skill with which Wackenroder rearranged and edited Vasari's material in such a manner as to bring out the character and higher qualities of the artists. In the decades following Wackenroder's work the artist figures so frequently as the hero of Romantic fiction that Friedrich Theodor Vischer complained, in a review of Eduard Mörike's *Maler Nolten* (1832), that the title was unfortunate because it suggested a genre that was already quite stale ("ganz abgelebt").[103]

· · ·

The immediate effect of Wackenroder's work is evident if we look at the genesis of *Franz Sternbalds Wanderungen* (1798). As early as 1795, under the fresh impact of Goethe's *Wilhelm Meisters Lehrjahre*, Tieck had conceived the plan of a *Bildungsroman*, which he began to write only a year later.[104] Tieck, who long cherished the desire to become an actor and had been obsessed with Shakespeare since boyhood, was especially captivated by the theatrical aspect of Goethe's novel, which was based on an earlier version called *Wilhelm Meisters Theatralische Sendung*. Accordingly he imagined the story of a young craftsman who sets out on his journey of apprenticeship and arrives at a palace, where his talent for acting is discovered. But suddenly, in the summer of 1796, Tieck put his novel aside (and completed it only some forty years later under the title *Der junge Tischlermeister*). On their walking trip to Dresden that summer Wackenroder had confided to Tieck for the first time the manuscript of his own work; impressed by that reading, Tieck immediately dropped everything else and arranged for the publication that very fall, with the addition of four pieces by his own hand, of the *Herzensergießungen*. One of those pieces, the "Letter of a Young German Painter in Rome to his Friend in Nürnberg," contains the basic situation of *Franz Sternbalds Wanderungen*. In constant conversations with his friend, Tieck developed the plan of his new novel, radically altering the emphasis of the original plan. The young craftsman-actor is transformed into a painter, and the time is shifted from the present back to the early sixteenth century of Raphael and Dürer. The action of the uncompleted novel, which lasts from the fall of 1520 to the spring of 1522, leads Franz Sternbald from Nürnberg by way of the Netherlands and Alsace-Lorraine to Florence and Rome, and brings him in touch with such contemporary artists as

Albrecht Dürer, Lucas van Leyden, and Andrea del Sarto. Tieck put aside his novel before he could achieve in the final volume the grand resolution of German and Italian art that was supposed to have been achieved by Franz on his return to Nürnberg.[105]

Tieck's novel owes a great deal to the contemporary Gothic romance with its complicated plot of confused identities and German-Italian family relations. Yet the novel is indisputably a *Malerroman*, which recapitulates and anticipates to an astonishing degree the typical Romantic views of art, and notably the tension between artist and bourgeois. Franz must repeatedly defend art against various detractors, who argue that it is useless; he does so by defining art as a kind of reverence, an expression of the human soul. He rejects the prevailing theory of art as imitation and establishes its legitimacy as a mode of symbolic expression independent of nature. He decries systematization as stifling to true creativity and advocates landscape painting as the purest form of absolute art. Finally, he defends the integrity of the individual against a shallow Roman academician who tells him that he is still young and when he matures he will learn "to venerate art rather than artists and to see how much every individual lacks."[106]

Given its embodiment of so many Romantic ideas, it is small wonder that the novel had the profound influence that it did.[107] It was not universally admired, to be sure. Caroline Schlegel was bored by it; her husband and Brentano were not amused; Goethe was provoked by it to utter his notorious condemnation of "das klosterbrudrisirende, sternbaldisirende Unwesen" threatening contemporary art.[108] But most young contemporaries were enthusiastic. Friedrich Schlegel insisted to his brother (March 1799) that it was a "divine" book—the first truly "Romantic" book since Cervantes and better by far than *Wilhelm Meisters Lehrjahre*. The young Philipp Otto Runge, who read the book immediately, wrote to a friend (June 3, 1798) that "nothing has ever gripped me so powerfully in the very depths of my soul." On February 23, 1800, Novalis wrote to Tieck that his own *Heinrich von Ofterdingen* would have much in common with Franz Sternbald. And Bettina Brentano was so greatly moved by the novel, as she wrote to Savigny (July 31, 1802), that her brother Clemens was annoyed. E.T.A. Hoffmann called it "this true artist's book" (September 26, 1805). Together with the *Herzensergießungen*, it constituted the manifesto for the school of young German artists in Rome who became known, a decade later, as the Nazarenes.

. . .

Under the circumstances it seems consistent that two of its earliest admirers—Friedrich Schlegel and his wife-to-be, Dorothea Veit—soon followed the lead of Tieck and Wackenroder by writing novels that, while
not set in the sixteenth century, nevertheless featured painters as their
heroes. Friedrich Schlegel's *Lucinde* (1799) is by no stretch of the imagination a *Malerroman* in the same sense as *Franz Sternbalds Wanderungen*.
Perhaps the most remarkable of Romantic novels, it is conspicuous above
all for two features.[109] Its new ethics, according to which human fulfillment is reached only through the love of man and woman, was recognized early by Schleiermacher in his *Vertraute Briefe über die Lucinde*
(1800). Later scholars have seen that Schlegel's "religion of love" amounts
to a radical revision of the dualism between spiritual and sensual love
that characterized most eighteenth-century thinking and writing. Second, it is important as the first and perhaps most successful embodiment
of Schlegel's theory of the novel as a genre that was to embrace and unify
all literary forms. *Lucinde* is constructed in the form of an arabesque in
which two groups of six shorter pieces—letters, allegories, idylls, reflections, dialogues—embrace a central narrative core entitled "Lehrjahre
der Männlichkeit." In the twelve surrounding pieces there is no overt
reference to painting, apart from the fact that the descriptions are often
written in what might be called a painterly fashion. The first sentence of
the first letter, for instance, represents Julius's perceptions in terms of
shape and color: "People and what they want and do appeared to me,
whenever I recalled it, like ash-gray figures without motion: but in the
sacred solitude around me everything was light and color and a fresh
warm breath of life and love caressed me and rustled and stirred in all
the branches of the voluptuous grove." However, such passages in themselves would not justify our consideration of the novel in this context.

   It is all the more remarkable, therefore, that in the heavily autobiographical narrative core of the work Schlegel presents his fictional persona, Julius, to us as a painter. Again, there are relatively few relevant
passages. Most of the account amounts to a catalogue of the women Julius
knew before he met Lucinde, and these sections contain only fleeting
references to art. One girl, Lisette, is conspicuous for the fact that she has
some good copies of the more sensual paintings of Correggio and Titian
in her boudoir. While this rather shallow creature has little appreciation
for most arts, she displays such a sense for the plastic arts that Julius often
talks with her about his works and ideas and executes some of his most

successful drawings while engaged in conversation with her. During these early years Julius "recognized in himself the lofty calling to divine art" (49);[110] but he was so alienated from himself and, in addition, so indolent that he had remained behind in his training and was incapable of any true exertion. Full of grand conceptions, his execution was crude: "the earnestness was forbidding, the forms deteriorated into monstrosities, antiquity became in his hands a hard mannerism, and his paintings, for all their thoroughness and insight, remained stiff and stonelike" (50).

It is the acquaintance with Lucinde, who is also a painter, that liberates him to true art. Lucinde's painting is precisely the opposite of Julius's: although the draftsmanship is vague and her training inadequate, her landscapes always betray a wholeness of vision, and all the parts coalesce into a unity. For her, painting is not a profession or even an art but a passion. She lacks the patience for oils, but with ink and aquarelles she is able to imbue her landscapes with a convincing reality and wildness. Under her influence Julius finally reaches fulfillment in his own art. "His paintings came to life, a stream of inspiriting light seemed to pour itself over them, and true flesh blossomed in fresh colors" (56). While Lucinde favors landscapes, Julius specializes in human figures that seem to resemble animated plants in human shape. In particular, his drawings of the embrace of love—Schlegel does not make it clear whether these are to be imagined as pornographic or not—succeeded in capturing the "fleeting and secret moment of highest life through a still charm" (57).

In these few pages, then, art serves a central liberating function. Not only are the two principal figures painters, not only does their love bring to maturity Julius's art, but, as we learn at the end of the "Lehrjahre der Männlichkeit," as his art matured and perfected itself, "so, too, his life became a work of art" (57). . . . It became light within him, he saw and surveyed all the masses of his life and the articulation of the whole clearly and correctly because he was standing in the center."

This principle of art becomes in turn the principle of organization for the entire novel: the integrated personality of the hero, represented in the central narrative portion, is now able to hold together in its painterly design the disparate parts that constitute the arabesque surrounding the "Lehrjahre der Männlichkeit." In one sense, Schlegel's *Lucinde* constitutes a fairly precise literary counterpart to the paintings of Philipp Otto Runge—especially the arabesques of the four *Tageszeiten*. While Schlegel shares the same lofty conception of art as Tieck and Wackenroder, his novel betrays a new emphasis: art is still the manifestation of religion, but it is now the secularized religion of love.

Dorothea Veit, who provided the model for Lucinde—so close a model, indeed, that many contemporaries were shocked at Schlegel's lack of discretion—was much more conventional in the *Malerroman* that she wrote in an effort to earn money to support her beloved Friedrich. *Florentin* was published anonymously, as "edited" by Schlegel, late in 1800. So dependent is the novel on *Wilhelm Meisters Lehrjahre* as well as *Franz Sternbalds Wanderungen* that Schiller, when he sent his copy to Goethe on March 16, 1801, warned him that in Madame Veit's novel "you will also see spooking the ghosts of old acquaintances."[111] This young Italian who, crossing Germany on his way to join the fight for independence in America, encounters new friends who turn out—or rather, because the novel remained unfinished, promise to be—related to him in mysterious ways cannot deny his pedigree as one of Wilhelm Meister's younger brothers.[112] However, it is in the encapsulated autobiographical sketch that Florentin provides for his new friends—a device reminiscent of the "Lehrjahre der Männlichkeit" in *Lucinde*—that the theme of the painter emerges.

Following a strange childhood and attempts to lock him away in a monastery, Florentin flees to Venice, where he first becomes seriously interested in art through his friendship with German painters in the city and his endeavors to show the works of art to his friends from England. Forced because of his complicity in a murder to leave Venice, he goes to Rome and first works as a guide to finance his art studies. When his career as a landscape artist begins to thrive, he marries a model and settles down to marital bliss. However, just as he begins to realize that he has no true calling for art, he is forced to flee once again because of the machinations of a sinister cardinal who has designs on his faithless wife. Making his way through France and England to Switzerland, Florentin ekes out an existence by painting portraits on commission and giving drawing lessons. Finally he decides to forsake his career in art. "It became increasingly difficult and finally quite impossible for me, now in my misfortune, to exploit like a servant girl the art which once had been the goddess, the bliss, and the companion of my lovely and fortunate days."[113] So Florentin has renounced art and is on his way to make a new life—as a great leader in the United States, the epilogue suggests—when we meet him during the weeks he spends in the palace of his friends in Germany. Again, however, the point to be noted is this: even in a work in which the career as a painter is not necessary for the plot, as it was in *Franz Sternbalds Wanderungen*, the mood of the times thrusts forward the painter as an interesting hero.

The new fascination with the figure of the artist produced another popular category of works that imitated the conception, if not always the spirit, of the *Herzensergießungen*: the fictionalized life or episode from the lives of famous painters. By far the most popular subject was Raphael, whose "divinity" had been certified by Wackenroder and Tieck in the *Herzensergießungen* as well as the *Phantasien über die Kunst*.[114] The generation of neoclassicists from Winckelmann through Lessing to Goethe had venerated the art of the mature Raphael, to which they devoted analyses and descriptions. (Both Benjamin West and Charles Willson Peale named sons after Raphael.) But the Romantics turned to his life in the form of drama, narrative poems, and novellas: e.g., Zacharias Werner's canzones "Raphael Sanzio von Urbine" and "Raphaels Stanzen," a five-act play by Georg Christian Braun (1819), and Achim von Arnim's tale "Raphael und seine Nachbarinnen" (1824), which is based on three episodes recounted by Vasari. Arnim, whose letters and journalistic writings, along with many poems, give ample evidence of his lifelong love of painting, also wrote a comic romance in rhymed couplets in which he describes how Rembrandt pretends to be dead in order to prove to an uncomprehending art dealer that his works will be more valuable, and not forgotten, after his death ("Rembrandts Versteigerung," in the collection *Landhausleben* of 1826).

Adelbert von Chamisso wrote a number of ballads based on the lives of artists. "Das Kruzifix" (1830) relates in terza rima the legend of a sculptor in despair because the figure in his Crucifixion scene appears so lifeless; a young man, out of his love for art, allows himself to be crucified as a model, enabling the sculptor to create his masterpiece, but for his sin he then undertakes a pilgrimage of atonement. In "Ein Kölner Maler" (1833) Chamisso retells from Ghiberti the tale of a fourteenth-century goldsmith who renounces art for a life of devotion when the wanton destruction of his masterpiece reveals to him the vanity of life. In "Francesco Francias Tod" (1834), finally, Chamisso relates, again in terza rima, the famous episode from Vasari (which Wackenroder had already used in the *Herzensergießungen*) concerning the aged painter who expires in ecstasy when he first sees Raphael's painting of Saint Cecilia.

The writer who recapitulated virtually every Romantic version of the painter's life, however, was E.T.A. Hoffmann, that phenomenally gifted man who, in addition to his literary genius and musical talent, was a graphic artist of no mean ability. Hoffmann began his literary career under the aegis of an artist, for his first collection of tales was entitled *Fantasiestücke in Callots Manier* (1814). The reference to the French engraver Jacques Callot (1592–1635) was meant in a very specific sense, as Hoffmann explained in his prefatory note, for he was striving in his writing to emulate Callot's ability to bestow upon the most commonplace scenes of everyday life the "shimmer of a certain romantic originality"[115] that would stir any mind predisposed to the fantastic. "Could not a poet or writer to whom the figures of ordinary life appear in the inner romantic kingdom of spirits, and who now represents them in the glitter by which they are there surrounded as in a strange and wondrous ornamentation, at least justify himself with reference to this master by saying he wanted to work in Callot's manner?" But Hoffmann did not restrict himself to working indirectly "in Callot's manner." In the novella "Signor Formica" (1819) he invented a delightful episode in which the painter Salvator Rosa helps his friend Antonio win the girl Marianna. Although the rather Boccaccian narrative has little to say about art or the landscapes of Salvator himself, the work conveys a sense of authenticity as a result of Hoffmann's scrupulous use of such contemporary sources as D'Argensville's *Leben der berühmtesten Maler* (Leipzig, 1767–1768), Hans Rudolf Füssli and Hans Heinrich Füssli's *Allgemeines Künstlerlexikon* (Zürich, 1812), and Jean Joseph Taillasson's *Observations sur quelques grands peintres* (Paris, 1807). The same interest in painters and their works is evident in several tales of Hoffmann that are based upon paintings: notably "Die Fermate" (1815), which was stimulated by a painting by Johann Erdmann Hummel, a professor at the Berlin Academy of Arts; "Doge und Dogaresse" (1817), elaborated from a painting by Karl Wilhelm Kolbe that Hoffmann saw at the Berlin Art Exhibition of 1816; and "Meister Martin Küfner und seine Gesellen" (1812), also based on a painting by Kolbe.

Hoffmann's most characteristic treatments of the painter as hero display an interesting development in the roughly two decades since Wackenroder and Tieck established the connection between art and religion and discovered the painter as representative of the pious artist. In several of Hoffmann's most important works, namely, the painter is exposed as a figure of confusion, sin, and shame, all the more shocking because of the expectation of piety conventionally attached to him. The first of these examples occurs in Hoffmann's Gothic thriller *Die Elixiere des Teufels*

(1815–1816). In this long and complicated tale of the renegade monk Medardus, the painter plays a small yet disproportionately important role. Some two-thirds of the way through the narrative the editor inserts a curious family chronicle labeled simply "the Parchment Sheet of the Old Painter" (bk. II, ch. 2). From this document—translated, we are told, from "Old Italian"—we learn that Medardus's great-great-grandfather had been a nobleman from Genoa who gave up his inheritance in order to devote himself to the study of art in the atelier of Leonardo da Vinci. As a young man Francesko embraced a lofty conception of art that would have stood him well in the company of Franz Sternbald or the pious Renaissance painters depicted by Wackenroder. When his father appealed to him to return to Genoa to take over the government, Francesko replied that "a prince, illumined by all the brilliance of the throne, seemed to him only a miserable creature in comparison with a competent painter and that the greatest deeds of war were nothing but an atrocious earthly game while the painter's creation was the pure reflection of the divine spirit inherent within him."[116]

Despite this nobility of spirit—or perhaps precisely on account of it— Francesko succumbs after Leonardo's death to a towering arrogance. Criticizing his former master, he falls in with a group of sculptors who venerate heathen antiquity and reject pious Christian art. Nevertheless, to earn money Francesko accepts the commission from a Capuchin monastery to execute a painting of Saint Rosalia for their church. Initially he intends as a blasphemous joke to replace the saint with an image of Venus; but in his overexcited imagination the two countenances vie until, drinking a potion given to him by one of his artist friends, he finally executes the face of a voluptuous Venus. Like a new Pygmalion, Francesko falls in love with his painting. Suddenly the living model appears to him—a girl who had secretly admired him, she says, while he was still an apprentice in Leonardo's atelier. They live together out of Christian wedlock in sinful happiness. When a son is born, however, the woman dies and shrivels into an ugly old hag, whereupon Francesko realizes that he has been under the spell of a witch of Satan. He flees into the wilderness with his child, where he prays to Saint Rosalia for intercession. Although he is cursed by God, Rosalia advises him to go to Prussia and decorate a church there. At this point the story of the ancestral painter ends. The child, adopted and raised by a nobleman, initiates several generations of the most blatant and complicated incest, which culminate in the birth of the monk Medardus. The painter, meanwhile, is redeemed

CHAPTER SIX

by Rosalia but condemned to wander the earth until the final expiation and extirpation of the family guilt that he initiated.

It is not necessary for our purposes to explore the perplexing question regarding the (fictional) authenticity of this family chronicle. Is it a fabrication or a true chronicle? Was it invented by Medardus (or by his editor?) in an attempt to justify his own crimes retroactively by attributing them to an ancestral curse? These questions, as intriguing as they are for our understanding of Medardus, are less relevant in our specific context than three other observations.[117] First, the figure of a painter was chosen to inaugurate the series of ancestral crimes and incests for simple shock value: the artist, who had emerged since Wackenroder and Tieck as archetypally pious, reveals himself to be susceptible to the most grievous crime and sin. Second, apart from vague hints at hubris the motivation is not explored; Francesko speaks several times of "dark powers" that have driven him and his family into guilt, but there is no real analysis: psychological motivation is left to Hoffmann's later works.

Finally, a remarkable parallel exists between Hoffmann's weird tale and another contemporary work that Hoffmann might well have known: Brentano's fragmentary *Romanzen vom Rosenkranz*. In a letter to Philipp Otto Runge, whom he hoped to persuade to create border designs for the work, Brentano described his epic as "a series of romantic fables, in which a heavy ancient ancestral sin is resolved by the creation of the rosary."[118] Indeed, the action of Brentano's epic, which goes back to an incident that allegedly occurred during the Holy Family's flight to Egypt, is even more obscurely complex than Hoffmann's *Elixiere des Teufels*.[119] What matters in our context, however, is the fact that the principal action of the epic, which takes place in thirteenth-century Bologna, shows certain conspicuous parallels to Hoffmann's novel. The inaugurator of this new incestuous action is again a pious painter, Kosme, who is the child of an incestuous union between Tannhäuser and his sister. Kosme becomes a painter and marries a singer and dancer named Rosalaeta, with whom he has three sons. When he is commissioned to paint a picture of the Madonna for a nunnery, he falls in love with his model, the doorkeeper named Rosatristis. Unaware that Rosatristis is the sister of his wife, Rosalaeta, and that the two sisters are also the children of an incestuous union, Kosme leaves his wife and, aided by Satan and Venus, seduces Rosatristis, with whom he has three daughters. When Kosme realizes what has happened, he retreats into solitude, where he spends the remainder of his life as a "pious" painter, watching the family fate work itself out—a fate that involves, almost predictably, incestuous unions between the three brothers and sisters.

Brentano started working on his epic in 1803, but he had written only nineteen of the projected twenty-four romances (in four-line trochaic strophes) when he broke it off in 1812. The work was published posthumously in 1852; we know, however, that a copy of the manuscript was circulating among Brentano's friends in Berlin just at the time when Hoffmann was working on the second half of his novel,[120] so it is not unlikely that he was aware of the fragmentary romances. In any case, the parallels are conspicuous: in both works a pious painter falls in love with the model for a sacred painting and produces a child (or children) who initiates a genealogy of sin and incest that the painter, eventually redeemed through his piety, must watch until it works itself out. The choice by Hoffmann and Brentano of a painter for this role seems in both cases to be a conscious response to the conception of the pious painter in early Romantic writings, and in both works the motivation is put down to the "dark powers" of destiny.

In two other tales written during these same years Hoffmann worked out the problem of the modern artist, as he saw it, much more fully. Both tales share a number of motifs, and in both cases the painter-hero is torn by the tension between reality and the envisioned ideal. But the outcome in one case is comic or at least Romantically ironic, while in the other it is tragic. The title of "Der Artushof" (1815) refers to a fourteenth-century guildhall in Danzig that, in more recent times, functioned as the stock exchange. It is here that the young Traugott, increasingly unhappy with his business career, steals time from his work to sketch the carved and painted figures that adorn the hall. After he meets the painter Godofredus Berklinger and his son, Traugott spends more and more time on his painting, making considerable progress with his work. In the home of his new friends he also sees and becomes infatuated with the painting of the deceased sister Felizitas. One day, entering the house unannounced, he finds Felizitas at the piano and realizes that the alleged son is none other than Felizitas dressed as a youth. Her father guards her so jealously because of a prophecy that he will die if she leaves him for love of another man. When Berklinger disappears with his daughter, Traugott hears that they have gone to "Sorrento." Leaving his job and his fiancée, he follows them to Italy, where among the German artists in Rome he achieves a considerable reputation and, in particular, arouses admiration for the portrait of the model he constantly paints: Felizitas. His friends discover a girl who resembles the painting, but she turns out to be Dorina, the daughter of a minor Italian painter—"the same image, painted by Raphael and Rubens," as Traugott puts it.[121] Despite his attraction to Dorina, he cannot bring himself to marry her because the image of Felizitas constantly interposes itself. He finally goes on to Sorrento and then, without success, back to Danzig. Here he learns that Felizitas and her father had been there the entire time—in a suburb known as "Sorrento." However, Felizitas has long since married a legal official, with whom she has produced many children, and her father has died. Traugott now realizes that, despite the loss of his living model, his ideal of art still survives in his imagination. Liberated, he returns to Rome to marry Dorina and devote his life to art.

Hoffmann's tale pays clear homage to Wackenroder and Tieck. Traugott's defense of art against his bourgeois acquaintances is reminiscent of a leitmotif in *Franz Sternbalds Wanderungen*. And Berklinger's name echoes an important name in *Herzensergießungen*—not of the painters, to be sure, but of the Romantic musician Joseph Berglinger. Like Berglinger, but unlike Wackenroder's painters, Traugott is a torn (*zerrissen*) figure: torn between artistic ambition and doubts in his own ability, between love of art and the claims of everyday life, between the ideal and reality. In this tale Hoffmann resolves the crisis with humor and irony. Traugott is not destroyed by disappointment in his earthly ideal; instead, he emerges from the experience with a renewed faith in his mission and his inner ideal of art, strong enough to look forward to a life both in art and in Rome with Dorina.

In "Die Jesuiterkirche in G." (1816), in contrast, Hoffmann shows what happens when the artist is unable to come to grips with reality. The tale is based upon Hoffmann's own experience in 1796, when during his law studies he helped with the interior decoration of the church in Glogau. The narrator encounters the forty-year-old painter Berthold, who has been reduced for unclear reasons to painting trompe-l'oeils and architectural illusions in the Jesuit church. The narrator's acquaintance in G., Professor Aloysius Walther, who represents the uncomprehending bourgeois mentality, shares with him a manuscript concerning Berthold written down by his former apprentice. As a young man in D[resden], Berthold had devoted himself principally to landscapes. In Rome, however, the contemporary enthusiasm for history painting caused him to doubt his painterly talent. Nevertheless, he went to Naples, where he made progress under the tutelage of the German landscape painter Philipp Hackert. Again his doubts were stirred by a mysterious Maltese, who pointed out that Hackert's landscapes, lacking all originality, are like "correct copies of an original written in a foreign language."[122] At this point, inspired by the face of a model that he glimpses in the sketchbook of his friend Florentin (surely a tribute to Dorothea Schlegel's novel), he experiences a mystical epiphany in a grotto outside Naples, in which Saint Catherine appears to him. From this moment on, Berthold is transformed, "as though inspired by divine power." Emerging from his depression, he studies the finest works of the old masters and succeeds gradually in painting a number of highly acclaimed altarpieces—mainly subjects from Christian legendry in which the image of his mystical ideal always shines forth.

Through a series of accidents produced by the Napoleonic siege of Naples, Berthold rescues the Princess Angiola, in whom he recognizes his ideal beauty. He succeeds in fleeing with her to M[unich], where he settles down to what ought to have been a life of bliss with the ideal of his artistic dreams. Hoping to establish his reputation, he sets out to paint a great canvas depicting Mary and Elisabeth with Jesus and John the Baptist. But his efforts fail; the image of Angiola always turns into a lifeless waxen figurine. Cursing his wife for having ruined his talent, he deserts her and their child and wanders around the countryside, supporting himself through church decorations. At this point the manuscript breaks off, and soon thereafter the narrator leaves town. But half a year later Professor Walther reports the end of the story to him. Berthold suddenly conquered his despair and completed his great altarpiece in a spectacular manner; then he disappeared and drowned himself in the river. The parallels between Traugott and Berthold are obvious: in both cases the pious painter falls in love with the image in a painting; in both cases the image materializes in the form of a real woman. But whereas Traugott is able through humor and irony to overcome his initial shock at the disparity between his aesthetic ideal and reality, Berthold is overcome by his despair and driven first to madness and then to death. But in both cases, and despite the difference in ending, Hoffmann is eager to demonstrate that the pious painter as conceived by Wackenroder and Tieck was too naive to be true. In reality, he suggests, the painter is subject to the same doubts and temptations as all other Romantic artists. In Hoffmann's hands the figure of the Romantic painter becomes more problematic and, at the same time, more emphatic.

• • •

One motif that occurs so frequently from the *Herzensergießungen* and *Franz Sternbalds Wanderungen* by way of *Florentin* down to Hoffmann's tales that it becomes a literary cliché is the association of German artists in Rome. And the motif, far from ending with Hoffmann, is still powerfully evident in such late Romantic classics as Eichendorff's *Aus dem Leben eines Taugenichts* (1826) and his novel *Dichter und ihre Gesellen* (1834). In this connection we should note, in conclusion, that conspicuous example of life imitating art—the German artists in Rome who have entered art history under the originally denigrating appellative "Nazarenes."[123]

The story of the group is picturesque enough to have occurred in a novella by Hoffmann. The tale begins in Vienna, where a group of six young students at the Academy of Art—Franz Pforr, Friedrich Overbeck, and four of their less well-known friends—became so disenchanted with the prevailing academic classicism that on July 10, 1809, they formed a confederation that they called the Brotherhood of Saint Luke, in memory of the patron saint of painters, whom August Wilhelm Schlegel had already canonized in a poem concluding his dialogue "Die Gemähble." The young idealists, inspired by the example of the art-loving friar and Franz Sternbald, intended to create a new art that would be motivated by moral and religious concerns rather than by purely aesthetic goals. Seceding from the Academy, they journeyed in May 1810 to Rome, where they moved into the monastery of Santo Isidoro, a former Irish Franciscan church and college. In sharp contrast to earlier generations of German artists who had pilgrimaged to Rome, they rejected the art of classical antiquity in favor of the Christian art of the late Middle Ages and Renaissance. In their effort to reenact the *Herzensergießungen* the young men, and others who gradually joined them, lived and worked all day in their monastic cells, coming together in the refectory for communal meals, readings, and drawing from models. They wore wide cloaks, let their hair grow long, and affected a generally archaic attire, as depicted in the portrait of Franz Pforr that Overbeck painted in 1810 just two years before his friend's early death or in the various portraits of one another that they liked to put into their historical and biblical scenes (e.g., the portrait of Overbeck in Pforr's painting *Shulamit and Maria*).

Just as the writers of the period featured painters in their novels and poems, the painters tended to draw their subjects from literary works (especially the Bible) and, in general, to cultivate a strong narrative style.

Rumohr perhaps put it most precisely when he observed, years later, that the painters did not simply borrow their subjects from literature; rather, the painters and writers were reflecting a common cultural source.[124] Overbeck is best known for his paintings of such biblical subjects as *The Raising of Lazarus* or the *Entry of Christ into Jerusalem*. Pforr tended to prefer literary subjects from Shakespeare (*Macbeth and the Witches*), Schiller (*Wallenstein at the Battle of Lützen*), or Goethe (illustrations to *Götz von Berlichingen*). Peter Cornelius, who joined the group shortly after Pforr's death, was already known for his illustrations of Goethe's *Faust* and the *Nibelungenlied*.

Their powerful narrative impulse, executed in a style dominated by crisp lines and primary colors, found its appropriate medium in the pure fresco technique (with no *a secco* modifications) that the Nazarenes rediscovered and executed with brilliant virtuosity in various Roman establishments. In 1815 the newly arrived Prussian General Consul, Jakob Salomon Bartholdy, commissioned a group of Nazarenes—Cornelius, Overbeck, Philipp Veit, Wilhelm Schadow, and Franz Catel—to decorate the reception room of his lodgings with scenes from the Old Testament story of Joseph. (The greatly admired works were moved in 1887 to the National Gallery in Berlin.) Encouraged by their success, in 1818 a leading Roman family commissioned the group—this time principally the older Joseph Anton Koch, along with Overbeck, Philipp Veit, and Julius Schnorr von Carolsfeld—to decorate the Villa Massimo with frescoes depicting scenes from the works of Dante, Tasso, and Ariosto.

It would be a mistake to allow subsequent neglect of this group to make us underestimate the recognition that they enjoyed for at least two decades. In the first place, they had close personal contacts with a number of leading figures. Peter Cornelius enjoyed both the friendship of Goethe and the patronage of Crown Prince Ludwig of Bavaria, who employed him to execute the frescoes of his new Glyptothek in Munich. Overbeck benefited from the sponsorship of Carl Friedrich von Rumohr, the consultant later for the Berlin museum. Philipp Veit was Friedrich Schlegel's stepson, and through him Schlegel became acquainted with many painters of the younger generation. Consul Bartholdy was the brother-in-law of Dorothea Schlegel's brother Abraham (the father of Felix Mendelssohn). On his trip to Rome in 1824 Schinkel became acquainted with some of the group and admired particularly Schnorr von Carolsfeld's frescoes in the Villa Massimo.[125] Even though their work was soon eclipsed as Romanticism gave way to realism, it survived in the work of foreign artists who were influenced by the Nazarenes and their conception of line and color, notably Ingres, Ruskin, Pugin, and Overbeck's friend William Dyce in his decoration of the Houses of Parliament. The public impact of the group can best be judged perhaps by the vehemence of the attacks launched against them, notably the notorious assault on "Neu-deutsche religios-patriotische Kunst" that Heinrich Meyer wrote in 1817, with Goethe's encouragement, for the periodical *Über Kunst und Alterthum.*[126] "The tendency or direction of taste that we propose to discuss has found adherents and supporters especially among Germans. The following remarks should therefore extend principally across Germany and all the way to Rome, where German artists along with traveling aficionados constitute a sort of academic collegiality since those who then return home, in accordance with the impressions they have received, truly guide the taste of the nation." Meyer's article, which begins with a rapid survey of German art since the 1790s, lays the blame mainly on Tieck, Wackenroder, and the Schlegels for the pernicious development of a naive, nationalistic, and Christian art that he sees as a threat to the classical tradition. And the controversy continued. The crown prince of Bavaria was such an enthusiast that he even adopted the archaic Germanic attire of the Nazarenes.

In conservative Austria the admiration was less effusive. In the spring of 1819, in honor of Emperor Franz's visit to Rome, the German artist community—some fifty painters, eight sculptors, and divers engravers and etchers—arranged an extensive display of German art in the Palazzo Caffarelli. To the artists' chagrin, the emperor and his entourage spent only one and a half disdainful hours in the exhibition, which was subsequently reviewed slightingly in the Austrian press. The reviews prompted a major vindication by Veit's stepfather, Friedrich Schlegel, "Über die deutsche Kunstausstellung zu Rom im Frühjahr 1819, und über den gegenwärtigen Stand der deutschen Kunst in Rom."[127] Following a survey of older taste in art, Schlegel devotes several pages to an appreciation of the two painters, Cornelius and Overbeck, whom even then he recognized as the leaders of the group. He goes on to note the significance of the Nazarene rediscovery of fresco painting and acknowledges their contributions to that genre. He concludes his piece by rejecting the mindless criticism of what he calls "mannered archaicism" ("manirierte Altertümlichkeit").

The fact that the Nazarenes soon dissipated as a group and that their achievement was displaced until the rediscovery in recent years of the masters among them is secondary to the fact that matters in our context. By the third decade of the nineteenth century, when Schinkel was designing his museum, public interest in the figure of the artist had been stirred up by writers from Wackenroder and Tieck to Hoffmann, maintained by reports concerning the activities of a colorful group of contemporary German artists in Rome, and inflamed by controversies involving the most important critics of the age. In the 1820s the public was conditioned to accept Schinkel's notion that a museum ought to be, in addition to a "temple of art," also a "pantheon" celebrating the figures and works of individual artists of past and present.

### THE GALLERY DIALOGUE AS GENRE

The Romantic museum was more than a temple of art and a pantheon of artists. It had also emerged par excellence as the locus for connoisseurs. This is not a trivial statement, for it changed the manner in which people looked at art and became able to understand it as a historical phenomenon. Art lovers had been looking at sculptures and paintings for centuries. But for the most part it was necessary to view such works either in the artists' studios, as Vasari often did, or in situ in the churches and palaces for which they had been commissioned. In either case the sense of historical continuity among works could easily be lost in the trek from place to place and in the haphazard arrangement of works. More recently the emergence of the Salon had created another opportunity to view art, but here the art, being inevitably contemporary, was by definition without a historical context; in addition, it was assembled in one place for only the brief duration of the exhibition and then dispersed again. As a result, Diderot often had to write his accounts of the Salons from catalogue notes jotted down hastily on the spot and expanded often weeks or even months later.[128]

Paintings by different artists and from different periods were of course assembled in private collections, ranging from the *Gemäldesaal* of local painters that Goethe's father owned in Frankfurt am Main to the great royal or papal collections.[129] In most cases, however, these collections were accumulated according to personal idiosyncrasy and taste and therefore did not provide a representative sample for historical study, and in any case they were private and not always accessible. Wherever paintings were assembled, however—either in private collections or public exhibitions—the gallery had emerged by the later eighteenth century as the place where culturally sophisticated travelers could expect to encounter the aesthetic elite of any town or city.[130] Diderot's Salon accounts, Heinse's gallery letters, and Goethe's *Italienische Reise* provide vivid accounts of the lively gallery life of Paris in the sixties, Düsseldorf in the seventies, and Rome in the eighties—not to mention the varied accounts from different hands of the frequent exhibitions in the Louvre after 1793.[131] It is hardly surprising that one of the most important episodes in Wackenroder's *Herzensergießungen* makes use of the gallery conversation as a cultural event.

It is the framework fiction of the work that the author is an elderly lay brother spending the last years of his life in the solitude of a monastery, where he recalls the experiences of his youth, which were devoted principally to art, and writes them down from time to time for the benefit of younger readers. The section entitled "Die Malerchronik," though it occurs toward the end of the volume, depicts an incident that stands at the beginning of the narrator's cultural consciousness and in a certain sense acts as a catalyst for all that follows.[132] The episode therefore deserves our particular attention. As he was traveling around as a young man in search of art, the narrator begins, he once found himself in a palace where he spent three days examining the extensive collections of paintings. Seeking to commit them all to memory, he managed merely to let his mind become confused by the wealth of pictures. On the third day an elderly gentleman appeared at the palace, an Italian priest whose name the narrator confesses that he has never succeeded in ascertaining. (The mysterious pater was a stock figure in the Gothic fiction of the time.) An astonishingly learned man, he had the physical appearance of a sage from the sixteenth century. Despite the narrator's youth, the older man struck up a friendly conversation with him and spent the entire day with him in the galleries.

Noting the younger man's interest in painting, he inquired if he knew the names of the masters who had created the works. The young man knew the names of the most famous artists, but it turned out that he knew virtually nothing more. "You have hitherto marveled at the lovely pictures, my dear son, as though they were wonderworks, fallen to the earth from heaven. But consider that they are all the work of human hands—that many artists were producing excellent things even at your age. What do you think now? Don't you have a desire to find out something more about the men who have excelled in painting?" (94–95). Having observed the youth's particular fascination with Raphael, the pater briefly tells him the story of Raphael's life and recounts a few examples of his gentle character. He goes on to point out that many men have written chronicles in which they describe the lives of the painters—the first and finest of whom was Giorgio Vasari. Thereupon the pater relates several other stories to illustrate how painting and personality flow together into what he calls "the artistic character." Above all, he stresses, the venerable painters of older times "made the art of painting into a faithful servant of religion and knew nothing of the color-vanity of present-day artists" (103–4). Following their dialogue in the gallery, the pater departs, leaving the narrator behind in a dreamlike state from all the tales he has heard. "I had been introduced into a wholly new, wonderful world" (105). He immediately sought out and read all the books about artists, especially Vasari's magnum opus, where he found again all the tales the pater had related. "It was this unforgettable man who led me to the study of the history of artists, which provides so much sustenance for the mind, the heart, and the imagination, and I am indebted to him for a great number of happy hours." The seminal conversation in the gallery, as it emerges here, provides the basis for the entire volume of *Herzenser-gießungen*, all of which are in one way or another either stories of the lives of the artists, based on such sources as Vasari, or else reflections on the relationship of art and religion.

It is not clear in which gallery this exemplary scene is supposed to be set—if indeed any specific gallery is intended. We know that Wackenroder was familiar with several important German galleries of his day, including Kassel, Salzthalen, and Pommersfeld.[133] However, the gallery that provided the locus for some of the most memorable occasions in German cultural history of the eighteenth century was the royal gallery in Dresden, which was popularly known as the Florence of Germany, not only for its renowned art collections and lively cultural life but also for its physical setting on the banks of the Elbe.[134] An epiphany in Dresden could be regarded as the beginning of the formal study of Western art since it was here that the young Winckelmann was inspired to his lifework by the paintings and sculptures and composed his first great study, *Gedanken über die Nachahmung der griechischen Werke in der Malerei und der Bildhauerkunst* (1755). It was also in Dresden that the student Goethe, traveling over for the occasion from the University of Leipzig, had his first encounter with a major collection of original paintings.[135] (At home in Frankfurt the originals to which he had been exposed were essentially second-rate local works; he knew the masterpieces only in the form of etchings or such miniaturized color copies as those in the famous Morgensternsche Gemälde-Kabinett.) It was during a visit to Dresden in 1789 that the seventeen-year-old Friedrich Schlegel first registered the profound impressions that constituted the foundation for all his subsequent studies of classical antiquity, as he noted in the preface to the 1822 edition of his collected art criticism. It was on a trip to Dresden in 1796 that Wackenroder first disclosed to Tieck the writings on art that eventually became the *Herzensergießungen* and inspired his friend to his own concern with art. The visit to the Dresden gallery constitutes a set piece in most of the autobiographical accounts of the times, as in Adolph Müller's *Briefe von der Universität*. Perhaps the most enthusiastic account is to be found in Henrich Steffens's autobiography.

It was on Goethe's recommendation that Steffens rode over to Dresden in 1799 from Freiberg, where he was pursuing his mining studies with Werner, to have his first look at a major gallery. Exhausted by the all-night ride and fortified by wine at breakfast, he hastened to the gallery. In a state of great agitation, Steffens absorbed hardly a word as he was guided through the galleries by the director, Friedrich Justus Riedel.

It had not occurred to us that a state of inner calm and sobriety, which we did not possess, is essential for the quiet contemplation of paintings. It seemed to me that the brightly colored pictures were tilting and moving around. The names of the painters, which mainly I was hearing pronounced for the first time, though they were in part quite familiar, were mixed just as chaotically and confusedly.[136]

After a considerable period viewing works from the Netherlands, they entered the Italian gallery, where Steffens anticipated great revelations. But as tired and sleepy as he was, he was unable to register any impressions or meanings. "The figures of the paintings hovered before me like visions, seemed to move, to step out of their frames and mingle with the visitors who were strolling about." Steffens became so agitated that he was sure everyone would notice his peculiar state. Then they stepped before a large painting that had been placed at eye level because it was being copied.

A female figure was hovering forth from the clouds bearing a wonderful child. The moment took me by surprise, the peculiar tension that gripped me had reached its peak, and I forgot where I was. A profound sensation penetrated me, and I broke into tears that flowed uncontrollably. . . . I looked around and saw that I was the object of general attention. I tried to get control of myself and now learned that the painting that had moved me so tumultuously was the most famous one in the gallery—it was Raphael's *Madonna*.

It is probably impossible to determine the extent to which the account in Steffens's memoirs is colored by fifty years of associations or even by his own fictionalizing: the same episode provided the basis for a considerably expanded description in the second novella of Steffens's cycle *Die vier Norweger* (written in 1828). In any case, it conveys a sense of the atmosphere in the great gallery at Dresden and the emotions with which members of the younger generation entered the premises that were almost ritually characterized as sacred or holy.

No occasion had more profound reverberations than the assembly of young Romantics who came together in Dresden in the late summer and early autumn of 1798 and spent many hours in the galleries, talking about sculpture and painting and developing what we now recognize as the Romantic theory of art.[137] We have several entertaining accounts of those memorable days—not all of them unbiased. Dora Stock, for instance, was the sister-in-law of Schiller's best friend, Körner, and hence predisposed against the Schlegels, who glorified Goethe at Schiller's expense, and especially against Caroline, who had contributed to the breakup of Dora's engagement. Stock, a painter who worked in the galleries as a copyist, was in a particularly good position to observe the goings-on. As she reported to Charlotte Schiller, the Schlegels spent almost every morning in the gallery, along with Schelling and the young translator Johann Diederich Gries.[138] "They took notes and expounded their theories so that it was a marvel to behold." The practicing painter speaks ironically about the critics with their incomprehensible theories. "Sometimes they chatted with me about problems of art and posed questions that I was incapable of answering. For I feel and I paint, but I understand nothing of professional talk, and I am all the more timid in the presence of those whose superior knowledge makes me sense my inadequacies." Dora Stock was not the only beneficiary of their theorizing. "They also initiated Fichte into the mysteries of art. You would have laughed to see the Schlegels drag him around everywhere and beleaguer him with their convictions." From another, more sympathetic source we hear the account of a mystical evening when a group of friends—Novalis, the Schlegels with their sister Charlotte Ernst, along with Karl August Böttiger, the Hellenist and director of the Weimar *Gymnasium*—assembled at the home of Wilhelm Gottlieb Bekker, the director of the sculpture gallery, to view the antiquities by torchlight.[139]

The immediate result of this Romantic art conference, which represents a summation of early Romantic thought on the subject, was the dialogue "Die Gemählde," written jointly by August Wilhelm and Caroline Schlegel and published the following year in the *Athenaeum*.[140] The dialogue begins in the antiquities room of the palace at Dresden, where Waller and Louise are discussing the aesthetic laws that govern the sculpture of classical antiquity. They encounter their friend Reinhold, who is annoyed because his sketch does not do justice to the sculpture he is trying to copy. His complaints prompt a discussion on the differences between the genres of art. Louise confesses that she enjoys painting more than sculpture because it addresses itself more directly to our senses. In response to the poet Waller, Reinhold argues that language is such an inadequate medium that it can never do justice to works of visual art. Louise and Waller object to Reinhold's notion that art exists simply for the benefit of the artist, who studies older works in order to bring forth new ones. "No, my friend, community and social interaction are the main purpose," Louise asserts (49). It turns out that Louise has been recording detailed descriptions of the paintings—to train her eye in critical vision but also, in an age before reproductions, to share her experiences with her sister, who was unable to accompany the group to Dresden.

Leaving the gallery, the three friends settle down on the bank of the Elbe, overlooking this Florence of the North, and Louise reads for their comment a few of her descriptions of paintings from the royal gallery in the Stallgebäude. The outdoor setting makes it natural to begin with descriptions of landscapes by Salvator Rosa, Claude Lorrain, and Ruisdael. In the course of the conversation it becomes clear that Waller is August Wilhelm himself and Louise is Caroline, while Reinhold expounds a synthesis of views of Friedrich Schlegel, Novalis, and other friends. The dialectical interplay of opinions, in other words, reflects the early Romantic aesthetic in all its facets. The discussion of landscape painting, which emerges from Louise's descriptions, produces the conclusion that it is "the loftiest genre because in it the pure phenomenon plays so important a role" (65)—because, that is, it becomes pure art and serves therefore as the most transparent medium for the expression of the artist's soul. (Today we recognize this view as characteristically Romantic, but in 1799—before the major works of Caspar David Friedrich and his followers or the theories of Philipp Otto Runge—it was amazingly prescient.)

The conversation then moves from landscape by way of German portraiture to paintings on biblical subjects by various Italian masters. Following Louise's description of works by Leonardo, Waller reads a few of his own depictions of canvases by Rubens, Poussin, Cignani, and Carracci. When the friends ask why Louise has so conspicuously omitted Raphael from her descriptions, she confesses that in this case Reinhold was right: words are not adequate to the challenge of the most sublime art. The three engage in a lively discussion of the *Sistine Madonna*, which culminates in a debate on the reciprocal relationship between the visual arts and poetry. While they do not share Wackenroder's mystical sense of art as religion, Waller points out that it is an inestimable advantage for artists and poets to have a shared mythic circle of belief in which the objects are familiar and, by tradition, organized in a painterly manner so that the attention can focus on the treatment rather than on the subject matter. For this reason, they agree, religion has once again become the main subject matter of painters despite a recent tendency to use matter from classical mythology and history or allegory or even Nordic mythology. The dialogue ends with what Louise calls a "transformation of paintings into poems" when Waller reads a series of sonnets based on paintings of various New Testament subjects.[141] The trio agrees that painting, in contrast to sculpture, is essentially a Christian art inasmuch as the Greeks had muses for all but the visual arts. The closest approximation to a semi-divine patron of art is Daedalus, and even he can be associated only with sculpture, not with painting. But Christians have a patron saint in the person of Luke the Evangelist. Waller reads in conclusion a poetic legend about Saint Luke and his portrait of the Virgin, which is completed by Raphael. Reinhold in return promises that the first Madonna that he succeeds in painting will be dedicated to Saint Luke and the Holy Raphael.

"Die Gemählde" contains *in nuce* all the central Romantic beliefs on art. The abrupt departure from the sculpture gallery and the ensuing conversation about painting exemplify dramatically the Romantic glorification of painting over sculpture—a striking shift away from the Classicist preference for works of sculpture prevailing since Winckelmann and Lessing. The recognition of painting as an essentially Christian art is

CHAPTER SIX

consistent with the new awareness of the historical development of art. Waller remarks at one point, for instance: "I don't know why Holbein strikes us as so old-fashioned since he lived precisely during the most blossoming period of Italian art. This is even more conspicuously the case with his predecessor Albrecht Dürer, who was also a contemporary of Raphael" (76). Again, this acknowledgment of historical differences differs from Winckelmann's attitude, which regarded classical antiquity as the perfection from which all other art is either a decline or an imitation. The essential unity and complementarity of all the arts are stressed; at the same time, the differences between the genres are acknowledged and the inadequacy of language to convey the impact of the visual arts is emphasized.

Finally, while the function of pure art in the form of landscape painting as a mirror of the artist's soul is accented, the notion of art for art's sake is rejected by Louise, who stresses the social and communal aspect of art—an argument that legitimizes the use of dialogue, in contrast to the treatise, as the appropriate genre in which to develop a theory of art that will do justice to the many facets of Romantic thought. In its shift of emphasis from sculpture to painting and its understanding of painting as a Christian art, "Die Gemählde" resembles the *Herzensergießungen*. In one essential, however, the Schlegels went beyond Wackenroder: his art-loving monk regarded the passive adoration of the artwork as a prayer, but for the three young Romantics in Dresden the contemplation of art should be a critical experience best undertaken actively through descriptive analysis and the lively exchange of views. Indeed, at the culmination of the dialogue—the response to Raphael's paintings—the descriptions already written down by Waller and Louise give way to the immediacy of dialogue, in which the views of the group can emerge spontaneously and, to use one of the favorite Romantic concepts, be shaped "progressively."

• • •

It is appropriate that August Wilhelm and Caroline chose the dialogue as the literary form in which to set forth their theory of painting, for the dialogue—as we have already observed in the remarks on Jena rhetoric—is in many senses the archetypal Romantic genre, the literary form in which the *sym*- of Friedrich Schlegel's ideal of *Symphilosophieren* becomes most apparent—or, to take another concept, the "fraternalization" (*Verbrüderung*) proclaimed in the preface of the *Athenaeum*. It is the literary form, moreover, in which it was easiest to capture the spirit of the gallery conversations that constituted such a characteristic aspect of German cultural life at the turn of the century. Yet it is not immediately obvious that the dialogue should have been available as a literary option. Following a long period of neglect, the dialogue was reintroduced into German letters as a mode of philosophical discourse by Moses Mendelssohn in his three dialogues on the immortality of the soul entitled *Phaedon* (1767).[142] In response to Mendelssohn's success many writers—including Lessing, Wieland, Herder, Jacobi, and Goethe—took up the graceful form. Especially for writers inspired by the popularizing impulses of the Enlightenment the form recommended itself as public and accessible. Under the influence of Kant's critical philosophy, however, the situation changed: the Platonic dialogue began to be regarded as inappropriate for the rigorous logic of systematic philosophy. A generation later Hegel continued to insist that dialectics was the only suitable mode for serious philosophical speculation. For the writers of the Romantic decades, therefore, to use the Platonic dialogue for philosophical discourse amounted to a polemical statement against Kant and his followers. Schleiermacher, himself a devoted translator and interpreter of Plato, treasured the dialogue as the truest expression of the social nature of man, to which he devoted the fourth of his *Reden über die Religion*. In several of his own works Schleiermacher used the philosophical dialogue, as did Schelling in *Bruno oder über das göttliche und natürliche Prinzip der Dinge* (1802). It also seems appropriate that the ultimate Romantic theory of aesthetics, Solger's *Erwin: Vier Gespräche über das Schöne und die Kunst* (1815), should have been expounded in the form of a dialogue.

Yet it was by no means only in formal philosophical works that the dialogue recommended itself to the Romantics with their passion for discourse. We have already noted that Friedrich Schlegel used the form for his "Gespräch über die Poesie" (1800). Moreover, in many Romantic novels the narrative gives way to pure dialogue, as in Schlegel's *Lucinde*. Other writers—notably Tieck in his *Phantasus* (1811) and E.T.A. Hoffmann in *Die Serapionsbrüder* (1818)—created for their story collections frameworks in which groups of friends engaging in dialogue develop theories of aesthetics. August Wilhelm and Caroline were therefore using an exemplary Romantic mode for their discourse on painting—a mode that was in this case doubly suitable because it enabled them to convey in their work the sense of the gallery conversation that had become so typical of the cultural life of the period and that, indeed, had specifically inspired their own "Gespräch." Largely as a result of the Schlegels' discourse, in turn, the gallery dialogue was recognized as such a representative genre that it could be parodied, as in the account that Achim von Arnim and Clemens Brentano wrote in 1810 of Caspar David Friedrich's exhibition of his seascape with a Capuchin monk.[143] Kleist, revising the article heavily and discarding the dialogue form, published the review under his own name in the *Berliner Abendblätter* on October 13, 1810, and it is his version that is usually cited in the history of the reception of Friedrich's works. But that fact should not obscure the popularity of the form that inspired Arnim and Brentano in the first place to write their parody in the form of a gallery dialogue among various groups of visitors.

Another literary genre needs to be specified also as a source for "Die Gemählde," for the Schlegels make use not only of the philosophical dialogue but also of the existing literary descriptions of paintings.[144] Here again they were drawing on a genre that had, in 1798, a short yet influential history. Essentially the literary description of painting was a product of the widespread new interest in painting in an age without reproductions. Goethe's experience is not unrepresentative: he was exposed to great art in the original only in a few vivid bursts of experience during his lifetime—in Dresden as a student, in Italy during his late thirties, and on a few other rare occasions. For most of his long life, however, he had access only to second- or third-rate collections in Frankfurt and Weimar or to crude reproductions of masterpieces.[145] Otherwise Goethe and his contemporaries were heavily dependent upon written descriptions that sought to refresh the memory or to communicate some sense of the work of art—and that focused, by necessity, on the theme and treatment of the subject matter more than on the painterly aspects. In response to this interest two related literary forms emerged around the middle of the eighteenth century and lasted until the development of adequate reproductions in the nineteenth century: the Salon report of the sort created and perfected from 1759 on by Diderot, and gallery letters of the sort written by Wilhelm Heinse in Düsseldorf, who has been called the first *"feuilletoniste* of art,"[146] and by Georg Forster in the course of his *Ansichten vom Niederrhein* (1791).

The Schlegels were well aware of their models. Before Louise begins reading her descriptions, Waller asks if she is familiar with Diderot's *Salon de peinture*. Louise replies that she does indeed know Diderot's work, but that she consciously distanced herself from his model—in part because of what she calls the "coquettish brusquerie" of the French style. Mainly, however, Louise stresses the difference of situation—between the

Salon exhibition, where good paintings can stand side by side with ap-
pallingly bad ones, and the leading permanent collections, where the
quality of the paintings is consistently high and the visitor has time
enough for peaceful contemplation. She disclaims any influence by Forster on the grounds that his aesthetic sense is so much weaker than his
ethical impulse. "He seeks out the nobility of the objects and in the process forgets the accomplishment of the treatment" (53). (It is this insistence on the value of pure form—the typically Romantic view—that
leads into the discussion of landscape painting as self-expression.)

In two important respects, however, the descriptions read by Louise as
well as Waller are related to the tradition that extends from Diderot by
way of Heinse (who is not cited) to Forster. First, they share the common
epistolary form, which preserves the casual sense of conversation. Indeed,
Diderot occasionally allows his Salon letters to slip into imagined dialogues with his friend Melchior Grimm.[147] Similarly, Heinse's descriptions of the gallery at Düsseldorf, published in Wieland's *Teutscher Mer-
kur* in 1776–1777, are presented in the form of letters to his friend Gleim.
And Forster's *Ansichten* preserves the tone of the letters—to his wife, his
father-in-law, his various friends—on which the descriptions were actually based. In short, the genre of descriptions tries consciously to capture
the sense of immediacy that is characteristic of the gallery dialogue itself.

At the same time—and this is the second point of similarity—almost
all the authors of these epistolary descriptions of paintings are keenly
aware of the inadequacy of language to express the essence of the paintings.[148] This produces in the earlier writers the tendency noted by Louise—to focus on theme and subject matter rather than on form, style, and
treatment. It should be noted, finally, that the literary description of
painting—while it had already been practiced for some forty years by
this time—conveyed in the 1790s the force of novelty. Diderot had been
turning out his accounts of the Salons ever since 1759, but they were
communicated through Grimm's *Correspondence littéraire* and not intended for a larger public.

These works were not published and made available to the general
public until long after Diderot's death: in 1796 an incomplete edition of
the *Salon de 1765* was published along with the *Essai sur la peinture*; in
1798 the complete *Salons* of 1765 and 1767 were published; and in 1799
Goethe translated part of the *Essai sur la peinture* for his *Propyläen*. Similarly, Forster's *Ansichten vom Niederrhein* did not appear until 1791, and
Forster had been recently brought to the attention of the younger Ro-

mantics by Friedrich Schlegel's admiring essay of 1797. Louise, therefore, is referring to two works that were virtually contemporary. (It is possible that the Schlegels were not familiar with Heinse's gallery letters since they had not been reprinted since their original publication some twenty years earlier.) In short, "Die Gemählde" was consciously practicing the most advanced and sophisticated literary form for dealing with art appreciation—the description.

It is important to stress the timing in order to appreciate the radical modernity of "Die Gemählde" and its synthesizing achievement. Here for the first time, in a form that was recognizably new, a synthesis was accomplished of the various aspects of connoisseurship that had been separated for most of the eighteenth century: a comprehensive theory of art that included painting as well as sculpture and that located the visual arts within general aesthetics; a critical apprehension of the individual work of art exercised in its presence; and the locating of the individual work in the context of a history of art extending from the sculpture of classical antiquity to the painting of modern Christian Europe. The adequate setting for this brilliant literary and critical accomplishment was a gallery—indeed, the gallery that, moving slowly toward the status of a public museum, had already established its place in the cultural consciousness of Germany. And the adequate form was a synthesis of the two recent genres that came closest to communicating the immediacy of art experienced in a gallery as well as the reciprocity of response in the gallery discourse—the dialogue and the letter. In "Die Gemählde," in sum, we see not just a landmark of Romantic aesthetic theory; it also constitutes a major document of German cultural history as well as a sophisticated use of literary form.

• • •

The significance of the Romantic art seminar that took place in the Dresden gallery in 1798 is most strikingly evident in "Die Gemählde," but there is also other testimony. After his return to Freiberg, Novalis wrote to Caroline and referred to an essay on the Dresden sculptures that he had agreed to write, apparently as a complement to "Die Gemählde."[149] Originally conceived in the conventional form of a gallery letter ("Der Brief über die Antiken"), it is now being recast, Novalis noted, in the form of a "romantic fragment" entitled "The Visit to the Antiquities" ("Der Antikenbesuch"). In short, had the essay actually been completed, it would have assumed the form of the genre gradually emerging as archetypally Romantic: the gallery conversation.

Unfortunately Novalis never finished the promised essay, but we can get a fair idea of his intentions from his notes, which display a remarkable parallel to the thoughts of "Die Gemählde."[150] Even though it was Novalis's assignment to deal with the sculptures, from the outset his thoughts kept straying to the realm of painting, and especially to the obsessive image of the *Sistine Madonna*. (His letter to Caroline closes with the flourish: "May the Madonna keep you healthy and protect our friendship.") The heading of the first major section of his notes is "*Antiquities. The Madonna.*" Following a weird—yet for Novalis characteristic—mélange of ideas concerning human history and physical chemistry, he jots down another major heading: "*Descriptions of paintings etc.*," which leads to the consideration of "landscape painting—and painting as opposed to sculpture in general." The idea of landscapes involves not only geometrical aspects ("Surfaces—structures—architectonics") but also topography with atmosphere, clouds, vegetation, and inorganic nature. From the notion that "sculpture and painting must be symbolic," Novalis goes on to observe that "the Painting Gallery is a storage room for indirect stimuli of every sort for the poet." The belief that "every work of art has an ideal a priori—has a necessity in itself to exist"—justifies the conviction that "a genuine criticism of painters is possible." Novalis returns once more to his initial assignment when he notes that "one is compelled by the antiquities to treat them as sacred objects."

Novalis got no further than these brief notes with what was to have been his contribution to the *Athenaeum* aesthetics, the gallery dialogue on classical sculpture. But it is clear from them that he shared with August Wilhelm and Caroline certain basic views regarding the differences between sculpture and painting, the historical development of art from classical to Christian, the primacy of landscape painting, the symbolic quality of art, the autonomy of art, the sacred nature of art, and the function of criticism. Above all, he took as given the conviction, which became central for his generation, that the proper study, appreciation, and understanding of the work of art—its theory, history, and criticism—take place most suitably in a gallery or museum by means of conversation among educated laymen (and not professional artists or scholars).

The meeting in Dresden produced a few other direct results—for instance, a sequence of six sonnets on religious paintings in the royal gallery written in 1798 by Gries.[151] However, the main product of that summer was the conclusion that the gallery should henceforth be the appropriate locus for the elaboration of thoughts about art—including history, theory, and criticism. This is instantly obvious if we look briefly at Friedrich Schlegel's most important contributions to the discussion. The four essays on painting that he wrote from 1803 to 1805 for his journal *Europa* occupy an important place in the emergence of the Romantic theory of art.[152] Indeed, the very title of his journal sheds any lingering traces of classicism that were still attached to the title of the earlier organ, *Athenaeum*. And following the widespread circulation among the Romantics of the manuscript of Novalis's discourse "Die Christenheit oder Europa," few readers could look at the title of the journal without hearing the resonance of association. It is wholly consistent with all the implications of the title, therefore, if Schlegel in his *Europa* essays elaborates the theory of painting already set forth in the *Athenaeum* dialogue as an essentially Christian art and in explicit opposition to the thoughts expressed in the *Propyläen* of the Weimar Friends of Art. Friedrich Schlegel did not merely reiterate, however; in a very important respect he went beyond August Wilhelm and Caroline. "Die Gemählde" concentrated mainly on Raphael and his followers during the High Renaissance. It was Friedrich Schlegel's contribution to expand the canon to include Italian primitives as well as older German painters as exemplary for a European Christian art.

Although his ideas are startlingly modern in their intertextual and hermeneutic approach, Schlegel chose to remain within the convention of the gallery letter to elaborate and communicate his views. This is evident in the opening sentences of the first piece, which is addressed "To a Friend in Dresden." (The unnamed friend is actually Ludwig Tieck, and the reference to Dresden instantly establishes a line of continuity for the initiate between the summer of 1798 in Dresden and the summer of 1802 in Paris.) "I shall first of all acquaint you as precisely as possible with the locale and then provide you with an overview of the paintings that at present are exhibited here."[153] Schlegel proceeds to give a detailed description of the Louvre as he first saw it in August 1802 when he arrived in Paris—a building, as we noted earlier, that struck him as utterly inadequate for the demands of a temple of art. He then cites the three catalogues to which he will refer in order to identify the works he discusses, warning his friend at the same time that the continual shifting of the objects—to make room for special exhibits, to send lesser items to provincial museums, to remove works for repair—causes constant distracting changes in the groupings. This, in turn, leads to the generalizing observation that "all the artworks of any single type belong together, and they best interpret one another reciprocally" (112). The imperfection of any collection, however, as well as the shiftings, reveals paintings to the observer in constantly new contexts and serves as a reminder that what one sees and knows is always only a part of the greater whole. All the descriptions of older Italian painting—"Titian, Correggio, Julio Romano, Andrea del Sarto, those are for me the last painters" (113)—are written in the context of this profoundly historical understanding of painting, which becomes possible only in a gallery.

The consciousness of being in a gallery is consistent with Schlegel's understanding of connoisseurship. At the beginning of the third article he notes the dangers of any aesthetic theory that is detached from actual critical experience. "Theory of art can never be separated from contemplation without inevitably degenerating into willful fabrications (*Hirngespinste*) or into empty generalities."[154] For this reason Schlegel justifies his procedure of providing not merely a broad outline but also detailed descriptions of old paintings. "Contemplation should in every case be the first order of business; the results arrange themselves from one viewing to the next into general principles whose coherence, as well as the inner unity of the view here presented, should be easily determined by anyone who thinks these thoughts to their conclusion." Hence Schlegel always provides his correspondent with the most vivid account of the surroundings where he has contemplated works of art—ranging from the great gallery of the Louvre to its restoration rooms, from the private collection of Lucian Bonaparte to exhibits in Brussels and Cologne. Schlegel has well absorbed the lesson that a suitable synthesis of theory, criticism, and history of art can be developed only in galleries where major collections of representative works are easily accessible to the experienced connoisseur.

It is fitting to conclude this discussion of the gallery dialogue as literary genre with mention of a work that in several senses rounds the circle. In 1819 Ludwig Tieck moved to Dresden, where, some twenty-five years earlier, he had been introduced by his friend Wackenroder to the world of Christian art. The following twenty years in Dresden marked a new stage in Tieck's life—a stage characterized by a public acclaim that linked him with Goethe as Germany's other great writer and by a steady production of works in the popular genre of the novella. One of his earliest novellas, and certainly one of the finest, revolves around his early interest in art: "Die Gemälde" (1823).[155] The story deals with four days in the life of Eduard, the prodigal son of a wealthy father who had accumulated both a magnificent library and an excellent collection of paintings. When Eduard returns home following his father's death, the paintings have disappeared; Eduard gradually sells off the library in order to support a life of conspicuous libertinage and, more clandestinely, generous welfare for the poor. The plot begins when Eduard attempts to assist his friend, the elderly painter Eulenböck, to sell off his skillful forgery of a Salvator Rosa landscape to his father's friend, the collector Walther. On that occasion he catches sight of Walther's daughter, Sophie, and it is love at first sight. However, the forgery is unmasked by a visitor to Walther's gallery, and Eduard, though given the benefit of Walther's doubt, is told in no uncertain terms that such a squanderer as he could entertain no hope of obtaining Sophie's hand in marriage. In the next two or three days several things happen. The haughty visitor who detected the forgery turns out to be a prince in whose entourage Eduard had hoped to achieve a position in order to recover his social standing. This hope is coldly dashed by the prince; but the prince is deceived, in turn, by a brilliant forgery of a Giulio Romano by Eulenböck, who assures himself a comfortable future in the prince's household. Eduard, a young man of considerable humor and equanimity, is happy for Eulenböck's success and amused at the prince's gullibility. At a farewell party, which deteriorates into a drunken brawl, the guests begin to tear down the paneling in Eduard's now empty library. It turns out to be a false paneling, behind which Eduard's father had hidden away his entire collection of paintings. Eager to integrate the two great collections, Walther now agrees to give his blessing to a marriage between Sophie and Eduard. Eduard has been sobered by recent events, and we have every reason to believe that the young couple will live happily ever after in the midst of the great collection of art as well as books, which Walther had secretly been buying up over the years in memory of his friend.

Tieck's graceful narrative also addresses a number of the liveliest topics and issues in the late Romantic world of art. The recent controversy surrounding the Nazarenes is summoned up both by a young painter with shoulder-length hair and an Old German cloak who paints religious subjects and by the prince, whose views parallel those of the academicians who attacked the exhibition of the Nazarenes in Rome. The pretenses of a society with aspirations to connoisseurship are exposed in the person of the prince, who is taken in by the skill of a shrewd forger. Eulenböck and Eduard engage in various discussions concerning the theory and criticism of art, e.g., on the question of authenticity and forgery. What matters in our context, however, is the fact that almost every important epi-sode takes place in a gallery, which emerges as the typical social and cultural locus. The catalytic incidents at the beginning—the detection of the Salvator Rosa forgery by the prince and Eduard's first glimpse of Sophie—take place in Walther's gallery. The dialogue on the proper sub-jects of painting and the detection of another forgery by Eulenböck take place midway through the story in the same gallery. The farewell ban-quet with its discussions of art takes place in a room that turns out to be the former gallery hidden behind the false paneling. And the final scene, in which Walther gives his daughter's hand to the now redeemed Edu-ard, takes place in a room where all the paintings have been exhibited in a grand display. It would be difficult to find a literary work that de-pended more heavily on the gallery setting for its symbolic effects.

We should note in conclusion two more general implications of Tieck's story. From Wackenroder's friar and his artistic pater to the var-ious figures in Tieck's tale we can see the emergence of the connoisseur as a typical figure in Romantic literature. (One could of course cite other contemporary examples, from Goethe's *Die Wahlverwandtschaften* to Im-mermann's *Die Epigonen*.) In this respect Tieck was faithful to the cul-tural life of his times. It is tempting to speculate that he had in mind such figures as Carl Friedrich von Rumohr, that famous eccentric and gastro-nome who personified the transition from eighteenth-century connois-seur to nineteenth-century art historian. In any case, the connoisseur is so typical for the decade of the 1820s that Wolfgang Hildesheimer properly chose this type as the central figure of his brilliant novel *Marbot* (1981), the "fictional biography" through which he sought successively to char-acterize that period and the first serious psychologist of art. Indeed, Ru-mohr, who appears in the novel as a character and receives many of An-drew Marbot's letters, is generally the model for Hildesheimer's young connoisseur. The fact that we should seize upon, however, is that the connoisseur qua art historian is largely dependent as a type on the exis-tence of public galleries and museums. Any systematic study or criticism would be difficult, if not impossible, as long as the work of art was tied closely to the often inaccessible locales of church and palace.

Tieck was fully aware of the changes taking place in the art world of his time. "Anyone who loves art and has collected," the prince observes at one point, "should sell his treasures for a reasonable price to princes or incorporate them in their wills and testaments into larger galleries" (22). This is precisely what happens in the course of Tieck's story: through the marriage between Eduard and Sophie the two family galleries are brought together into a major collection. Tieck knew that the great private collections of the times, like those of Giustiniani, Solly, and the Boisserées, were beginning to be sold to enrich the great public museums that were gradually taking shape in Berlin, Munich, and elsewhere in Europe. His work reflects these institutional developments in fictional form.

It is fitting, finally, that the genre of the gallery dialogue, in which Romantic aesthetic theory was largely shaped, should have provided the formal basis for one of the finest novellas of the period. If life imitated art in the careers of the Nazarenes, in Tieck's story art tended to imitate the forms of Romantic life. "Die Gemälde," published in the very year when Schinkel was drafting his proposal for the new museum in Berlin, exemplifies the fictional adaptation of the gallery dialogue—a mode of discourse that Schinkel's museum was designed to accommodate.

## SCHINKEL'S MUSEUM: INSTITUTIONALIZATION OF THE MUSEAL IMPULSE

It can be argued that Schinkel's Altes Museum in Berlin embodies architecturally the most important new attitudes toward art that had emerged during the Romantic decades. By means of its temple design Schinkel stated that art is sacred, and by locating his temple with respect to the cathedral and palace he implied that art is equal to church and state in authority and value. His use of the rotunda, which he explicitly called a "pantheon," reflected the interest in the figure of the artist, which had dominated Romantic literature for some twenty-five years. And the radically new organization of the galleries was undertaken in accordance with the Romantic conception of the museum as the place where the nation was to be educated through culture to an understanding of art in its historical sequence as well as its aesthetic integrity.[156] To comprehend Schinkel's building in all its dimensions, both architectonic and intellectual, is in a very precise sense to understand some of the main tendencies of German culture in the period from 1789 to 1830.

However plausible the arguments of the preceding pages may seem, they depend on our ability to demonstrate that Schinkel was actually aware of the intellectual and cultural currents of his day and not simply tied to his drawing board. Clearly, architecture has its own history and powerful traditions, and Schinkel was well aware of them through his studies and his travels. Like all his other buildings, the Altes Museum is unimaginable without an architect steeped in the history of building types. At the same time, Schinkel's buildings can be read as a reliable index to the *Zeitgeist* precisely because he was so profoundly involved with the leading thinkers of his time.[157] Schinkel was personally acquainted with the principal architects of his day: he had been a fellow student in Berlin under Gilly *père et fils* with both Leopold von Klenze and Haller von Hallerstein. He also knew many of the major figures from the contemporary art world. On his first trip to Italy he had met the leaders of the older generation of painters and sculptors: Joseph Anton Koch, Philipp Hackert, Christian Daniel Rauch, Bertel Thorvaldsen, and others. On the occasion of his second trip twenty years later he met a younger generation of German painters in Rome and, in particular, admired the frescoes of the Nazarenes. Although Schinkel never encountered Caspar David Friedrich personally, he knew Friedrich's landscapes from the Berlin exhibitions. Schinkel first met Wilhelm von Humboldt in 1803 in Italy, and their acquaintance extended through the years of their collaborative work on the museum until Humboldt's death in 1835. Schinkel remodeled the lovely little Schloss in Tegel where Humboldt spent the last years of his life. (Schinkel also knew Alexander von Humboldt, whom he met on a trip to Paris and later saw in Berlin.) The collectors and connoisseurs also figure conspicuously in his life. He knew the brothers Boisserée for many years and closely followed their scheme to complete the cathedral at Cologne. He worked closely with Gustav Waagen, the leading young art historian of the age and the first art historian to become curator of a major museum. (In 1844 Waagen published the first biography of Schinkel, a rich source of detail concerning the architect's role in the cultural life of Berlin.) The two of them learned much, in turn, from Carl von Rumohr, generally regarded as the greatest connoisseur of his day.

But Schinkel's acquaintances were not limited to the world of art and architecture. He was a friend of the Prussian royal family for decades—Friedrich Wilhelm III, the popular Queen Luise, Crown Prince Friedrich Wilhelm IV, whom he tutored—and worked closely with a number of ministers of state. As an active participant in the cultural life of the city and a member of the Christlich-Deutsche Tischgesellschaft, he knew Arnim, Brentano (who wrote a poem about him), Bettina von Arnim, Savigny, Solger (a onetime schoolmate), Immermann, and other Berlin writers and intellectuals. He attended Fichte's lectures (where he took detailed notes) and chatted with Schelling in the Salons. He designed the stage setting for the premiere of Hoffmann's opera *Undine* in 1816. Indeed, through his connections with opera and theater (for which he also designed a building on the Gendarmenmarkt) Schinkel was acquainted with the leading figures of music, drama, and dance. Outside Berlin he also met Goethe, and through Gustav Waagen, who was Ludwig Tieck's nephew, he met the other most famous writer of the day. (Tieck's brother, Friedrich, executed the finest bust of Schinkel.)

The typically Romantic view of art, which Schinkel shared with most of his contemporaries and embodied in his work, is clearly evident in a brief note that he wrote on "Bestimmung der Kunst" (a title that betrays the influence of Fichte's rhetoric):

What is the vocation of art? The various mechanical, chemical, organic forces of nature are intimately connected not only among themselves but also with the spontaneous forces that constitute the realm of freedom; and to that extent they shape totality. Every human being without exception has a more or less clear premonition of this totality. The compulsion aroused by this premonition to investigate the interrelationships of a given number of phenomena has produced science; the compulsion aroused by the same premonition to contemplate in context as large a group of phenomena as possible has produced art. Therefore the vocation of art is a representation of its object in a manner that makes evident as many of its connections as possible.[58]

If we take Schinkel at his word and interpret his museum in the light of this statement, then it implies not only that the museum must accommodate works of art in such a manner as to bring forth their multiple interconnections (the main thrust of Rumohr's disposition of the works) but also that the building itself should exemplify as extensively as possible the cultural forces that contributed to its creation. In sum, Schinkel's life and thought suggest that he was fully aware of the characteristic ideas of his age and that their instantiation in his design can be regarded as anything but random.

• • •

In a certain sense the art museum represents simply one institutionalized aspect of the general "museal impulse" that has been identified by some critics as one of the salient characteristics of the nineteenth and twentieth centuries: a conservative tendency that represents society's attempts to store up its heritage against the threat of economic and technological ravages[159]—an impulse that throbbed powerfully during a revolutionary era that threatened to sweep away the values of traditional European culture. At the beginning of the nineteenth century this impulse manifested itself in the efforts of men like Goethe, Wilhelm von Humboldt, and Sir John Soane to make museums of their own homes. Going a step further, Ludwig I even sought in Munich to make an architectural museum of an entire city. And one of the greatest eccentrics in an age of eccentrics, Hermann von Pückler-Muskau, squandered one of the greatest fortunes of Europe in his attempt to convert his vast estates near Cottbus into a museum of gardens and landscape architecture. Nor has the museal impulse abated in the twentieth century. Many of the cathedrals of Europe have been transformed for all practical purposes into museums, which many visitors enter for no other reason, and the relics within the churches and cathedrals have undergone a corresponding transformation from sacral to museal objects. In many countries, as Ernst Jünger has observed, the nobility have been metamorphosed into museum curators, who earn a living by selling tickets of admission to their palaces and estates.

If the museal impulse is to preserve things—castles, villages, forests, houses, objets d'art—from the depredations of time and neglect, one of its effects is to separate works of art from any function they may originally have had. Hans Sedlmayr has spoken in this connection of the "desocialization" (*Entgesellschaftung*) of art[160]—a trend that had already become a cliché of cultural history by the time André Malraux noted that museums, by suppressing the model of every portrait, "did away with the significance of Palladium, of Saint and Saviour; ruled out associations of sanctity, qualities of adornment and possession, of likeness or imagination."[161] This concern, however, is by no means a product of the twentieth century.

The trend began with two nearly simultaneous events in the first years of the French Revolution. Through a decree of August 21, 1791, the Assembly opened the Salon for the first time to all artists, French or foreign, whether or not they were members of the Academy.[162] That single act liberated art from the control of the Academy, which had hitherto used its authority to maintain the fine arts essentially as an "emanation of the throne" and to favor those themes of myth and Bible that could generally be understood as allegories of power. At the same time, the exhibition of art being assembled in the Louvre from all over Europe brought about a change in the relationship of the art object to society. Although many of the works were eventually returned to their countries of origin, the traditional association of art objects with a specific location had been broken, with the result that many of them came increasingly to be regarded as objects per se.[163] Goethe, for one, profoundly regretted this development. At the end of his introduction to the *Propyläen* he recalled the recent time when, with few exceptions, works of art tended to remain in the same place and became associated in the education of artists and connoisseurs with specific cultural locations. "Now, however, a great change has taken place that will have important consequences for art generally as well as specifically."[164] People were beginning to realize, he continued, that Italy had hitherto constituted a great aesthetic corpus (*Kunstkörper*), the whole of which amounted to far more than the sum of its parts. Now that totality has been destroyed by the removal of too many parts. It is too early to determine, he sadly concludes, whether the new *Kunstkörper* being assembled in Paris will play a similarly important role in European cultural history.

The confrontation of aesthetics with the newly desocialized art contributed to the concept of "uselessness" as a criterion for art. The appreciation of "uselessness" began with such pre-Romantic thinkers as Rousseau.[165] In *Les Rêveries du promeneur solitaire* (1782) Rousseau claimed, "I have found true charm in the pleasures of the spirit only when I have completely lost sight of the interests of my body."[166] No delights, he continues, can match those offered by "a pure and disinterested contemplation." When Rousseau speaks of "une contemplation pure et désintéressée," he is using precisely the term that Kant was to employ a few years later in the *Kritik der Urteilskraft* (1790) to make a distinction between the Good, the Pleasant, and the Beautiful (bk. 1, §5). In contrast to moral and sensory gratifications, which are attached to one's personal interest, the satisfaction that we receive from beauty is "disinterested" ("Wohlgefallen ohne alles Interesse"). Schiller immediately appropriated Kant's idea that art is at home in a purely aesthetic realm beyond all crass human needs. Art is in such a sorry state at present, he argued in the second of his letters *Über die ästhetische Erziehung des Menschen* (1795), because "functionality [*Nutzen*] is the great idol of the times." Art, however, is a "daughter of freedom": she must transcend the constraints of material reality and elevate herself boldly above necessity.

This notion of "uselessness" appealed to the Romantic theorists. Franz Sternbald defends himself and his art repeatedly against attacks on its "uselessness." "What do you mean by 'usefulness'?" he asks on one such occasion.

"Does everything have to be reduced to eating, drinking, and clothing? . . . I will say it again: whatever is truly lofty may not and cannot be functional; usefulness is quite alien to its divine nature, and to demand that it be useful means to debase its sublimity and to reduce it to the common needs of mankind."[167]

A similar argument shows up, as we have seen, in the dialogue "Die Gemählde." It would be instructive to trace the notion of "uselessness" as a criterion in the new theory of landscape painting from Philipp Otto Runge's letters to Goethe's late notes for an essay on landscape painting, which he designates as "a useless world" ("eine unnütze Welt").[168] So widespread was the revolt against functionality in art that it soon came to be regarded as a characteristically German phenomenon. In his essay on "The State of German Literature" (1827) Thomas Carlyle recapitulated the Romantic view that "Art is to be loved, not because of its effects, but because of itself; not because it is useful for spiritual pleasure, or even for moral culture, but because it is Art, and the highest in man, and the soul of all Beauty. To inquire after its *utility*, would be like inquiring after the *utility* of a God, or, what to the Germans would sound stranger than it does to us, the *utility* of Virtue and Religion."[169]

But if art is "useless" and "desocialized," then it requires a setting that makes explicit its non-functionality: not a cathedral or a palace, where its religious or political purpose would be evident, but a building where it can be contemplated reverentially in its sacral autonomy, where the viewer can engage himself or herself directly with the work in its aesthetic historicity and approach a greater understanding through dialogue with like-minded thinkers—a setting, in short, precisely like the temple of art that Schinkel presented to the city of Berlin with the construction of the Altes Museum.

CHAPTER SEVEN

# Conclusion

IN THE PRECEDING chapters we have observed five social institutions as they assumed a new shape and significance during the age of Romanticism in Germany. While we began in each case with an attempt to account for their emergence on historical grounds, we focused chiefly on the interaction between these institutions and contemporary literary culture. Has this institutional approach opened perspectives on German Romanticism that would otherwise be inaccessible or not readily evident by means of traditional literary criticism or literary history? I believe that our study has both corroborated certain existing views from a new theoretical standpoint and exposed certain common aspects of Romantic literature—of language, substance, and theme—that were hitherto not manifest.

While all five institutions affected the literature of the day, each one exhibited its influence in a different way. Mining tended to supply images—primarily for the descent into the psyche but also in other connections, e.g., for the university as the "Mount of the Muses." The law, in contrast, provided a rich variety of plots for writers as well as a focal point for patriotic poetry during the wars of liberation and the post-Napoleonic reaction. The fascination with the madhouse, and notably the new understanding of mental illness that it implied, opened literature to a broader range of characters and a greater depth of psychological analysis. The debates concerning the nature of the university supplied a new realm of subject matter for literature and expanded the modes of discourse favored by the Romantics. The emergence of the museum, finally, paralleled the turn to the history and criticism of art as well as a growing interest in the figure of the artist.

At the same time, it became evident that most of the five institutions were themselves reciprocally shaped by Romantic cultural and intellectual activity. Savigny's success against Thibaut in reinstating in Germany a form of Roman law was possible only in a society that had turned, as the Romantics did, to history and to a belief in the organic growth of institutions. The shape that psychiatry gradually assumed in Germany, in contrast to France and England, can be explained largely as a result of the Romantic interest in extremes of personality and the attempt to integrate the practical reforms of Pinel and Crichton with Romantic *Naturphilosophie*. The Romantic university, as conceived in Jena and realized fleetingly in Berlin, was based on the philosophical conception of a *Wissenschaft* that was both unified and progressive. And the conception of the museum as a temple of art emerged from the Romantic belief in the sacral nature of an autonomous art.

Surveying the material that thrust itself upon our attention in the preceding chapters, we see now that the five institutions sum up several representative themes of German Romanticism. The mine exemplifies the descent into the realm of the psyche, where the forces of history, religion, and sexuality are at work. The concern with law reflects the growing awareness of history and deliberations concerning the relationship between individual freedom and the constraints of the state. The madhouse symbolizes the contemporary fascination with exotic states of consciousness as well as the conviction that "madness" is sometimes an expression of truths inaccessible to Philistine reason. The university instantiates the Romantic belief in the unity and integrity of knowledge. The museum represents the appropriate response to the apotheosis of art.

However, it is not the case that these five institutions simply existed autonomously side by side during the period from the French Revolution to the post-Napoleonic restoration. In fact they were closely interrelated both by the people involved in them and the themes that they embodied. It is clear, as we recapitulate our survey of the five institutions, that many of the same names kept recurring. Brentano's peregrinations as a student are exemplary. He first studied mining in Bonn in 1794 and then law at Halle in 1797; during his enrollment at Jena from 1798 to 1800 he was a medical student; and he finished his university career at Göttingen in the faculty of philosophy. While few other students made so many career shifts, most of them display enough interest in the various institutions to suggest their appeal to the Romantic consciousness. Thus while Adolph Müller was on his way to Halle in 1803, where he was to study medicine, he stopped off at Celle to visit the madhouse and write an account for his father and sister of the "most pleasant entertainment" that it afforded;

later he made the ritual pilgrimage to the galleries at Dresden and also toured the mines of the Harz with Steffens. Kleist began as a student of law at Frankfurt an der Oder; on his trip to Würzburg in 1800 he passed through Freiberg in too much of a hurry to descend into the mines, but he did visit the famous asylum of the Julius Hospital and reported on it at length. To his pen we also owe a vivid account of the Louvre in 1801 as well as of Caspar David Friedrich's exhibition in Berlin. E.T.A. Hoffmann was a trained lawyer and practicing judge who wrote one of the classic tales of mining, defended academic freedom against the reactionaries of the Metternich era, and brought a humane understanding of madness into the legal definition of mental competence. In all these cases, in short, we can document—and explicitly for the most prominent writers—the pervasive Romantic interest in most of the representative institutions. To appreciate the point, we need only to remind ourselves how few contemporary French or English writers had studied law, visited a madhouse, or descended a mine shaft. Indeed, most of them, as we noted, never attended a university, and there is nothing in the mythology of French and English Romanticism to match the art symposium at Dresden in 1798.

It is truly astonishing to recall how many figures of the age were actively involved with these representative institutions, which expose their personal and intellectual interrelationships in often surprising new configurations. Goethe was a lawyer by training; during his administrative career at Weimar he supervised mining operations of the duchy and belonged to the overseers of the University of Jena; he was himself a painter and a biographer of artists as well as a frequent commentator on the arts and collections of his day; and while, unlike many of his contemporaries, he did not like to visit madhouses, he was acquainted with several of the "mad-doctors" (notably Langermann) and contemporary works on the subject. In his preface to the second edition of *Die unsichtbare Loge* (1821) Jean Paul called Goethe, admiringly, the writer "who among all known writers combines the most basic knowledge in himself, from the exercise of imperial government and legal theory by way of all the arts to mining and botany and every natural science."[1]

Friedrich Anton von Heynitz (1725–1802) is not a name that figures prominently in the history of German Romanticism. Indeed, one looks in vain for his name in the indices of the standard works. And why, indeed, should it occur there? This engineer and national economist, who moved ever higher in the administrative hierarchies in Brunswick, then

Saxony, and finally Prussia, where he was a trusted minister under three kings, is not conspicuous even in political histories. Yet Heynitz is one of those curious figures of the age who are unobtrusively involved in many of the most salient developments of the times. His quiet professionalism, through the institutions in which he was involved, had a lasting impact on so many people of the age that his name keeps cropping up in the most varied contexts. Related by marriage to Novalis and the Prussian minister Karl von Hardenberg, he became a father figure for his protégé, Stein. The founder of the mining academy at Freiberg, he was also instrumental thirty years later in expediting the earliest plans for the institution that subsequently grew into the museum in Berlin. And in his involvement with many institutions he is by no means alone among that group of brilliant Prussian administrators that of course included Wilhelm von Humboldt, who established the University of Berlin and was involved in the planning of the museum.

In light of this involvement by writers and other intellectuals, it is no wonder that many literary works of the period also display various configurations of the same institutions. Justinus Kerner's loosely organized set of fictional scenes entitled *Reiseschatten* (1811) introduces a "mad poet" named Holder (based on Kerner's clinical observation of Hölderlin while he was a medical student in Tübingen); it contains two long sections of university satire and ends with a vision of Albrecht Dürer's funeral inspired by the works of Old German painting that the narrator views in the Sebaldus church. Similarly, the anonymous *Nachtwachen von Bonaventura* (1804), in which a madhouse provides one of the principal scenes, contains extended passages of satire on universities, museums, and the law. Many other poets of the age dealt with the various institutions in separate works—and often expressly in what are now regarded as the major works of Romantic literature. Brentano celebrated the opening of the University of Berlin and inscribed a paean to Schinkel's architecture as well as a report on Friedrich's painting; he used the image of the mine as the basis for one of his greatest poems; and the history of law provided the setting for major sections of his *Romanzen vom Rosenkranz*. Novalis gave us in *Heinrich von Ofterdingen* the most glorious apotheosis of mining in Romantic literature; but he also planned a dialogue on the sculpture gallery in Dresden, and he allegorized the new conception of the university in *Die Lehrlinge zu Sais*. Hoffmann's tales, finally, cover the spectrum from the university setting of "Der Sandmann" and "Klein Zaches" to the spectacular mines of "Die Bergwerke zu Falun," from the madness of Anselmus, "Ritter Gluck," and Krespel to the ambivalent "pious painters" and the omnipresent lawyers of his later fiction.

In a large sense it can be maintained that social institutions provide the common denominator linking contemporaries of the period who often held quite diverse views. Goethe and Fichte, for all their differences of opinion, were united in their commitment to the university, just as Savigny and Thibaut—or Brentano and Kleist—shared a profound faith in *law*, albeit radically different kinds of law. Heine makes fun of the mines that Novalis idealizes, but both acknowledge their centrality as a Romantic image. Kant and Reil took wholly different paths to the mutual goal of providing humane care for the mentally ill. Goethe and the Romantics held sharply divergent views of art, but they all began with an epiphany in the Dresden galleries. An institutional approach, then, exposes many of the issues that unified the age—the common questions to which different responses were proposed.

It was not simply the people who tied together the five institutions through their interest, their participation, and their activity. The institutions are linked by common themes of the period that they share and exemplify. We observed that one of the three dimensions of experience encountered through the descent into the mine of the soul was history. History was of course also the force that motivated the quest for Roman law (in contrast to the theoretical timelessness of natural law) and that informed the new approach to art embodied in the organization of the museum in Berlin. Its historical etiology, finally, differentiated Romantic psychiatry most clearly from rationalist psychology with its conception of an incurable madness produced by physical causes. The Romantic understanding of these four institutions, in short, is colored significantly by the awareness of progress and movement through time that characterizes virtually every aspect of human endeavor—from Fichte's "productive imagination," through which the *Ich* incessantly posits the *Nicht-Ich*, and Hegel's phenomenology, through which the spirit gradually arrives at ever greater self-awareness, to Schleiermacher's understanding of the evolution of positive religions and the Grimms' conception of the emergence of language.

The Romantic insistence on the "uselessness" of art corresponds to the conviction, from Schiller to Schelling, that a university *Bildung* must have no career-oriented goal and their abhorrence of the *Brotgelehrte* and narrow-minded specialist. But it is also reflected in the belief that the pious miner works beneath the earth not for sordid personal gain but for knowledge of nature and the welfare of mankind.

Finally, the insight into the unity of art as expressed in the aesthetics of A. W. Schlegel, Hegel, and Solger and exemplified in the design of Schinkel's museum parallels the insistence on the unity of knowledge in the thought of Fichte, Schelling, Novalis, and Humboldt that provided the theoretical basis for the Romantic university. This same Romantic belief in the unity of all being shows up in Savigny's understanding of law as the expression of social integrity of the people, in Novalis's perception of the unity of nature toward which the stones strive in *Die Lehrlinge zu Sais*, and in Reil's conception of insanity, which is distinguished from sanity only by degree, not by quality.

The belief in the fundamental unity of all social, natural, and intellectual being; the conviction that knowledge, like art, is an absolute value; and the understanding of nature and society and knowledge as the product of historical development—these three factors that link the institutions of the age reveal themselves as basic characteristics of the Romantic view of the world: the belief in history, the autonomy of art, and the unity of being. To understand the prominence of these institutions, therefore, is to appreciate central forces motivating the age.

• • •

At the end of the introduction I suggested that an institutional approach to the understanding of a society and its literature is a typically Romantic enterprise. But it is at the same time an equally modern endeavor. During the years immediately following World War II, when German writers were seeking what they called a "zero point" from which to make a radically new beginning, they turned away from Romanticism because they had come to believe that the traditional bourgeois culture of which it constituted a major part had been contaminated through its cooptation by National Socialism. The past ten years, in contrast, have seen an almost obsessive return to Romanticism not only in scholarship but by many novelists as well.[2] Peter Härtling published a highly regarded biographical novel on *Hölderlin* (1976). In *Kein Ort. Nirgends* (1979) Christa Wolf used excerpts from letters, diaries, and other contemporary sources to portray an imaginary yet plausible encounter in 1804 beween Heinrich von Kleist and the poet Karoline von Günderode, both of whom were to die by their own hands a few years later. In *Marbot* (1981) Wolfgang Hildesheimer produced the biography of a Romantic art critic that is factual in almost every detail except the existence of the totally fictional central character. And in *Hoffmanns Erzählungen: Aufzeichnungen eines verwirrten Germanisten* (1983), an epistolary novel that intertwines past and present, Peter Henisch tells the story of a lecturer in German literature who, in his obsession with the life and works of E.T.A. Hoffmann, encounters a man who claims to be the reincarnation of the Romantic writer and purports to acquaint the narrator with the "true" circumstances of Hoffmann's life.

Now what is relevant in all these cases is not simply the fascination with Romanticism but also the evidence that contemporary writers sense a close parallel between that age and their own circumstances. On the first page of her story Christa Wolf, addressing Kleist and Günderode as "Vorgänger ihr" ("you predecessors"), introduces her central theme: the tension between the individual and the state, which was as urgent in Prussia of 1804 as in the German Democratic Republic of 1979.[3] Peter Härtling begins his account with the qualifying statement:

—I am not writing a biography. Rather, I am writing perhaps an approximation. . . . I am making an effort to encounter realities. I know that they are more my own than his. I can find him, invent him, only to the extent that I ally my memory with the transmitted memories. To a great extent I am transferring information into a context that I alone create.[4]

And Peter Henisch's narrator—who, like Hoffmann's major character, is named Kreisler—is explicitly concerned, as the title of his lecture indicates, with "Late Romanticism and Its Relation to the Present with Particular Reference to Schizoid Structure in the Works of E.T.A. Hoffmann."[5] But it is not just the personal identification of the contemporary narrator with the historical figure that is established. As "Hoffmann" points out to the narrator with reference to the social ideologies of Romanticism:

"Well, Kreisler, since then we have learned how such dreams end. The revolution of consciousness and the march through the institutions have also been a topic of conversation in the recent past— both frequently and, ultimately, in vain. But in those days we still didn't know it." (120)

At this point, in conclusion, it is appropriate to point out that the five Romantic institutions have lived on into the present in various ways. In one case, mining, the fact that it took shape in pre-industrial Germany meant that the institution itself had to change radically as the nation became heavily industrialized during the nineteenth century; as a result, the "Romantic" institution of mining achieved the status of a purely literary image that had little bearing on external reality in succeeding ages. We noted its survival in the works of Rilke, Musil, Graß, and others. But the concept of a unified nature that informed Romantic science has experienced a conspicuous resurgence in the quest for a unified field theory that has dominated modern physics and for the fundamental principles governing biology at the molecular level.

The Roman law that was restored in most German-speaking lands under the influence of Savigny and his supporters prevailed until 1900, when a new code of law for the German Empire was promulgated. But the powerful "natural-law movement" that, in recent decades, has challenged codification in Germany and other countries resuscitates a controversy whose classic positions were defined in Germany during the Napoleonic era. The fictional analyses and depictions of madness provided material for modern theories of psychoanalysis: both Freudians and Jungians have come to grips with Hoffmann in their studies, while psychoanalysis has confirmed the dream theories of G. H. Schubert and the Romantic narrators who followed him. And the Romantic view of the madhouse as an asylum for the liberated spirit shows up frequently in postwar German literature, where the "view from the madhouse" is often equated with the voice of a sane humanity in the midst of a cruel and inhumane world.[6]

The Romantic conception of the university, especially as instantiated in the University of Berlin, provided the model for the modern research university that subsequently emerged in the United States as well as Germany. Appropriately, therefore, the debates concerning the nature of the institution in Germany during the turmoil of the 1960s returned almost obsessively to the discussions underlying the establishment of that first Romantic university. Ernst Anrich justified his 1964 edition of the seminal texts by Fichte, Schelling, Schleiermacher, and Steffens by reference to the earlier crisis of the university around 1800.[7] Both Wilhelm Weischedel (1960) and Otto Rühle (1966) hark back to the founding of the University of Berlin in the prefaces of their respective undertakings. Weischedel begins his celebration of the Free University of Berlin by observing that "a university cannot acknowledge its predecessor more appropriately than through the endeavor to raise for renewed discussion the spirit in which it lived."[8] And Rühle states his intention to begin his analysis of the Marxist premises of universities in the German Democratic Republic "with the neo-Humanistic university, with the guiding image that Wilhelm von Humboldt and other idealists sketched out."[9] Through a paradox of which they were largely unaware, the German students of the 1960s (and, by extension, their compatriots in France and the United States) who sought to overthrow the institution that justified their existence were reenacting the Romantic renewal of the German university—a renewal that produced the very institution that came under siege a hundred and fifty years later.

Schinkel's building, finally, still stands in Berlin—next to the extensively damaged and unused cathedral and facing, instead of the palace, the contemporary seat of state power, the Parliament of the German Democratic Republic—where it serves its museal function as an exhibition space. But the institution that was so extensively reshaped in the course of its establishment in the early nineteenth century has spread throughout the world as a model for public education in art.

In sum, to study these representative Romantic institutions means, in most cases, coming to grips with institutions that still define the society in which we live. Indeed, when we engage in public debate regarding the nature of our institutions—for higher education, health care, public culture, and other social needs—we are often criticizing and revising institutions that assumed their recognizably modern form during the era of Romanticism. If our age is newly fascinated by Romanticism and its institutions, it is not just because we have learned from Romanticism that the surest approach to understanding society as a whole, as well as the factors linking its individual representatives, is by way of its institutions. It is also because we sense more or less consciously that we live in a time analogous to Romanticism to the extent that traditional institutions are being challenged and modified in response to a new *Zeitgeist* or, to use a more timely term, model or paradigm. An institutional approach not only provides new insights into the structure of Romanticism as a historical phenomenon and into the language, substance, and ideas of Romantic literature. It also offers the thoughtful observer startling glimpses into the problematics of our own post-Romantic society.

# NOTES

## Chapter One

1. The painting is featured, for instance, as the cover illustration on the paperback reprint of Erich Heller's *The Artist's Journey into the Interior and Other Essays* (New York: Random House-Vintage, 1968), as the back-cover illustration on Roger Cardinal's *German Romantics in Context* (London: Studio Vista, 1975), and on the dust jacket of Mark Kipperman's *Beyond Enchantment: German Idealism and English Romantic Poetry* (Philadelphia: Univ. of Pennsylvania Press, 1986). Heller (77) called it "the most Romantic painting in the gallery" at the 1959 Tate Gallery exhibition of "The Romantic Movement."

2. "Der Regierungsrat Joseph von Eichendorff: Zum Verhältnis von Beruf und Schriftstellerexistenz im Preußen der Restaurationszeit," *Internationales Archiv für Sozialgeschichte der deutschen Literatur* 4 (1979): 37–67.

3. "Die Berufslaufbahn Friedrich von Hardenbergs (Novalis)," *Jahrbuch der deutschen Schillergesellschaft* 7 (1963): 253–312.

4. "Hoffmanns Auffassung vom Richteramt und vom Dichterberuf," *Jahrbuch der deutschen Schillergesellschaft* 11 (1967): 62–138.

5. "Literature as an Institution," *Accent* 6 (1946): 159–68; cited here from the reprint in *Literary Opinion in American*, ed. Morton Dauwen Zabel, rev. ed. (New York: Harper, 1951), 66. The substance of this essay was reprinted as the introduction to Levin's *Gates of Horn: A Study of Five French Realists* (New York: Oxford, 1966).

6. *Theory of Literature* (New York: Harcourt-Harvest, 1956), 216.

7. "Institutional Control of Interpretation," *Salmagundi* 43 (1979): 72.

8. Stanley Fish, *Is There a Text in This Class? The Authority of Interpretive Communities* (Cambridge: Harvard Univ. Press, 1980), 331–32.

9. Gerald Graff, *Professing Literature: An Institutional History* (Chicago: Univ. of Chicago Press, 1987).

10. Alvin B. Kernan, *The Imaginary Library: An Essay on Literature and Society* (Princeton, N.J.: Princeton Univ. Press, 1982), 13–14.

11. See Peter Uwe Hohendahl, *The Institution of Criticism* (Ithaca: Cornell Univ. Press, 1982), 11–43; and Hohendahl, *Literarische Kultur im Zeitalter des Liberalismus 1830–1870* (München: Beck, 1985), 11–54.

12. *Die Kunst. Ihr Wesen und ihre Gesetze* (Berlin: Schuhr, 1891), 117.

13. "Das Kunstwerk im Zeitalter seiner technischen Reproduzierbarkeit," in Benjamin's *Gesammelte Schriften* (Frankfurt am Main: Suhrkamp, 1974), I/2, 431–70.

14. Max Horkheimer and Theodor W. Adorno, *Dialectic of Enlightenment*, trans. John Cumming (New York: Seabury, 1972), 120–67.

15. *Strukturwandel der Öffentlichkeit* (Neuwied: Luchterhand, 1962).

16. Peter Bürger, *Vermittlung—Rezeption—Funktion: Ästhetische Theorie und Methodologie der Literaturwissenschaft* (Frankfurt am Main: Suhrkamp, 1979), 182–83.

17. "Literary Institution and Modernization," *Poetics* 14 (1985): 432.

18. *Poetics* 12 (1983): 290.

19. Peter Bürger, *Vermittlung*, 174.

20. Ralph Waldo Emerson, *Essays. 1st and 2nd Series* (New York: Dutton-Everyman, 1906), 39.

21. James K. Feibleman, *The Institutions of Society* (London: Allen & Unwin, 1956), 162.

22. Talcott Parsons, *The Social System* (Glencoe, Ill.: The Free Press, 1951), 39 and 43.

23. *International Encyclopedia of the Social Sciences* (New York: Macmillan, 1968), XIV, 410.

24. Bronislaw Malinowski, *Freedom and Civilization* (New York: Roy, 1944), 153–71 ("Freedom Through Organization").

25. Lloyd Vernor Ballard, *Social Institutions* (New York: Appleton-Century, [1936]), 3.

26. *Wörterbuch der Soziologie*, ed. Wilhelm Bernsdorf, 2nd ed. (Stuttgart: Enke, 1969), 466.

27. My characterization of the two types is intentionally sharp. I am aware that Raymond Williams in *Culture and Society* (London: Chatto and Windus, 1958) anticipates several of the themes of the German social theorists, and that Christa Bürger in *Der Ursprung der bürgerlichen Institution Kunst im höfischen Weimar* (Frankfurt am Main: Suhrkamp, 1977) has applied the more general theory to specific cases after the fashion of literature as an institution.

28. John Bender has analyzed the interaction between a single institution and a single genre in *Imagining the Penitentiary: Fiction and the Architecture of Mind in Eighteenth-Century England* (Chicago: Univ. of Chicago Press, 1987).

29. *Werke*, XVIII, 74.

30. *Werke*, XII, 69.

31. *Denkwürdigkeiten*, II, 382.

32. *Schriften*, II, 437 (#65).

33. *Kritische Ausgabe*, I, 206.

34. *Kritische Ausgabe*, V, 191.

35. Giambattista Vico, *Il Diritto Universale*, II, pt. 2, ch. I, §1; *Opere*, ed. Fausto Nicoline (Bari: Gius, Laterza & Figli, 1936), II/2, 308. See Michael Mooney, *Vico in the Tradition of Rhetoric* (Princeton, N.J.: Princeton Univ. Press, 1985), xiv–xv, 185, and 220.

36. *De la littérature*, ed. Paul van Tieghem (Paris: Minard, 1959), I, 17.

37. *Sämmtliche Werke*, VI, 320–21.

38. Friedrich Carl von Savigny, *Vom Beruf unsrer Zeit für Gesetzgebung und Rechtswissenschaft*; in Hattenhauer, 171.

39. Hamburg edition, IX, 524.

40. See W. H. Bruford, *Culture and Society in Classical Weimar, 1775–1806* (1962; London: Cambridge Univ. Press, 1975), 293–388 ("Weimar Cultural Institutions and Their Creators").

41. Weimar edition, LIII, 175–92.

42. *Das Zeitalter der deutschen Erhebung, 1795–1815* (Bielefeld & Leipzig: Velhagen & Klasing, 1913), 23.

43. See Theodor Steinbüchel, ed., *Romantik: Ein Zyklus Tübinger Vorlesungen* (Tübingen and Stuttgart: Rainer Wunderlich, 1948); and Richard Brinkmann, ed., *Romantik in Deutschland: ein interdisziplinäres Symposion* (Stuttgart: Metzler, 1978).

44. *German Romantics in Context* (London: Studio Vista, 1975), 11.

45. "The Counter-Enlightenment," in his *Against the Current: Essays in the History of Ideas* (London: Hogarth, 1979), 20.

46. *Schriften*, II, 419.

## CHAPTER TWO

1. Julius Voigt, *Goethe und Ilmenau* (Leipzig: Xenien, 1912); and Josef Dürler, *Die Bedeutung des Bergbaus bei Goethe und in der deutschen Romantik* (Frauenfeld-Leipzig: Huber, 1936), 78–110.

2. Gerhard H. Weiss, "An Interpretation of the Miners' Scene in Goethe's *Wilhelm Meisters Lehrjahre*," in *Lebendige Form*, Festschrift für Heinrich E. K. Henel, eds. Jeffrey L. Sammons and Ernst Schürer (München: Fink, 1970), 83–88; and Monika Wagner, "Der Bergmann in *Wilhelm Meisters Wanderjahren*," *Internationales Archiv für Sozialgeschichte der deutschen Literatur* 8 (1983): 145–68.

3. Richard Samuel, "Der berufliche Werdegang Friedrich von Hardenbergs," in *Deutsche Vierteljahresschrift*, Buchreihe 16: *Romantik-Forschungen* (Halle: Niemeyer, 1929), 83–112; and Dürler, *Die Bedeutung des Bergbaus*, 110–54.

4. Merete van Taack, *Königin Luise: Eine Biographie* (Stuttgart: Deutsche Verlags-Anstalt, 1985), 30.

5. *Werke*, I, 507; see Dürler, *Die Bedeutung des Bergbaus*, 154–70.

6. *Sämtliche Werke*, III, 138.

7. *Deutscher Geist: Ein Lesebuch aus zwei Jahrhunderten*, eds. Oskar Loerke and Peter Suhrkamp (Berlin and Frankfurt am Main: Suhrkamp, 1953), I, 523.

8. Wackenroder, *Dichtung*, 20–21.

9. Letter of 10/11 Sept. 1799 to Georg Friedrich and Leonhard Creuzer; rpt. in *Reisebriefe deutscher Romantiker*, ed. Rudolf Walbiner (Berlin: Rütten & Loening, 1979), 97–98.

10. Diary entry for 13 Sept. 1805; *Werke und Schriften*, III, 115.

11. *Briefe von der Universität in die Heimat*, 248 and 233.

12. See Jost Hermand's notes to Heine, *Gesamtausgabe*, VI, 520 and 603.

13. *Die Harzreise*, in *Gesamtausgabe*, VI, 94.

14. Karl Alfred von Zittel, *History of Geology and Palaeontology to the End of the Nineteenth Century*, trans. Maria M. Ogilvie-Gorden (New York: Scribner, 1899), 46.

15. Charles C. Gillispie, *Genesis and Geology: A Study in the Relations of Scientific Thought, Natural Theology, and Social Opinion in Great Britain, 1790–1850* (1951; rpt. New York: Harper Torchbooks, 1959), 184–216.

16. Marjorie Hope Nicolson, *Mountain Gloom and Mountain Glory: The Development of the Aesthetics of the Infinite* (1959; rpt. New York: Norton Library, 1963); and Theodore Ziolkowski, *The Classical German Elegy, 1795–1950* (Princeton, N.J.: Princeton Univ. Press, 1980).

17. *Caspar Wolf (1735–1783): Landschaft im Vorfeld der Romantik*, Exhibition Catalogue (Kunstmuseum Basel, 1980), esp. 93–97 ("Die Höhlenbilder Caspar Wolfs").

18. *Gallerie der unterirdischen Schöpfungswunder und des menschlichen Kunstfleisses unter der Erde* (Leipzig, 1806), I, 26; cited by Barbara Maria Stafford, "Toward Romantic Landscape Perception: Illustrated Travels and the Rise of 'Singularity' as an Aesthetic Category," *Art Quarterly*, N.S. 1 (1977–1978): 89–124.

19. David S. Landes, *The Unbound Prometheus: Technological Change and Industrial Development in Western Europe from 1750 to the Present* (Cambridge: Cambridge Univ. Press, 1969); and John Temple, *Mining: An International History* (New York: Praeger, 1972).

20. Nicolson, *Mountain Gloom and Mountain Glory*, 341–45; also David Daiches and John Flower, *Literary Landscapes of the British Isles* (New York: Penguin, 1971), 172–95 ("The Blackening of England"); and Margaret Drabble, *A Writer's Britain: Landscape in Literature* (London: Thames and Hudson, 1979), 195–245 ("The Industrial Scene").

21. In *The Poetry of Industry: Two Literary Reactions to the Industrial Revolution* (New York: Arno, 1972), 1–2.

22. *The British Poets in One Hundred Volumes* (Chiswick: Whittingham, 1822), IV, 194–95.

23. "Colebrook Dale," in *The Poetical Works of Anna Seward*, ed. Walter Scott (Edinburgh: Ballantyne, 1810), II, 314–19.

24. Letter of 10 Oct. 1811 to Francis Hodgson; in *Byron's Letters and Journals*, ed. Leslie A. Marchard (London: John Murray, 1973), II, 109.

25. H. C. Robinson, *Diary, Reminiscences, and Correspondence*, ed. Thomas Sadler, 2nd ed. (London: Macmillan, 1869), I, 88–89.

26. Landes, *Prometheus Unbound*, 142; see also Kurt Borchardt, *Grundriß der deutschen Wirtschaftsgeschichte* (Göttingen: Vandenhoeck & Ruprecht, 1978).

27. Heinrich Winkelmann, *Der Bergbau in der Kunst* (Essen: Verlag Glück-auf, 1958), 16.

28. On Freiberg see *Festschrift zum hundertjährigen Jubiläum der Königl. Sächs. Bergbauakademie zu Freiberg am 30. Juli 1866*, 2 vols. (Dresden: Meinhold, 1866–1867); Frederick Gleason Corning, *A Student Reverie: An Album of Saxony Days* (New York: Frederick G. Corning, 1920); and *Bergakademie Freiberg: Festschrift zu ihrer Zweihundertjahrfeier am 13. November 1965*, vol 1: *Geschichte der Bergakademie Freiberg* (Leipzig: Deutscher Verlag für Grundstoffindustrie, 1965).

29. The 1866 *Festschrift* contains a complete register of students enrolled at the Academy during its first century (221–95).

30. G. B. Tennyson, *Sartor Called Resartus: The Genesis, Structure, and Style of Thomas Carlyle's First Major Work* (Princeton, N.J.: Princeton Univ. Press, 1965), 21–22 and 26.

31. LeRoy Wiley McCoy, "My Student Days in Germany," *Journal of Chemical Education* 7 (1930): 1081–99.

32. On Werner and his role in the history of geology and mining see B. von Cotta, "Die Geologie seit Werner," in the 1866 Freiberg *Festschrift*, II, 99–120; Dürler, *Die Bedeutung des Bergbaus*, 12–29; S. F. Mason, *A History of the Sciences: Main Currents of Scientific Thought* (London: Routledge and Kegan Paul, 1953), 319–32; von Zittel, *History of Geology*, 46 ff.; Frank Dawson Adams, *The Birth and Development of the Geological Sciences* (1938; rpt. New York: Dover, 1954), 209–38; Samuel, "Der berufliche Werdegang Friedrich von Hardenbergs"; and *Abraham Gottlob Werner*. Gedenkschrift aus Anlaß der Wiederkehr seines To-destages nach 150 Jahren am 30. Juni 1967 (Leipzig: Deutscher Verlag für Grundstoffindustrie, 1967).

33. Alexander M. Ospovat, "Romanticism and German Geology: Five Students of Abraham Gottlob Werner," *Eighteenth-Century Life* 7 (1982): 105–17; and esp. the Werner *Gedenkschrift*, passim.

34. Mining as an institution and mining education developed quite differently in France, where the national École des Mines at Paris (1783) was established according to the pattern of the military engineering school at Mézières rather than emerging from the ancient craft and practice of mining. See Charles C. Gillispie, *Science and Polity in France at the End of the Old Regime* (Princeton, N.J.: Princeton Univ. Press, 1980).

35. *Novellen*, VIII, 26.

36. "The Drunken Boat: The Revolutionary Element in Romanticism," in *Romanticism Reconsidered*. Selected Papers from the English Institute, ed. Northrop Frye (New York: Columbia Univ. Press, 1963), 16.

37. Walter A. Strauss, *Descent and Return: The Orphic Theme in Modern Literature* (Cambridge, Mass.: Harvard Univ. Press, 1971), 20–49; and Albert B. Smith, "Variations on a Mythical Theme: Hoffmann, Gautier, Queneau and the Imagery of Mining," *Neophilologus* 63 (1979): 179–86.

38. Adams, *The Birth and Development of the Geological Sciences*, 77–136 ("On the 'Generation of Stones' "); and Paul Sébillot, *Les Travaux publics et les mines dans les traditions et les superstitions de tous les pays* (Paris: Rothschild, 1894), 392–402.

39. Mircea Eliade, *Forgerons et alchimistes* (Paris: Flammarion, 1956), 34–56.

40. *Handwörterbuch des deutschen Aberglaubens*, ed. Hanns Bächtold-Stäubli (Berlin: De Gruyter, 1927), VI, 207–11 ("Metalle, Erze").

41. Georgius Agricola, *Ausgewählte Werke*, ed. Hans Prescher (Berlin: Deutscher Verlag der Wissenschaften, 1956), III, 161.

42. Bern Dibner, *Agricola on Metals* (Norwalk, Conn.: Burndy Library, 1958), 21.

43. Zedler, *Universal-Lexikon*, XXI, 340–44.

44. Fritz Paul, *Henrich Steffens: Naturphilosophie und Universalromantik* (München: Fink, 1973), 140–48.

45. *Ansichten*, 200–1.

46. *Schriften*, I, 245–46.

47. *Schriften*, I, 252.

48. *Schriften*, I, 253–54.

49. *Gesammelte Novellen*, VIII, 186–87.

50. *Gesamtausgabe*, VI, 94.

51. Adams, *The Birth and Development of the Geological Sciences*, ch. 8: " 'Figured Stones' and the Birth of Palaeontology"; and Stafford, "Toward Romantic Landscape Perception."

52. III, 399; cited by Stafford, 93.

53. *Schriften*, III, 335, and III, 340.

54. *Novellen*, VIII, 11.

55. *Novellen*, VIII, 12.

56. Erwin Rohde, *Psyche: The Cult of Souls and Belief in Immortality among the Greeks* (1890), trans. W. B. Hillis (1925; rpt. New York: Harper & Row, 1966), I, 88–114 ("Cave Deities: Subterranean Translation").

57. Wolfgang Kemp, "Die Höhle der Ewigkeit," *Zeitschrift für Kunstgeschichte* 32 (1969): 133–52.

58. See the rubric "Bergentrückt" in *Handwörterbuch des deutschen Aberglaubens*, I, 1056–71.

59. *Schriften*, I.

60. *Was ich erlebte*, 153.

61. Wilhelm Dilthey, *Das Leben Schleiermachers* (Berlin: Reimer, 1870), I, 354.

62. Jean-Bertrand Barrère, "Sénèque et Rousseau: Le Thème des Mines," in *Mélanges d'histoire littéraire offerts à Daniel Mornet* (Paris: Nizet, 1951), 155–62.

63. *Les Rêveries du promeneur solitaire*, 95–96.

64. The first Latin edition of *De re metallica* was printed in 1556, and the first (unsatisfactory) German translation followed the next year. The first translation into English (London, 1912) was published by Herbert Hoover and his wife, Lou Henry Hoover, both of whom studied mining engineering and geology at Stanford University. An abridgment with a useful introduction was edited by Bern Dibner, *Agricola on Metals* (Norwalk, Conn.: Burndy Library, 1958).

65. The intellectual and moral superiority of miners is a topos that extends from Agricola by way of Goethe, Novalis, and Steffens down into the nineteenth century. See Corning, *A Student Reverie*, 29; and "Das Bergmännische Studium," in the 1866 *Festschrift*, I, 89–138.

66. *Werke und Schriften*, I, 375. Eichendorff used mining motifs in other poems as well, e.g., "Glück auf" (I, 306), but it is nowhere so consistently maintained as here.

67. *Sämmtliche Werke*, 30.

68. *Sämmtliche Werke*, 39–40.

69. *Sämmtliche Werke*, 30–35.

70. *Sämmtliche Werke*, 296–308.

71. Werner's drama constitutes vol. VI of his *Ausgewählte Schriften*.

72. *Werke*, II, 341–51.

73. Dürler, *Die Bedeutung des Bergbaus*, 200–11.

74. *Werke*, I, 223–24.

75. *Werke*, I, 329–32.

76. See Stafford, "Toward Romantic Landscape Perception"; and J. Christopher Middleton, "Two Mountain Scenes in Novalis and the Question of Symbolic Style," in *Literary Symbolism* (Austin: Univ. of Texas Press, 1965), 85–106, esp. 99–100.

77. *Schriften*, I, 247.

78. *Gesamtausgabe*, VI, 94.

79. *Werke*, II, 61.

80. Among many treatments see Karl Reuschel, "Über Bearbeitungen der Geschichte des Bergmanns von Falun," *Studien zur vergleichenden Literaturgeschichte* 3 (1903): 1–28; and John Neubauer, "The Mines of Falun: Temporal Fortunes of a Romantic Myth of Time," *Studies in Romanticism* 19 (1980): 475–95.

81. *Ansichten*, 215.

82. *Ansichten*, 216.

83. *Poetische Werke*, 252–55.

84. *Poetische Werke*, III, 220.

85. Frederick Burwick, "Demonic Seduction: Sexual Dreams on Holy Nights," in *The Haunted Eye: Perception and the Grotesque in English and German Romanticism* (Heidelberg: Winter, 1987), 137–204, esp. 177–87. Burwick does not mention Hoffmann's tale among his various examples for the Eve of Saint John's.

86. See Winkelmann, *Der Bergbau in der Kunst*; and Gerhard Heilfurth, *Der Bergbau und seine Kultur: Eine Welt zwischen Dunkel und Licht* (Zürich: Atlantis, 1981).

87. Kurt Ringger and Christof Weiand, "Aspects littéraires de la mine," *Revue de Littérature Comparée* 58 (1984): 417–41.

88. *Versuch über die Gräbersymbolik der Alten*, in Johann Jakob Bachofen, *Mutterrecht und Urreligion: Eine Auswahl*, ed. Rudolf Marx (Stuttgart: Kröner, 1954), 43.

89. Sigmund Freud, *Die Traumdeutung*, 5th ed. (Leipzig und Wien: Franz Deuticke, 1919), 247–49.

90. E. F. Lorenz, "Die Geschichte des Bergmanns von Falun, vornehmlich bei E.T.A. Hoffmann, Richard Wagner und Hugo von Hofmannsthal," *Imago* 3 (1914): 250–301.

91. E.g., "The Phenomenology of the Spirit in Fairytales," in *The Archetypes and the Collective Unconscious*, trans. R.F.C. Hull, 2nd ed. (Princeton, N.J.: Princeton Univ. Press, 1968), 223, where Jung cites, among others, "the metallic men who dwell in the mines, the crafty dactyls of antiquity, ... the gnomic throng of hobgoblins, brownies, gremlins, etc."

92. Paul Sébillot, *Les Travaux publics et les mines*, 446–78.

93. R. M. Rilke, *Sämtliche Werke*, ed. Ernst Zinn (Wiesbaden: Insel, 1955–1956), I, 542.

94. *Sämtliche Werke*, I, 723.

95. Thomas Mann, *Gesammelte Werke in zwölf Bänden* (Frankfurt am Main: Fischer, 1960), VI, 263.

96. See Margaret Jacobs, "Hugo von Hofmannsthal: Das Bergwerk zu Falun," in *Hofmannsthal: Studies in Commemoration*, ed. F. Norman (London: Institute of Germanic Studies, 1963), 53–82; and Gotthart Wunberg, *Der frühe Hofmannsthal: Schizophrenie als dichterische Struktur* (Stuttgart: Kohlhammer, 1965), 68–91.

97. Robert Musil, *Gesammelte Werke in neun Bänden*, ed. Adolf Frisé (Reinbek bei Hamburg: Rowohlt, 1978), VI, 252.

98. Among the many studies of the novel the one that comes to grips with its mythic aspects is Gundi Wachtler, "Der Archetypus der Großen Mutter in Hermann Brochs Roman *Der Versucher*," in *Hermann Broch: Perspektiven der Forschung*, ed. Manfred Durzak (München: Fink, 1972), 231–50.

CHAPTER THREE

1. See "Fausts Pakt mit Mephistopheles in juristischer Beleuchtung," *Goethe-Jahrbuch* 24 (1903): 113–31, with opinions by two prominent jurists (E. Landsberg and J. Kohler); Georg Müller, *Das Recht in Goethes Faust: Juristische Streifzüge durch das Land der Dichtung* (Berlin: Heymann, 1912); and the survey of research in Eugen Wohlhaupter, *Dichterjuristen*, ed. H. G. Seifert, 3 vols. (Tübingen: Mohr, 1953–57), I, 356–85.

2. Kleist's tale has elicited an extensive bibliography of legal treatments, beginning with Rudolf von Jhering's famous tract *Der Kampf ums Gesetz* (1872), trans. John J. Lalor: *The Struggle for Law* (Chicago: Callaghan and Company, 1879), and extending to Peter Horn, "Was geht uns eigentlich der Gerechtigkeitsbegriff in Kleists Erzählung 'Michael Kohlhaas' noch an?" *Acta Germanica* 8 (1973): 59–92. See the overview in Paul Michael Lützeler, "Heinrich von Kleist: Michael Kohlhaas," in *Romane und Erzählungen der deutschen Romantik. Neue Interpretationen*, ed. P. M. Lützeler (Stuttgart: Reclam, 1981), 213–39.

3. William Seagle, *The History of Law* (New York: Tudor, 1946) and *Men of Law from Hammurabi to Holmes* (New York: Macmillan, 1948).

4. Richard Weisberg and Jean-Pierre Barricelli, "Literature and the Law," in *Interrelations of Literature*, eds. Jean-Pierre Barricelli and Joseph Gibaldi (New York: The Modern Language Association of America, 1982), 150–75; Hans Fehr, *Das Recht in der Dichtung* (Bern: Francke [1931]); Klaus Kanzog, "Literatur und Recht," in *Reallexikon der deutschen Literaturgeschichte*, 2nd ed. (Berlin: De Gruyter, 1965), II, 164–95; *The Law in Literature*, vol. I of *The World of Law*, ed. Ephraim London (New York: Simon and Schuster, 1960).

5. Richard H. Weisberg, *The Failure of the Word: The Protagonist as Lawyer in Modern Fiction* (New Haven, Conn.: Yale Univ. Press, 1984). For further examples see Karen L. Kretschman, *Legal Novels: An Annotated Bibliography*, Tarlton Law Library Legal Bibliography Series 13 (Univ. of Texas School of Law, 1976).

6. For relevant biographical information see Wohlhaupter, *Dichterjuristen*. Wohlhaupter is less useful for the discussion of literary works.

7. Franz Finke, "Gustav Hugos Laudatio auf Heine," *Heine-Jahrbuch* 7 (1968): 14.

8. Oliver Wendell Holmes, Jr., *Collected Legal Papers* (New York: Harcourt, 1920), 164–65.

9. "Catalogue of the Works of Sir William Blackstone," in [D. Douglas], *The Biographical History of Sir William Blackstone* (London, 1782), 3–7.

10. Robert A. Ferguson, *Law and Letters in American Culture* (Cambridge, Mass.: Harvard Univ. Press, 1984).

11. John Marshall Gest, *The Lawyer in Literature* (Boston: Boston Book Co., 1913), 113–55.

12. Charles E. McClelland, *State, Society, and University in Germany, 1700–1914* (Cambridge: Cambridge Univ. Press, 1980); Dietrich Rueschemeyer, *Lawyers and Their Society: A Comparative Study of the Legal Profession in Germany and in the United States* (Cambridge: Harvard Univ. Press, 1973); Roscoe Pound, *The Lawyer from Antiquity to Modern Times* (St. Paul, Minn.: American Bar Association, 1953).

13. Michael Mooney, *Vico in the Tradition of Rhetoric* (Princeton, N.J.: Princeton Univ. Press, 1985), 76 (n. 94).

14. *Dichtung und Wahrheit*, bk. ii, ch. 6; Hamburg edition, ix, 246.

15. Gertrud Schubart-Fikentscher, *Goethes sechsundfünfzig Strassburger Thesen vom 6. August 1771: Ein Beitrag zur Geschichte der deutschen Rechtswissenschaft* (Weimar: Böhlau, 1949), 6.

16. When Goethe arrived in Strassburg, he immediately learned that the study of law in that French-oriented university differed radically from the law he had studied at Leipzig. Here all training was geared to the practical. It was made clear to him that the philosophical and historical approach to law to which he was accustomed counted for little in comparison with memorization of the laws required for practice. See bk. 9 of *Dichtung und Wahrheit*; Hamburg edition, ix, 359.

17. Franz Eulenberg, *Die Frequenz der deutschen Universitäten von ihrer Gründung bis zur Gegenwart*, Abhandlungen der Philologisch-historischen Klasse der Königl. Sächsischen Gesellschaft der Wissenschaften xxiv/11 (Leipzig, 1904).

18. Wolfgang Leppmann, *Winckelmann* (New York: Knopf, 1970), 43.

19. McClelland, *State, Society, and University*, 39ff.

20. Happel, *Der akademische Roman*, 277.

21. Alfred R. Neumann, "Werther the Lawyer," in *Husbanding the Golden Grain. Studies in Honor of Henry W. Nordmeyer*, eds. Luanne T. Frank and Emery E. George (Ann Arbor: Dept. of Germanic Languages and Literatures, The University of Michigan, 1973), 218–22.

22. Goethe himself had been criticized for his frivolous style by the court in Frankfurt. See Wohlhaupter, *Dichterjuristen*, i, 229–30.

23. Letter of 27 Nov. 1792; *Dichtung*, 402–3.

24. Letter of 1 May 1795; *Briefwechsel*, i, 62.

25. John Henry Merryman, *The Civil Law Tradition: An Introduction to the Legal System of Western Europe and Latin America* (Stanford, Calif.: Stanford Univ. Press, 1969); Alan Watson, *The Making of the Civil Law* (Cambridge, Mass.: Harvard Univ. Press, 1981).

26. Karl Bader, "Deutsches Recht," in *Deutsche Philologie im Aufriß*, ed. Wolfgang Stammler, 2nd ed. (Berlin: Erich Schmidt, 1962), iii, 1971–2023.

27. See Bader, "Deutsches Recht"; also Paul Koschaker, *Europa und das römische Recht* (Berlin/München: Biederstein, 1947).

28. Hamburg edition, ix, 530.

29. Otto Gierke, *Natural Law and the Theory of Society 1500 to 1800*, trans. Ernest Barker (Cambridge: Cambridge Univ. Press, 1950); *Naturrecht oder Rechtspositivismus*, ed. Werner Maihofer, 3rd ed. (Darmstadt: Wissenschaftliche Buchgesellschaft, 1981).

30. Schubart-Fikentscher, *Goethes sechsundfünfzig Strassburger Thesen*, 3. The statement is a quotation from Ulpian, which stands at the beginning of the *Digesta* in the *Corpus Juris Civilis*.

31. Ernst Landsberg, *Geschichte der Deutschen Rechtswissenschaft* (München-Leipzig: Oldenbourg, 1898); the entire first "half-volume" is devoted to natural law.

32. *Sämtliche Werke*, I, 222–23.

33. *Werke und Schriften*, II, 1047.

34. See Hans Hattenhauer's introduction to his edition: *Thibaut und Savigny: Ihre programmatischen Schriften*, 9–51; Klaus Epstein, *The Genesis of German Conservatism* (Princeton, N.J.: Princeton Univ. Press, 1966), 372–87 ("The Controversy about the Allgemeine Landrecht"); and Uwe-Jens Heuer, *Allgemeines Landrecht und Klassenkampf: Die Auseinandersetzungen um die Prinzipien des Allgemeinen Landrechts Ende des 18. Jahrhunderts als Ausdruck der Krise des Feudalsystems in Preußen* (Berlin: VEB Deutscher Zentralverlag, 1960).

35. Hattenhauer, 12: "Das Projekt des Corporis Juris Fridericiani, das ist Seiner Königlichen Majestät in Preußen in der Vernunft und Landesverfassungen gegründetes Landrecht, worinnen das Römische Recht in eine natürliche Ordnung und richtiges System . . . gebracht."

36. Reinhart Koselleck, *Preußen zwischen Reform und Revolution. Allgemeines Landrecht, Verwaltung und soziale Bewegung von 1791 bis 1848* (Stuttgart, 1967), 26 (note 12).

37. *Briefe an Savigny 1803–1831*, 143.

38. Elisabeth Fehrenbach, *Traditionale Gesellschaft und revolutionäres Recht: Die Einführung des Code Napoléon in den Rheinbundstaaten* (Göttingen: Vandenhoeck & Ruprecht, 1974).

39. Hattenhauer, 40.

40. Cited according to Hattenhauer, 61–94.

41. On Thibaut's role in the history of musicology see Wohlhaupter, *Dichterjuristen*, I, 120–66 ("Thibaut und Robert Schumann").

42. *Arnims Briefe an Savigny*, 143.

43. Cited according to Hattenhauer, 98–192.

44. See Hattenhauer, 193–298, for a selection of representative documents.

45. On Kant and natural law see esp. Landsberg, *Geschichte der Deutschen Rechtswissenschaft*, I, 503–11.

46. On the influence of Kant's monograph see Gerhard Schulz, *Die deutsche Literatur zwischen Französischer Revolution und Restauration* (München: Beck, 1983), I, 159–80.

47. *Werke*, IX.
48. *Werke in fünf Bänden*, I.
49. *Sämtliche Werke*, II, 959.
50. *Sämtliche Werke*, VI, 78.
51. *Sämtliche Werke*, VI, 249.
52. *Sämtliche Werke*, II, 38.
53. Kleist, *Sämtliche Werke und Briefe*, II, 491.
54. Gerd Heinrich, "Die Geisteswissenschaften an der brandenburgischen Landesuniversität Frankfurt/Oder um 1800," in *Kleist-Jahrbuch 1983* (Berlin: Erich Schmidt, 1983).
55. *Sämtliche Werke und Briefe*, II, 683.
56. Bonaventura, *Nachtwachen*, ed. Paulsen.
57. This conclusion is consistent with the suggestion by Franz Heiduk— "Bonaventuras 'Nachtwachen': Erste Bemerkungen zum Ort der Handlung und zur Frage nach dem Verfasser," *Aurora* 42 (1982): 143–65—that the anonymous author was the legally trained Erfurt writer Theodor Ferdinand Kajetan Arnold.
58. Hattenhauer, 24.
59. *Schriften*, II, 487.
60. *Kritische Ausgabe*, V, 399–400.
61. *Kritische Ausgabe*, V, 341.
62. Müller, *Briefe von der Universität*, 473.
63. *Gedichte*, 74.
64. *Gedichte*, 79.
65. See Varnhagen, *Denkwürdigkeiten*, III, 217–382, for a useful firsthand account of the legal situation in Baden and Württemburg.
66. Hamburg edition, IX, 361.
67. On Brentano and Savigny see Wohlhaupter, *Dichterjuristen*, I, 3–96.
68. *Werke*, II, 454–55.
69. *Werke*, IV, 545.
70. *Werke*, I, 795–97.
71. On Savigny and Arnim see Wohlhaupter, *Dichterjuristen*, I, 97–119.
72. *Arnims Briefe an Savigny*, 108.
73. Arnim, *Gedichte*, 116–21.
74. On Eichendorff see Wohlhaupter, *Dichterjuristen*, II, 99–190; and Wolfgang Frühwald, "Der Regierungsrat Joseph von Eichendorff," *Internationales Archiv für Sozialgeschichte der deutschen Literatur* 4 (1979): 37–67.
75. These essays—e.g., "Preußen und die Konstitutionen" or "Über Verfassungsgarantien"—amount to variations on the same basic theme; see *Werke und Schriften*, IV, 1275–1353.
76. *Werke und Schriften*, II, 1035–36.
77. *Werke und Schriften*, II, 127.

78. Egon Schwarz has pointed out that each of the three books of the novel represents a different realm of experience: personal-poetic, social-political, and philosophical-religious. See his essay on *Ahnung und Gegenwart* in *Romane und Erzählungen der deutschen Romantik*, 308.

79. See *Briefe der Brüder Grimm an Savigny*; Gunhild Ginschel, *Der junge Jacob Grimm, 1805–1819* (Berlin: Akademie, 1967); and Gerhard Dilcher, "Jacob Grimm als Jurist," in *Die Brüder Grimm: Dokumente ihres Lebens und Wirkens*, ed. Dieter Hennig and Bernhard Lauer (Kassel: Weber & Weidemeyer, 1985), 25–41.

80. Ginschel, *Der junge Jacob Grimm*, 38.

81. Grimm, *Kleinere Schriften*, VI, 153.

82. *Die Brüder Grimm: Dokumente ihres Lebens und Wirkens*, 271–72.

83. Schubart-Fikentscher, 82–85.

84. See Carl Maria von Weber, *Der Freischütz: Texte, Materialien, Kommentare*, eds. Attila Csampai and Dietmar Holland (Reinbek bei Hamburg: Rowohlt, 1981), 9–30.

85. Peter A. Kroner, "Adelbert von Chamisso," in *Deutsche Dichter der Romantik: Ihr Leben und Werk*, ed. Benno von Wiese (Berlin: Erich Schmidt, 1971), 385.

86. *Chamissos Werke*, I, 437.

87. *Werke*, II, 806.

88. Wolfgang Frühwald, "Clemens Brentano," in *Deutsche Dichter der Romantik: Ihr Leben und Werk*, ed. Benno von Wiese (Berlin: Erich Schmidt, 1971), 280–309.

89. Karl Marx and Frederick Engels, *Collected Works* (London: Lawrence & Wishart, 1975), I, 12–15.

90. *Collected Works*, I, 203–10.

91. *Gesamtausgabe*, VI, 9.

92. The following paragraphs are based on analyses that I develop more fully in "Kleists Werk im Lichte der zeitgenössischen Rechtskontroverse," in *Kleist-Jahrbuch 1987* (Berlin: Erich Schmidt, 1987), 28–51.

93. *Sämtliche Werke und Briefe*, II, 323.

94. Hans-Peter Schneider, "Justizkritik im 'Zerbrochenen Krug,' " in *Kleist-Jahrbuch 1988–89* (Berlin: Erich Schmidt, 1988), 309–26.

95. Hans Kiefner, "Species facti. Geschichtserzählung bei Kleist und in Relationen bei preußischen Kollegialbehörden um 1800," in *Kleist-Jahrbuch 1988–89* (Berlin: Erich Schmidt, 1988), 13–39.

96. *Sämtliche Werke und Briefe*, II, 491.

97. Letter of 25 Oct. 1807, to Ulrike von Kleist; *Sämtliche Werke und Briefe*, II, 793.

98. Letter of 13 Feb. 1811, to Karl von Hardenberg; *Sämtliche Werke und Briefe*, II, 851.

99. *Sämtliche Werke und Briefe*, II, 458.

100. Hartmut Boockmann, "Mittelalterliches Recht bei Kleist: Ein Beitrag zum Verständnis des *Michael Kohlhaas*," and Klaus Lüderssen, "Recht als Verständigung unter Gleichen in Kleists *Prinz von Homburg*—ein aristokratisches oder ein demokratisches Prinzip?" in *Kleist-Jahrbuch 1985* (Berlin: Erich Schmidt, 1985).

101. Hans Höller, *Der 'Amphitryon' von Molière und der von Kleist. Eine sozialgeschichtliche Studie*, GRM-Beiheft 3 (Heidelberg, 1982), 28 and 60–61.

102. This confirmation of the positive law has been noted by several legal historians: e.g., Joachim Bohnert, "Positivität des Rechts und Konflikt bei Kleist," in *Kleist-Jahrbuch 1985* (Berlin: Erich Schmidt, 1985), 46.

103. Wohlhaupter, *Dichterjuristen*, II, 35–98; Wulf Segebrecht, "E.T.A. Hoffmanns Auffassung vom Richteramt und vom Dichterberuf," *Jahrbuch der deutschen Schillergesellschaft* 11 (1967): 62–138; E.T.A. Hoffmann, *Juristische Arbeiten*, ed. Friedrich Schnapp (München: Winkler, 1973); and Wulf Segebrecht, "Beamte, Künstler, Außenseiter: Analogien zwischen der juristischen und der dichterischen Praxis E.T.A. Hoffmanns," in *Imprimatur: Ein Jahrbuch für Bücherfreunde*, N. F. 11 (1984): 295–307.

104. *Briefwechsel*, I, 62.

105. Letter of 23 December 1808; *Briefwechsel*, I, 254.

106. Letter to Hippel of 12 March 1815; *Briefwechsel*, II, 45.

107. *Briefwechsel*, II, 27.

108. *Briefwechsel*, II, 47.

109. Letter of 3 April 1817, to Friedrich de la Motte Fouqué; *Briefwechsel*, II, 127.

110. In the annual report for 1816 by Friedrich von Trützschler und Falkenstein, vice-president of the Kammergericht; quoted in *Juristische Arbeiten*, 30.

111. *Juristische Arbeiten*, 53 and 519.

112. *Poetische Werke*, III, 15.

113. *Briefwechsel*, III, 259.

114. *Poetische Werke*, II.

115. *Poetische Werke*, II, 449.

116. *Poetische Werke*, VI, 271.

117. *Briefwechsel*, III, 259.

118. *Poetische Werke*, II, 634–35.

119. *Poetische Werke*, II, 582.

120. *Poetische Werke*, VI, 634.

121. *Poetische Werke*, V, 19.

122. The relevant documents are reprinted in Hoffmann's *Briefwechsel*, III, 117–213; here 150–51.

123. *Briefwechsel*, II, 263.

124. Mark Pavlyshyn, "Interpretation of Word as Act: The Debate on E.T.A. Hoffmann's *Meister Floh*," *Seminar* 17 (1981): 196–204.
125. *Poetische Werke*, VI, 86.
126. *Briefwechsel*, III, 236.
127. *Poetische Werke*, II, 558.

CHAPTER FOUR

1. The history of administrative sequestration, principally in France, has been traced by Michel Foucault, *Madness and Civilization: A History of Insanity in the Age of Reason* (1961), trans. Richard Howard (New York: Pantheon, 1965). The development of Prussian "therapeutic idealism" has been outlined by Klaus Doerner, *Madmen and the Bourgeoisie: A Social History of Insanity and Psychiatry* (1969), trans. Joachim Neugroschel and Jean Steinberg (Oxford: Blackwell, 1981), 164–291.

2. H. A. Korff, *Frühromantik*, vol. III of *Geist der Goethezeit*, 3rd ed. (Leipzig: Koehler & Amelang, 1959), 162: "Der Wahnsinn gehört zu den charakteristischen Motiven der Goethezeit." This notion was first developed more extensively by Albrecht Schöne, "Interpretationen zur dichterischen Gestaltung des Wahnsinns in der deutschen Literatur" (diss., Münster, 1951). Recently several useful studies have appeared: Anke Bennholdt-Thomsen and Alfredo Guzzoni, *Der "Asoziale" in der Literatur um 1800* (Königstein: Athenäum, 1979), esp. 165–214; Jutta Osinski, *Über Vernunft und Wahnsinn: Studien zur literarischen Aufklärung in der Gegenwart und im 18. Jahrhundert* (Bonn: Bouvier, 1983); Franz Loquai, *Künstler und Melancholie in der Romantik*, Helicon: Beiträge zur deutschen Literatur 4 (Frankfurt am Main: Peter Lang, 1984). Georg Reuchlein, *Bürgerliche Gesellschaft, Psychiatrie und Literatur: Zur Entwicklung der Wahnsinnsthematik in der deutschen Literatur des späten 18. und frühen 19. Jahrhunderts*, Münchner Germanistische Beiträge 35 (München: Wilhelm Fink, 1986), provides a valuable survey of secondary works on madness and literature (14–35). Despite its title, Lothar Pikulik's *Romantik als Ungenügen an der Normalität* (Frankfurt am Main: Suhrkamp, 1979) has little to say about madness.

3. See especially Dieter Jetter, *Grundzüge der Geschichte des Irrenhauses* (Darmstadt: Wissenschaftliche Buchgesellschaft, 1981). For architectural design see the chapter on "Hospitals" in Nikolaus Pevsner, *A History of Building Types*, Bollingen Series XXXV/19 (Princeton, N.J.: Princeton Univ. Press, 1976), 139–58.

4. *Madness and Civilization*, 9.

5. *Universal-Lexikon*, XLIII, 1140, and LXIII, 1007–14.

6. Franz G. Alexander and Sheldon T. Selesnick, *The History of Psychiatry: An Evaluation of Psychiatric Thought and Practice from Prehistoric Times to the Present* (New York: Harper & Row, 1966), 115. In this connection see also An-

drew T. Scull, "From Madness to Mental Illness," *Archive européenne de sociologie* 16 (1975): 218–51.

7. Alexander and Selesnick, 112.

8. Martin S. Staum, *Cabanis: Enlightenment and Medical Philosophy of the French Revolution* (Princeton, N.J.: Princeton Univ. Press, 1980).

9. Jetter, 120–28.

10. Werner Leibbrand and Annemarie Wettley, *Der Wahnsinn: Geschichte der abendländischen Psychopatholgie* (Freiburg/München: Karl Alber, 1961), 341; Doerner, *Madmen and the Bourgeoisie*, 74–75.

11. Doerner, *Madmen and the Bourgeoisie*, 207–12; Leonard Krieger, *The German Idea of Freedom: History of a Political Tradition* (Chicago: Univ. of Chicago Press, 1957), 139–65.

12. Jetter, 34–35.

13. Anke Bennoldt-Thomsen and Alfredo Guzzoni, "Der Irrenhausbesuch: Ein Topos in der Literatur um 1800," *Aurora* 42 (1982): 82–110; and Osinski, 59–75.

14. "Der Irrenhausbesuch," 85.

15. *Sämtliche Werke und Briefe*, II, 561.

16. "Der Irrenhausbesuch," 88.

17. On psychiatry during the Romantic period see generally, in addition to the relevant chapters in Doerner, *Madmen and the Bourgeoisie*, Leibbrand/Wettley, *Der Wahnsinn*; Alexander/Selesnick, *The History of Psychiatry*; George Rosen, *Madness in Society: Chapters in the Historical Sociology of Mental Illness* (Chicago: Univ. of Chicago Press, 1968); Erwin Ackerknecht, *A Short History of Psychiatry*, trans. Sula Wolff, 2nd rev. ed. (New York: Hafner, 1968); *Psychiatrie zur Zeit Hölderlins*, Ausstellungskataloge der Universität Tübingen 13, Gerhard Fichtner, ed. (Tübingen: Universitätsbibliothek, 1980); Geza Wunderlich, *Krankheits- und Therapiekonzepte am Anfang der deutschen Psychiatrie* (Husum: Matthiesen, 1981); and Gunter Herzog, "Heilung, Erziehung, Sicherung: Englische und deutsche Irrenhäuser in der ersten Hälfte des 19. Jahrhunderts," in *Bürgertum im 19. Jahrhundert: Deutschland im europäischen Vergleich*, ed. Jürgen Kocka (München: Deutscher Taschenbuchverlag, 1988), II, 418–46.

18. *Inquiry*, I, i.

19. *Traité*, li. The only English translation—*A Treatise on Insanity*, trans. D. D. Davis (Sheffield, 1806)—is also available in a modern reprint with an introduction by Paul F. Cranefield (New York: Hafner, 1962), but Pinel's important introduction to the first edition is missing, and the translation is misleadingly free in many passages.

20. *Werke*, x, 529.

21. On Crichton see Leibbrand and Wettley, *Der Wahnsinn*, 355–60.

22. On Cullen see Leibbrand and Wettley, *Der Wahnsinn*, 341–50.

23. On Pinel see Doerner, *Madmen and the Bourgeoisie*, 127–38; Leibbrand and Wettley, *Der Wahnsinn*, 418–23; and Ackerknecht, *Short History*, 41–47.

24. On Kant's view of madness see Doerner, *Madmen*, 180–87; and Leibbrand and Wettley, *Der Wahnsinn*, 361–68.

25. The term "psychosis" entered the English language through the translation of Feuchtersleben's work, *The Principles of Medical Psychology*, trans. H. Evans Lloyd, rev. and ed. B. G. Babington (London: The Sydenham Society, 1847), ch. 5, §123ff.; the volume is now conveniently available in the series "Classics in Psychiatry" published by the Arno Press (New York, 1976).

26. Sander L. Gilman, *Seeing the Insane: A Cultural History of Madness and Art in the Western World* (New York: John Wiley, 1982); and the useful dissertation by Jane E. Kromm, "Studies in the Iconography of Madness, 1600–1900" (Emory University, 1984).

27. Marianne Thalmann, *Der Trivialroman des 18. Jahrhunderts und der romantische Roman* (Berlin, 1923), 64–66.

28. Friedrich von Blanckenburg, *Versuch über den Roman* (1774; rpt. Stuttgart: Metzler, 1965), 461.

29. Herman Meyer, *Der Sonderling in der deutschen Dichtung* (1943; rpt. München: Hanser, 1963), 101 and 22–23.

30. Ackerknecht, *Short History*, 52; and Alexander and Selesnick, *History of Psychiatry*, 134.

31. Ackerknecht, *Short History*, 60.

32. *Traité*, 54–57.

33. Gerhard Schulz, *Das Zeitalter der Französischen Revolution*, vol. 1 of *Die deutsche Literatur zwischen Französischer Revolution und Restauration* (München: Beck, 1983), 283–96.

34. On Spiess's life see Wolfgang Promies's afterword to his edition of *Biographien der Wahnsinnigen* (Neuwied: Luchterhand, 1966), 317–32; on his work see also Osinski, *Über Vernunft und Wahnsinn*, 59–75 and 141–46; and Reuchlein, *Bürgerliche Gesellschaft*, 98–130.

35. For convenience specific page references are cited according to Promies's edition, which includes only eight of the eighteen episodes in the original four-volume edition (Leipzig: Voss, 1795–1796).

36. In addition to Thalmann, *Der Bundesroman*, see James Trainer, *Ludwig Tieck: From Gothic to Romantic* (The Hague: Mouton, 1964), 26–49.

37. See Victor Lange, "Zur Gestalt des Schwärmers im deutschen Roman des 18. Jahrhunderts," in *Festschrift für Richard Alewyn*, eds. Herbert Singer and Benno von Wiese (Köln: Böhlau, 1967), 151–64.

38. See Eric Blackall's discussion in *The Novels of the German Romantics* (Ithaca, N.Y.: Cornell Univ. Press, 1983), 151–59.

39. For a discussion of the images of the novel see William J. Lillyman, *Real-*

*ity's Dark Dream: The Narrative Fiction of Ludwig Tieck* (Berlin: De Gruyter, 1979), 21–41.

40. Tieck revised the novel twice during his lifetime: once in 1813 and then again for his collected works in 1828. Since the first edition has not been reprinted and is not conveniently available, I refer to the third edition as reprinted in *Werke*, I.

41. See Alfred Anger's afterword to *Franz Sternbalds Wanderungen*, 550.

42. See Gerhard Schulz's discussion of Tieck and *William Lovell* in *Das Zeitalter der Französischen Revolution*, 371–98; here 376.

43. Marianne Thalmann, *Die Romantik des Trivialen: Von Grosses "Genius" bis Tiecks "William Lovell"* (München: List, 1970), 108–9.

44. My undertaking—to interpret the novel in the light of contemporary psychiatric theory—is quite different from that of Walter Münz, *Individuum und Symbol in Tiecks "William Lovell": Materialien zum frühromantischen Subjektivismus* (Frankfurt am Main: Peter Lang, 1975), 105–32, who analyzes the madness in the novel according to modern psychological theories of endogenous depression; and also from the largely social interpretation of Bennholdt-Thomsen and Guzzoni, *Der "Asoziale"*, 195–96 and 208–15.

45. Hamburg edition, vol. VII.

46. In this connection see Frederick J. Beharriell, "The Hidden Meaning of Goethe's 'Bekenntnisse einer Schönen Seele,'" in *Lebendige Form*, Festschrift for Heinrich E. K. Henel, eds. Jeffrey L. Sammons and Ernst Schürer (München: Fink, 1970), 37–62.

47. See Eric Blackall's discussion in *Goethe and the Novel*, 111–36; Osinski, *Über Vernunft und Wahnsinn*, and Bennholdt-Thomsen and Guzzoni, *Der "Asoziale,"* 180–88. Reuchlein, *Bürgerliche Gesellschaft*, 131–80, discusses several of Goethe's works (notably *Faust*, *Wilhelm Meisters Lehrjahre*, and *Iphigenie*) under the rubric "Psychologisierung der Literatur und Moraldidaxe."

48. Dorothea Flashar, *Bedeutung, Entwicklung und literarische Nachwirkung von Goethes Mignongestalt* (Berlin: Ebering, 1929), 53–71.

49. See Paul Krauss, "Mignon, der Harfner, Sperata: Die Psychopathologie einer Sippe in *Wilhelm Meisters Lehrjahren*," *Deutsche Vierteljahrsschrift für Literaturwissenschaft und Geistesgeschichte* 22 (1944): 327–54. My emphasis differs significantly from Reuchlein, *Bürgerliche Gesellschaft*, 149–61, who sees little development in the figure of the harpist from the earlier version to the later one.

50. The two main scenes with the harpist occur in bk. IV, chs. 12–13 of the *Theatralische Sendung*.

51. See Gloria Flaherty, "The Stage-Struck Wilhelm Meister and 18th-Century Psychiatric Medicine," *MLN* 101 (1986): 493–515. Also relevant is Gottfried Diener, *Goethes "Lila": Heilung eines "Wahnsinns" durch "psychische Kur"* (Frankfurt am Main: Athenäum, 1971).

52. *Goethe in vertraulichen Briefen seiner Zeitgenossen, 1749–1803*, ed. Wilhelm Bode (Berlin, 1921), 517.

53. Friedrich Husemann, *Goethe und die Heilkunst: Betrachtungen zur Krise in der Medizin* (Dresden: Emil Weise, 1936), 148–50, is mistaken when he states that the methods described by Goethe were not put into practice until the twentieth century under Rudolf Steiner. In fact, Goethe is describing the moral management common in England in the late eighteenth century.

54. Letter of 20 Oct. 1797; *Der Briefwechsel zwischen Schiller und Goethe*, I, 171.

55. *Athenaeum*, I/2, 354 and 346.

56. *Werke*, V, 44–46.

57. On Reil see Doerner, *Madmen*, 198–207; Leibbrand and Wettley, *Der Wahnsinn*, 387–99; Alexander and Selesnick, *History of Psychiatry*, 135–37; Osinski, *Über Vernunft und Wahnsinn*, 222–26; and *Dictionary of Scientific Biography*, XI, 363–65.

58. Cited in Leibbrand and Wettley, *Der Wahnsinn*, 395.

59. *Rhapsodieen*, 31.

60. A. Mechler, "Das Wort 'Psychiatrie,' " *Nervenarzt* 34 (1963): 405.

61. Ackerknecht, *Short History*, 49–50.

62. See Hans Söhnlein, "Die Fabel des *Titan*: Ein Versuch zu ihrer Entschlüsselung," *Hesperus* 24 (1962): 32–43. For an exhaustive discussion of the novel see H. A. Korff, *Geist der Goethezeit*, III, 122–69; for more recent discussions with bibliography see Eric Blackall, *The Novel of the German Romantics*, 84–90; and Gerhard Schulz, *Das Zeitalter der Französischen Revolution*, 350–60; Reiner Matzker, *Der nützliche Idiot: Wahnsinn und Initiation bei Jean Paul und E.T.A. Hoffmann* (Frankfurt am Main: Peter Lang, 1984), attempts to locate Jean Paul within a framework of philosophy of religion and not, despite its title, within the contemporary discussion of madness.

63. *Werke*, III.

64. See Lucie Stern, *"Wilhelm Meisters Lehrjahre* und *Titan"* (1922), rpt. in *Jean Paul: Wege der Forschung*, ed. Uwe Schweikert (Darmstadt: Wissenschaftliche Buchgesellschaft, 1974), 41–42.

65. See Emil Staiger's discussion of *Titan* in his *Meisterwerke deutscher Sprache aus dem neunzehnten Jahrhundert* (1945; rpt. München: Deutscher Taschenbuch Verlag, 1973), esp. 66–67.

66. See Eduard Berend's introduction to his edition of *Titan* in Jean Paul, *Sämtliche Werke*, I. Abt., VIII, lix and lxxv.

67. "Roquairol: Eine Studie zur Geschichte des Bösen," in his *Begegnungen und Probleme: Studien zur deutschen Literaturgeschichte* (Bern: Francke, 1957), 155–242.

68. See the detailed account of the genesis of the novel in Berend's introduction to his edition of *Titan*: on Schoppe esp. xvii, lv, lxxvi, and lcviii.

69. Bennholdt-Thomsen and Guzzoni, *Der "Asoziale,"* 196–97.

70. *Sämtliche Werke*, Abt. 3, v, 20.

71. For summaries of the existing theories see Gerhart Hoffmeister's chapter on the *Nachtwachen* in *Romane und Erzählungen der deutschen Romantik*, ed. Paul Michael Lützeler, 194–212; and Jeffrey L. Sammons, "In Search of Bonaventura: The *Nachtwachen* Riddle 1965–1985," *The Germanic Review* 61 (1986): 50–56. Most studies of the work begin almost ritually with a consideration of the authorship—and often do not get beyond that point. A recent article by Ruth Haag—"Noch einmal: Der Verfasser der Nachtwachen von Bonaventura," *Euphorion* 81 (1987): 286–97—brings the most compelling evidence to date for the authorship of August Klingemann and has perhaps laid the controversy finally to rest.

72. *Nachtwachen*, 83.

73. In this connection see Hoffmeister, 204–8.

74. See Lillian Feder, *Madness in Literature* (Princeton, N.J.: Princeton Univ. Press, 1980); and Theodore Ziolkowski, "The View from the Madhouse," in *Dimensions of the Modern Novel: German Texts and European Contexts* (Princeton, N.J.: Princeton Univ. Press, 1969), 332–61.

75. Franz Loquai, *Künstler und Melancholie in der Romantik*, 5–8. Loquai presents his evidence more extensively in "Der Nachtwächter im Irrenhaus. Zum Thema des Wahnsinns in den *Nachtwachen von Bonaventura*," *Internationales Archiv für Sozialgeschichte der deutschen Literatur* 12 (1987): 134–55.

76. Loquai, *Künstler und Melancholie*, 280–81, stresses Bonaventura's familiarity with the principal psychiatric writings of the day.

77. See the letter of 23 Dec. 1796, which Langermann wrote to Novalis to report on Sophie's progress; Novalis, *Schriften*, iv, 466–67.

78. On Langermann, see Doerner, *Madmen*, 212–15; Leibbrand and Wettley, *Der Wahnsinn*, 499–501; and *Allgemeine Deutsche Biographie*, xvii, 682–83.

79. The relevant documents are summarized by Doerner, *Madmen*, 212–15.

80. Jetter, *Grundzüge der Geschichte des Irrenhauses*, 36–37. This development continued until about 1840, when many of these new institutions were again combined into the typically German *Heil- und Pflegeanstalten* under a new generation of psychiatrists led by Christian Friedrich Wilhelm Roller.

81. The best account is Horn's own *Oeffentliche Rechenschaft über meine zwölfjährige Dienstführung als zweiter Arzt des Königl. Charité-Krankenhauses zu Berlin* (Berlin, 1818), written in response to his dismissal from that institution for the suffocation-death of an inmate caused by the notorious "sack" that he invented for therapeutic purposes.

82. Karl Jaspers, *Allgemeine Psychopathologie* (Berlin-Heidelberg: Springer, 1948), 703–16.

83. *Schriften*, i, 344.

84. *Werke*, iv, 362.

85. *Psychiatrie zur Zeit Hölderlins*, 51–86.
86. Waiblinger, *Die Tagebücher 1821–26*, 216–217.
87. *Werke und Briefe*, I, 394.
88. Conversation with Riemer on 1 Feb. 1813; *Gedenkausgabe*, XXII, 680–81.
89. *Werke*, I, 19.
90. *Poetische Werke*, III.
91. Friedhelm Auhuber, *In einem fernen dunklen Spiegel: E.T.A. Hoffmanns Poetisierung der Medizin* (Opladen: Westdeutscher Verlag, 1986), 2.
92. Wulf Segebrecht, "Krankheit und Gesellschaft: Zu E.T.A. Hoffmanns Rezeption der Bamberger Medizin," in *Romantik in Deutschland: Ein interdisziplinäres Symposion*, ed. Richard Brinkmann, (Stuttgart: Metzler, 1978), 267–90.
93. Auhuber, *In einem fernen dunklen Spiegel*, 10–12.
94. *Poetische Werke*, VI, 735.
95. *Poetische Werke*, II, 385 and 390; III, 219.
96. *Poetische Werke*, II, 553.
97. *Poetische Werke*, II, 553–54.
98. This is one of the principal theses argued persuasively by Auhuber.
99. Auhuber, 100–8, who follows Claudio Magris, *Die andere Vernunft: E.T.A. Hoffmann* (Königstein: Athenäum, 1980).
100. James M. McGlathery, "The Suicide Motif in E.T.A. Hoffmann's 'Der goldne Topf,' " *Monatshefte für deutschen Unterricht* 58 (1966): 115–23; and Maria M. Tatar, *Spellbound: Studies on Mesmerism and Literature* (Princeton, N.J.: Princeton Univ. Press, 1978), 145–46.
101. *Poetische Werke*, II, 344.
102. *Poetische Werke*, III, 41.
103. *Poetische Werke*, II, 408.
104. *Poetische Werke*, I, 350.
105. *Poetische Werke*, III, 37.
106. Reprinted in *Juristische Arbeiten*, 83–120.
107. Wulf Segebrecht, "E.T.A. Hoffmanns Auffassung vom Richteramt und vom Dichterberuf: Mit unbekannten Zeugnissen aus Hoffmanns juristischer Tätigkeit," *Jahrbuch der deutschen Schillergesellschaft* 11 (1967): 92–93. See also Georg Reuchlein, *Das Problem der Zurechnungsfähigkeit bei E.T.A. Hoffmann und Georg Büchner: Zum Verhältnis von Literatur, Psychiatrie und Justiz im frühen 19. Jahrhundert* (Frankfurt am Main: Lang, 1985), 20–44.

## CHAPTER FIVE

1. *Was ich erlebte*, 91.
2. *Lebenserinnerungen*, I, 47–75; here 71–72.
3. Quoted in Novalis, *Schriften*, IV, 632.
4. Novalis, *Schriften*, IV, 633.

5. Rudolf Haym, *Die romantische Schule: Ein Beitrag zur Geschichte des deutschen Geistes* (1870; rpt. Darmstadt: Wissenschaftliche Buchgesellschaft, 1961), 371.

6. Karl Jaspers, *Schelling: Größe und Verhängnis* (1955; rpt. München: Piper, 1986), 275.

7. Gert Ueding, *Klassik und Romantik: Deutsche Literatur im Zeitalter der Französischen Revolution, 1789–1815* (München: Deutscher Taschenbuch Verlag, 1988), 1, 65–139.

8. Roger Cardinal, *German Romantics in Context* (London: Studio Vista, 1975), 14–15.

9. S. F. Mason, *A History of the Sciences: Main Currents of Scientific Thought* (London: Routledge & Kegan Paul, 1953), 352–63 ("Scientific Institutions in France and Britain during the Nineteenth Century").

10. Paul Farmer, "Nineteenth-Century Ideas of the University: Continental Europe," in *The Modern University*, ed. Margaret Clapp (Ithaca, N.Y.: Cornell Univ. Press, 1950), 3–26.

11. Sheldon Rothblatt, "The Student Sub-culture and the Examination System in Early 19th Century Oxbridge," in *The University in Society*, ed. Lawrence Stone (Princeton, N.J.: Princeton Univ. Press, 1974), 1, 247.

12. Arthur Engel, "Emerging Concepts of the Academic Profession at Oxford 1800–1854," in *The University in Society*, 1, 307–8.

13. *The Universities in the Nineteenth Century*, ed. Michael Sanderson (London and Boston: Routledge & Kegan Paul, 1975), 35.

14. John Henry Cardinal Newman, *The Idea of a University* (Westminster, Md.: Christian Classics, [n.d.]), ix.

15. Letter of 10 Sept. 1817; John Keats, *Complete Poems and Selected Letters*, ed. Clarence DeWitt Thorpe (New York: Odyssey, 1935), 510.

16. Herbert Nimtz, *Motive des Studentenlebens in der deutschen Literatur von den Anfängen bis zum Ende des achtzehnten Jahrhunderts* (Würzburg: Triltsch, 1937). Unfortunately this Berlin dissertation is not useful for the later eighteenth century.

17. Theodore Ziolkowski, "Faust and the University: Pedagogical Ruminations on a Subversive Classic," in *Texte, Motive und Gestalten der Goethezeit. Festschrift für Hans Reiss*, eds. John L. Hibberd and Hugh B. Nisbet (Tübingen: Niemeyer, 1989), 65–79.

18. Georg Rudolf Widmann, *Fausts Leben*, 67–69.

19. *Oeuvres de Frédéric le Grand*, xiv, 308.

20. On student life during this period see Friedrich Schulze and Paul Ssymank, *Das deutschen Studententum von den ältesten Zeiten bis zur Gegenwart*, 4th ed. (München: Verlag für Hochschulkunde, 1932), 181–222; and Henri Brunschwig, *Enlightenment and Romanticism in Eighteenth-Century Prussia*, 77–81.

21. Kortum, *Die Jobsiade*, 42.

22. Salzmann, *Carl von Carlsberg*, I, 155.

23. René König, *Vom Wesen der deutschen Universität* (1935; rpt. Darmstadt, Wissenschaftliche Buchgesellschaft, 1970), 17–47; R. Steven Turner, "University Reformers and Professorial Scholarship in Germany 1760–1806," in *The University in Society*, II, 495–531.

24. Laetitia Boehm, "Einführung," in *Universitäten und Hochschulen in Deutschland, Österreich und der Schweiz*, eds. Laetitia Boehm and Rainer A. Müller (Düsseldorf: ECON, 1983), 23.

25. Zachariä, *Scherzhafte Epische Poesien*, canto I.

26. Helmut Henne and Georg Objartel, *Historische deutsche Studentensprache* (Berlin/New York: De Gruyter, 1982), 12.

27. Schulze and Ssymank, 199–200.

28. *Universitäten und Hochschulen*, 213.

29. *Magister F. Ch. Laukhards Leben und Schicksale*, I, 50.

30. Schulze and Ssymank, 196.

31. *Dichtung und Wahrheit*, bk. 20; Hamburg edition, vol. x, 174.

32. Hans Tümmler, *Goethe der Kollege: Sein Leben und Wirken mit Christian Gottlob von Voigt* (Köln/Wien: Böhlau, 1970), esp. chs. 5, 9, and 15.

33. Fritz Hartung, *Das Großherzogtum Sachsen unter der Regierung Carl Augusts 1775–1828* (Weimar: Böhlau, 1923), 165.

34. Goethe's official reports concerned with Jena University, along with useful notes, are reproduced in vol. 53 of the Weimar edition; here 275.

35. *Briefe*, I, 401.

36. *"Der Universitäts-Bereiser" Friedrich Gedike und sein Bericht an Friedrich Wilhelm II*, ed. Richard Fester. Supplement no. 1 of the *Archiv für Kulturgeschichte* (Berlin: Duncker, 1905), 78–85; here 78.

37. See esp. Fritz Hartung, *Das Großherzogtum Sachsen*, 159–72; and Karl-Heinz Hahn, "Im Schatten der Revolution—Goethe und Jena im letzten Jahrzehnt des 18. Jahrhunderts," in *Jahrbuch des Wiener Goethe-Vereins* 81–83 (1977–1979): 37–58.

38. Paul Ssymank, "Die Jenaer Duellgegner des Jahres 1792 und Karl Augusts Kampf gegen die geheimen Studentenverbindungen," in *Quellen und Darstellungen zur Geschichte der Burschenschaft und der deutschen Einheitsbewegung*, ed. Herman Haupt (Heidelberg: Carl Winter, 1913), IV, 1–30.

39. Weimar edition, LIII, 285–90.

40. Hahn, "Im Schatten der Revolution," 43 (note 9).

41. Letter of July 1796 to Karl Schlegel and his wife: *Caroline: Briefe aus der Frühromantik*, I, 393.

42. *Briefe*, II, 291.

43. *Was ich erlebte*, 70.

44. *Lebenserinnerungen*, 63.

45. *Crabb Robinson in Germany*, 118.

NOTES TO CHAPTER FIVE

46. *Alma mater Jenensis: Geschichte der Universität Jena*, eds. Siegfried Schmidt, Ludwig Elm, and Günter Steiger (Weimar: Böhlau, 1983), 127–75 ("Die Klassische Zeit der Universität Jena").

47. Fritz Hartung, *Das Großherzogtum Sachsen*, 137–48.

48. *Briefe*, I, 403.

49. *"Der Universitäts-Bereiser,"* 79.

50. *Alma mater Jenensis*, 164.

51. "Bericht an den Marschall Alexandre Berthier über die wissenschaftlichen und künstlerischen Institute in Weimar und Jena," Weimar edition, LIII, 243–49.

52. *Crabb Robinson in Germany*, 115.

53. Fritz Hartung, *Das Großherzogtum Sachsen*, 148–59; *Alma mater Jenensis*, 140–55.

54. *Briefe*, I, 397.

55. Fritz Hartung, *Das Großherzogtum Sachsen*, 156; *Alma mater Jenensis*, 157. In all fairness it should be noted that Schiller was also widely reputed to be a terrible, stilted, declamatory lecturer who was uncertain of his historical facts. See Gedike, 84.

56. "der Stolz unsres Jahrhunderts," in the petition to Duke Karl August of 20 Apr. 1799; in *Die Schriften zu J. G. Fichtes Atheismus-Streit*, ed. Frank Böckelmann (München: Rogener & Bernhard, 1969), 213.

57. Paul Raabe, "Das Protokollbuch der Gesellschaft der Freien Männer in Jena 1794–1799," in *Festgabe für Eduard Berend*, eds. Hans Werner Seiffert and Bernhard Zeller (Weimar: Böhlau, 1959), 336–83.

58. *Die Schriften zu J. G. Fichtes Atheismus-Streit*, 217.

59. *Crabb Robinson in Germany*, 103.

60. *Briefe*, II, 289–94.

61. *Sämtliche Werke*, IV.

62. *Gesamtausgabe*, I/3, 3–22; and *Fichtes Schriften zur Gesellschaftsphilosophie*, II, 1–32.

63. *Gesamtausgabe*, I/3, 19.

64. *Sämtliche Werke*, VI, 152.

65. *Gesamtausgabe*, I/3, 13.

66. *Gesamtausgabe*, I/3, 37.

67. *Gesamtausgabe*, I/3, 14.

68. All three lecture series are conveniently reproduced in vol. II of *Fichtes Schriften zur Gesellschaftsphilosophie*.

69. Text cited according to *Gesamtausgabe*, I/3, 25–68.

70. *Der Briefwechsel zwischen Friedrich Carl von Savigny und Stephan August Winkelmann (1800–1804)*, ed. Ingeborg Schnack (Marburg: Elwert, 1984), 40. For a more negative assessment of Fichte's ideas see Frederic Lilge, *The Abuse of*

*Learning: The Failure of the German University* (New York: Macmillan, 1948), 37–56.

71. See *Die Schriften zu J. G. Fichtes Atheismus-Streit*.

72. Rpt. in Anrich, *Die Idee der deutschen Universität*, 1–123. A translation by E. S. Morgan, edited and with an introduction by Norbert Guterman, has been published under the title *On University Studies* (Athens: Ohio University Press, 1966).

73. *Schriften*, III, 518.

74. *Schriften*, III, 249.

75. *Schriften*, III, 280.

76. *Literary Notebooks*, 185.

77. *Werke*, IV, 9.

78. René Wellek, "The Concept of Romanticism in Literary History" and "Romanticism Re-examined," in *Concepts of Criticism*, ed. Stephen G. Nichols, Jr. (New Haven, Conn.: Yale Univ. Press, 1963), esp. 161 and 220.

79. See the editor's notes in Brentano's *Werke*, II, 1209.

80. *Werke*, II, 983–84.

81. See *Schriften*, IV, 22–23, and Schlegel's letter to his brother of Jan. 1792 (quoted in *Schriften*, IV, 572).

82. *Schriften*, II, 413.

83. *Schriften*, IV, 251.

84. See Jurij Striedter, "Die Komposition der 'Lehrlinge zu Sais,'" *Der Deutschunterricht* 7 (1955): 5–23; Géza von Molnar, "The Composition of Novalis' *Die Lehrlinge zu Sais*: A Reevaluation," *PMLA* 85 (1970): 1002–14; Nicholas Saul, *History and Poetry in Novalis and in the Tradition of the German Enlightenment* (Institute of Germanic Studies: University of London, 1984), 126–40.

85. *Kritische Schriften*, 341.

86. *Schriften*, I, 79.

87. *Schriften von 1794–1798*, 337.

88. On Schlegel's university career see Josef Körner's introduction to his edition of Schlegel's *Neue Philosophische Schriften* (Frankfurt am Main: Schulte-Bulmke, 1935), 35–45.

89. See Ernst Behler's introduction to *Kritische Ausgabe*, XI, xxxi–xxxiv.

90. "Ideen zu Gedichten (VI: 46)," in *Kritische Ausgabe*, XVI, 198.

91. Konrad Polheim, "Studien zu Fr. Schlegels poetischen Begriffen," *Deutsche Vierteljahrsschrift* 35 (1961): 363–98, esp. 378–89; revised in Polheim's *Die Arabeske: Ansichten und Ideen aus Friedrich Schlegels Poetik* (München: Schöningh, 1966), 72–95.

92. *Kritische Ausgabe*, XVI, 292.

93. *Kritische Schriften*, 98.

94. René Wellek, *A History of Modern Criticism*, II, 35.

95. Wellek, II, 35.

96. *Kritische Ausgabe*, II.

97. For this paragraph see Friedrich Paulsen, *Geschichte des gelehrten Unterrichts auf den deutschen Schulen und Universitäten vom Ausgang des Mittelalters bis zur Gegenwart*, 3rd ed. (Berlin/Leipzig: De Gruyter, 1921), II, 226, 258–59, 271.

98. Rpt. in Anrich, *Die Idee der deutschen Universität*, 125–217.

99. *Alma mater Jenensis*, 141.

100. *Briefe an Ludwig Tieck*, ed. K. von Holtei (Breslau, 1864), III, 65.

101. See Fritz Hartung, 172–88; Hans Tümmler, *Goethe der Kollege*, 100–118; Ernst Borkowsky, 220–34; and *Alma mater Jenensis*, 162–67.

102. Rpt. by René Wellek, "Ein unbekannter Artikel Savignys über die deutschen Universitäten," *Zeitschrift der Savigny-Stiftung für Rechtsgeschichte*, Germanistische Abteilung 51 (1931): 529–37.

103. *Briefe von der Universität*, 75 and 363.

104. *Denkwürdigkeiten*, I, 203.

105. *Werke und Schriften*, II, 1044–45.

106. Börne, *Sämtliche Schriften*, I, 597–609.

107. *Was ich erlebte*, esp. 174–202.

108. Peter Classen and Eike Wolgast, *Kleine Geschichte der Universität Heidelberg* (Berlin: Springer, 1983), 35–45.

109. Loeben, *Gedichte*, x.

110. See *Joseph und Wilhelm von Eichendorffs Jugendgedichte*, passim.

111. Karl Bartsch, *Romantiker und germanistische Studien in Heidelberg 1804–1808* (Heidelberg: Hörning, 1881); and *Heidelberg im säkularen Umbruch: Traditionsbewußtsein und Kulturpolitik um 1800*, ed. Friedrich Strack (Stuttgart: Klett-Cotta, 1987).

112. Roger Paulin, *Ludwig Tieck: A literary biography* (Oxford: Clarendon Press, 1986), 164–65.

113. *Werke und Briefe*, I, 217.

114. *Werke*, I, 173–84.

115. See Hartmut Fröschle, *Der Spätaufklärer Johann Heinrich Voss als Kritiker der deutschen Romantik*, Stuttgarter Arbeiten zur Germanistik 146 (Stuttgart: Akademischer Verlag Hans-Dieter Heinz, 1985).

116. *Schriften*, I, 207–8.

117. *Werke*, I, 307.

118. *Werke*, III, 113–14.

119. *Poetische Werke*, V, 27.

120. *Werke und Schriften*, II, 731.

121. On the founding of the University of Berlin see Rudolf Köpke, *Die Gründung der königlichen Friedrich-Wilhelms-Universität zu Berlin* (Berlin, 1860); Max Lenz, *Geschichte der Königlichen Friedrich-Wilhelms-Universität zu Berlin* (Halle: Verlag der Buchhandlung des Waisenhauses, 1910), vol. I; *Idee und Wirklichkeit einer Universität: Dokumente zur Geschichte der Friedrich-Wilhelms-Uni-*

NOTES TO CHAPTER FIVE

*versität zu Berlin*, ed. Wilhelm Weischedel (Berlin: De Gruyter, 1960); Charles E. McClelland, *State, Society, and University in Germany 1700–1914* (Cambridge: Cambridge Univ. Press, 1980), 101–49; Ulrich Muhlack, "Die Universitäten im Zeichen von Neuhumanismus und Idealismus: Berlin," in *Beiträge zu Problemen deutscher Universitätsgründungen der frühen Neuzeit*, eds. Peter Baumgart und Notker Hammerstein, Wolfenbüttler Forschungen 4 (Nendeln/Liechtenstein: KTO Press, 1978), 299–340.

122. Max Lenz, *Geschichte*, I, 78.

123. Weischedel, *Idee und Wirklichkeit*, 11–15.

124. Max Lenz, *Geschichte*, I, 85–92.

125. Rpt. in Anrich, *Die Idee der deutschen Universität*, 219–308.

126. Herbert Scurla, *Wilhelm von Humboldt: Werden und Wirken* (1970; rpt. Düsseldorf: Claassen, 1976), 131–84.

127. On the influence of the Jena theorists on Humboldt's educational theory see Otto Rühle, *Idee und Gestalt der deutschen Universität: Tradition und Aufgabe* (Berlin: Deutscher Verlag der Wissenschaften, 1966), 92–120; and Günter Steiger, "*Brotgelehrte* und *Philosophische Köpfe*: Universitäten und Hochschulen zwischen zwei Revolutionen," in *Magister und Scholaren, Professoren und Studenten: Geschichte deutscher Universitäten und Hochschulen im Überblick*, eds. Günter Steiger und Werner Fläschendräger (Leipzig-Jena-Berlin: Urania, 1981), 72–102.

128. Humboldt's writings on the university are conveniently collected in vol. IV of his *Werke*.

129. Max Lenz, *Geschichte*, I, 287.

130. *Werke*, III, 418–20.

131. Max Lenz, *Geschichte*, I, 301.

132. *Werke*, I, 218.

133. Reinhold Steig, *Heinrich von Kleists Berliner Kämpfe* (Berlin and Stuttgart: Spemann, 1901), 289–324.

134. *Berliner Abendblätter*, 7.

135. Steig, *Berliner Kämpfe*, 302.

136. *Briefwechsel*, II, 157.

137. Steig, *Berliner Kämpfe*, 296.

138. *Wilhelm und Caroline von Humboldt in ihren Briefen*, III, 399.

139. On this phase of the history see Max Lenz, *Geschichte*, I, 305–468.

140. *Sämmtliche Werke*, 3. Abtheilung, I, 449–76.

141. Weischedel, *Idee und Wirklichkeit*, 252–56.

142. Weischedel, *Idee und Wirklichkeit*, 260–61.

143. Ekkehart Mühlenberg, "Der Universitätslehrer," in *Friedrich Schleiermacher 1768–1834*, ed. Dietz Lange (Göttingen: Vandenhoeck & Ruprecht, 1985), 39.

144. Max Lenz, *Geschichte*, I, 496.

145. *Briefe*, 376.
146. Weischedel, *Idee und Wirklichkeit*, xxviii.
147. Weischedel, *Idee und Wirklichkeit*, 310.


CHAPTER SIX

1. Letter of 29 Dec. 1822; cited in *Karl Friedrich Schinkel 1781–1841*, a cata-
logue published by the Staatliche Museen zu Berlin on the occasion of the DDR
Exhibition in the Altes Museum from 23 Oct. 1980 to 29 Mar. 1981 (rpt. Berlin:
Westberlin Verlag Das Europäische Buch, 1981), 135.

2. Henry-Russell Hitchcock, *Architecture: Nineteenth and Twentieth Centuries*,
4th ed. (Baltimore: Penguin, 1977), 57–61.

3. Nikolaus Pevsner, *A History of Building Types*, The A. W. Mellon Lectures
in the Fine Arts 1970, Bollingen Series xxxv/19 (Princeton, N.J.: Princeton Univ.
Press, 1976), 127.

4. Johnson's (unpaginated) introduction to Karl Friedrich Schinkel, *Collection
of Architectural Designs* (Chicago: Exedra Books, 1981)—a reprint (with translations) of Schinkel's *Sammlung architektonischer Entwürfe* (Berlin: Ernst und
Korn, 1866).

5. On the early history of the museum see Volker Plagemann, *Das deutsche
Kunstmuseum, 1790–1870: Lage, Baukörper, Raumorganisation, Bildprogramm*
(München: Prestel, 1967), 66–81. A convenient summary of the relevant dates
and materials is available in Hans Ebert, "Daten zur Vorgeschichte und Ge-
schichte des Alten Museums," *Forschungen und Berichte* (Staatliche Museen zu
Berlin [DDR]) 20/21 (1980): 9–22.

6. *Denkwürdigkeiten*, II, 728–29.

7. For information relating to the construction of Schinkel's museum see his
*Sammlung architektonischer Entwürfe*, 41–42 and plates nos. 37–48; *Aus Schinkel's
Nachlass*, III, 217–327; Hans Kauffmann, "Zweckbau und Monument: Zu Frie-
drich Schinkels Museum am Berliner Lustgarten," in *Eine Freundesgabe der
Wissenschaft für Ernst Hellmut Vits*, ed. Gerhard Hess (Frankfurt am Main: Fritz
Knapp, 1963), 135–66; Hermann G. Pundt, *Schinkel's Berlin: A Study in Environ-
mental Planning* (Cambridge, Mass.: Harvard Univ. Press, 1972), 138–57; and
Erik Forssman, *Karl Friedrich Schinkel: Bauwerke und Baugedanken* (München:
Schnell und Steiner, 1981), 110–26.

8. Cited in Pevsner, *A History of Building Types*, 126.

9. "Über Lehranstalten, zugunsten der bildenden Künste," *Propyläen* II/2
(1799): 153.

10. *Aus Schinkel's Nachlass*, III, 272–83.

11. *Drey Reisen nach Italien*, 295–96.

12. *Universal-Lexikon*, XXI, 1375.

13. On the history of museums see Plagemann, *Das deutsche Kunstmuseum*;

the chapter "Museums" (111–38) in Pevsner's *History of Building Types*; Luc Benoist, *Musées et muséologie* (Paris: Presses universitaires de France, 1960); Gudrun Calov, *Museen und Sammler des 19. Jahrhunderts in Deutschland* (Berlin: De Gruyter, 1969); Wolfgang Becker, *Paris und die deutsche Malerei 1750–1840* (München: Prestel, 1971); and Kenneth Hudson, *A Social History of Museums* (London: Macmillan, 1975).

14. Pevsner, *History of Building Types*, 117–18; Hudson, *Social History*, 6–9.

15. *Gesammelte Schriften*, xiv, 383–84.

16. Letter of Nov. 1801 to Adolfine von Werdeck; *Sämtliche Werke*, ii, 702.

17. "Nachtrag italiänischer Gemählde," *Europa* 2 (1803): 97.

18. *Briefe von der Universität*, 438–39.

19. *Denkwürdigkeiten*, ii, 93–95.

20. *Sammlung architektonischer Entwürfe*, 41.

21. Friedrich Stock, "Urkunden zur Vorgeschichte der Berliner Museum," *Jahrbuch der preussischen Kunstsammlungen* 51 (1930): 209–14; also cited by Pevsner, 128.

22. *Gesammelte Schriften*, xii, 539–66; also rpt. in *Aus Schinkel's Nachlass*, iii, 298–327. On Humboldt's role in the organization of the museum see Hermann Lübbe, "Wilhelm von Humboldt und die Berliner Museumsgründung 1830," *Deutsche Vierteljahresschrift* 54 (1980): 656–76.

23. *Sammlung architektonischer Entwürfe*, 41. Many early galleries were located in former stables, which were suitable both in terms of spaciousness and lighting. The great collection at Dresden was long housed in the Stallgebäude, and the Augustina Collection in Vienna still occupies the building of the onetime royal stables.

24. *Sammlung architektonischer Entwürfe*, 41–42.

25. *Aus Schinkel's Nachlass*, iii, 241–43.

26. Boullée, *Architecture. Essai sur l'art*, ed. Jean-Marie Pérouse de Montclos (Paris: Hermann, 1968), 81.

27. *Aus Schinkel's Nachlass*, iii, 248.

28. *Aus Schinkel's Nachlass*, iii, 231–32.

29. The combination of colonnade and rotunda, while actually constructed for the first time in Schinkel's building, was not unique in museum design. The influential French architect Durand favored the same combination for various public edifices: not only the museum but also the public treasury, the institute, and the library. But Durand's museum design (which was never executed) differs significantly from Schinkel's in two respects: the colonnade covers only two-thirds of the frontal plane, and the rotunda is not masked by a rectangular attic. The total effect of the design is therefore wholly unlike that of Schinkel's museum. See J.N.L. Durand, *Précis des leçons d'architecture données à l'École Polytechnique* (Paris, 1805), ii, 56–57 and planche 11.

30. Schinkel, *Reisen nach Italien*, 126.

31. *Reisen nach Italien*, 170.

32. *Gesammelte Schriften*, XII, 543.

33. *Sammlung architektonischer Entwürfe*, 42.

34. Stock, "Urkunden," 209.

35. *Gesammelte Schriften*, XII, 556.

36. Plagemann, *Das deutsche Kunstmuseum*, 22–23.

37. *Sammlung architektonischer Entwürfe*, 42.

38. On Rumohr's plan see his *Drey Reisen nach Italien*, 277–302. On Rumohr see Wilhelm Waetzoldt, *Deutsche Kunsthistoriker von Sandrart bis Rumohr* (Leipzig: Seemann, 1921), 292–318.

39. Pevsner, *History of Building Types*, 128; Stock, "Urkunden," 209–214.

40. *Gesammelte Schriften*, XII, 556–57.

41. *Gesammelte Schriften*, XII, 549–50.

42. Plagemann, *Das deutsche Kunstmuseum*, 30.

43. Pevsner, *History of Building Types*, 20.

44. See Paul Ortwin Rave, *Karl Friedrich Schinkel* (1953), ed. Eva Börsch-Supan (München: Deutscher Kunstverlag, 1981); and Wolfgang Herrmann, *Deutsche Baukunst des 19. und 20. Jahrhunderts* (1932; rpt. Basel: Birkhäuser, 1977), 35–48.

45. Robert Rosenblum, *Transformations in Late Eighteenth Century Art* (Princeton, N.J.: Princeton Univ. Press, 1967), 138.

46. Pevsner, *A History of Building Types*, 16, cites the passages from Milizia and Semper.

47. Boullée, 41.

48. Pevsner, 293.

49. August Grisebach, *Carl Friedrich Schinkel: Architect, Städtebauer, Maler* (1924; rpt. Frankfurt am Main: Ullstein, 1983), 178.

50. *Werke*, I, 342.

51. Pevsner, *History of Building Types*, 124. On neoclassicism see also the special number of *Architectural Design* (vol. 49, No. 8–9), ed. Geoffrey Broadbent; and Paul Klopfer, *Von Palladio bis Schinkel. Eine Charakteristik der Baukunst des Klassizismus* (Esslingen: Paul Neff, 1911).

52. Pevsner, *History of Building Types*, 11–26.

53. Pevsner, *History of Building Types*, 18.

54. Gerhart Rodenwaldt, *Griechisches und Römisches in Berliner Bauten des Klassizismus* (Berlin: De Gruyter, 1956), 28–29.

55. Letter of 5 June 1788; *Briefe*, Hamburg edition, vol. II, 94.

56. Hubert Schrade, *Deutsche Maler der Romantik* (Darmstadt: Wissenschaftliche Buchgesellschaft, 1967), 41; and *The Triumph of Art for the Public*, ed. Elizabeth Gilmore Holt (Garden City: Doubleday-Anchor, 1979), 12–16 and 52–57.

57. Goethe's writings on art are most conveniently collected in vol. XIII of the *Gedenkausgabe*; here 136–37.

58. *Gedenkausgabe*, XIII, 276.

59. Bk. II, ch. 8; Hamburg edition, IX, 320.

60. Letter of 15 Nov. 1798; in *Caroline: Briefe aus der Frühromantik*, I, 472–73.

61. *Athenaeum*, I/2 (1798): 222.

62. *Dichtung*, 201.

63. *Europa*, I, 108.

64. Schlegel's writings on art are most conveniently collected in vol. IV of the *Kritische Ausgabe*, ed. Hans Eichner; here 244.

65. Letter of 28 Dec. 1808; in Helen Marie von Kügelgen, *Ein Lebensbild in Briefen*, 6th ed. (Stuttgart: Belser, 1912), 147.

66. Letter of 27 Mar. 1809; *Lebensbild*, 154.

67. *Nachtwachen*, 107.

68. *Erwin: Vier Gespräche über das Schöne und die Kunst*, 272.

69. *Vorlesungen über Ästhetik*, 335–39.

70. *Werke*, XIII, 116–19.

71. I disagree with Plagemann, *Das deutsche Kunstmuseum*, 25–26, who regards the notion of the "temple of art" as a meaningless metaphor, a "rhetorical flourish," and rejects any association of religion and art among the Romantics. Plagemann is overreacting to the exaggerated view of art as religion in Hubert Schrade's early book *Schicksal und Notwendigkeit der Kunst* (1936). In a more recent volume, *Deutsche Maler der Romantik* (20–21), Schrade takes a moderate view that is not incompatible with my own interpretation.

72. In this context it is irrelevant that the title as we know it today was formulated not by Wackenroder himself but by his friend, the composer Reichardt; the basic image of the art-loving friar is present in Wackenroder's earliest conception of the work. For a survey of the debate see Martin Bollacher's collective review, *Wackenroder und die Kunstauffassung der frühen Romantik* (Darmstadt: Wissenschaftliche Buchgesellschaft, 1983), 102–14.

73. *Dichtung*, 191.

74. *Dichtung*, 193.

75. *Dichtung*, 201.

76. *Dichtung*, 232.

77. In the translation by Terrence N. Tice: *On Religion: Addresses in Response to Its Cultured Critics* (Richmond, Va.: John Knox Press, 1969), 206.

78. *Über die Religion* (1799).

79. *Schriften*, III, 562.

80. *Schriften*, III, 521.

81. *Schriften*, II, 441.

82. *Athenaeum* 3 (1800): 6.

83. Haym, *Die romantische Schule*, 459.

84. *Sämmtliche Werke*, x, 365.

85. *Sämmtliche Werke*, I, 87–96.

86. Runge, *Leben in Selbstzeugnissen*, 151. On Runge see Rudolf M. Bisanz, *German Romanticism and Philipp Otto Runge: A Study in Nineteenth-Century Art Theory and Iconography* (Dekalb: Northern Illinois Univ. Press, 1970).

87. Letter of 3 Sept. 1802; *Leben in Selbstzeugnissen*, 126.

88. Letter of 18 Dec. 1802; *Leben in Selbstzeugnissen*, 146.

89. Letter of 9 Mar. 1802; *Leben in Selbstzeugnissen*, 110.

90. *Reden über die Religion*, 38.

91. Friedrich, *Bekenntnisse*, 102–5.

92. On Hegel's aesthetics see René Wellek, *A History of Modern Criticism, 1750–1950*, vol. II: *The Romantic Age* (New Haven: Yale Univ. Press, 1955), 318–34; and Ernst Gombrich, "Hegel and Art History," in the symposium "On the Methodology of Architectural History," ed. Demetri Porphyrios, *Architectural Design* (1981): 3–9.

93. *Vorlesungen über Ästhetik*, 344.

94. *Vorlesungen über Ästhetik*, 345.

95. *Aus Schinkel's Nachlass*, III, 25.

96. See Rosenblum, *Transformations in Late Eighteenth Century Art*, 107–45; and Carroll L. V. Meeks, "Pantheon Paradigm," *Journal of the Society of Architectural Historians* 19 (Dec. 1960): 135–44.

97. *Aus Schinkel's Nachlass*, III, 244–45.

98. In this connection see Hans Sedlmayr, *Verlust der Mitte: Die bildende Kunst des 19. und 20. Jahrhunderts als Symptom und Symbol der Zeit* (1948; rpt. Berlin: Ullstein, 1965), 27–30; and Hans Kauffmann, "Zweckbau und Monument," 159.

99. See Lionello Venturi, *History of Art Criticism*, trans. Charles Marriott. New rev. ed. (1936; rpt. New York: E. P. Dutton, 1964).

100. See Käte Laserstein, *Die Gestalt des bildenden Künstlers in der Dichtung* (Berlin: De Gruyter, 1931); and G. Bebermeyer, "Malerroman," in *Reallexikon der deutschen Literaturgeschichte*, eds. Paul Merker and Wolfgang Stammler (Berlin: De Gruyter, 1926–1928), II, 328–32.

101. In this connection see Mary Hurst Schubert's introduction to her translation of Wackenroder's *Confessions and Fantasies* (University Park: Pennsylvania State Univ. Press, 1971), 44–52.

102. *Sämmtliche Werke*, x, 366–67.

103. F. T. Vischer, *Kritische Gänge*, ed. Robert Vischer, 2nd ed. (Leipzig: Verlag der Weißen Bücher, 1914), II, 4.

104. See Alfred Anger's afterword to his edition, 557–58; and Roger Paulin, *Ludwig Tieck: A Literary Biography* (Oxford: Clarendon, 1986), 91–97.

105. On Tieck's unsuccessful efforts in 1815–1816 to revise and complete his novel, see Paulin, *Ludwig Tieck*, 202–3.

106. *Franz Sternbalds Wanderungen*, 392.

107. For the following references see Anger's edition, 503–33.

108. In a paragraph that he added to J. H. Meyer's essay "Über Polygnots Gemälde" (1805); *Gedenkausgabe*, XIII, 451.

109. See Hans Eichner's introduction in the *Kritische Ausgabe*, V, xvii–xlvi; and Eric A. Blackall, *The Novels of the German Romantics*, 21–43.

110. *Kritische Ausgabe*, V.

111. *Briefwechsel*, II, 361.

112. Jürgen Jacobs, *Wilhelm Meister und seine Brüder: Untersuchungen zum deutschen Bildungsroman* (München: Fink, 1972). Jacobs, curiously, does not take up *Florentin*.

113. *Florentin*, 121.

114. See Wilhelm Hoppe, *Das Bild Raffaels in der deutschen Literatur von der Zeit der Klassik bis zum Ausgang des 19. Jahrhunderts* (Frankfurt am Main: Moritz Diesterweg, 1935).

115. *Poetische Werke*, I, 63.

116. *Poetische Werke*, II, 288.

117. For a discussion of the critical debate see James M. McGlathery, "Demon Love: E.T.A. Hoffmann's *Elixiere des Teufels*," *Colloquia Germanica* I (1979): 61–76.

118. Letter of Feb. or Mar. 1810; *Werke*, I, 1206. Because Runge died in 1810 the collaboration never took place.

119. *Werke*, I, 649–1010. Indeed, the plot of the fragmentary work must be pieced together from the sections that were actually completed as well as Brentano's paralipomena for its continuation.

120. *Werke*, I, 1209.

121. *Poetische Werke*, III, 208.

122. *Poetische Werke*, II, 497.

123. See Keith Andrews, *The Nazarenes: A Brotherhood of German Painters in Rome* (Oxford: Clarendon, 1964); William Vaughn, *German Romantic Painting* (New Haven, Conn.: Yale Univ. Press, 1980), 163–90; and W. D. Robson-Scott, "German Romanticism and the Visual Arts," in *The Romantic Period in Germany*, ed. Siegbert Prawer (London: Weidenfeld, 1970), 259–81.

124. "Über den Einfluß der Litteratur auf die neueren Kunstbestrebungen der Deutschen," in Athanasius Raczynski, *Geschichte der Neueren Deutschen Kunst* (Berlin, 1841), III, 371–82.

125. Schinkel, *Reisen nach Italien*, 179.

126. Heinrich Meyer, *Kleine Schriften zur Kunst*, ed. Paul Weizsäcker (Stuttgart: Göschen, 1886), 97–131. The introduction to this edition contains much useful material on Meyer, Goethe, and the Weimar *Kunstfreunde*. The text of Meyer's essay is also reprinted in the *Gedenkausgabe*, XIII, 708–27.

127. *Kritische Ausgabe*, IV, 237–62.

128. Albert Dresdner, *Die Entstehung der Kunstkritik im Zusammenhang der Geschichte des europäischen Kunstlebens* (München: Bruckmann, 1915), 263.

129. See Goethe's descriptions in books I–III of *Dichtung und Wahrheit*; Hamburg edition, vol. IX, 10–114.

130. Wilhelm Waetzoldt, *Deutsche Kunsthistoriker*, 234.

131. See *The Triumph of Art for the Public*, ed. Elizabeth Gilmore Holt, for a selection of lively accounts of salons and galleries in the period 1785–1848.

132. *Dichtung*, 217–28. The book contains another gallery dialogue, which takes place in the dream scene entitled "Ehrengedächtnis unsers ehrwürdigen Ahnherrn Albrecht Dürers" (182–90).

133. See Tieck's preface to the 1814 edition of *Phantasien über die Kunst*.

134. Hans Joachim Neidhardt, *Die Malerei der Romantik in Dresden* (Leipzig: Seemann, 1976), 7–11.

135. See the account in bk. VIII of *Dichtung und Wahrheit*; Hamburg edition, vol. IX, 320. On the essentially "black-and-white" acquaintance with painting that prevailed from the seventeenth to the nineteenth centuries, see André Malraux, *The Voices of Silence*, trans. Stuart Gilbert (1953; rpt. Princeton, N.J.: Princeton Univ. Press, 1978), 15–16.

136. *Was ich erlebte*, 141–42.

137. For an excellent account of this period see Albert Schlagdenhauffen, *Frédéric Schlegel et son groupe: le doctrine de l'Athenaeum, 1798–1800* (Paris: Les belles lettres, 1934), 195–237; and Emil Sulger-Gebing, *Die Brüder A. W. und F. Schlegel in ihrem Verhältnisse zur bildenden Kunst* (München: Carl Haushalter, 1897), 31–80.

138. Letter of 24 Oct. 1798; in *Charlotte Schiller und ihre Freunde* (Stuttgart: Cotta, 1865), III, 25.

139. Schlagdenhauffen, *Schlegel et son groupe*, 219.

140. *Athenaeum* 2 (1799): 39–151.

141. While there existed a long tradition of poems on secular paintings (notably with classical themes), Schlegel's sonnets initiated the popular genre of poems, especially sonnets, on *religious* paintings. See Gisbert Kranz, *Das Bildgedicht in Europa: Zur Theorie und Geschichte einer literarischen Gattung* (Paderborn: Schöningh, 1973), 96–98.

142. Rudolf Hirzel, *Der Dialog: Ein literarhistorischer Versuch* (Leipzig: Hirzel, 1895), II, 418–37; Wolfhart Henckmann's epilogue to his edition of Solger's *Erwin*, 492–501; and Rudolf Wildbolz, "Dialog," in *Reallexikon der deutschen Literaturgeschichte*, 2nd ed. (Berlin: De Gruyter, 1955), I, 251–55.

143. "Verschiedene Empfindungen vor einer Seelandschaft von Friedrich, worauf ein Kapuziner," in Brentano's *Werke*, II, 1034–38.

144. Christian Schuster, "The Work of Art in German Literature: Methods and Techniques of Description from 1755–1830 (diss. Columbia, 1948).

145. See Christian Beutler's introduction to Goethe's *Schriften zur Kunst*; *Gedenkausgabe*, XIII, 1087–1100.

146. Waetzoldt, *Deutsche Kunsthistoriker*, 131.

147. *Oeuvres complètes* (Paris, 1821), VIII, 328–40.

148. Waetzoldt, *Deutsche Kunsthistoriker*, 236.

149. Letter of 9 Sept. 1798; *Schriften*, IV, 260.

150. "Studien zur bildenden Kunst," in *Schriften*, II, 648–51.

151. J. D. Gries, *Gedichte und poetische Übersetzungen* (Stuttgart: Löflund, 1829), 212–17.

152. Henri Chélin, *Friedrich Schlegels Europa* (Frankfurt am Main: Lang, 1981), 81–94; and especially Hans Eichner's introduction to *Kritische Ausgabe*, IV, xi–lvi.

153. *Europa*, I, 108.

154. *Europa*, II/2, 1.

155. *Werke*, III, 7–74.

156. On the redefinition of the cultural role of the museum from 1816 to 1848 see Plagemann, *Das deutsche Kunstmuseum*, 30; and Bernhard Knauss, *Das Künstlerideal des Klassizismus und der Romantik* (Reutlingen: Gryphius, 1925).

157. See Wolfgang Herrmann, *Deutsche Baukunst des 19. und 20. Jahrhunderts*, 35–48, for a chapter on Schinkel as expressive of the times. On Schinkel's life see Rave, *Karl Friedrich Schinkel*; Grisebach, *Carl Friedrich Schinkel*; and Max Neumann, *Menschen um Schinkel* (Berlin: De Gruyter, 1942).

158. *Aus Schinkel's Nachlass*, II, 207.

159. Ernst Jünger, "In den Museen," from the second edition of *Das abenteuerliche Herz* (1938); in Jünger's *Werke* (Stuttgart: Klett, 1960–1963), VII, 280–85.

160. *Verlust der Mitte*, 27.

161. Malraux, *The Voices of Silence*, 14.

162. *The Triumph of Art for the Public*, ed. Elizabeth Gilmore Holt, 40.

163. Holt, *The Triumph of Art*, 79.

164. *Gedenkausgabe*, XIII, 155.

165. Werner Strube, "Interesselosigkeit," *Archiv für Begriffsgeschichte* 23 (1980): 148–74.

166. *Rêveries du promeneur solitaire*, 94.

167. *Franz Sternbalds Wanderungen*, 177.

168. "Landschaftliche Malerei," in *Gedenkausgabe*, XIII, 790.

169. Thomas Carlyle, *Critical and Miscellaneous Essays* (New York: Alden, 1885), 60.

## CHAPTER SEVEN

1. *Werke*, I, 17.

2. See Theodore Ziolkowski, "Das Nachleben der Romantik in der modernen deutschen Literatur: Methodologische Überlegungen," in *Das Nachleben der Romantik in der modernen deutschen Literatur*, ed. Wolfgang Paulsen (Heidel-

NOTES TO CHAPTER SEVEN

berg: Lothar Stiehm, 1969), 15–31; and Per Öhrgaard, "Die Romantik als Bezugspunkt in der deutschen Gegenwartsliteratur," in *Aspekte der Romantik*, ed. Sven-Aage Jörgensen, Per Öhrgaard, and Friedrich Schmöe (Kopenhagen-München: Fink, 1983), 128–45. This phenomenon does not occur only in German literature, of course. In Robertson Davies's novel *The Lyre of Orpheus* (1989), "ETAH"—the shade of Hoffmann—plays a major role, commenting from Limbo on the actions of the characters in contemporary Toronto, who are completing and staging an opera entitled *Arthur of Britain, or the Magnanimous Cuckold*, that Hoffmann allegedly left unfinished at the time of his death. In the course of the novel numerous parallels emerge between Romanticism and the present, as well as between the plot of the opera and the plot of the novel.

3. *Kein Ort. Nirgends. Erzählung* (Berlin: Aufbau, 1979), 5; see Alexander Stephan, *Christa Wolf*, Autorenbücher 4, 2nd ed. (München: Beck, 1979), 128–34.

4. *Hölderlin. Ein Roman*, Sammlung Luchterhand 260 (Darmstadt and Neuwied: Luchterhand, 1978), 7.

5. *Hoffmanns Erzählungen: Aufzeichnungen eines verwirrten Germanisten* (München: Nymphenburger, 1983), 15.

6. Theodore Ziolkowski, "The View from the Madhouse," in *Dimensions of the Modern Novel: German Texts and European Contexts* (Princeton, N.J.: Princeton Univ. Press, 1969), 332–62.

7. *Die Idee der deutschen Universität*, vii–x.

8. *Idee und Wirklichkeit einer Universität*, vii.

9. *Idee und Gestalt der deutschen Universität*, 7.

# EDITIONS CITED

Agricola, Georgius. *Ausgewählte Werke*. Ed. Hans Prescher. 8 vols. Berlin: Verlag der Wissenschaften, 1956–1974.
*Allgemeines Landrecht für die Preußischen Staaten von 1794*. Ed. Hans Hattenhauer. Frankfurt am Main: Metzner, 1970.
Anrich, Ernst, ed. *Die Idee der deutschen Universität*. Darmstadt: Wissenschaftliche Buchgesellschaft, 1964.
Arnim, Bettina von. *Werke und Briefe*. Eds. Gustav Konrad and Joachim Müller. 5 vols. Frechen-Köln: Bartmann, 1959–1963.
Arnim, Ludwig Achim von. *Briefe an Savigny*. Ed. Heinz Härtl. Weimar: Böhlau, 1982.
———. *Gedichte*. Zweiter Teil. Eds. Herbert R. Liedke and Alfred Anger. Tübingen: Niemeyer, 1976.
———. *Sämtliche Romane und Erzählungen*. Ed. Walther Migge. 3 vols. München: Hanser, 1962–1963.
———. *Werke*. Ed. Reinhold Steig. 3 vols. Leipzig: Insel, [1911].
*Athenaeum. Eine Zeitschrift*. 3 vols. Facsimile edition with an afterword by Ernst Behler. Darmstadt: Wissenschaftliche Buchgesellschaft, 1960.
*Berliner Abendblätter*. Facsimile edition. Ed. Georg Minde-Pouet. Leipzig: Klinkhardt & Biermann, 1925.
Börne, Ludwig. *Sämtliche Schriften*. Eds. Inge and Peter Rippmann. 5 vols. Düsseldorf: Melzer, 1964–1968.
Bonaventura. *Nachtwachen*. Ed. Wolfgang Paulsen. Stuttgart: Reclam, 1964.
Brentano, Clemens. *Werke*. Eds. Wolfgang Frühwald, Bernhard Gajek, and Friedhelm Kemp. 4 vols. München: Hanser, 1963–1968.
*Caroline. Briefe aus der Frühromantik*. Ed. Erich Schmidt. 2 vols. Leipzig: Insel, 1913.
Chamisso, Adelbert von. *Chamissos Werke*. Ed. Heinrich Kurz. 2 vols. Leipzig and Wien: Bibliographisches Institut, [n.d.].
Crichton, Alexander. *Inquiry into the Nature and Origin of Mental Derangement*. London, 1798. Facsimile edition. Ed. Richard Ellenbogen. New York: AMS, 1976.
Eichendorff, Joseph Freiherr von. *Werke und Schriften*. Ed. Gerhart Baumann. 4 vols. Stuttgart: Cotta, 1957–1958.

Eichendorff, Joseph Freiherr von. *Joseph und Wilhelm von Eichendorffs Jugendgedichte*. Ed. Raimund Pissin. Berlin: Frensdorff, [n.d.].

*Europa. Eine Zeitschrift*. Facsimile edition with an afterword by Ernst Behler. Darmstadt: Wissenschaftliche Buchgesellschaft, 1963.

Fichte, J. G. *Gesamtausgabe der Bayerischen Akademie der Wissenschaften*. Eds. Reinhard Lauth and Hans Jacob. 4 parts. Stuttgart–Bad Cannstadt: Frommann, 1962ff.

———. *Schriften zur Gesellschaftsphilosophie*. Ed. Hans Riehl. 2 vols. Jena: Fischer, 1928–1929.

———. *Sämmtliche Werke*. Ed. J. H. Fichte. 8 vols. Berlin: Veit, 1845–1846.

Frederick II of Prussia. *Oeuvres de Frédéric le Grand*. 31 vols. Berlin: Decker, 1846–1857.

Friedrich, Caspar David. *Bekenntnisse*. Ed. Kurt Karl Eberlein. Leipzig: Klinkhardt & Biermann, 1924.

Goethe, Johann Wolfgang von. *Goethes Werke*. Ed. Erich Trunz. 14 vols. Hamburg: Christian Wegner, 1948–1960.

———. *Gedenkausgabe der Werke, Briefe und Gespräche*. Ed. Ernst Beutler. 24 vols. Zürich: Artemis, 1948–1960.

———. *Goethes Werke*. 143 vols. Weimar: Böhlau, 1887–1919.

———. *Der Briefwechsel zwischen Schiller und Goethe*. Eds. Hans Gerhard Gräf and Albert Leitzmann. 3 vols. Leipzig: Insel, 1955.

Gries, J. D. *Gedichte und poetische Übersetzungen*. Stuttgart: Löflund, 1829.

Grimm, Jacob. *Kleinere Schriften*. 8 vols. Berlin: Dümmler, 1864–1890.

———. *Briefe der Brüder Grimm an Savigny*. Ed. Wilhelm Schoof. Berlin: Erich Schmidt, 1953.

Happel, Eberhard Werner. *Der akademische Roman*. Bern-Stuttgart-Wien: Scherz, 1962.

Hattenhauer, Hans, ed. *Thibaut und Savigny: Ihre Programmatischen Schriften*. München: Franz Vahlen, 1973.

Hebel, Johann Peter. *Poetische Werke*. Ed. Theodor Salfinger. München: Winkler, 1961.

Hegel, G.W.F. *Werke*. Eds. Eva Moldenhauer and Karl Markus Michel. 20 vols. Frankfurt am Main: Suhrkamp, 1969–1971.

Heine, Heinrich. *Historisch-kritische Gesamtausgabe der Werke*. Ed. Manfred Windfuhr. Hamburg: Hoffmann und Campe, 1973ff.

———. *Sämtliche Werke*. Ed. Ernst Elster. 7 vols. Leipzig und Wien: Bibliographisches Institut, 1887–1890.

Hölderlin, Friedrich. *Sämtliche Werke*. Ed. Friedrich Beißner. Kleine Stuttgarter Ausgabe. 6 vols. Stuttgart: Cotta, 1944–1962.

Hoffmann, E.T.A. *Briefwechsel*. Ed. Friedrich Schnapp. 3 vols. München: Winkler, 1967–1969.

———. *Juristische Arbeiten*. Ed. Friedrich Schnapp. München: Winkler, 1973.

————. *Poetische Werke*. Ed. Gerhard Seidel. 6 vols. Berlin: Aufbau, 1958.

Humboldt, Wilhelm von. *Gesammelte Schriften*. Eds. Albert Leitzmann and B. Gebhardt. 17 vols. Berlin: Behr, 1903–1936.

————. *Werke in fünf Bänden*. Eds. Andreas Flitner and Klaus Giel. 3rd ed. 5 vols. Darmstadt: Wissenschaftliche Buchgesellschaft, 1980–1981.

————. *Wilhelm und Caroline von Humboldt in ihren Briefen*. Ed. Anna von Sydow. 7 vols. Berlin: Mittler, 1907–1918.

————. *Briefe*. Ed. Wilhelm Rößle. München: Hanser, 1952.

Kant, Immanuel. *Werke in zehn Bänden*. Ed. Wilhelm Weischedel. 10 vols. Wiesbaden: Insel, 1960–1964.

Kerner, Justinus. *Werke*. Ed. Raimund Pissin. 6 vols. Berlin–Leipzig: Deutsches Verlagshaus Bong, [n.d.].

Kleist, Heinrich von. *Sämtliche Werke und Briefe*. Ed. Helmut Sembdner. 2nd rev. ed. 2 vols. München: Hanser, 1961.

Körner, Theodor. *Sämmtliche Werke*. Ed. Karl Streckfuß. 3rd ed. Berlin: Nicolai, 1838.

Kortum, Carl Arnold. *Die Jobsiade. Ein komisches Heldengedicht in drei Teilen*. Leipzig: Insel, 1906.

*Magister F. Ch. Laukhards Leben und Schicksale*. Ed. Viktor Petersen. 6 vols. Stuttgart: Lutz, 1908.

Loeben, Otto Heinrich Graf von. *Gedichte*. Ed. Raimund Pissin. 1905. Darmstadt: Wissenschaftliche Buchgesellschaft, 1968.

Müller, Adam. *Die Elemente der Staatskunst: Sechsunddreißig Vorlesungen*. Meersburg–Leipzig: Hendel, 1936.

[Müller, Adolph]. *Briefe von der Universität in die Heimat*. Ed. Ludmilla Assing. Leipzig: Brockhaus, 1874.

Novalis. *Schriften. Die Werke Friedrich von Hardenbergs*. Eds. Paul Kluckhohn and Richard Samuel. 2nd ed. 4 vols. Stuttgart: Kohlhammer, 1960–1975.

Pinel, Philippe. *Traité médico-philosophique sur l'aliénation mentale ou la manie*. Paris, 1800. Facsimile edition. Ed. François Asouvi. Genève-Paris: Slatkine, 1980.

*Propyläen. Eine periodische Schrift*. Facsimile edition. Ed. Wolfgang von Löhneysen. 3 vols in one. Stuttgart: Cotta, 1965.

Reil, Johann Christian. *Rhapsodieen über die Anwendung der psychischen Curmethode auf Geisteszerrüttungen*. Halle, 1803. Facsimile edition. Amsterdam: E. J. Bonset, 1968.

Richter, J. P. Friedrich. *Jeans Pauls Werke*. Ed. Norbert Miller. 6 vols. München: Hanser, 1960–1963.

————. *Sämtliche Werke*. Ed. Eduard Berend. 24 vols. Weimar: Böhlau, 1927ff.

Rist, Johann Georg. *Lebenserinnerungen*. Ed. G. Poel. 3 vols. Gotha: Perthes, 1880–1888.

*Crabb Robinson in Germany 1800–1805*. Extracts from his correspondence. Ed. Edith J. Morley. London: Oxford Univ. Press, 1929.

Rousseau, Jean-Jacques. *Rêveries du promeneur solitaire*. Ed. Henri Roddier. Paris: Garnier, 1960.

Runge, Philipp Otto. *Sein Leben in Selbstzeugnissen und Berichten*. Ed. Karl Privat. Berlin: Propyläen, 1942.

Salzmann, Christian Gotthilf. *Carl von Carlsberg oder über das menschliche Elend*. 6 parts in 3 vols. Leipzig: Crusius, 1783–1788.

Schelling, Friedrich Wilhelm Joseph. *Schriften von 1794–1798*. Darmstadt: Wissenschaftliche Buchgesellschaft, 1967.

———. *Werke*. Ed. Manfred Schröter. 1927. 6 vols. München: Beck, 1958–1959.

Schiller, Friedrich. *Briefe*. Ed. Fritz Jonas. 7 vols. Stuttgart: Deutsche Verlagsanstalt, 1892.

———. *Sämtliche Werke*. Eds. Gerhard Fricke and Herbert G. Göpfert. 5 vols. München: Hanser, 1965–1967.

Schinkel, Karl Friedrich. *Aus Schinkel's Nachlass: Reisetagebücher, Briefe und Aphorismen*. Ed. Alfred Freiherr von Wolzogen. 4 vols. Berlin: Decker, 1862–1864.

———. *Reisen nach Italien: Tagebücher, Briefe, Zeichnungen, Aquarelle*. Ed. Gottfried Riemann. Berlin: Rütten & Loening, 1979.

———. *Sammlung architektonischer Entwürfe*. Berlin: Ernst & Korn, 1866. Facsimile edition. Eds. Kenneth S. Hazlett, Stephen O'Malley, and Christopher Rudolph. Chicago: Exedra, 1981.

Schlegel, August Wilhelm von. *Sämmtliche Werke*. Ed. Eduard Böcking. 12 vols. Leipzig: Weidmann, 1846–1847.

[Schlegel, Dorothea]. *Florentin. Ein Roman hrsg. von Friedrich Schlegel*. Ed. Paul Kluckhohn. In Deutsche Literatur in Entwicklungsreihen, Reihe Romantik 7, pp. 89–244. Leipzig: Reclam, 1933.

Schlegel, Friedrich. *Kritische Friedrich-Schlegel-Ausgabe*. Ed. Ernst Behler with Jean-Jacques Anstett and Hans Eichner. 35 vols. München–Paderborn–Wien: Schöningh, 1958ff.

———. *Kritische Schriften*. Ed. Wolfdietrich Rasch. München: Hanser, 1956.

———. *Literary Notebooks 1797–1801*. Ed. Hans Eichner. Toronto: Univ. of Toronto Press, 1957.

Schleiermacher, Friedrich. *Über die Religion. Reden an die Gebildeten unter ihren Verächtern*. Ed. Carl Heinz Ratschow. Stuttgart: Reclam, 1980.

Schubert, Gotthilf Heinrich. *Ansichten von der Nachtseite der Naturwissenschaft*. Dresden, 1808. Facsimile edition. Darmstadt: Wissenschaftliche Buchgesellschaft, 1967.

Solger, Karl Wilhelm Ferdinand. *Erwin: Vier Gespräche über das Schöne und die Kunst*. Ed. Wolfhart Henckmann. München: Fink, 1971.

———. *Vorlesungen über Ästhetik*. Ed. K.W.L. Heyse. Leipzig: Brockhaus, 1829.

Spiess, Christian Heinrich. *Biographien der Wahnsinnigen*. Ed. Wolfgang Promies. Neuwied: Luchterhand, 1966.

Steffens, Henrich. *Novellen*. Gesammt-Ausgabe. 16 vols. Breslau, 1837–1838.

———. *Was ich erlebte*. Ed. Willi A. Koch. München: Winkler, 1956.

Tieck, Ludwig. *Werke in vier Bänden*. Ed. Marianne Thalmann. 4 vols. München: Winkler, 1963–1966.

———. *Gesammelte Novellen*. 12 vols. Berlin: Georg Reimer, 1852–1854.

———. *Franz Sternbalds Wanderungen*. Studienausgabe. Ed. Alfred Anger. Stuttgart: Reclam, 1966.

———. *Kaiser Oktavianus*. Jena: Frommann, 1804.

Uhland, Ludwig. *Gedichte*. Ed. Hans-Rüdiger Schwab. Frankfurt am Main: Insel Taschenbuch, 1987.

Varnhagen von Ense, Karl August. *Denkwürdigkeiten des eignen Lebens*. Ed. Konrad Feilchenfeldt. 3 vols. Frankfurt am Main: Deutscher Klassiker Verlag, 1987.

Varnhagen, Rahel. *Briefwechsel*. Ed. Friedhelm Kemp. 2nd ed. 4 vols. München: Winkler, 1979.

Wackenroder, Wilhelm Heinrich. *Dichtung. Schriften. Briefe*. Ed. Gerda Heinrich. München: Hanser, 1984.

Waiblinger, Wilhelm. *Die Tagebücher 1821–1826*. Ed. Herbert Meyer. Stuttgart: Klett, 1956.

Werner, Zacharias. *Ausgewählte Schriften*. 12 vols. Rpt. Bern: Lang, 1970.

Widmann, Georg Rudolf. *Fausts Leben*. Ed. Adelbert von Keller. Bibliothek des Litterarischen Vereins in Stuttgart 146. Tübingen, 1880.

Zachariä, Friedrich Wilhelm. *Scherzhafte Epische Poesien nebst einigen Oden und Liedern*. Braunschweig und Hildesheim: Schröder, 1754.

Zedler, Johann Heinrich. *Großes Vollständiges Universal-Lexikon aller Wissenschafften und Künste*. 64 vols. Halle und Leipzig: Zedler, 1732–1750.

# INDEX